**Confronting
Social
Problems**

Confronting
Social Problems

Ronald A. Hardert

Sociology Department
Arizona State University

Leonard Gordon

Sociology Department
Arizona State University

Mary R. Laner

Sociology Department
Arizona State University

Mark Reader

Political Science Department
Arizona State University

West
Publishing
Company
St. Paul
New York
Los Angeles
San Francisco

**Library of Congress
Cataloging in Publication Data**

Main entry under title:

Confronting social problems.

Includes index.
1. Social problems—Addresses, essays, lectures.
I. Hardert, Ronald A., 1938–   .
HN27.C66   1984   361.1   83-21819
ISBN 0-314-78013-0

Copy Editor: Joan M. Torkildson
Cover Photos: Clockwise from upper right: © F. B.
Gruenzweig; U.S. Navy; © Geoffrey Cove. All
from Photo Researchers, Inc.
Artwork: Editing, Design & Production, Inc.
Compositor: The Clarinda Company

PHOTO CREDITS

1 Glenn Short;   8 Glenn Short;   16 © Pam
Hasegawa, Taurus Photos;   19 United Press
International;   23 AP/Wide World;
35 AP/Wide World;   39 Mike Peters, Dayton
Daily News;   40 United Press International;
45 United Press International;   49 AP/Wide
World;   57 Magnum Photos;   65 AP/Wide
World;   68 United Press International;
73 United Press International;   84 United Press
International;   91 Bert Glinn, Magnum
Photos;   93 L. M. Shea, Freelance Photographers
Guild;   99 Chester Higgins, Jr., Photo
Researchers;   103 AP/Wide World;
111 HUD;   113 Reprinted by courtesy of *New
Woman* magazine copyright © 1982 by *New
Woman.* All rights reserved throughout the
world.   116 Chester Higgins, Jr., Photo
Researchers;   122 Julie Jensen;   129 Alice
Kandell, Photo Researchers;   129 Frank
Siteman, EKM Nepenthe;   132 Alice Kandell,
Photo Researchers;   137 David M. Grossman,
Photo Researchers;   141 Bohden Hrynewych,
Stock, Boston;   150 Frank Siteman, EKM
Nepenthe;   158 © George W. Gardener, Stock,
Boston;   161 Photo Researchers;   172 AP/Wide
World;   173 AP/Wide World;   177 Photo
Researchers;   185 AP/Wide World;   189 Rene
Buru, Magnum Photos;   192 Ellan Young, Photo
Researchers;   197 AP/Wide World;   201 United
Press International;   206 © The New Yorker,
1979;   213 United Press International;

Photo Credits continued on page 489.

To our families:
Past, present, and future

Preface

Economist Robert Heilbroner, writing in *Inquiry into the Human Prospect*, tells us that humanity faces three major challenges to survival. Population growth is the first challenge, having grave environmental and political implications. The threat of nuclear war—the result of nationalism and of unequal distribution of resources around the world—is the second challenge. Finally, we are also faced with devastating environmental deterioration, as a result of inadequate controls on industrial activity.

In order to address the problems we face, we must approach them realistically and with a willingness to alter our behavior. Heilbroner's concern is that adequate responses may not be mounted in time. Capitalism and socialism, the world's major economic systems, have not yet adequately solved our problems. Can democratic societies meet these challenges, or can only totalitarian governments obtain the obedience and rapid reactions to social and political changes that are required for survival? Nationalistic allegiances may replace the understanding that we are all in the global lifeboat together. In times of crisis and personal insecurity, authoritarian leadership is sometimes welcomed. Are we, as a society, moving toward surrendering our democratic rights and freedoms? Can we resolve the challenges facing us in creative ways that do not abridge human rights?

Social scientists hold different views as to how social problems may be defined, analyzed, and resolved. In the prologue that follows, we present background assumptions and the special perspectives that sociologists bring to the study of social problems. Those who have had an Introductory Sociology course may find it a useful review; those for whom this is a first exposure to viewing the world in sociocultural terms will be formally introduced to sociological concepts which are basic to this approach.

Recognizing that students from very different backgrounds and at different educational levels may be enrolled in any Social Problems course, our text steers a middle course. We have limited our use of sociological "jargon" and have defined all necessary terms briefly when they first appear in the text, and in more detail in the Glossary. Our goals, however, are broad. We focus your attention on a number of social problems, introduced first by a current news item, which shows the relevance of the problem to daily life. Next follows a consistent form of presentation which includes (1) the definition of each problem, (2) how society views the problem, (3) how sociologists analyze the problem, and (4) suggested policies for resolving the problem. Each chapter follows this format.

Beyond providing a basic acquaintance with the complexity and diversity of the sociocultural world, we hope to increase comprehension of the conflict, rapid change, and especially of the ambiguities and contradictions that seem to be accelerating. Some of the problems and challenges we face may not be solvable in our time; however, we

advance ideas for reducing their negative effects. Finally, we hope to foster interest in the sociological approach and in sociology as a discipline.

Ronald A. Hardert
Leonard Gordon
Mary Riege Laner
Mark Reader

Tempe, Arizona

Acknowledgments

An editor once said (in regard to textbook development): "Good books are not *written*, they *evolve*." If that is true, this text ought to be a winner because its total development and execution spanned a period of about five years.

Special thanks go to everyone in the College Division of West Publishing for their professionalism and for believing in our project. Our editor, Denise Simon, was a constant source of good ideas, encouragement, and inspiration. Our copy editor, Joan Torkildson, did a masterful job ironing out the rough spots and unifying the writing styles of four co-authors. Our production editor Marta Fahrenz showed the patience of Job, especially on days when the ice and snow of St. Paul stood between her and the office. Finally, we want to thank Beth Hinzman for her confidence and creative advertising of the book, and also Tamborah Moore for finding such appropriate and interesting photos.

The following people should receive acknowledgments for helping with various chapters of the book. For research on Chapters 14 and 15, our thanks go to Beth Sand, Raymond Wrabley, and Fran Reader. Paul S. Charnetsky (physical health), Majel Dominguez (elites), Alicia M. Gonzalez (population and food), Lawrence Rosen (suicide), and Con Alan Wilson (Epilogue) also contributed research in the areas indicated. Opal Blalock, Rena Gordon, Professors Dickinson McGaw and Stephan Walker (both of the Political Science Department at Arizona State University), and Nina Mohit (Committee for a Non-Nuclear Future) provided timely references. Linda Hardert helped edit various versions of the manuscript and proofread most of the galleys and page proofs. Sue Alonzo, Peggy Cowan, Bonnie Goforth, Cecelia Obenstine, Diane Popple, Debbie Sult, and Sandra Woodard supported us with speedy and expert typing—usually on very short notice. Thanks also to Fran Reader for preparing the Instructor's Manual, to Tim Danielson for editing it, and to Chris Ptuhl for film research.

A number of professional reviewers read and critiqued the manuscript in various stages. We appreciate very much, and tried to incorporate, contributions of all of our reviewers, especially the following persons:

Diane Mitsch Bush
Colorado State University

D. J. Call
Western Washington University

Colin B. Campbell
University of York—England

Walter Cartwright
Texas Tech University

Don A. Gibbs
Portland Community College

David Graeven
California State University, Hayward

Joan Huber
University of Illinois

Robert Hunter
University of Colorado

Cary S. Kart
University of Toledo

Philip H. Kuhn
University of Arkansas

Henry W. Peddle
Elgin Community College

Eleanor M. Vanderhaegen
Keene State College

Evan Vlachos
Colorado State University

Arthur S. Wilke
Auburn University

Contents

CHAPTER 8
Crime and Punishment 213

CHAPTER 9
Physical and Mental Health 241

PROLOGUE

Confronting Social Problems

CONTENTS

Teens found willing to take stand on social movements

By George Gallup

PRINCETON, N.J.—American teen-agers are willing to get involved in causes they believe in, according to the latest Gallup Youth Survey.

At least one teen-ager in six already is actively engaged in at least one movement.

Nationwide, a solid majority of teen-agers say they would like to become champions for certain social issues such as efforts to bring world peace, better government, conservation of natural resources, racial harmony and environmental concerns.

The issue with the greatest potential for teen involvement is world peace. In an age when nuclear war is an ever present threat, it is not surprising to find seven in 10 teens willing to rally behind a peace movement. Gallup pollsters found an almost equal proportion of teens, 68 percent, eager to work toward the improvement of government.

Interest in becoming involved in these two issues is highest among boys and girls with an above-average academic standing, those who live in the center cities and teens who attend church regularly. In addition, black youngsters show a greater desire to get involved in these causes than do white teens.

Concern for Earth and Mother Nature is also high on the teens' list of causes worth fighting for. For example, 62 percent said they would like to get involved with the conservation of natural resources, and 52 percent mention environmental issues.

The drive for racial harmony also drew a great deal of interest among all teen-agers. Black teens have greater expectation of participating in a cause that furthers racial equality than their white schoolmates.

Women's rights is the only issue that less than a majority

TEEN INVOLVEMENT
Would like to get involved in:

	Racial Harmony	Environmental Issues	Women's Rights
NATIONAL	58	52	42
Boys	55	52	32
Girls	61	52	52
Whites	57	51	39
Blacks	68	56	58
Protestants	56	50	38
Catholics	59	50	43
East	55	52	46
Midwest	59	49	38
South	59	55	44
West	59	51	41
Churchgoers	60	51	40
Not regular churchgoers	56	53	44

	Peace Efforts	Better Govt.	Conserving Resources
NATIONAL	70	68	62
Boys	68	70	64
Girls	72	67	59
Whites	69	67	63
Blacks	76	79	58
Protestants	70	66	61
Catholics	70	70	61
East	70	69	60
Midwest	69	69	64
South	72	67	60
West	67	69	64
Churchgoers	73	71	65
Not regular churchgoers	67	66	59

©1982, The Associated Press

of teen-agers, 42 percent, would like to align themselves with. However, among girls, 52 percent are willing to work for women's rights compared with 32 percent of boys. This 20-point spread represents the greatest divergence of opinion found for all the issues tested.

Finally, teen groups showing the highest levels of involvement in at least one social cause are those living in the South, 21 percent; Protestants, 20 percent; blacks, 20 percent; and boys and girls who attend church regularly, 19 percent.

The survey showed 17 percent of the teens in the Midwest are involved in at least one issue; whites, 16 percent; nonregular churchgoers, 14 percent; East, 14 percent; and Catholics, 14 percent.

The question asked was:

"In the past, there have been certain issues which have captured young people's attention, or have served as a rallying point, such as the Vietnam War. Please tell me which of the following issues or causes, if any, you are now actively involved in or would like to become involved in: Efforts to bring peace in the world, the conservation of natural resources, environmental issues, women's rights, racial harmony, getting better government."

The survey findings are based on telephone interviews with a representative national cross section of 1,010 boys and girls.

Source: Gallup Youth Survey. In *Phoenix Gazette, 25 June 1982.*

IDENTIFYING SOCIAL PROBLEMS

Defining Social Problems: The Issue of Bias

As George Gallup's Youth Survey reveals, a majority of America's teenagers thinks that something can be done to solve a number of our social problems, and they are willing to involve themselves in the effort. The survey also reveals some differences among the teenagers surveyed: More girls than boys would lend their support to women's rights issues, and more blacks than whites are interested in working toward racial harmony. These differences may be called biases by sex and by race, respectively.

Similarly, the General Social Surveys conducted annually by the National Opinion Research Center (NORC) find that older adults also differ in their attitudes toward various social issues. Often, these differences appear as geographical biases, and the annual NORC surveys show that the boundaries of geographic regions, relative to attitudes, tend to remain stable over time.

According to the report of a NORC survey in the *Wall Street Journal* (3 February 1981, 25), opinions of adult Americans differ by geographic region on the topic of sexual orientation: "Fewer than 60 percent of New Englanders think that adult homosexuality is always wrong, while almost 90 percent of the people in the East South Central states . . . think so." On many social issues, New Englanders are the most liberal, with the Pacific Coast region usually a close second. Parts of the South tend to be the most conservative. While almost 60 percent of New Englanders and those from the Pacific Coast area support a married woman's right to an abortion, in the east south central states (such as Kentucky and Tennessee), only one-third of those surveyed support that right. On political and religious topics, NORC surveys find that tolerance of Communists and atheists is far lower throughout the South than in the New England and Pacific regions. Apparently, the most trusting people live in the west north central states (such as

Minnesota, the Dakotas, Iowa, and Kansas). More than any other area, respondents from this region believe that "most people try to be fair in dealing with others" (*Wall Street Journal* 1981, 25).

Are social scientists more objective regarding social issues than others (as some people believe), or are they also prone to subjective biases? Sociologists' opinions also differ by region of their native countries, by sex, by race, by religion, and by other factors. Forty years ago, sociologist C. Wright Mills (1943, 165–80) analyzed the ideologies of his colleagues who studied social problems. By **ideologies**,[1] Mills meant the particular sets of ideas that members of various groups use to explain things. He concluded that both the selection and the description of social problems were affected by predetermined community standards for acceptable social behavior. At the time Mills wrote (mid-1900s), the majority of sociologists came from small towns or rural areas, and their ideas, he found, tended to reflect the values and attitudes of white, Anglo-Saxon, Protestant America.

Today's sociologists come from more varied backgrounds and are highly sensitive to the issue of scientific objectivity. Since personal values derived from ideologies can distort understanding of social problems, most contemporary sociologists make strong efforts to counteract such biases. That is, they try to eliminate the influence of preconceived ideas on their work. Sociological training typically includes considerable emphasis on eliminating personal biases, both in the selection of problems for study and in the way they are studied.

Earlier sociologists did not always agree on the definition of a social problem. Identification of a social problem might depend on (1) the number of persons affected by a social condition, (2) the number of people defining the condition, (3) the special interests and social power of those doing the defining,

---

1. For a more complete definition of terms printed in boldface, see the Glossary at the back of the book.

(4) the consequences of the condition for individuals, groups, societies, or the world, or (5) a combination of these factors. The variability in these defintions indicates that social problems were seen, to some extent, as "what people think they are" (Fuller and Myers 1941, 320). Contemporary sociologists, in contrast, agree that *all* of the factors identified above may be involved in defining a social problem.

As Fuller and Myers point out, every **social problem** consists of an objective (verifiable) condition and a subjective (personal) evaluation of that condition. Today's sociologists, however, are less likely to be subjectively biased by personal factors, such as their race, sex, or native region, than they are by their theoretical (explanatory) views of the social world. The discipline of sociology includes several schools of thought regarding its subject matter, as do virtually all the sciences. Each school claims to have the best perspectives for explaining some aspects of the social world and to have the best techniques for studying those aspects (Gusfield 1979, 5).

Is it Possible to Transcend Bias?

Sociologist Karl Mannheim argues that sociologists and other scholars come from such diverse backgrounds that together they constitute a scientific community that is more objective than any community of nonsociologists (Christodoulou, 1965, 65–69). Mannheim also believes that theoretical knowledge, resting on scientific criteria, has little to do with social class or other biasing factors and could therefore be more objective. In contrast, practical knowledge is more likely to be influenced by biases related to social class or other social factors such as age or religious affiliation.

Although Mannheim's views have been criticized by some—especially by Marxists—his argument is attractive to many others. In the effort to overcome or at least control subjectivity, the most objective approach to social problems takes into account the max-

imum range of possible definitions of and approaches to social problems. Scholars who view all social problems with only one theoretical or methodological (techniques for study) approach are, in contrast, hampered by a "partiality of knowledge." The study of social problems requires flexibility, open-mindedness, cooperation, and adaptation (Bronowski 1973). These characteristics are also the prerequisites for social and personal survival.

Another answer to the problem of subjectivity lies not in eliminating such evaluations, but in an awareness of them and in stating them up front. Others may then judge the merit of explanations for and solutions to problems within the framework through which they were studied and by comparing the results of different approaches to the same problems. Awareness of subjective biases first requires reflection on the extent to which personal **values** (how we think things ought to be) enter into the selection, definition, analysis, and interpretation of any social problem (Weber 1949, 49–112). Second, any arguments brought to bear on a problem should be supported by current data (up-to-date, verifiable evidence) from the greatest possible variety of quantitative (numerical) and qualitative (descriptive) sources.

As in all other sciences, there is no single, overarching sociological theory that explains all of social behavior, and no single, agreed-upon method of study that provides the "best" data. (Medical science, for instance, relies on clinical observation, laboratory testing, and on any of several theories of physiological functioning. Moreover, such theories are continually modified or revised, informed by newly developed data.) In the study of social problems, as in other areas of study, our best hope for containing the errors to which personal biases lead is to follow the techniques described above. In this text, we present the problems we have selected for study through several theoretical perspectives and through research data collected by a variety of methods.

ANALYZING SOCIAL PROBLEMS

Problem Levels: The Individual versus Interpersonal, Societal, and Global Levels

In addition to identifying the biases among sociologists of his time, C. Wright Mills (1959) makes an important distinction between personal troubles and public issues.

Personal troubles may include difficulties that lie in the domain of psychology, that is, problems that require changes *within* the individual. Public issues—problems involving relationships *between* individuals or groups (including groups as small as two persons and as large as whole societies)—are likely to have social solutions. Mills's lesson is that the level of the solution and the level of the problem are the same. These

This photo of a domestic dispute demonstrates the interpersonal and conflict aspects of some social problems. Police are frequently injured and sometimes killed in attempting to quell domestic disputes.

levels may involve groups, organizations, or whole societies; they may also be inter-societal or global, for larger issues such as war. Occasionally, social issues bridge several levels and require multilevel approaches.

Mills also points out that individuals' feelings of alienation, inadequacy, and powerlessness result from beliefs that the problems they face (such as unemployment) are their personal troubles. However, some troubles that seem personal to those experiencing them, or to bystanders, can often be explained by the influence of group, societal, or even global factors. These problems, then, are not psychologically based. Social conditions influence our feelings about ourselves and about the world.

Labeling and Blaming the Victim as Substitutes for Analysis

William Ryan (1978, 35) points out the danger of labeling any behavior as a social problem:

We must particularly ask: "To whom are social problems a problem?" And usually, if truth were to be told, we would have to admit that we mean they are a problem to those of us who are outside the boundaries of what we have defined as the problem. Negroes are a problem to racist whites, welfare is a problem to stingy taxpayers, delinquency is a problem to nervous property owners.

An example may be useful to illustrate the labeling process. Before Adolf Hitler came to power in the early 1930s, no "Jewish problem" existed. However, Hitler laid blame for Germany's economic troubles on German Jews, and because Hitler was a charismatic (inspiring) leader for the Nazis, the "Jewish problem" was defined into existence. In this way, some behaviors or conditions or groups are made problematic merely by labeling (i.e., on the basis of personal beliefs rather than evidence). Social problems, in short, may refer to actual social conditions or to a stigmatizing (degrading or devaluing) label attached to social actors individuals, events, or conditions.

Conversely, labeling may benefit a social condition. For example, child abuse was not considered a social problem until many people were made aware of and reacted to an objective fact that had long been in existence. Thus, at its best, labeling may be the first step in reducing or eliminating an objectively harmful condition; at its worst, it may merely pit one group or set of values against another, and may be the first step toward oppression.

A word of caution: The labeling *process* discussed in this section should not be confused with labeling *theory*, to be discussed below. These are distinct—one a process, the other a theory—but easily confused because of the similarity of terms.

Another dangerous substitute for analysis rests on a logical fallacy which Ryan calls "blaming the victim" (1978, 31–38). This situation occurs when the victims of a problem with *social* origins are blamed as *individuals* for the problem. For instance, in social arrangements that exclude women from educational, occupational, and political opportunities to control their own destinies, some blame women for being devious and manipulating in order to meet their needs. The problem actually lies in the social arrangements rather than in women's responses to those arrangements. Problems arising from the behaviors of the sexes toward one another cannot be resolved through psychological (individual level) solutions; the social arrangements that generate the behaviors must be changed. As mentioned earlier, what appear to be personal troubles are often the result of demonstrable social conditions.

Can All Social Problems Be Solved?

Interpersonal, societal, and global problems may be more readily solvable than some individual problems. Personal problems may require the individual's total cooperation for their resolution. In contrast, interpersonal, societal, or global issues may require only a large or strong enough proportion of the whole for their resolution. Thus, closing down nuclear power plants and ending nuclear weapons production might be possible if a meaningfully large or sufficiently powerful proportion of the public were convinced, before the damage becomes irreversible, that radiation from the entire nuclear fuel cycle is damaging to health (Caldicott 1978; Sternglass 1981). Conversely, individual "deviants," such as child abusers, may do permanent damage or even destroy victims before they can be detected and stopped. Even then, those whose behavior is identified as harmful may not be willing to give up such behaviors if given the opportunity to continue them.

Given sufficient knowledge and concern, even social problems that cannot be completely resolved can be reduced. For instance, the conditions under which coal miners work could be improved so that they might avoid black lung disease and accidents in the mines (Wooley and Reid 1975); and worker alienation could be reduced by introducing practices that give workers a larger share of company profits and decision making (Schumacher 1975; 274–82). Creative measures are already being undertaken to reduce or alleviate some identified problems. When the people of Chelan County, Washington, for instance, thought that they were being gouged by the local utility company, members of the community bought out the privately owned utility and ran it themselves. This locally managed public utility district now sells more than $28 million worth of electricity annually, using three-fourths of the income to retire the bonded indebtedness of the original loans; the remaining $7 million pays for social services and public facilities to enhance the quality of life in the county (Caudill 1976; 52–56).

GENERAL EXPLANATORY PERSPECTIVES

We noted earlier that sociologists, like all other scientists, have no single, overarching explanation of the problems they study (Ja-cobs 1983, 4). In method, theory, and scope, sociological approaches can be specific versus general, qualitative versus quantitative, and theoretical versus atheoretical (Jacobs 1983, 4–20). In this section, we present three general sociological theories that have been used to analyze social problems.

Three General Social Problems Theories

Three theoretical perspectives are useful for understanding social problems. They are functional theory, conflict theory, and interactionist theory (Henry 1978, 39–47). According to sociologist Kenneth Henry, structural-functionalism (or just functionalism) is the most objective approach, conflict theory includes both objective and subjective approaches, and interactionist theory is the most subjective. Henry points out that the basic ideologies of these perspectives differ. Functionalism holds that things are as they are because a certain amount of societal balance needs to be maintained; change comes about in the disruption and restoration of the basic social state of equilibrium. Conflict theory, in comparison, holds that things are as they are because of the successful domination of one group by another; change comes about because of conflict between groups, and stability is maintained only as long as one group maintains dominance. Interactionists believe that things are only what individuals in any given situation think they are; change comes about through shifts in meaning attributed by individuals to situations. (For those who have had a course in introductory sociology, the names of Talcott Parsons and Robert Merton may be familiar as functionalists, Karl Marx and Ralf Dahrendorf as conflict theorists, and Erving Goffman and George Herbert Mead among the interactionists.)

Functionalism.   The functional perspective is often used for the study of system-based problems of large groups or whole societies.

Functionalism can be either conservative or radical in its political aspects (Wright and Hilbert 1980, 215), but its implications are often conservative because of its focus on equilibrium maintenance as the basic task of social systems. Functionalists observe how changes in one part of a system influence its other parts and the system as a whole. For example, technological and economic changes are known to have effects on social institutions such as religion and the family. Sociologists using a **macrofunctional approach** (studying whole societies or large systems within societies) and those using a **microfunctional approach** (focusing on the study of smaller groups within societies) are often more interested in the consequences of change than in its origins. Their goal is to distinguish between the intended effects of change and its actual effects.

To illustrate, at the end of the Carter administration the Federal Reserve Board attempted to decrease the rate of inflation by raising the interest rates that banks charge investors. The change was intended to "cool off" the economy by discouraging overly rapid spending. The positive function of the government's effort was to partially lessen inflation; its negative consequences included recession, increased unemployment, losses of homes and farms, and increased suicide rates.

The term *function* not only refers to the positive and/or negative effects that system elements have on other system elements or on the system as a whole, but also refers to aspects of systems that facilitate adaptation or adjustment of the whole (Nagel 1961, 524). Between nations, for example, a peaceful gesture made by one side may be functional in that it has a survival-enhancing effect on both nations, on the relationship between those nations, and on the rest of the world.

A large majority of sociologists still consider themselves structural-functionalists (Gouldner 1970, 168) in spite of criticisms that theoreticians of other schools of thought have leveled at this perspective. Critics maintain that functionalists have not responded adequately to the overemphasis they place on **societal consensus** (shared values) (Nagel 1961, 520–35; Hempel 1971, 179–210; Martindale 1981, 510–11). Conflict theorists, for instance, think that functionalists neglect social conflict as an area of study. The conflict perspective differs from functionalism in other important ways, as we shall see below.

Conflict theory. Conflict theorists focus on disequilibrium (imbalances) between aspects of societies or between other social groups or both. Karl Marx, who is considered a classical conflict theorist, believes that economic factors involved in the struggle between social classes consitute the basic structure of all societies. Marx uses the term **false consciousness** (not acting in one's own behalf) to explain how the producers (workers) are led to support interests that are not their own but are those of the owners. In contrast, Northern Ireland is a modern example of people acting in their own behalf against outside rule, and the situation illustrates how social unrest and even open conflict can result from the failure of the mechanisms that those in power use to maintain workers' false consciousness.

Another important concept in Marx's conflict theory (1964, 108ff.) is alienation. Economic alienation, Marx maintains, is the result of private ownership of property. When privately owned, the means of production (land, natural resources, machinery) enhance selfish interests, promote indifference to workers, and limit production and profits which, according to Marx, rightfully belong to all. As populations grow, owners find it more difficult to control all the profits and at the same time persuade workers to participate in the production of those private profits. This Marxian idea is illustrated in contemporary American industry, where worker motivation is increased when profit-sharing incentives are introduced.

Although Marx's political ideas are better known, his sociological theory and its important propositions regarding conflict are relevant to contemporary issues. These propositions can be summarized as follows:

1.   The totality of the production structure [economic institutions] in a society determines the characteristics of the social structure [institutions such as family, education, and the state] and the personality of the people.

2.   Social change in a society is a consequence of changes in property relations [i.e., who owns what] and the production structure.

3.   Social class conflict [capitalists versus workers] exists in all spheres of the society and is based on class interests. (Zeitlin 1967, 79)

Later conflict theorists have modified Marx's economic determinism form of conflict theory in a number of ways. Introductory sociology students may recall the critical theory of Herbert Marcuse and the reflexive sociology with which Alvin W. Gouldner is identified. Marx and his followers were interested not only in the societal level of analysis but also in the effects of social conditions on individuals. However, the third general perspective, discussed below, places more emphasis on individual responses to social life than either functionalism or conflict perspectives.

Interactionist theory.   Earlier we noted that most sociologists strive for objectivity either by conscious awareness and suppression of personally held biases or by stating their biases openly. Interactionists are less concerned with such matters than are structural-functionalists or conflict theorists.

The general term *interactionist* includes several perspectives, each of which focuses on processes by which individual reality is socially constructed. Among these perspectives are symbolic interactionism, phenomenology, and ethnomethodology. Each of these frameworks shares an underlying assumption that the meanings that social actors assign to aspects of their lives are the appropriate subject matter for sociological study. These perspectives also believe that objectivity is not possible, that appearances are deceptive, and that "truth" lies between the lines and can be discovered by studying subjective perceptions, including those of the sociologists who do the studying. The unit of analysis (the object of study) in these perspectives is often the *language* of social interaction. Interactionists believe that there are multiple realities and that behavior, from any actor's point of view, is never irrational. For example, the attempted assassination of a politician in order to gain media attention may be seen as "rational" in that the assailant's behavior constitutes a personal adaptation to the situation (Hardert and Parker 1977, 4). In contrast, the psychiatrist who examines the assailant may see reality differently, arguing that assaultive behavior is not a constructive adaptation.

Symbolic interactionists are particularly interested in language and self-development. This includes not only the language of social interaction, but also the individual capacity to respond to what we say to ourselves (Mead 1934, 140) and to develop a sense of identity.

Ethnomethodologists, rather than assuming common sense rules as guides for social behavior, investigate the basic properties of common sense itself. This includes analysis of the situational meanings attached to language use in the society.

Phenomenologists note that individuals' subjective realities are a mix of the culturally inherited social context and their individual experiences. Together, these comprise the interpretations of reality that enable individuals to function (Berger and Luckmann 1967). Phenomenology is the study of phenomena that human consciousness generates, and rests on the belief that those who do the studying are also influenced by "inescapable subjectivity" (Holzman and Pines 1982, 97).

A theoretical framework is a perspective or point of view that includes not only where the observer stands, but also his object of study. Structural-functionalists stand somewhat farther back from everyday life, and usually study interactions between larger system parts—especially interactions that tend to produce social stability. Conflict theorists stand a little closer and study interactions between system parts—especially interactions that tend to produce or inhibit social change. Interactionists stand closest of all and study interactions between still smaller parts of the system—especially those that produce varying definitions of reality.

A word of caution: As with all attempts to encapsulate complex matters in a few sentences, this description of perspectives is a considerable oversimplification. Still, the description may help to explain why sociologists do not always agree in their analyses of social problems or on how to resolve them.

Earlier we suggested that multiple approaches to problems, taken together, would produce the most objective view of those problems. Thus, rather than present any one of the three major perspectives as the guiding framework for this text, we have used the theory that seems most appropriate to each social problem discussed, as determined by the level at which the problem exists. Table P–1 shows how two of the general theories are related to selected social problems at the interpersonal, societal, and global levels.

Note that the individual level of analysis and the interactionist theory are not represented in Table P–1. The interactionist focus on meanings and on the construction of social reality is woven throughout the chapters as appropriate (i.e., wherever such individual-level considerations are relevant).

Beyond the application of the broad, general theories displayed above, a number of social issues have been addressed through special theories of deviance. These are derivations of the three major perspectives already presented, as we show in the following section.

SPECIAL THEORIES OF DEVIANCE

Social Disorganization and Anomie Theories (Functionalism)

The study of social deviance may be approached by attempting to locate factors in structural arrangements that produce strains, that is, areas in which the fit between system parts is imperfect. *Social disorganization theory* views problematic behavior as a consequence of variable rates of social and cultural change. Society is composed of different types of structures: roles, groups, statuses, institutions, organizations, and other elements. Deviance, in this view, arises because some parts of the system change more slowly than others. Those caught between these different rates of change tend to display forms of behavior that are seen as unconventional and hence deviant. Earlier theorists of this persuasion focused on the prevalence of deviance in central cities undergoing rapid change, and

TABLE P–1 General Sociological Theories as Frameworks for the Study of Selected Social Problems, by Level of Problem

LEVEL OF PROBLEM	GENERAL SOCIOLOGICAL THEORIES	
	Functionalism	*Conflict*
Interpersonal	Singleness, Cohabitation, and Divorce	Aging in a Youth-oriented Society
Societal	Gender Roles in Transition	Work, Elites, and Economics
Global	The Urban Crisis	Energy, Civilization, and the Future

often studied delinquency, gambling, suicide, and various forms of vice.

The second perspective on deviance within the functional orientation, *anomie theory*, was developed by Robert Merton (1957, chap. 4 and 5). Merton maintains that cultural goals are similar for all in terms of material and social rewards. Not all of us, however, have equal access to the socially approved means to achieve those goals (e.g., education). Lack of legitimate means, coupled with the desire for culturally valued goals, places strain on low-income groups to achieve goals through non-normative (illegitimate) means. In Merton's view, pressure to deviate stems from the structural arrangements of society and not from individuals themselves. The disparity between goals and means leads to **anomie**—the general breakdown of norms and their constraining effects on behavior. Sociologist Albert Cohen (1955) uses this perspective to explain the emergence of low-income gangs and their delinquent behaviors. According to Cohen, gang members, unable to compete effectively because of insufficient skills, reject middle-class norms for achieving their goals and substitute their own norms. The norms of the gang set them apart as a **subculture** (a group whose norms and behaviors may come into conflict with those of the larger society).

Value Conflict Theory (General Conflict)

The value conflict approach also focuses on environmental conditions rather than individual characteristics in the production of deviance. This approach holds that problems arise when incompatible values come into contact (Fuller and Myers 1941, 24ff.). In a heterogeneous (highly diverse) society such as ours, groups often organize around special interests, values, and goals, which may be incompatible with those of other groups. This practice leads not only groups but also the individuals within them into potential conflict situations. From the perspective of each group, the other group is deviant.

An example of the conflictful situation can be found in the issue of abortion. Prochoice groups argue that decisions on abortion should be left to expectant mothers and their doctors. Prolife groups call for restrictions on such decisions, and advocate amending the Constitution in favor of their values. Another example of values in conflict involves the issue of marijuana smoking. The use of marijuana is accepted and approved by a large segment of American society (National Institute on Drug Abuse 1983). To those in power, however, marijuana smoking is unacceptable and defined as illegal—at least at present. Powerful tobacco industrialists and their government supporters and subsidizers define marijuana use as deviant.

Labeling and Differential Association Theories (Interactionist)

Howard Becker, the theorist most often associated with the labeling or societal reaction approach to deviance, calls deviance a social creation, meaning that "social groups create deviance by making rules whose infraction constitutes deviance, and by applying those rules to particular people and labeling them as outsiders" (Becker 1963, 9). Making a similar point but using the term *tagging*, Frank Tannenbaum (1937, 17ff.) contends that deviance is a matter of definition. Behaviors that children define as exciting or exhilarating forms of play, for instance, are often defined by adults as delinquent or evil or both. Stealing, truancy, and vandalism are examples. Another contributor to the labeling perspective, John Kitsuse, calls for a change in focus—from studying forms of behavior labeled deviant (e.g., suicide, drug abuse, and alcoholism) to studying processes by which people and behavior are labeled deviant. Kitsuse (1962, 248) sees deviance as a three-phase process in which a "group, community, or society: (1) interpret behavior as deviant, (2) define persons who so behave as deviant, and (3) accord them treatment considered appropriate." The labeling perspective differs from

TABLE P–2. Special Theories of Deviance as Frameworks for the Study of Selected Social Problems

I. STRUCTURAL-FUNCTIONAL THEORIES	II. GENERAL CONFLICT THEORY	III. INTERACTIONIST THEORIES
A. Social disorganization theory (War, Peace, and Government) B. Anomie theory (Poverty and Class Conflict)	A. Value conflict theory (Population, Environment, and Resources)	A. Labeling theory (Unconventional Sexuality) B. Differential association theory (Crime and Punishment)

others in that it is concerned with how behavior and people come to be defined as deviant; other perspectives study the causes of deviance, and take the labeling process for granted.

The differential association approach to deviance is articulated by Edwin H. Sutherland, who maintains that criminal behavior, for instance, is learned through the same process as noncriminal behavior. Several propositions taken from his theory (Sutherland and Cressey 1974, 75–76) express this view:

1. Criminal behavior is learned.

2. Criminal behavior is learned in interaction with other persons in a process of communication.

3. The principal part of the learning of criminal behavior occurs within intimate personal groups.

4. A person becomes delinquent because of an excess of definitions favorable to violation of the law over definitions unfavorable to violation of the law.

5. The process of learning criminal behavior by association with criminal and anticriminal patterns involves all of the mechanisms that are involved in any other learning.

Thus, both deviant and nondeviant behavior can be explained as learning processes. The only distinctions among the learned behaviors of a banker, a teacher, a nurse, and a criminal are *what is learned* and the *groups with whom they associate*. In a group within which one learns criminal behaviors, views of reality lead to definitions favoring

violation of the law more than to definitions favoring law-abiding behaviors.

Table P–2 shows how several of the social issues addressed in this text are related to these special theories of deviance.

Tables P–1 and P–2 display how all but four of the social problems that later chapters discuss are related to a major theoretical perspective. We have left it to readers to identify the appropriate approaches to interpersonal violence, drug abuse, physical and mental health, and racial and ethnic minorities, although it is safe to say that conflict *and* interactionist theories are involved. A worthwhile exercise is to try to identify the relevant frameworks before reading those chapters, and to check those decisions afterward.

In the final section of this overview, we present our plan of organization for the social issues we have selected for study.

THE STRUCTURE AND CONTENT OF THE BOOK

Our major goal in this overview has been to present and explain our approach to identifying, analyzing, and resolving social problems. We have stressed that ideology—a personal system of value-laden ideas—can distort perceptions of social reality and our ability to adequately define or resolve social problems. The general human tendency is to construct social reality to fit our own socioemotional needs. Even the most conservative sociological approach, claiming the greatest degree of objectivity, has been accused of bias in defending present social arrangements. Any sociological perspective, if applied inappropriately, may distort reality and, in any case, provides only a partial view of its subject matter.

A second goal of this overview has been to present three well-known general theoretical perspectives and several special theories of deviance.

Our last goal is to explain our plan for the structure and content of the chapters that follow. We present a consistent format in each chapter, providing (1) a definition of each social problem, (2) a view of how society has confronted the problem, (3) data based on sociological analysis of the problem, and (4) suggested policies for resolving or reducing the problem. Each chapter begins with a relevant news item indicating the contemporary aspect of the issue involved. We have also included tables, photographs, and cartoons that provide additional illustrations.

The content of the book is divided into three major sections. Part I, Human Development and Sociocultural Change, deals primarily with social problems at the interpersonal level. Part II, Social and Economic Justice, deals with problems of injustice at the societal level. Part III, The Question of Survival, presents global issues, and the "Epilogue" considers possible future directions of our society and world. We hope that this format, structured to progress from familiar to complex levels, will provide greater understanding of our social world and the social problems that can be reduced or eliminated only through our best efforts.

REFERENCES

Becker, H. S. 1963. *Outsiders: Studies in the sociology of deviance.* New York: Free Press.

Berger, P. L., and T. Luckmann. 1967. *The social construction of reality.* New York: Doubleday.

Bronowski, J. 1973. *The ascent of man.* Boston: Little, Brown.

Caldicott, H. 1978. *Nuclear madness.* Brookline, Mass.: Autumn.

Caudill, H. M. 1976. *A darkness at dawn.* Lexington, Ky.: Univ. of Kentucky Press.

Christodoulou, S. 1965. *Twentieth century sociologists.* New York: Monarch.

Cohen, A. 1955 *Delinquent boys: The culture of the gang.* Glencoe, Ill.: Free Press.

Fuller, R. C., and R. R. Myers. 1941. The natural history of a social problem. *American Sociological Review* 6 (June): 320.

Gouldner, A. W. 1970. *The coming crisis of western sociology.* New York: Basic.

Gusfield, J. 1979. Buddy, can you paradigm? The crisis of theory in the welfare state. *Pacific Sociological Review* 22:3–22.

Hardert, R. A., H. A. Parker, E. H. Pfuhl, and W. A. Anderson. 1977. *Sociology and social issues* Hinsdale, Ill.: Dryden.

Hempel, C. G. 1971. The logic of functional analysis. In *Readings in the philosophy of the social sciences,* ed. M. Brodbeck, 179–210. New York: Macmillan.

Henry, K. 1978. Three kinds of theory. In *Social problems,* ed. K. Henry, 39–47. Glenview, Ill.: Scott, Foresman.

Holzman, H. R., and S. Pines. 1982. Buying sex: The phenomenology of being a john. *Deviant Behavior* 4(1): 89–116.

Jacobs, J. 1983. *Social problems through social theory: A selective view.* Houston: Cap & Gown.

Kitsuse, J. 1962. Societal reaction to deviance: Problems of theory and method. *Social Problems* 9 (Winter): 248.

Martindale, D. 1965. Limits of and alternatives to functionalism in the social sciences. In *Functionalism in the social sciences,* ed. D. Martindale, 148ff. Philadelphia: American Academy of Political and Social Sciences (February) Monograph 5.

————. 1981. *The Nature and types of sociological theory.* Boston: Houghton Mifflin.

Marx, K. 1964. *Economic and philosophic manuscripts of 1844.* New York: International Publishers.

Mead, G. H. 1934. *Mind, self, and society.* Chicago: Univ. of Chicago Press.

Merton, R. K. 1957. *Social theory and social structure.* Glencoe, Ill.: Free Press.

Mills, C. W. 1943. The professional ideology of social pathologists. *American Journal of Sociology* 49 (September):165–80.

————. 1959. *The sociologcal imagination.* New York: Oxford Univ. Press.

Nagel, E. 1961. *The structure of science.* New York: Harcourt, Brace.

National Institute on Drug Abuse. 1983. *NIDA capsule* (February).

Ryan, W. 1978. The art of savage discovery: How to blame the victim. In *Social problems: Institutional and interpersonal perspectives,* ed. K. Henry, 31–38. Glenview, Ill.: Scott, Foresman.

Schumacher, E. F. 1975. *Small is beautiful.* New York: Harper & Row.

Sternglass, E. J. 1981. The lethal path of T.M.I. fallout (part II). *The Nation* (7 March):267–73.

Sutherland, E. H., and D. Cressey. 1974. *Criminology.* Philadelphia: Lippincott.

Tannenbaum, F. 1937. *Crime and the community.* Boston: Ginn.

Wall Street Journal. 3 February 1981.

Weber, M. 1949. *On the methodology of the social sciences.* Ed. and trans. by E. A. Shils and H. A. Finch. Glencoe, Ill.: Free Press.

Wooley, B., and F. Reid. 1975. *We be here when the morning comes.* Lexington, Ky.: Univ. of Kentucky Press.

Wright, C., and R. E. Hilbert. 1980. Value implications of the functional theory of deviance. *Social Problems* 28: 205–19.

Zeitlin, I. M. 1967. *Marxism: A reexamination.* Princeton, N.J.: Van Nostrand.

PART I

Human Development and Sociocultural Change

As you learned in the "Prologue," social problems exist at different levels of reality and may be explained from various theoretical perspectives. The theme of this section is that some problems are best understood at the *interpersonal* level, employing mainly *interactionist* theory and concepts. The five problem areas discussed in Part One are explained by theories and concepts describing how people influence one another in everyday life. Beyond this, each chapter analyzes the reaction of conventional society to those involved in, or afflicted by, the particular problem focused on in the chapter. Society's negative reaction to people's interpersonal problems generally isn't constructive and may actually tend to reinforce deviant behavior.

Specifically, Chapter 1 distinguishes interpersonal violence from societal and global violence (the latter of which will be discussed later in the book), in an attempt to find creative policy alternatives for containing the many types of violence expressed in American life. Chapter 2 explores the world of drug use and drug abuse, stressing the importance of peer group and parental influences as a key to understanding the motives behind drug use. Why has drug education been largely a failure in this country, and is it possible to get young people turned on to life instead of drugs?

Chapter 3 deals with interactionist as-

pects of sexual variance and with society's mostly negative reaction to those who engage in unconventional sexual behavior. Perhaps society would do well to *transcend* its concern for sexual variance by focusing on more pressing social problems of the day. Chapter 4 examines the special problems of the aged in our youth-oriented society, concluding that many positive things can be done to make the lives of older people more meaningful.

Finally, in Chapter 5, we explore singlehood, divorce, and cohabitation as interpersonal alternatives to traditional courtship and marriage relations in the society. Rather than referring to the *collapse* of the family in America, we should be thinking in terms of the *changing form* of the family during a period of tremendous social and economic transition.

CHAPTER 1

Interpersonal Violence

CONTENTS

The tavern rape: Cheers and no help

No one came to her aid. No one called the police. Some of the men even cheered as a 21-year-old woman, drinking in a bar in New Bedford, Mass., was assaulted and raped repeatedly for more than an hour before the eyes of at least 15 other male customers, police say. As details of the appalling incident emerged last week, the historic whaling town of New Bedford found itself at the center of a nationwide furor. The local women's center reported calls from hundreds of people who were outranged over the incident—and a candlelight vigil was scheduled at New Bedford's city hall this week to protest not only the vicious gang rape but the callousness of those who witnessed it. "This woman was treated like a piece of meat," said Debra Robbin of the women's center.

Pleas: The young mother of two entered Big Dan's—a seedy bar in the city's predominantly Portuguese North End—to buy cigarettes. Never having been there before, she was apparently unaware of its reputation in the neighborhood for gambling and brawling. But when she met a woman she knew in the bar, she stayed on for a drink. According to police accounts of the events that followed, it was after her friend departed that a man grabbed her, stripped off her clothes—except a pink sweater—and raped her on the barroom floor. Then two other men forced her to perform oral sex. As she struggled—screaming, "Stop . . . I want to get out," and pleading for help from the drinkers at the oval bar—several of them reportedly lifted her onto the pool table and raped her again and again to the cheers and applause of other bar patrons. "Knock it off—this is getting out of hand," one patron insisted, but no one listened. Finally able to flee, the woman flagged down a passing van whose occupants called the police. "I've been a cop for 18 years and investigating rapes for 10 years," said Detective Sgt. Ronald Cabral, "and I've never seen anything like this."

Police acted quickly, arresting four men between the ages of 22 and 26, all of whom pleaded not guilty to charges of rape. They were released on $1,000 bail—later increased to $200,000 for one of the men after he allegedly tried to buy a plane ticket to the Azores. District Attorney Ronald Pina also was investigating whether some of the bar's other patrons that night could be charged as accomplices. Many of those present said they were too scared to call for help. A hearing in the case was delayed until this week, but the fate of Big Dan's may already have been decided. The bar closed two days after the incident, the owner handed in its liquor license, and workmen moved in—cutting up Big Dan's oval bar with a chainsaw and removing tables, chairs, video games—and the infamous pool table itself.

Source: Newsweek 21 March 1983, 25.

DEFINING THE PROBLEM: WHAT IS VIOLENCE?

We all have heard about crimes of violence, such as "The Tavern Rape" just presented, and we have heard that the use of force and violence is increasing in Western society. Defining the various types of violence and making the point that *human* violence is always expressed in traditional (recognizable) ways is therefore necessary.

Suzanne Steinmetz and Murray Straus (1974, 4) define **physical violence** as "the intentional use of physical force on another person." Wife battering is an example of violence in a physical sense. The term **psychological violence** is used to connote the use of mental force or coercion on another person. Examples of psychological violence include assaulting a person verbally with abusive language and deliberately ignoring someone one has known for a long time. Treating people in inhumane ways through the use of psychological force can be just as violent and destructive as using physical force.

While both physical and psychological violence are applied to others at the *interpersonal* level of social relations, structural (institutional) violence occurs at the *societal* level. **Structural violence** is aggression expressed through institutional means in which people who have power and authority over others can either bestow or withhold rewards, goods, and services—even the necessities of life (Turner 1982, 286–301). Structural violence is possible because some persons are vested with status positions and social roles that carry differential **authority** (legitimate power) in various social institutional settings, such as the family or place of work. Children are punished and people are fired for "institutional" reasons. Other examples of structural violence include institutionalized (i.e., structured and somewhat permanent) societal inequality, such as poverty, racism, sexism, and ageism. We sometimes do structural violence to the poor and to minorities because available

goods and services are not fairly distributed throughout the society.

As you will learn in this chapter, some interpersonal violence is expressed within conventional group settings, and some is not. An example of interpersonal violence in a conventional setting is sports violence. Being mugged on the way to the grocery is an example of interpersonal violence outside a conventional setting. This chapter focuses mainly on the physical and psychological aspects of interpersonal violence, using conflict theory as the major explanatory principle. The discussion of structural violence, such as war and terrorism, is reserved for chapter 14, War, Peace, and Government.

Another way of viewing human violence in general is through the concept of **aggression,** defined as "the fighting instinct [drive] in beast and man which is directed against members of the same species" (Lorenz 1970, ix). The aggressive nature of humans is hard to dispute. With the exception of certain rodents, no other vertebrate habitually destroys members of its own species (Storr 1970, i). No other animal takes pleasure in the exercise of cruelty upon another organism of its own kind. All of us seem to harbor within ourselves the same aggressive impulses that have led to murder, torture, and war throughout history.

One difficulty in conceptualizing what is meant by aggression is that no clear dividing line exists between those forms of human aggression that most of us deplore and those that have survival value. For example, we disapprove of killing a person during an armed robbery (interpersonal violence), but condone killing a human being on the battlefield (institutional violence). A child's rebellion against authority is a sign of aggression, but also a sign that the child is displaying a drive toward self-development, which is a necessary part of growing up.

A tragic paradox is that those qualities that have led to human success are also the traits most likely to destroy us (Storr 1970, iv). Since humans think and communicate about abstract concepts symbolically, their capacity both for respecting life and for destroying it is greater than other members of the animal kingdom.

To explore the problem of interpersonal violence as a possible outgrowth of institutional violence, we will examine such diverse topics as violence in the family, schools, media, professional sport, cults and sects, among the nation's youth, and as it is expressed in growing homicide and suicide rates.

CONFRONTING THE PROBLEM: INTERPERSONAL VERSUS INSTITUTIONAL VIOLENCE

As comforting as it is for civilized people to think of barbarians as violent, Western civilization and various forms of institutional violence have been close partners (Tilly 1969, 4). Historians and political scientists believe that a certain amount of institutional violence is normal. The "right of resistance" was a part of the English legal tradition on which the American colonists insisted in the act of separating themselves from the mother country (Tilly 1969, 7). This realization (i.e., the right of revolution) makes recent civil strife and terrorism in such places as South and Central America, Ireland, Italy, Spain, and the Middle East more understandable.

Institutional violence did not fade out after the American Revolution, the French Revolution, and the American Civil War. Since these events, we have had violent railroad, trucking, and mining strikes, vigilante and protest movements, racial and urban violence, two world wars, and the wars in Korea and Vietnam. Western history since 1800 is violent—full of revolutions, coups, and civil wars, and scarred with conflict on a smaller scale. This violence is reflected in our folklore and literature, such as the war novels of Stephen Crane, Ernest Hemingway, and Dalton Trumbo. Hemingway's early novels and stories express a far more cruel and degrading war experience than the

Civil War depicted in Crane's *The Red Badge of Courage* (Lynn 1969, 229). Dalton Trumbo (1970, vi) describes the increasing violence and pointlessness of more recent war:

Proportionately, Viet Nam has given us eight times as many paralytics as World War II, three times as many totally disabled, 35% more amputees. Senator Cranston of California concludes that out of every hundred army veterans receiving compensation for wounds received in action in Viet Nam, 12.4% are totally disabled. Totally.

Recently, Americans have become concerned with the increase in interpersonal violence, such as family and youth violence, media violence, and mass murder. These newer forms of aggression may be related to institutional violence in that they all show a tendency toward **anarchy,** or a loss of social and political control, in Western society.

Let us now turn to analysis of the problem of interpersonal violence and how it differs from structural or institutional violence.

ANALYZING THE PROBLEM: A SOCIOLOGICAL PERSPECTIVE

Youth Violence

What is happening in our larger American cities exemplifies youth violence: young muggers who rob, rape, and sometimes kill people on or near subway platforms in New York City is one example. In the first seven months of 1980, 7,234 New York subway crimes were reported—an increase of 8.4 percent over the same period of time in 1979 (*Associated Press* 5 October 1980). In addition, sixteen people including three transit police officers were slain in that time span, compared with sixteen in all of 1979. One youth slashed subway riders with a meat cleaver. Such stories of violence along the subway make crime a grim, daily preoccupation for riders.

Other bizarre cases of youth violence include a boy and girl who paid to have their father killed so they could "smoke pot" and go on a spending spree; a fifteen-year-old boy who shot subway riders in the head because he "got a kick out of blowing them away"; and a twelve-year-old boy charged with shooting his mother, two sisters, and a niece because he felt deprived of "material things." According to a report by the Ford Foundation (Dreyfuss 1980, 38), juvenile arrests for violent crimes such as homicide, rape, robbery, and assault increased 293 percent between 1960 and 1975.

When a ten-year-old stabs an eight-year-old to death during a minor argument (Dreyfuss 1980, 38), it is time to stop and take stock of where we are going. According to psychiatrist Dr. Daniel Jacobs, "The greatest contributor to violent adolescence is child abuse, since those children who become violent usually have a history of violence done to them" (Dreyfuss 1980, 40, 58). Educational psychologist Abraham Avesar thinks that violence is a sign that a child is not getting what he or she needs to grow up: someone who cares (Dreyfuss 1980, 60). Sociologists Marvin E. Wolfgang and F. Ferracutti (1967, 158) hypothesize that violence is part of the normative (value) system of a subculture, and that this system is reflected in the psychological traits of participants in the subculture. Sociologist Timothy Hartnagel (1980) found partial support for this sub-

One type of youth violence is seen in this attempt to intimidate another person. Parks, unlighted areas, and out of the way places tend to attract young people and, hence, become natural settings for youth violence.

culture of violence hypothesis, using survey data collected from delinquent adolescents.

Street gangs and outlaw motorcycle groups tend to attract older youth, from fourteen to thirty years old. In Los Angeles, youth gangs are said to be responsible for 15 to 20 percent of all murders, assaults with deadly weapons, robberies, and shootings into inhabited dwellings (*Arizona Republic* 20 August 1978). Much of this gang behavior is related to the use of alcohol, cocaine, and other drugs.

In Ohio, motorcycle gangs have graduated from heavy drinking and mayhem to dealing in drugs, prostitution, and murder for hire. According to the *Cleveland Plain Dealer*, bikers began selling pot and heroin in the early 1970s and now handle LSD, PCP (Angel Dust), and methamphetamine (speed). The Hell's Angels and the Outlaws are said to have a powerful nationwide network of motorcycle gangs, some of which have hidden interests in bars and other businesses (Wiessler 1982, 65). The leader of a biker gang in southern Ohio describes violence with a rival gang in the following way:

They shoot up a car, you shoot up a car and it goes from there. They machine gun my house. We shoot a guy on the street. . . . The funny thing about a *war* [italics ours] is that it just stops. That's it. It's over. Everything goes back to the way it was before (*Cincinnati Enquirer* 31 July 1973).

Violence in the Media

Hidden violence also is pervasive in our society. Americans seem to have a tremendous attraction to violence in both its overt and covert forms. Much of our literature deals with the topics of sex and violence. These topics are also stressed in advertising, sport, television, movies, humor, and pop art. Many children's cartoons and films for young people depict violence in the act of someone (or some animal) being hurt or put down. Compared with most British humor, American humor tends to be the exaggerated, slapstick variety.

The media's glorification of sex, aggression, and various types of deviant behavior may be contributing to interpersonal violence in our society. Newspapers, for example, probably had much to do with creating the outlaw image of motorcycle groups. The first biker incident picked up by the media was the American Motorcycle Association races ("gypsy tour") held in Hollister, California, over the Fourth of July weekend in 1947. The *Press* describes the cyclists as having "taken over the town," racing and performing stunts along Main Street (*New York Times* 7 July 1947). "Wino Willie," one of the founders of the Boozefighters club, denies that Hollister was "taken over" by the bikers. Further, while the *Times* cites thirty-eight arrests, the Boozefighters recall only about ten.

Distortion in the press is one problem, but movies that may incite gang violence are another. *The Warriors*, a movie about rival street gangs in New York City, was linked to fatal attacks on 2 persons during and after its initial showing (*Chicago Sun-Times* 20 February 1979). In Oxnard, California, an eighteen-year-old was stabbed to death in a gang fight in the lobby of the theater showing the movie. In Boston, two youths charged with a murder had just seen *The Warriors* before the murder occurred. A *selective* process may be operating in these cases, however, wherein a film like *The Warriors* tends to attract more aggressive individuals. Hence, rather than causing their violent behavior, this kind of film could tend to reinforce those already disposed to violence.

Regarding TV violence, researchers Patricia B. Higgins and Marla W. Ray (1979, 26) raise another interesting question about our apparent desensitization to violence. They found an "inordinate number" of hand-held weapons on prime-time "action shows," but very few people depicted as injured. That is, 84 percent of the shots from handguns and 81 percent of the shots from rifles and shotguns were misses. Hence, Higgins and Ray wonder if this unrealistic depiction of violence on TV will lead viewers to believe that weapons use is not very severe.

Regarding the hypothesis that TV violence leads (unconsciously) to aggressive behavior in children or adults or both, the results are mixed; that is, *some research supports the violence hypothesis, and some does not.* Psychiatrist Roderick Gorney found (Nietzke 1978, 14) that viewing violent shows like "Hawaii Five-O" led to a "slight increase in aggressive mood" for adult males. Conversely, viewing helpful or "prosocial" shows, like "The Waltons," led to a "significant decrease in aggressive mood" for those adult male viewers. Further, the wives of the males who watched violent shows reported that their husbands exhibited a high level of hurtful behavior, while the prosocial viewers showed less hurtful behavior. Again, a selective process may be operating.

Other research tends to confirm the hypothesis that TV violence leads to aggressive behavior in children and adolescents. A report (Liebert and Neale 1972, 38) by an advisory committee to the United States surgeon general concludes that experimental and survey evidence suggests that viewing filmed violence observably increases some children's aggressive behavior. A study by the University of Pennsylvania's Annenberg School of Communications indicates that children who spend more than four hours a day watching television believe the world is more violent than do children who watch less TV. The study also found that almost 90 percent of the characters in television shows aimed at children are involved in violent acts (i.e., hurting or killing a person or threatening harm).

A six-year study of 1,565 British teenagers by researcher William Belson indicates that "the evidence was very strongly supportive of the hypothesis that long-term exposure to violence increases the degree to which boys engage in violence of a serious kind" (Muson 1978, 50). Belson also found that stories that present violence in a very realistic way tend to produce more *actual* violence (Muson 1978, 53). Conversely, he found that

slapstick violence, violent cartoons, sports other than boxing or wrestling, and science fiction violence do not appear to promote serious violence (Muson 1978, 53–54). Ironically, Belson's research was supported by a $290,000 grant from the Columbia Broadcasting System, which has not been eager to publicize his results.

Finally, a report released in May 1982 by the National Institute of Mental Health (NIMH) says that "violence on television does lead to aggressive behavior by children and teenagers who watch the programs" (*U.S. News & World Report* 1982, 27). In one five-year study of 732 children, several kinds of aggression—including fighting and delinquency—were positively correlated with the total amount of television viewing.

Other studies, however, do not lend as much support to the hypothesis that TV violence leads to aggressive attitudes or behavior or both among young people. Social scientist Bradley S. Greenberg (1975) studied British school children to see if the frequency of watching TV programs with "recurrent violent themes" related to aggressive attitudes. He concluded that only a moderate relationship existed between watching TV programs high in violent themes and possessing aggressive attitudes toward others. Similarly, sociologists Timothy Hartnagel, James Teevan, and Jennie McIntyre (1975) found "only minimal support" for the hypothesis that exposure to violent TV programming is related to aggression among adolescents.

Perhaps the NIMH findings are stronger than some of the other findings because the NIMH studies extended over a longer period of time. At any rate, the NIMH data leave us thinking that violent television is still on trial.

Now that we have analyzed two of the newer forms of force and violence in Western society—youth violence and media violence—traditional types of aggression may be easier to understand. Here we have in mind sociological analysis of violence in the schools, in sports, and in the family, along with rape, homicide, suicide, and terrorism.

Violence in the Schools

Protest, violent disruption, and some other kinds of collective behavior have increased in American society since the early 1960s. Most institutions in the society—perhaps the educational system more than any other—felt the effects of violence either directly or indirectly. An estimated 1,000 to 3,000 underground newspapers sprang up in the schools, and many students rejected education for a drug-oriented environment.

A new wave of unrest and violence seems to be sweeping through the schools of urban and suburban America. School violence is now moving to the suburbs, which troubles both educators and parents. Handguns, ice picks, explosives, and other weapons are turning up at schools in wealthy suburbs of Los Angeles, Denver, Washington, D.C., and New York. The National Institute of Education estimates that 5,200 teachers are attacked and 6,000 are robbed *each month* in the United States (*U.S. News & World Report* 1979b, 63). Drugs, violence, and turmoil are several important reasons for the surge in teachers' strikes and the loss of many capable teachers (*U.S. News & World Report* 1983, 41).

Recent school violence includes the following specific examples (McGuire 1980): a high school student in Virginia bit off a third of his teacher's ear during a scuffle; a third-grader in rural Missouri twisted a teacher's thumb, tearing several ligaments; and students in California, angry over low grades, set their teacher's hair on fire. Other examples (*U.S. News & World Report,* 1979b) include two boys in New Orleans who threw a smaller child off a second-floor balcony, and a thirteen-year-old who shot and killed his English teacher because he received a failing grade. Further, rape in school hallways and restrooms is no longer recorded as a rare event (*United Press International* 30 August 1979), students on drugs rob other students to pay for their drugs, and some students consume alcoholic drinks in the parking lots and then beat up other students. Today's teenagers run a greater risk of personal violence in schools than on the streets, particularly in the junior high schools.

Violence and vandalism have altered the face of American schools. Educator Willard McGuire says that school vandalism costs $600 million a year, which is about the same amount spent yearly on the nation's school textbooks (*Arizona Republic* 25 September 1976). Over a six-year period, Los Angeles County schools lost an estimated $100 million as a result of muggings, lawsuits, theft, and vandalism (*Time* 1980).

Much has been written about schools that casts light on possible reasons for the growing disruption and protest. Some argue that teaching needs to be made more "professional." Others contend that teaching is already too professional (i.e., too encrusted with bureaucratic requirements and too bogged down in its own technical jargon) (*Time* 1980). Charles E. Silberman (1970, 10–11) charges that America's system of public education is "intellectually sterile." He further says that a general "mindlessness" of those in authority blocks educational reform in this country. Silberman is an advocate of the open classroom, in which students work at their own pace.

Violence in Sports

Jon Morris, a center for professional football's Chicago Bears and later for New England's Patriots, retired recently after fifteen seasons in the National Football League. His retirement speech contained some telling comments about the game he loved so much:

Violence . . . is going to kill the game. The competition for jobs and big money is making the game immensely more violent. You see it especially among the younger players. They'll do anything to get into the NFL. . . . I think the league is in serious trouble unless something is done (Underwood 1980, 57).

When Morris referred to the increasing violence in professional football, he could have been referring to any of the following incidents: the "hit" (i.e., tackle) Oakland's Jack Tatum put on the Patriots' wide receiver Darryl Stingley, which left Stingley paralyzed from the neck down; the Cardinals' Tim Kearney "clothes lining" Eagle running back Dave Hampton, crashing a forearm into Hampton's neck; Mel Morgan of the Bengals throwing a forearm into the face of Steeler receiver John Stallworth; Pittsburgh's tackle "Mean Joe" Greene punching Denver center Mike Montler, after he had already punched guard Paul Howard; and the Cardinals' Conrad Dobler hitting linebacker Bob Matheson in the head.

In almost every case, a rationalization (instead of a reason) is given for the aggressive behavior. Tatum is quoted (*United Press International* 11 January 1980) as saying, "I like to believe that my best hits border on felonious assault." Kearney defends his blow as "perfectly legal," and Greene says he was "being held illegally" and thus "had to go outside the rules" (Underwood 1978b, 35–36). If the sport had been professional basketball instead of football, Jon Morris's concern likely would have focused on Rudy Tomjanovich, whose face was crushed by a Kermit Washington punch in December 1977 (*Chicago Sun-Times* 14 February 1978). Tomjanovich has never completely recovered from that violent blow, which ended his career.

The greatest number of serious injuries are sustained in football, however—not basketball. Underwood (1978a, 71–72) estimates that yearly the great American game (1) injures a million high school players at approximately 20,000 schools, (2) injures 70,000 college players at more than 900 schools, and (3) inflicts a 100 percent yearly casualty rate (i.e., at least one injury for every player) on the National Football League. Considering knee injuries alone, 25 percent of lost-time injuries to pro football players involve the knee (Underwood 1978b,

37), which is the most vulnerable part of an athlete's body and unsuitable for football. The Detroit Lions, for example, had twenty-two knee operations over a three-year period.

In 1976, psychiatry professor Arnold Mandell wrote a book about his experiences as an unpaid locker-room analyst for the San Diego Chargers (Underwood 1980). In *The Nightmare Season*, Dr. Mandell details professional football players' use of amphetamines (speed) and his attempts to wean players from dangerous street speed by giving them prescription drugs. This attempt backfired when Mandell was banned from further contact with players, but he continued his crusade to get amphetamines out of football. He said amphetmaines were "the single factor that causes unnecessary violence in pro football today" (Underwood 1980, 71). Doses as high as 150 milligrams result in a kind of "pre-psychotic paranoid rage." This five-hour temper tantrum produces the late hits, fights, and assaults on quarterbacks that are ruining pro football.

Another issue in the sport arena is that of violent acts committed by fans—against one another and against players (*Arizona Republic* 27 March 1983). In professional baseball, players have to slug their way through the fans to get off the field after the big games. During some of the regular games, outfielders duck everything from bottles to firecrackers, thrown by the fans. From time to time, Pittsburgh's Dave Parker (now with Cincinnati) refused to play in front of hometown fans after being hit, and nearly hit, with numerous flying objects. All-Star players Pete Rose and Steve Garvey have been subjected to similar fan violence during their lengthy careers.

Sociologist Harry Edwards says that violence in sports tends to be magnified by television (*Associated Press* 17 November 1977). Television fans can identify with violence in place of what they cannot do on the sports field. Fan violence is a way for spectators to break out of their normally passive roles and become as competitive as the stars they applaud and emulate. Thus, as long as people watch sports instead of participating, there will probably be violence in the stands. What is frightening is that we are now being asked by sport to respect its violence (Gilbert and Twyman 1983, 62–74).

Family Violence

The term **family violence** includes child neglect and abuse, incest, wife and husband battering, and battering of the elderly, including parent abuse. According to a survey by sociologists Murray Straus, Richard Gelles, and Suzanne Steinmetz (1980), victims of family violence in the United States in 1975 totaled about 8 million persons, or roughly the population of New York City. These sociologists also found that within the span of one year (1) 16 out of every 100 couples have violent confrontations of one kind or another (2) 3 of every 100 children are kicked, bitten, or punched by their parents, and (3) more than one-third of all brothers and sisters severely attack each other.

Violence among family members used to be something that occurred frequently but was seldom discussed. This began to change in the mid-1960s, however, as one form of family violence after another was exposed. In the early 1970s, the focus shifted from child beating and abuse to the topic of sexual abuse of children. In the mid-1970s, the focus turned to wife beating, and in the late-1970s and early 1980s, husband beating became a topic of discussion. Other recent topics of interest include sibling abuse, parent abuse, and abuse of the elderly, which the British call "granny bashing" *(Los Angeles Times* 6 June 1979).

Child abuse and neglect.   According to the survey by Straus, Gelles, and Steinmetz (1980), the rate of child abuse is 129 percent higher in families in which abuse of either the wife or the husband takes place. Gelles estimates that in 1975, between 1.4 and 1.9

million children were subjected to physical injury at the hands of family members. These numbers seem to be very high, but some family experts say that the amount of family violence has probably decreased since colonial times, when both wives and children were considered slaves (DeMause 1975; Dobash and Dobash 1977–78). Further, we learn that the highly fluctuating child abuse rates (60,000 reported cases in 1972,[1] compared with over a million reported cases in 1975) may not be trustworthy. The reported rates skyrocketed after Congress passed the Child Abuse and Prevention Act in 1974, which granted $85 million for the treatment of child abuse. Hence, actual child abuse rates may not have fluctuated much over the years. Mainly, our *perception* of the amount of child abuse may have changed, and that view is highly influenced by political, economic, and media events.

The fact of widespread child abuse and neglect remains, however, in spite of conflicting perceptions from one decade, or one year, to the next. **Child abuse** refers to any type of physical or psychological abuse inflicted on a child. This type of injury includes everything from bruises and welts (most common) to poisoning (least common). The most common manner of inflicting child abuse is through beatings with various instruments; the least common method is by drowning. Typical instruments used in physical abuse of children range from fists to guns.

Typical forms of **child neglect** include abandonment for long periods of time; lack of supervision; nutritional, medical, dental, and educational neglect; inappropriate or insufficient clothing; shelter and emotional neglect; and moral neglect (i.e., not providing ethical guidance).

The following quotation from an early child abuse report demonstrates that the

---

1. An estimate from the University of Colorado School of Medicine.

forms of child abuse have not changed much in recent years:

Seven out of ten battered children are under 5, and many of them are less than a year old. Most often, the child suffers injury to the head from repeated blows, as well as broken arms and legs from violent pulling and shaking. The commonest serious injury is a skull fracture accompanied by the formation of a hematoma, or blood clot, on the brain. X-rays of the limbs often show multiple breaks in various stages of healing, indicating that the child has been subjected to repeated assaults (Helfer and Kempe 1974).

Initially, these researchers noted, the parent usually blames the injuries on a fall or declares that the child "bruises easily."

While most experts believe that child abuse is learned behavior (i.e., most child abusers were abused as children), the reasons for child abuse are a mixture of psychological, sociological, and situational factors (*Time* 1979b). One psychological factor is the emotional immaturity of the parent, which is usually associated with a lack of knowledge about parenting. A sociological factor is the patriarchal notion that "sparing the rod will spoil the child" (i.e., discipline is the traditional privilege and responsibility of a father, and he should exercise it over his children). Situational factors include such stressful life crises as loss of a job, extended illness, divorce and separation, and moving into a new area. Inflation, recession, and other economic difficulties may tend to aggravate the child abuse problem.

Sociologists have no easy answer to the reasons for child abuse and neglect. According to Straus, Gelles, and Steinmetz (1980), the incidence of family violence is highest among the urban poor, blue-collar workers, people under thirty or without religious affiliation, families with a jobless husband, and those with four to six children. High-income families exhibit less *physical* violence toward one another. Families with incomes over $20,000 per year seem able to handle more stress before they begin to abuse each other (*Knight-Ridder News Service* 27 No-

vember 1979). The families who live on marginal incomes are those who take the brunt of any recession and have higher levels of family violence. Violence does occur, however, among affluent, educated families as well.

Battered women.   Violence by men against women is not a new phenomenon. What is new is the public admission that beating of women occurs in civilized countries and the insistence by women and men that such violence is no longer acceptable. With the emergence of the women's movement, battered women have become much less tolerant of violence against them, as evidenced by the increase in the number of retreat shelters for battered women throughout the United States and England (Gelles 1974, 14).

In 1971, women in the United Kingdom raised an outcry about violence against women so that authorities could no longer turn their heads away from the problem. Erin Pizzey helped found Chiswick's Women's Aid, now renamed Chiswick Family Rescue. The need for refuge was so great that the shelter was immediately overflowing with battered women and their children. Pizzey wrote about her experiences and made a short film to alert women around the world to the problem. By 1973, reports of wife-battering occasionally appeared in newspapers, but very little research had been published about violence directed at wives. In 1975, the National Organization for Women (NOW) proclaimed marital violence a major problem and established a national task force on battered women and household violence. In addition, the International Tribunal on Crimes Against Women was held in Brussels, Belgium in 1976.

Finally, the research findings began to accumulate. According to the national survey by Straus et al. (1980), 3.8 percent (1.8 million) of American wives were beaten by their husbands in 1975. In one month of 1980 alone, thirty-one cases of wife abuse were reported in Raleigh, North Carolina

(Leavy 1981, 96). Some maintain that American women are safer outside their homes, as more of them die in their own bedrooms than anywhere else (*Knight-Ridder News Service* 27 November 1979).

In Scotland, sociologists Dobash and Dobash (1977–78, 436–37) studied police records in Glasgow and Edinburgh for 1974 and found that (1) only 15 percent of female victims were assaulted by persons outside their families; (2) 38.7 percent of reports of all violence involved males against unrelated males, while 26 percent involved violence by husbands against their wives; and (3) only 1.1 percent of reported family assaults involved wives against husbands, compared with 76 percent involving husbands against wives.

Dobash and Dobash (1983) recently found that 75 percent of 109 battered women they interviewed experienced violence *within the first year of marriage*. In the beginning, the violence was trivial, but it gradually became more severe. If domestic violence continued, these Scottish women usually went to family and friends first and then to police or a shelter home. The police, however, rarely arrested men for domestic violence, and the women were told to "seek private solutions" (Dobash and Dobash 1983).

Why does a woman stay married to someone who beats her? Most important are the debilitating effects of depression and loss of self-esteem. The husband may have told his wife repeatedly that she is homely, a bad wife or mother or both, a bad lover or can't cook. In other words, emotional abuse is frequently tied to physical abuse. Traditional social constraints against divorce, along with the stigma of admitting to past beatings, keep some couples together. The attitudes of police are not always helpful, since police are injured more often in responding to "domestic disturbance" calls than any other complaint category. The FBI estimates that about 20 percent of American police deaths and 28 percent of assaults on police officers occur while officers are intervening in family fights (*Los Angeles Times* 6 June 1979).

Social workers and clergy also are not always responsive to the problems of battered women. Their "hands are tied" in some states where battering one's wife is not illegal. Tennessee, Rhode Island, and Hawaii have special statutes that make most spouse abuse a misdemeanor. Some wives refuse to press charges against their husbands, attack the police or social workers when they arrive, or do both. If the wife does press charges, the husband can return home and beat her again after he is released. Dobash and Dobash (1979, 28) summarize the battered wife's predicament in the following way:

Regardless of the source of the unhelpful response, women find it very difficult to leave a violent husband: she is often threatened with severe reprisals if she attempts to leave, has few places she might go even temporarily, and setting up a permanent household is beset with enormous problems of finding accommodation, employment and child care facilities and exacerbated by isolation and lack of adult company. A woman does not stay because of her "need" for excitement or violence, but because she becomes trapped in the relationship.

Other factors related to why women stay with men who beat them involve their emotional dependency and the tendency to rationalize the husband's behavior. Many women in our society are economically and emotionally dependent because they marry early, lack advanced education related to specialized job skills, and may be living in a new area in which they have few friends or relatives who might help. Battered women rationalize the husband's behavior the way abused children often do—in order not to lose the "love" of the abusive person. Abused persons can fall into a type of dependency called **learned helplessness** (Walker 1977–78). This concept is based on experiments in which caged dogs did not prevent themselves from being shocked and young rats did not save themselves from drowning, after they had learned in earlier experiments that their efforts to escape were fruitless. The theory of learned helplessness focuses on the psychological reasons why a battered woman becomes dependent on her husband and does not leave a violent relationship (Dobash and Dobash 1983).

The types of men who abuse their spouses appear to come from all kinds of backgrounds and income groups, and to be of all ages and races. As in the case of family violence in general, lower-income persons with limited education and lower-status jobs are more highly represented among wife abusers than are high-income persons (Straus et al. 1980). Alcohol is definitely a factor in most households in which husbands batter women and children (Leavy 1981, 95). Further, the opening of 170 new shelter homes for abused women and children in America between 1975 and 1979 (*U.S. News & World Report* 1979a) underscores the dimensions of the problem.

Rape

Another form of aggression against women, usually committed by a stranger to the victim, is rape. We say "usually" a stranger, because cases of rape and beatings within marriage have occurred, such as that of Greta Rideout versus her husband, John (New York Times, 1978). Further, some women are raped by persons who could be termed acquaintances. In one study of rape, sociologist Sharon McCombie (1978, 241) found that 28 percent of the women raped were in the company of their assailants before the actual assault. Nevertheless, in the highest proportion of cases, the assailant is unknown to the victim before the assault.

McCombie (1978, 237) defines **rape** as "a total attack upon the person which affects physical, psychological, and social well-being." Her sample was composed of seventy rape victims who received crisis counseling at Beth Israel Hospital in an urban residential area of Boston. The women in

her study were mainly middle-class whites who represented a segment of the rape victim population about which little is known. The women in McCombie's sample tended to be young (fifteen to twenty-five years old), single, and well-educated. Forty percent were students and 50 percent had attended college or graduate school. The background of these women appears to destroy the myth that most women who are raped are "asking for it" (i.e., doing something provocative to encourage the rapist at the time of the assault).

McCombie did find (1978, 240) that eleven women, or 15 percent of the sample, had been raped or sexually assaulted before—in several cases by the same man. Approximately half of McCombie's sample said they were afraid of reprisal from their assailants (1978, 242), and most of the women felt "terrified and shaken" or "numbness and disbelief" after the attack (1978, 244). The most prevalent response immediately after the assault was to seek out a friend or relative. Regarding long-term counseling, 74 percent of the victims said they would turn to family members for emotional support (McCombie 1978, 248). Clearly, traditional sex role socialization does not prepare women for rape, and some men know this. McCombie found (1978, 244) that 35 percent of the women in her sample offered no resistance. We are not suggesting that there is a right way to react during an assault, but the Center Against Sexual Assault (CASA) in Phoenix, Arizona recommends that if a woman is going to resist during a confrontation, she should resist *during the first several minutes or not at all.* CASA also recommends that more women learn self-defense techniques and avoid putting themselves in defenseless positions and locations.

Who rapes others? Rapists seem to come from all walks of life; no link to social class background is apparent, and their personalities are similar to those of the average male in the population (*Cincinnati Horizons* 1978, 10). Rapists seem to be motivated more by a need to express power, domination, and exploitation of women than by the idea of sexual gratification. Many of these "anger" rapists are sexually impotent in both normal and rape situations.

According to the *Uniform Crime Reports* (U.S. Department of Justice 1981) a forcible rape occurs every six minutes in the United States. Many such attacks are never reported, however, and the actual rates are thought to be five to ten times higher than the official statistics. Further, rapes ending in murder are not recorded as rapes but as homicides. Thus, a rape actually occurs about every two minutes in America. Feminist leader Deborah Flick concludes (*Associated Press* 28 September 1980) that one of every four girls born in the United States will be raped or molested by the time she is eighteen years old. Author Flick says that *all* women are victims of violence, whether they are raped or are simply afraid to walk alone at night.

Homicide and Suicide

Homicide (murder of another) and suicide (self-murder) can be viewed as expressions of two different types of aggression—the first directed against others and the second against the self. Sociologists Andrew F. Henry and James F. Short, Jr. (1964, 14–17) examined the relationship of suicide and homicide to the business cycle in the United States. Their theory of suicide and homicide is an elaboration of sociologist Emile Durkheim's earlier theory of anomie (i.e., normlessness). Durkheim (1951) proposed that an increase in the rate of suicides follows any disturbance in the societal order. Henry and Short were concerned primarily with economic crises as reflected in periods of both economic depression and prosperity.

Henry and Short's (1964) data show that while suicide rates tend to rise in economic depression and fall in prosperity, rates for murder and other types of violent crime tend to rise in prosperity and fall during economic depression. Although suicide rates increase in most social status levels during economic depression, with the exception of elderly, poor black women (*United Press International* 19 March 1983), the degree of increase is greatest in the higher-status categories in which the relative loss of social status is greater than in the lower-status categories. Further, homicide rates among high-status whites also increase during economic recession, while homicide rates among low-status blacks decrease. Thus, the murder data suggest that high-status categories suffer a greater relative loss of social status during business recession and depression than do the low-status categories. As we move down the social class scale, the response of suicide to business depression decreases and the response of homicide to business prosperity increases. Henry and Short tentatively assume that suicide and homicide are alike in that *they are both aggressive reactions to frustration.*

Durkheim suggested earlier that subordinate social status works to provide immunity against suicide, as in the case of elderly black women, because poverty is a restraint in itself. This is especially true when other external restraints (e.g., family and religion) on the individual are strong. In this case, aggression generated by frustration may be directed *outwardly against another person.* Conversely, when external constraints are weak, aggression generated by life's frustrations may be directed *against the self* (Henry and Short 1964, 17).

Because of the positive correlation between higher-status position and higher suicide rates, persons of high social status are assumed to be more sensitive to economic disturbances than persons of low status. Hence, during periods of economic instability, males, whites, some categories of young people, and persons with high incomes tend to have higher suicide rates than women, most ethnic and racial minorities, elderly, poor black women, and persons with low incomes.

The general trends stated above have exceptions, however. One exception is in the area of age, in which the elderly are becoming a more highly suicidal group (Greenbaum 1983). Apparently, health considerations and the feeling of uselessness are related to increasing suicide rates with age.

Another exception occurs among the ethnic and racial minorities, such as blacks (Seiden 1970, 24) and native Americans (National Institute of Mental Health 1974), where suicide rates for younger males are much higher than the national averages controlling for age groups. The suicide rate among white, adolescent females has also increased recently. Note, however, that nearly three times as many males as females *commit* suicide, but nearly ten times as many females as males *attempt* suicide (Greenbaum 1983).

Although America's overall suicide rate has not varied much in the past fifty years, the rate for all young people nearly tripled between 1955 and 1978, and the rate in the 1980s is even higher, as shown in figure 1–1 (Greenbaum 1983). Among all fifteen-to twenty-four-year-olds, the suicide rate rose from 5.2 per 100,000 in 1960 to 12.4 in 1978 (*Arizona Republic* 14 November 1982). For white males, the rate went from 8.2 to 20.8 in that same time period. Fear of economic

FIGURE 1–1. Deadly Trend

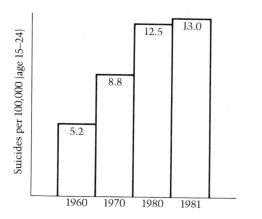

Source: U.S.N. & WR. 20, June 1983, 65.
Data from U.S. Dept. of Health and Human Services.

hard times seems to be a key factor in the national trend toward higher rates of youth suicide (*Associated Press* 30 September 1982). Actual suicides by children under fourteen years of age are still rare, but researchers are finding that attempted suicides and psychological depression are common among emotionally disturbed youth (*Time* 1978, 82).

Other categories of Americans are also considered more likely to commit suicide. Called "high-risk" groups, they include persons with serious physical ailments and those who are single, divorced, and widowed. Any sudden increase in suicide rates, however, suggests that a factor may be operating that has general influence over large numbers of people in the society, including the high-risk groups. Such a variable is the relative economic prosperity of the society. At least some of the general increase in American suicide rates is due to recent increases in unemployment and underemployment.

More than 50,000 persons commit suicide in the United States each year (Greenbaum 1983). Many actual suicides are disguised as being related to alcohol or drug abuse, workaholic behavior that leads to cancer or heart attacks, and various types of risk-taking behavior—for example, hazardous driving. If it were not for the fact that only *acknowledged* suicides are listed on death certificates, the suicide rate would be higher. Alleged suicides are not classified by medical examiners as *official* suicides.

Psychologist Edwin S. Shneidman (1976) defines **suicide** as "the human act of self-inflicted, self-intentioned cessation." Shneidman (1976, 604–19) summarizes much of what is generally known about suicide in the following way:

1. Women tend to *attempt* suicide more often, while men tend to *complete* it more often.

2. For whites, young adulthood and middle age tend to be the most common times for suicide; blacks and other minorities tend to

commit suicide during their twenties or earlier.

3. People who threaten or attempt suicide
are more likely than others to actually complete suicide.

4. Suicidal persons generally find it difficult to have "normal" social relationships.

5. An increase in suicide rates generally
follows economic depression in a society.
Further, as the world becomes more complex, thoughts of suicide seem to be more
prevalent.

6. Suicide is more common among those
who have a history of psychological disorder; however, suicidal people are not necessarily mentally ill.

7. With the possible exception of Quaaludes (or methaqualone, a depressant) no
evidence exists that any one drug directly
causes suicide.

Suicide is clearly not a simple problem to
understand from either a societal or an interpersonal point of view. Yet, suicide does
not often occur without warning. Some categories of people are more susceptible than
others. Individuals who are suicide risks
give warnings that those close to them can
recognize. Suicidal behavior often forms a
logical pattern and is potentially understandable, as we will see in the next section
on Jonestown.

Violence in a Sect: Jonestown

Cults are usually defined as small groups
that are innovative in purpose, informal, and
spontaneous, and that lack a definite hierarchy of authority (Richardson 1979, 159–60).
The Manson Family is an example of a cult
that degenerated into violent behavior.

Following the definition of a **sect** as more
authoritarian, elitist, and crystallized than a
cult, the People's Temple can be viewed as a
sect attempting to become a **commune** or
intentional community at Jonestown, Guyana. The San Francisco chapter of the People's Temple began in 1971, but its leader,
Jim Jones, moved it to Guyana in mid-1977

after stories of his excesses began to appear
in the press.

Initially, the activities of the People's
Temple appeared socially and religiously
conventional, peaceful, and law-abiding.
Reverend Jones, preaching against racism,
sexism, and ageism, was viewed as epito-
mizing the American dream. He had opened
the first People's Temple in Indianapolis in
1955 and had been successful there, being
named head of that city's human rights
commission six years later (*Associated Press*
26 November 1978). After stints in Brazil,
Indiana (again), and Okiah, California, Jones
moved his flock to San Francisco. With his
long sideburns and dark glasses, his appearance was not typically ministerial, but his
success continued.

Gradually, however, Jones's behavior became more eccentric and violent. He increasingly worried that a nuclear holocaust
would destroy the world (*Phoenix Gazette*
21 November 1979). Then, like Charles
Manson, Jones shifted to the idea that a gi-
gantic race war would destroy the world
(Kilduff and Javers 1978, 55). Jeannie Mills,
a former member of the People's Temple, was
frightened the first time she heard Jones, but
her husband and daughter liked him, and
the family continued to attend church. Still,
certain things about the church continued
to bother her, such as the orchestrated way
in which twenty-five people simultaneously
and immediately lined up on the platform to
give their testimonials. Others noted the
unique social structure of the church that
divided the membership into four hierarchical levels, with Jones at the top. The second
level consisted of from twelve to twenty in-
ner-circle advisers called the Angels, a large
majority of whom were white women. The
third level was the planning commission,
and the fourth level was the security force—
Jones's armed guards.

Soon Jones began to use sex to win converts to his church (*Phoenix Gazette* 23 November 1979). About a dozen advisers, both
men and women, admitted to Mrs. Mills
that they had had sex relations with Jones.
Mike Cartmell, another former member of

the People's Temple, gave the following account:

Jones realized the power of sex in destroying stable family relationships. In some cults you have communal living. In People's Temple, Jones . . . made himself the only legitimate object of sexual desire. (Kilduff and Javers 1978, 55).

After a few other incidents, the Mills family announced that they would be leaving the church. Leaving, however, did not turn out to be as simple as they had hoped. For nearly two years they were threatened by phone calls, anonymous letters, and personal visits from advisers. They were told they would be beaten or killed if they ever spoke out against the church (*Phoenix Gazette* 24 November 1979). Further, friends of the late Reverend Jones confirmed to federal officials that Jones had kept a hit list of persons to be murdered in case he was ever arrested or killed (*Los Angeles Times* 6 December 1978).

Even after the Mills family had departed, the situation at the People's Temple grew more intense. Jones was holding six- to eight-hour planning commission meetings on Wednesday nights. Important politicians who publicly supported Jones didn't know what was going on behind locked doors.

Jones wanted parishioners to call him "Dad" so that he could paddle them for such sins as smoking or leaving a stove burning. Deviants were told to box with opponents Jones had selected, and nurses stood by to help the injured. The beatings increased in severity, Jones resumed his cancer "cures," and the first suicide drill was held in 1973 after eight members defected. When some of these practices leaked out to the public, Jones realized the Temple would be attacked by the authorities and decided it was time to move the church to Guyana in South America. Once in Guyana, Jones was reported to have told an associate:

If we ever get the members over here, I'll be able to keep them in line. While they're in the states, they can always make trouble if they go out and complain about discipline. But when they're in the jungle there'll be no place for them to go (*Phoenix Gazette* 24 November 1979).

The rest of Jones's story is history. By the evening of 18 November 1978, over 900 members of the People's Temple had died after Representative Leo Ryan of California, three newsmen, and a sect defector were shot from ambush as they prepared to fly out of Guyana. Jones told the sect members that some of his guards planned to kill Ryan

Victim of mass "suicide" at Jonestown, Guyana. Guyana's leading pathologist believes that murder, not suicide, claimed more than 700 of the 911 persons who died at Jonestown.

at the airstrip and that the sect would be attacked "by parachute" in retaliation. He convinced his parishioners that the children would be tortured and that everyone would be killed. Jones pleaded with his followers to "die in dignity" (*Time* 1979a, 27).

Guyana's leading pathologist believes that murder, not suicide, claimed more than 700 of the 911 persons who died in Jonestown (*Associated Press* 17 December 1978). Dr. C. Leslie Mootoo, the first doctor at the scene of the tragedy, does not believe the suicide theory, either for Jones or for most of the others. He thinks that Jones was too "power-drunk" to kill himself and that "most cult members were forced to drink the poison" (*Associated Press* 17 December 1978). His conclusions are based on "70 autopsies performed on victims, as well as his examination of other bodies and an inspection of the scene" (*Associated Press* 17 December 1978). Others presume that Jones shot himself (*Time* 1979a, 28), but no gun was found with his body (*Associated Press* 17 December 1978).

Cult Violence: The Manson Family

Before his last arrest, Charles Manson spent fourteen years in and out of various jails (Bugliosi 1974). While in jail, he started to believe in **Scientology,** which is "a reincarnationist religion that claims to train individuals to experience past lives, to leave their bodies, and to achieve great power and immortality" (Sanders 1971, 29). When Manson left jail, he began to gather new friends—at first only young women. Manson became a sort of "hostel keeper" for runaways, and he likened himself and the women to Christ and the disciples. From 1961 through 1967, Manson and his friends traveled up and down the West Coast, referring to themselves as a "family." Like gypsies, they survived by working at odd jobs for a time and then moving on. The Manson Family stayed together, arguing that separateness would be a sin. They stressed group experiences (e.g., LSD trips and mystical discus-

sions led by Manson). Manson began to see himself as Jesus, and his followers, who now included a few men, as his "children" (similar to Jim Jones). The people who joined the Family at this point were down and out—young girls, runaways, and those just released from jail. Many had been in jail on drug-related charges and, like Manson, were still checking in with their parole officers.

Like Reverend Jim Jones, Manson had an unusual ability to manipulate people and obtain favors from them. This included sexual favors, which were an essential part of the group's daily activities. Manson won over women with his love-making skills, and they wanted to join the Family to be with him. Other than the main core of members, most stayed only a short period of time. The rule was, "If you fit in, you can stay" (Sanders 1971, 67).

By 1967, Manson began to live a more sophisticated life. He began to associate increasingly with the children and other relatives of celebrities, in an attempt to get some of his music published. The Family was becoming larger, however, and since they no longer could migrate in a Volkswagen bus, they camped near friendly houses and set up tents for the extra people. Once Manson won over a few children of entertainment personalities, others followed. This practice helped him to obtain free credit cards, money, and hospitality at nice homes (Hotchner 1976). He even obtained jobs on and off Sunset Boulevard, performing both alone and in groups.

Soon Charlie began to want younger girls. He told the other women that if they really loved him, they would bring him younger girls—which they did. Childbirth was encouraged, as no birth control was used. Infants were thought to be the ideal, for they were not "cursed by the culture" and acted spontaneously—from the soul. By this time, the cult believed in reincarnation and in monitoring past lives; therefore children became the total culmination of the life chain of evolution (Sanders 1971, 67).

The Manson Family changed drastically in

1968. After the life of flowers and sexuality came violence, devil worship, and satanism. Violence was rationalized as being from the soul; the women became witches and Manson was the Devil. He now believed in a state of mind termed *coyotenoia:* "Christ on the cross, the coyote in the desert—it's the same thing. He is aware of everything, as he moves through the desert delicately. He is always in a state of total awareness" (Sanders 1971, 129).

Manson wanted the cult to live in The Hole in Death Valley to avoid "Helter Skelter." He picked up the term Helter Skelter (which refers to a slide in an English amusement park) from the song by the Beatles and thought it meant a race war that would be won by the blacks. (Jim Jones thought a forthcoming race war would be won by the whites.) Manson told his cult members that killing actress Sharon Tate and the La Bianca family, among others, would set off a war between blacks and whites. Manson also believed that the Beatles were whispering to him in their album, telling him to come to London. He tried to telephone them, but apparently they didn't return his call. He interpreted the Beatle album as racist doom songs, including songs like "Piggies," "Happiness Is a Warm Gun," and "Rocky Raccoon." This experience apparently changed Manson's life, and murder replaced mind games as his favorite topic of conversation (Sanders 1971, 150).

In the final stages, Manson gave lessons in knife throwing to his women, and the cult made preparations for the end of the world or for Helter Skelter. He became obsessed with the idea of blending violence into his transactions with others. Male members of the cult, especially, became fearful for their lives. Some of them left the group and didn't return. Like Jim Jones, Manson became fearful that those who left might talk, so he pressured some of them to return. Manson put out contracts on people's lives, and the Family became a band of murderers. On 1 December 1969, final evidence was gathered to arrest the remainder of the Manson Family and Charles Manson himself (Sanders 1971, 412).

Although their family backgrounds were different, some similarities exist between Manson and Jim Jones. Both men had a tremendous capacity to control others, and both had a drug problem. A major difference was that Jones could hide some of his sadistic behavior behind an established sect's cloak of respectability, while Manson worked with a tattered and loosely knit cult. Hence, Jones's behavior *appeared* somewhat more respectable, even in retrospect. Beneath the surface, however, lurks another major similarity in their attitudes: the emphasis on oneness and the absolute self just discussed. This attitude appears in Reverend Jones's last pleading with his followers to "die in dignity" by sipping the poisoned drink:

Lay down your life with dignity. Don't lay down with tears and agony. It's just *stepping over into another plane.* Stop this hysterics . . . it's just something to put you to rest. . . . Keep your emotions down. . . . I don't care how many screams you hear; death is a million times preferable to spend[ing] more days in this life. If you knew what was ahead of you, you'd be *glad to be stepping over tonight* (italics ours) (Time 1979a, 28).

This attitude, coupled with Jones's admission that Representative Ryan's airplane was about to be attacked, fits Manson's statement: "If you are willing to be killed, then you should be willing to kill" (Zaehner 1974, 55).

Interpersonal Violence and the Larger Society

Many explanations have been offered for why Jonestown occurred. One of the most plausible explanations comes from Dr. Hardat A. S. Sukhdeo, a social psychiatrist and native of Guyana. Sukhdeo heads the Center for the Study of Coercive Persuasion in Newark, New Jersey and is chief of psychiatry at the Newark branch of the College of Medicine and Dentistry of New Jersey. He has had considerable experience with cults, which includes helping a friend who kidnapped his son back from the Moonies, (i.e., members of the Unification Church of Reverend Sun Myung Moon). He finds an intellectual flaw in some young persons who join cults, gangs, and biker groups, which is a tendency to see "all of life in either black or white." There are not enough "grays"; he thinks we need more of them. As he attempts to explain how people can surrender their self-identity to a cult or sect to find meaning, Sukhdeo's friends and neighbors consistently doubt him:

They cannot understand any sensible human being doing this and letting themselves be killed. They want to Blame the Victim, saying he was mentally ill or intellectually underdeveloped. "It can't happen to me," is what they're really saying. Ah, well, the cultists aren't "crazies," and it can happen to any of us, providing a certain combination of idealism and rootlessness overtakes us. There is much that's wrong with life, and a commitment to change is understandable (*New York Times* 16 December 1978).

Relative to Jonestown, however, Dr. Sukhdeo points out that the *nature* of the commitment must be fully understood, i.e., what kind of leader is being followed. Parents should provide material things, and the schools can provide knowledge, "but at the same time we should provide our children the opportunity to learn wisdom." Such wisdom frequently comes through what is termed "the school of hard knocks" (i.e., experience).

Beyond the use of mind-expanding drugs, what caused the Manson cult to go wrong?

R. C. Zaehner (1974, 50–58), a professor of comparative religion, thinks that morality (for many) seems to be out, while ecstasy is very much in. This results in many no longer believing that a fixed frame of reference exists from which to make sense of their lives. Traditional religion, as taught by the churches, seems "diminished in every way" and Eastern mysticism appears to have "bewitched the minds of so many of the young." Neither modern Christianity nor Buddhism nor Hinduism are able to overcome the concept of *moral relativity*, i.e., the idea that there are no *universal* (cross-cultural), ethical, or religious standards. Hence, some begin to think of themselves as immortal and free—beyond good and evil.

This attitude made it possible for Manson and his followers to show *no* remorse when they were caught and brought to trial. It made it possible for them to kill Sharon Tate, her unborn child, and her associates with no feelings of guilt. It also made it possible for them to justify torturing Shorty Shea, a minor associate, in the process of killing him. After Manson and the others had gotten rid of all sense of ego and replaced it with the absolute self, they were able to murder to their heart's content and feel no remorse at all. As Zaehner (1974, 55) explains:

The end and goal of both Hinduism and Buddhism is to pass into a form of existence in which time and space and all the opposites that bedevil human existence are totally transcended, and in which one is literally "dead" to the world but alive in a timeless eternity. This ritual death Charles Manson had already experienced; and, as a result of this experience, he had taught his disciples that they must kill themselves in this way in order to kill others and be free from remorse. At the trial when Linda Kasabian . . . appeared as the principal witness for the prosecution, Susan Atkins, the most egoless of them all, "mouthed the words, 'You're killing us.' " To which Linda replied, "I'm not killing you. You've killed yourselves." She had heard it so often before. "Yes," she said again, in that interminable cross-examination, "he used to say, 'If you are willing to be killed, then you should be willing to kill'. . . ." Charles Manson *had* "killed" himself. But at the trial he had come to life again, not as a superman, or a god, but as a very human being, the son of a teen-age prostitute, a "country boy who never grew up" as he once described himself.

In summary, this chapter has come full circle. We began with the idea that institutional violence, such as war, may indirectly encourage interpersonal violence. We end the analysis section with the thought that the various types of interpersonal violence described here may be having negative effects on the larger society and its institutions.

POLICY ALTERNATIVES FOR INTERPERSONAL VIOLENCE: IS THE PROBLEM SOLVABLE OR NOT?

Numerous suggestions have been advanced for containing interpersonal violence including youth and urban violence. Although they have been referred to as paramilitary **vigilantes** (persons who take the law into their own hands), Curtis Sliwa and his Guardian Angels have had some success

protecting people in New York's sprawling subways.

Sliwa's patrols have been expanded to Central Park, the Staten Island Ferry, buses, and even to other cities, such as St. Louis. These self-styled enemies of crime and criminals are karate experts who carry no weapons and receive no pay. They believe that crime in the big cities has gotten out of hand and that the police need help whether or not they will admit it.

Violent crime has been described (*New York Times* 11 February 1981) as "one of the nation's most serious problems." Justice Department officials are studying the following proposals: (1) making murder for hire a federal offense, (2) having Congress establish a

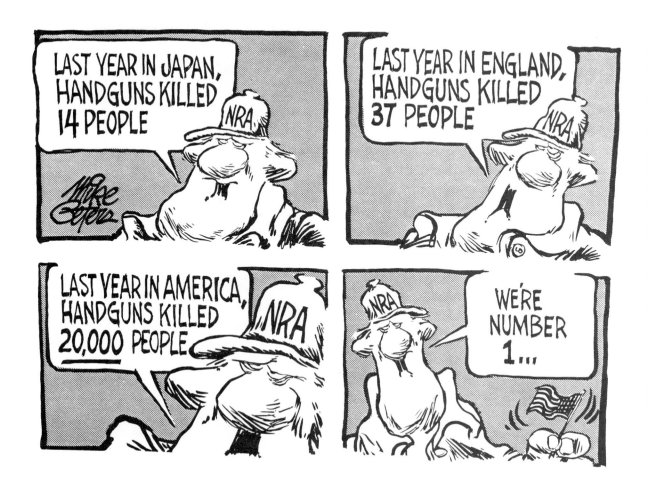

"victim compensation fund," (3) passing federal laws to provide new protections for crime victims and witnesses, and (4) passing federal laws that might provide an increased or mandatory sentence for any crime in which a weapon was used or a person was injured due to violence.

Should handguns be outlawed? Michael Beard, executive director of the National Coalition to Ban Handguns, says yes, and Neal Knox, executive director of the National Rifle Association, says no (*U.S. News & World Report* 1980, 23–24). Beard is espe-

cially concerned about the 32,000 lives lost each year in America due to handguns and thinks there ought to be national legislation to outlaw the manufacture, sale, transportation, and possession of handguns (only) by private citizens. Conversely, Knox does not think the ban on handguns would work, because people wouldn't obey a gun law.

In partial defense of Beard's position, considerable evidence exists that most Americans favor regulating handguns (*Los Angeles Time* 23 March 1978). In a total of twelve opinion polls taken between 1959 and 1976,

American citizens being trained in the use of firearms. Other Americans think that handguns either should be outlawed or carefully regulated. Handguns and their users take about 32,000 lives each year in the United States.

a large majority of respondents—68 percent to 78 percent said they favored requiring gun purchasers to obtain police permits for their weapons. Also in favor of Beard's argument is that stricter firearms control laws appear to be curbing gun-related crimes in Canada (*Associated Press* 29 March 1980). In support of Knox's position, some argue that the man arrested for John Lennon's murder brought his gun to the mainland from Hawaii and violated New York's highly restrictive gun law, which requires police permission to possess a firearm.

This will be a difficult issue to resolve, but the fact remains that about 50 percent of murders in the United States are committed with handguns (*U.S. Department of Justice* 1981, 12). Members of Congress know that a sizable majority of the American public favors various forms of gun control (*Nashville Banner* 7 August 1978), but the intense pressure coming from the anti gun-control lobby seems to be decisive.

For those who think the media may be having a negative impact on their children, citizen Diana Green publishes *Parents Choice*, a bimonthly guide to acceptable media for children (*New York Times* 3 October 1980). The purpose of her publication is to provide parents with a central source of information about the movies, television programming, games, records, and books to which their children are exposed. Unlike many other publications and groups concerned about the effects of television on children, *Parents Choice* stresses the positive media experiences available to children rather than what is deemed negative.

Sociologists have no easy answer to family violence. As long as violence is viewed as an acceptable solution to problems in America, family violence will persist (*Time* 1979b, 55). However, the reduction of aggressive themes on television, the outlawing of corporal (bodily) punishment in schools, and the elimination of the seldom-employed death penalty might be helpful in reducing family violence. The opening of shelters for battered women and the establishment of the National Center for Child Abuse and

Neglect have already proven beneficial. Some states have initiated a family court arrangement to handle family violence cases. This new court system is designed to keep family violence cases out of the criminal courts, as a way to offer counseling instead of sentencing. Merely passing laws is not the answer. If the courts and the police do not take the problem seriously, not much can be accomplished. Cynthia Hutto, who was acquitted for killing her abusive husband in self-defense, offers two pieces of advice to women. First, don't get married too young, and second, if you are battered, turn to someone outside the immediate situation for help (Rockmore 1980). Regarding violence in the schools, the National Education Association passed a resolution in 1979 to protect school personnel from physical attacks and to reimburse them for loss of time due to injury (McGuire 1980:19G). Further, a committee to study the causes of school violence has been established by the Los Angeles district Board of Education (*Los Angeles Times* 14 March 1978). School violence in Los Angeles has been increasing in two important categories—student attacks on teachers, and assault and battery incidents involving students or school employees.

More encouraging reports include a Texas high school teacher who won damages of $2,396 from a student who hit him. This is considered a landmark verdict in that it could lead to greater protection of teachers and students in Texas and around the nation. In Cincinnati, Ohio, high school school administrators discovered that limiting the total population of schools to 500 students has reduced much of the alienation and violence that occur when schools are allowed to contain two or three thousand students.

In the area of sport, Congress is considering a sport violence bill that would make it a federal felony to use excessive force in sport (Lowenstein 1980). The bill is based mainly on the work of Richard Horrow, who wrote a thesis on sport violence and the law while he was a student at Harvard Law School. Horrow defines excessive violence as any conduct that "has no reasonable relationship to the competitive goals of the sport," is "unreasonably violent," and "could not be reasonably foreseen, or consented to" by the injured player (*Cox News Service* September 1980). Horrow contends that the absence of a legal definition of "excessive violence" makes state and local law enforcement officials reluctant to take action in the area of sport violence.

Regarding suicide, students of human nature believe that the urge toward self-destruction is always present in society and that a certain amount of suicide is unavoidable, especially during economic recession. If human unhappiness could be prevented, then suicide would be almost nonexistent. In general, suicide prevention relates to principles of good mental hygiene.

Suicide intervention refers to the treatment and care of a person during a suicidal crisis. Suicide prevention centers should really be termed suicide *intervention* centers. Many practical techniques for effective suicide intervention are known. A great deal of literature on therapy and treatment of suicidal persons has been gathered in various settings such as suicide prevention centers, outpatient offices, and medical and mental hospitals. Suggestions for care include working with significant others in the suicidal person's life, using available community resources for referral, and focusing on the reduction of the person's hostility during the period of suicidal crisis.

Many kinds of people, including volunteers, are trained and supervised to be lifesaving agents in the prevention of suicide. Professionally trained individuals, such as psychiatrists, psychologists, and social workers, perform the primary roles in suicide prevention services and in suicide research.

SUMMARY

In this chapter, we have attempted to define, confront, and analyze the problem of interpersonal violence, and have outlined policies suggested for resolving the growing problem of interpersonal force and violence in America and the rest of Western society. The topics covered included a variety of problem areas, such as youth, biker gang, and urban violence, media violence, violence in sport and in the schools, family violence, rape, homicide, suicide, and cult violence. These are problem areas that resist speedy solutions. At best, we can only hope for a drop in the general level of violence in the United States and throughout the world as societies continue to mature.

How is this proposed reduction in the total amount of force and violence to be achieved? We might begin by studying cultures and societies that have alternatives to violence, and begin to emulate them. For example, in countries such as England and Scotland, the murder rate is much lower than it is in America. Why do those societies have a general distaste for violence, and why have they been able to establish such strict gun-control laws? Why are the police generally unarmed in England, and why do the English think of guns as "tacky?" Finally, why do pacifists have such a gentle view of humanity?

When we find the answers to these and similar questions, we may be on our way toward resolving problems of force and violence in the society and world around us. There are elements of violence in our own language, folk literature, and music. We might consider replacing our national anthem—which contains a number of war-glorifying phrases ("the rockets' red glare, the bombs bursting in air")—with "America the Beautiful," a song with a much gentler and more positive message.

STUDY QUESTIONS

1. Write a brief essay in which you address the question, Is America a violent society or not?

2. Summarize and discuss the research findings in the area of family violence. What are the major social factors related to the perpetuation of family violence?

3. Briefly explain the history of either the Manson Family or the People's Temple, as well as the similarities between Charles Manson and Jim Jones.

4. Discuss the research findings related to the effects of media violence or human behavior.

5. Distinguish between interpersonal violence and institutional (structural) violence in American society. Support your discussion with examples.

6. What policies are suggested at the end of the chapter to reduce the amount of interpersonal violence in society?

REFERENCES

Arizona Republic. 25 September 1976; 20 August 1978; 14 November 1982; 27 March 1983.

Associated Press. 17 November 1977; 26 November 1978; 17 December 1978; 24 April 1979; 28 September 1980; 5 October 1980; 30 September 1982.

Bugliosi, V. 1974. *Helter skelter.* New York: W. W. Norton.

Chicago Sun-Times. 14 February 1978; 20 February 1979.

Cincinnati Enquirer. 31 July 1973.

Cincinnati Horizons. 1978. *Rape.* (June): 10.

Cox News Service. September 1980.

DeMause, L. 1975. Our forebears made childhood a nightmare. *Psychology Today* 8: 85–88.

Dobash, R. E., and R. P. Dobash. 1977–78. Wives: The "appropriate" victims of marital violence. *Victimology* 2: 426–42.

———. 1979. If you prick me do I not bleed? *Community Care* (3 May): 26–28.

———. 1983. Battered wives. Paper presented at Arizona State University, 24 March.

Dreyfuss, J. 1980. Our violent children. *Family Circle* (13 May).

Durkheim, E. 1951. *Suicide.* New York: Free Press.

Gelles, R. 1974. *The violent home.* Beverly Hills: Sage.

Gilbert, B., and L. Twyman. 1983. Violence: Out of hand in the stands. *Sports Illustrated* (31 January): 62–74.

Greenbaum, A. 1983. Suicide. *Psych Talk* 1 (4).

Greenberg, B. S. 1975. British children and televised violence. *Public Opinion Quarterly* 38: 531–47.

Hartnagel, T., J. Teevan, Jr., and J. McIntyre. 1975. Television violence and violent behavior. *Social Forces* 54: 341–51.

Hartnagel, T. 1980. Subculture of violence: further evidence. *Pacific Sociological Review* 23: 217–242.

Helfer, R. E., and C. H. Kempe. 1974. *The battered child.* Chicago: Univ. of Chicago Press.

Henry, A. F., and J. F. Short, Jr. 1964. *Suicide and homicide.* Glencoe, Ill.: Free Press.

Higgins, P. B., and M. W. Ray. 1979. The media: Plastic killings, painless deaths. *Human Behavior* (March): 26.

Hotchner, A. E. 1976. *Doris Day: Her own story.* New York: Morrow.

Kilduff, M., and R. Javers. 1978. *The suicide cult.* New York: Bantam.

Knight-Ridder News Service. 27 November 1979.

Leavy, W. 1981. Battered women. *Ebony* (February): 94–98.

Liebert, R. M., and J. M. Neale. 1972. TV violence and child aggression: Snow on the screen. *Psychology Today* (April): 38–40.

Lorenz, K. 1970. *On aggression.* New York: Bantam.

Los Angeles Times. 14 March 1978; 23 March 1978; 6 December 1978; 6 June 1979.

Lynn, K. 1969. Violence in American literature and folklore. In *Violence in America,* eds. H. D. Graham and T. R. Gurr, 219–33. New York: New American Library.

McCombie, S. L. 1978. Characteristics of rape victims seen in crisis intervention. In *Social problems: Institutional and interpersonal perspectives,* ed. K. Henry, 237–50. Glenview, Ill.: Scott, Foresman.

McGuire, W. 1980. Violence in the schools. *Today's Education* (April–May): 18G–19G.

Muson, H. 1978. Teenage violence and the telly. *Psychology Today* (March): 50–54.

Nashville Banner. 7 August 1978.

National Institute of Mental Health. 1974. *Indian suicide: Suicide, homicide, and alcoholism among American Indians.* Rockville, Md.: National Institute of Mental Health.

New York Times. 7 July 1947; 16 December 1978; 3 October 1980; 11 February 1981.

Nietzke, A. 1978. TV violence. *TWA Ambassador* (June): 14.

Phoenix Gazette. 21 November 1979; 23 November 1979; 24 November 1979.

Richardson, J. T. 1979. From cult to sect. *Pacific Sociological Review* 22 (April): 159–60.

Rockmore, M. 1980. Should battered women hit back? *Rockmore Company* (25 October).

Sanders, E. 1971. *The family.* New York: E. P. Dutton.

Seiden, R. H. 1970. We're driving young blacks to suicide. *Psychology Today* (August): 24.

Shneidman, E. S. 1976. Suicide. *Psychiatric Annals* 6 (November): 604–19.

Silberman, C. E. 1970. *Crisis in the classroom.* New York: Random House.

Steinmetz, Suzanne K. 1977. The Cycle of Violence. New York: Praeger.

Steinmetz, S. K., and M. Straus, eds. 1974. *Violence in the family.* New York: Dodd, Mead.

Storr, A. 1970. *Human aggression.* New York: Bantam Books.

Straus, M., R. Gelles, and S. K. Steinmetz. 1980. Behind closed doors: *Violence in the American family*. New York: Doubleday.

Tilly, C. 1969. Collective violence in European perspective. In *Violence in America*, eds. H. D. Graham and T. R. Gurr, 4–42. New York: New American Library.

Time. 1978. Release dated 25 September: 82 under "Behavior."

———. 1979a Release dated 26 March: 27–28 under "Nation."

———. 1979b Violent families. (9 July): 55.

———. 1980. Education. (16 June): 63.

Trumbo, D. 1970. *Johnny got his gun*. New York: Bantam Books.

Turner, J. H. 1982. *The structure of sociological theory*. Homewood, Ill.: Dorsey.

Underwood, J. 1978a. An unfolding tragedy. *Sports Illustrated* (14 August): 68–82.

———. 1978b. Punishment is a crime. *Sports Illustrated* (21 August).

———. 1980. The death of an American game. *Book Digest Magazine* (April): 57–75.

United Press International. 30 August 1979; 11 January 1980; 19 March 1983.

U.S. Department of Justice. F.B.I. 1981. *Uniform crime reports*. Washington, D.C., 26 August.

U.S. News & World Report. 1979a. Battered families: A growing nightmare. (15 January): 60–61.

———. 1979b. Now it's the suburbs where school violence flares. (21 May): 63–64.

———. 1980. Should handguns be outlawed? (22 December): 23–24.

———. 1982. What is TV doing to America? (2 August): 27–30.

———. 1983. Want better teachers? Raise pay, stop classroom violence. (4 March): 41.

Walker, L. E. 1977–78. Battered women and learned helplessness. *Victimology* 2: 528–31.

Wiessler, D. A. 1982. Motorcycle gangs go gray flannel. *U.S. News & World Report* (20 September).

Wolfgang, M. E. and F. Ferracutti 1967. *The subculture of violence*. London: Tavistock.

Zaehner, R. C. 1974. The wickedness of evil: on Manson, murder and mysticism. *Encounter* (April): 50–58.

CHAPTER 2

Drug Abuse

CONTENTS

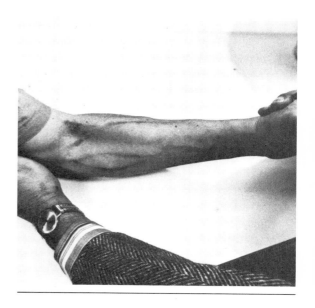

America's new moonshiners

Michael Reese with Pamela
Abramson in northern
California, Stryker McGuire in
Texas, Donna Foote in Illinois
and Susan Agrest in New York

A decade ago marijuana farmers tended to be spaced-out counterculture horticulturists who grew a few plants for their own consumption. But today marijuana is big business—and those attracted to it range from legitimate farmers who can't make a living growing corn and soybeans to the kind of rapacious entrepreneurs who made it big bootlegging liquor during Prohibition. Indeed, says Sheriff Bud Cook of Monterey County, Calif., "You can't always tell who a grower might be." NEWSWEEK profiles five of today's modern-day marijuana farmers:

The McCoys (not their real names) are middle-aged descendants of GTT (Gone to Texas) Kentuckians. They live in a two-room, tumble-down house on what an acquaintance calls 110 "sorry-assed dirt acres" in northeast Texas. Fifty years ago the land might have been used to grow cotton, 30 years ago, grain sorghum, 10 years ago, soybeans. Now it's marijuana.

"They are tough, tough mountain folk, harder than a night in jail," drawls the acquaintance. "The woman works in an all-night gas station. The old man and his son have got 50 to 75 junk cars in the yard." But now they're supplementing their income with marijuana. "I know for a fact that not one of them has ever used the stuff," says the friend. "Their idea of a good time is to get a six-pack of beer and a pack of Marlboro reds."

David used to make $25,000 a year growing marijuana in California. But not anymore. Two years ago he and a partner were held up at gunpoint, and David—who was never sure that marijuana farming was a proper profession for a nice Jewish boy from the suburbs—went out of business. "I never felt secure about what I was doing," says David, 33. "I'd see planes flying over, and I'd wonder all day what they saw."

But David's business was so profitable that he was able to put himself through college. He's now a doctoral candidate at a major university—and, not surprisingly, his field of study is plant breeding. In fact, if marijuana is ever legalized, the first thing David plans to do is travel the world for seed samples. "Right now, farmers don't have access to a fraction of what's out there. The possibilities are endless."

"I'm a hustler," says Steve, 29. "I've always been, and I decided that being sharp and having a little ingenuity can go a long way." Steve, a native of rural New York who "grew up poor and didn't like it," started growing marijuana five years ago to supplement his regular $45,000-a-year income. He now makes $50,000 a year on his "hobby" alone. "It's a question of living good—a matter of keeping up with the big boys and living in the fast lane," he explained.

Steve insists he works hard for his money. He spends at least four hours a day on the plants that he tends by hand and irrigates with water pumped from his pond. "Totally organic," he says proudly. He doesn't even begrudge having to sit up at night to guard his crop from intruders. "It's a really personal experience, and I take a lot of pride in growing it." And he does not believe that what he's doing is wrong. "We're outlaws," he concedes. "But I'm not a criminal screwing up somebody's mind with some deadly drug."

For 30 years Melvin Shaw was a respected farmer and businessman in rural Steeleville, Ill. (population: 2,249). Until 1970 he successfully ran a local sorghum mill and introduced several innovations into the processing of molasses. After the mill closed, Shaw devoted most of his time to farming. But recently the 60-year-old farmer started padlocking both entrances to his 216-acre Paradise Valley farm, and he boasted that he had forsaken the cultivation of wheat and corn for "health food."

But what Shaw calls "health food," the authorities call "cannabis." And when they raided Shaw's farm earlier this month, they discovered 3,000 pounds of the stuff—estimated at $3 million in street value. It seems that Shaw had converted his farm into a marijuana factory, using a secluded field, an old pole barn, a greenhouse and two tin storage sheds as his base of operation. When Shaw was asked about his motives, he explained that domestic grain crops no longer paid enough to sustain the average farmer and that he was in debt. "It was a way to raise a little money," he told police.

They love the land, the fresh air and the joy of rural life. For that reason, Sue and Gary didn't mind the half-mile hike through thick brush to get to their one-room cabin in the Sierra foothills—base of operations for their 100-acre marijuana farm. They grew only 40 plants, enough to earn the couple close to $50,000 a year over the past five years. Their product was good—so good that they were able to barter it for everything from dental work to stained-glass windows. Most recently, they tried to barter it for legal services after they were arrested last summer and authorities confiscated all but 10 of their plants.

From the dirt beneath her fingernails to the moccasins on her feet, Sue is every inch a farmer—committed to her customers and, more importantly, to the quality of her product. So is Gary, who vows he will be back in business—on somebody else's property—within the year. "You're a fool to do it," concedes Gary, "but you're a fool not to."

Source: Newsweek 25 October 1982.

DEFINING THE PROBLEM: A BRIEF HISTORY OF DRUG USE

Although the preceding article contains an element of humor, many Americans believe that drug abuse is a monster that was born in the 1960s. These people contend that the monster's parents were the hippies and that no drug problem existed in the distant past. They also claim that drug abuse symbolizes the way our country is going to hell due to a general decay of moral values (Shorter and McDarby n.d.).

Actually, drugs have been used throughout the world since the beginning of human history, and alcohol and marijuana have been part of American culture for centuries. Marijuana use on this continent probably predates Columbus, and the early colonists introduced alcohol (U.S. Department of HEW 1979, 1). During this long period of time, alcohol has been one of our most popular recreational drugs. In 500 B.C., the Greek historian Herodotus described drug use by Siberian tribes, who were advanced hunters and gatherers. They burned marijuana in open stone bowls, inhaled the vapors, and got high. Greeks and Romans used alcohol, and their excesses and triumphs are clearly recorded in art and literature. They were the early alcohol abusers; other drugs were used infrequently.

As history progressed, societies diversified, expanded, and interacted. Trade lanes opened to distant lands, so that exotic drugs filtered into various subcultures and became fashionable almost everywhere. Between 1300 and 1500 A.D., a so-called insidious drug spread through the Middle East, Yemen, and Arabia. That drug was coffee (caffeine), which was previously used for medicinal purposes only, but soon became popular as a beverage for daily consumption. Middle Eastern political and religious leaders termed coffee houses "centers of sin and sedition." In 1511, a week-long reign of terror against the brew failed, and coffee remained as popular as before. The bean became an important source of revenue for the Ottoman Empire, and its use spread to Europe about 1600. Similarly, the Europeans brought back tobacco, coca (the leaves of which yield cocaine), and cocoa from the New World.

In America, a proportion of alcohol and other drug use gradually became characterized as abusive. Over the years, many people condemned alcohol and sought its suppression. Such vigorous protest movements as the Women's Temperance Union and Carrie Nation's saloon-smashing campaign are examples of periodic reactions. These and other factors led to the passage of the Volstead Act in 1919, which outlawed all alcoholic beverages. Prohibition, however, did not solve the problems of alcohol abuse, just as passage of the Harrison Act in 1914 (which made "narcotics" use illegal) did not stop that drug use. Almost overnight, the Volstead and Harrison acts created new populations of technical lawbreakers. Repeal of Prohibition swept away the apparatus that had served the illegal alcohol market, but the restoration of alcohol to a legal status did not bring a solution to the problem of alcoholism. Alcoholism has now been associated with a wide variety of serious health problems including liver damage, ulcers, heart disease, and sterility.

Conventional groups and powerful individuals have led the United States through various antidrug campaigns. By 1924, heroin manufacturing and importation were banned, and Bayer Pharmaceutical had stopped advertising heroin as cough medicine in leading magazines. Soon after 1924, cigarette smoking was attacked for reasons of "morality." Marijuana was attacked as an "evil weed" smoked primarily by jazz musicians, black stevedores and Mexican laborers. In 1933, the FBI urged adoption of the Uniform State Narcotic Drug Act to control marijuana use, which it termed "reefer madness." The Marijuana Tax Act of 1937 bolstered marijuana prohibition and provided for a prohibitive tax and strict regulation of the drug.

Why Drugs Are a Problem

This chapter addresses a societal (group) problem through the use of value conflict and interactionist theory. **Drug abuse** may be defined as the compulsive (excessive) use of drugs or alcohol to a degree that is harmful to the individual and others. Thus, drug *use* becomes drug *abuse* when it becomes intensive (e.g., daily use) and is characterized by dependency.

Physiological (bodily) addiction is a form of drug abuse, but not all persons who use a drug—including alcohol—become either physiologically or psychologically dependent on the drug. People called "chippers" are able to snort heroin on a fairly regular basis without becoming addicted. Many people who experiment with heroin use, however, *do* become physically dependent on it.

These persons become aware of their physiological addiction to heroin when they realize that not using it is accompanied by withdrawal symptoms, e.g., nausea, pain, and vomiting (Lindesmith 1965). Since the use of drugs without debilitating effects is possible, the *abuse* of drugs—not the use—is what creates problems.

The use of any given drug does not impose the same effects on every individual who takes it. In discussing narcotics addiction, sociologist Alfred Lindesmith (1966, 67) notes: "The addict's evaluation of the effects of the drug is not inherent in the drug itself, but rather is a learned reaction." Lindesmith also points out that the individual addict may appreciate the dizziness and nausea that a large initial injection of heroin or morphine sometimes produces, because the effects provide evidence of the injec-

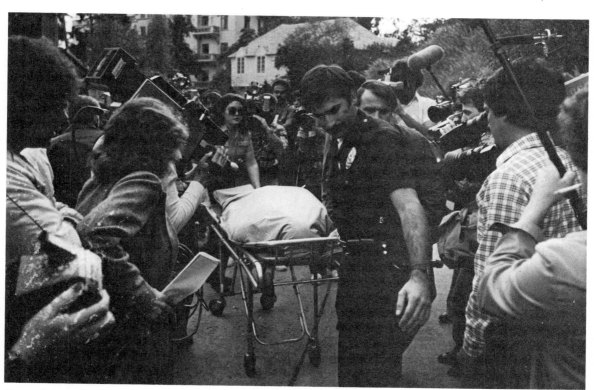

Drug abuse affects all segments of the society, as depicted in the death of comedian John Belushi. The death of Belushi and recent arrests of other celebrities and sport figures underscore the fact that drug use/abuse is fashionable among upper-middle-class and upper-class individuals who have more money available to buy drugs.

tion's potency. Similarly, responses to non-addictive drugs, such as marijuana, are often varied. After their first experience of smoking marijuana, some persons react with fear or sickness—others with pleasure. The effects vary according to *how they are defined* by the individual (Becker 1963, 41–58). Subjective or "phenomenological" aspects are therefore involved in most drug use.

The number of Americans reportedly abusing different types of drugs, as well as their varied reactions to the drugs, constitutes a social problem. The prevalence of experience with drugs that abuse the body is widespread in the general population, as the National Institute on Drug Abuse (February 1983) continues to point out. A recent Gallup Poll (*Associated Press* 16 November 1982) revealed that one-third of Americans believe alcohol abuse is a problem in their families. Thus, America's biggest drug abuse problem involves alcohol, which 93 percent of our high school students have used by the time they are seniors (National Institute on Drug Abuse February 1983).

The National Survey on Drug Abuse has also established that millions of Americans currently use marijuana (U.S. Department of HEW 1979, V). After marijuana, with at least 16 million users, cocaine is by far the most widely used illegal drug. About 10 million Americans have tried cocaine at least once, and about 2 million have taken it within the last month. Cocaine, which is expensive, is fashionable among upper-middle-class and upper-class individuals, including professional athletes and film makers. Numerous celebrities have been arrested for possessing cocaine, and actor Robert Blake has been quoted as saying, "The whole town of Hollywood is coked out of its head" (*Associated Press* December 1978).

Further, some estimate that there are about 400,000 heroin addicts and at least 500,000 heroin users in America (Abelson et al. 1977). Heroin use is thought to be decreasing now, but physical problems remain for those addicted, and organized crime continues to be involved in its distribution and sale. Finally, reports indicate that from 2 million to 20 million American women are medication junkies who take tranquilizers, sleeping pills, painkillers, or stimulants daily (Nellis 1981, 7). As in the case of alcohol, large numbers of people are victimized.

Newer Illicit Drugs

Newer illicit drugs of concern in America include PCP (phencyclidine hydrochloride), fentanyl, and amyl and butyl nitrite.

PCP, or Angel Dust, is also sold under the names Cannabinal, Crystal, THC, Dust, TIC, TAC, Erth, Green, KW, KJ, Hog, and Sheets (Shorter and McDarby). It may be taken orally, smoked, snorted, and injected. In an NBC (1980) documentary on Angel Dust, description of the drug's violent effects included a man who pulled out his own teeth with a pair of pliers and a woman who fried her baby in cooking oil.

Fentanyl is a new synthetic narcotic (depressant) that has been described by some as "worse than heroin," due to the number of deaths it has caused in a very short period of time (*Associated Press* 20 December 1980). Fentanyl is sometimes sold on the street as China White, a prized kind of heroin that comes from Southeast Asia. However, fentanyl is "80 times more potent than any morphine on the market," (*Associated Press* 20 December 1980), faster acting than China White, and difficult to trace in urinalysis.

Amyl nitrite is a cardiac stimulant once recommended for angina (heart) patients but now used by a growing number of persons for the intense high it provides when inhaled. Amyl's chemical cousin, butyl (or isobutyl) nitrite, or poppers, produces the same high but has no current medical application. Amyl nitrite is also referred to as poppers because it is sold in ampules that produce a popping sound when snapped. White, middle-class children, ages eight to twelve years, are becoming increasingly fond of snorting butyl nitrite. As amyl and butyl nitrite's abuse grows, so do the legal and medical controversies that surround it (*New York Times* 23 November 1978).

Other relatively common drugs, especially in the barrios and ghettos, are inhalants: glue, paint, and gasoline. Low-income young people (twelve to seventeen years of age) favor sniffing these chemicals because they produce a quick and cheap high. Inhalation bypasses the gastrointestinal system, and the large surface of the respiratory system rapidly absorbs the chemical. Symptoms of intoxication include relaxation, giddiness, lessening of inhibitions, and sometimes unconsciousness. **Drug tolerance,** the need to inhale more chemicals to reach the same high, develops with prolonged use.

In addition, the use of lookalikes among young Americans has skyrocketed (Do It Now Foundation 1981a) over the past few years. The drugs are called lookalikes because they are deliberately made to look like legally controlled substances, particularly speed. Most often, lookalikes contain, either singly or in combination, over-the-counter stimulants (especially caffeine), decongestants, and antihistamines. While the ingredients are usually legal, lookalikes are proving to be more dangerous than the prescription drugs they are meant to resemble. They pose particular dangers to persons with heart problems, high blood pressure, diabetes, or thyroid disease. Serious side effects of lookalikes include sleep disturbances, chronic anxiety, heart disease, and even death in susceptible users (Do It Now Foundation 1981a).

So far, we have dealt mainly with the drug problems of young and middle-aged persons. Older people tend to have problems with prescription drugs: Valium, sedatives, and stimulants, as well as with tranquilizers other than Valium, as you will see in the next section. Table 2–1 presents a summary discussion of many of the major drugs covered in this chapter.

Conventional versus Nonconventional Drugs

Up to this point, we have focused mainly on nonconventional or unlawful drug abuse. Prescription (doctor-prescribed) drugs, such as tranquilizers, can also present serious problems. The three top-selling prescription tranquilizers are Valium, Librium, and Dalmane; chemically, they are known as benzodiazepines. In a year's time Valium, either alone or in combination with other drugs, will kill about 900 Americans (*Newhouse News Service* 27 September 1979). Valium's critics say the drug is misused and overprescribed, with yearly prescriptions running at a rate of slightly under 50 million, including refills (*Associated Press* 18 March 1979). About 15 percent of the adult American population takes tranquilizers, and annual sales of Valium alone are placed at about $250 million (*Associated Press* 18 March 1979).

The widely sold painkiller Darvon is of little medical value, is no more effective than aspirin, and causes numerous deaths each year in the United States (Shorter and McDarby, 13). Experts disagree on the exact number of Darvon deaths and whether they are suicides or accidents.

Because over-the-counter drugs can be bought at drugstores and supermarkets without prescriptions, most Americans do not consider them as drugs (Gorrell 1978, 8–13). These nonprescription drugs include cold pills and capsules, cough syrups, asthma and bronchitis medicine, and bromides for nervous disorders. Taken in excess, any of these drugs can be dangerous; even too much aspirin can cause stomach or intestinal damage or both. Many people are not aware that most pain medicines already contain aspirin or acetaminophen (a nonaspirin pain reliever) or both (Gorrell 1978, 9). Either acetaminophen or aspirin can be bought at a fraction of the cost of pain medicines at almost any drugstore.

A further complication with over-the-

TABLE 2–1. Controlled Substances: Uses and Effects

	DRUGS	OFTEN PRESCRIBED BRAND NAMES	MEDICAL USES	DEPENDENCE PHYSICAL
NARCOTICS	Opium	Dover's Powder, Paregoric	Analgesic, antidiarrheal	High
	Morphine	Morphine	Analgesic	High
	Codeine	Codeine	Analgesic,	Moderate
	Heroin	None	None	High
	Meperidine (Pethidine)	Demerol, Pethadol	Analgesic	High
	Methadone	Dolophine, Methadone, Methadose	Analgesic, heroin substitute	High
	Other narcotics	Dilaudid, Leritine, Numorphan, Percodan	Analgesic, antidiarrheal	High
DEPRESSANTS	Chloral hydrate	Noctec, Somnos	Hypnotic	Moderate
	Barbiturates	Amytal, Butisol, Nembutal, Phenobarbital, Seconal, Tuinal	Anesthetic, anti-convulsant, sedation, sleep	High
	Glutethimide	Doriden	Sedation, sleep	High
	Methaqualone	Optimil, Parest, Quaalude, Somnafac, Sopor	Sedation, sleep	High
	Tranquilizers	Equanil, Librium, Miltown, Serax, Tranxene, Valium	Anti-anxiety, muscle relaxant, sedation	Moderate
	Other depressants	Clonopin, Dalmane, Dormate, Noludar, Placydil, Valmid	Anti-anxiety, sedation, sleep	Possible
STIMULANTS	Cocaine†	Cocaine	Local anesthetic	Possible
	Amphetamines	Benzedrine, Biphetamine, Desoxyn, Dexedrine	Hyperkinesis, narcolepsy, weight control	Possible
	Phenmetrazine	Preludin	Weight control	Possible
	Methylphenidate	Ritalin	Hyperkinesis	Possible
	Other stimulants	Bacarate, Cylert, Didrex, Ionamin, Plegine, Pondimin, Pre-Sate, Sanorex, Voranil	Weight control	Possible
HALLUCINOGENS	LSD	None	None	None
	Mescaline	None	None	None
	Psilocybin-Psilocyn	None	None	None
	MDA	None	None	None
	PCP‡	Sernylan	Veterinary anesthetic	None
	Other hallucinogens	None	None	None
CANNABIS	Marijuana Hashish Hashish oil	None	Pain reduction	Degree unknown

†Designated a narcotic under the Controlled Substances Act.
‡Designated a depressant under the Controlled Substances Act.

Source: U.S. Department of Justice, Drug enforcement Administration. Drugs of abuse. (Washington, D.C.: Government Printing Office, n.d.).

TABLE 2–1. (continued)

POTENTIAL: PSYCHOLOGICAL	TOLERANCE	DURATION OF EFFECTS (IN HOURS)	USUAL METHODS OF ADMINISTRATION
High	Yes	3 to 6	Oral, smoked
High	Yes	3 to 6	Injected, smoked
Moderate	Yes	3 to 6	Oral, injected
High	Yes	3 to 6	Injected, sniffed
High	Yes	3 to 6	Oral, injected
High	Yes	12 to 24	Oral, injected
High	Yes	3 to 6	Oral, injected
Moderate	Probable	5 to 8	Oral
High	Yes	1 to 16	Oral, injected
High	Yes	4 to 8	Oral
High	Yes	4 to 8	Oral
Moderate	Yes	4 to 8	Oral
Possible	Yes	4 to 8	Oral
High	Yes	2	Injected, sniffed
High	Yes	2 to 4	Oral, injected
High	Yes	2 to 4	Oral
High	Yes	2 to 4	Oral
Possible	Yes	2 to 4	Oral
Degree unknown	Yes	Variable	Oral
Degree unknown	Yes	Variable	Oral, injected
Degree unknown	Yes	Variable	Oral
Degree unknown	Yes	Variable	Oral, injected, sniffed
Degree unknown	Yes	Variable	Oral, injected, smoked
Degree unknown	Yes	Variable	Oral, injected, sniffed
Moderate	Yes	2 to 4	Oral, smoked

counter drugs involves the number of medical patients who are taking many different prescription drugs at the same time. Older patients may not be told why they are given the medications. The reasons are written on patients' charts at clinics and hospitals, but not on personal drug containers. Older patients, some of whom suffer serious memory losses, also tend to become forgetful and confused about what they may or may not have swallowed. This is especially true of senile patients who live alone (Gorrell 1978, 8).

Legal tobacco (nicotine) abuse is another seldom-discussed health problem. American scientists did not take the potential health hazards of tobacco seriously until the 1930s, when they first linked smoking with an alarming increase in the incidence of lung cancer (Do It Now Foundation n.d.). In the 1950s, a number of British and American studies produced strong evidence that cigarettes contributed to the increase. The U.S. surgeon general's committee came to these conclusions: (1) smoking does cause lung cancer, (2) it is associated with heart disease, (3) it is the most common cause of chronic bronchitis, and (4) it substantially increases the risk of premature death (Do It Now Foundation n.d.).

The great number and variety of mind-altering drugs ingested in America appear to relate largely to two factors: (1) people's reaction to stress in the society and (2) a health care system based on an unbreakable drug-dispensing circle. A drug seems to exist for every thought, feeling, and need.

Next, we consider the medical effects of taking America's most popular recreational drugs: alcohol, marijuana, and cocaine.

Medical Effects of Major Problem Drugs

Alcohol. Alcohol or ethanol, in the form of beer, wine, and whiskey, is so widely and traditionally used that people tend to forget that it is a drug. Alcohol is the most widely abused drug in the United States, with at least 10 million Americans currently esti-

mated to be alcoholics (Do It Now Foundation 1980b). Long-term alcohol use can produce serious and irreversible damage to the liver, brain, stomach, and heart. Alcohol does not have to be abused to cause adverse effects. Among expectant mothers, even one or two drinks per week can increase the chance of stillbirth or adversely affect fetal growth and development (Do It Now Foundation 1981b). Smoking more than a pack of cigarettes a day can result in infant-nursing problems. Mothers who are both heavy smokers and drinkers deliver babies that are smaller than would be expected if only one substance were abused.

Three stages of alcohol metabolism take place in the first hour after having one drink (Hymes 1983). The most critical of the three stages in this process is the second stage, because here the chemical acetaldehyde is produced, due to the reaction between the enzyme aldehyde DH and ethanol (alcohol). Acetaldehyde is ten times more toxic to the body than the original alcohol! High levels or prolonged use of alcohol (for example, over a period of fifteen to eighteen years) can cause mental as well as physical damage. Other effects on the body are disturbed sleep patterns, enlargement of the heart, memory loss, personality changes, interference with blood clotting, the tendency to bruise more easily, decreased sex drive, water retention, and disturbance in the release of male and female hormones. Since alcohol irritates the stomach and intestines, absorption of nutrients, vitamins, minerals, and proteins is bypassed. This can result in malnutrition and susceptibility to illness and disease.

Not all alcohol-related problems are physical, however, and one does not have to be an **alcoholic** (i.e., a person addicted to alcohol) to experience them. Alcohol changes the way people feel and act, even if they don't drink more than an ounce or two. In many cases, even a few drinks can be deadly if the person drinking is driving a car. In 1982 alone, more than 25,000 persons died in American auto accidents, and an additional 1.5 million persons were injured. A disproportionate number of those killed were under twenty-five years of age, and 50 percent of our auto fatalities are alcohol-related. These deaths and injuries ought to be viewed as *medical* problems related to the use and abuse of alcohol. Beyond the lives lost, the cost of drunk-driving accidents amounts to over $24 billion every year in property damage, loss of wages, and medical and legal fees—not to mention the emotional pain to victims' families and friends.

Marijuana.   As we pointed out earlier, the second most abused drug in America is marijuana (the flowering tops, stems, and leaves of the cannabis plant). One of the 421 active ingredients in marijuana, and the chief intoxicant, is THC (technically, Delta 9-tetrahydrocannabinol). THC enters the bloodstream through the lungs, attaches to fats in the body, and remains there from five to seven days—although chemical analyses have shown that the THC from just one joint (marijuana cigarette) may remain in the body for as long as twenty to thirty days. THC accelerates the existing mood of the user, distorts concepts of time and distance, impairs judgment, and affects memory. The effects of one joint can last as long as seven to eight hours. Not only does marijuana affect the body's immune system, but also some researchers believe that marijuana contains more cancer-causing chemicals than tobacco (Do It Now Foundation 1981c). Like tobacco, marijuana has been shown to inhibit lung functioning with extended use and may be linked to lung cancer and other respiratory ailments.

Marijuana's effects pose particularly serious hazards for pregnant women. THC and other chemicals in marijuana pass through the placenta and are stored in the fetus. Exposure to the drug before birth has been associated with a wide variety of physical and behavioral problems in infants, and may also increase chances of miscarriage or stillbirth (Do It Now Foundation 1981c). While marijuana has not been confirmed as a

cause of birth defects, the drug does produce changes in chromosomes (Nahas 1979, 130–34), which may alter normal patterns of fetal growth and development.

Young people using marijuana constitute a second high-risk group. Disruption of hormone levels in the critical growth years of adolescence may delay or change normal maturation patterns. During this period of greatest emotional and psychological development, heavy use of marijuana may also lead to personality and behavior changes.

Because some persons who try marijuana use it repeatedly, and because use on a near-daily basis is common among current users, the behavioral consequences of marijuana use are of special concern. The 1979 National Survey on Drug Abuse examined reduced performance of automobile driving and loss of personal motivation among marijuana users with various histories of use. Large numbers of regular marijuana users believe that "getting really high" impairs their driving performance (Miller and Cisin 1979, 22). Among regular users, 30 percent of the young adults and 26 percent of the older adults report that at one time they "stopped caring about hard work and did not try as hard" because of steady or daily marijuana use (Miller and Cisin 1979, 23).

 The issue of safe marijuana use is highly controversial. Psychiatrist Lester Grinspoon (1977, 372–99) thinks that the "marijuana menace" has been somewhat exaggerated. Grinspoon, citing the results of various studies, rejects the hypothesis that even heavy use of pot, in the long run, causes mental, physical, or personality deterioration. He tends to emphasize the positive aspects of marijuana, such as its therapeutic use with glaucoma patients and with cancer patients receiving chemotherapy. Several states have recently passed laws allowing doctors to prescribe marijuana cigarettes or THC pills for the treatment of glaucoma—an eye disease—and to relieve pain and nausea in cancer patients.

Despite the controversy surrounding the marijuana issue, a growing consensus on some of its dangers is apparent (U.S. News & World Report 26 November 1979, 72). Most researchers agree that occasional use rarely leads to serious social or medical problems for healthy adults who are not pregnant. Regular use however, especially in combination with other drugs or alcohol, may be dangerous. Smoking marijuana at typical social levels impairs physical performance and brain functions, such as classroom learning. The National Institute on Drug Abuse cautions against driving while intoxicated with marijuana. An intake of five to ten milligrams of THC (about one marijuana cigarette) into the bloodstream is enough to induce cannabis intoxication (Russell 1980, 11).

Although a number of reports suggest that heavy use of marijuana can damage the brain, the National Institute on Drug Abuse maintains that the evidence is inconclusive (U.S. News & World Report 26 November 1979, 72). Although chromosome breaks have been reported in the blood cells of marijuana users, the NIDA holds that most of the genetic research—on both humans and animals—has been negative (U.S. Department of HEW 1979, 154).

We believe a safe conclusion is that marijuana and alcohol use is not without risk. That alcohol use is culturally accepted in America, with marijuana use not far behind (*Newsweek* 25 October 1982, 38) means that education concerning the dangers of these two drugs is vital.

Cocaine.   **Cocaine** is a bitter, odorless powder extracted from the leaves of the coca plant. Although legally classified as a narcotic, cocaine is actually a central nervous system stimulant (see table 2-1) with effects similar to those of the amphetamines. For about $2,000 an ounce, cocaine produces several minutes of intense stimulation and euphoria. Its relative scarcity, pleasurable yet fleeting effects, and exorbitant prices (some users spend as much as $10,000 *per month* to support their habit) all contribute to cocaine's reputation as a status drug.

Most commonly, users sniff coke, but freebase cocaine—a powerful preparation of the drug that users smoke—is rapidly amassing a following of its own. Preparation of freebase can be risky, as the solvents used (e.g., ether) are usually highly flammable and can explode in the presence of heat or flame. Cocaine can also be taken orally, but most users consider this method wasteful, as the drug is not absorbed readily through the digestive system. Finally, injection of cocaine is the most rapid means of absorption and produces an instantaneous and intense stimulation.

Although cocaine is not addicting in the *physical* sense, long-term use of the drug, particularly in its freebase form, can produce strong *psychological* dependence. As in heroin use, however, the most serious danger associated with cocaine use is that cocaine is one of the most often-adulterated illegal drugs. The tremendous assortment of powders or cutting agents that are regularly mixed into cocaine and heroin to increase dealer profits can pose serious health risks. For the unwary buyer, cocaine can be—and often is—a rip-off. Yet, the abundance of adulterated cocaine and the potential dangers that some of these adulterants present have not detracted from the drug's desirability and allure.

Prolonged use of cocaine can produce a number of serious physical side effects (Do It Now Foundation 1981d). Because cocaine is a stimulant, heavy use can severely strain the heart, disrupt blood pressure, and cause insomnia and weight loss. Cocaine's anesthetic action produces a constriction of blood vessels in the nose from sniffing the drug. Over a period of time, vasoconstriction can damage nose tissues and produce perforation of the nasal septum, the tissue that separates the nasal cavities.

Overdosing on cocaine is possible but unlikely in most cases, due to the impurity of the street drug (Do It Now Foundation 1981d). Most deaths from cocaine occur from a single large dose that the body rapidly absorbs (usually from injection into the bloodstream), causing respiratory depression and cardiac arrest. Fortunately, the extraordinary expense involved in using cocaine limits major toxic effects of the drug. Additionally, cocaine has one of the highest "turn-off" rates of all street drugs; only one in eight individuals who have tried the drug continue to use it.

Next we turn to discussion of society's varied reactions to drug abuse.

CONFRONTING THE PROBLEM: DRUG ABUSE

As with other social problems in America, people are divided on the seriousness of the drug abuse issue. The brief history of drug use given at the beginning of this chapter points out the tension that drug use creates in conventional society. The criminal justice system's intervention against drugs has its roots in a fairly puritanical and self-righteous past. Today, however, this model is supported by scientific, medical, and sociopsychological data. Still, some important issues are being overlooked. One of these issues is whether altering one's consciousness (i.e., having new experiences) is an innate, human drive. Researcher Andrew Weil (Shorter and McDarby n.d., 7) claims that consciousness alteration "is an innate, normal drive analogous to hunger or the sexual drive." He further contends that drug use history and the natural availability of mind-altering substances to all cultures, in all areas of the world, tend to support his thesis.

Weil's viewpoint however, is in the mi-

It appears that a higher percentage of young people than ever before are using drugs to alter their consciousness in some way. Close to one third of all youths twelve to seventeen years of age have tried marijuana.

nority, since many others in society view drug abuse as deviant (nonconventional) behavior. Celebrities may revel in snorting cocaine, but that is not the behavior of most conventional Americans. The media consistently present a dim view of various types of drug use. Politicians and the Pentagon are concerned about increasing levels of alcohol abuse in the military and with alcoholism in Veterans Administration hospitals (*United Press International* 5 March 1979).

Humanists are appalled that the Central Intelligence Agency (CIA) performed experiments with hallucinogenic drugs in a federal drug-treatment facility in 1963. Similarly, sport fans are concerned that some players in the National Basketball Association use drugs. Coaches and players are speaking out against drug use in college and professional football.

Other negative reactions to drugs include an Ohio doctor's reference (*United Press International* 27 November, 1980) to marijuana as "the most horrendous single health problem in pediatric practice." Dr. Ingrid Lantner, a member of the International Council on Drug Abuse, adds:

Teen-agers used to be our healthiest generation. Now more and more kids come to see me with chronic chest pains and coughs. . . . To me it's not a moral issue, but a medical one (*United Press International* 27 November 1980).

Dr. Lantner sees an increasing number of young people with marijuana use symptoms, including short-term memory loss, lowered motivation, fatigue, lack of concentration, depression, and impaired sexual function.

In response to these concerns, a group of celebrities including Carol Burnett, has begun encouraging entertainers to speak out against drugs. Further, black intellectuals are speaking out against "black alcoholism," feminists are concerned about the rising proportion of female drug users, and Jews are troubled by the growing problem of alcoholism among Israelis (*United Press International* 1 April 1979).

The Consumers Union (Brecher et al.

1972, ix) and others associated with it, conclude:

1. The various mind-altering drugs have become readily and increasingly available on the illicit market in most parts of the country.

2. The use to illicit drugs, especially by young people, appears to be increasing year by year.

3. The United States has based its efforts to curb illicit drug use primarily on punishment—everything from arrest to social contempt. These penalties, however, have damaged our society in numerous ways and have labeled and alienated large numbers of young people.

4. Programs designed to warn children and young people have failed to accomplish their purpose; some programs actually may have contributed to the rising tide of drug use.

Most likely, a safe conclusion is that a higher percentage of young people than ever before are altering their consciousness in some way, on a daily to weekly basis. No simple answers to the drug abuse problem exist, and the amount of misinformation on illegal drugs is overwhelming. A new body of information, however, tends to be more accurate. In spite of the Consumers Union report previously cited, early education still appears to be the best remedy for discouraging drug use.

ANALYZING THE PROBLEM: DRUG USE AND ABUSE

A review of the research literature on adolescent alcohol and drug use demonstrates that although the number of young people using strong drugs may have already stabilized, adolescent use of alcohol and marijuana is only beginning to level off (Radosevich et al. 1979, 15–35). The study of adolescent substance abuse has advanced greatly in the past twenty years, and we now have **longitudinal research** (the study of behavior over an extended period of time) and the use of national samples. The National Survey on Drug Abuse, discussed next, is one such study (Miller and Cisin 1979).

Drug Use among Youth, Young Adults, and Older Adults

The National Survey on Drug Abuse summarizes and interprets the most recent findings of a continuing research effort that the National Institute on Drug Abuse (NIDA) sponsors. This survey provides data on the use of a wide variety of both legal and illegal substances. It covers three major population groups: youth (twelve to seventeen years of age), young adults (eighteen to twenty-five years of age), and older adults (twenty-six years of age or older). The primary focus of the study is on those illicit drugs that large numbers of young people have now used: marijuana, alcohol, cocaine, and the hallucinogens. The survey consists of personal interviews with over 7,000 respondents, randomly selected from the household population of the United States. Five earlier surveys provide the basis for reporting trends in drug use across the decade of the 1970s.

The two measures of drug use prevalence (i.e., extent of use) most often used in the National Survey are lifetime experience and current use. The prevalence of **lifetime experience** with a particular drug is defined as the percentage of respondents who report ever having used the drug. The prevalence of **current use** refers to the percentage of respondents who report having used the drug during the month previous to the interview.

The National Survey results can be generalized to the larger American population from which the sample was drawn. In *any* sample survey, however, a degree of statistical uncertainty is present. For this reason, tables 2-2 and 2-3 include estimates of ranges (e.g., 6 percent to 9 percent) of drug use prevalence, as well as actual percentages of use (e.g., 7 percent). The ranges are re-

TABLE 2–2. **Prevalence of Lifetime Experience with Selected Illicit Drugs, in Three Major Age Groups: 1979**

PERCENTAGE WHO EVER USED EACH DRUG OR DRUG CLASS

	Major Age Groups[a]		
Drug/Drug Class	Youth	Young Adults	Older Adults
MARIJUANA/HASH (95 percent confidence interval)[b]	31% (29% to 33%)	68% (66% to 71%)	20% (18% to 21%)
COCAINE (95 percent confidence interval)	5% (4% to 7%)	28% (25% to 30%)	4% (4% to 5%)
HALLUCINOGENS (95 percent confidence interval)	7% (6% to 9%)	25% (23% to 28%)	5% (4% to 6%)
HEROIN (95 percent confidence interval)	1% (* to 1%)	4% (3% to 5%)	1% (1% to 2%)

Source: Judith Droitcour Miller and Ira H. Cisin, *Highlights from the National Survey on Drug Abuse* (Rockville, Md.: National Institute on Drug Abuse, 1979).

[a]*Youth are aged 12 to 17 years; young adults are aged 18 to 25; older adults are 26 years of age or older.*
[b]*The logic of the 95 percent confidence interval is explained in the text. In some cases, the upper or lower confidence limit may be the same as the sample estimate, because of rounding.*
Less than one-half of one percent.

ferred to as "95 percent confidence intervals," because if corresponding ranges were calculated for all possible similar samples, the population value (percentage of use) would be included in the range 95 out of 100 times. Hence, we can be 95 percent certain that the range presented includes the value that would be obtained in a complete census of the population.

Lifetime Experience in Drug Use

Opportunity is an important factor in the process of beginning illicit drug use. Persons who have "ever used" substances such as marijuana and cocaine are a subsample of all those who ever experienced the *chance* to try these drugs. Complex analyses of National Survey data reveal the process of how people begin using drugs. The typical potential user does not seek out the chance to try an illicit drug. Rather, acquaintance with a user precedes the first opportunity experience—and most persons who experience a chance to try an illicit drug do not take advantage of their first opportunity (Somerville

and Miller 1980). Many who pass up their first chance to use a particular drug do, however, try it at a later date. These patterns seem to apply both for marijuana and for stronger drugs.

Presently, the opportunity structure of drug users is strongly related to age. Young adults, eighteen to twenty-five years of age, are most likely to have experienced the chance to try an illegal drug. Opportunity experiences are also widespread among older teens and adults twenty-six to thirty-four years of age, but are considerably less common among younger teens and persons thirty-five years of age or older. As shown in table 2-2, the "ever used" category of illicit substances is most strongly concentrated among young adults eighteen to twenty-five years of age. About two-thirds of all young adults have now tried marijuana, and substantial numbers report experience with cocaine and hallucinogens such as LSD or PCP (Miller and Cisin, 1979).

Many persons who have experience with strong drugs have also used marijuana, and many have tried both cocaine and hallucino-

TABLE 2–3. Prevalence of Lifetime Experience with Legally Obtainable Substances, in Three Major Age Groups: 1979

PERCENTAGE WHO EVER USED EACH DRUG OR DRUG CLASS

	Major Age Groups[a]		
Drug/Drug Class	Youth	Young Adults	Older Adults
NONMEDICAL Rx[b]	7%	30%	9%
(95 percent confidence interval)	(6% to 9%)	(27% to 32%)	(8% to 11%)
INHALANTS	10%	17%	4%
(95 percent confidence interval)	(8% to 12%)	(15% to 19%)	(3% to 5%)
ALCOHOL	70%	95%	92%
(95 percent confidence interval)	(68% to 73%)	(94% to 96%)	(90% to 93%)
CIGARETTES	54%	83%	83%
(95 percent confidence interval)	(52% to 57%)	(81% to 85%)	(81% to 85%)

Source: Judith Droitcour Miller and Ira H. Cisin, *Highlights from the National Survey on Drug Abuse* (Rockville, Md.: National Institute on Drug Abuse, 1979).

[a]*Youth are aged 12 to 17 years; young adults are aged 18 to 25; older adults are 26 years of age or older.*
[b]*Includes recreational (nonmedical) use of stimulants, sedatives, etc., that are legally obtainable only under a doctor's prescription.*

gens. Hence, the population of young adults may be divided into three lifetime experience groups: (1) those who have never used any illegal drug, (2) those who have used marijuana only, and (3) those who have used cocaine or hallucinogens or both, as well as marijuana. These categories of lifetime experience represent the chronological order of most drug use histories. That is, young adult users typically report that marijuana was the first illicit drug used. Among those who began with marijuana, about half report later trying cocaine or hallucinogens or both. For the majority of young adults, illicit drug use began during the teen years. As table 2-2 indicates, close to one-third of all youth twelve to seventeen years of age have tried marijuana.

Table 2-3 presents lifetime prevalence data on legally obtainable substances that may be subject to abuse. As in the case of the illicit substances previously discussed, the recreational (nonmedical) use of prescription drugs is strongly related to age. The same is true for substances like glue, gasoline, and "locker room" odorizer, which are inhaled for kicks or to get high. Conversely, lifetime experience with alcohol and cigarettes is about equally prevalent in all adult age groups.

Drug Use among High School Seniors in the United States

In a study conducted by the University of Michigan's Institute for Social Research, NIDA reports information on the drug use and related attitudes of high school seniors in the United States (Johnston et al. 1979). The basic research design involves data collections during the spring of each year, beginning with the class of 1975. Each data

TABLE 2–4. High School Senior Drug Use: 1975–1982

	PERCENTAGE HAVING EVER USED[a] DRUGS							
				Class of				
	'75	'76	'77	'78	'79	'80	'81	'82
Marijuana	47	53	56	59	60	60	60	59
Inhalants	NA[b]	10	11	12	13	12	12	13
Amyl & Butyl nitrites	NA	NA	NA	NA	11	11	10	10
Hallucinogens	16	15	14	14	14	13	13	13
LSD	11	11	10	10	10	9	10	10
PCP	NA	NA	NA	NA	13	10	8	6
Cocaine	9	10	11	13	15	16	17	16
Heroin	2	2	2	2	1	1	1	1
Other opiates	9	10	10	10	10	10	10	10
Stimulants	22	23	23	23	24	26	32	36
Sedatives	18	18	17	16	15	15	16	15
Barbiturates	17	16	16	14	12	11	11	10
Methaqualone	8	8	9	8	8	10	11	11
Tranquilizers	17	17	18	17	16	15	15	14
Alcohol	90	92	93	93	93	93	93	93
Cigarettes	74	75	76	75	74	71	71	70

Source: Student Drug Use in America: 1975–1982. Rockville, Md.: National Institute on Drug Abuse, February 1983).

[a]*"Ever used" means used one or more times.*
[b]*"NA" indicates not available.*
Note: Table shows percentage of high school seniors from classes of 1975–1982 who have used drugs of abuse. Numbers were gathered in annual nationwide surveys conducted by Univerisity of Michigan Institute for Social Research for the National Institute on Drug Abuse (NIDA). Seven surveys involved more than 100,000 high school seniors from both public and private schools. Separate questions about the use of PCP (Angel Dust) and amyl and butyl nitrites (poppers) were not asked until 1979.

collection takes place in approximately 125 to 130 public and private high schools selected to provide an accurate cross section of high school seniors throughout the United States.

Table 2-4 summarizes recent trends in lifetime use of sixteen types of drugs, comparing the classes of 1975 through 1982 (National Institute on Drug Abuse February 1983). While 47 percent of the class of 1975 had used marijuana at least once during their lifetime, 60 percent of the classes of 1979 through 1982 had done so. Hence, marijuana use among high school seniors has apparently leveled off starting about 1980. The use of inhalants, alcohol, and cigarettes also seems to have stabilized for this group of students.

The overall proportion of students using illicit drugs other than marijuana, such as LSD, heroin, other opiates, sedatives, and poppers, has remained relatively stable over the last few years. Some changes have occurred, however, for other drugs within the illicit class. Cocaine use, for example, has exhibited a dramatic increase in popularity, with lifetime prevalence rising from 9 percent in the class of 1975 to 17 percent in the class of 1981. While about half of these seniors use cocaine only once or twice during the year, a number of frequent users are now detectable. Further, use of stimulants, which remained relatively unchanged between 1975 and 1978, is now beginning to show evidence of a gradual increase. Finally, the decline in hallucinogen use in the middle of the 1970s has halted except for PCP use, which continues to decline. Use of the sedative methaqualone leveled off for several years, but now appears to be rising again.

On the positive side, the *overall* pattern of drug use among high school seniors over the past few years has been one of declining involvement with most types of drugs.

On the negative side, the overall pattern of drug use among older adults between 1979 and 1982 was one of increasing involvement with most types of drugs—especially marijuana and cocaine (National Institute on Drug Abuse February 1983).

Drug Use in the Military, the Medical World, and among College Students

So far, we have discussed drug use among youth in the general population and among high school seniors. Next we turn to a review of research on alcohol and drug abuse in the military and among physicians, nurses, and college students.

The use of hard drugs by military personnel has declined over the past five years, according to a worldwide drug abuse survey conducted in the spring of 1980 (*Retired Officer* 1981). The Department of Defense study, conducted by a private research firm, could not determine any trend in alcohol use, because of a lack of earlier, comparable data. The study found, however, that alcohol use by service members is slightly higher than that of civilians. Eighty-four percent of the military reported consuming alcohol in the past thirty days compared with 82 percent of civilians. The specific rates for alcohol use were: the army, 80 percent; air force, 82 percent; and navy and Marine Corps, both 86 percent.

Although military and civilian drug use rates were comparable, the military had the higher drug abuse rate for marijuana and hashish. By service, the air force was lowest in overall drug abuse, with 14 percent reporting use within the previous thirty days. For the army, the figure was 29 percent; for the navy, 33 percent; and for the Marine Corps, 37 percent. Twenty-one percent of the more than 15,000 randomly selected military personnel said their work had been impaired during the past year because of drug abuse, and 27 percent said their work had been impaired at least once by alcohol (*Air Force Times* 1981, 32).

An air force spokesman said the survey findings closely matched the results of surveys the air force had taken earlier. The spokesman also said that the lower rates of alcohol and drug use in the air force may be due partly to its active drug abuse prevention program.

A Marine Corps spokeswoman said the Corps plans to use the survey results to redirect its drug abuse and alcoholism programs. She said the marines considered the sampling techniques in the survey accurate and added that the findings "were no surprise" (*Air Force Times* 1981, 32). She further noted that the Corps attributes its relatively high drug use rate to a younger and less highly educated population, with more single men than the other services.

A navy spokesman said the navy is studying the survey data and is planning to analyze computer tapes from the Department of Defense survey. The navy declined to discuss the survey directly.

Another drug study indicated that the greatest increase in the use of almost all drugs in the year after high school occurred in a subsample of graduates who went on to domestic military service in that year (Johnston 1974, 195–196). During the high school years, that group (composed of 144 respondents) had a very similar profile of drug use to the one found for those who entered civilian employment. The military sample, however, showed one of the highest rates of conversion to drugs, while the civilian-employed group showed one of the lowest, making for very different drug use profiles one year after high school.

Finally, the drug use problem in the air force took on an interesting twist in the summer of 1979, when marijuana was found in the control room of an underground missile silo (*Associated Press* 14 July 1979)!

Within the professions, doctors and nurses have had more than their share of drug-related problems. According to statistics from the American Medical Association, one of every ten physicians in the United States abuses alcohol, drugs, or both (*Arizona Republic* 14 February 1983). The problem is of growing concern to various boards of medi-

cal examiners around the country, who must either put drug abusers on probation or, in extreme cases, revoke their licenses to practice.

The various state boards of nursing appear to take even harsher action by suspending or revoking the licenses of a much higher proportion of nurses suspected of drug abuse. This tougher discipline standard is applied to nurses because nurses, unlike doctors, "are with patients all day" (*Arizona Republic* 14 February 1983).

Hospitals, fellow doctors, and even patients, are reporting those they believe are drinking too much or are taking too many drugs. Nurses sometimes steal pills from patients or obtain drugs by substituting water for tranquilizers being administered intravenously to patients. Drugs missing from hospital pharmacies are often traced to doctors or nurses on duty. Hence, determining drug abuse is usually easier than uncovering alcohol abuse.

Instead of condemning these doctors and nurses, the boards attempt to rehabilitate them with terms of probation of up to five years. Many doctors are released from probation after the third year, however. Reasons given for doctors and nurses having such high rates of involvement with drugs range from the great amount of occupational stress to the easy access these professionals have to most drugs.

The good news regarding drug use on American college campuses is that the number of students who drink alcohol—estimated at 82 percent of about 12 million college students in the nation—may have leveled off for the first time in twenty years (*College Press Service* 9 February 1983). Further, alcohol abuse and the side effects of heavy drinking may also have steadied for the first time in years, according to sociologist David Hanson and health professor Ruth Engs. The number of college students who drink, however, has been rising steadily since the early 1950s. The bad news is that substitution of other drugs, including marijuana, might be the reason for the leveling off of student drinking.

Other findings in this study of more than 5,000 students in all fifty states are: (1) white students drink more than black students, (2) religious students drink less than nonreligious ones, and (3) students with lower grades are more likely to be heavy drinkers.

Even if student drinking has leveled off, however, college officials still have to deal with significant alcohol and other drug abuse problems on campus.

In the next section, we discuss various factors that seem to contribute to drug abuse throughout American society.

Motivations for Drug Use

The general consensus is that much youthful drug abuse is initiated through the peer group (friends) social-learning process (Johnston et al. 1979, 72). Research has shown a high correlation between an individual's illicit drug use and that of his or her friends. Such a correlation probably reflects various causal patterns: (1) a person with friends who use a drug will be more likely to try the drug, (2) conversely, the individual who is already using a drug will be likely to introduce friends to the experience, and (3) one who is already a user is more likely to establish friendships with others who are also users.

Analyses of data from the National Survey On Drug Abuse have revealed some special ways in which the family influences drug use behavior among teenagers, young adults, and older persons in their thirties and forties (Miller and Cisin 1979, 10–12). The example of older family members appears to influence teenagers. Drug use behavior is more likely among teenagers whose mothers smoke cigarettes or drink alcoholic beverages moderately or both than among youth whose mothers do not drink. This general pattern holds for teenage use of marijuana and stronger illegal drugs as well as for youthful alcohol and cigarette consumption.

Drug use is also more likely among teenagers whose older brothers or sisters use alcohol or illicit drugs or both, and less likely among those whose older siblings avoid alcohol and drugs. Conversely, the father's substance use does not appear to be related to a son's or daughter's drug use (Miller and Cisin 1979, 10).

The prevalence of illegal drug use is very high among young adults who do not live within a family group (Miller and Cisin 1979, 10). Over 80 percent of young adults who live alone have tried marijuana, as have almost 90 percent of those who live with friends, "roommates" or "spouse-type" partners. Current marijuana use is reported by 45 percent of young adults who live alone and by 65 percent of those who live with roommates. Hence, during the young adult years, residence apart from family members appears conducive to substance abuse. Peer-group living may also intensify this tendency toward drug use.

Among married persons in the twenty-six to thirty-four age group, the presence of children in the home is an influence against drug use (Miller and Cisin 1979, 11). Sixty-two percent of the married persons who have no children have tried marijuana, and 24 percent are current users. In contrast, 40 percent of the married persons with children have tried marijuana, and only 10 percent are current users. Apparently, having children in the home tends to insulate adult parents against drug use. However, a mother's current marital status (i.e., whether a father or stepfather lives in the home) appears to have little or no influence on teenage drug use.

Sociologist Patricia Brennan (1973, iii and 69–70) studied the personal characteristics of twenty-three former heroin addicts and discovered the importance of peer-group pressure in heroin addiction. All twenty-three of the ex-addicts she studied (1) were influenced by a peer group both prior to and while addicted, (2) had their first experience with heroin in a social atmosphere, (3) were introduced to the drug by a "friend," and (4) had pleasurable effects during their first experience. Brennan concluded that the independent variable (factor) in becoming a heroin addict is peer-group pressure, and the intervening variable is the person's subjective definition of first use of the drug as pleasurable. Conversely, this was not always the case among nonaddicts.

Educators Donald and Muriel Samuels (1974, 421–28) have isolated other factors related to drug use in general. Their research shows that 75.5 percent of their subjects (thirty-seven adolescent members of a drug rehabilitation program) considered low self-concept to be one cause of their turning to drugs. However, 91.9 percent of the subjects believed that boredom and curiosity were other factors, 67.5 percent blamed peer pressure, and 64.8 percent said that pleasure

seeking was a problem. These results show that boredom and curiosity were the leading reasons given for drug abuse among the subjects studied. While low self-concept was also a factor to be considered, the impact was less than researchers originally suspected. The implications of the Samuels's study were for preventive programs aimed at keeping adolescents busy and interested in alternative activities, and at building strong self-concepts.

Similarly, in a study of rebellion in high school, Arthur Stinchcombe (1964) found that "short-run hedonism" (a short-run pleasure-seeking attitude toward one's life) and "extensive boredom" were important factors in adolescent rebellion in the school. Although 14 percent of both boys and girls who had been well behaved found their

The use of airplanes makes enforcement against illicit drug traffic difficult. This plane contained 640 pounds of cocaine, and seven men were arrested. Unlike most other types of drug use, cocaine and marijuana use among older adults continues to grow in popularity.

classes boring, 59 percent of the "rebellious boys" found most of their classes dull and boring (Stinchcombe 1964, 19). These findings are important in that they give insight into degrees of adolescent alienation in the schools, if not in the larger society.

In summary, factors related to drug use among young persons and others in America include (1) peer-group pressure (possibly coupled with resentment against family authority), (2) emulating certain family members or older adults, (3) social status involved in being able to buy and use drugs, (4) a weak self-concept struggling to establish its own identity, (5) recreation, (6) curiosity, and (7) alienation and role confusion, which express themselves as boredom with life in general.

Next we turn to discussion of policy in the alcohol and drug abuse areas. The areas of emphasis will include alcohol, marijuana, and narcotics (rather than cocaine abuse), since narcotics abuse usually involves coping with the difficult problem of physiological addiction.

ALTERNATIVE POLICIES FOR RESOLVING THE PROBLEM: CONTAINING DRUG ABUSE

Alcohol

Our knowledge of alcohol abuse is probably greatest in the areas of *how many* young people drink and why, but we know much less about *problem* drinking and what to do about it. Currently, young people are being raised in societies in which nearly all adults drink, and both per capita consumption and alcoholism are increasing around the world. Young people's lower tolerance for alcohol, due to their inexperience, makes drinking more hazardous for them. The policy potential for coping with alcohol abuse is somewhat limited by the following findings (Hymes 1983, 22–23):

1. Drinking has increased steadily among young Americans since about 1968 and is most common among males, Catholics, high-income groups, and those who do not attend church. Almost all persons twenty to twenty-four years of age (92.5 percent) list themselves as drinkers. *Frequent* drinking among young people is not common, however, as only 7.7 percent of young people, compared with 18.4 percent of older adults, list themselves as daily drinkers.

2. Most drinking begins in family settings, but drunkenness tends to occur outside the family.

3. The reasons for drinking among young people are complex and involve such factors as curiosity and the desire to socialize, to relieve psychological stress, to be like friends and parents, and to just "grow up."

4. Young people who resist pressures to drink tend to be more conventional, ambitious, cautious, and church- and family-centered. Hence, policies directed toward reducing alcohol abuse ought to emphasize programs that will strengthen religious, family, and societal values.

5. Young people tend to drink in a fashion similar to their parents; however, many do not automatically follow their parents' example. Boys often drink regardless of peer pressure and family example. Some evidence suggests that such child-rearing practices as lax maternal control and rejection by the father are more important than mere parental drinking in creating youthful drinking.

6. Children of alcoholics tend more often— but not always—to have drinking problems.

7. Studies of the childhood experiences of problem drinkers suggest that male overassertiveness, as well as many social and financial problems, appears as a strong negative influence.

Unfortunately, not much professional interest has been taken in treating the problems of young people affected by their own or others' drinking. Part of this is due to the general acceptance of alcohol as a traditional part of our culture. Young alcoholics, however, are apparently not more difficult to treat and have about the same recovery rates as older alcoholics (Hymes 1983, 23). The new lower drinking-age laws have led to increases in adolescent drinking and alcohol-related auto accidents, although public drunkenness records show no real trend toward increased incidence.

The policy of alcohol education in the schools has never been very extensive or popular. Strong parental response in some areas, however, is an indication that early (elementary-level) alcohol education could be more popular and successful than in the past. Alcohol education programs have been developed and tested for students in grades seven through ten, but it is too early to evaluate the outcome of those programs. Parents may need to increase their own knowledge about alcohol and its effects before they can become a reliable source of information for their children. Some parents may need to review their own drinking habits or child-rearing practices before their adolescents' drinking can be modified.

Various policies have been employed in the treatment of alcoholism, from the use of the clergy as counselors to crash educational programs directed at teenage drinking. For example, the Distilled Spirits Council of the United States (DISCUS) is spending several million dollars a year on an advertising campaign to educate young people who drink to do so "responsibly" (U.S. News & World Report 18 September 1978, 64). In addition, the issue of raising the legal age for drinking is being fervently debated.

In Sweden, billboards warn Swedish parent not to purchase liquor for their children, and sale of medium beer (3.6 percent alcohol by weight) has been restricted to state liquor stores to keep it out of the hands of minors (Do It Now Foundation 1980a). Sweden now ranks twenty-eighth highest in the world in yearly average consumption of alcohol at 5.9 quarts per person, while the United States

ranks nineteenth highest with an average of 9 quarts per person.

Alcoholics Anonymous tries to keep alcoholics "on the wagon" (sober) by getting them to admit to themselves that they *are* alcoholics and then encouraging them to discuss this problem with others. Another helpful policy is to have well-known former alcoholics or problem drinkers or both speak out against the condition. These persons are aware that alcoholism is treatable but not fully curable, and that they can regain control over their lives at any time. Whatever programs and policies are used, alcohol and other drug detoxification is apparently more successful when the persons being treated are encouraged to understand why they began to abuse drugs in the first place.

Marijuana

Of the many thousands of marijuana users, we now know that some of them, after an initial exposure, will develop panic reactions to the drug, and a few will develop toxic psychosis. Others, finding their initial exposures pleasurable, will continue to indulge. If their use remains casual or occasional, they will continue to obtain a "social high" and perhaps avoid any of the previous reactions. *Those who become regular users, however* (i.e., smoking two or more times weekly) *run the risk of developing the types of intellectual impairment reactions described earlier.* Unfortunately, the development of such reactions is usually slow and subtle. Neither the subject nor casual observers (parents, teachers, friends) notice the early changes. After all, adolescence is a time of change, sensitivity, rebellion, awkwardness and self-consciousness. How can one be expected to sort out adolescent upheavals from the change that marijuana initiates? If progressive downward trends are noted—in personal habits, school performance or attendance, or social relationships—possible drug effects should be considered (Gordon 1983, 14). These effects include an interruption of normal adolescent growth processes following moderate or heavy regular use of marijuana. This interruption occurs in adolescents without predisposition to serious mental disturbance. This point should put to rest the spurious argument that suggests that if you are "emotionally together," you can smoke all the marijuana you wish—that only those who are emotionally unstable have problems with smoking marijuana.

Finally, any discussion of marijuana that claims it is completely safe or completely harmful is invalid and biased. Marijuana is a relatively mild intoxicant, and if used judiciously, most people will experience no ill effects. Used regularly or compulsively, many people will demonstrate some deterioration of higher mental and psychological functioning.

Use and possession of small amounts of marijuana have been decriminalized in some U.S. states in recent years. At the same time, however, the Reagan administration recently waged a war on marijuana and other drugs (*U.S. News & World Report* 7 June 1982, 45–46). This "war" includes a crackdown on suppliers of marijuana and promotes the idea that penalties for use should not be lifted altogether, as this could undermine federal policy to discourage marijuana use (*Newsweek* 25 October 1982, 38). Further, FBI statistics show that local (U.S.) arrests for violation of marijuana laws ran at more than 400,000 a year for over six years—up from only 18,000 in 1965. Of those 400,000 arrests per year, 87 percent are still for possession of the drug.

Some experts contend that letting people grow small amounts of their own marijuana

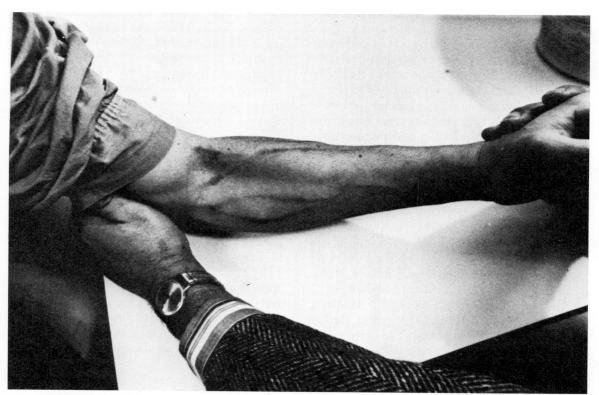

The arm of this heroin addict in a methadone program shows track marks for needles. Many heroin addicts end up on dialysis machines as the drug ruins their kidneys, creating the potential for a widespread social and economic problem.

might be better than forcing them to buy from and support the underworld—at very high prices. Thus, a great burden could be taken off the FBI, police, courts, attorneys, and taxpayers (*Newsweek* 25 October 1982, 41–43).

Narcotics

The one overwhelming objection to heroin, morphine, opium, and other narcotics is that they are physiologically addicting. The time has come to recognize that heroin addicts continue using the drug despite long prison terms, repeated cures that don't work, and risks of disease and even death (Brecher 1972, 528). The treatment of narcotics addiction includes such methods as the punitive, medical-psychiatric, communal, religious, chemotherapy (cyclazocine and methadone maintenance), and the use of "rational authority" (Brill 1972, 141–48). Although no permanent cure for most heroin addiction exists, the use of methadone maintenance can be helpful. It frees persons from being labeled heroin addicts and turns many of them into law-abiding citizens. **Methadone maintenance** is a method of treatment aimed at replacing the addict's craving for heroin with methadone, stabilizing his or her drug needs, and giving the person a chance to live a relatively normal life (Shorter and McDarby n.d., 13). One of the advantages of methadone is what is termed a "blocking action." That is, methadone not only eliminates the need to use heroin but also prevents the high from being produced if heroin is used.

Methadone maintenance is not a panacea, however, and the British system of making drugs available to addicts to cut the profits of illegal sales has been criticized in some quarters (O'Donnell and Ball 1966, 198–209). **Buprenorphine,** a drug used in Europe as a painkiller, could replace methadone for treating heroin abuse because it causes fewer withdrawal problems, is nonaddictive, and addicts liked it in a recent test (*Associated Press* 21 May 1981).

Other negative effects of narcotics addiction are largely the results of outmoded laws and policies. Before 1914, many morphine and heroin addicts led fairly healthy, productive, and respectable lives. Enforcement of the Harrison Act of 1914, however, brought the underworld into action with black market, high-priced narcotics (Brecher et al. 1972, 528). Presently, the business in paraphernalia for illegal drugs (e.g., "head shops," and record stores) is booming. Some American business executives appear to be profiting from their involvement in illegal drug traffic and prostitution (*U.S. News & World Report* 11 September 1978). And, finally, the United States seems unable to stem the flow of all types of illicit drugs across our borders (*United Press International* 18 February 1983).

What, if anything, is being done about these conditions? A Mexican program to destroy the poppy fields has somewhat cut the flow of low-grade brown heroin from Mexico (*Newhouse News Service* December 1979). No such heroin eradication programs exist in Iran, Pakistan, or Afghanistan, however. Further, bureaucratic infighting between the custom service's Office of Investigations and the newly formed Drug Enforcement Administration has reportedly diminished U.S. defenses against illicit drugs (*U.S. News & World Report* 8 December 1980). According to a former customs worker, Drug Enforcement Administration officials are more interested in making "buys" of narcotics from street dealers, for the sake of statistics, than in intercepting significant loads of contraband at the border, the credit for which might go to another agency: customs (*U.S. News & World Report* 29 December 1980). Making matters worse, the customs service's own investigators are presently barred from gathering drug-trafficking intelligence themselves. Hence, border inspectors must often rely on intuition and luck rather than inside information to catch smugglers.

With regard to narcotics users, the Consumers Union (Brecher et al. 1972, 530) recommends the following policies: (1) that United States drug policies be promptly revised to ensure that narcotics addicts will not need to obtain their drugs from the black market, (2) that methadone maintenance, or the equivalent, be made available under medical direction (as it is in England and other United Kingdom countries) to every addict who applies for it, and (3) that other forms of narcotics maintenance, including heroin maintenance, be made available along with methadone maintenance under medical supervision on an experimental basis. The third recommendation reasons that addicts are better off addicted to legal, low-cost, medicinally pure heroin than they are addicted to high-priced, dangerously contaminated, black market heroin.

The Consumers Union (Brecher et al. 1972, 509) also contends that many youth drug centers have had success getting youthful drug users to try alternative, nonchemical ways of "turning on." These alternatives to drug use include sensitivity training, Zen Buddhism, yoga, transcendental meditation, hypnosis, and self-hypnosis. Transcendental meditation has reportedly been especially helpful as an alternative to the use of marijuana, LSD, barbiturates, and even narcotics. In one study, 49 percent of those studied said that their drug use changed after transcendental meditation "because life became more fulfilling" (Brecher et al. 1979, 511), not because of any deliberate effort on their part to stop drug use.

Drug Abuse Policy in the High Schools

The extensive use of both legal and illegal drugs among high school students in the United States is regarded as a serious social problem, and the nation's educators have assumed a major role in its relief.

Many societal explanations have been offered in response to why the high school drug problem exists. These explanations include everything from peer-group influence to rock music to the economics of dealing in the drug market. However, what about explanations that deal directly with the edu-

cational system itself? One such explanation is that too many schools have taken an "it can't happen here" attitude and have simply ignored the problem (Jones 1971, 3). Those schools that have faced the problem too often have used one of two extreme approaches: the "overkill" or the "underkill."

The overkill approach uses scare tactics such as lectures and films on the dangers and illegality of drugs. Of 100 films on drug abuse reviewed by the National Coordinating Council on Drug Abuse Education and Information, 36 were labeled "contrived, exaggerated, inaccurate, and unrealistic" (Jones 1971, 15). The danger posed here is that overkill may not only fail to curb drug use, but it may also have the opposite effect. Some of these films paint a glamorized picture of the "underdog" drug user, stirring empathy among high school viewers. Teenagers also resent the failure of society to distinguish between marijuana and the addictive, hard drugs.

The underkill approach consists of the use of an informal drug education program. Speakers are brought into the schools occasionally, and the students are herded to the lectures to be "cured." Evidently, such a loosely organized approach has also not contributed much to a decline in usage rates (Kandel et al. 1976). The best approach may reside in beginning the various drug education programs earlier in the lives of young people, before drug habits are allowed to develop.

In the area of curriculum, some persons believe more practical courses should be offered, which provide a "nonchemical high" and an improved student self-concept. Drugs could be studied, perhaps, on a more scientific or historical basis, with students working on individual study projects related to topics that interest them (Morse 1976, 48–49). Alternative modes of education are needed that will meet the needs of each individual, including alternative learning centers. Scientific subjects could be studied on an ethical basis of inquiry, as well as on a factual basis. The creation of family groups within the school environment might help compensate for the decay of traditional family solidarity. On-the-job training for students in cooperation with vocational education programs is another suggestion for changing the traditional format in response to the drug problem.

Educators Thomas A. Brodie and William O. Manning (1976) think that "schools should not become treatment centers, but they certainly can and should play an active role in motivating treatment and in sustaining recovery." Schools are developing drug abuse programs in which trained staff intervene personally to help chemically dependent students and employees recognize their problems and find sources of assistance.

Insofar as our education system assumes responsibility for alleviating the drug use problem among high school (and some elementary) students, all schools in the country need to take corrective measures. Minimal information is available so far on the results of such programs mentioned previously, yet this information remains our final hope for the educational system in dealing with the problem of drug abuse.

SUMMARY

The extensive use of both conventional and nonconventional drugs among persons of all ages in the United States has been the subject of this chapter. To see whether descriptions of drug abuse as "cancerous" and "capable of destroying the society" were warranted, reviewing the statistics summarizing the extent of the drug use problem and its recent decline in many areas was necessary. We then discussed some factors that contribute to the overall drug problem and reviewed what policies have been suggested to relieve it.

Explanations offered for why young people use drugs included: (1) the poor example set by the adult drug culture, (2) boredom with school and with life in general, (3) emotional problems of youth, (4) peer-group influence, (5) the search for pleasure, (6) the search for deeper insights into the meaning of life, (7) weakened family patterns, and (8) the economics of dealing in the drug market. Many thousands of teenagers, preadolescents, and young adults use marijuana and alcohol. Most of them use these drugs because they are available and they enjoy using them. As in almost everything else relating to the nature of being human, peer pressure plays a big role in initial and continuing use.

We are cautioned, however, against interpreting both the national prevalence statistics on drug use and people's reported motives for using drugs. The use of many drugs seems to be experimental and sporadic rather than regular and permanent; persons described as "heads" constitute the minority of users. We should also be reminded that social concern toward illicit drug use may be somewhat misdirected, when the use of legal drugs such as alcohol, tobacco, and prescription medicines is clearly greater overall and perhaps more damaging.

STUDY QUESTIONS

1. Write a brief essay in which you demonstrate that drugs have been used throughout the world since the beginning of human history. Then discuss the sociological implications of your essay.

2. Briefly discuss the difference between the terms *drug use* and *drug abuse*. Why is this an important distinction?

3. Explain the difference between prescription and over-the-counter drugs, with examples of each.

4. Discuss the medical effects of taking each of the following drugs: alcohol, marijuana, and cocaine. What are the implications of these effects for the larger society?

5. Among high school seniors in the United States, what have been the recent drug use trends for marijuana, alcohol, cocaine, and stimulants?

6. What policies are suggested that might alleviate drug abuse problems in America? Do you think they will work? Why or why not?

REFERENCES

Abelson, H., P. Fishburne, and I. Cisin. 1977. *National survey on drug abuse*, Vol 1. Rockville, Md.: National Institute on Drug Abuse, Division of Research.

Air Force Times. 5 January 1981.

Arizona Republic. 14 September 1980; 15 September 1980; 14 February 1983.

Associated Press. December 1978; 18 March 1979; 14 July 1979; 4 December 1980; 20 December 1980; 21 May 1981; 16 November 1982.

Becker, H. 1963. *Outsiders: Studies in the sociology of deviance*. New York: Free Press.

Brecher, E. M., and the editors of *Consumer Reports*. 1972. *Licit and illicit drugs*. Boston: Little, Brown.

Brennan, P. 1973. Characteristics of heroin addicts. Master's thesis, Arizona State University.

Brill, L. 1972. *The de-addiction process*. Springfield, Ill.: Charles C. Thomas.

Brodie, T. A., and W. O. Manning. 1976. In the Wayzata schools they do more than just talk about alcohol and drugs. *American School Board Journal* (November).

College Press Service. 9 February 1983.

Do It Now Foundation. N.d. *Tobacco abuse*. (Report 117).

———. 1980a. *Drug Survival News* 9 (3) (November–December).

———. 1980b. *Alcohol, drug, and apathy abuse.*

———. 1981a. *Lookalikes: The new "speed."*

———. 1981b. *Alcohol, tobacco, caffeine and pregnancy.*

———. 1981c. *Marijuana and health.*

———. 1981d. *Cocaine papers: From Freud to freebase.*

Gordon, B. 1983. Marijuana. In *Chemical use/abuse prevention project*, ed. H. Hymes. Scottsdale, Ariz.: Informed Parents, Inc.

Gorrell, R., M.D. 1978. The legal drug problem. *Arizona Magazine* (March).

Grinspoon, L. 1977. *Marijuana reconsidered*. Cambridge: Harvard Univ. Press.

Hymes, H., ed. 1983. *Chemical use/abuse prevention project*. Scottsdale, Ariz.: Informed Parents, Inc.

Johnston, L. 1974. *Drugs and american youth*. Ann Arbor, Mich.: Institute for Social Research.

Johnston, L. D., J. G. Bachman, and P. M. O'Malley. 1979 *Highlights: Drugs and the nation's high school students*. Rockville, Md.: National Institute on Drug Abuse, Division of Research.

Jones, W. J. 1971. *Drug crisis: Schools fight back with innovative programs*. Washington, D.C.: National School Public Relations Association.

Kandel, D., et al. 1976. Epidemiology of drug use. *American Journal of Public Health* 66 (1) (January).

Lindesmith, A. 1965. *The addict and the law*. Bloomington, Ind.: Indiana Univ. Press.

———. 1966. Basic problems in the social psychology of addiction and a theory. In *Narcotic addiction*, eds. J. A. O'Donnell and J. C. Ball. New York: Harper & Row.

Miller, J. D., and I. H. Cisin. 1979. *Highlights from the national survey on drug abuse*. Rockville, Md.: National Institute on Drug Abuse.

Morse, J. 1976. Why kids use drugs and what that means for schools. *Educational Digest* (December).

Nahas, G. G. 1979. *Keep off the grass*. Oxford, England: Pergamon.

National Broadcasting Co. 1980. "Angel Death." A documentory on PCP (February).

National Institute on Drug Abuse. 1983. *NIDA capsule. (February).*

Nellis, M. 1981. Hooked! A sobering report on women and drugs. *Family Weekly* (1 March).

New York Times. 23 November 1978.

Newhouse News Service. 27 September 1979; December 1979.

Newsweek. 1982. Guns, grass—and money. (25 October).

O'Donnell, J. A., and J. C. Ball, eds. 1966. *Narcotic addiction*. New York: Harper & Row.

Radosevich, M., L. Lanza-Koduce, R. L. Akers, and M. D. Krohn 1979. The sociology of adolescent drug and drinking behavior: A review of the state of the field: Part I. *Deviant Behavior* 1 (1) (October).

Retired Officer. January 1981.

Russell, G. K. 1980. *Marijuana today*. New York: Myrin Institute.

Samuels, D. J., and M. Samuels. 1974. Low self-concept as a cause of drug abuse. *Drug Education* 4 (4) (Winter).

Shorter, M. A., and D. McDarby. N.d. *Chemical survival: A primer for Western man and woman*. 2d ed. Phoenix, Ariz.: Do It Now Foundation.

Somerville, S. M., and J. D. Miller. 1980. Opportunity and decision: An analysis of drug use entry. In *National survey on drug abuse during the seventies: A social analysis*, ed. J. D. Rittenhouse. Washington, D.C.: U.S. Government Printing Office.

Stinchcombe, A. L. 1964. *Rebellion in a high school*. Chicago: Quadrangle.

United Press International. 5 March 1979; 1 April 1979; 27 November 1980; 18 February 1983.

U.S. Department of Health, Education and Welfare. Public Health Service, Alcohol, Drug Abuse, and Mental Health Administration. 1979. *Consequences of alcohol and marijuana use.*

U.S. News and World Report. 11 September 1978; 18 September 1978; 26 November 1979; 8 December 1980; 29 December 1980; 7 June 1982.

CHAPTER 3

Unconventional Sexuality

CONTENTS

A survival of the least fit

By Wesley G. Pippert

WASHINGTON (UPI)—Many teen-age girls who turn to prostitution do so out of desperation, but some of the boys who ply the street-corner sexual trade do so for the money and excitement, a new government report says.

The report by the General Accounting Office also says that commercial child pornography has declined since 1977, but the number of children involved in prostitution and private pornographic enterprises probably has increased.

The GAO, a watchdog agency for Congress, was asked 13 months ago by Rep. Austin J. Murphy, D-Pa., chairman of a House education subcommittee, to study the two problems.

Its 63-page report, released this week, was based on questionnaires to the 50 states and the mayors and police departments of all 22 cities over 500,000 in population.

The GAO said speculation about the number of teenage prostitutes varies widely. One respected estimate is that as many as one-fourth of the nation's 450,000 prostitutes are juveniles.

"Officials . . . generally believed the number of teen-age prostitutes had increased during the last five years," the report said.

One study found that some young male prostitutes "are gay-identified and become prostitutes as a means of exploring their homosexuality. They consider themselves entrepreneurs, entertainers and sexually desirable partners."

Another study showed that some gay-identified teen-age prostitutes "claim to enjoy prostitution (and) do not have pimps but operate as independent street hustlers or freelance call boys."

GAO said another study found that male prostitutes are usually 8 to 17 years of age, underachievers in school or at home, without previous homosexual activity, underdeveloped physically and from a low-income background.

But the report said by far most of the causes and effects of teen-age prostitution were grim.

"Generally, teen-agers become prostitutes as a means of survival after they have run away to escape a poor home environment. Children often enter pornography for the same reason," it said.

"Many teen-age female prostitutes are products of a poor home environment characterized by violence, lack of parental love and affection, and drug and alcohol abuse.

"Many have been the victims of sexual abuse, including incest and rape . . . They often see prostitution as a life of adventure, glamour and excitement and as an easy way to earn money."

Source: San Diego Union 23 April 1982. Reprint permission from United Press International.

DEFINING THE PROBLEM: PORNOGRAPHY, PROSTITUTION, AND HOMOSEXUALITY

As reporter Pippert's article indicates, juvenile involvement in pornography and prostitution is an issue of special concern to members of Congress and others. The General Accounting Office's report to a congressional subcommittee contends that highly negative home environments have led youngsters to seek escape along paths that seem to promise rewards, but which have punishing consequences for society and for the children themselves. As with other problems of the young, such as illiteracy and high teenage suicide rates, the nation worries that its children's life chances are diminishing or being destroyed and that family life is in a state of decay.

Reports such as the GAO's fan the fires of moral outrage. When the young choose or are led into high-risk behaviors, and whether they exploit themselves or others exploit them, indignant citizens are sometimes led into what may be called "crisis mentality." They may search for quick solutions to complex problems, often led by persons whose positions in society provide them with an aura of moral authority.

The sex-related problems of some American youth raises the larger focus of concern in this chapter—to examine the broader topics of unconventional sexuality as they conflict with the morality of a sexually conventional society.

We begin by presenting definitions of each of our three topics—pornography, prostitution, and homosexuality—as adapted from the *Encyclopedia of Sociology* (1981).

Pornography is often equated in general usage with the term *obscenity* and is sometimes confused with the term *erotica*. A precise definition of pornography that will withstand legal challenges and court tests has not yet been developed. Most attempts to define pornography refer to the portrayal of sexual acts in some form, which includes an emphasis on violence or a disregard for conventional sexuality.

Prostitution is defined as allowing sexual access for money, goods (such as drugs), or favors. It may be seen as the antithesis of a romantic ideology that considers love between partners as the only basis for sexual access, and as the antithesis of private, marital sexuality.

Homosexuality is sexual interest in or sexual contact with a person of one's own sex. It is known to occur in many mammalian species and in most—if not all—societies, even those in which it is strictly prohibited.

These definitions contain no explicit value judgments and thus identify no moral problems. Beliefs about the morality of each of these topics, however, reveal their problematic aspects, and when spokespersons for various value-laden positions voice their beliefs, they indicate the lengths to which some are willing to go to stamp out pornographers, prostitutes, and homosexuals. For example, David Bianculli (1982), a *Knight-Ridder News Service* reporter, notes that a documentary series that the Christian Broadcasting Network produced for cable television warns of the "growing encroachment" of pornography and decries prostitution and homosexuality in statements that are "undeniably inflammatory." A CBN spokesperson has said, "I believe that homosexuality is one of those [things] that could be coupled with murder and other sins" (*Knight-Ridder News Service* 24 October 1982).

People for the American Way, headed by television producer Norman Lear, counterattacked such inflammatory statements. In its program "Life and Liberty . . . for Those Who Believe," this group contends that the Christian Broadcasting Network itself is a threat to the American way of life in its packaged efforts to impose its own restrictive value judgments on all.

As reporter Bianculli points out, whichever side's position outrages us depends on our own beliefs. Opponents of pornography see it as a degradation of "normal" sexuality and as a means of increasing males' acceptance of violence against women, as well as men's acceptance of "rape myths"—the belief that women enjoy being forced into sexual acts. Opponents of both homosexuality and prostitution have seen these behaviors as disruptive to conventional society. Same-sex attraction and the sale of sexual favors appear to undermine the high esteem in which we hold conventional family roles—husband-father for men and wife-mother for women.

Such views, however, are not universally shared. Some see neither homosexuality nor prostitution as social problems. Such behaviors, they argue, are "nobody else's business" as long as no one is demonstrably hurt (Smith and Pollack 1976) or unless such behaviors constitute a public nuisance (*Roanoke Times* 6 February 1976). Pornography also inspires debate even among those who oppose it. According to researcher Susan H. Gray (1982), some believe that protection of the First Amendment, which guarantees freedom of speech and the press, takes precedence over efforts to suppress pornography. Others, who believe that pornography leads to violence and moral decay, support actions to reduce its market.

Today, many states have laws prohibiting certain forms of sexual behavior even between consenting adults. Even where such laws are not in force, informal **sanctions** (punishments, in the negative case; rewards, if sanctions are positive) are sometimes imposed on those whose behavior is seen as unconventional. Frequently, overt action is not even-handed in its application. For instance, although some may oppose **lesbianism** (sexual attraction or sexual behavior between women), overt discrimination has been much more severe against **gay men** (homosexual men who have publicly affirmed their sexual orientation) than against lesbians. Conversely, although conventional ideology may not look with favor on male patrons of prostitutes, overt action has been primarily directed against prostitutes themselves. For example, in a recent year, the city of San Francisco reported arrests of 7,560 prostitutes, but of only twelve of their male customers.

Cultural Ideals and Everyday Realities

The Judeo-Christian part of our heritage supports the position that all sexual activity should be confined to marriage and should take place only between male-female pairs of adults. However, marital sexual activity as an ideal conflicts with an everyday reality in which unmarried persons of all ages engage in sexual intercourse and other forms of sexual activity. Our feeling of shock at such unconventional behavior as the sexual involvement of children is at odds with our popular support of displaying children as sexual objects in advertising and movies, among other media (Rush 1980).

With regard to prostitution, thirteen of seventeen Nevada counties do not have laws against it; everywhere else in America, prostitution is illegal. Despite its illegality, prostitution continues in many forms. Data on its prevalence are difficult to obtain because such sources as jail and arrest records do not tell us what the ratio of arrests to actual incidents might be (Adler 1975, 64; James 1978, 176). According to a report prepared for the American Civil Liberties Union a few years ago, more than 100,000 arrests are made in America each year for prostitution and related crimes (*Roanoke Times* 6 February 1976). Of the various kinds of prostitution, adult female prostitutes who sell their erotic favors to male patrons are by far the most numerous. Other kinds of prostitution include child prostitutes, both male and female, adult male prostitutes for both male and female patrons (Harris 1973), and female prostitutes who provide commercial sex for female clients (Pomeroy 1965).

The incidence of homosexuality is also difficult to ascertain, primarily because such activity is condemned. According to the *Encyclopedia of Sociology* (1981, 128), and contrary to stereotypes, fewer than 15 percent of homosexual males are identifiably effeminate, and only a small proportion of lesbian women are identifiably masculine. And, a large majority of those who have homosexual experiences also have heterosexual experiences at some time in their lives.

Researcher Susan H. Gray (1982) cites earlier studies of pornography and provides the following information. Violence in photos, drawings, and cartoons found in *Playboy* and *Penthouse* magazines has been increasing in recent years, although violent portrayals are found only in a minority of such materials. One scholar suggests that increasing violence in pornography is part of a patriarchal response to women's gains in social power (Diamond 1980). Another study examined "adults only" paperback fiction available in "adult" bookstores and found violent themes in about a third of the 428 books reviewed (Smith 1976). The violence, usually committed by men against women, included such themes as mental coercion and blackmail as well as physical violence. Two additional investigations of the early 1970s cited by Gray indicate that the primary consumers of pornography are young, married men. They are college educated, politically liberal, and high consumers of mass media in general. According to these studies by Nawy (1973) and Wilson and Abelson (1973), about one-fourth of all men have been exposed to **sadomasochistic** materials in which inflicting pain or having pain inflicted are shown as pleasurable. The investigations cited above all deal with print media. According to Gray, however (1982, 395). "Dienstbier [1977] has pointed out the irony in U.S. society's massive exposure to violence in the media with lower exposure to violence in real life, coupled with society's lower exposure to pornography in the media and higher exposure to sex in real life."

Problematic Definitions

In addition to civic and religious spokespersons, both the law and the public tend to look to psychiatric opinions for justification of their attitudes and beliefs (Weinberg 1973). Until 1975, psychiatrists classified homosexuality as a form of mental illness. Then, a committee of the American Psychiatric Association reclassified it (Gagnon 1977, 368). Not long afterward, the American Psychological Association supported the psychiatrists' action, adopting the following resolution:

Homosexuality per se implies no impairment in judgment, stability, reliability, or general social or vocational capabilities. Further, the American Psychological Association urges all mental health professionals to take the lead in removing the stigma of mental illness that has long been associated with homosexual orientations (Conger 1975).

Despite these proclamations, biases against homosexuals persist. Those who are morally indignant about homosexuality feel distrust and repugnance toward gays, believe that homosexuals have mannerisms of the opposite sex, and believe that homosexuals can be "cured" of their "sickness." Such persons tend to be (1) of rural origin or rural residence, (2) Caucasian, (3) claim religious affiliation with some tendency toward fundamentalist Protestantism, and, in general, tend to be (4) relatively conservative in attitude toward *any* sexual behaviors (Levitt and Klassen 1974). Moreover, those who are antigay tend not to support equality between men and women, and tend to be **authoritarian** in personality type (MacDonald and Games 1974). "The authoritarian personality" is defined as one whose mind is closed to new ideas and who advocates punitiveness as a response to deviance (*Encyclopedia of Sociology* 1981, 25).

In contrast to their about-face in defining homosexuality, psychiatrists have continued to attribute many types of "mental pathology" to prostitutes. This view contrasts sharply with the assessment, for instance, of Masters and Johnson (1966), who used prostitutes as surrogate partners in their early studies of human sexuality. After working with 118 female and 27 male prostitutes, Masters and Johnson described them as generally knowledgeable, obviously intelligent, verbally effective, and highly cooperative and helpful. As the contrast between mental health practitioners and these sex researchers illustrates, the value orientation of the observer may color interpretations of what is being observed. Observers may also influence those being studied in such a way that observees respond in accordance with observers' biases (Laner 1974).

Defining pornography is also problematic. As Supreme Court Justice Stewart Potter noted, although he could not define hardcore pornography, he knew it when he saw it. In the famous case of *Roth v. Alberts* (1957) the Court ruled that laws forbidding obscenity were constitutional, and a three-part test was developed to judge whether materials were obscene. First, the dominant theme of the material taken as a whole must appeal to a prurient interest in sex. Second, the material must be patently offensive because of its affront to contemporary community standards. Third, the material must also be completely without any redeeming social value. In application, this three-part test proved to be complicated and controversial.

The Supreme Court changed the second and third parts of the pornography test in 1972. The Court decided that "community standards" should be determined locally rather than nationally, and that material did not need to be completely devoid of redeeming social value to be found pornographic. Taken as a whole, materials that were found to lack serious artistic, literary, political, or scientific value could be considered pornographic. This decision, many thought, opened the door to repressive action at local community levels.

As Gray (1982, 388) has shown, "defining pornography is the key problem in the debate over, and study of, its effects." Further, as we learn from the *Encyclopedia of Sociology*, the National Commission on Obscenity and Pornography has recommended that most anti-obscenity laws be repealed, arguing that most obscenity laws were vague and unenforceable. The commission also found that pornography had no demonstrable negative relationship to crime, sexual deviation, or other commonly cited fears. The National Commission on the Causes and Prevention of Violence, however, found that exposure to pornography can cause harm. Thus, the debate over the effects of pornography on society and individuals continues, with one side advocating increased legal controls and the other supporting the repeal or loosening of such laws (*Encyclopedia of Sociology* 1981, 214).

America's Sex Negativity

From time to time, the antigay movement in America has taken on the characteristics of a witch hunt (Becker 1963; *Arizona Republic* 8 June 1978). In witch hunts, members of the group defined as the target of the hunt are rounded up and tormented in some way. In 1978, the Briggs Initiative in California, also known as Proposition 6, was such an effort. It advocated terminating the employment of homosexually oriented public school teachers and administrators. The initiative was soundly defeated (*Los Angeles Times* 1978). Supporters of Proposition 6 thought that homosexuals should not be employed in schools—not because of any incompetence, but solely on the basis of their sexual orientation (whether actively practiced or not). Opponents thought that Proposition 6 would open the door to accusations by, for instance, children who received a poor grade, that their teacher was homosexual (*Arizona Republic* 21 September 1978).

Senator Briggs, the author of the Initiative, had been a campaigner against gay rights in Florida with entertainer Anita Bryant's Protect America's Children campaign (Keerdoja 1978). Opponents of the Briggs Initiative challenged the Senator's assertion that homosexual teachers might be harmful role models for children. Existing laws, they pointed out, already enabled school boards to fire teachers who flaunted their sexuality or who attempted to "recruit" students, whether heterosexually or homosexually (*Newsweek* 2 October 1978).

Many types of sexual behavior attract explanations of psychological abnormality in

America. One explanation for this phenomenon is what psychologist Richard Smith has called America's "sex negativity" (1975b). Smith points out that in an underpopulated society, prohibiting masturbation, homosexuality, prostitution, contraception, or any activity that would decrease the likelihood of births would be "functional." Sex-negative norms would flourish to preserve family stability, since families would be needed to care for and educate the children that these norms based only on reproductive sex would produce.

Smith maintains, however, that in our time concern has shifted from under- to overpopulation. Agents and agencies outside the family have supplemented many of the tasks that the family formerly handled, such as education, health maintenance, and entertainment. A variety of family forms now coexist. (As we will see in chapter 5, the idealized conventional family is now a numerical minority.) In this changed context, Smith writes, many who were previously opposed to birth control practices are now strong advocates of contraception. Laws have changed to permit abortion under specified circumstances. Even marriage is no longer automatically considered the permanent bond it once was. All these changes are "functional" under current overpopulated conditions.

Why, then, does sex negativity toward nonreproductive forms of sexual expression continue to exist? It is a carry-over from earlier eras and, Smith contends, is now **dysfunctional** (e.g., is antithetical to the interests of society as a whole).

Over twenty years ago, Ira Reiss (1960) identified at least four coexisting standards regarding sexual expression outside of marriage: (1) abstinence for both men and women; (2) permissiveness toward nonmarital sex for men, but not for women (the "double standard"); (3) permissiveness toward nonmarital sex when there is affection between partners; and (4) permissiveness toward nonmarital sex, regardless of affectional aspects. The fourth standard (the

"playboy" philosophy) governs such play-oriented behaviors as patronage of prostitutes and erotic behavior between same-sex persons. This philosophy, however, is the least strongly held of the four co-existing standards—at least publicly. Note that three of the four standards are marriage, family, and reproduction oriented, and thus sex-negative regarding play-oriented erotic expression. Given the strength of our cultural heritage, sex negativity is not likely to disappear overnight, despite conditions that no longer support it.

CONFRONTING THE PROBLEM: HOMOSEXUALITY AND PROSTITUTION AS EVILS IN THE PUBLIC EYE

According to the Model Penal Code drafted more than twenty years ago by a commission of the American Law Institute, prostitution spreads venereal disease; is used by organized crime in combination with illegal trade in drugs, liquor, and gambling; leads to corruption in government and among the police; and is a significant factor in social disorganization because it encourages delinquency and undermines marriage, the home, and individual character. These traditional concerns are reflected today in the many laws that are used to arrest "bad girls." Since prostitution and prostitutes tend to be defined as evil, police make efforts to stop or at least slow down activity in red light districts (areas in which prostitutes are known to operate).

Similarly, harassment of and violence against homosexual men is relatively widespread. In San Francisco, attacks on gays recently have increased four-fold. One victim said, "Almost every gay I know has been mugged. It's random, senseless fag bashing by young kids who think they can get away with it." Many assaults are not reported, so the full extent of such assaults is not known (*Newsweek 1981* 23 March: 30).

Why have crimes against homosexuals increased? Some psychiatrists think that those who commit such assaults, themselves either gay or straight, are motivated by their own unresolved feelings about homosexuality. Gays may seem easy targets since they are perceived (stereotypically) as effeminate and thus unlikely to fight back. It has also been thought that a more conservative climate and anti-gay groups like the Moral Majority may have fueled the increase in crimes against gays.

Gays are starting to fight back. In San Francisco, a group patrols the streets in an effort to protect gays. Activists in some cities are lobbying police for more protection. Community groups also try to reduce friction between gays and their adversaries. In San Francisco, for instance, teenagers are taught about gay life styles, and self-defense workshops are held in gay communities (*Newsweek* 23 March 1981: 30). As social commentator William Raspberry has warned, the attitude that homosexuals are "bad" and should be punished is held not only by those who think that homosexuality is a learned preference but also "by those who think gays are born gay" (*Arizona Republic* 8 June 1978).

In spite of his admission that no evidence exists that homosexual men do any harm, Raspberry expresses worry about what he considers the dangers of homosexuality—especially the alleged danger of "recruitment" of young people into the "ranks" of homosexuals. Those who oppose gay rights legislation, says Raspberry, believe that any such legislation is tantamount to a government certification that homosexuality is "perfectly all right." The use of inflammatory language, as in such terms as *recruitment* and *into the ranks*, implies that a vast army of male homosexuals is on the march.

The controversy about whether homosexuality is inborn or learned has not been resolved. Scientific evidence regarding a possible inborn disposition toward **homoeroticism** (sexual behavior with a same-sex partner) is inconclusive, as is evidence for an entirely learned sexual orientation (Bar-

field 1976; Evans 1978). Regardless of whether "nature," "nurture," or some combination of these factors is most influential, all sexual orientations are known to resist change, whether they follow or go against cultural expectations (Barfield 1976). In spite of this fact, and even though there is no evidence that association with a homosexual adult can make a (presumably) heterosexually oriented young person "turn gay," (Hunt 1978), fundamentalist religious leaders lean toward the nurture side of the nature versus nurture debate (*Newsweek* 23 February, 1981, 23–24). That is, they believe that homosexuality is a learned orientation and therefore can be unlearned.

An unspoken but closely connected belief appears to be that heterosexuality is very weak in the young. In this view, homosexual **role models** (persons on whose behavior we may pattern our own) can effectively destroy erotic interest in members of the other sex.

Antigays consider homosexuality a disaster that is running rampant throughout America. As evidence for this view, one senator noted that over a third of the states have passed laws guaranteeing gay rights. He also called homosexuality a "revolutionary force" working toward the "abolition of the family" (Von Driska 1978). Fundamentalist Christian antihomosexuals have mustered considerable support for their point of view. Relying on selected biblical passages as their authority for pursuing the matter, and linking their antigay "war" with patriotism, anti-Communism, and a "Mom and apple pie" view of the family, these **true believers** brought about the repeal of laws that forbade discrimination against homosexually oriented persons in several American cities in the late 1970s. The *Dictionary of Sociology* (1969) defines a true believer as one who has a deep need to belong to something larger than himself or herself. Because of this need, such persons show a strong tendency to become enthusiastic members of social movements, especially those that are extremist (Hoult 1969).

Paradoxical Beliefs

The antigay movement, as we have seen, considers gay men dangerous. This belief, however, is not confined to members of "crusades." It has also been found in college students (Steffensmeier 1970) and in members of the general public (Simmons 1969), and is even carried over to persons who are believed to have reoriented themselves from homosexuality to heterosexuality (Bobys and Laner 1979). This belief is paradoxical in view of the stereotype of homosexual men as passive, effeminate, and "like the weaker sex." Regardless of the large body of evidence that the great majority of gay men (and lesbian women) do not show gender characteristics of the other sex,[1] such stereotypes persist (Weinberg 1973; MacDonald and Games 1974; Tripp 1975).

Another paradox may be seen in the concern over AIDS (auto-immune deficiency syndrome), a disease in which homosexuals and others who are affected lose the ability to ward off infections. Some have argued that this disease, which affects only a small proportion of homosexuals, is a reason for avoiding all homosexual encounters. Yet, little similar concern is voiced regarding venereal disease as a rationale for avoiding all heterosexual encounters.

Efforts to remove homosexuals from positions of authority also persist. Several cases of discrimination against gays in the military are illustrative. According to a report in *Civil Liberties* (December 1981, 7), the army knew that Sergeant Perry Watkins was gay when it drafted him in 1968. During his thirteen years of service Watkins was open about his homosexuality, and the army itself ruled that his orientation in no way affected his performance; indeed, it granted him security clearances more than once. In March of 1981, however, the Department of Defense issued new rules stating that as a matter of policy, homosexuality is incompatible with military service, regardless of a soldier's military record. The army stripped Watkins of his security clearance and moved to discharge him for homosexuality, although his commanding officer had commended him for outstanding performance. A lawsuit filed on his behalf charged the army with violating his rights to due process and freedom of speech. In another case, ten women and two men sailors were charged with homosexuality by the U.S. Navy (*National NOW Times* October 1982).

With regard to efforts to remove homosexually oriented teachers from their jobs, Samuel P. Hunt, writing in *Medical Aspects of Human Sexuality* (1978, 103–4) noted that:

Homosexual men, more often than not . . . make good teachers because they tend to be humane and empathetic with young people of both sexes. It goes without saying that . . . good teachers, whatever their orientation, keep their personal life private . . . to deprive pupils of a good teacher solely because of homosexuality may do far more harm than good to all concerned, especially to the children.

We have noted that dread of homosexuals is paradoxical. Another paradox is found in society's simultaneous support and condemnation of prostitution (Velarde 1975; James 1978). Yet another paradox of prostitution was identified many years ago by sociologist Kingsley Davis, who noted that "purely from the angle of economic return, the hard question is not why so many women become prostitutes, but why so few of them do" (1937).

In recent years, we have seen the rise of the "massage parlor" phenomenon. Several types of massage parlors have been identified: genuine massage parlors operating as or with health clubs, and service establishments that provide only physical therapy and exercise; parlors whose advertising is seductive and where decor and conversation are sexually suggestive but where no sexual

---

1. See Abbott and Love 1972; Bell 1971; Corzine, Glassner, and Moreno 1977; Goldstein 1970; Hooker 1965; Laner 1978, 1979; Pierson and D'Antonio 1974; Reiss 1976; Robinson, Skeen, and Flake-Hobson 1982; Shaver and Freedman 1976; Simpson 1976; Sonenschein 1968; Tourney 1975; and Walum 1977, among others.

services are actually provided; parlors that are really disguised brothels, where "anything goes" in sexual terms; and finally, massage-and-masturbation parlors, which are believed to be the most prevalent type (Bryant and Palmer 1977). As Armstrong remarks, "the massage parlor as a locale of commercialized sex is constituted to a significant degree by the *customer's* wishes and the extent to which *he* is willing to offer financial reward" for their fulfillment (1978, 118) (italics ours).

Clearly, not all Americans decry prostitution or prostitutes. The "whore with a heart of gold" has been a staple of fiction in America and elsewhere. Hypocrisy is revealed in the proliferation of movies, plays, books, and humor about prostitution. A highly popular Broadway stage play, *The Best Little Whorehouse in Texas*, inspired a highly popular movie of the same name. Both play and movie were based on the story of the famed Chicken Ranch brothel that operated for years in La Grange, Texas until it was closed in 1973. When the movie opened in Austin, Texas in July 1982, a newspaper report commented that it was heralded "with all the bright lights and stars of a Hollywood opening night." The report continued:

Burt Reynolds and Dolly Parton, who portray a small-town Texas sheriff and the madame of the Chicken Ranch, headline the cast that will be on hand for a parade that will wind through downtown Austin and stop in front of the historic Paramount Theatre. The premiere is a benefit for the 67-year old theatre. The premiere showing, with tickets at $100, $200 and $500, was sold out (*Arizona Republic* 11, July, 1982).

Victimless Crimes?

Some believe that homosexual behavior and prostitution, each taking place between consenting adults, are victimless crimes. With regard to prostitution, opinions differ as to who is victimized. Some feminists believe that since prostitution degrades all women, its practice constitutes a crime against all women. Other feminists think that all women in a **patriarchal** (male-dominated)

society sell themselves in one way or another, and that prostitutes are a group that is unfairly punished for what all women do.

There are a number of other views on prostitution, none of which is totally consistent with the rest. A panel of "experts" not long ago argued that prostitution is not a victimless crime since customers, prostitutes, and the community itself is victimized by it; that punishment victimizes only poor and minority culture prostitutes; and, that any crimes connected with prostitution should be dealt with on their own, but that prostitution should be decriminalized (Medical Aspects of Human Sexuality, 1978). In a more recent view, it has been observed that prostitution constitutes an occupational pyramid with streetwalkers at its base. As one descends the pyramid, chances increase that a client will contract a venereal disease or become the victim of a crime that a prostitute perpetrates. Yet, since pimps force prostitutes into committing such crimes as assault and robbery, this raises the question of whether the prostitute or the pimp is the real criminal (Medical Aspects of Human Sexuality, 1981). Still another commentator notes that our society uses sex as a marketing commodity in the media, and encourages women to view themselves as sexual objects who can acquire material possessions or relationships by being seductive. From this perspective, it is ironic that the social system encourages prostitution but punishes its practitioners (Medical Aspects of Human Sexuality, 1978).

Finally, some argue that prostitutes are victims of sex stereotyping. That is, they are punished for earning their living with behaviors that are considered unacceptable for members of their sex only (James 1978, 1980). Men who patronize prostitutes are considered normal even though their behavior is also outside the law; the difference in status between male customer and female prostitute "tends to protect these men from the possibility of involvement in the criminal justice system" (1978, 177).

Homosexual behavior between consenting adults is also sometimes seen as a victimless crime. Adding to the seeming paradoxes that characterize both prostitution and homosexuality, researchers Brian Miller and Laud Humphreys have found that "closeted" gay men are more likely to be crime victims than are gay men who are open about their homosexuality. Miller and Humphreys investigated the murders of 161 gay men during a five-year period. "Almost two-thirds of the victims were highly secretive about their homosexuality," said Professor Humphreys. "In fact, 36% of the gay men were heterosexually married, with wives and children at the time of their deaths" (*San Francisco Sentinel* 12 December 1980). Male prostitutes and hustlers killed 64 percent of the gay victims in the study; the rest were murdered by "gay-bashing gangs." Miller and Humphreys (1980, 182) comment that

moral entrepreneurs and other agents who promote social conformity prescribe that homosexuals get married, settle down family-style, and fit in. For married homosexuals who are unable to relinquish same-sex activity, this prescription directs them into a singularly risky lifestyle. . . . What he may gain in avoidance of stigma, he loses in susceptibility to crime victimization. . . . Movement of homosexual marginals into openly gay lifestyles appears to *decrease* their vulnerability to violent crime. The gay world not only offers a variety of social, affectional, and cultural opportunities but also tends to protect members from those who may victimize them.

Captain Jerry Feinberg of the Los Angeles Police Department's Hollywood division has pointed out that "there are people out there who may not even be gay, who are letting themselves be picked up by gays to rob them" or to murder them (*San Francisco Examiner and Chronicle* 4 January 1981).

Threats to the Family?

Strongly negative attitudes toward homosexual men, some argue, may stem in part from heterosexuals' envy of homosexuals' unfamilial lives. Since conventional sexuality makes being a responsible head of a household the requisite for "sex or family pleasures," and since courtship is thought of as

the "minimum payment" for sex, "it vexes people to see others apparently matching the profits without having to pay as dearly for them" (Weinberg 1973, 14). Adversaries of homosexuals, writes Weinberg (1973, 17),

have done what they could to make homosexuals appear as outright enemies of the family. . . . Observe how preoccupation with the nuclear family, and the blind faith in reproduction as the standard for sexuality, and the religious motive, tie together. Reproduction and children and the promise of an afterlife are used by some as magical devices to cope with their fear of death. To many, the homosexual, who does not appear to be wearing these amulets, evokes this fear.

Any or all of these fears may lead to **homophobia,** which has been defined as feelings of personal anxiety, disgust, and avoidance of homosexuals (Milham, San Miguel, and Kellogg 1976). Apparently, no parallel term for prostitution exists (such as prostiphobia), possibly because a great many American men experience no personal anxiety or disgust about what these "bad girls" do, nor do they necessarily avoid their company. Because both homosexuality and prostitution are thought to be antifamily, however, members of both groups can be inferiorized in the name of profamily conservatism. As with other low-status groups, when outgroups are identified, judgments can be made about the superiority of one group over another, and members of the group or groups defined as inferior can then be targeted for oppression. For example, "it has been observed that women as an oppressed minority have a scapegoat status not unlike that suffered by Jews, blacks, religious heretics," and others defined as "deviant" members of the community (Saltzman 1978, 272). From the point of view of these so-called deviants, however, they are not the problem; rather, they see themselves as victims of hypocrisy, bigotry, and oppression. Homosexuals, for example, have been discriminated against in the areas of public employment, public accommodations, private employment, housing, education, real estate practices, credit practices, immigra-

"Parents of Gays" have formed organizations in support of their gay children. Movement of homosexuals into openly gay lifestyles appears to decrease their vulnerability to violent crime.

tion laws, and union practices, among many other areas of community life.

Neither prostitution nor homosexuality has always been considered antifamily. Similarly, the behaviors of prostitutes and homosexuals have not always been seen as unconventional. Evidence for these claims is presented in the following section.

ANALYZING THE PROBLEM: HOMOSEXUALITY AND PROSTITUTION: HISTORICAL AND CONTEMPORARY PERSPECTIVES

Historical Perspectives

Prostitution has not always been seen as encouraging social disorganization. The prominent fourth century churchman St. Augustine warned, "Suppress prostitution and capricious lusts will overthrow society."

As late as the nineteenth century, moralist William Lecky declared that the prostitute "is ultimately the most efficient guardian of virtue" and contended that if it were not for the social functions performed by prostitutes, the chastity of other women, the stability of the family, and the preservation of those social institutions that depend on sexual abstinence would be in jeopardy (Adler 1975, 57).

In other times and places, the activities of prostitutes were considered neither illegal nor scandalous, according to scholar Frieda Adler. The ancient Hebrews did not strongly disapprove of prostitution, and the Greeks elevated courtesans to positions of esteem. Such women, Adler writes, like the Japanese geisha, were well educated, of high artistic ability, and schooled in social graces.

Another contemporary scholar observes that prostitution of young girls under religious auspices may have promoted prostitution in the public sphere. Donald Shoemaker cites a large body of literature regarding numerous forms of prostitution that have been accepted in earlier times and in other societies (1977, 242). Clinard and Abbot (1973) tell us that prostitutes in India were known as temple dancers and entertainers, and that even today, Indian prostitutes equate their profession with such activities. As early as 300 B.C.E. (Before the Christian Era), temple prostitution was fully developed and highly esteemed in the Orient (Benjamin and Masters 1965).

In medieval times, the Church accepted and regulated prostitution, and derived part of its financial support from houses of prostitution (Adler 1975, 56). At the end of the fifteenth century, however, tolerance for prostitution declined.

The Protestant backlash against the sexual permissiveness among the Catholic clergy and laity, together with the Protestants' emphasis on the virtues of hard work, self-discipline, and abstinence, were antithetical to a climate of sexual freedom (Adler 1975, 56).

By the end of the eighteenth century, the prostitute, seen either as "sinner" or as "victim" could be considered a boundary marker between "bad" and "good" women (Gagnon 1977). Note that in the nineteenth century, the age of consent for sexual activity was thirteen years, and young prostitutes were apparently still widely available (Shoemaker 1977).

In the present century, commercialized, organized prostitution was at its height in the 1920s and 1930s, according to the American Social Health Association. Since that time, prostitution has continued to flourish, but the occupation has attracted many part-timers including former models, jobless actresses, runaway juveniles, and even housewives (Adler 1975, 65). Although the elaborate high-class brothel is, for practical purposes, no longer on the American scene, says Adler, houses of prostitution continue to operate under one guise or another—as massage parlors, for instance (Heyl 1977).

A review of the history of homosexuality, as we shall see next, reveals several parallels with the history of prostitution. For instance, like prostitution, homosexuality has been found throughout the historical record and in all parts of the world, although the meaning that various cultures have assigned to homosexuality has differed (Katchadourian and Lunde 1972).

The Old Testament condemns homosexuality explicitly. Reviewing the biblical story of Onan, who spilled his semen on the ground rather than complete sexual intercourse with his dead brother's wife, historian-sociologist Vern L. Bullough comments that it is not clear whether the Lord slew Onan for "wasting" semen or for his refusal to obey the custom that he take his sister-in-law as wife. "Generally, throughout Christian culture," Bullough writes, "this passage has been taken to justify the condemnation not only of contraception but of masturbation and homosexuality, since none of these activities results in procreation" (1979, 18). The story of Onan, however, says Bullough, clearly describes coitus interruptus. Following out Jewish history, Bullough notes that later tradition continued to emphasize the procreative aspects of

sex and to condemn male homosexual behavior.

Extreme hostility toward male homosexuality was characteristic of many later commentators, "who equated homosexuality with Greek influences and were attempting to keep Israel pure from Greek ideas in general and sexual ideology in particular" (1979, 18–19). Bullough contends that it is not so much what the scriptures say about homosexuality that has dominated Western thinking, but what they were interpreted to mean. Antihomosexual aspects of the story of Lot, for instance, seem to have been added much later than the original writing, as part of an anti-Greek campaign in Palestine (1979, 20). Even the word *sodomy* does not have its origins in the sins of Sodom, for which that city was destroyed. Rather, the clearest association of the destruction of Sodom with homosexuality appears in the writings of Philo Judaeus, a hellenized Egyptian Jew. Bullough notes that the Jewish concern with homosexuality was at its height when Christianity appeared on the scene, and Judaeus' interpretation was current at that time. Yet, "in spite of such hostility, there is no evidence that the Jews mounted a large-scale campaign against homosexuality" (1979, 22).

The prevalence and acceptance of homosexual relationships in classical antiquity, on the other hand, is well known, i.e., the sexual component of tutorial relationships between older and younger Greek men. Psychiatrists Katchadourian and Lunde note that "some Greek cities had regiments of lovers fighting side by side" (1972, 275). Another historian tells us that while the Greeks seem to have been almost free from "perversion" (sadomasochism), they wholeheartedly accepted "inversion" (homosexual behavior), recognizing "that the sexual nature of every human being contains both homosexual and heterosexual elements" (Taylor 1973). Love relationships between men were absolutely general and highly valued.

Tripp, the psychologist-historian author of *The Homosexual Matrix* (1975) briefly describes the history of homosexuality in several other societies. Among these, several require young men to be sodomized during puberty rites "to make them strong." Tripp also tells us that

even the Hebrews practiced religious **fellatio** [oral-genital sexual contact] until after the Babylonian exile. . . . Among the eastern Peruvian natives . . . homosexuality was dominant to the point of heterosexual contacts being relegated to only two or three ceremonial occasions a year. (1975, 64) (italics ours)

An example closer to home is the native American tribal practice of *berdache,* in which boys are raised to have some of the qualities of women and are available for sexual use by the men of the tribe (Tripp 1975).

Our own society, Tripp writes (1975, 71), contains some cultural contradictions. On the one hand, we derive a brand of individualism and personal striving from our Greco-Roman heritage. This kind of society, which rates men on an individual basis, emphasizes winner-loser distinctions, and creates "heroes" is conducive to "homosexual motivations." On the other hand, from later sources (the biblical-Christian), we derive a rule book and a philosophy that are antihomosexual. These combined contradictory elements, writes Tripp, may account for both the prevalence of homosexuality and the strong feelings against it. Thus, the very qualities we think of as the province of "real men" or "men's men" (i.e., heroism and winning the game) may be those that inspire or encourage some men to be "men's men" in the less conventional sense.

Given our Judaic-Catholic-Protestant historical routing, coupled with Puritan ideals emphasizing hard work and denying today's pleasures for the sake of tomorrow, it is little wonder, perhaps, that today's fundamentalist Christians and some others find both homosexuality and prostitution an affront. However, although no homoerotic act exists that cannot be performed—and indeed, is not performed—as a heteroerotic act, and al-

though such heteroerotic acts are not reproduction oriented, *such acts are condemned only when they occur between persons of the same sex.* Why some and not others are condemned for identical behaviors is explained by a definition of socially valued sexual activity:

Socially useful acts are heterosexual ones (which, in the past, were needed to keep the birthrate high enough to overcome the astronomical child death rate, and to instantly distinguish males from females . . . so that division of labor by sex was simple and psychologically compelling). So, most people have been taught to regard socially wasteful gender acts . . . as pathological, or loathsome or sinful. (Smith 1975a, 91)

Insofar as prostitutes and their customers are not engaged in "socially useful" sex activity, some can also define prostitution as pathological, loathsome, sinful, or a combination of these.

Contemporary Perspectives

Although the psychiatric and psychological professional organizations are committed to a nonpathological view of homosexuality, some of their members remain unconvinced. Weinberg comments with regard to this reluctance: "You can lead an expert to the source of his fear and disgust, but you cannot always make him drink of his observations" (1973, 39). Illustratively, Smith (1975a, 90) relates a tale of two psychiatrists, both panelists at a professional conference. After a speech in which one of these men had discussed homosexuality, he was asked whether he believed homosexuality and **transvestism** (dressing in the clothing of the other sex) to be illnesses. He responded:

As much as I agree with the aims of gay liberation—to end social discrimination . . . I still believe that both of those conditions are forms of sickness. I've had over a thousand homosexual and transvestite patients in my practice and *every* single one—*without exception*—has had some kind of psychological hang-up—often a *serious* psychological hang-up. Therefore, it is obvious to me that homosexuality and transvestism either *are* mental illnesses, or they *cause* mental illness, or they are the *results* of mental illness. No other hypothesis fits the facts.

After the applause had subsided, the second psychiatrist spoke: Although I am now retired, I practiced psychiatry for over forty years. I have had over *two* thousand *heterosexual* and *non*-transvestite patients in my practice. Every single one—*without exception*—had some kind of psychological hang-up—often a *serious* psychological hang-up. Therefore, it is obvious to me that *heterosexuality* and *non*-transvestism either *are* mental illnesses, or they *cause* mental illness, or they are the *results* of mental illness. No other hypothesis fits the facts (italics in original).

As the comments of the second psychiatrist make clear the absurdities in the statements of the first psychiatrist, so recent research has countered several of the purportedly negative aspects of prostitution listed in the Model Penal Code of 1959, described earlier. For example, on the question of whether prostitution is controlled by organized crime, a 1967 presidential commission demolished the notion that organized crime is heavily involved. Rather, the commission argued, organized crime has turned to more lucrative areas such as politics and the stock market (Lindsey 1976). The 1959 Code held that prostitutes are responsible for the spread of venereal disease. A United Nations study, however, found that in America, only 5 percent of all venereal disease cases were traceable to prostitutes (Lindsey 1976, 20). As one psychiatrist put it, "more venereal disease is probably spread by promiscuous amateurs than by professionals" (Marmor 1978, 101). The Model Penal Code of 1959 worried that prostitution would lead to corruption among the police, referring to "payoffs" and the like. Police behavior in dealing with prostitution may be criticized on other grounds, however. Occasionally, efforts at entrapment of prostitutes may have tragic results, as in a 1982 case described as "police lawlessness" (Davidson 1982, 7). In that case, an undercover policewoman's bullet paralyzed a twenty-four-year-old male from the neck

down. Donald Collier was sitting in his car when he was approached by the officer:

The policewoman's assignment was to dress provocatively and then walk the streets trying to fool men into believing she was a prostitute. It is part of a regular operation by the Denver Police Department. Whenever the policewoman succeeds, she charges the man with the misdemeanor of patronizing a prostitute or soliciting for prostitution. In other operations, men on undercover assignment seek to fool prostitutes into thinking they are customers. All of the officers in this decoy operation volunteer for duty (Davidson 1982, 7).

Davidson raises a number of questions. Why was an unarmed man shot as he sat in his car? Why was pulling a gun necessary to write a ticket for a petty offense? Further, as Davidson puts it, "Most fundamentally, why was a police officer on the streets of Denver trying to lure people into committing a victimless crime?" The issue of police corruption in this regard was addressed some time ago by New York City Police Commissioner Patrick V. Murphy, who said, "By charging our police with the responsibility to enforce the unenforceable, we subject them to disrespect and corruptive influences" (Davidson 1982). In this view, it is not prostitution that leads to police corruption; rather, it is inappropriate law enforcement.

Prostitution has endured despite centuries of attack. The Bible contains innumerable references to "whores" and "harlots." Prostitutes do not see themselves as a threat to marriage or family life, and often characterize their services as therapeutic as much as sexual. As one prostitute put it, "There will always be a need for us. As long as the world has lonely, unhappy, or bored men, they will seek us" (Auerback 1978, 11).

Such statements may be seen as efforts to counter negative self-images that prostitutes, and indeed all women, derive from common socialization into the "whore-madonna" ideology; that is, we teach young females a sharp distinction between "bad" and "good" girls.

Homosexuality also suffers the stigma of

the "bad" label, but more often the term *un-natural* is applied to same-sex orientation. Yet, some years ago, Ford and Beach (1951) published extensive data indicating that some form of homosexual behavior occurs in almost all species, which calls the label *unnatural* into question. In human societies, Ford and Beach found homosexual behavior virtually everywhere, including societies that maintain strict negative sanctions against it. Gebhard (1976) has summarized a number of studies of the incidence of homo-sexuality published in America and in West-ern European countries. He reports that between one-quarter and one-third of all adult males, including the college educated, have had overt homosexual experience since puberty. This estimate is similar to those reported by Alfred Kinsey and his co-work-ers well over a quarter of a century ago (Kin-sey et al. 1948; Kinsey et al. 1953). Kinsey and his associates found that homosexuality and heterosexuality are not distinct entities. Rather, in their exclusive forms, they define the endpoints on a continuum of sexual ori-entations. More recent research has gener-ally confirmed the findings of the Kinsey reports, despite a number of criticisms about their sampling procedures and other aspects of these early surveys.

Male homoaffectional behavior is not ac-ceptable in public, with certain exceptions, one of which is in sport contact. Homoaffec-tional behavior is typical of locker-room and other more public sport settings. We may think, for instance, of the acceptability of men patting one another's buttocks, and of their hugging and lifting one another with close body contact. Garner and Smith (1977) have shown that homosexuality is prevalent among male members of college athletic teams to a far greater extent than had previ-ously been believed. Other societies do not draw such sharp lines between arenas in which such behaviors may or may not be displayed between men. In many Western countries (e.g., Spain, France, and Italy), hugging and kissing between men on greet-ing and parting is expected and accepted.

Members of the antigay movement see

questions of "recruitment" of the young by adult male homosexuals as extremely press-ing. Yet, considerable evidence exists indi-cating that the use of the young for sexual purposes is primarily a heterosexual, not a homosexual, phenomenon.

The question of a special interest of adult gay men in young boys is directly addressed in several recent studies that approach the topic from different research-issue perspec-tives. Some light on the question, for in-stance, is shed through an examination of homosexual personals ads in newspaper and magazine columns. As in similar ads placed by heterosexuals, these ads typically seek partners as companions, dates, permanent mates, and for sexual encounters. Advertis-ers are anonymous except for the informa-tion they choose to reveal about themselves to readers. Because of this anonymity, such ads are less likely to be untruthful or to contain defensive statements than might face-to-face interviews or questionnaires on sensitive topics. Two recent studies of such ads indicate that homosexual advertisers of both sexes show no particular interest in so-liciting young partners (Laner 1978, 1979). This finding is consonant with the conclu-sion MacFarlane (1978) reached after exten-sive study of reports on sexual abuse of children: "Although some **pedophiles** [those whose primary sexual gratification involves contact with children] are homosexuals, the correlation in many people's minds between homosexuality and child molesters is a fal-lacious one that is unsubstantiated by fact. The vast majority of known child abusers are heterosexual (1978, 87) [italics ours].

Another study also reports that between 85 and 90 percent of cases of child sexual abuse involve heterosexual males misusing female children (Herjanic 1978). Research conducted at the Massachusetts Center for the Diagnosis and Treatment of Sexually Dangerous Persons resulted in findings de-scribed by psychologist Richard Smith:

Heterosexual males, with their interest in female partners who have soft musculature, hairless bodies, and relatively high-pitched voices, would sometimes regress (under psychological duress) to being aroused by pre-pubertal children, whereas gay men, with their eye to sexual partners having solid muscles, hairy chests and legs, and lower pitched voices, found it nearly impossible—whether under duress or not—to lust after immature youngsters (1978, 2).

Despite the considerable evidence to the contrary, antigay spokespersons continue to believe that homosexual men characteristically prey on the young. On the basis of such fallacious claims, fear of homosexual men is kept high among the unknowledgeable, resulting in "widespread disapproval of homosexuals [who] often experience discrimination and physical abuse as a result" (Bryant 1977, 6).

Prostitutes as Victims

Although capital punishment has not been suggested for prostitutes, they are victims not only of discriminatory law enforcement practices (James 1978) but to some extent by the nature of "the life" itself.

The prostitute's life is highly competitive (Stone 1976). Relationships with other prostitutes are poor; even at the upper levels of the profession, prostitutes are highly distrustful of their co-workers, and disloyalty and mutual exploitation mark their relationships (Bryan 1965). Yet, the economic rewards of prostitution are higher than those of most other "female" occupations, especially for the young and those at the upper levels (Benjamin and Masters 1965, 93). The prositute is paid not only for sexual service but also for loss of social status (James 1978, 177). At lower levels, financial rewards are not as great, and they lessen even more as time passes. Life for the prostitute has been called a "downward spiral" in which drug use, dealings with pimps and police, distrust, and other problems mount (Stone 1976, 24).

Most researchers agree that a basic causative factor in entering prostitution is to be found in childhood experiences, especially in unsatisfactory relationships with parents (Barry 1959), which lead to low feelings of personal worth *as female*. Compensation for such feelings is sought in a life-style where worth *as female* is reaffirmed through the payment for sexual service that can be obtained elsewhere (e.g., from wives or girlfriends) without charge.

James and Meyerding (1978) compared prostitutes with nonprostitute women and found significant differences between groups: prostitutes had learned less about sex from their parents, had experienced more sexual advances from older persons (only a small proportion of whom were strangers), were more often the objects of incest, initiated sexual activity at an earlier age, and experienced a higher incidence of rape (over half the sample) than did nonprostitute women.

Harold Greenwald (1958) found an "amazing similarity" in the backgrounds of the "call girls" he studied: not one said that she came from a family in which there was a permanent, well-adjusted relationship between her parents, and over 90 percent said that they felt rejected by both parents, which led to feelings of being unwanted, unloved, and unworthy of being wanted or loved.

Over 70 percent of the prostitutes in still another study reported that one or both parents—most often the father—were absent in childhood (James 1978, 193). Wallace's (1978) study of over 300 arrestees (primarily streetwalkers and massage parlor employees) also found that incest was a common experience early in these women's lives, and was often followed by their running away.

Since teenage runaways often have no means of emotional or financial support, prostitution seems to provide an alternative—a measure of security and identity—and such young women are emotionally vulnerable to pimps (Adler 1975, 171). Almost all women are brought up to believe that they need a man to care for them, love them, and make a home for them. As such, women's socialized need for men is reinforced by a woman's status being determined by that of her man (James 1978, 189, 191).

Taking into account these kinds of observations, one theory of why women enter prostitution is based on (1) early life experiences, (2) sex stereotyping, and (3) societal discrimination against women (James 1978). Another theory suggests that all women use sex to equalize status differences between themselves and men. "Philosophically, at least, prostitutes may be only contractually removed from the sexual ploys a . . . designing wife might use to seduce financial favors from her husband" (Adler 1975, 69). This idea is not far from the formula advanced by Marabel Morgan in her widely read "advice to housewives" book, *The Total Woman* (1973). Morgan urged wives to

A prostitute and a potential "john." Most researchers agree that basic causative factors for entering prostitution are found in childhood experiences.

make themselves into seductresses to keep their husbands happy at home, pointing out that a sexually happy man will give up his money for a new fur coat or a vacation trip—a notion that is clearly a "play for pay" scheme. Yet, Morgan characterized herself as a promoter of Christian virtues associated with home and hearth.

At the upper levels of prostitution, part-timers, homemakers-turned-prostitute, and full-time call girls may look and act enough alike to be virtually indistinguishable, and may lead economically secure, arrest-free lives (Adler 1975, 72). At the lower levels, however, prostitutes' lives are so marked by "psychosocial pathology that it is difficult to know what part, if any, prostitution contributes to their many difficulties" (Adler 1975, 73).

Differences in status between men and women appear to be at the root of much of the problem of prostitution. The following passage, written many years ago, indicates how status differences translate into discriminatory laws and differential law enforcement. Readers may judge whether these realities have changed meaningfully in the years since Kingsley Davis wrote this passage:

The professional prostitute being a social outcast may be periodically punished without disturbing the usual course of society; no one misses her while she is serving out her term—no one, at least, about whom society has any concern. The man [customer] however, is something more than a partner in an immoral act; he discharges important social and business relations. . . . He cannot be imprisoned without deranging society (1937, 752).

In an earlier section, we examined how homosexual males are victimized for their sexual preference or behavior or both. Although this victimization continues, signs of change are evident. These signs, and policies for resolving the problems of unconventional sexuality, are addressed in the final section of this chapter.

ALTERNATIVE POLICIES FOR RESOLVING THE PROBLEM: CHANGING VIEWS AND ELIMINATING OPPRESSION

Labeling pornography, prostitutes, and homosexuals as "deviant" has not resolved the problems associated with unconventional forms of sexuality. As psychiatrist Thomas Szasz (1970) contends, the term merely draws an artificial boundary between "us" and "them," which is used to justify their social control, oppression, persecution, or even destruction. Further, as sociologist Howard Becker put it, "social groups create deviance by making those rules whose infraction constitutes deviance" (1963, 8–9).

One alternative to continuing the "us" versus "them" distinction is to change the rules. Another is to educate the public. These alternatives are already in motion, in a number of ways, with regard to prostitution and homosexuality, as we shall see. Other alternatives have been suggested with regard to pornography, on which our discussion focuses first.

Pornography: Suppression or Change?

Recent studies have shown that sexual violence in the mass media is on the increase, that viewing pornographic films, reinforces men's acceptance of violence against women, that men exposed to pornography have a lowered belief in victim trauma resulting from rape, that sexually violent depictions on record album covers are associated with a lowered belief in rape as a violent crime, and that depictions of rape increase males' aggression against females (Check 1981, 14). The studies reviewed here were all conducted after the Commission on Obscenity and Pornography (1970) concluded that there were no antisocial effects of exposure to pornography. Gray's (1982) study of the effects of pornography notes that although some have argued that pornography consumption is a cathartic device through which aggressive impulses might be discharged without harm to others, "pornog-

raphy can also be a tool for validating a deeper anger toward women" (1982, 394). Gray argues that men's unresolved anger toward women is more the problem than pornography. Insofar as some find the images of women in pornography repulsive, says Gray, it is futile to

try to change images of women by reducing the amount of pornography available. Suppression rarely changes social images over time; more often it drives them underground, thereby giving them a tantalizing flavor. Suppression could even encourage a more extreme pornographic genre (1982, 394–95).

Gray (1982, 387) calls attention to the division of opinion as to what should be done about pornography, even among those who are opposed to it. Some think that protection of the First Amendment, which guarantees freedom of speech and the press, is more important than suppressing pornography, while others try to educate the public about pornography's harmful effects and encourage boycotting such materials.

What are the alternatives to suppression? We present several, all cited in Gray (1982). Johnson and Goodchilds (1973) have recommended a pornography more clearly in line with both feminist and humanist values. Neither sex would be manipulated or used as a sex object, as they are in conventional pornography. English (1980) suggested a pornography in which older women pair with younger men, in which there would be a greater variety of body types, and in which sexual expression would be less phallus centered. Gray herself recommends cultural mechanisms to encourage socially acceptable forms of anger resolution, in an effort to improve communication in interpersonal relations as antidotes to pornography that evokes anger against women, which she believes is unlikely to be eliminated even if alternate forms are developed. She also recommends (as antidotal)

changes in the rigid sex role expectations and notions of masculinity which lead to pain and anger when they cannot be lived up to, and improved education for men about the nature of being a woman and about female sexuality. Without these, violence toward women can find its expression with or without pornography. With these mechanisms, pornography may . . . be viewed as just another form of fantasy, probably not dangerous and maybe no longer attractive to men who are no longer angry (1982, 395–96).

The Gay Rights Movement

An effort to bring our values, norms, and laws in line with contemporary reality is the most recent reemergence of the gay rights movement. Gay rights activists (and others) contend that norms against homosexual behavior between consenting adults serve neither the society's interests nor those of specific minority groups within it. For that reason, the National Gay Task Force formed several years ago to spearhead the effort of homosexuals to educate the public toward tolerance of the unconventional and toward "enlightened legislation" (*Free Spirit Newletter* 1978). The increased visibility of gay men and lesbian women in recent years, as they have formed into lobbying groups, has produced general reexamination of biases against homosexuality— except among far-right fundamentalist religionists.

As sociologist Frederick L. Whitam has explained, homosexuality is neither a "condition" nor a "role." Rather, it is a nondominant, regularly occurring sexual orientation (1975, 1977, 1978). Relative to the heterosexually oriented majority, this fact puts homosexuality into perspective, analogous to the regular occurrence of left-handedness in a predominantly right-handed world. The National Gay Task Force has embarked on an educational campaign called "We ARE Your Children," in an attempt to counter erroneous images of homosexuality projected in Moral Majority "crusades" (*National Gay Task Force Newsletter* 1977, 3).

The gay liberation movement has been effective in producing legislation in various cities to bar antigay discrimination. Some cities now have affirmative action programs protecting gay rights, among them, Boston,

New York City, Portland, Oregon, and Urbana, Illinois.

While full acceptance of homosexuality may not yet have taken place, some evidence for partial acceptance exists. Ward (1979), for instance, has found that compared with a similar study conducted some years ago, "sinful lust" is less often attributed to homosexuals, but "sensitive intellectual" characteristics are attributed more often.

Television programming more often includes homosexual characters in either neutral or sympathetic portrayals: Jody on "Soap" and Sidney on "Love, Sidney" are examples. Movies treat homosexual themes more often. *Personal Best* dealt with a lesbian romance as a subsidiary theme, and *Making Love* dealt with male homosexuality as a central theme. Occasional negative portrayals are also shown, as in the film *Cruising*.

Weekly newsmagazines such as *Newsweek* and *Time* have discussed homosexuality in feature articles, and magazines produced especially for the college audience deal straightforwardly with "gays and straights" on campus (Gustaitis 1982). *TV Guide* produced a two-part series dealing with the changes the gay lobby has produced in television programming (30 May 1981, 6 June 1981) and documentaries about various aspects of homosexuality have appeared a number of times in recent years (*TV Guide* 11 October, 1979; CBS's "60 Minutes" 9 January 1983).

Gay men and lesbians have formed groups within various churches, including "Integrity" and "Affirmation" in mainline Protestant denominations. They have also

inspired similar organizations among Mennonites, Pentecostals, Mormons, Christian Scientists, Seventh-Day Adventists and Jews. In many cities, gays have organized their own churches, synagogues, and even Zen Buddhist centers. The first gay Christian denomination—the Universal Fellowship of Metropolitan Community Churches— has applied for membership in the National

Council of Churches (*Newsweek* 1982c, 113–114).

Other church-based associations have been formed within the Catholic church and among the Quakers. The American Friends Service Committee of the Quakers has recently adopted an affirmative action policy, which includes the involvement of homosexuals in committees and on staff. "One aspect of affirmative action is to let those who are not part of the minority which has been discriminated against learn more about the discrimination" (*Spotlight*, 9 January 1982), claims the AFSC, noting two books it recommends: *Is the Homosexual My Neighbor?* by Scanzoni and Mollenkott and *The Men with the Pink Triangle* by Heger, the latter dealing with the treatment of homosexuals in Nazi concentration camps during World War II.

Legal gains in recent years have included passage of a lesbian-gay rights law in Wisconsin, prohibiting discrimination against homosexuals in all areas regulated by the state (*National NOW Times* April 1982, 17), and repeal the Texas sodomy law, enacted in 1974. U.S. District Judge Jerry Buchmeyer stated in his ruling that the law violated both the fundamental right of privacy and the right to equal protection of the law guaranteed by the U.S. Constitution (*National NOW Times* September 1982, 9). Gay marriage unions are now discussed in textbooks for college courses in marriage and the family (Scanzoni and Scanzoni 1981) and in law journals (*University of Pennsylvania Law Review* 1978, 193–216).

This educative effort has predictably produced backlash, which is located primarily in lower middle class strata employed in bureaucratic or-

The porno district in New York City's Times Square. Studies done on the effects of pornography reveal conflicting opinions. Some researchers feel that there are no antisocial effects from exposure to pornography, while others have argued that it may encourage violence towards women.

ganizations or in highly competitive small businesses. In a period of economic stagnation and rising prices, these strata are excluded from participation in a life style of affluence or hedonistic indulgence, and they resent those they believe do so. Thus antagonism toward homosexuality in these strata has the same roots as the tax revolt, and opposition to abortion, contraception, and the women's movement (Greenberg and Bystryn 1978).

On the other hand, the positive changes, which signal understanding and a lessening of persecution and oppression, are the focus of another scholar's comments:

In recent years, the public posture toward homosexuality has changed considerably in the direction of more tolerance if not permissiveness. . . . Social discrimination is eroding informally, as well as formally. Coping with residual hostile public responses is still traumatic for many homosexuals, however. . . . Not only is homosexuality becoming more accepted as an alternate sexual mode, but concomitantly, bisexuality is also becoming relatively prevalent and even "chic" in some avant-garde circles (Byrant 1977, 11–12).

Women and Self-Definition

Women who have been objects of male definitions (Adler 1975, 83) have begun to define themselves. This effort is part of the most recent revival of the women's liberation movement. For example, many contemporary women are unwilling to accept sexual activity as the measure of female morality, and do not approve of standards that permit a promiscuous male to be admired while a promiscuous female is denigrated (Ader 1975, 83).

Adler believes that legalization of prostitution, along with social acceptance of female sexuality, will take prostitution out of the "nether world of vice" to which it has been assigned. Legalization, however is not a goal that prostitutes themselves seek. Rather, they advocate decriminalization. In recent years, prostitutes have formed unions, hoping not only to destigmatize their work but also to enhance their working conditions. One such union, PUMA (Prostitutes Union

of Massachussetts) consists largely of streetwalkers. Among their aims are the provision of day-care centers for their children, public education about prostitution, and the development of a lobby for decriminalizing prostitution (Lindsey 1976, 20). Other similar unions formed in other cities include PONY (Prostitutes of New York), ASP (Association of Seattle Prostitutes), DOLPHIN in Hawaii (Dump Obsolete Laws; Prove Hypocrisy Isn't Necessary), and, perhaps the most well known of these unions, COYOTE (Call Off Your Old Tired Ethics) in San Francisco.

COYOTE, started in 1972 by Margo St. James, a former madam, claimed 8,000 members only four years after its founding (Lindsey 1976, 20). In 1976, the first world meeting of prostitutes took place; its theme was decriminalization of prostitution (MacLean 1976).

Decriminalization has been held to be the least abusive method of dealing with prostitution. Rasmussen and Kuhn (1976, 292) believe that the newer forms of sex-for-money, such as massage parlors, will be fully decriminalized in the near future. "Decriminalization differs from legalization in that, instead of creating more legal involvement, it removes prostitution from the criminal code entirely" (James 1978, 198).

In decriminalizing prostitution, America would be following the pattern of most of the member nations of the United Nations that have eliminated the crime of prostitution and have abandoned attempts to regulate it (United Nations 1951). "The criminal laws in those countries seek instead to control public solicitation and to discourage the pimps and procurers who live off the earnings of prostitutes" (James 1978, 198). In James's view, the least abusive form of community control that might be exercised over prostitutes would be to require each woman to obtain a small-business license and a health card. Has decriminalization been successful in other countries? In Sweden, prostitution is "a woman's own affair, unless she becomes a public nuisance. In Amsterdam, prostitution flourishes openly without apparent impairment of personal security, economic prosperity, or moral decay" (Greenblatt 1978, 106).

The future of COYOTE's effort to decriminalize prostitution may depend on its ability to find allies in the women's movement, law reform groups, and other sectors that are committed to opposing the oppression of minorities, says sociologist John Gagnon (1977, 293). Another potential source of acceptance is the business community, which gives increasing evidence of courting the homosexual market (*Business Week* 3 September 1979).

If COYOTE and other similar organizations are successful, future generations may see less and less of a line between so-called good and bad women. This may lead, in turn, to a focus on individual behaviors rather than on "categorical crimes" and may reduce victimization of all women.

SUMMARY

This chapter has focused on three forms of unconventional sexuality: pornography, prostitution, and homosexuality. Both prostitutes and homosexuals may be seen as members of oppressed social groups. Although their behavior is labeled as deviant or unnatural or both, prostitution and homosexuality have been found in virtually all societies throughout history. Laws against the sexual activities of prostitutes and homosexuals exist in spite of the widespread view that their behaviors are often victimless crimes. Such laws may be seen as carryovers from an earlier era when they were functional, and as part of America's generally negative attitude toward those who are overtly sexually "different." (If all sex-negative laws were fully enforced, *most* Americans would be in jail. The affront of homosexuals and prostitutes, it appears, is in being forthright about what many others hide.)

Homosexuals have been recognized as a major force in the marketplace, and today many businesses not only do not discrimi-

nate against them but also court the spendable dollars they represent. Prostitutes are organizing, lobbying in Washington, and working toward decriminalization of the so-called world's oldest profession.

Fundamentalists, however, strongly oppose granting homosexuals civil rights and oppose in general any sexuality that is not reproduction oriented. These attitudes are based on the belief that both homosexuality and prostitution are antifamily. The falsity of such beliefs has been demonstrated repeatedly. In any case, neither prostitution nor homosexuality will cease to exist— whether society ignores them, accepts them, or rejects them. At present, some see them as appropriate subjects for oppression by those with more power in society.

STUDY QUESTIONS

1. You are a member of a debating team. Develop an argument for the following position: To include homosexuality and prostitution in the same chapter is demeaning to homosexuals.

2. You are a member of a debating team. Develop an argument for the following position: To include homosexuality and prostitution in the same chapter is demeaning to prostitutes.

3. What would the effect or effects of legalizing marriage between homosexuals be? On homosexuals themselves? On the heterosexual majority?

4. Argue for or against the notion that exposure to pornography leads to decreased direct violence against women.

5. Argue for or against the position that men who patronize prostitutes should be arrested and given the same sentence as the arrested prostitute receives.

6. America has been called sex-negative. Yet on television, in movies, and in other media, we seem obsessed with sexual themes. In view of this, how does it make sense to call America sex-negative?

REFERENCES

Abbott, S., and B. Love. 1972. *Sappho was a right-on woman: A liberated view of lesbianism.* New York: Stein & Day.

Adler, F. 1975. Sisters in crime: *The rise of the new female criminal.* New York: McGraw-Hill.

Arizona Republic. 8 June 1978; 21 September 1978; 11 July 1982.

Auerback, A. 1978. Secrets of prostitutes' success. *Medical Aspects of Human Sexuality* 12(9):11.

Barfield, A. 1976. Biological influences in sex differences in behavior. In Sex differences: Social and biological perspectives, ed. M.S. Teitelbaum. Garden City, N.Y.: Anchor.

Barry, J. V. 1959. Prostitution: A report from Australia. *British Journal of Delinquency* 9(3): 182–91.

Becker, H. S. 1963. *Outsiders: Studies in the sociology of deviance.* New York: Free Press.

Bell, R. R. 1971. *Social deviance.* Homewood, Ill.: Dorsey.

Benjamin, H., and R.E.L. Masters. 1965. *Prostitution and morality.* London: Souvenir.

Bobys, R. S., and M. R. Laner. 1979. On the stability of stigmatization: The case of ex-homosexual males. *Archives of Sexual Behavior* 8(3): 247–61.

Bryan, J. H. 1965. Apprenticeships in prostitution. *Social Problems* 12 (Winter): 287–97.

Bryant, C. D. 1977. *Sexual deviance in social context.* New York: New Viewpoints.

Bryant, C. D., and C. E. Palmer. 1977. Tense muscles and the tender touch: Massage parlors, "hand whores," and the subversion of service. In *Sexual deviance in social context,* ed. C. D. Bryant. New York: New Viewpoints.

CBS. 1983. "Gay men and women in the military." On "60 Minutes" (9 January).

Bullough, V. L. 1979. *Homosexuality: A history.* New York: Meridian.

Business Week. 1979. Gays: A major force in the marketplace. (3 September): 118–20.

Check, J. V. P. 1981. Antisocial effects of violent pornography. *Medical Aspects of Human Sexuality* 15(8): 14–15

Civil Liberties. 1981. Army moves to discharge gay sergeant after 13 years. (December): 7

Clinard, M. B., and D. J. Abbot. 1973. *Crime in developing countries: A comparative perspective.* New York: Wiley.

Commission on Obscenity and Pornography. 1970. The report of the commission on obscenity and pornography. Washington, D.C.: U.S. Government Printing Office.

Conger, J. J. 1975. Proceedings of the American Psychological Association, Inc., for the year 1974: Minutes of the Annual Meeting of the Council of Representatives. *American Psychologist* 30: 620–51.

Corzine, J., B. Glassner, and J. Moreno. 1977. The gay movement and social change. Paper presented at the annual meeting of the American Sociological Association, Chicago, September.

Davidson, D. E. 1982. Police lawlessness: An obscene ending for a youngman. *Civil Liberties* (February): 7

Davis, K. 1937. The sociology of prostitution. *American Sociological Review* 2: 744–55.

Diamond, I. 1980. Pornography and repression: A reconsideration. *Signs* 5: 686–701.

Dienstbier, R. A. 1977. Sex and violence: Can research have it both ways? *Journal of Communication* 27: 176–88.

Encyclopedia of Sociology. 1981. Guilford, Conn.: DPG Reference Publishing.

English, D. 1980. The politics of porn. *Mother Jones* 5(April): 44–45.

Evans, R. B. 1978. Factors in the genesis of homosexuality. *Medical Aspects of Human Sexuality* (October): 87.

Ford, C., and F. Beach. 1951. *Patterns of sexual behavior.* New York: Harper & Row.

Free Spirit Newsletter. 1978. (September).

Gagnon, J. H. 1977. *Human sexualities.* Glenview, Ill.: Scott, Foresman.

Garner, B., and R. W. Smith. 1977. Are there really any gay male athletes? *Journal of Sex Research* 13(1): 22–34.

Gebhard, P. H. 1976. Incidence of overt homosexuality. In *Homosexuality: Final report and background papers,* ed. J. M. Livingood. Rockville, Md.: National Institute for Mental Health.

Goldstein, F. J. 1970. Sex identity, deviation, and inversion. In *Sex roles in a changing society,* ed. G. H. Seward and E. C. Williamson. New York: Random House.

Gray, S. H. 1982. Exposure to pornography and aggression toward women: The case of the angry male. *Social Problems* 29(4): 387–98.

Greenberg, D. F., and M. H. Bystryn. 1978. Social sources of the prohibition against male homosexuality. Paper presented at the annual meeting of the Society for the Study of Social Problems, San Francisco, September.

Greenwald, H. 1958. The call girl: A social and psychoanalytic study. New York: Ballantine.

Gustaitis, R. 1982. At issue: Gays and straights. *Nutshell* (Fall): 73–76.

Harris, M. 1973. *The Dilly boys: The game of male prostitution in Picadilly.* Rockville, Md.: New Perspectives.

Herjanic, B. 1978. Medical symptoms of sexual abuse in children. *Medical Aspects of Human Sexuality* 12(9): 139–140.

Heyl, B. S. 1977. The madam as teacher: The training of house prostitutes. *Social Problems* 24(5): 545–55.

Hooker, E. 1965. An empirical study of some relations between sexual patterns and gender identity in male homosexuals. In *Sex research: New developments,* ed. J. Money. New York: Holt, Rinehart & Winston.

Hoult, T. F. 1969. *Dictionary of modern sociology.* Totowa, NJ: Littlefield, Adams.

Hunt, S. P. 1978. Influence of a homosexual father. *Medical Aspects of Human Sexuality* 12(9): 103–4.

James, J. 1978. The prostitute as victim. In *The victimization of women,* eds. J. R. Chapman and M. Gates. Beverly Hills: Sage.

James, J., and J. Meyerding. 1978. Early sexual experience as a factor in prostitution. *Archives of Sexual Behavior* 7(1): 31–42.

Johnson, P., and J. D. Goodchilds. 1973. Pornography, sexuality, and social psychology. *Journal of Social Issues* 29: 231–38.

Katchadourian, H. A., and D. T. Lunde. 1972. *Fundamentals of human sexuality.* New York: Holt, Rinehart & Winston.

Keerdoja, E. 1978. Anita and the gays. *Newsweek* (13 March).

Kinsey, A. C., W. B. Pomeroy, and C. E. Martin. 1948. *Sexual behavior in the human male.* Philadelphia: Saunders.

Kinsey, A. C., W. B. Pomeroy, C. E. Martin, and P. Gebhard. 1953. *Sexual behavior in the human female.* Philadelphia: Saunders.

Knight-Ridder News Service. 24 October 1982.

Laner, M. R. 1974. Prostitution as an illegal vocation: A sociological overview. In *Deviant behavior: Occupational and organizational bases,* ed. C. D. Bryant. Chicago: Rand McNally.

———. 1978. Growing older male: Heterosexual and homosexual. *Gerontologist* 18: 496–501.

———. 1979. Growing older female: Heterosexual and homosexual. *Journal of Homosexuality* 4(3): 267–75.

Levitt, E. F., and A. D. Klassen, Jr. 1974. Public attitudes toward homosexuality: Part of the 1970 national survey by the Institute for Sex Research. *Journal of Homosexuality* 1(1): 29–43.

Lindsey, K. 1976. Streetwalkers organize in Boston, *Ms.* 5(3): 20.

Los Angeles Times. Nov. 9 1978.

MacDonald, A. P. Jr., and R. G. Games. 1974. Some characteristics of those who hold positive and negative attitudes toward homosexuals. *Journal of Homosexuality* 1(1): 9–27.

MacFarlane, K. 1978. Sexual abuse of children. In *The victimization of women,* ed. J. R. Chapman and M. Gates. Beverly Hills: Sage.

MacLean, F. 1976. The first world meeting of prostitutes. *Ms.* 5(3): 24.

Marmor, J. 1978. Is prostitution a victimless crime? *Medical Aspects of Human Sexuality* 12(8): 94, 101, 108.

Masters, W. H., and V. E. Johnson. 1966. *Human sexual response.* Boston: Little, Brown.

———. 1981. Prostitution and crime. *Medical Aspects of Human Sexuality* 15(8): 16–17.

Milham, J., A. L. San Miguel, and R. Kellogg. 1976. A factor-analytic conceptualization of attitudes toward male and female homosexuals. *Journal of Homosexuality* 2(Fall): 3–10.

Miller, B., and L. Humphreys. 1980. Lifestyles and violence: Homosexual victims of assault and murder. *Qualitative Sociology* 3(3): 169–85.

Morgan, M. 1973. *The total woman.* New York: Pocket.

National Gay Task Force Newsletter. 1977. 4(3): 3.

———. 1980 7(5): 4.

National NOW Times. 1982. Wisconsin first state to pass lesbian/gay rights law. (April): 17.

———. 1982. In brief. (September): 9.

———. 1982. In brief. (October): 11.

Nawy, H. 1973. In the pursuit of happiness? Consumers of erotica in San Francisco. *Journal of Social Issues* 29: 147–61.

Newsweek. 1978. Gay teachers. (2 October): 56.

———. 1979a. Sex and the homosexual. (30 April): 81–82.

———. 1979b. Voice against gay rights (30 July): 19.

———. 1981. Jerry Falwell's troubles. (23 February): 23–24.

———. 1982a. Gays and lesbians on campus. (5 April): 75–77.

———. 1982b. Newsmakers. (12 July): 35.

———. 1982c. Homosexuals in the churches. (11 October): 113–14.

Pierson, E. C., and W. V. D'Antonio. 1974. *Female and male: Dimensions of human sexuality.* Philadelphia: Lippincott.

Pomeroy, W. P. 1965. Some aspects of prostitution. *Journal of Sex Research* 1(3): 177–87.

Rasmussen, P. K., and L. L. Kuhn. 1976. The new masseuse: Play for pay *Urban Life* 5(3): 271–92.

Reiss, I. L. 1960. *Premarital sexual standards in America: The social context of premarital sexual permissiveness.* New York: Free Press.

———. 1976. *Family systems in America.* 2d ed. Hinsdale, Ill.: Dryden.

Roanoke Times. 6 February 1976.

Robinson, B. E., P. Skeen, and C. Flake-Hobson. 1982. Sex role endorsement among homosexual men across the life span. *Archives of Sexual Behavior* 11(4): 355–59.

Roth v. Alberts. 1957. 354 U.S. 476.

Rush, F. 1980. *The best kept secret: Sexual abuse of children.* New York: McGraw-Hill.

Saltzman, K. 1978. Women and victimization: The aftermath. In *The victimization of women,* ed. Chapman and M. Gates. Beverly Hills: Sage.

San Francisco Examiner and Chronicle. 4 January 1981.

San Francisco Sentinel. 12 December 1980.

Scanzoni, L. D., and J. Scanzoni. 1981. *Men, women, and change.* 2d ed. New York: McGraw-Hill.

Shaver, P., and J. Freedman. 1976. Your pursuit of happiness. *Psychology Today* 10(3): 26–32, 34.

Shoemaker, D. J. 1977. The teeniest trollops: "Baby pros," "chickens" and child prostitutes. In *Sexual deviance in social context,* ed. C. D. Bryant. New York: New Viewpoints.

Simmons, J. L. 1969. *Deviants*. Berkeley: Glendessary.

Simpson, R. 1976. *From the closets to the courts: The lesbian tradition*. New York: Viking.

Smith, A. B., and H. Pollack. 1976. Deviance as a method of coping. *Crime and Delinquency*. (January): 3–16.

Smith, D. D. 1976. The social content of pornography. *Journal of Communication* 26: 16–24.

Smith, R. W. 1975a. Is biology destiny? Or is culture? (A new look at transvestism and homosexuality). *Counseling Psychologist* 5(1): 90–91.

———. 1975b. Why are many societies sex negative? A social-functional theory. *Counseling Psychologist* 5(1): 84–89.

———. 1978. Sex research, sex education, and Proposition 6: A teacher's dilemma. Unpublished manuscript.

Sonenschein, D. 1968. The ethnology of male homosexual relationships. *Journal of Sex Research* (May): 69–83.

Spotlight. 1982. New understandings: Books, books, books. Pasadena: American Friends Service Committee.

Steffensmeier, D. J. 1970. Factors affecting reactions toward homosexuals. Master's thesis, Iowa State University.

Stone, E. 1976. How to make trouble. *Ms.* 5(3).

Szasz, T. S. 1970. *The manufacture of madness*. New York: Harper & Row.

Taylor, G. R. 1973. *Sex in history: The story of society's changing attitudes to sex throughout the ages*. New York: Harper & Row.

Time. 1979a. Homosexuality: Tolerance vs. approval. (8 January): 48–51.

———. 1979b. How gay is gay? Homosexuality in America. (23 April): 72–79.

Tourney, G. 1975. Aggressive vs. passive homosexuals. *Medical Aspects of Human Sexuality* (January): 139.

Tripp, C. A. 1975. *The homosexual matrix*. New York: McGraw-Hill.

T.V. Guide. 1979. Homosexuals: ABC News Closeup Special (advertisement). (11 October).

———. 1981 How the Gay Lobby has changed TV. 30 May.

———. 1981 Our only allies now are our worst enemies. (6 June).

United Nations. 1951. *International Convention for the Suppression of the White Slave Traffic*. New York: United Nations Publishing.

University of Pennsylvania Law Review. 1978. Homosexuals' right to marry: A constitutional test and a legislative solution. 128(1): 193–216.

Velarde, A. J. 1975. Becoming prostituted: The decline of the massage parlour profession and the masseuse. *British Journal of Criminology* 15(3): 251–63.

Von Driska, M. B. 1978. Emotional appeals surfaced in debate. *State Press* (Arizona State University) (15 November): 6.

Wallace, A. S. 1978. Is prostitution a victimless crime? *Medical Aspects of Human Sexuality* 12(8): 109.

Walum, L. R. 1977. *The dynamics of sex and gender: A sociological perspective*. Chicago: Rand McNally.

Ward, R. A. 1979. Typifications of homosexuals: A replication and extension. Paper presented at the annual meeting of the American Sociological Association, Chicago, September.

Weinberg, G. 1973. *Society and the healthy homosexual*. Garden City N.Y.: Anchor.

Whitam, F. L. 1975. Homosexuality as emergent behavior. Paper presented at the annual meeting of the Pacific Sociological Association, Victoria, British Columbia, April.

———. 1977. The homosexual role: A reconsideration. *Journal of Sex Research* 13(1): 1–11.

———. 1978. A comment on the sociology of politics and homosexuality. Unpublished manuscript.

Wilson, W. C., and H. I. Abelson. 1973. Experience with and attitudes toward explicit sexual materials. *Journal of Social Issues* 29: 19–39.

CHAPTER 4

Aging in a Youth-Oriented Society

CONTENTS

Government's big spending digs pauper's grave for our posterity

Scott Burns, Register and Tribune Syndicate

Some columns provoke more response than others.

A recent column on the elderly as "haves" and the young as "have-nots" brought this note from a reader in Waltham, Mass.:

". . . I am a senior citizen, but also a mother, and I find myself much more concerned about our young citizens. They are certainly paying for the 'graying of America' who I feel monopolize the low-rent housing, free entertainment and food. Discounts on almost everything. I feel emphasis should be put on our young parents who are struggling to raise future citizens and certainly give them a break.

"Thank you for writing such an enlightening column and God bless you. Could you run for office sometime in the future? You would have my vote."

Alas, most of the letters urged me to run, but for cover, not for office.

One reader wrote, "I don't believe your mother would be very proud of the column you wrote on old people being the 'haves.' "

Unfortunately, we cannot solve the problem of rising Social Security costs and/or the federal deficit by shooting the messenger.

Worse, there is no way anyone who is elderly can overcome the fundamental feelings of vulnerability that come with old age and retirement. All we can do, together, is try to understand how we feel and comprehend the underlying economics of what we do as human beings. Then we can take a look at what government spending is doing to all of us.

What is this thing we call economy?

The most important economy is the one made of our relationships and what one generation does for the next. As a parent, I like to think I will do as much for my children as my parents did for me. There is nothing even vaguely unusual in this. It comes with the territory.

As adults, retired or still working, we like to think that we have contributed to the base of knowledge, skills and tools that will help those who succeed us. We do this by educating our children as best we can, by saving, and by building the enterprises that serve other people.

Those who are now retired can rightfully look with great pride on the sacrifices they made to create and transmit the knowledge and skills that make the world work. There is no way, simply no way, that those retired can be looked upon as unworthy, spend-thrifts, etc.

Unfortunately, while all of us have been working to create value—in our children, in our society—our government has been busy borrowing against it.

If you had added up the value of everything all Americans possess—houses, cars, washing machines, corporate stocks, bonds, bank deposits, etc.—as recently as 1975, you would have come up with a staggering $2.5 trillion net worth. Much of that value was created by people who are now retired.

In the same year, the discounted present value of future Social Security commitments—what pension actuaries would call "unfunded liabilities"—was the same amount, $2.5 trillion. This means that if the government were to take everything you and I own, everything that we have worked so hard to create and accumulate, it would have had just enough to satisfy the claims of Social Security.

And things have gotten worse since 1975.

Right now, the unfunded liabilities of the Social Security system are two or three times greater than everything all of us have. In other words, while you and I have been working, saving and trying to create value for ourselves and future generations, our government has been making spending commitments that exceed our ability to create and save.

The excess is not small.

It is mind boggling, almost beyond comprehension.

Rather than trying to think in billions or trillions, let me suggest another way: Right now, for every dollar you and I save, invest or commit to the education of our children, our government is borrowing two or three dollars for them to pay off.

There is nothing you and I can do for our children that will compensate for the debts and payment commitments our government is creating every minute, every day.

The appropriate object of anger is not the elderly for the young, the young for the elderly, or this writer.

It is our politicians and the circus of the Potomac.

Source: Arizona Republic 16 January 1983.

DEFINING THE PROBLEM: TROUBLED TIMES AND RESENTMENTS

Scott Burn's column lays the blame for current economic trouble♪ and intergenerational resentments at the feet of the federal government. In an earlier column (Register and Tribune, 9 December 1982), Burns noted what he called the beginnings of a bitter intergenerational war stemming from government spending practices that, in his view, turned America's elderly into a generation of "haves" while the younger generations became "have-nots":

It is the young who no longer have access to home ownership; who no longer have government loans for education; who no longer receive Social Security benefits to go to college; who must work but are coming of age in an economy that is incapable of employing them; who must pay the rising burden of employment taxes while seeing the elderly reap capital gains on their housing sales, tax-free, or capital gains on their stock sales at reduced rates.

Other sources, however, paint a far less rosy picture of America's elderly in the 1980s and beyond. A report that the research firm Data Resources, Inc. a prepared for the National Retired Teachers Association and the American Association of Retired Persons states that over the next several decades, there will be a

decline in the relative share of income going to the elderly. Real incomes of the elderly will rise, but at a slower rate than those of younger cohorts, and the elderly will receive a smaller share of society's resources (Christian Science Monitor 29 January 1980).

Under the Reagan administration, Congress made cuts in Social Security benefits (contrary to presidential campaign promises) in an effort to counterbalance enormous federal budgetary deficits. An Associated Press report 23 August 1981) pointed out that by cutting widows' benefits, delaying the date at which early retirees might claim benefits, limiting the amount that workers in their

seventies could earn without losing Social Security benefits, reducing eligibility for death benefits, and reducing disability benefits, among other changes, the government "saved" over $9 million in 1982, and was expected to generate "savings" of $10 billion through 1986. The giant's share of these savings were at the expense of the elderly, many of whom live on fixed incomes, which are about half of their preretirement earning level (Soldo 1980, 21). This drop in income, coupled with the eroding effects of inflation and the higher proportion of their income that the elderly must spend for the necessities of life, means that retirement, for many, is an introduction to poverty. Adding the near-poor and the "hidden" poor to those whose incomes are below the official (governmental) poverty level, over one-fourth of all persons age sixty-five and over are impoverished.

Government cutbacks in support have negatively affected both younger and older citizens. Why, then, is the resentment of the young focused on the old? For the answer to this question, we must turn to other aspects of socio-cultural change.

Demographic Change and Stereotypic Images

America is a graying society. Unlike its demographic profile during the baby-boom years following World War II and ending in the late 1960s, the present and projected profile of America shows increases in the size and proportion of the old. This fact alone inspires uneasiness in some and outright fear in others. Writer Michael Thacher (1978) discusses the possibility that the future may bring advances in techniques for prolonging life, and expresses the fears of those who believe that "society would sag under the weight of its elderly population." What consequences would increases in the older population bring? Thacher offers this view:

The proliferation of old folks would exacerbate social tensions and create a powerful political bloc. Pension and retirement funds would be milked dry. Even today, the 25-to-55 year old work force is increasingly supporting the aged. . . . Society is breaking up into competing groups—unemployed youth, a burdened work force, and unproductive oldsters. . . . In no time, Earth might be ruled by a gerontocracy and the thinking of the very old tends to lack imagination and flexibility (1978, 21).

Thacher's fears are echoed by Alan Otten writing in the *Wall Street Journal* (23 February 1978). Otten worries that older people are already beginning to flex their political muscle. As he sees it, no one knows just how many older people the rise in mandatory retirement age (to seventy), which Congress passed in 1978, will permit to continue working, either full- or part-time. According to Otten, however, whether the actual figures are thousands, hundreds of thousands, or a million or more, "there will be that many fewer job openings." To Otten, Thacher, and those with similar fears, the handwriting is on the wall, and it spells trouble.

Some interesting inconsistencies are embedded in this fearful view of the near future. For example, do we fear a larger older generation because it contains many *productive* persons who would take jobs away from the young? Or are the old feared because they are *unproductive,* draining away the incomes of younger workers through taxation for support of this growing group of dependents? In contrast to fears of a **gerontocracy** (rule by the old), which might enact legislation in its own favor and thus against the rest, *New York Times* columnist Pete Hamill shows just the opposite (16 January 1982). According to Hamill, President Reagan—a man in his seventies during his presidency—was guilty of attacking his own contemporaries, to the benefit of hustlers, con men, Medicaid racketeers, and "those who just don't care about other people's pain." Far from gerontocratic rule, Hamill notes that Reagan, who spent billions yearly on national defense, believed that the nation could not "afford to defend the lives, dig-

nity, and sanity of its old people in nursing homes," even though nursing home residents comprise only a miniscule proportion of the nation's population as a whole and only about 5 percent of those sixty-five years of age and over, at any point in time (Soldo 1980, 18).

Those who fear gerontocracy, however, point to the rise of senior citizen organizations whose purpose, they say, is to promote causes that will enhance and benefit the old. Among such organizations is the 13 million member American Association of Retired Persons. The AARP does work to eliminate existing age barriers in a society that discriminates against older people in a number of ways. However, *Washington Post* columnist Neal Peirce points out (3 October 1982) that "Local debates on elderly issues suggest that seniors aren't afflicted with tunnel vision for their own causes." Politicians' fears that the elderly may act as a single-minded force at the polls, striking down those who oppose positions taken by their lobbies, are "political mythology" and the

Maggie Kuhn, founder and leader of the Gray Panthers. The organization is devoted to eliminating discrimination against all age groups, not just the old.

existence of a "geriatric juggernaut" is doubtful, says Peirce.

Another political association, the Gray Panthers, founded in 1970 under the leadership of Maggie Kuhn, is a nationwide organization with a membership of about 50,000. Gray Panthers fight for social changes that will benefit America's older population, but their interest is in improving social conditions in general—not in ruling society. Members come from *all* age groups. (The organization's original name was the Consultation of Older and Younger Adults for Social Change, but it adopted the name that the media tagged it.) The published goals of the Gray Panthers are:

1. To promote a positive attitude toward aging;
2. To expose inequities and injustices, based on age, and force them into the public policy arena;
3. To make an impact on social policies that often reinforce negative stereotypes of aging;
4. To organize grass roots Gray Panthers "networks" that will tackle these issues in their communities where the potential for impact is greatest.

"Our society," says Maggie Kuhn, "is infected with an epidemic of gerontophobia," which is the unreasoned and illogical fear of the old. "We are the one group that has been successful in bringing young and old together," she asserts (*Arizona Senior World* September 1981). Kuhn believes that political mobilization of the elderly against others is not only wrong but is "unworthy for older Americans to endorse." The Gray Panthers challenge age discrimination at *all* age levels—not just against the old.

Why, then, does the belief persist that the nation's older citizens represent something to fear? The fears are paradoxical, as we have seen, and not supported by evidence. Such irrational fears suggest that to some extent, the problem of aging in a youth-oriented society lies in assigning a scapegoat function to older people (Butler 1978). Scapegoating occurs when a social majority that is having difficulty solving its survival problems projects blame for some or all of those problems onto a group that can be identified as an "outsider." Concerns over inflation, unemployment, and other serious matters—such as the possibility of nuclear war—suggest to some people that someone or some group must be the cause of things going wrong. If that someone or that group can be held back, kept down, or even eliminated in some way, things may get better.

Are Older People Being Scapegoated?

Thinking about the language we used to describe older Americans, we may notice that although we have constructed some pleasant-sounding terms in recent years (such as Golden Agers, Senior Citizens, and the New Generation), negative terms such as *oldsters*, *the aged*, and *the elderly* are much more common, as linguistics professor Frank H. Nuessel, Jr. has pointed out (1982). The negative terms imply incapacitation and devalued status. Sometimes we refer to older individuals in terms that indicate what they have lost or given up, such as *widow* and *retiree*. These labels imply that such persons are not full participants in social life. Still other terms such as *old battle-ax*, *old fogey*, *old timer*, and *old codger*, and the lack of counterpart terms (such as young battle-ax or young geezer), make clear that we talk—and therefore think—negatively about the old. To call someone an "old fool" means that the person has learned little from life's experiences, has little time left to compensate for past failures, and isn't worth much investment. On the other hand, a "young fool" is thought to be foolish only from lack of experience. He or she has a lifetime ahead in which to learn and is worth, we believe, investments of many kinds. In some societies, such as among Jews and Orientals, the term *elder* is applied, indicating deference and valued status

(Eckstein 1977). The more common American term *elderly* is seldom applied to respected older persons (Kinchella 1977). What attitudes toward older persons underlie our terms for them, and what do those attitudes imply about our behavior toward our elders?

CONFRONTING THE PROBLEM: ATTITUDES TOWARD THE OLD

Although we may value specific older *individuals*—a dear relative, a longtime friend, a film star, or someone who is politically powerful—we do not seem to value old people in general. Not long ago, an opinion survey (*What's Happening to the American Family* 1978), to which over 300,000 "middle Americans" responded, indicated that we may not value our own older family members. Ninety-six percent of those surveyed said contact with older people was important for a child's development, and 87 percent said that most children growing up today do not have enough contact with their elders. Yet, 72 percent believed that older people are "generally forgotten by their families." Most telling of all, perhaps, when asked where older relatives who are no longer able to take care of themselves should live, respondents divided evenly between "nursing home placement" and "living with their own children." Apparently, the thought of having an elder relative living with the family is more palatable than the reality, if that relative is in need of help.

Our nation's nursing homes, where half the survey respondents were willing to place their infirm relatives, have long been considered a disgrace to society (*United Press International* 16 April 1979). Yet, in 1982, the Reagan administration moved to repeal federal laws regulating nursing homes—laws forbidding such homes from employing people with communicable diseases, requiring such homes to be safe and sanitary, and requiring operators to respect the privacy and dignity of patients (*New York Times* 16 January 1982). Passage of such deregulations

would render the disgraceful and scandalous a "triumph of the obscene," according to one observer. Also of interest is that the General Accounting Office in Washington, D.C. has calculated that home health care instead of nursing home placement would save millions of dollars annually. Home health care services over a period of three years for an individual cost one-fourth of that for the same care provided in a nursing home, according to the National Association for Home Care newsletter. Moreover, institutional care costs come from private insurance, Medicare, Medicaid, and community funds, while home health care, when physician-ordered is covered entirely by Medicare, says the same newsletter (*Arizona Republic* 1 December 1982). Why, then, would half of those surveyed opt for placing their infirm relatives in nursing homes?

Survey respondents who deplored the lack of contact between children and elders may not have been aware that various media presentations distort images of old people in a negative direction, and thus serve to distance the young from the old. Children's literature, for instance, has been found to contain discriminatory images of old people. A typical description of "Grandpa" notes that "He likes soft-boiled eggs best. Second best is soup." A review of such books, intended for children ranging from preschool through third grade, found that the old play only a minor role in stories. Moreover, old people are shown as talking, teaching, and communicating in other ways less than other adults:

The aged were depicted in realistic social activities in just 18 of 2,501 drawings. Their work activities described them as janitors, storekeepers, or servants, but did not show them in positions that required mental sharpness. Overall, they were presented as more passive, sickly, and less self-reliant than other adults (Barnum 1977).

Another medium that distances us from old people is television. "American commercial television—like a large segment of American society—is uncomfortable with aging and the aged" (*United Press International* 10 November 1978). Jules Power, producer of "Over Easy," a Public Broadcasting System series geared to the interests of those fifty-five years of age and over, comments that commercial television usually does not deal with older people at all. In prime-time programming, says Power, "men and women are very young and sexy in young terms. Every attitude is in young terms . . . even the adult shows don't have older people on them" (*United Press International* 10 November 1978). As Nancy Schlossberg has argued, the media communicate trend-setting views of aging which, in turn, influence attitudes about aging. What picture of our elders does television provide? In general, research shows that

1.   The elderly are underrepresented;

2.   Older men outnumber older women three to one;

3.   Proportionately fewer older characters are "good" and proportionately more older characters are "bad," especially older men;

4.   When the success of a character is measured, more older women are unsuccessful than successful; and

5.   Elderly women are disproportionately portrayed as victims and as persons in poor health (Schlossberg 1982, 22).

Schlossberg also asserts that heavy television viewers tend to believe, contrary to fact, that older adults are a disappearing group and that women age faster and earlier in life than men. Findings indicate, she states, that heavy viewers think that the elderly are "for the most part unhealthy, financially distressed, sexually inactive, and stubborn and intolerant."

Television advertising also discriminates against older people. A congressional House committee has urged advertising executives to avoid making fun of older people in their sales pitches, but the television industry has defended its portrayal of the elderly (*Associated Press* 27 January 1978). The House committee's report notes that although older people constitute more than a $60 billion market, television commercials tend to portray aging as an affliction.

Age Negativity

Humor, which can reveal basic attitudes, thoughts, and feelings, tends to be age-negative. One study has found that jokes about older people portray them in uncomplimentary ways in 78 percent of such humor, while aging as a valued aspect of life is the theme of only 12 percent of the jokes studied (Richman 1977). Among negative themes in jokes related to age are loss of attractiveness, physical or mental decline, loss of sexuality, and death (Richman 1977, 212). A connection between **ageism** (discrimination against persons on the basis of age) and sexism is apparent in much of this humor as well:

The emphasis on older men/younger women in sexual jokes, the negative jokes about old maids, and the sexual bias in age-concealment jokes demonstrates a strong difference in attitude toward aging of the sexes. Male aging is considered much more positively than female aging, in particular for sexual functioning. The negative stereotype of the old unmarried women is very strong (Davies 1977, 244).

These findings are not surprising, since they reflect the male-dominant bias of our culture, which includes greater emphasis on male sexuality. The stereotype of older women as "sick, sexless, and single" is also pervasive (Payne and Whittington 1976).

Negativism toward older women is of special interest, since women constitute a much larger proportion of all older persons—six out of every ten. For those age seventy-five and over, male mortality takes an even greater toll, leaving only 56 men for every 100 women (Soldo 1980, 18). These older women are generally healthy; in fact, when males survive to old age, far higher proportions of men than women report that they are unable to carry out major life activities (29.9 percent of the men compared with only 9 percent of the women). In spite of their generally better health status, however, fewer older women than men are employed outside their homes. This means that a subgroup of old, poor women within the sixty-five-and-over population exists, whose needs constitute a special problem. Yet, attitudes toward this needy group are generally uncomplimentary, as we have seen.

Negativism toward older people in general is at least partly rooted in the American value system—a set of values that have characterized us as a society virtually since the nation began.[1]

American Values and Old Age

Most American values may be thought of as "continuous," while others are more recent and may be either short-term fluctuations or the beginnings of long-term trends (Inkeles 1977). Among the qualities we have continuously valued are self-reliance, individualism, autonomy, and independence. These interrelated values include the belief that one's own efforts account for success or failure in life. If failure occurs, the individual rather than social conditions is blamed. In this view, our attitudes toward the older generation can be translated as follows: If they cannot take care of themselves and get along on their own, it is their own fault.

Another American characteristic is optimism—the belief that one can succeed if one tries. This value sometimes negatively affects the older generation, i.e., if they do not want to be poor, alone, sick, helpless,

unmarried, and the like, they should try to help themselves.

Among the more recent value changes is a lessening of the hard-work ethic and of the emphasis on frugality that characterized Americans in earlier times. As Inkeles (1977) puts it, the previously put-away society has become the throw-away society. This value change applies to older people in that perhaps instead of taking care of them—let alone treasuring them—they can be more or less discarded.

Another change has to do with political confidence. The belief that institutions are capable of carrying out their intended functions has eroded. What has this to do with older Americans? If we have lost faith in governmental assistance programs such as Social Security and Medicare, then the burden of caring for those older people who have low incomes and higher than average medical bills would fall directly on the rest of us, as individuals and as families. In spite of our loss of faith in governmental agencies, we may retain the belief that they *should* provide for those who need help, even if we can no longer believe that they will.

Another observer of continuities and changes in American values has found that although warm, close-knit families are still important to us, they are no longer believed to be essential to our happiness. Researcher Margaret Zube studied concepts of morality displayed over time in the *Ladies Home Journal*, a widely read magazine. With regard to our elders, Zube found that

the older generation is [portrayed as] unable to recognize changes in institutions or roles or to recognize the implications of such changes and . . . they therefore apply traditional formulas to altered circumstances (1972, 391).

Apparently, readers of this "home" magazine are provided with a portrait of home life that renders Grandma and Grandpa (or Aunt Millie and Uncle Tim) irrelevant or annoying or both.

---

1. Earlier in our history, however, old people as a group were not seen as negatively as they are today; their position in society was different. Life expenctancy was considerably shorter. There was little if any retirement period as we now know it (no years of enforced leisure). Men and women remained part of the social mainstream until they died. Today, life expectancy is in the seventies, compared with less than fifty years at the turn of the century, and today many workers retire early—a trend that has been increasing in recent years, especially among men (Singer 1978).

Generational Value Differences

Each generation makes its own modifications in the common core of values we all hold. If we divide the population into the young, the middle-aged, and the old (an artificial distinction, but useful for our purposes), these groups clearly grew up under very different historical conditions, which led to the adoption of somewhat different outlooks on life. Each group's slightly modified value system seems relevant to its own time (Payne, Summers, and Stewart 1973).

People now past age sixty-five were born during or prior to World War I—a time when the country was more rural than urban, when large families were the norm, when the rate of change was slower than at any time since, and when about half of all males were already in the labor force by age fifteen. For additional perspective, consider that in 1916, the ratio was one automobile to every 200 Americans. "Getting close to nature" was an everyday experience for many, often connected with hard labor, and a very different matter than taking the family camper to a crowded national park. Nationwide radio broadcasts did not come into being until after 1920.

By the time today's younger generation was born, our society was very different. America was fully industrialized, urbanized, and bureaucratized. Television brought the world (and previously unexplored parts of the universe) into the living room, along with the message that those over thirty years of age were not to be trusted. For some time following World War II, schoolchildren were drilled, along with such subjects as the "new math," in saving themselves from atomic bomb blasts by crouching under their desks. The move to suburbia often left elders behind in the city. Further, by the late 1960s, the birthrate began to drop, and small nuclear families provided different interaction settings from that of the larger families of the past, who had to cooperate closely in order to survive.

That the oldest, the middle, and the younger generations see the world differently is not surprising. The oldest has had the most experience with change of all kinds; the youngest has no direct experience beyond its own social context. The middle generation is sandwiched between the others and may feel the pressure of dependency (or potential dependency) from both sides as both the life expectancy of the old and the length of time preparing for work among the young increase.

Most observers, however, see generational antagonisms as pitting the older generation against all who are younger. At the beginning of the 1970s, for instance, *Time* magazine (3 August 1970) produced a special report called "The Old in the Country of the Young," in which a primary theme was concern with whether, given increased health, education, and vigor in the older generation, "vigorous octogenarians [would] keep the reins of politics, business, and family finances, frustrating the powerless younger generations."

In settings in which older people interact directly with younger people, as in age-integrated classrooms, negativism may increase. Not long ago, a study found that typical college students who had older classmates grew to like them less over time (Auerbach and Levenson 1977). Younger students reported that they did not like competing with older students and did not like the older students' enthusiasm for class work. Further, the tendency of older students to bring "irrelevant" elements into the classroom (i.e., references to their own lives and past experiences) irritated them, and what they saw as a tendency on the part of older students to segregate themselves also irritated them. Older students, on the other hand, said that they were afraid to "interfere" with the younger ones.

The young sometimes think of the old as domineering, competitive, and aggressive (Fitzgerald 1978). Such descriptions may be related to younger persons' concerns about control over their own lives. "The older individual who tries to be helpful and cooperative may be misread as being power oriented and controlling by a younger individual," notes Fitzgerald (1978, 401), and this kind of misperception may lead to conflict—not so much because of what is actually done, but more because of why people think things are done. Younger people also have more negative attitudes toward old age than do older people (Chiriboga 1978).

Unfortunately, although much of the preparation for later life occurs in the family, families do little to **socialize** (that is, to teach social identity) younger family members into the roles they will play as they age. Further, little instruction is given to family members as to how to relate to older persons. As a result, the young may be unresponsive to older persons' needs. In a special report for *Newsweek* (Gelman 1982), writer David Gelman concludes that although it has become more possible than ever before to "grow old gracefully" in America,

the young avert their eyes and ears from the elderly, as uncomfortable reminders of their own mortality. It remains a basic anguish for most of them that they hope for long life and dread the deprivations it may bring. The new old themselves, the first generation of full-timers, may have to challenge that image—to assert their continued humanity in a culture that hails old age as an achievement and treats it as a failure (1982, 60).

Arthur S. Fleming, as chairman of the U.S. Commission on Civil Rights, told a House subcommittee that the Civil Rights Commission was "shocked at the cavalier manner in which our society neglects older persons" (U.S. Department of HEW, 1978). The commission investigated implementation of the Age Discrimination Act of 1975 and reported that (1) discrimination on the basis of age in the delivery of federally supported services and benefits existed to some extent in every federal program examined; (2) members of minority groups, women, and handicapped individuals were often victims of compounded discrimination based on age, sex, race, national origin, and handicap; (3) age discrimination was facilitated by federal, state, and local program administrations who developed policies based on narrow interpretations of goals. In their application, these goals limited participation in programs, so that some age groups were excluded; and (4) age discrimination was facilitated by the federal government's establishment of performance standards (required for eligibility), which effectively excluded participation by certain age groups. Who was Fleming complaining about? Typically, the administrators of such programs are not the old themselves.

ANALYZING THE PROBLEM: CHALLENGING THE STEREOTYPES

Who *are* the elders that encounter the negativism of younger adults? This is a difficult question because those sixty-five and over are an extremely **heterogeneous** (widely varied) group. Linda K. George of the Center for the Study of Aging and Human Development at Duke University puts it this way: "If you think of a 15-year-old and a 30-year-old, you'd never consider lumping them together. Yet we tend to generalize that everyone over age 60 is the same" (*Arizona Republic* 10 December 1978). *Are* a sixty-five-year-old and an eighty-five-year-old more alike than they are different? Some authorities call those from fifty-five to seventy-four the "young old," and those seventy-five and over the "old old." When asked to label their own age category, the young-old are less likely to call themselves "old" than are the old-old. These self-identifications do not match well with the stereotype that treats all older persons alike, but coincides well with life expectancy calculations. Recent figures put average life expectancy at 73.3 years (Soldo 1980, 16)—somewhat longer for women and somewhat less for men. This means that as one approaches the upper end of the current life expectancy or lives beyond it, the label *old* realistically applies. That is, one has outlived the "expected" number of years.

Among those sixty-five and over, some are still working, some are not, and still others have never worked for wages. Most are healthy, some are ill, and some are incapacitated sufficiently, so that they require institutional care. Some are financially well off, and some live in the direst poverty. While these and other differences might characterize almost any subgroup of Americans, such characteristics vary more in older persons than in younger persons of any age group. In spite of their many differences, however, we have not lost our old-fashioned tendency to judge all persons sixty-five and older by their **master status** (a characteristic that overrides all others): age. To see the situation more realistically, we offer the following facts.

Realities of the Sixty-Five-and-Over Minority

Size.   We have already noted that this subpopulation is rapidly growing. Between 1900 and 1980, the proportion of Americans sixty-five and over almost tripled (4.1 percent to 11.2 percent). At the same time, their number increased about eightfold (from 3 million in 1900 to 25 million in 1980). At present death rates, an increase to about 32 million is expected by the year 2000—out of a total population that, depending on birth rates, may be as large as 260 million or as small as 246 million (Soldo 1980, 6–7).

Health.   We have already noted that only 5 percent of those sixty-five and over are institutionalized at any given time. In nursing homes, the average patient age is eighty-two years, and two-thirds of such residents are women. Only half have surviving spouses or children, in contrast to four-fifths of those who are not institutionalized (Brody 1982, 5). Jacob A. Brody of the National Institute on Aging states that deaths from heart disease and stroke have declined dramatically. However, optimism about long, healthy lives must be tempered by National Center

for Health Statistics data, which show that from 1966 to 1976, there were increases in *all* age groups (but most notably among those between ages forty-five and sixty-four) in (1) inability to carry out normal activities, (2) number of days of restricted or limited activity per year, and (3) the presence of chronic diseases or conditions. The middle-aged and young-old to whom these data apply will not necessarily produce an enormous increase in disabled elderly, however. Brody points out that

our world contains more scientists, physicians, and politicians than have ever existed. They themselves are all growing older and they have elderly parents and relatives. What appears today to be a formidable *status quo* or even a loss of ground must inevitably yield to forces already in the making with the massing of energy, dedication, and intellect. We will probably not empty out the nursing homes . . . but awareness, familiarity, and commitment will probably lead to appropriate new insights and to changes that will make our tasks easier (1982, 5).

Work.   Due in part to the development of pension systems, participation of older persons in the labor force has changed markedly since the turn of the century. Prior to 1900—specifically, between the revolutionary and Civil wars—America, struggling to build a nation, depended on people of all ages to contribute their work to that effort. Reliance was also placed on the experience and wisdom of the elders. However, from the Civil War until the start of the First World War in 1914, changes in science, economics, and other sectors tended to undermine the generally favorable assessment of the worth of older people. During this time, however, their numbers and occupational involvement changed very little. After the turn of the century, Americans began to become aware of the diminished status and life circumstances of older persons, whose number had begun to grow. We began to think of elders as no longer useful—indeed, as an economic burden. The federal government (through the Social Security Act of 1935 and other measures designed to alleviate the plight of older persons) increasingly involved itself in the lives of elders. Families came to rely on government assistance more and more for the support of their older members. This aspect of government involvement paralleled other efforts to shore up a nation struggling with the multiple burdens of the Great Depression. To Americans growing accustomed to relying on institutions outside the family for jobs, housing, and other essentials, it seemed reasonable that care of elders, formerly the province of the family, should increasingly be taken over by "someone else."

In 1900, two out of three men sixty-five and over worked for wages. By 1979, this figure had dropped to one out of five. For women, proportionate participation in the labor force remained about the same

through 1979 as it was in 1900—about one in twelve older women worked outside the home for wages (Soldo 1980, 20).

Interestingly, during America's involvement in the Second World War, the work force participation of older people changed. Older men and women were called into the labor market to work in defense plants. They were urgently needed to replace the young men who had held such jobs previously but had gone into military service. Both young and old women and older men successfully accomplished the "hard work" that supposedly only the strongest young males could manage. After the war, when young men returned seeking civilian jobs again, younger women and older persons of both sexes were displaced. The notion that they could not do such difficult work as

A pleasant nursing home setting, which quite often is not the norm. Having someone nearby who cares can create a sense of well-being among the elderly.

welding and riveting (or that they should
not be required or allowed to do it) once
again found its way into our beliefs.

Finances.   Older people generally live on
less money than do younger adults. Among
couples with a husband sixty-five years or
older, the median income in a recent year
was only 53 percent of the median income
of families with a head of household under
age sixty-five. A similar relationship exists
between the incomes of those sixty-five and
over who live alone or with nonrelatives
and the incomes of those in the same circumstances who are under sixty-five years
of age. According to a publication of the
Population Reference Bureau,

elderly people's financial status depends a great
deal on where their money comes from. Most
rely on a mix of sources—Social Security benefits, pensions (both public and private), wages,
and income from savings, real estate, or investments. Social Security is by far the most important. Since almost all retired elderly are covered
by the system, monthly Social Security checks
alone account for nearly four of every ten dollars
of money income among older persons. . . . In
part to counteract high rates of poverty among
the elderly and particularly among those entirely
dependent on Social Security, the Supplemental
Security Income (SSI) program was instituted in
1974. This guarantees a minimum income for
older Americans; however, the maximum payment is a scant $208 a month for an individual
and $312 for a couple with no other income.
About 11 percent of all those 65 and over now
depend in part on public assistance programs,
mostly SSI (Soldo 1980, 21–23).

The following summarizes the realities of
life across the several dimensions we have
examined briefly for those sixty-five and
older.

First, older persons constitute only 11 percent of the population. Despite the rapid
growth of this subgroup compared with the
rest of the population, it will remain a minority. Even when the baby-boom cohort
reaches age sixty-five, setting off a "senior
boom," the Census Bureau projects the proportion of the elderly at 18.3 percent of the
population. After the year 2030, the low
birth rates of the 1960s and 1970s will produce a sharp fall in the rate of growth of the
older population.

Second, most older people are sufficiently
healthy to function as productive members
of society. Although most elders have favorable attitudes toward retirement, low incomes and inflationary times might result
in some returning to work if sufficient part-
time jobs were available and if ageist practices were eliminated. Only a minority work
for wages. Of these, most work in low-paying, white-collar, and service jobs (Soldo
1980, 19).

Third, only about one-fourth of the old
live below or near the poverty line. Most of
these are women, and they are likely to be
the victims of lifelong discriminatory practices in education and the job market.
Within this group, whose members need
special help, many are also nonwhite and
have also suffered a lifetime of discrimination. Poor health—often the result of inadequate medical and dental care earlier in
life—coupled with poverty and ongoing discrimination renders late life considerably
less than a "golden age" for this subgroup.

Clearly, the sixty-five and over population
is not all disadvantaged. While the old face
common problems such as age discrimination in the labor market and reduced incomes, the vast majority appears to be doing
well or at least adequately. However, since
older people *in general* are stereotypically
seen as problematic—either lording it over
or draining the pockets of the rest—con-
trasting some additional myths with the
realities of life among those sixty-five and
over may be useful. The findings of several
studies that examined the quality of life and
the well-being of elders are discussed in the
following section.

Quality of Life and Well-Being

Beliefs about older persons, when compared
with their own assessments of their lives,
show considerable distortion. The findings

"So you'd like to help an old lady across the street? If I see one, I'll tell her."

of a Harris poll (Harris et al. 1975) showed, for instance, that half or more of the general public thought that most people over sixty-five found the following problems "very serious": fear of crime, poor health, not having enough money to live on, not having enough medical care, and not feeling needed. In actuality, however, only 23 percent thought fear of crime was a serious problem; 2 percent were very seriously concerned with poor health; 15 percent had very serious concerns about lack of money; 12 percent said that lack of sufficient medical care was a very serious problem; and only 7 percent had very serious worries about not feeling needed. Ten percent or less of the older people surveyed had very serious problems with education, poor housing, lack of things to do, lack of friends, and lack of job opportunities. However, from 20 to 45 percent of the general public thought that all these matters were of very serious concern to those sixty-five and older.

In 1977, Mohamed Abdel-Ghany (1977) reported the findings of a study of 961 adults who were all at least sixty-five years of age. They were asked about their housing, health, social relationships and activities, life satisfaction, independence, and eco-nomic conditions. The study revealed that social and physical isolation and economic achievement concerns were the salient factors affecting the quality of satisfaction with life.

Social and physical isolation were related to such matters as dissatisfaction with the inconvenience of traveling to public libraries, shopping, banks, doctors and clinics, parks, restaurants, post offices, and places of worship. Social and physical isolation are, in part, a function of transportation inadequacies. Many services and goods that older people must have are no longer available within walking distance from their homes.

Factors related to economic achievement concerns were years of schooling, family income, family financial assets, assessment of money or other assets available to meet needs, and problems connected with obtaining heat and electricity for the home.

Health was also of concern to these elders and was also related to both social and physical isolation and to economic problems.

If help was offered in these areas to meaningfully improve perceptions of the quality of life, would older people accept it? Moen (1978) found that rural elders, who may have more trouble than others with the kinds of problems Abdel-Ghany's study (1977) identified, are reluctant to admit need or accept help when it is offered. Moen's findings show that older people's thinking about services places "help" in one of the three following categories: services that are "earned," those that require a "donation," and those that are "available to all." Those available to all are considered the most acceptable. Those requiring public declarations of poverty are the least acceptable. The poor, apparently, have lost neither their pride nor their sense of dignity.

Liang and Fairchild (1977) report that older people's sense of financial well-being is less dependent on their actual level of income than on the comparison of present with past, or on comparisons of the situation one faces with one's assessment of how others are faring, or both. If America has bred pride into its children—pride in accomplishment, mastery, individualism, and self-reliance—a negative payoff is apparent later in life. The very pride that helped to produce a strong nation may prevent those whose work helped to build the nation from admitting that they need assistance. Little wonder, then, that needy elders may experience **alienation,** that is, feelings of powerlessness, meaninglessness, cynicism, cultural estrangement, social isolation, and even self-estrangement (Seeman 1971, 94).

Additionally, feelings of powerlessness have been found to inhibit learning across a wide range of situations, for instance, learning about how to care for one's health or learning about options available for finding new and fulfilling roles at retirement. We have taught our citizens to love accomplishment and to abhor failure (i.e., the inability to manage one's own life). In view of this, Moen's (1978) finding of reluctance to admit need or to ask for help is not surprising. If learning to "change gears" is as necessary in later life as it seems to be, and if feelings of powerlessness hamper such learning, perhaps we as a nation have overemphasized the winner-loser, powerful-powerless distinctions.

Another major study that may serve to reduce the mythological aspects of old age is Reed Larson's (1978) survey of thirty years of research on the well-being of older people. Larson concluded that well-being is most strongly related to health. Socioeconomic factors and the degree of social interaction, however, are also implicated. Larson reported that poor health and low income create greater vulnerability to the impact of other negative conditions. That is, persons with greater financial resources can

circumvent negative life situation conditions to which persons of lower SES [Socio-economic status] are directly vulnerable. . . . Further consideration needs to be given to the implication that the effects of negative life situations are multiplicative. (1918, 117)

In all of the studies that Larson surveyed, the salient themes reported in Abdel-Ghany's research were affirmed. Of particular interest, however, was a typical finding: *Age by itself did not account for the low quality of life reported by some elders* (see Edwards and Klemmack 1973; Larson 1975; and Kivett 1976.) Another important finding was that although no consistent differences between the sexes were found in reports of the quality of life, differences were found in well-being reported by race. These differences, Larson explains, were probably due to income differences between racial groups (1978, 114). Larson summarizes his findings (which are only briefly outlined above) as follows:

[F]olk lore has it that health, wealth, and love are the basis of happiness. The studies reviewed . . . suggest that a similar formula is applicable to older Americans. Level of education, occupational status, marital status, availability of transportation, housing, and nonamorous forms of social interaction also appear to be related to subjective well-being. These findings are generally consistent with the findings of similar research on the well-being of adults of *all* ages (1978, 116).

All of us need good health to be able to carry on daily activities, enough money to ensure that our needs can be met, and social contact to ensure against problems associated with isolation. Older people, then, are not different from the rest of us when it comes to determining the factors that make up our sense of well-being.

Special Problems of Aging: Minority Groups

Although Larson's study found no consistent difference in well-being among older persons on any measure, other investigators have repeatedly drawn attention to the special problems that older women face. (Older women, as we have seen, are far from a numerical minority. Like all women in a society that favors males educationally, occupationally, and in virtually every other sphere of social life, however, they have minority status.) *National Business Woman* makes the point this way:

If the plight of the elderly poor is abysmal, the plight of the poor and aged woman is a horror story. For her, the general problems that accompany longevity are compounded. In a society that idealizes youth, the older woman is cast aside; if women in America have been second-class citizens in general, the aging women has been relegated to third-class citizenship at best. A society that until recently placed particular value on women as sex objects is not likely to treat kindly those women whose prime has passed. Simone de Beauvoir has said that a man can be treated like a man in old age only if he has been treated by society like a man during his entire life. The same applies to women in their older years. Only if society regards women as "people" during their lifetime will society have the empathy to treat them like "people" in their old age (1975, 25).

Contrary to popular opinion, which holds that women do not have as great an interest in work outside the home as men do, older working women seek work as one of their principal reasons for living (Sokolowska 1965). They have also been shown to have less positive attitudes toward retirement than do men (Jacobson 1974). Yet, as we have seen, older women are underrepresented in the work force—a fact that undoubtedly contributes to their overrepresentation among the elder poor. At a conference, "The Maturing Women in America Today" (U.S. Department of HEW 1977), the pressing and unmet needs of this subgroup were discussed—especially needs for reforms in the Social Security system and for expanded employment opportunities. *National Business Woman* (1975) has also emphasized the need for telephone reassurance programs, transportation, nutrition programs, and escort services.

The problems of older women are in some ways both like and different from the problems of those who have been handicapped throughout their lives by racism (see chapter 10)—the Asian-American, black, American Indian, and Hispanic elders. For these groups, one problem is simply living long enough to collect Social Security benefits. The most recent issue of a government publication called *Facts About Older Americans* (U.S. Department of HEW 1978) shows that 11 percent of Caucasians were sixty-five and over in a recent year, as compared with 8 percent of Blacks and only 4 percent of "persons of Spanish origin." Members of racial minority groups suffer from double jeopardy; they are discriminated against both because they are old and because they are members of inferiorized groups (Hill 1978). If more older than younger people, proportionately, are poor, older members of racial minority groups are even more likely to be poor. In a recent year, the median value of housing units that elderly persons owned was about two-thirds the value of homes that younger adults owned. For black elderly, however, the median value of their homes was about half that of all older people (U.S. Department of NEW 1978, 5).

Interestingly, even in old age, minority group members contribute significantly to maintaining stability and cohesion in family life. As Robert Hill puts it,

four times as many families headed by elderly black couples take younger relatives into their households than do similar white families. Almost half of the black families headed by elderly women have related children living with them—in contrast to only one-tenth of comparable white families (1978, 273).

Although life expectancy for blacks is about seven years less than for nonblacks, "after age 75, nonwhite mortality is lower than white. Thus, although fewer blacks survive to reach age 75, those who do may, on the average, expect a remaining lifetime of about 2.5 years longer than the whites" (Davis 1978). Davis counsels that because of the history and the reality of the lives of elder black Americans, special assistance is imperative. "Their future, like the future of

Blacks, in later life, may be more "familial" as a group than whites. Because of this reliance on the extended family, minorities are sometimes less vulnerable to various life crises than whites.

the Mexican American and the American Indian, is inextricably linked to efforts of this society to discharge its responsibility to all its members" (1978, 276). The same can be said of the Asian-American old.

To reduce the special problems of women and of non-Caucasian elders to the few summarizing statements we have made here is to underemphasize the multitude of problems they face. To be old, nonwhite, *and* female is a situation of triple jeopardy.

Why *All* the Old Are Stigmatized

Robert Atchley of the Scripps Foundation Gerontology Center has suggested that all older persons suffer the stigma of age; that is, old age in and of itself has a negative, disqualifying character in our society. The old are seen as "expendable" (1977, 18). Further, as Richard Kalish has pointed out, in modern, industrial societies, death usually occurs late in life. In societies in which death rates are high, death comes at all ages and can thus be considered separately from old age. In societies like ours, in which death is associated with the later years, younger people may shun older ones who remind them of their own mortality (Kalish

1976). Our educational system adds to the stigma of old age in that we focus our educational efforts on the young. With each year that passes after graduation, knowledge becomes more and more obsolete. No mechanism exists for systematically updating knowledge. In Atchley's words, "People whose education and job skills have grown obsolete are treated exactly like those who have never gained an education or job skills and are not encouraged or given the opportunity to begin anew" (1977, 18). Finally, the stigma of age is related to the ability to perform. As Atchley explains it, "Because a few older people are unable to perform in normal adult roles, society has been quick to jump to the conclusion that aging is the cause of their inability" (1977, 18).

Atchley (1976) has provided a valuable way to view the relationships among age, stages of the life cycle, occupational cycle, economic cycle, and family cycle. Although these relationships may vary among individuals and for various social categories such as ethnic groups or social classes (Atchley 1977, 89), the comparisons shown in figure 4–1 help us to see why the old are devalued and seen as a social problem.

Atchley defines the life course as an idealized, age-related progression or sequence of roles and group memberships that individuals are expected to follow. Note that old age, shown on the life course line, begins about age eighty (figure 4–1).

Following out the occupational cycle line, we see that just before later maturity begins (approximately ages sixty to eighty), a "phasing out" period occurs, followed by retirement. Phasing out indicates less than maximum productivity, and retirement is defined primarily as nonproductivity. While they may have some positive connotations, lowered productivity and leisure living do not fit well with our belief in activity maintenance as a desirable goal—especially productive activity.

The family cycle line shows that negatively valued events take place later in life. The home is emptied of young voices (the "empty nest") and widowhood (or widowerhood) becomes likely. The economic cycle line shows that maintenance purchasing and dependency are characteristic of later life stages, neither of which fits well with the American emphasis on consumerism and self-sufficiency.

Although Atchley reminds us that these **ideal-typical** (abstracted from reality) cycles may not describe any particular person's life accurately, they do describe what many *think* later life is like. Thus, figure 4–1 helps us to see why the negative term *elderly* is more commonly used than the positive term *elder*. For older people who experience voluntary or involuntary withdrawal from full social participation—indeed, for older people in general—Barbara Meyerhoff's description is appropriate:

Old people in America go through a deculturation, a process in which the habits of a lifetime are reversed. Instead of growing up into society

. . . they must learn how to make their exit from it, and this period of life may well last as many years as it takes to become an adult. Indeed, some can succeed in remaking their lives with little or no help from our society, their support coming from one another and their shared traditions and history. But for the many who cannot fall back on such resources, old age has come to be associated with pain, confusion, loss, and terror (Meyerhoff quoted in Kessler 1976).

Even in the context of a supportive community, says Meyerhoff, survival for the older person depends on his or her ability to live alone, to function independently (including walking, preparing meals, getting to stores and services, and performing other similar essential tasks), and to deal with the complexities of life, such as transportation, health care, and other agents and agencies. All this is critical when ties with family have eroded or if children do not live nearby.

FIGURE 4–1. Relationships among Age, Life Cycle, Occupational Cycle, Family Cycle, and Economic Cycle

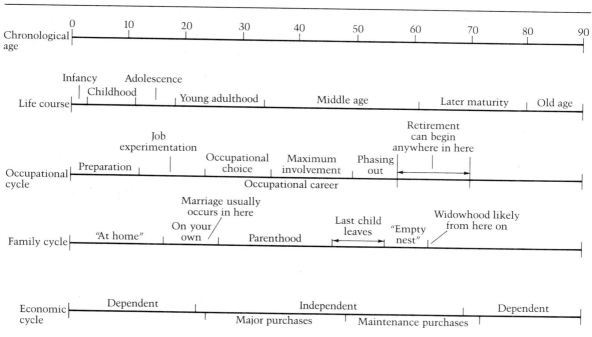

Data from Robert C. Atchley, The life course, age grading, and age-linked demands for decision-making. In *Life-Span Developmental Psychology: Normative life crises*, ed. Nancy Datan and Leon H. Ginsberg, pp. 261–78. (New York: Academic Press, 1976).

The Need for Reforms

Government officials have been aware of the special needs of our older population for some time. Programs developed to meet those needs, however, do not always succeed in their goals. The Older Americans Act of 1965 was intended to be the centerpiece of the federal commitment to elders. The goals of the Older Americans Act declare that older Americans have the right to

1. An adequate income,
2. The best possible physical and mental health,
3. Suitable housing,
4. Full restorative services,
5. Opportunity for employment with no age discrimination,
6. Retirement in health, honor, and dignity,
7. Pursuit of meaningful activity,
8. Efficient community services,
9. Immediate benefit from proven research knowledge, and
10. Freedom, independence, and the free exercise of individual initiative (Soldo 1980, 28–29).

Federal programs for elders have proliferated and include at least the following agencies and acts. The Administration on Aging, which is within the Department of Health and Human Services (a network of state and area agencies on aging has also developed); the Comprehensive Older Americans Act Amendments of 1978 (which provides for the distribution of funds through Title III for social services, senior centers and nutrition services, Title IV for demonstration projects, Title V for community service employment programs, which are administered by the Department of Labor, and Title VI for the development of services to older Native Americans by Indian tribal organizations); and the Social Security Administration (also part of the Department of Health and Human Services), which provides disability and Medicare payments and is financed through three trust funds. The Social Security Administration also conducts research on issues related to aspects of retirement. Further, it directs the Supplemental Security Income (SSI) program, which began in 1974 to replace state welfare programs for the aged. Title XX was included in the social service amendments of the Social Security Act in 1974 and has decentralized the planning and delivery of social services. Because of the broadly defined guidelines, the number and types of Title XX services vary from state to state, but most attempt to shore up independent functioning through such services as adult day care, homemaker services, and help with chores. The Health Care Financing Administration's primary programs are Medicaid and Medicare, but it also supports research and demonstration projects. The Department of Housing and Urban Development directs the Housing Assistance Payments Program and administers various subprograms known as Section 8, Section 202, and Section 312. The Department of Labor administers the Senior Community Service Employment Program and other employment services and opportunities. The Department of Transportation attempts to ensure access of the elderly (and other) disabled to all forms of transportation, and the Department of Agriculture administers the food stamp program on which many low-income elderly depend. It also supervises the donation of surplus food to the Title III nutrition program, which provides hot meals to people over sixty.

Suppose that you are relatively young and in reasonably good health. Suppose further that for whatever reason, you are asked to understand and be able to use any or all of the agencies and services listed above. Would you experience any difficulty? The government booklet from which the preceding list was taken (Soldo 1980, 28–30) continues for another 1½ pages, listing other federal programs for elders, including the Farmers Home Administration, the Department of Energy programs, the Veterans Administration, the Federal Council on the Aging, the National Institute on Aging, the President's Commission on Pension Policy, the Pension Benefit Guaranty Corporation, the U.S. Commission on Civil Rights, the Special Committee on Aging and the Subcommittee on the Aged (both Senate committees), and the Select Committee on Aging (in the House of Representatives).

Soldo's evaluation of the public sector response to America's older citizens is as follows:

The above review only hints at the extent of the federal involvement in programs benefitting the elderly. The House Select Committee on Aging has identified 48 major federal programs directed specifically at the elderly. If all programs that affect the elderly in some way are included in the inventory, there are at least 135 and perhaps as many as 200 programs at the federal level. They come under the jurisdiction of 49 Congressional committees and subcommittees and are administered by seven Executive departments and five independent agencies. . . . Clearly there is no shortage of federal programs for the elderly (1980, 31–32).

The problem with the federal response has been described in congressional hearings as one of "fragmentation, duplication, and total lack of coordination" (U.S. Congress 1980). As Soldo (1980, 32) writes, if an older person needs help, he or she must struggle through a maze of separate applications for various services, which often requires traveling to various state and local service agencies that may be located "all over town." The individual's responsibility is to determine what kind of services are needed, where they are available, and how to put together a comprehensive service package. "This lack of coordination, coupled with limited program funding, helps to explain why many of the elderly in need go without services."

The private sector response to the needs of elders includes a number of large-scale, sometimes voluntary, organizations. In a recent year, more than 270,000 volunteers, age sixty and over, participated in various ACTION programs (such as the Older Ameri-

can Volunteer program, which provides foster grandparents and senior companions, and the Retired Senior Volunteer Program, or RSVP, in which elders act as resource persons for the improvement of life in the community). Professional organizations with various goals have also developed, among them the National Council on Aging, which maintains the Center for Public Policy, the Gerontological Society of America, the Western Gerontological Society, the American Geriatrics Society, the International Federation on Aging, and a number of lobbying groups such as the National Caucus on the Black Aged, the National Association of Retired Federal Employees, the National Association for Spanish Speaking Elderly, the National Indian Council on Aging, the American Association for Retired Persons, the National Council of Senior Citizens, and the Gray Panthers.

Since 1950, the federal government has sponsored four national meetings, each called a White House Conference on Aging. The most recent of these conferences was held in 1981. Delegates are provided with a forum in which to air their concerns and perhaps provide some guidance to policymakers in both public and private sectors (Soldo 1980, 33–34).

We have uncovered, in this list of governmental and private sector responses to the needs of elders, another cause of scapegoating of the elder minority. The size of the federal involvement alone leads some to argue that the sixty-five-and-over population receives far more attention than other minority groups who are also in need—far more attention than the health and financial stability of the majority of elders warrant. Yet, problems of coordination clearly continue to plague the delivery of social services to the minority of elders who need them most. "A comprehensive 'aging network' continues to be an elusive objective of public policy" (Soldo 1980, 35). The need for reform is critical. What theory of social aging might guide reform? We turn to this question in the next section.

ALTERNATIVE POLICIES FOR RESOLVING THE PROBLEM: THEORIES OF SOCIAL AGING AND VISIONS OF THE FUTURE

Social scientists who study aging are called social gerontologists. These scientists consider aging as problematic—not from biological, physical, or psychological points of view, but in how sociocultural factors affect elders. Some social gerontologists have developed theoretical perspectives that purport to explain the relationship between social systems and the aging subpopulations within them. In this section, we will examine several of these perspectives in highly abbreviated form. We will also attempt to extract whatever implications the theories may contain for social policy or its reform or both.

Disengagement Theory

This theory, first presented by Cumming and Henry (1961) contends that social aging involves a mutually beneficial withdrawal of the individual from society and of society from the individual. As individuals age, they reduce social roles and social interaction in preparation for the final disengagement (death). Societies encourage this "easing out" of their oldest members so that death will not disrupt the social equilibrium. This two-sided withdrawal process is said to be universal and inevitable, and functional both for the society and for the individual. It is a structural-functional effort to explain the behavior of aging individuals and the societal response to them. Successful aging, then, is successful disengagement.

This perspective has been criticized harshly in a number of ways. Its policy implications have been attacked by Alex Comfort:

Disengagement in our culture is often, alas, sludge language for being ejected, excluded or demeaned, and liking it—an attribute wished on the newly created old to plaster our guilt and provide a piece of jargon to excuse our conduct. Age-proof people will have none of it (1976, 65).

Activity Theory

In this perspective, a direct relationship exists betwen activity and life satisfaction. Activity theory argues that although aging individuals may experience physiological and health status changes, psychological and social needs are ongoing. These needs may be harder to meet if the social world withdraws from aging persons. Since successful aging is defined as staying active and resisting societal withdrawal, however, the individual who ages optimally does so by maintaining involvement through the replacement of lost roles with substitute roles. Lemon, Bengston, and Peterson (1972) are the researchers whose names are most closely identified with the original formulation of activity theory.

As may be readily apparent, activity theory can be criticized as applying only to those who are able to exert some control over their social environment, and not to those whose losses are debilitating (for instance, those who are financially impoverished by retirement or those who are physically unable to carry on activities). Further, as Kart (1981, 96) asks, can "activities *of any kind* substitute for lost involvement in work, marriage, parenting, and so on"? In social policy, activity theory would encourage volunteerism among the elderly, replacing lost work roles (paid) with unpaid involvement.

Note that activity theory retains the concept of societal withdrawal (from disengagement theory), although the concept is not proposed as either inevitable or universal. Activity theory is oriented to the social structure, but insofar as it assumes that individuals can influence the larger system and vice versa, the theory lies close to the social interaction theory perspective.

Exchange Theory

Dowd (1975) has been credited with placing aging within the broader exchange theory framework. (Exchange theory may be considered a variant of the even broader conflict theory perspective.) A basic assumption of this theory is that each of us attempts to maximize rewards and reduce costs, and this effort is what motivates our behavior. Dowd sees the problem of elders in modern society as one of decreased power; in exchanges between the society and the old, the latter lose power as income declines and social dependency increases.

Emerson (1962) has spelled out policy implications, noting that power balances can be restored by using a number of tactics or strategies, among them (1) withdrawal from the scene, (2) developing alternative sources of reward, (3) developing skills that are useful to the power holders, and (4) forming coalitions among the powerless. Withdrawal on the part of the old is tantamount to disengagement. Alternative sources of reward might include Grandmother's cookie-baking talents or Grandfather's knowledge of cabinetmaking. Skills useful to power holders might include offering one's services without charge, as in volunteerism. Coalition formation would involve elders recognizing their common social and economic outgroup status, and banding together to change social conditions. Successful aging, in the exchange theory framework would be defined as the capacity to maintain or create conditions in which the older do not suffer deprivations because of power imbalances favoring the younger.[2]

Possibilities for the Future

In addition to the implications of the social gerontological theories we have examined, **global** (comprehensive; all-encompassing) visions have been advanced for the purpose of "mainstreaming" America's elders. A sampling of these practical plans for removing

older people from their outgroup or scapegoat status is presented in this section.

In *Looking Forward: The Abundant Society* (1966), R. N. Iyer described what he considered the optimal life-style of the future. In place of the "succession principle"—first education, then work, finally leisure—Iyer recommended what he called the "simultaneity principle" involving education, work, and leisure in combination throughout life. Is this unlikely to occur? Rochelle Jones (1977), writing in *The Other Generation: The New Power of Older People*, believes that this solution is not beyond reach:

In many parts of the country, people are already experimenting with new mixes of work, leisure, and education. Alternative work patterns, such as shortened work weeks, staggered work hours, and flexible working hours, known as flexitime, are being tried with beneficial results for both employees and employers. They prove that the lockstep of education, work, and leisure can be broken. These people are pioneering the future. What is the life-style of some of us today may be the life-style of all of us tomorrow (1977, 191).

Jones observes a new political pressure group composed of outraged older adults emerging. She points to multiple organizations, lobbying efforts, and the voting power of older Americans as a "nationwide movement nourished by impatience, frustration, and fear" (1977, 218). This movement would seem to approach the "coalition formation" solution to powerlessness that the exchange theory perspective suggests. As we have seen, however, the many private sector groups working toward bettering conditions for elders are somewhat fragmented. As Dowd (1975) has argued, older people have not yet developed a sufficiently extensive awareness of their common social and economic plight to form a genuinely powerful coalition.

Moreover, as Jones envisions the situation, the economic "pie" is limited. To say yes to expanded or improved programs for older Americans is to say no to the needs of other sectors of the population. The belief in a limited pie sets up a competitive scenario in which one generation is pitted against

---

2. The theories presented here are only a sampling of those developed to explain aging in its social context. Others, as listed by Kart (1981), are socioenvironmental theory (Gubrium 1973, 1975), subculture theory (Rose 1965), modernization theory (Cowgill 1974), and age stratification theory (Riley 1971, 1977; Riley et al. 1972; Foner 1975). Students may wish to pursue the policy implications of any or all of these, but space does not permit us to describe each of them here.

others. Must we accept the notion that economic or political limits exist? In the job market, for instance, the young and the old would unlikely compete for the same jobs. Erdman Palmore suggested some years ago that

the idea that society can provide only a limited number of jobs and that therefore it cannot provide enough jobs for aged workers is no longer accepted by most economists. Society could create a useful role for every adult if it were willing to devote the necessary attention and resources to this end. Certainly there would be major economic and political problems involved. But there is an unlimited amount of goods and services needed and desired in our American society (1969).

Although pressures exerted on legislative bodies through the several organizations representing elders' interests have brought about some beneficial changes, a critical need remains to reduce negative stereotypes of old age. Dissemination of the findings of social scientists through a wide-ranging reeducative effort may help (Neugarten 1973). Programs to educate children about what it means to be old and to reduce negative images of aging have recently been developed (Sorgman et al. 1979). The education of older adults is now also being taken seriously.

Optimistic media presentations are more frequent. For example, revised thinking about elders is reflected in special features such as *U.S. News and World Report's* (1980) "Life Begins at 55," *Newsweek's* (1982) "Living Longer, Living Better," and economist Sylvia Porter's article, "Aging of America promises to solve productivity woes" (*Arizona Republic* 26 January 1981). In the arts, a Broadway musical called *My Old Friends*, dealing with romance in the late years of life, received high praise (*Time* 1979), and the movie *On Golden Pond* enjoyed great box office success. Popular entertainment industry figures such as George Burns are heralded for their refusal to disengage (*United Press International* 18 January 1981).

Still, much remains to be done, says Robert Butler, former head of the National Institute on Aging, to change the attitudes we hold about older people (Henig 1979). Conventional "wisdom" still has it that aging brings inevitable senility, memory loss, dependence, and rigidity. According to Butler, these notions about old age are born of "stark terror. We base our feelings on primitive fears, prejudice and stereotypes rather than on knowledge and insight" (Henig 1979, 44–45). As a result, we remain to some extent **gerontophobic** (fear of the old or of old age or both). The recent spate of books dealing with life crises or "passages" leads us to believe that growing older is a series of painful hurdles and ordeals. This focus escalates negativism toward our own aging and toward the currently old as well.

Experts in aging provided policy agenda for the 1980s in a recent issue of *National Forum* (1982), in which the following recommendations were offered.

As the Gray Panthers demonstrate, they are a coalition of "Age and Youth in Action." Because of their wisdom and their growing numbers, the elderly represent an important political force in America.

1. Regarding health, "Basic research on chronic diseases is most urgently needed. . . . Further elucidation of the reported increase in diseases and disabilities at all age is essential" (Brody 1982, 5). If the increase is real, writes Brody, it has implications for the quality of life as life expectancy increases.

2. Regarding federal programs, Kutza (1982) identifies four important issues: (a) What changes can be made to make the public more responsive to those groups of the elderly who are disadvantaged by our current strategies? (b) Which activities are best carried out by the federal government and which by state and local governments? (c) What changes in public programs will be needed to attend to the next group of citizens who will join the ranks of the elderly? (d) What are the limits of government intervention?

3. Shanas (1982, 11) argues that we must study the form of families in which older people live, not all of which are "traditional," because "We . . . need to know what services these pseudo-families can and cannot perform for their members and what supports they need to function effectively." In the near future, writes Shanas, more and more older persons will be living in families that differ from the norm.

4. Regarding work and retirement, James T. Sykes offers numerous recommendations leading to an enlightened national policy (1982, 15–16). Among these are disseminating information about the value of retaining older workers and removal of the mandatory retirement age limit. He also advocates an affirmative action program for middle-aged and older workers to assure access to jobs.

5. Morrison H. Beach's recommendations (1982, 17–18) echo those of Sykes. Beach argues for removal of the greatest barrier to employment: lack of choice. He also notes that company-sponsored financial planning programs can be designed to help employees plan and save for retirement as well as for other goals such as home buying and college education for children.

6. Harold R. Johnson, director of the Institute of Gerontology at the University of Michigan, Ann Arbor, speaks to problems of education in an aging society (1982, 19–21). He offers a number of recommendations to implement the "three E's"—enrichment, expertise, and enlightenment. Enrichment refers to the benefits of education for elders; expertise refers to the goal of education for personnel who serve the elderly; and enlightenment refers to the necessity to educate the public—of all ages—about processes or normal aging and what it is like to grow old in America.

7. Regarding the mass media, Nancy K. Schlossberg offers three broad recommendations. First, a national council for mass media should be created to serve as a watchdog and advocate for most honest portrayals of elders. Second, new technology should be used to promote mental health and education:

Older people face many situations which seem unmanageable, confusing, or unexpected. The media can aid adult socialization, the process through which adults learn to perform the roles and behaviors which are expected and which they expect of themselves. The media also can link people to available resources, a service of growing importance as the numbers of older people increase (1982, 22).

Schlossberg's third recommendation is that knowledge of adult development should be imparted to those in control of the media, so as to reduce stereotypic presentations of elders and increase fairness and accuracy.

8. Fay Lomax Cook (1982, 23–25) and Bernice L. Neugarten (1982, 25–27) both recommend age-neutral policies and programs—programs that are directed to all who need them, regardless of age. Cook reports evidence that the public is willing to provide support for the old when it can see a clear link between a service and a need. However, "the public does not overwhelmingly support age alone as the criterion by which eligibility for services should be decided" (1982, 25). Douglas W. Nelson's arti-

cle underscores these recommendations. (1982, 27–30). Nelson also advocates defining elders not by needs and interests but as a heterogeneous group that has spent a lifetime contributing, earning, and sacrificing. "Being old is thus seen as warranting, if not requiring, socially conferred and age-triggered prerogatives, privileges, and protections . . . as *earned* entitlements" (1982, 30) (italics in original).

9. Both Henry J. Pratt and Robert B. Hudson focus on the "gray lobby." Pratt (1982, 31–33) cautions such lobbies about the risks of potential lack of spontaneity and political imagination as organizations develop. Hudson (1982, 33–35) notes that the "maintenance of adequate and balanced programs for older people lies, most likely, in the presence and pressures of . . . organized groups" although, as he sees it, today's policy toward the elderly boils down to a budget question (regarding Social Security and other programs): "Will we balance the budget on the backs of the elderly?"

Several factors, some assert, will contribute to a decline in negative attitudes toward old people. According to Clark Tibbits (1979), they are the growing positive conceptions that most older people have of themselves, the desires they have for continuing growth and participation, the eagerness of increasing numbers of elders to find fulfillment through broader—often contributory—social roles, and finally, advancing knowledge of the persistence of physical and cognitive capacities in late life. As with other groups in the 1960s and 1970s, older Americans are increasingly "getting their act together"—often in concert with younger Americans. Both their credibility and their credentials may be on the rise.

SUMMARY

As the older population has grown in size and proportion, predictions of trouble ahead have appeared. Envisioned problems often focus on political or economic woes or both. We have examined some of these predictions and found them contradictory, leading to the observation that our elders are being scapegoated or seen as an outgroup onto which our survival problems are projected.

Attitudes toward the old are also contradictory. Although we may think of growing old as something of a praiseworthy feat, we also take negative views of older persons. These are more often based on misinformation than on mere bigotry. Negative views, however, may translate into policies that work against elders, diminishing the quality of their lives.

Factual information about elders reveals that they are likely to remain a minority well into the forseeable future, that most older people are healthy enough to carry on daily activities, and that large numbers of elders could work for wages if policies allowed it. Retirement policies and plans, however, can lead to a life of enforced leisure—sometimes welcome, but often producing hardships of various kinds, including poverty and isolation. The circular effect of our policies has been a vision of the old as unproductive and dependent. Such attitudes and policies have not always characterized Americans, but have emerged in relatively recent years. Older women constitute a minority within a minority that suffers special hardships, partly as a result of lifelong discrimination.

Theories of social aging, when examined for their policy implications, have been seen to support various lines of action for or by elders. Among these are withdrawal by and from them, the maintenance of an active life through substitute roles for those lost (e.g., in widowhood and retirement), and coalition formation to negate loss of power in later life. Revisions in federal programs, now fragmented and difficult to access, are needed, and recommendations for change suggest appropriate revisions—not only at the federal level but also throughout the social spectrum.

Changing the way we think about human development and especially about late life could eliminate much of what is seen as the problem of aging in a youth-oriented society. Older people themselves are growing aware of their common problems and taking steps to lobby for remedies. A massive educational effort aimed at all sectors of the population could enhance the quality of life for those now old and for those who will be old tomorrow.

STUDY QUESTIONS

1. What is the difference between ageism and gerontophobia?

2. Why do younger college students think that the personal stories that older college students tell are irrelevant to the educational experience?

3. Would you be willing to have an older relative live permanently in your family home? What would be the advantages? The disadvantages?

4. Why was a national pension system instituted in 1935?

5. Knowing nothing but their ages, you are asked to predict the typical behavior of a two-year-old and a seventy-two-year-old. Which would be easier (more accurately predictable) and why?

REFERENCES

Abdel-Ghany, M. 1977. Quality of life from the perspective of the elderly. *Home Economics Research Journal* 6: 38–47.

Arizona Republic. 10 December 1978; 26 January 1981; 1 December 1982.

Arizona Senior World. September 1981.

Associated Press. 27 January 1978; 23 August 1981.

Atchley, R. C. 1976. The life course, age grading, and age-linked demands for decision-making. In *Life-span developmental psychology: Normative life crises,* ed. N. Datan and L. H. Ginsberg. New York: Academic.

———. 1977. *The social forces in later life.* 2nd ed. Belmont, Calif.: Wadsworth.

Auerbach, D. N., and R. L. Levenson, Jr. 1977. Second impressions: Attitude change in college students toward the elderly. *Gerontologist* 17: 362–66.

Barnum, P. W. 1977. Discrimination against the aged in young children's literature. *Elementary School Journal* 4: 301–6.

Beach, M. H. 1982. The economy in an aging society. *National Forum* (Fall).

Brody, J. A. 1982. Length of life and health. *National Forum* (Fall).

Butler, R. N. 1978. Age-ism: Another form of bigotry. In *Social problems of aging: Readings,* ed. M. Seltzer, S. L. Corbett, and R. C. Atchley. Belmont, Calif.: Wadsworth.

Chiriboga, D. A. 1978. Evaluated time: A life course perspective. *Journal of Gerontology* 33: 388–93.

Christian Science Monitor. 29 January 1980.

Comfort, A. 1976. *A good age.* New York: Simon & Schuster.

Cook, F. L. 1982. Public support for services. *National Forum* (Fall).

Cowgill, D. O. 1974. Aging and modernization: A revision of the theory. In *Communities and environmental policy,* ed. J. Gubrium. Springfield, Ill.: Charles C. Thomas.

Cumming, E., and W. Henry. 1961. *Growing old: The process of disengagement.* New York: Basic.

Davies, L. J. 1977. Attitudes toward old age and aging as shown by humor. *Gerontologist* 17: 220–26

Davis, D. L. 1978. Growing older black. In *Social problems of aging: Readings,* ed. M. M. Seltzer, S. L. Corbett, and R. C. Atchley. Belmont, Calif.: Wadsworth.

Dowd, J. 1975. Aging as exchange: A preface to theory. *Journal of Gerontology* (30 September): 584–94.

Eckstein, S. L. 1977. Elder = Respect. *Gerontologist* 17: 276.

Edwards, J. N., and D. Klemmack. 1973. Correlates of life satisfaction: A re-examination. *Journal of Gerontology* 28: 497–502.

Emerson, R. 1962. Power-dependence relations. *American Sociological Review* 27: 31–41.

Fitzgerald, J. M. 1978. Actual and perceived sex and generational differences in interpersonal style: Structural and quantitative issues. *Journal of Gerontology* 33: 394–401.

Foner, A. 1975. Age in society: Structures and change. *American Behavioral Scientist* 19(2): 289–312.

Gelman, D. 1982. Growing old; feeling young. *Newsweek,* (1 November).

Gubrium, J. 1973. *The myth of the golden years: A socioenvironmental theory of aging.* Springfield, Ill.: Charles C. Thomas.

———. 1975. *Living and dying at Murray Manor.* New York: St. Martin's.

Harris, L., et al. 1975. *The myth and reality of aging in America.* Washington, D.C.: National Council on Aging.

Henig, R. M. 1979. Ageism's angry critic. *Human Behavior* (January): 43–46.

Hill, R. B. 1978. Excerpts from *The black elderly.* In Social problems of aging: Readings, ed. M. M. Seltzer, S. L. Corbett, and R. C. Atchley. Belmont, Calif.: Wadsworth.

Hudson, R. B. 1982. Accounting for old-age policy: A review essay. *National Forum* (Fall).

Inkeles, A. 1977. American perceptions. *Change* (August): 25–32.

Iyer, R. N. 1966. The social structure of the future. In *Looking forward: The abundant society*, ed. R. N. Iyer. Santa Barbara, Calif.: Center for the Study of Democratic Institutions.

Jacobson, D. 1974. Rejection of the retiree role: A study of female industrial workers in their 50s. *Human Relations* 27: 477–92.

Johnson, H. R. 1982. Education in an aging society. *National Forum* (Fall).

Jones, R. 1977. *The other generation: The new power of older people*. Englewood Cliffs, N.J.: Prentice-Hall.

Kalish, R. A. 1976. Death and dying in a social context. In *Handbook of aging and social sciences*, ed. R. Binstock and E. Shanas. New York: Van Nostrand.

Kart, C. S. 1981. *The realities of aging: An introduction to gerontology*. Boston: Allyn & Bacon.

Kessler, J. B. 1976. Aging in different ways. *Human Behavior* (June).

Kinchella, C. A. 1977. When do you get "elderly"? *Gerontologist* 17: 276.

Kivett, V. 1976. *The aged in North Carolina: Physical, social and environmental characteristics and sources of assistance*. No. 237 of *Technical bulletin*. North Carolina Agricultural Experiment Station.

Kutza, E. A. 1982. The impact of federal programs on older persons. *National Forum* (Fall).

Larson, R. 1975. Is satisfaction with life the same in different subcultures? Unpublished manuscript.

———. 1978. Thirty years of research on the subjective well-being of older Americans. *Journal of Gerontology* 33: 109–25.

Lemon, B. W., V. L. Bengston, and J. A. Peterson. 1972. Activity types and life satisfaction in a retirement community. *Journal of Gerontology* 27: 511–23.

Liang, J. and T. J. Fairchild. 1977. Relative deprivation and perception of financial adequacy among the aged. Paper presented at the annual meeting of the American Sociological Association, Chicago, September.

Moen, E. 1978. The reluctance of elderly to accept help. *Social Problems* 25: 293–303.

National Business Woman. 1975 Aging in America. (March): 25–28.

Nelson, D. W. 1982. The meanings of old age for public policy. *National Forum* (Fall).

Neugarten, B. L. 1973. Patterns of aging: Past, present, future. *Social Service Review* 47: 571–80.

———. 1982. The aging society. *National Forum* (Fall).

New York Times. 16 January 1982.

Newsweek. 1982. Living longer, living better. (1 November).

Nuessel, F. H. Jr. 1982. The language of ageism. *Gerontologist* 22: 273–276.

Palmore, E. 1969. Sociological aspects of aging. In *Behavior and adaptation in later life*, ed. E. Busse and E. Pfeiffer. Durham, N.C.: Duke University Press.

Payne, B. and F. Whittington. 1976. Older women: An examination of popular stereotypes and research evidence. *Social Problems* 23: 488–504.

Payne, S., D. A. Summers, and T. R. Stewart. 1973. Value differences across three generations. *Sociometry* 36: 20–30.

Pratt, H. J. 1982. The "Gray Lobby" revisited. *National Forum* (Fall).

Register and Tribune. 9 December 1982.

Richman, J. 1977. The foolishness and wisdom of age: Attitudes toward the elderly as reflected in jokes. *Gerontologist* 17: 210–19.

Riley, M. W. 1971. Social gerontology and the age stratification of society. *Gerontologist* 11: 79–87.

———. 1977. Age strata in social systems. In *Handbook of aging and the social sciences*, ed. E. Binstock and E. Shanas. New York: Van Nostrand.

Riley, M. W., M. Johnson, and A. Foner. 1972. *Aging and society*. Vol. 3 of *A sociology of age stratification*. New York: Russell Sage Foundation.

Rose, A. M. 1965. The subculture of aging: A framework in social gerontology. In *Older people and their social worlds*, ed. A. M. Rose and W. A. Peterson. Philadelphia: F. A. Davis.

Schlossberg, N. K. 1982. Older adults and the media. *National Forum* (Fall).

Seeman, M. 1971. Alienation: A map. *Psychology Today* (August).

Shanas, E. 1982. The family relations of old people. *National Forum* (Fall).

Singer, J. W. 1978. Jobs: A later retirement, more opportunities. In *The economics of aging: A national journal issues book*. Washington, D.C.: U.S. Government Printing Office.

Sokolowska, M. 1965. Some reflections on the different attitudes of men and women toward work. *International Labor Review* 92: 35–50.

Soldo, B. A. 1980. *America's Elderly in the 80s*. Vol. 35(4) of *Population bulletin*. Washington, D.C.: Population Reference Bureau, Inc.

Sorgman, M., M. Sorensen, and M. Johnson. 1979. What sounds do I make when I'm old? A hands-on approach to ageism. *Social Education* 43: 135–39.

Sykes, J. T. 1982. Needed: An enlightened national policy on work and retirement. *National Forum* (Fall).

Thacher, M. 1978. Cosmic culture shock. *Human Behavior* 7: 18–22.

Tibbits, C. 1979. Can we invalidate negative stereotypes of aging? *Gerontologist* 19: 10–20.

Time. 1970. The old in the country of the young. (3 August) 49–54.

———. 1979. Geriantics: A review of "My Old Friends." (5 February): 142.

United Press International. 10 November 1978; 16 April 1979; 18 January 1981.

U.S. Congress. House. Subcommittee on Human Services of the Select Committee on Aging. *Future Directions for Aging Policy: A Human Service Model*.

Cong. sess., 1980. Committee Publication No. 96–226. Washington, D.C.: U.S. Government Printing Office.

U.S. Department of Health, Education, and Welfare. Office of Human Development, Administration on Aging. 1977. *Aging*, no. 275-276. Washington, D.C.: U.S. Government Printing Office, September–October.

———. 1977. *Aging*, no. 281–282. Washington, D.C.: U.S. Government Printing Office, March–April.

U.S. Department of Health, Education, and Welfare. 1978. *Facts about older Americans: 1978.* Washington, D.C.: U.S. Government Printing Office.

U.S. News & World Report. 1980. Life begins at 55. (1 September): 50–61.

Wall Street Journal. 23 February 1978.

Washington Post. 3 October 1982.

What's Happening to the American Family? 1978. A report from the editors of *Better Homes and Gardens.* Des Moines: Meredith Corp.

Zube, M. 1972. Changing concepts of morality: 1958-1969. *Social Forces* 50: 385–93.

CHAPTER 5

Singleness, Cohabitation, and Divorce

CONTENTS

Married households are still majority, census study shows

By Spencer Rich
Washington Post

WASHINGTON — The Census Bureau said Thursday that 73 percent of the nation's population lives in households headed by married couples, down from 82 percent in 1970.

The percentage would be higher if the bureau had made some allowance for such groups as unmarried young adults and elderly widows and widowers, who traditionally have been more likely to live alone.

The new census survey was taken in March 1982 and excluded people who were institutionalized.

The new figures show that, for all the talk of new lifestyles, the traditional family is still the norm in this country. If divorce is common, so is remarriage, and about three-fourths of all children younger than 18 live in traditional two-parent households.

The bureau also found that since 1970 there has been a sharp drop in the size of the average household, from 3.14 persons to 2.72 in 1982.

The bureau said relatively low birth rates, declining marriage rates and high levels of separation and divorce caused this decline.

In its basic figures on the settings in which people live, exluding those living in nursing homes and other institutions, the bureau reported that in March 1982:

● About 165.2 million people, or 72.8 percent of the population, lived in married-couple households, consisting of 49.6 million couples (99.3 million people), 46.3 million children younger than 18, and 19.6 million others, both relatives and unrelated.

● Another 35 million people, 15.4 percent of the population, also lived in families, but families headed by one man or woman with no spouse present. About three-quarters of these were families headed by women, often single parents with several small children.

● In addition, 19.4 million people lived alone, 8.5 percent of the non-insititutional population, up from 6 percent in 1970.

● Nearly 7.4 million (3.3 percent) lived in households of two or more persons not related by family ties. In a large number of cases, these households consisted of people of the same sex sharing living quarters, such as group houses of young men or women banding together to cut down rent, friends sharing an apartment and the like.

The bureau said that in March 1982 there were about 1.9 million unmarried couples consisting of a man and a woman living together; in four-fifths of these cases one or both parties was younger than 35. But some cases, the bureau said, involve other types of situations, such as an elderly widow renting a room to a young male student.

Source: Washington Post 21 November 1982.

DEFINING THE PROBLEM: A "MARRIED WORLD" AND "THOSE OTHERS"

Spencer Rich's optimistic report, based on Census Bureau data, implies that in the area of family life, America is doing well. "For all the talk of new lifestyles," he writes, "the traditional family is still the norm." Others, focusing on different aspects of the same data, see a growing problem. In its own publication, the U.S. Bureau of the Census (1982) highlights the following changes over recent years:

1. The median age at first marriage for both men and women has increased by 1½ years since 1970.

2. In 1981, 22 percent of the women ages twenty-five to twenty-nine had never married. This figure is double the percentage in 1970.

3. Since 1970, the divorce ratio has climbed from 47 to 109 persons per 1,000 married persons with spouse present.

4. Children living in one-parent families accounted for 20 percent of all children under eighteen years old, compared with 12 percent in 1970.

5. The number of persons living alone has risen by 75 percent since 1970.

These changes, some think, indicate that although marriage and conventional family life *is* still "the norm," the future of these institutions is in question.

Scholars, as well as others, have expressed concern. They cite the increased attention paid to family violence in all its forms, the rise in the profession of marriage and family therapy, and other aspects of the social scene as possible indicators of trouble. Some conclude that the family is "alive but not well," while others believe that the family is a robust institution "here to stay" (Laslett 1978, 476).

Before we can confront singleness, unmar-ried cohabitation, and divorce meaningfully, we need clear definitions of these terms. **Divorce** is relatively simple to define: the legalized union of two persons has been legally dissolved. Typically, each person has taken up (at least temporarily) a single life again. For either or both of the former partners, that life may include children of the former marriage, or may include a nonmarital cohabiting relationship with another adult. Divorce is a legal process.

The categories of "single" and "divorced" overlap. **Singleness** may refer to those who have not yet married, or it may mean those who have been married (perhaps more than once) but are not married now because of divorce or widowhood. Singleness may also include those who choose not to marry, such as members of religious orders, among others. For simplicity's sake, we will use the term *singleness* to indicate the state of being unmarried, whether prior to or after a marriage, and regardless of how any marriage or other relationship may have ended (e.g., through desertion, separation, divorce, or death). The category will also include those with no plans to marry.

Being unmarried, however, may not be the same as living alone. Unmarried persons may cohabit with other adults, may live with children (from earlier marriages or other circumstances) or may live in any number of other arrangements. Clearly, we are not dealing with only one life-style but with a category that may include many life-styles. Moreover, to many people, to be unmarried is to belong to a residual category, with emphasis on the *un*.

Cohabitation is also somewhat complex in its definition. Those who live together without having legally (and perhaps religiously) acknowledged the bond between them have been categorized into several types. For example, some cohabitants have a sexual relationship, but others do not. One categorical scheme for cohabitation that Eleanor Macklin (1978) developed includes (1) *temporary casual convenience*, in which two persons share living quarters primarily because it is expedient, (2) *affectionate dating-going together*, which includes those who live together as an extension of the dating (especially steady dating) relationship, (3) *temporary alternative to marriage*, which includes partners who are committed to staying together but are waiting for a more convenient time to marry, (4) *trial marriage*, which includes those "engaged to be engaged" couples who, according to Macklin, are consciously testing the relationship before making a permanent commitment, and (5) *permanent alternative to marriage*, which includes couples living together in long-term committed relationships similar to marriage but without religious or legal sanctions. Each of these types may have a

different meaning to the participants than to society. Macklin's scheme is only one of several ways of categorizing cohabitants, as we shall see.

Another way to view singleness, cohabitation, and divorce might be to group them together as the "unmarried," and then discuss various subtypes, e.g., the once-or-more previously married and the never-married. Further subtypes might include those who live with another adult (cohabitants), those who live with one or more children but without any other adult, and those who live alone. These groupings, which avoid overlaps across categories, may make sense; however, they do not parallel current views of the unmarried.

Cohabitors may bring children of previous marriages along into the new relationship. This practice may or may not lead to problems in the new relationship.

Politics, Religion, and the Family

Why should the unmarried be considered a social problem? Sociologists Jerry Pankhurst and Sharon Houseknecht (1983, 5–34) offer two perspectives that explain this phenomenon. The first, or "profamily" perspective points out that at the end of the 1970s, the New Christian Right made the family one of its special interests. Subsequently, the political New Right became intertwined with the evangelistic movement. As part of the major goals of its 1980 party platform, the Reagan administration included strengthening the traditional family structure—the first time in history that an administration took an official position favoring a single family type. All other forms but the patriarchal family thus became problematic.

The second perspective, which is not incompatible with the familial emphasis of the New Right (both religious and political), sees the problematic aspects of the family (such as alternative life-styles) as a reaction against worldwide changes, both social and technological. The patriarchal (male dominated) family has become impractical and difficult to maintain. The "old individualism" that favored only males has given way to a "new individualism" that is more egalitarian. "It relates to each member of the family and allows variations in lifestyle patterns that the traditional patriarchal forms oppose. . . . The New Right in many ways can be interpreted as striking out against this new individualism" (Pankhurst and Houseknecht 1983, 27).

From the structural-functional perspective, changes have taken place that render the patriarchal family dysfunctional. From the value conflict perspective, as Pankhurst and Houseknecht (1983, 8) point out,

social change in family relations requires adaptation of traditional patterns, but the sentiments and values that have been established in support of the traditional forms are not easy to overturn. To the bearer they are important on their own terms and not as a means of adaptation. They are, therefore, clung to, even grasped at, as they recede from the scene, and sometimes they are reconstructed in a distorted form after their essential basis has evaporated. It is these reactions to social change in the family sphere that provide the impetus for the current conservative profamily movement.

Although we cannot hope to cover all important aspects of the lives of the unmarried in this chapter, we will examine how mainstream America sees (or misinterprets) them, and will look at some dimensions of their lives. Finally, we will suggest a way to transcend the social problem that unmarried persons appear to pose.

CONFRONTING THE PROBLEM: WHAT IS GOING ON OUT THERE?

According to James Ramey (1978), many Americans are unaware of family **pluralism**—the variety of forms in which people actually live. Ramey cites Bureau of Labor statistics showing the distribution of adults in United States household during a recent year (see table 5–1).

Ramey contends that with the exception of the final category, these are all merely variant family forms. (Experimental or alternative forms, he states, include contractual

TABLE 5–1. Distribution of Adults in U.S. Households

CATEGORY	PERCENTAGE
Heading single-parent families	16
Other single, widowed, separated, or divorced persons	21
Living in childfree or postchildrearing marriages	23
Living in dual-breadwinner nuclear families	16
Living in single-breadwinner nuclear families	13
Living in no-breadwinner nuclear families	1
Living in extended families	6
Living in experimental families or cohabiting	4
	100

Source: James Ramey, "Experimental family forms—The family of the future," *Marriage and Family Review* 1(1)(1978).

marriages, homosexual marriages, sexually open marriages, family clusters, intimate groups and networks, multiadult households, consensual and nonconsensual adultery, swinging, communes, and other forms such as the incestuous family.)

Notice that the idealized version of the family, in which the husband-father works and the wife-mother stays at home caring for the children, makes up 13 percent of the adult population or less, since the 13 percent shown in table 5–1 includes mothers who work outside the home and fathers who are house-husbands. Yet, in spite of its relative infrequency in the population, the idealized version of the family is one that many consider the standard way of life. For these people, variant categories and alternative and experimental forms simply do not exist. Even those who believe in sexual freedom may have difficulty envisioning the pluralistic nature of family life, as well as difficulty thinking about the future family if it differs from their beliefs about what is right. "We may want to rid ourselves of the repressions of a romantic past but we fear emotional emptiness in a deromanticized future, even while we anticipate its greater freedom" (Ramey 1978, 5).

Divorce Rates and What They Mean

Underlying many of the variant forms shown in table 5–1 is our high divorce rate. Marriages per 1,000 persons in the population compared with divorces per 1,000 persons across recent years are shown in table 5–2.

These raw statistics are widely reported in the popular press. Such data, along with accompanying commentaries, make it clear that America's divorce rate is among the highest in the world. The statement is often made that one of every two marriages ends in divorce—a statement presumably based on figures such as those shown in table 5–2. The correct conclusion, however, is that for every two marriages that take place, one divorce takes place. (If the difference between those two statements is not clear at first reading, it may help to realize that the marriage and divorce rates shown in such tables include both multiple marriages and multiple divorces. Thus, the 2,495,000 marriages and 1,180,000 divorces that took place in 1981, for instance, were not all first-time occurrences for the individuals involved.)

According to the Population Reference Bureau, Inc., living-together arrangements have been on the upswing in recent years. Demographers report that between 1960 and 1970, unmarried cohabitation rates rose by 19 percent; however, between 1970 and 1977, they rose 83 percent (Population Reference Bureau 1977). Moreover, in the decade between 1970 and 1980, "unmarried-couple households" increased from 523,000 to 1,808,000—an increase of 246 percent (U.S. Bureau of the Census 1982).

These astonishing increases are sometimes cited to support the belief that American marriage ideals are "going to hell in a handbasket." However, the Census Bureau report reveals that "unmarried-couple households . . . include a variety of living arrangements such as that of an elderly

TABLE 5–2. **Marriages and Divorces in the United States per 1,000 Persons: 1976–82**

	1982	1981	1980	1979	1978	1977	1976
Marriages	10.8	10.6	10.6	10.4	10.3	9.9	9.9
Divorces	5.1	5.3	5.3	5.2	5.1	5.0	5.0

Source: National Center for Health Statistics, *Births, marriages, divorces, and deaths for 1982,* vol. 31 (12), DHHS Publication no. (PHS) 83–1120. (Hyattsville, Md., March 1983).

woman who rents a room to a male college student or that of an elderly man who employs a live-in female nurse or housekeeper" (U.S. Bureau of the Census 1982, 6). The same source tells us that although the increase in unmarried-couple households has been dramatic, these households, however composed, make up only 2 percent of all households in the United States.

The rise in divorces, however, is meaningful. Glick and Norton (1977, 4), the well-known demographers, observe the following:

1. Since 1972, both first marriage rates and remarriage rates have fallen substantially.
2. The U.S. divorce rate in recent years has been far above that of any other country. Further, 40 percent of marriages of women now in their late twenties are likely to end in divorce.
3. Although four out of five divorced persons now remarry, projections indicate that this proportion may soon fall to three out of every four.

Despite these data, Glick and Norton do not conclude that marriage is heading toward extinction. They state, "Some two of every three first marriages taking place today are expected to last 'until death do them part' " (1977, 4).

This optimistic view is not necessarily shared by the general public. Not long ago, a survey of more than 302,000 adults revealed that well over 75 percent thought that family life is in trouble (Meredith Corporation 1978). The primary threats to family life, according to these respondents, were seen as one or more of the following: inattentive parents, the absence of religious or spiritual foundations, materialism, financial pressures, both parents working, permissive attitudes about sex, television, drug or alcohol abuse or both, and crime (1978, 10). Asked to look ten years ahead to predict future threats to family life, those surveyed suggested one or more of the following: war, inflation, the energy shortage, pollution,

crime, recession or depression, a food shortage, changing weather patterns, and moral decay (1978, 12).

Differences in Attitude: The Older Versus the Younger

Moral decay is a general term that can cover "a multitude of sins." It usually includes such concerns as divorce rates, unmarried cohabitation, and high rates of voluntary singleness. All of these are seen as against conventional morality. Almost half of the respondents under age thirty-five, and two-thirds of those age fifty-five and over, thought that moral decay threatened family life. The idea of a lifetime marriage commitment was important to over 80 percent of the survey respondents, although more than half thought that most couples marrying now do not expect to remain married "forever" (1978, 33–34). The primary cause of marital failure, most thought, was the immaturity of the partners, with selfishness running a close second (1978, 34, 37).

Most of these survey respondents were married. Asked their thoughts about unmarried cohabitation, less than half approved of it if the question referred to living together *before* marriage. Less than a fourth approved when the question referred to living together *instead* of marriage (1978, 206).

In contrast to these older, conventional Americans, a survey of younger, single college students at a large southwestern university (Laner and Housker 1980) showed that twice as many of these young adults (almost 80 percent) approved of couples living together *before* marriage, and just over 68 percent approved of living together *instead* of marrying. Younger and older adults—or single and married adults—apparently do not think alike regarding unmarried cohabitation, either temporary or permanent.

Teenagers have also been found to place a lower priority on marriage than their elders might wish. In one survey, girls ranked marriage fourteenth after such goals as "getting a job I enjoy" and "making it on my own"; for boys, marriage ranked sixteenth in importance after goals similar to those that the girls endorsed (*New York Times* 6 March 1978). These teenagers, surveyed as part of the Youth Values Project, came from every ethnic and socioeconomic background.

In giving marriage relatively low priority, these young people were not necessarily choosing to live alone, although some positive reasons for living alone may have influenced their choice. Robert T. Michael and his colleagues identified some characteristics (Michael, Fuchs, and Scott 1978) of those who endorse this option. They tend more often to be white, mobile, well educated, and relatively unconcerned with the "social climate," but neither the degree of urbanization nor the male/female ratio in specific age groups was a significant factor in the decision to live alone. As Peter Stein (1978) has observed, those who cater to the singles market through singles bars, clubs, and vacations have become big business. Interestingly, these profit-making efforts are geared toward coupling the uncoupled. Still, as Stein points out, the increase in goods and services intended for singles makes life easier for them. Other observers have suggested that such factors may have contributed to the increased numbers of those who postpone marriage (Allon and Fishel 1973).

As we have seen, relatively less disapproval of unmarried cohabitation exists among younger adults. Little disapproval of nonmarital sexual activity is also evident. Over 80 percent of college students in one study said that premarital sex between people who are in love is all right, and almost the same proportion believed that premarital sex may contribute to a happy marriage later on (Laner and Housker 1980). Older adults are less likely to approve. Responses to the same questions in the national survey mentioned earlier (Meredith Corporation 1978) showed that only 41 percent of older adults approved of premarital sex between those in love, and 57 percent thought it could or might contribute to a happy marriage later on (1978, 48–49).

Differences among Singles

As we mentioned earlier, single persons are not all of one type. Peter Stein's (1978, 3–4) description of four types of singleness is helpful in distinguishing differences within this group. Stein has identified the following major distinctions.

The voluntarily temporarily single.   The voluntarily temporarily single are the younger never-marrieds and the divorced, who are postponing marriage for some period of time. For them, the search for a mate has low priority compared with other activities such as work, education, career, politics, and the like. This category also includes men and women who have lived together but who plan to marry at some future time.

The voluntarily stable single.   The voluntarily stable single category includes those who have never been married and are satisfied with that choice, those who were formerly married but do not want to marry again, cohabitants who do not wish to marry, and those whose life-style has made marriage highly unlikely, e.g., priests and nuns. This category also includes single parents (both formerly married and never married) who are raising their children alone or with the help of others, but who are not seeking mates.

The involuntarily temporarily single.   According to Stein, the involuntarily temporarily single category consists mostly of men and women whose marriages were terminated (the widowed and divorced) and who are seeking mates, single parents seeking mates, and younger, never-married persons who are also actively seeking marriage partners. These people, says Stein, believe in marriage.

The involuntarily stable single.   Stein includes in the involuntarily stable single category older, divorced, widowed, and never-married persons who had wanted to marry (or remarry) but have not found partners.

They have come to accept their single status as probably permanent. The category also includes those who have physical or psychological problems that prevent them from being successful in the marriage market.

In addition to these four general types, there are other aspects of life that crosscut singleness, namely, sexual activity and sexual preference. As Stein puts it, single persons may be heterosexually, bisexually, or homosexually oriented, and may range from the totally abstinent (celibate) to the sexually active. Among the sexually active, there are those who may be involved with only one regular partner and those who may have many partners.

Still another crosscutting dimension is the social. Stein (1978, 4) notes that some persons have social relationships with members of both sexes, while "others live in a same-sex world." Still others may live in a world primarily composed of members of the other sex.

One final difference that is critical in the life-styles (and perhaps the life chances) of those who are single is the matter of children, either living with or not living with a single parent. Stein (1978, 4) writes, "The presence or absence of children crucially shapes and alters the patterns of interaction and the emotional and social relationships of single adults." Clearly, single parents face restrictions in time, money, and a multitude of other factors that do not burden nonparent singles. They also have opportunities, through their children, that are not available to nonparent singles.

Individuals today appear forced into a search for satisfying lives in a society that offers increasing options but does not prepare them, either emotionally or intellectually, to take advantage of available opportunities. Pluralism and increasing complexity make it a necessity for alternative life-styles to be legitimated, and with time, "legislation, policies, and practices will become more in consonance with the needs and aspirations of members of these various forms" (Sussman and Cogswell 1972, 13). The next section examines var-

Single parents face many problems, as well as many opportunities, that are not available to non-parent singles. Single parents probably have more role conflict built into their lives than non-parent singles.

ious groups of singles to better understand their "needs and aspirations."

ANALYZING THE PROBLEM: SINGLENESS, COHABITATION, AND DIVORCE

Singleness: Research Findings

Why are deliberate efforts being made to evolve legitimate alternatives to life in the nuclear family? In this section, research findings are examined for the light they may shed on this question. As we shall see, the singles studied are of several different kinds.

Elmer Spreitzer and Lawrence E. Riley (1974) have studied "bachelors and spinsters." Persons included in the research were all applicants for Social Security disability benefits. Although such individuals may not seem typical of all older singles, Spreitzer and Riley point out that the medical conditions that led to their applications for benefits began, on the average, at age fifty-two. Thus, whatever the medical problems were, they were not conditions that kept these persons from marrying earlier in life. Since the median (average) age of this sample was fifty-five years, Spreitzer and Riley considered members of the group highly unlikely to marry in the future; thus, they may be seen as the "stably single." The study included 2,454 persons who came from different parts of the country (New Orleans, Minneapolis-St. Paul, and twenty-one counties in central Ohio). The researchers were interested in establishing the relationship between certain variables, such as race and sex, and being "stably single."

Spreitzer and Riley found that rates of singleness did not vary by race (white or black) for men, but that white women tended to remain single more than did black women. Catholic men and women were less likely to marry than were Protestants of either sex. High education level was associated with the tendency to remain single among women, as was a high level of intelligence; for men, the higher the intelligence level, the less likely they were to remain single. Occupational status also had different effects for each sex. Men with higher occupational achievement were least likely to remain single, but women with higher occupational achievement were most likely to remain single.

The connection between single status in women and high educational, intelligence, and occupational status has been found in a number of other studies and has been interpreted in different ways. Spreitzer and Riley proposed that any of the following interpretations might be correct:

1. High-status women experience greater pressure to avoid "marrying beneath themselves" than do high-status men. Thus, more of such women remain single (David 1973; Hollingshead 1950).

2. Women of high educational, intelligence, and occupational status tend to be rejected in the "marriage market," because men do not want to compete for status with such wives (who may also have strong, independent personalities) (Srole et al. 1962).

3. Women with this cluster of characteristics tend to be more selective about their marital partners, i.e., they are less willing to marry or to stay in marriages (Havens 1973).

The factors that Spreitzer and Riley studied (i.e., race, religious affiliation, sex, education, and the like) were objective. Other researchers have taken different approaches to factors associated with singleness, and have studied samples of persons different from those in Spreitzer and Riley's research. We have selected three of these approaches for examination.

Peter Stein (1975) examined subjective factors associated with the choice of a single life—"reasons" that his respondents gave for their singleness. In marked contrast to Spreitzer and Riley's (1974) sample, Stein's was small and relatively young. Stein notes that the selection of this sample for in-depth interviewing was designed so that it "deliberately favored persons who at some time in their lives have been involved in exclusive relationships, in or out of marriage" (1975, 492). Such persons, Stein thought, would be able to assess their preference for singleness on the basis of comparative experience. His interviewees had "clearly chosen, at least for the forseeable future, the single state as the more viable life style for the fulfillment of their needs" (1975, 492). None was currently seeking a mate, and most believed that they would not ever marry.

From his interviews, Stein extracted what he called "pushes" and "pulls" toward marriage and singleness. (Pulls are attractions to either life-style; pushes are negative aspects of the alternative life-style.) Stein found that the the *primary pull* toward singleness was the satisfaction of economic independence and the options it represents. The *primary push* (away from marriage and toward singleness) was the feeling that marriage restricts personal growth or is an obstacle to it. The *second pull* toward singleness was the belief that it could create conditions through which individuals might attain confidence and self-respect. The *second push* toward singleness was the sense of isolation and loneliness that interviewees said they often felt in exclusive relationships. Although Stein's respondents identified several other pushes and pulls, we will limit ourselves here to noting that the *third pull* toward singleness was the sexual availability factor, and the *third push* was the belief that marriage restricts opportunities. "The dominant view was that marriage is an entrapment, requiring constant accommodation and compromise and cutting off variety of experience" (1975, 494).

Stein was not able to assess the relative importance that each of the push and pull factors had to the individuals he interviewed. Two follow-up studies, however, attempted to determine what weight they carried in larger and different samples.

Mary Laner and her associates (1979) arranged Stein's list of push and pull factors in questionnaire form, and distributed them to 217 unmarried college students at two large southwestern universities. The students were asked to rate the push and pull factors (fourteen of each) in importance to their decision making about their future life-style. These investigators believed that college students, who were between eighteen and twenty-four years of age in the study, were less likely to be "soured" on marriage or by failed relationships of other kinds than were the group of singles Stein studied.

Laner and her colleagues found that "love," "desire for a family," and "economic security" were the three strongest motivators toward marriage (the first two factors are pulls, and the third is a push away from singleness). Over 95 percent of both male and female students endorsed love; over 70 percent of both sexes endorsed the next two motivators.

Regarding motivators toward singleness, over 70 percent of both sexes endorsed "variety of experiences" and the desire for "self-sufficiency." The "freedom to change and experiment" was the third most strongly cited factor in both sexes. All of these factors were pulls toward (attractions to) the single life.

Male and female differences were found in this study, as were differences by age and school level of the respondents. For instance, more of the younger, freshman and sophomore women were motivated toward marriage by factors (such as "desire for a family" and "the influence of parents") that had less effect on older, junior and senior women.

Across all factors studied, Laner and her colleagues found that with the exception of love, respondents more strongly supported the motivators associated with singleness than those associated with marriage. Yet, most of the students said that they expected to marry. In this regard, the importance that both male and female students placed on love is telling: the most compelling factor associated with motivation to marry is a transitory one, at least in its initial, romantic aspect. What happens to the future marriages of these respondents as romantic love fades? From the overall findings of the study, the investigators concluded that future marriages among these students would very likely be of the "companionate" (equalitarian and individualistic) rather than the conventional, authoritarian (male-dominant) type.

In another follow-up study to Stein's original work, Nancy Greenwood (1978) used Stein's list of pushes and pulls to assess motivations toward marriage and singleness in a noncollege group of unmarried adults. She studied 167 Californians who were characterized by a variety of life-styles and occupations but had never married or cohabited. Greenwood thought that more men than women would favor singleness over marriage, but this prediction was not supported. She also thought that more older than younger respondents would favor singleness over marriage, and that more lower socioeconomic status (SES) respondents than higher SES respondents would choose marriage over singleness. Again, these predictions were not supported. Greenwood did find the same strong relationship between love and motivation to marry. Further, she reported that those whose friends were mostly other single people (or a mix of marrieds and singles) were less likely to support the motivators toward marriage than were those whose friends were mostly married couples.

In a different type of study, Leonard Cargan (1978) compared groups of the never-married (single), the divorced, those married for the first time (once-married), and those married two or more times (the remarried). He was interested in similarities and differences that might be uncovered regarding family background factors, feelings of happiness, sexual activities, and other factors. Cargan's samples were drawn in the Dayton, Ohio metropolitan area, which is considered one of the "ten typical demographic areas of the country" (1978, 3).

Regarding family background, Cargan found that more of the divorced came from stable but conflict-ridden or "cold" families, or from one-parent families, than did members of the other three groups. (The parents of divorced persons were also less communicative with their children.) Further, the divorced, more than the other three groups, tended to "fight" or "fight a lot" with their parents. This finding also tended to be more often true of the never-married than of either of the two married groups.

More of the married respondents reported that they were happy most of the time (85 percent) than did the unmarried (72 percent). A clear majority of both groups, however, reported themselves as generally happy. Similarly, majorities of both married and unmarried groups reported themselves satisfied with their sex lives, but the distinction between groups on this topic was greater (80 percent of the married, 55 percent of the unmarried). Frequency of sexual activity was

least for the never-married and most for the divorced. The divorced were also twice as likely as other groups to claim to have had more sexual partners.

Thirty-three percent of the divorced said they were either very or moderately lonely in their activities, while other groups making this claim ranged between 20 percent and 24 percent. (Fewer of either married group said that they had feelings of loneliness than did members of the unmarried groups.) Finally, higher proportions of the never-married and the divorced said that they got drunk once a week or more often.

In recent years, special groups of singles whose needs and aspirations had previously been overlooked have received attention. Among these, John R. Porter (1979) has focused on black singles as their lives may compare with and differ from white singles' lives. Porter's work includes an effort to provide Christian guidelines for young blacks. A broader focus is found in Robert Staples's *The World of Black Singles* (1981), in which the author addresses "changing patterns of male/female relationships." Other groups of singles, such as lesbian women and gay men, have also received attention. Homosexual life-styles are addressed, for instance, in *The Lesbian Community* (Wolf 1980) and *The Social Organization of Gay Males* (Harry and DeVall 1978), among others. (Note that not all homosexually oriented men and women consider themselves as singles. Despite society's obvious reluctance to legalize unions between persons of the same sex, many live as long-term committed couples, sometimes with children. Some seek and obtain religious sanction for their unions; others do not.)

Limited space prevents displaying research findings regarding black, homosexual, or other subgroups of singles. To some extent, such groups are still neglected in the scholarly literature, but within the last decade, interest has increased as the complexity of our society has generated increasing attention to these subgroups.

In the following section, we turn to the display of a somewhat larger group of studies of the living-together experience and its outcomes. Discussion of each of these investigations, however, is somewhat more brief than were our reviews of singleness studies.

Living Together Unmarried

Most sociologists, among them Eleanor Macklin (1972), whose categories of cohabitants we reviewed earlier, see cohabitation as a form of courtship rather than as a marriage-like arrangement. The late anthropologist Margaret Mead, however, and some psychologically oriented commentators think that cohabitation and common-law marriage are similar. This view assumes that all cohabitants intend to remain together permanently. As we already know, however, not all those who live together have such intentions. Moreover, the legal system, which is far from uniform across the United States, does not always recognize common-law marriage, much less cohabitation. In Arizona, where unmarried cohabitation is illegal, couples living together are guilty of a misdemeanor, which carries a (generally unenforced) penalty of thirty days in jail, a $200 fine, or both. Nonetheless, an early writer (Berger 1971) contended that

Most sociologists agree that cohabiting is a part of courtship, rather than a marriage-like arrangement. However, cohabitation could be evidence that the form of the traditional family is changing, rather than its function.

"trial marriages" in one form or another have been with us over time and across cultures. Berger reviewed a large body of literature about such arrangements in other societies as well as in our own, and recommended that a socially acceptable alternative to dating should be available as marriage preparation. Berger also raised the question of the possibility of exploitation in nonlegal arrangements, and raised the "critical issue" of whether *any* type of trial marriage was a valid preparation for marriage. Since the time that Berger wrote (1971), a number of studies have been undertaken in an attempt to resolve these issues.

Carl A. Ridley, Dan J. Peterman, and Arthur W. Avery (1978) tried to assess the effect of cohabitation on marriage. Their analysis, which is more psychological than sociological, provides us with another categorical scheme based on what the authors call "commonly observed" types. These are (1) the Linus Blanket type, in which the primary goal is the search for emotional security (a fragile relationship); (2) the Emancipation type, characterized by individuals who are using cohabitation in their struggle against strict sexual standards imposed by family or church or both (a tenuous relationship); (3) the Convenience type, which allows for regular sexual access and other aspects of domestic living without marital responsibilities (a relationship that precludes deep commitment); and (4) the Testing type, which is somewhat like Macklin's (1971) Trial Marriage type. In this type, partners are committed to exploring themselves and one another in an intimate arrangement that may lead to marriage. Of the four types, Ridley and his colleagues believe that the Testing type has the most potential for leading to a better marriage later, less because of the cohabitation than because of the general maturity level and interpersonal skills of those who are likely to be involved. Cohabitation, however, doesn't always lead to marriage, even following such "testing." The investigators state:

It would seem unfortunate to conclude that cohabitation is inherently good or bad preparation for marriage, but rather, it should be viewed as having the potential for both, with the characteristics of the individuals and the relationship being of critical importance in determining the effects of cohabitation (1978, 134).

Peterman, Ridley, and their colleague Scott Anderson (1974) suggested that given increased opportunity to cohabit in recent years, about a third of all college students simply experiment with short-term, limited-commitment living together. In their study of 1,100 college students, cohabitants were compared with noncohabitants on various background factors as well as on intellectual and emotional functioning. These investigators found few differences between groups on any of the factors studied.

Somewhat contradictory to Peterman, Ridley, and Anderson's study, Donald Bower and Victor Christopherson's (1977) sample of 1,191 students revealed both similarities and differences between cohabitants and noncohabitants. Moreover, only one-fourth of these students had cohabited. These investigators found that cohabitants were more likely than noncohabitants to show willingness to engage in a variety of nontraditional living styles. Those who had cohabited intended to marry at about the same rate as those who had not cohabited, but the cohabitants expected to marry somewhat later and wanted fewer children when they did marry. Bower and Christopherson believe that cohabitation appears "to have become a durable American courtship phenomenon" (1977, 452) but that it poses no serious threat to conventional marriage and childbearing norms—at least not in the form or forms in which it is currently being practiced.

Richard R. Clayton and Harwin J. Voss conducted an extensive, nationwide survey of noncollege cohabitants, but their sample was composed of men only. These 2,510 men's names were randomly chosen from Selective Service records for the years 1962 through 1972. Clayton and Voss (1977) reported that almost one-fifth of the men they studied had lived (unmarried) with a woman for six months or more. At the time they were interviewed, however, only 5 percent were cohabiting. The authors suggest that cohabitation rates would probably increase as these men grow older. With regard to background variables, Clayton and Voss's research found the following:

1. The older the man, the more likely it is that he has cohabited;

2. Those who grow up in metropolitan areas are more likely to engage in unconventional activities (such as cohabitation) than are those who grow up in areas with smaller populations;

3. Men whose fathers are college educated are more likely to cohabit than are men whose fathers did not complete high school;

4. Blacks are more likely to cohabit than are whites or members of other ethnic groups;

5. Those who attend church more frequently are less likely to cohabit than those who attend less frequently; and

6. The earlier the age at first sexual intercourse, the greater the likelihood of cohabitation.

Clayton and Voss cautioned readers against drawing conclusions about nationwide rates of cohabitation from studies of college student cohabitation. Recently, Roy E. L. Watson (1983) compared persons who had been married for one year—divided into those who had cohabited prior to marriage and those who had not—on their level of marital adjustment in that first year of marriage. His sample was drawn from the general community rather than from college students. Unlike an earlier study that Jeffrey M. Jacques and Karen Chason (1979) conducted, in which the investigators found that marital success was not affected by whether partners had or had not cohabited

prior to marriage, Watson found higher marital adjustment scores for those who had *not* cohabited prior to marriage. Watson suggested two explanations for his findings. Either the higher adjustment scores were the result of prior noncohabitants being in the honeymoon phase of marriage during the first year (while the prior cohabitants had already lived through the honeymoon phase together), or the difference might be explained as follows:

Far from being a mere rite of passage, the act of becoming formally married may have deep and quite different meaning for those who marry after cohabiting or after traditional courtship. To the latter, marriage is a liberating ritual through which new possibilities, notably, the public establishment of a common household, are opened to a couple and are celebrated. Cohabiters have already established common residence and have had to define their roles to each other and before friends and, often, to defend their action before parents. To them, the aspect of marriage which is emphasized is not the freedom it brings but the assumption of new responsibilities. It is this which . . . leads to their lower scores (1983, 146).

Watson contends that if the latter explanation is correct, the premarital behavior (whether cohabitation or not) would have progressively less effect on marital adjustment with the passage of time. If the earlier explanation is correct, says Watson, the differential would very likely persist if couples were surveyed again at a later date. In this case, "the principal significance of cohabitation lies in the duration of the period during which the partners become habituated to one another" (1983, 146).

To many scholars who study intimate relationships, as Macklin (1978) points out, a degree of commitment is assumed necessary for success. Most scholars also agree that cohabitation involves insufficient commitment. Macklin explains that researchers tend to see commitment as having two components: a *personal* commitment regarding the extent to which one is dedicated to continuing the relationship and a *behavioral* commitment involving the consequences of living with someone that make it more likely one will continue to do so (1978, 5).

Commitment: The Critical Factor?

From studies of college students on four campuses where questions about commitment in cohabitation were raised, Macklin (1978) reports that most students believe a long-term commitment to the partner is not necessary; rather, respondents indicated that the necessary relationship is merely one in which there is a "strong, affectionate, preferably monogamous relationship between the two persons" (1978, 3). Macklin also provides us with the following summary of research dealing with commitment:

1. On both personal and behavioral dimensions, unmarried cohabitants indicate significantly less commitment than do married couples. Married couples report a stronger dedication to continuing the relationship and more external constraints against separating (Budd 1976; Johnson 1973).

2. Unmarried cohabitants tend to be as personally committed to their partners as are engaged couples, but are less committed to the idea of marrying their partner (Lewis, Spanier, Storm, and Lettecka 1975).

3. There is a tendency for cohabiting women to have higher commitment scores than their partners (Budd 1976; Johnson 1973; Kieffer 1972; Lyness, Lipetz, and Davis 1972).

This last finding is the basis of the concern that cohabitation is sometimes exploitative of the female partner by the less emotionally involved and less personally committed male partner.

Cohabitants often express the belief that they will be able to learn much more about each other while living together, and thus can make more sensibly informed decisions about marriage than can those who do not cohabit. They have also had an opportunity to go beyond the typical "gameplaying" of conventional courtship (Jacques and Chason 1979). Such reasons, however, do not convince those who see cohabitation as a social problem. As Jacques and Chason remark, detractors argue that cohabitation is merely a way to avoid commitment and responsibility and amounts to a "copout."

Whether cohabitants know what marriage will be like is open to question. In a recent popular article, "Couples Who Live Together: The Surprises After Marriage," reporter Susan Jacoby comments on what can happen between people who think they know all there is to know about one another. After interviewing couples who had cohabited before marriage, she concluded that

the deeper level of commitment represented by marriage affects everything, from the way long-established couples handle their money to their relationships with relatives and friends. . . . The shorter the period of time a couple has lived together, the greater the change after marriage. The younger the people are, the greater the change (1978, 82).

As if in echo of Jacoby's findings, Jacques and Chason's report concluded that "premarital cohabitation may not provide types of learning experiences that significantly alter—in either a positive or negative direction—an individual's preparation for marriage" (1979, 38).

Marriage and Divorce: Contemporary Complications

In *The Divorce Experience* (1977), Morton and Bernice Hunt contend that divorce is a vehicle for remaining happily married, in that partners can be changed to meet the individual's needs as those needs change over the life span. This view is contrary to the attitude held by those who see marriage as a permanent relationship. The Hunts' statement represents a relatively *romantic* view—one that sees the happiness of individuals as a paramount concern. Those who consider marriage indissoluble hold a more *conventional* view—one that is based on what we believe to be the traditional religious perspective. A third view, the *rational*, suggests that decisions about divorce should be based on information, or the rational assessment of "the facts." Our cultural heritage includes all three ways of considering the meaning of divorce (Martinson 1960), which leads to some confusion. Feelings, faith, and reason, as bases of judgment, are often incompatible. In this section, we adopt a rational approach and examine factors that have been found to contribute to high divorce rates.

Attorney Norman Sheresky and writer Marya Mannes (1972) have observed that Americans marry with less knowledge of what they are undertaking than they have when they buy cars. Marriage is a legal contract, an agreement undertaken between the two individuals and the state (Melville 1977, 159). Sociologist Lenore Weitzman advises that

the provisions of the marriage contract are unwritten, its penalties are unspecified, and the terms of the contract are typically unknown to the "contracting" parties. . . . One wonders how many men and women would agree to the marriage contract if they were given the opportunity to read it and consider the rights and obligations to which they are committing themselves (1975, 531).

The four provisions of the marriage contract are based on the assumption that some privileges and obligations are the province of men, while others are assigned to women— regardless of personal preferences or capabilities (Melville 1977, 159–60). These provisions, which Weitzman believes are inapplicable to contemporary life, are:

1. The husband is the head of the household,
2. The husband is responsible for support,
3. The wife is responsible for domestic services, and
4. The wife is responsible for child care.

When people marry, says sociologist Keith Melville, the state steps in and partially defines the nature of their relationship (1977, 165). When people divorce, the state steps in again, presumably representing the interests of society as a whole. In recent years, the state, through its laws, has grown more and more intrusive. For instance, judges in forty of the states have almost complete discretion over a divorcing couple's property (*Newsweek* 10 January 1983, 42). As a feature story on the woes of marital and family breakup warns:

With no-fault laws in 48 of the 50 states, leaving a spouse is now nearly as easy as getting a marriage license. And yet, as divorce has become easier, it has also become harder—for both the legal system and the splitting partners. Couples who cannot resolve their disputes now face boundless official intrusions into their lives. Their property and their children are fair game for judicial fiat (*Newsweek* 10 January 1983, 42).

Thinking about divorce most often focuses on the emotional disruption to the concerned parties, or on the consequences of marital breakup in the area of religious beliefs (i.e., on the feeling and faith levels), or on both. The realities of divorce, at the rational level, involve consideration of the legal consequences. Increasingly, as awareness of these latter complications grows, agents of the court have forced divorcing partners to seek a mediator who will help them negotiate their own settlements. Further, those who understand the complications are using marriage contracts as a preventative for court intrusion, should marriages later dissolve. We shall further discuss mediation and contracts in the last section of this chapter. First, however, we will examine two views of the causes of divorce—one microsocial, the other macrosocial.

Roy Tamashiro (1978) has developed a microsocial view of the causes of divorce, based on what he calls criteria for marital success. In Tamashiro's view, marriage involves a set of developmental stages that follow a definite sequence, although married couples may progress through the stages at different rates (1978, 238). In each of the four stages, different criteria for success apply.

In the *first stage*, physically observable symbols are important, and criteria for success involve concrete aspects of marriage, such as money, sex, and children (1978, 239–40). In the *second stage*, success is gauged by how well social rules or conventionalities are followed, and the relevant rules are those standards that the couple's **reference group** holds—a group whose standards are seen as "right" (1978, 240). In the *third stage* the criteria for success change from external rules to satisfactions based on personal preferences. The focus turns to developing a sense of self and to individual growth. Marriage is seen as a worthwhile means to reach these ends (1978, 240–41). In the *final stage*, one moves away from one's own conscience, values, and emotions as guides to the "good life" as individuals realize that personal standards are often inconsistent, changeable, and may lead to confusion, uncertainty, and ambiguity. In this last stage of development, confusions and conflicts are faced directly, and partners make meaning of their marriage without relying on outward symbols, social conventions, or personal standards (1978, 241).

Tamashiro points out that each stage has characteristic limitations, problems, and weaknesses. Moreover, problems from earlier stages do not always disappear with movement to later stages (1978, 242). In this microsocial formulation, divorce may be seen as an outcome of failure to meet the criteria of any of the four stages. "Causes" in the first three stages might be attributed to inability to resolve problems associated with the outward symbols and concrete aspects of marriage, or to inability to meet reference group standards, or to the belief that the marriage hampers personal growth. The following principles and concepts from exchange theory help to explain how this happens.

Exchange theory, especially as developed by Thibaut and Kelley (1959) rests on the basic principle that individuals seek to maximize rewards and minimize costs in their relationships—that is, we are motivated to get the largest possible "net profit." In relationships that provide large net profits, individuals think of themselves as happy.

Exchange theory also includes a set of useful concepts known as the comparison level and the comparison level for alternatives. For our purposes, we may think of an individual's comparison level as the "fit" between what one has and what one thinks one ought to have (in Tamashiro's terms, one's "criteria for success"). When the fit is good, individuals consider themselves satisfied with things as they are. When the fit is not good, and conflict between partners escalates without resolving the problem, individuals' comparison level for alternatives comes into play. That is, partners assess what alternatives are available to them and whether any of them promise greater happiness or satisfaction than the current relationship. If another relationship (or even being without a relationship) promises either greater net profit (happiness) or greater likelihood of meeting one's criteria for suc-

TABLE 5–3. Combinations of Happiness and Satisfaction Assessments and Their Outcomes

		ASSESSMENTS OF HAPPINESS	
		Sufficient Net Profit	*Insufficient Net Profit*
ASSESSMENT OF SATISFACTION	*Criteria for Success Met*	Relationship Stable	Relationship Unstable
	Criteria for Success Unmet	Relationship Unstable	Relationship Dissolution Prone

cess (satisfaction) than the existing relationship, the outcome is likely to be a move toward dissolving the present relationship. Table 5–3 displays the several combinations of happiness and satisfaction assessments and their outcomes, from an individual point of view.

The microsocial view appears to be individual-oriented and, as such, may seem to some readers out of place in a sociologically oriented text. Yet, individualism itself can be seen as a sociological phenomenon. In contemporary America, we are the inheritors of an individualistic orientation that has been with us since our earliest days as a nation. The "frontier mentality," the "everyone for himself/herself" philosophy, and our belief that individuals must be judged on their own merits all reflect our tendency to focus away from collectivity and toward the individual. In the 1970s, individualism seemed to some observers to have reached a peak. The "Me Generation" label reflected a tendency to place personal considerations of happiness and satisfaction above the social good. This individual focus is not characteristic of all societies; in many, the welfare of the group—whether as small as the married pair or the family, or as large as the state—comes first (Chester 1971).

Returning for a moment to Tamashiro's framework with its emphasis on "stages" in which individuals change in meaningful and basic ways over time, we may ask whether any evidence supports such a theory. One psychologist's investigation conducted some years ago studied couples who had been married for at least twenty years. Kelly (1955) reported that on the average, 52 percent of his respondents said their values had changed; 55 percent said their vocational interests had changed; 69 percent acknowledged changes in their personal characteristics; and 92 percent said that their attitudes had changed. As Melville comments, it would be a surprise if people could "wake up on their twentieth wedding anniversary to find that they are the same as they were when they married" (1977, 285). Even if personal characteristics remained

the same over time, says Melville, the changing demands of life would produce considerable change in the marital relationship—demands such as those involved in occupations, childrearing, and the regained freedom of the postparental years (1977, 285).

Melville's comments lead us to consider factors operating beyond the individual that affect marriages for better or worse. First, however, we can dramatize the impact of marriage, divorce, and remarriage on our lives and those around us. Figure 5–1 shows the median age at various marital events for Americans born between 1900 and 1959 (Glick and Norton 1977).

As family demographers Glick and Norton advise, divorce after first marriage is now occurring sooner for those who obtain divorces. Half of those who remarry do so within three years after divorce. Those who divorce a second time tend to do so between a year and a half and two years sooner than it took them to obtain their first divorce:

The upshot is that young adults have been entering first marriage later and shortening the intervals not only between marriage and divorce but also between remarriage and redivorce. Thus, marital events are being compressed into a shorter span of years (Glick and Norton 1977, 8).

What factors beyond the individual level are associated with divorce and redivorce? On the basis of evidence from a large and complex body of research, sociologist Mary Laner (1978) summarized factors known to contribute to marital dissolution. Some of these factors operate at the cultural level, some at the societal level, some are dyadic (dealing with the marital pair), and some are individual-level factors. Laner's summary is useful for displaying determinants of divorce macrosocially as well as microsocially.

Cultural-level factors. High divorce rates are associated with societies such as ours in which values have changed from predominantly "sacred" to predominantly "secular" (Kirkpatrick 1955). Sacred indicates a focus on otherworldly concerns such as salvation, and secular means a this-worldly focus, e.g., on getting ahead, winning the game, and similar goals. High divorce rates are also associated with societies (like ours) that have changed from traditional male-dominance patterns toward more equalitarian patterns (Kirkpatrick 1955), and that have high rates of female employment outside the home (Kinzel 1974). Populations in such cultures are less **homogeneous** (similar or alike) and more **heterogeneous** (dissimilar or pluralistic) (Burgess and Locke 1953), and show high intermarriage rates among dissimilar persons (Cavan 1963). Such cultures are also characterized by **neolocal** residence (in which newlyweds move away from their parents to begin their new homes) and by relatively independent nuclear families (Johnson 1971).

In such cultures, permissive attitudes toward individual behavior (the "individualism" mentioned earlier) have been accompanied by an emphasis on subjective factors as the basis for mate selection (Sirjamaki 1960), a rise in the importance of the emotional relationship between wives and husbands (Dennis 1962), and raised expectations of emotional intensity between married partners (Parsons and Fox 1960).

Where there are high rates of social change in any culture such as ours, disruption of marriages seems less important, socially and economically, than it would be in relatively unchanging cultures (Schwartz 1959). The trend toward equalitarianism brings with it equalization of access to divorce-granting agencies; thus, for "the masses," divorces are easier to obtain (Goode 1962). As more people obtain divorces, disapproval of divorce lessens (Cavan 1963).

Finally, when the emphasis in a culture shifts from childbearing and childrearing to the quality of life for the husband-wife pair, the strain on the marital relationship and on the nuclear family increases (Parsons and

FIGURE 5–1. Median Age at Marital Events for U.S. Men and Women Born 1900–1959

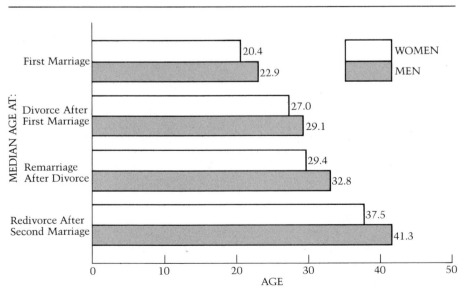

Courtesy of the Population Reference Bureau, Inc., Washington, D.C.

Bales 1955), and the likelihood of high divorce rates also increases.

Societal-level factors. High divorce rate societies are those that are highly urbanized and industrialized (Goode 1962). Such societies also have high residential mobility (Burgess and Locke 1953), high geographic mobility (Christensen and Meissner 1953), and high social mobility (Thorner 1943). Labor, formerly allocated by the sex of the persons who perform it, becomes more equalitarian, and so does decision making in the husband-wife pair (Kandel and Lesser 1972; Kirkpatrick 1955).

Dyadic (marital-level) factors. Two kinds of factors are associated with divorce proneness at this level: the *structural* and the *dynamic*. Structurally (i.e., built into the nature of our courtship and marriage institutions), each of the following factors is independently associated with divorce proneness:

1. Short periods of acquaintance before marriage (Goode 1956);
2. High heterogeneity within couples (i.e., a poor fit on social background factors such as religion, social class level, and the like) (Goode 1964);
3. Either very few (or no) children or a large family (Chester 1972; Christensen 1959)—in the former case because of less disapproval of divorce for such couples, and in the latter case because of the additional strains on marriage that large families produce;
4. Low income, low economic status, and low occupational level (Goode 1951, 1962; Kephart 1955); and
5. A low degree of "familism" (the feeling of embeddedness within family life—less typical of men than of women) (Fisher 1974).

The dynamic factors associated with divorce proneness have to do with the degree of adjustment (problem-solving ability) between partners and the degree of conflict they experience. Being married requires continual readaptation to change. This means making changes in one's roles, or in the way one relates to a partner, or both. Such changes require both the motivation to make changes and the capacity to empathize (the ability to "put yourself in the other person's shoes") (Kieren and Tallman 1972). Where degree of conflict is high—especially conflict over the basic aspects of the relationship—problem-solving ability is likely to be low. Before solutions are worked out, especially in the earlier years of marriage, the cost of such conflicts may seem too high a price to pay. Low problem-solving ability and high unresolved conflict both predict dissolution proneness in marital relationships.

Individual-level factors. At this level, the following factors affect men and women alike, and contribute to divorce proneness:

1. Low age at marriage (Glick and Norton 1977);
2. Poor childhood environment in their family-of-origin homes (Gurin, Veroff, and Feld 1960) as contrasted with emotional security in the early years and strong feelings of personal worth; and
3. High achievement training or motivation or both (Blake 1955). Marriage requires cooperation, not competition, between partners. Excessive striving is costly to marital relationships.

The next two factors operate in different ways for men and for women.

4. Educational level: Women at higher educational levels tend to marry less often and to stay married less often. In contrast, men with higher educational levels experience a greater tendency to marry and to stay married. In general, however, midlevel education (neither very high nor very low) is

associated with divorce proneness (Goode 1956, 1964).

5. Socioeconomic status: Women with higher SES backgrounds tend to marry less and to stay married less. For men, higher SES backgrounds predict the tendency to marry and to stay married (Goode 1951, 1962; Kephart 1955).

When the individual-level variables are negative, they result in low capacity for flexible, adaptive behavior. Yet, flexibility and adaptability are necessary if marriages are to remain intact. Persons low in flexibility or adaptability or both are unlikely to rate their marriages successful, as Tamashiro has suggested.

At all four levels, much of our sociocultural environment and, as a consequence,

much of what we ourselves are like, operates against the ideals we still hold about marriage. The times and conditions in which those values and ideals developed were vastly different from today's world. We still believe that marriage should last until death, for instance, but death comes, on the average, twenty-five years later today than it did as recently as the beginning of this century. Marriages, if they last, are potentially double their length at any previous time in history. Yet, we would like to think that marriages of fifty years' duration (and more) can be successfully negotiated on the basis of choices made in our early twenties—choices, as we have seen, primarily informed by romantic love over other considerations.

Large, interdependent families are a his-

When we marry, we envision "walking hand in hand into the sunset." In contemporary societies, however, many factors combined to elevate marital dissolution rates.

torical fact rather than a meaningful reality for most. Families of the past often served multiple functions for their members: employer, doctor and nurse, educator, and religious guide, among others. Today, most of those functions have been given over to outside agencies. Today's small families have become more specialized and their importance increased as sources of personal identity and meaning (Laslett 1978, 478). Many marriages last, in spite of such strains, but some contend that success is unlikely in today's world (Lasch 1977; Slater 1970, 1977).

We emphasize individualism, yet are surprised and even dismayed when individuals exercise their rights as choices for singleness rather than for marriage, cohabitation, or divorce. As sociologist-historian Barbara Laslett contends:

Perhaps the most important question to be asked about the modern family is not whether it is "here to stay" but whether it can sustain and satisfy the search for meaning and the weight of expectation that it has come to have. The contradiction implied by saying that the contemporary family is "here to stay, but not well" can be understood only when the . . . question . . . has been answered: Does, and can, the family have the resources—both material and emotional—to satisfy the demands which are placed upon it in contemporary American society? (1978, 487).

ALTERNATIVE POLICIES FOR RESOLVING THE PROBLEM: TRANSCEND AND ASSIST, NOT RESIST

If we are not willing to change virtually everything about our culture and our society, are we willing to change our attitudes instead? We need not abandon values that support marital permanence and loving marriages and homes, but so that the "reals" may more closely match the "ideals," both material and emotional resources must be devoted—not only to intact families but also as supports to those for whom the choice lies elsewhere, whether temporarily or permanently.

As we noted in chapter 4, the life cycle need not be considered, as it has been in the past, as a standardized, inevitable movement through marriage, parenthood, and subsequent "crises" of aging (Gubrium 1978). Alternative routes through life have always been available, but for the most part, we have tried to invest life with certainty by downgrading differences and lauding similarities. The label *deviant*, however, is not helpful to adaptation, whether imposed by others or by one's self. We continue to think of the average family as composed of a father who works outside the home, a mother who takes care of house and children, and (ideally) two children—the older, a boy; the younger, a girl. As we have seen, such families constitute only a small minority. As social scientists, we have sometimes contributed to the solidification of distorted views of the world in our definitions of "healthy" or "normal" families or both, and in our failure to turn our attention to unvarnished realities. Over the past decade, however, social scientists have broadened their field of vision and shed light not only on the structural actualities but also on identifying valuable survival techniques in a world that requires increasing flexibility and adaptability.

Emotional Supports

Elizabeth Cauhapé's (1978) study of long-term marriages that ended in divorce has shown that when divorce is defined positively, the transition out of a long-standing status into a new and unfamiliar one (singleness) is made easier through the development of adaptive strategies.

Using survey data collected in 1957 and 1976, Alfreda Iglehart (1978) compared working mothers who experienced a nonsupportive environment at the earlier date with those whose environment was supportive. The 1957 mothers reported feelings of personal inadequacy as parents, and the younger their children, the less positive were the mothers' feelings about themselves. By 1976, sufficient evidence had accumulated about working mothers, so that negative attitudes toward them were much less prevalent. By 1976, the attitudes of working mothers toward themselves also reflected the positive social attitude change. Clearly, negative societal views benefited neither the mothers nor husband-fathers nor children of the 1957 cohort.

As Seymour Leventman (1978) has counseled, as long as we drag our heels by blaming problems on the passing of traditional structures, we serve neither our understanding of society nor the individuals within it. Leventman notes that we continue to be defensive about change, trying to legitimate the "traditional" in a world where it may no longer be completely appropriate. Divorce, cohabitation, and singleness may be adaptive rather than problematic. Laslett (1978, 487) contends that the "specialized and bureaucratic organization of modern life has made the family one of the few locations where the expression of strong feeling is legitimate," but as she also points out, this legitimation increases the likelihood that emotionally charged interaction—both positive and negative—will occur within families.

Stein (1975) has argued that the choice of the single life-style is a movement that lacks an ideology such as that supporting the choice for marriage. Ida F. Davidoff (1977) sees unmarried cohabitation not merely as a cultural variant but rather as the striving of a portion of the population to come to terms with some basic issues of the change from childhood to maturity—an additional "rite of passage" which, she believes, can be a creative alternative rather than evidence of "moral disintegration." Even demographers Glick and Norton (1977) have noted that relaxation of social pressures toward marrying and staying married

may have its good points. The delay in first marriage, the downturn in remarriage, and growing experimentation with premarital intimacy may mean eventual greater stability for those marriages that do take place.

Public opinion about divorce is already changing, although the pendulum has not yet swung to full acceptance. In a 1978 national survey, 75 percent of the respondents thought it was all right for couples who could not get along to divorce, even where children were involved; where no children were involved, 84 percent said it was all right (Meredith Corporation 1978: 38). However, in answer to the question "Do you feel there's a social stigma attached to being divorced?" half of the respondents said that in their opinion, there was (1978, 39).

Perhaps because they are reluctant to marry while they are still inexperienced (Abeel 1979, 3), some who have chosen cohabitation have devised contracts for self-protection. Such contracts may be simple, merely specifying how property is to be acquired and how it is to be divided if the relationship dissolves. Contracts have received considerable attention in the popular press, and lawyers have encouraged both married and unmarried cohabitors—especially women—to undergird their self-confidence with such contracts (*Los Angeles Times*, 1 April 1982). Further,

as state courts across the country begin to uphold property agreements made by persons living together though unwed, and as cohabitation is no longer illegal in most states, lawyers report a rush by unmarried couples to draw up contracts protecting their property rights (Population Reference Bureau 1977, 9).

Material Resources

Divorce laws are extremely inequitable at present, and the chief victims of these laws are women (and their children). Efforts at reform have been less than completely successful. Children are involved in divorce more than half the time, and only a third of divorced mothers receive child support payments, "an epidemic of lawlessness that is rivaled, perhaps, only by income-tax cheating" (*Newsweek*, 10 January 1983, 42). Alimony is rarely awarded and often lasts for only a brief time until the recipient obtains a job. For homemakers who have never worked or who have low-paying jobs, the situation may be desperate; divorced women with children have become the "nation's new poor" (1983, 42).

Divorce mediation, to which we referred earlier, is now in use in the courts of twenty three states. Mediation deals only with how couples want to settle their property, and although it appears more promising than the system of hiring an attorney to fight a court battle over property, it is also seen as a "mixed bag:"

Not everyone is sold on the idea. Even mediators doubt the value of laws that require it, since the negotiating process depends on the spirit of cooperation. Divorce lawyers . . . worry that a bullying spouse may dominate negotiations. They also doubt the skills of mediators in complicated financial cases and fear that some lawyers who mediate may unethically seek to represent both sides (*Newsweek* 10 January 1983, 45).

The many problems associated with divorce, in law and in other dimensions, do not indicate the undesirability of divorce as much as they indicate that society has not caught up with its own needs. Full reform of the structure of family law is required so that all parties concerned receive fair and equitable treatment. Are we willing to make the necessary sweeping changes?

We noted earlier that life is not necessarily characterized by a rigid movement across predetermined events. Sociologists Henry Etkowitz and Peter Stein make this point:

The nature and extent of social changes affecting the lives of adult men and women and the emergence of new adult roles calls into question the validity of the life cycle model composed of a sequence of stages. If the stage theory of . . . life . . . is accurate, the overwhelming proportion of the population would experience these stages in the pattern prescribed; if there are life course stages in the adult years, then every individual should go through the same set of stages . . . with a minimum of strain (1978, 435).

As the authors point out, however, more and more adults do not conform to any set sequence of stages; the pattern is merely the statistically prevalent pattern which, Etkowitz and Stein contend, has been rigidified into a set of "oughts" regarding how people should live (1978, 437). Their study of intimacy in adulthood has led these researchers to identify four different patterns among American adults:

1. A sequence of traditional roles, such as those involved in the life cycle model;

2. Shifts between traditional and alternative patterns, including marriage, divorce, and singleness; married parenting to single parenting; shifts in sexual identity from single partnership to multipartnership; and from conventional marriage to open marriage. "For many," they write, "there is a subsequent movement back to traditional roles. One example involves marriage, divorce, and remarriage" (1978, 437).

3. Movement from early nontraditional patterns to later traditional ones; for example, early communal living, to living alone, to unmarried cohabitation, to marriage; and,

4. Remaining single and choosing singleness as a life-style, long-term communal membership, women or men or both who choose to be single parents, or those who choose cohabiting parenthood.

Etkowitz and Stein reviewed data obtained from interviews with a sample of middle-class unmarried women and men between twenty four and forty five years of age. They wrote:

In the absence of marriage, these single adults noted the importance of substitute networks of human relationships that met their needs for intimacy, sharing, and continuity. While pressures from external sources to leave singlehood continued, their membership in various support networks and in validating reference groups enabled them to discount negative evaluations. Such support networks included women's and men's groups, political groups, therapy and encounter groups, and organizations formed around specialized interests. Although not restricted to singles, they were particularly well adapted to meet the needs of single people. These groups were cited as helpful in legitimizing alternative roles and dealing with critical life events (1978, 440).

Etkowitz and Stein make the point that human needs can be met through a variety of traditional and alternative roles (1978, 438). Studies of marital satisfaction, separation, divorce, and family therapy suggest that "marriage and family structures do not meet the intimacy needs of many adults" (1978, 439). The authors recommend that we accept both traditional and alternative life-styles and patterns. Rather than viewing them as "good" and "bad" or as "normative" and "deviant," they argue for transcending such value judgments and viewing alternatives merely as the choices of persons who are attempting, in a variety of ways, to meet their adult needs.

In times of increasing change, moving away from prejudgments about how people ought to live and focusing instead on how they do live seems only good sense. Increasingly, the taken for granted lockstep life cycle model has been questioned in the face of employment and career changes, in challenging conventional role definitions, and in expanding opportunities for relating in meaningful ways to others. "Social problems" such as divorce, cohabitation, and singleness could disappear by definition. Attention might be more profitably focused on the outcomes, rewards, and costs of those alternatives and on how best to support them—both emotionally and with material resources.

although most men and women choose marriage rather than unmarried cohabitation, those who cohabit, divorce, or opt for the single life are seen as deviant and threatening to the institutions of marriage and the family.

We have examined the pluralism in family forms that characterizes our society, noting the the "ideal version" of the family is also a minority. We have seen that younger adults consider alternative life-styles less critically than do older adults, although both groups hold a similar set of values affirming the stability of marriage and family life. We have attempted to show that both uncohabiting and cohabiting singles constitute a variety of types, and that motivations for adopting these life-styles also vary. Finally, we have displayed both micro- and macro-level explanations for divorce.

If we cannot turn back the clock to earlier ways of living that supported long-term marriages, we can modify our attitudes about whether divorce, unmarried cohabitation, or singleness constitute social problems. If we accept contemporary social realities, the advantages to be gained are at least understanding how alternate life-styles can enhance survival and what their negative consequences may be. Divorce, for example, can play havoc with lives—especially those of women and children; singles risk isolation; unmarried cohabitants and sexually active noncohabitants risk venereal diseases and the complications of childbearing outside marriage. None of these negative outcomes is necessary if we are willing to provide both the emotional supports and the material resources for those whose adult needs are best met in nonmarital arrangements.

SUMMARY

Singleness, unmarried cohabitation, and divorce rates are increasing. Although most marriages last "until death," although single adults are still a minority of all adults, and

STUDY QUESTIONS

1. Of the three alternatives to married life discussed in this chapter, which is the most troubling from society's point of view? Why?

2. If persons who value many aspects of the single life eventually marry, what do their values suggest about the kinds of marriages they are likely to have? What are the possible outcomes?

3. Why do most sociologists agree that unmarried cohabitation is more courtship-like and less marriage-like?

4. Why is there a tendency for many of today's young to postpone marriage?

5. What factors contribute to today's high divorce rates?

6. Explain the difference between micro- and macrosociological levels of approach.

REFERENCES

Abeel, E. 1979. Divorce fever: Is it an epidemic? In *Choice and challenge.* 2d ed., ed. C. E. Williams and J. F. Crosby. Dubuque, Iowa: Wm. C. Brown.

Allon, N., and D. Fishel. 1973. Urban courting patterns: Singles' bars. Paper presented at the annual meeting of the American Sociological Association, New York City, August.

Berger, M. E. 1971. Trial marriages: Harnessing the trend constructively. *Family Coordinator* 20: 38–43.

Blake, J. 1955. *The family structure in Jamaica.* Glencoe, Ill.: Free Press.

Bower, D. W., and V. A. Christopherson. 1977. University student cohabitation: A regional comparison of selected attitudes and behavior. *Journal of Marriage and the Family* 39: 447–53.

Budd, L. S. 1976. Problems, disclosures, and commitment of cohabiting and married couples. Ph.D. diss., University of Minnesota.

Burgess, E. W., and H. J. Locke. 1953. *The family* 2d ed. New York: American Book Co.

Cargan, L. 1978. Singles: Are they different? Paper presented at the annual meeting of the Society for the Study of Social Problems, San Francisco, September.

Cauhapé, E. S. 1978. Mid-life singles: Upper middle-class adults after long-term marriage. Paper presented at the annual meeting of the Society for the Study of Social Problems, San Francisco, September.

Cavan, R. S. 1963. *The American family.* New York: Thomas Y. Crowell.

Chester, R. 1971. The duration of marriage to divorce. *British Journal of Sociology* 22: 172–82.

———. 1972 Is there a relationship between childlessness and marital breakdown? *Journal of Biosocial Science* 4: 443–54.

Christensen, H. T. 1959. Selected aspects of child spacing in Denmark. *Acta Sociologica* 4: 34–45.

Christensen, H. T., and H. H. Meissner. 1953. Studies in child spacing, III: Premarital pregnancy as a factor in divorce. *American Sociological Review* 18: 641–44.

Clayton, R. R., and H. J. Voss. 1977. Shacking up: Cohabitation in the 1970s. *Journal of Marriage and the Family* 39: 273–83.

David, D. 1973. *Career patterns and values: A study of men and women in science and engineering.* Columbia University: Bureau of Applied Social Research.

Davidoff, I. F. 1977. "Living together" as a developmental phase: A holistic view. *Journal of Marriage and Family Counseling* 3: 67–76.

Dennis, N. 1962. Secondary group relationship and the preeminence of the family. *International Journal of Comparative Sociology* 3: 80–90.

Etkowitz, H., and P. Stein. 1978. The life spiral: Human needs and adult roles. *Alternate Lifestyles* 1(4): 434–46.

Fisher, E. O. 1974. *Divorce: The new freedom.* New York: Harper & Row.

Glick, P. C., and A. Norton. 1977. *Marrying, divorcing, and living together in the U.S. today.* Population bulletin 32 (5). Washington, D.C.: Population Reference Bureau.

Goode, W. J. 1951. Economic factors and marital stability. *American Sociological Review* 16: 808–12.

———. 1956. *Women in divorce.* Glencoe, Ill.: Free Press.

———. 1962. Marital satisfaction and instability: A cross-cultural analysis of divorce rates. *International Social Science Journal* 14: 507–26.

———. 1964. *The family.* Englewood Cliffs, N.J.: Prentice-Hall.

Greenwood, N. A. 1978. Attitudes toward marital options among singles: Singleness as a positive lifestyle. Paper presented at the annual meeting of the Society for the Study of Social Problems, San Francisco, September.

Gubrium, J. F. 1978. Life cycle theorizing and marital status. Paper presented at the annual meeting of the Society for the Study of Social Problems, San Francisco, September.

Gurin, G., J. Veroff, and S. Feld. 1960. *Americans view their mental health.* New York: Basic.

Harry, J., and W. B. DeVall. 1978. *The social organization of gay males.* New York: Praeger.

Havens, E. M. 1973. Women, work, and wedlock: A note on female marital patterns in the United States. *American Journal of Sociology* 78 (January): 975–81.

Hollingshead, A. 1950. Cultural factors in the selection of marriage mates. *American Sociological Review* 15 (October): 619–27.

Hunt, M., and B. K. Hunt. 1977. *The divorce experience.* New York: McGraw-Hill.

Iglehart, A. P. 1978. Working mothers: No longer a social problem? Paper presented at the annual meeting of the Society for the Study of Social Problems, San Francisco, September.

Jacoby, S. 1978. Couples who live together: The surprises after marriage. *McCalls* (June).

Jacques, J. M., and K. L. Chason. 1979. Cohabitation: Its impact on marital success. *Family Coordinator* 28(1): 35–39.

Johnson, M. M. 1971. The structural-functional theory of family and kinship. *Journal of Comparative Family Studies* 2: 133–44.

Johnson, M. P. 1973. Commitment: A conceptual structure and empirical application. *Sociological Quarterly* 14: 395–406.

Kandel, D. B., and G. S. Lesser. 1972. Marital decision-making in Danish and American urban families. *Journal of Marriage and the Family* 34: 134–38.

Kelly, E. L. 1955. Consistency of the adult personality. *American Psychologist* 10: 654–81.

Kephart, W. M. 1955. Occupational level and marital disruption. *American Sociological Review* 20: 456–65.

Kieffer, C. M. 1972. Consensual cohabitation: A descriptive study of the relationships and sociocultural characteristics of eighty couples in settings of two Florida universities. Master's thesis, Florida State University.

Kieren, D., and I. Tallman. 1972. Spousal adaptability: An assessment of marital competence. *Journal of Marriage and the Family* 34: 244–56.

Kinzel, R. 1974. The connection between the family circle and divorce rates: An analysis based on divorce rates. *Journal of Marriage and the Family* 36: 379–88.

Kirkpatrick, C. 1955. *The family as process and institution*. New York: Ronald.

Laner, M. R. 1978. Love's labors lost: A theory of marital dissolution. *Journal of Divorce* 1(3): 213–32.

Laner, M. R., and S. L. Housker. 1980. Sexual permissiveness in younger and older adults. *Journal of Family Issues* 1(1): 103–24.

Laner, M. R., R. H. Laner, and C. E. Palmer. 1978. Motivated to marry or satisfied with singlehood? Stein's "pushes" and "pulls" revisited. *Cornell Journal of Social Relations* 14(1): 59–74.

Lasch, C. 1977. *Haven in a heartless world: The family besieged*. New York: Basic.

Laslett, B. 1978. Family membership, past and present. *Social Problems* 25(5): 476–90.

Leventman, S. 1978. Social problems and mass society theory. Paper presented at the annual meeting of the Society for the Study of Social Problems, San Francisco, September.

Lewis, R. A., G. B. Spanier, V. L. Storm and C. F. Lettecka. 1975. "Commitment in married and unmarried cohabitation." Paper presented at the annual meetings of the American Sociological Association, San Francisco, August.

Los Angeles Times. 1982. Making a business of romance: Lawyer advises a partnership agreement. April 1, Part V (5).

Lyness, J. F., M. E. Lipetz, and K. E. Davis. 1972. Living together: An alternative to marriage. *Journal of Marriage and the Family* 34: 305–11.

Macklin, E. D. 1972. Heterosexual cohabitation among unmarried college students. *Family Coordinator* 21: 463–72.

———. 1978. Nonmarital heterosexual cohabitation. *Marriage and Family Review* 1(2).

Martinson, F. M. 1960. *Marriage and the American ideal*. New York: Dodd, Mead.

Melville, K. 1977. *Marriage and family today*. New York: Random House.

Meredith Corporation. 1978. *What's happening to the American family? A report on the American family from the editors of Better Homes and Gardens*.

Michael, R., V. R. Fuchs, and S. R. Scott. 1978. Research cited in *Marriage and Divorce Today* 4(4) (11 September): 2.

National Center for Health Statistics. 1983. *Births, marriages, divorces, and deaths for 1982*, vol. 1(2). DHHS Publication no. (PHS) 83-1120. Hyattsville, Md., March.

New York Times. 6 March 1978.

Newsweek. 1983. Divorce American style. (10 January): 42–48.

Pankhurst, J. G., and S. K. Houseknecht. 1983. The family, politics, and religion in the 1980s: In fear of the new individualism. *Journal of Family Issues* 4(1): 5–34.

Parsons, T., and R. F. Bales. 1955. *Family: Socialization and Interaction Process* Glencoe, Ill. Free Press.

Parsons, T., and R. C. Fox. 1960. Illness, therapy, and the modern American family. In *Modern introduction to the family*, ed. N. W. Bell and D. F. Vogel. Glencoe, Ill.: Free Press.

Peterman, D. J., C. A. Ridley, and S. M. Anderson. 1974. A comparison of cohabiting and non-cohabiting college students. *Journal of Marriage and the Family* 36: 344–54.

Population Reference Bureau. 1977. *Intercom: The international newsletter on population*. Washington, D.C. (October).

Porter, J. R. 1979. *Dating habits of young black Americans: And almost everybody else's too*. Dubuque, Iowa: Kendall-Hunt.

Ramey, J. 1978. Experimental family forms—the family of the future. *Marriage and Family Review* 1(1).

Ridley, C. A., D. J. Peterman, and A. W. Avery. 1978. Cohabitation: Does it make for a better marriage? *Family Coordinator* (April): 129–37.

Schwartz, M. J. 1959. Sexuality and aggressiveness on Romonum, Truk. *American Anthropologist* 60: 467–86.

Sheresky, N., and M. Mannes. 1972. A radical guide to wedlock. *Saturday Review* (12 July).

Sirjamaki, J. 1960. Cultural configurations in the American family. In *Modern introduction to the family*, ed. N. W. Bell and E. F. Vogel. Glencoe, Ill.: Free Press.

Slater, P. 1970. *The pursuit of loneliness: American cul-*

ture at the breaking point. Boston: Beacon.

———. 1977. Footholds: Understanding the shifting sexual and family tensions in our culture. New York: E. P. Dutton.

Spreitzer, E., and L. E. Riley. 1974. Factors associated with singlehood. Journal of Marriage and the Family 36: 533–42.

Srole, L., T. Langer, S. Michael, M. Opler, and T. Rennie. 1962. Mental health in the metropolis: The midtown Manhattan study. New York: McGraw-Hill.

Staples, R. 1981. The world of black singles. Westport, Conn.: Greenwood.

Stein, P. J. 1975. Singlehood: An alternative to marriage. Family Coordinator 24: 489–503.

———. 1978. The lifestyles and life chances of the never-married. Marriage and Family Review 1(4).

Sussman, M. B., and B. E. Cogswell. 1972. The meaning of variant and experimental marriage styles and family forms in the 1970s. In Non-traditional family forms in the 1970's, ed. M. B. Sussman. Minneapolis: National Council on Family Relations.

Tamashiro, R. T. 1978. Developmental stages in the conceptualization of marriage. Family Coordinator (July): 237–44.

Thibaut, J. W., and H. H. Kelley. 1959. The social psychology of groups. New York: Wiley.

Thorner, I. 1943. Sociological aspects of affectional frustration. Psychiatry 6: 157–73.

U.S. Bureau of the Census. 1982. Marital status and living arrangements: March, 1981. Current population reports, ser. P-20, no. 372. Washington, D.C.: U.S. Government Printing Office.

U.S. Department of Health and Human Services. Public Health Service. Office of Health Research, Statistics, and Technology. 1981. Monthly vital statistics report 29(12) (18 March).

Watson, R. E. L. 1983. Premarital cohabitation vs. traditional courtship: Their effects on subsequent marital adjustment. Family Relations 32: 139–47.

Weitzman, L. 1974. Legal regulation of marriage: Tradition and change. California Law Review 62: 1169–1288.

———. 1975. To love, honor, and obey? Traditional legal marriage and alternative family forms. Family Coordinator (October): 531–48.

Wolf, D. G. 1980. The lesbian community. Berkeley: Univ. of California Press.

PART II

Social and Economic Justice

It is almost a truism to say that human-kind's most serious flaw is that we are poorly organized. Social relations are never as well structured (arranged) as they could be. Better social organization might alleviate many social problems inherited from our not-too-distant ancestors.

This section presents and analyzes a number of problems that relate to differences in power and authority in our society. We interact with others through *networks* of status positions (jobs) that contain great distinctions in their rights and obligations. The existence of these social *structures* implies that some persons receive either more or less social and economic justice than others on a daily basis. Thus, in a society as competitive as our own, structural arrangements can create problems not found in more cooperative social systems.

In Part Two, we describe a set of problem areas with recognizable structural components and suggest a number of policy alternatives that might alleviate them. Chapter 6 explores interrelationships among societal elites, economic theories, how work gets done in society, and who does it. Chapter 7 focuses on the persistence of poverty in America and its relationship to social class conflict. Chapter 8 deals with crime and delinquency, punishment, and injustice within the criminal justice system, including inconsistent sentencing, police violence and

corruption, and conditions in the prisons. Chapter 9 describes problems in the mental and physical health care systems of the society, with suggestions for their improvement. Chapter 10 spells out the special problems of racial, ethnic, and political minorities and the ways in which they might be brought back into the economic and political systems. Finally, in Chapter 11, we analyze social change in gender roles and what this might mean to the future of the society. The underlying theory which seems best able to explain the diverse structural problems encountered in Part Two is *conflict* theory, although other theories are presented as well.

CHAPTER 6

Work, Elites, and Economics

CONTENTS

After months out of work: "I feel betrayed"

Government Officials say that the country is on the road to economic recovery, but hundreds of thousands of unemployed workers see no quick end to their bitter troubles.

One of them is John Worrall, 37, a Pittsburgh-area steelworker laid off for more than a year. Below, he tells how joblessness has changed his outlook and the plans he had for his wife and children.

McKEESPORT, Pa.—Having put 17 years of my life into the mill, I can't help but be angry as I sit here out of work, with no prospects of a job, and a wife and two kids to support. Except for a couple of weeks' work at the mill last Christmas, I haven't seen a paycheck since August of 1981.

I don't know who to blame—myself, the government, the company or the union. One thing's for sure: I feel betrayed.

When I first got on with the company, I was just 20 years old. My father had been a steelworker, and I was told by relatives that I'd be set for life if I went into the mill. All I had to do was keep my nose clean, and I'd always have a job—just like my dad did. Those steady paychecks, good health-insurance benefits and nice vacations every year all looked very attractive.

Because I started work at the mill so young, I figured by the time I reached 50, I'd have my 30 years in and could retire. My kids would be grown by then, and between the equity I'd have in my home and savings, I could start my own business. With a pension check, I thought I'd have a good chance of success, too, because I could afford to plow everything right back into the business.

But now I regret that decision. At the time, I was working in a filling station, and I wish I hadn't let my relatives talk me out of the plans I had to buy my own station. By now I would have had 17 years in business and some real security—instead of having to scratch for my next meal.

Now I'm in the final 13 weeks of unemployment compensation, which means I have $198 coming in each week until December, in addition to the $57 in food stamps we've been getting right along each month.

I want us to avoid more welfare as long as possible. It's not that I think it's wrong. If I have to accept welfare to put food on the table, I'll do it. But taking welfare is a big step for me. I've always thought that people on welfare didn't want to work and that anyone who

wanted a job in this country could find one. Now I'm not so sure.

I've been spending a lot of time putting applications in for work all over the place, and I've concluded that there are a lot more people hunting work than there are jobs. It used to be that when one steel mill slacked off, you could find work at another. But this entire valley is dead. I can't even get a job pumping gas and, believe me, I've tried. Even my wife, who has been a full-time housewife since we were married, can't find a simple waitress job.

I don't know what we would have done without our family and friends. It seems like they take turns helping us with a little bit of food or money to tide us over.

When our hot-water tank burst and flooded the basement, we didn't know how we'd manage because we no longer have any credit. But a friend who is also a laid-off steelworker bought one for us on his credit and trucked it over. This guy's struggling to survive himself, but he didn't think twice about doing it. That's the kind of thing that keeps you going when you're down.

When I look around at friends from the mill who are

getting divorced or losing their homes, I wonder, "Am I next? Am I going to lose the home I've worked for all my life?"

I can't help but be depressed. I've felt unneeded and useless—that this family is being supported by the government, not by me. I get embarrassed going to the bank for food stamps and standing in line to redeem them at the market. It digs into your pride.

I know that all of this has made me miserable to live with and that I haven't been a very good husband or father since this began.

It seems like all I ever have on my mind are bills and how I'm going to pay them. I wake up in the morning thinking about them, and the collection agencies don't make it any easier. They hound me by mail and telephone day after day, wanting to know why I'm not paying. Telling them your situation and promising to pay a little bit each month does no good. They won't listen.

My top priority has been to make the mortgage payments of $370 a month on our house and keep up with the utilities, because I want my wife and kids to have a roof over their heads. But that means I've slipped behind on other debts. I'm six months behind on the car payments, and I know that any day now it will be repossessed.

Sometimes the problems seem so overwhelming that I think about leaving home, that maybe my family would be better off without me. But I've never been a quitter, and I'm not going to start now.

If worst comes to worst and I'm not called back to the mill, I'll just start all over again. I'm not sure how, exactly. I know we won't leave the area. Our families are here, and from what I read in the newspapers, things aren't much better anywhere else. I'm always hearing about people who've spent every last dime they had to move away and then come back in worse shape than when they left.

Maybe we'll sell everything we have and try to start that business I've always wanted. I feel like I built my life the same way you build a house. I built the foundation, the walls and then the roof. But now I'm back in the basement again. The only thing I haven't lost is faith in myself.

Source: U.S. News & World Report 18 October 1982. © 1982 U.S. News and World Report, Inc.

DEFINING THE PROBLEM: THE SOCIOLOGY OF WORK

As the U.S. economy tries to pick up speed, laid off industrial workers, like John Worrall, are in danger of being left behind permanently. Steelworkers, mechanics, welders, assemblers, and textile workers are among those who occupy a million jobs that may never return (*U.S. News & World Report* 1982, 53). From the gray steel towns of Pennsylvania to cities all over America, the new unemployed have tales of shopping bag ladies, street people, and swelling numbers of other "walking wounded."

The problem of the homeless in the United States is suddenly critical. In New York City alone, an estimated 36,000 homeless persons sleep in hallways, abandoned factories, parks, and the doorways of prestigious department stores and offices (Parker 1982, 14). An estimated 22,000 persons are homeless in Los Angeles, including an increasing number who sleep in the public restrooms of Los Angeles International Airport (Parker 1982, 14). On a recent trip west, one author of this book spotted about two hundred migrant workers living in cardboard boxes near Bakersfield, California. Our most recent recession seems to have created more desperation than ever among the unemployed.

The Demographics of Employment and Unemployment

From a sociological point of view, those who counsel the unemployed report seeing more white-collar workers and small-business owners among the "disaffiliated" than ever before. By Winter 1983, the unemployment rate in the U.S. seemed to be leveling off at about 8.4 percent of the civilian work force.

In a civilian labor force of 110.7 million workers (see figure 6–1), the total number of unemployed seems to be increasing by smaller numbers. If more people continue to come into the labor force than there are new

jobs, however, unemployment will rise again. Further, if the Federal Reserve Board and neighborhood banks do not continue to lower interest rates, thereby creating more housing starts and other business investments, permanently high unemployment rates of 8 to 10 percent are a strong possibility.

The myth that large numbers of Americans do not want jobs was dispelled when more than 15,000 Chicagoans braved the cold to apply for 2,800 full-time and 1,000 part-time jobs (*Associated Press* 7 January 1983), and when St. Louis police dispersed 4,500 teens seeking minimum wage summer jobs offered by that city (*Associated Press* 29 March 1983). We are a work-oriented society, and the great *majority* of Americans would rather work than be given handouts. These workers tend to believe in our competitive political and economic system even when it fails them.

Relations Between Workers and Owners

One of the earliest students of industry-labor relations was Karl Marx. In his *Economic and Philosophical Manuscripts of 1844*, he observed that economic alienation results from ownership of private property because it limits the means of production available to the whole society (Marx 1964). In Marx's view, land, other natural resources, and machinery are vital to everyone's survival and should not be manipulated by self-interest or personal indifference. The ownership of property should be a relationship developed among all people, since the motives that make it personally desirable to own property result only from the value society places upon such goals.

According to Marx, alienation can occur for the person controlling the means of production as well as for the workers. He says that economic alienation occurs when the employer is in control of land or industry and the workers are treated as tools to be manipulated to the advantage of the individual owner. In this type of relationship, workers are first alienated from the product they produce and then from themselves as the creators of the product. Thus dehumanized, they work only to gain subsistence, taking little pride in the work itself. The result is alienation, unemployment, and economic markets saturated with goods that workers cannot afford to buy. Industrial monopolies are responsible for alienating scientific, professional, and artistic people, according to Marx (1964, 108ff.).

This economic alienation may be the reason for some of our present quality control problems. Even in modern capitalism with its worker incentives, quality control is a continuing problem. Automakers, for example, are constantly searching for ways to keep assembly line workers from falling asleep on the lines. For a time, Volvo of Sweden had a small team of workers build

each car to reduce monotony and to foster pride in their work. Judging from Volvo's recent high marks in reliability (*Consumer Reports* 1983, 208), this practice has been helpful.

Conversely, the quality and reliability of most American cars has dropped off markedly since about 1978 (*Consumer Reports* 1983, 202–8)—a major reason why Japanese cars, the most reliable autos in the world, now account for almost one-third of all automobiles sold in the United States every year. The loss of sales of so many American cars contributes greatly to our balance of payment deficits in the world trade market. As safety recalls of domestic cars increase year after year, however, (U.S. Department of Transportation 1981, 50–54), some Americans still continue to buy Japanese cars. Currently, General Motors is hoping to avoid a recall of up to 5.3 million cars, due to lost rear wheels and axles on some of its

FIGURE 6–1. U.S. Total Labor Force, 1800–1983

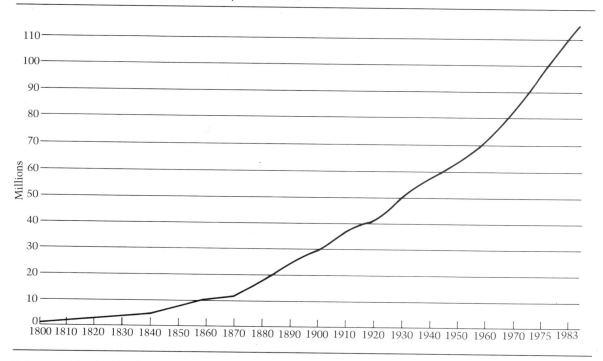

Data prepared for the Joint Economic Committee by the Council of Economic Advisors, *Economic Indicators*, June 1983. (Washington, D.C.: U.S. Government Printing Office, May 1983), p. 11.

1978–80 model cars. GM is trying to convince the federal government that "it isn't dangerous for a car's rear wheel and axle to fall off" (*Wall Street Journal* 8 April 1983, 4). This arrogance and isolation from reality is precisely what contributes to our quality control problems.

While industry's problems appear to concentrate in the areas of quality control, slowdowns, strikes, absenteeism, rising wages, and increased material costs, labor also has problems. Workers who struck at Chevrolet's Lordstown factory complained that assembly line tasks were speeded up and that "supervisors authorized shipment of defective cars" (Rothschild 1979, 331). The company complained that workers "attacked the paint, body, upholstery, and controls of the Vegas" they were building (Rothschild 1979, 331). Amid accusations and counteraccusations, Emma Rothschild (1979, 332) wrote this vivid account of Lordstown's "Fordism":

From the days when Vegas were XP-887 experimental cars, and Lordstown workers built Chevrolet Impalas, GM's Lordstown policy was determined by Fordist exigencies: mechanization of jobs, reorganization of factory life, time, and space around skilled work, and the modern auto imperative of cutting all costs, everywhere. Henry Ford's production had required the transfer of skills and jobs from workers to machines, and the "rationalization" of those jobs that could not be mechanized, and work was now so organized to be as precise, as predictable, and as machine-like as possible. In the Fordist "unity" of "men and machines," jobs followed the rhythms of mechanical production—as at Highland Park, so at Lordstown with its robots and computer controls.

So much had efficiency and impersonality been stressed at Ford plants that workers there began to refer to the "Ford whisper" and "Fordization of the face" (Flink 1976, 87).

Hazards for Men and Women in the Workplace

Along with problems of monotony and impersonality, workers also complain of dangers on the job that management ignores. In writing about a thirteen-month strike at the Brookside and Highsplint coal mines (Harlan County, Kentucky), Bryan Woolley and Ford Reid (1975) describe the killing of a miner, controversial court orders, arrests of miners' wives, the threat of open warfare between union supporters and "scabs," and the final capitulation (i.e., giving-in) of the company.

As the miners put it, the "mainest" issue in the strike was safety in the mines. They insisted on their right to shut down a mine if unsafe conditions existed, a demand the owners found distasteful. The authors' portrayal of this situation is perhaps biased toward the miners. Yet, the following description of conditions in the Harlan County mines is haunting:

The miner [a huge machine resembling a praying mantis] runs on a big electrical cable, you know, about as big around as a man's arm. It carries four hundred and forty volts of electricity. I've been in there three or four times when that big cable would blow, and the inspector standing right there. You know, to do a good splice job on that cable takes a good forty-five minutes to an hour. And the boss would say, "Don't bother to splice that cable. The next shift will take care of it." And the inspector standing right there. And the next shift wouldn't take care of it (Woolley and Reid 1975, 45).

Woolly and Reid describe other negative conditions in the Brookside mine: (1) hot-wired power boxes blew up with workers sitting next to them; (2) roofs in the mines are only thirty-six to forty-eight inches high, which forced the men to squat or kneel under them all day; (3) some men worked alone in the mines against regulations, became exhausted, and caught an arm in heavy machinery; and (4) the Southern Labor Union contract at Brookside didn't provide for a safety committee. As one worker put it, "All they [the owners] was interested in was running another ton of coal, just as fast as we could. They didn't want to take time for no safety" (Woolley and Reid 1975, 42–50).

Other types of industrial work are also

dangerous. Atlantic Nuclear Services (1980) job description for steam generator inspectors and repair operators in nuclear power plants includes the following warnings for prospective employees:

1. While on duty, *"your exposure to radiation will be constantly monitored"*; however, by completing our application and accepting employment, "you acknowledge *and release* Atlantic Nuclear Services, Inc., and its customers, employees, and agents, *from liability* due to such hazards."

2. The working area inside a steam generator is a warm and highly "constricted" space. "Most work is done in a *crouching position* looking directly overhead."

3. When workers go into the steam generator, they are often required to *wear a full face respirator* through which they receive forced air in order to breathe.

4. Jumpers work in special anticontamina-tion clothing, which is *very warm*, and "individuals usually *perspire freely* after a small amount of exertion." Workers are known as "jumpers" because they are expected to "jump" quickly in and out of the generator "in order to *minimize their exposure* to radiation." (italics ours).

Total radiation exposure of U.S. nuclear reactor workers jumped 35 percent in 1980, according to the Environmental Policy Institute (*United Press International* 3 September 1981). The institute, using Nuclear Regulatory Commission data, concluded that "the upward trend in total workforce-radiation dose signals chronic maintenance problems with atomic reactors" (*United Press International* 3 September 1981).

In "Women Working," Studs Terkel (1979, 343–58) describes work conditions of women who suffer on the job. Grace Clements works in the luggage division of

TABLE 6–1. 10 Suspected Hazards in the Workplace

As cited by federal agencies, here are some of the major agents linked to on-the-job diseases.

POTENTIAL DANGERS	DISEASES THAT MAY RESULT	WORKERS EXPOSED
Arsenic	Lung cancer, lymphoma	Smelter, chemical, oil-refinery workers; insecticide makers and sprayers—estimated 660,000 exposed
Asbestos	White-lung disease (asbestosis); cancer of lungs and lining of lungs; cancer of other organs	Miners; millers; textile, insulation, and shipyard workers—estimated 1.6 million exposed
Benzene	Leukemia; aplastic anemia	Petrochemical and oil-refinery workers; dye users; distillers; painters; shoemakers—estimated 600,000 exposed
Bischloromethylether (BCME)	Lung cancer	Industrial chemical workers
Coal dust	Black-lung disease	Coal miners—estimated 208,000 exposed
Coke-oven emissions	Cancer of lungs, kidneys	Coke-oven workers—estimated 30,000 exposed
Cotton dust	Brown-lung disease (byssinosis); chronic bronchitis; emphysema	Textile workers—estimated 600,000 exposed
Lead	Kidney disease; anemia; central-nervous-system damage; sterility; birth defects	Metal grinders; lead-smelter workers; lead storage-battery workers—estimated 835,000 exposed
Radiation	Cancer of thyroid, lungs, and bone; leukemia; reproductive effects (spontaneous abortion, genetic damage)	Medical technicians; uranium miners; nuclear-power and atomic workers
Vinyl chloride	Cancer of liver, brain	Plastic-industry workers—estimated 10,000 directly exposed

Source: U.S. News & World Report, 5 February 1979. © 1979 U.S. News and World Report, Inc.

ARMCO Corporation in a tank six feet deep and eight feet square. The tank is filled with pulp made of ground wood, ground glass, fiberglass, and a mixture of chemicals and water. A new piece of luggage must be processed out of the die every forty seconds, which means Grace is constantly standing, bending, and moving. If she talks while working, the work foreman reprimands her. She works eight straight hours, with two ten-minute breaks and one twenty-minute break for lunch, including a trip to the washroom. Mrs. Clements produces between 800 and 850 pieces of luggage a day. Like other women who work in this shop, she has numerous scars and burns that sometimes require medical leaves of from two to three months to heal. Grace has arthritis in the joints of her fingers and in one shoulder. She must endure noise around her workplace and summer temperatures that range from 100 to 150 degrees Fahrenheit.

Other accidents have occurred in the luggage division of ARMCO (Terkel 1979, 344). One woman lost two fingers when part of a hydraulic lift broke and dropped on her hand. Workers slip on the floors when wooden platforms around the tanks get wet from water and from oil that leaks out of hydraulic presses. Mrs. Clements is chairwoman of the shop grievance committee, and worker complaints are numerous. Although the company is "obstinate," many of the grievances eventually are won through arbitration.

Another complaint from American labor is lack of company loyalty, even to workers with seniority. A classic case is that of news commentator Edward R. Murrow, who was gradually squeezed out of CBS after his documentary on the political excesses of Senator Joseph McCarthy. Murrow gradually realized he was "skating on thin ice" with CBS and remarked to his friend Charles Collingwood, "You're only important around here as long as you're useful to them, and you will be for a time. And when they're finished they'll throw you out without another thought" (Halberstam 1979, 150). Bill Shirer, at the point of his exodus from CBS, previously warned Murrow, "It's okay for me. I've been through this before with newspapers. But you're going to get it too. Don't kid yourself" (Halberstam 1979, 134).

In October 1958, Murrow went before a meeting of radio and television news directors in Chicago:

And if there are any historians . . . a hundred years from now and there should be preserved the kinescopes for one week of all three networks, they will find recorded, in black and white or color, evidence of decadence, escapism and insulation from the realities of the world in which we live. . . . If we go on as we are then history will take its revenge and retribution will [catch] up with us (Halberstam 1979, 151).

In leaving CBS, Murrow escaped what Marx termed "false consciousness." That is, Murrow finally defined management in *his* own best interests instead of *theirs*.

Next we turn to discussion of the power elite—those who control politics, the military, the means of production, and the work lives of other Americans.

CONFRONTING THE PROBLEM: WHAT THE CONTROLLERS ARE DOING

The Military-Industrial Complex

In this section, we focus on elitist aspects of what former President Dwight D. Eisenhower termed the **military-industrial complex.** He was referring to such power elites as the military, big business, and big government. The term **power elite,** as used by sociologist C. Wright Mills (1956, 296ff.), refers to persons who occupy positions that control the major political, economic, and military institutions of our society. The social and attitudinal similarities of the men and women who occupy these positions of power interested Mills. Since **power** is defined sociologically as "the ability to make others dependent" (Emerson 1962, 32), an awareness of societal elites and how they sometimes operate at the expense of those who are dependent is necessary. **Authority** is a special form of legitimate power, in which members of a group or society agree that persons occupying given social statuses (positions) may exercise power over them in certain social situations (Weber 1947, 328ff.). Hence, government officials have the authority to create and enforce laws, but the public utilities, for example, have the power to raise prices on natural gas and electricity for the home, even though local corporation (rate) commissions are *supposed to control them.*

Concepts such as social power and the power elite help us understand the rise to power of the military, on which we now spend nearly $250 billion annually, and the increasing influence of large corporations in a technologically (machine) oriented society. These concepts further help us understand the overlapping interests of our economic and political institutions. The main goal of this chapter is to analyze power elites in the hope of understanding how their behavior relates to the areas of work and economics. This goal will carry us into the following areas: societal reaction to power elites; sociological analysis of work, elites, and economics; and alternative policies for improving work and economic conditions in the society.

Judging from the number and variety of news articles on the subject, America's interest in its various elites has been enormous. We have always had public curiosity surrounding the exploits of the rich, the jet-setters, and movie stars. America's most recent response to power and authority, however, has been more in the areas of scandal, lawsuits, and congressional investigations. Here, we refer to the rise of consumer protection groups, societal awareness of corporate fraud and political corruption, and a general feeling that all is not well with our so-called free enterprise system. We have had social welfare programs for the poor and needy for a long time. Now we have welfare for the rich as well (Tussing 1974). The latter fact can be seen in the government's "bailing out" of certain industries (e.g., Chrysler), in special tax breaks for corporations, and in the practice of passing rising operation costs to consumers in the form of ever-higher prices. When a public utility, for example, passes the costs of building nuclear power plants directly to the customer, where is the *company's* element of financial risk? Small business and the self-employed individual appear to be the only modern examples of our once-proud free enterprise system.

Politicians Under Attack

Fear of failure in the competitive marketplace seems to underlie much scandal in the business and political worlds. American companies are under heavy public and governmental scrutiny for everything from consumer fraud to giving bribes to foreign diplomats. In the political arena, state and local officials are being brought into court on charges of abusing public authority for personal gain. The federal crackdown includes mayors, sheriffs, and state treasurers. Further, in a survey of over 13,000 U.S. banks, about 15 percent of the banks admitted they "frequently" waive overdraft charges for public officials (*Los Angeles Times* 27 March 1978).

In another area, our government dropped its perjury case against an International Telephone and Telegraph Corporation official because "it could not go to trial without exposing CIA secrets." That particular official was accused of concealing the company's efforts to influence Chile's 1970 election. Further, the Environmental Protection Agency was recently accused of the following problems and improprieties: mismanagement, including missing funds and destruction of incriminating documents; various conflicts of interest; use of political influence in firing environmentalists from the agency; personal financial gain; and unethical conduct with a chemical company accused of dumping toxic wastes (*U. S. News & World Report* 1983a, 25).

"Spoiled Identity" in Government and Business

Spoiled identity is a concept from sociologist Erving Goffman that refers to the feeling of ego deflation people get when they know they have done something unethical. Politicians and some business people currently suffer from feelings of spoiled identity. The major problem areas are white-collar (middle-class) crime and various antitrust activities, including bribery and cover-ups; price fixing; windfall profit taking; and consumer and computer fraud.

Specifically, we can refer to the following examples of white-collar crime:

1. Bribery or taking kickbacks was evidenced in payoffs by the Lockheed Corporation in Japan, Italy, and the Netherlands (Deming and Field 1976, 57). In June of 1979, Lockheed pleaded guilty to concealing payoffs to the Japanese government and to business officials, including a $1.8 million bribe to former Prime Minister Kakuei Tanaka, who was convicted of bribery in the fall of 1983. These scandals were not confined to Lockheed alone, as other American firms acknowledged giving payoffs abroad. R. T. Paret, Jr., chairman of Upjohn Company, implied that such payments may have seemed "necessary." He added that the payoff custom is "beyond question . . . a demeaning cost of business" (*Associated Press* 2 June 1979), which translates, "Everybody else is doing it, why not us?"

2. Specific antitrust suits. Major corporations, eager to diversify their holdings, are buying up other large and small businesses. Federal trustbusters are afraid that too much economic power will fall into the hands of fewer and fewer companies (*U.S. News & World Report* 1978, 44). Even the churches

are suspect, as the U.S. attorney general was asked to investigate the Mormon church and its many corporations for possible antitrust violations (*United Press International* 9 April 1979).

Price-fixing examples include an antitrust suit against B. F. Goodrich for setting artificially high prices for its tires (*Phoenix Gazette* 24 February 1979) and a government suit against American Airlines for attempting to get Braniff to join them in raising fares (*Time* 1983, 66). Possible price fixing is indicated in a government report that shows that America's "beef prices are set by a few large meatpackers that report daily sales to market-reporting services, primarily one called the Yellow Sheet" (*Associated Press* 13 December 1978). Further, only *five* companies buy and sell grain on an international basis (Morgan 1979, vii), and they control the prices that American farmers receive for grain.

3. Windfall profit taking is reflected in American banks that conspire to drive down the value of the dollar on foreign money markets to reap windfall profits. Citibank, among others, has been accused of capitalizing on the dollar's weakness abroad by "selling short" one day and buying back dollars the next day after they decline in value. When bankers "sell short," they borrow U.S. dollars, sell them at the going price, and replace them later at a lower cost to the banks. This practice may be illegal if it can be shown that the banks "acted together to drive down the price of the American currency" (*Associated Press* 2 November 1978) in relation to foreign money.

Similarly, the federal government has accused the Atlantic Richfield Company of $18 million worth of price control rule violations from August 1973 to July 1977 (*United Press International* 27 February 1979). The government also indicted two smaller oil companies and five individuals for gaining $3.8 million in excess profits by selling lower priced "old" oil as higher priced "new" oil (*Associated Press* 8 March 1979).

Next we turn to sociological analysis of other economic problems that societal elites have created.

ANALYZING THE PROBLEM: THE POWERS THAT BE

Who Are the Rich and Powerful in American Society?

Today, according to a number of social scientists, a new elite class has arisen in the United States at least several million strong. Its members are the brain workers—highly educated planners, policymakers, and communicators (e.g., media persons) who run our technological society. This "new class" is a new cultural bourgeoisie (middle class) whose capital is not its money but its control over valuable knowledge, according to sociologist Alvin W. Gouldner (*Newsweek* 1979, 91–92). The new class individual is the type of person who is in a position to commit white-collar crime, because he or she has access to power and authority in the form of public trust. "In 1940, only 9 percent of 18-to-24-year-olds were enrolled in college. By 1978, that figure reached 25 percent" (*Newsweek* 1979, 91). For the first time in history, a critical mass of individuals has emerged who survive through the use of their wits.

Standing in the background, but often manipulating members of the new class, are those who have inherited wealth and power over several generations. These persons comprise what sociologists term the "upper upper class" in America. Most of us do not know who many of these truly wealthy people are. They remain inconspicuous to the general public for various reasons, including fear of family members being kidnapped and held for ransom.

Which is the wealthiest family in America? According to the *World Almanac*, the choice is between the DuPonts of Wilmington, Delaware and the Mellons of Pittsburgh, with each family being worth

between $3 and $5 billion. It should be noted, however, that the various descendants (heirs) of Pierre Samuel DuPont are worth a *combined* $9 billion (Gissen 1983, 151). The richest individual in the United States is reported to be Gordon Peter Getty, one of the sons of oilman John Paul Getty (Gissen 1983, 74). His personal wealth is estimated at between $2 and $3 billion, or more than that of the entire Rockefeller family. Another of America's 400 wealthiest individuals is Nelson Bunker Hunt, whose total worth is reported to be $1.4 billion (Gissen 1983, 75). Most of Hunt's inheritance is based on oil and energy resources.

America is a land of millionaires, since we have about 200,000 of them (*Town and Country* 1978)—approximately one millionaire out of every 1,200 people. Further, *Town and Country* magazine lists seventy-four American individuals and families worth more than $200 million each. Among the names "are oilionnaires and cattle barons, investment bankers and industrialists" and "makers of greeting cards, pet foods and baby shampoo" (*Town and Country* 1978).

Our implication is not that all families with inherited wealth and power obtain their great influence through unethical means. A brief look at the histories of a few of these individuals and families, however, is certainly instructive. For example, the Fords, Mellons, Rockefellers, and Pews have been criticized for removing hundreds of billions of dollars worth of raw materials from Appalachia; the Mellons alone reportedly have taken $6 billion from the region (Caudill 1976, 68). Similarly, the conservative Chandler family and its *Los Angeles Times* newspaper controlled California politics for about ninety years, with the result that Jerry Brown became only the third Democratic governor of California in this century (Halberstam 1979, 94–108). Today, the city of Los Angeles continues to resist the power of labor unions, because Harry Chandler fought unions "in a constant ongoing struggle that was nothing short of war" (Halberstam 1979, 95).

A final example of the enormous power that a few individuals wield is the case of William C. Durant, founder of General Motors. Durant and a few of his friends (for example, entrepreneur J. P. Morgan) are known to be partly responsible for the crash of the stock market in 1929 (Flink 1976, 136). Durant himself had $1.2 billion in the market by 1928, and he directly controlled about $4 billion in investments. He and a few other speculators decided to sell their stock in the spring of 1929 when the market began to look shaky. Because of Durant's personal influence in the market place, his decision to "unload" stock had considerable impact on the subsequent market crash in October 1929. Some also contend that "Durant's main brainchild, General Motors, has come to symbolize much that is wrong with contemporary American institutions and values" (Flink 1976, 136).

Sociological Research into Power Elites

The point of departure for much recent research on power elites is C. Wright Mills's 1946 study, *Small Business and Civic Welfare*. The main goal of this study was to evaluate the effect that concentrated (centralized) economic power has on people and cities. Mills found that a few large companies can dominate a community. Contemporary examples of this kind of dominance are Proctor and Gamble in Cincinnati, Ohio, Cummins Diesel in Columbus, Indiana, the Ball Company in Muncie, Indiana, and the

Dallas attorney Ivan Irwin, Jr., left, leans over to confer with his client, billionaire Nelson Bunker Hunt, right. At center is Nelson's brother, William Herbert. The brothers told a House Government Operations subcommittee in Washington that they had attempted to corner the silver market when they purchased massive amounts of the precious metal as an investment.

Los Angeles Times. Mills (1946) discovered that by 1944, 2 percent of all manufacturing concerns employed 60 percent of America's industrial workers, and further noted that

1. Big-business cities experience explosive jumps in population and related urban sprawl, while small-business cities experience more planned and gradual growth.
2. Income is more equally distributed in small-business cities than in big-business cities.
3. Civic welfare is greater in small-business cities than in big-business cities. (This may be because people know and identify more closely with one another in small-business communities.)

Ralph Nader and Mark Green (1973) refer to Mills's small-business research as one of the few studies of the local effects of corporate power. They think it unfortunate that social scientists have not pursued this issue more thoroughly, especially today when large companies control a disproportionate amount of important decision making in many cities. Nader and Green suggest that while corporations are not going to give up this type of power, they will gradually be forced to recognize their moral obligations to local communities. As Nader points out in another study, however, most company presidents and chairpersons of top corporations are unknown to the general public (Nader and Ross 1971, 23). They are deliberately insulated from public scrutiny. Nader and Green advocate community-level cooperation in fighting these elitist problems, since they fear that trying to check corporate power through federal intervention may lead to parallel growth of the federal bureaucracy. The latter development would mean still another impersonal power elite with which to contend.

G. William Domhoff's *Who Rules America* is a study that locates the power elite of the United States in our upper social

Consumer advocate Ralph Nader addressing a group of Congressional interns on Capital Hill. Nader can be characterized as a person with a great deal of prestige, only moderate power, and very little personal wealth, but he has done much to make business and big government accountable to the public.

classes. Focusing on the relatively small number of prep schools and private universities, clubs, and resorts that upper-class persons frequent, Domhoff reasons that this common background leads to shared interests, values, goals, and world views. His investigation of the backgrounds of U.S. presidents, members of Congress, cabinet members, and members of boards and bureaus indicates that most of these persons either had upper-class backgrounds or were linked to corporations or institutions that the upper class controlled (Domhoff 1967).

Research into Community Power

At the level of community power analysis, Edmund McLaughlin (1975, 185–95) describes connections between influential people and the enterprises that constitute the apparent power network in Phoenix, Arizona. His study determined how 125 business, educational, legal, governmental, and charitable organizations in Phoenix are interrelated. Four types of "linkages" were used in the research: (1) shared officers-directors, (2) shared family officers-directors, (3) shared law firms, and (4) shared club memberships. The resultant analysis shows the relative closeness of each of the 125 enterprises to each and all of the others (McLaughlin 1975, 188). All of the banks and law firms, and the two savings and loan associations, are part of a tight circle of heavily interlocked enterprises at the center of the power structure. Near this center are thirty-two closely related enterprises, with another thirty-two less closely related enterprises around the periphery.

With respect to influential names, McLaughlin (1975, 190) found that "31 people probably make up the core of the power network" in the Phoenix metropolitan area. These persons represent twenty-five of the thirty largest and most important enterprises, as measured by net worth, sales, control of funds, and number of employees. Of the thirty-one "multiple interlockers," only one individual showed as many as four interlocks; however, eight persons showed three interlocks and the remaining twenty-two key influentials had two interlocks.

While McLaughlin confirmed the importance of banks in the Phoenix power structure, another recent study shows a direct relationship between the size of banks and the percentage of bank loans to business agencies. Richard Ratcliff (1979) discovered that the top five banks in the United States (out of seventy-seven major banks) have 46.9 percent of all commercial and industrial loans. This implies that five banks have a tremendous amount of impersonal control over a highly dependent business community.

Regarding power and dependency relations, business life in America is also becoming more impersonal at the national level. The goal of big business in a capitalist economy is to continue making increasing profits. This goal is sometimes accomplished by dominating various markets. One form of domination, **monopoly capitalism** involves industry gaining control over sources of raw materials, wherever these sources might be (Baran and Sweezy 1966). American corporations find vast new areas of business when they invest in foreign countries. By developing a foreign market for one kind of product, new demands are created for related products. For example, building an auto factory in Brazil or Mexico will create a demand for other automotive products.

Owners of American companies also form multinational corporations, which means simply that they find it more profitable to set up factories on foreign soil where workers' wages are much lower. Multinationals, such as Motorola of Mexico and Ford of England, mean that the total amount of capital available in the United States is depleted, at least in the short run. In addition, development of multinational corporations causes higher interest rates, less money for local investment, and higher unemployment in the United States. This may be one reason why one public opinion poll indicates that two out of every three Americans favor "radical changes" in the country's economic system (*Associated Press* 1 September 1975).

Power in Smaller Communities: The "Good Ol' Boy" Network

To make the point that power and status are pervasive (all-encompassing) in American society, we turn to sociologists Majel Dominguez and Terry Lundgren's study of power in small towns.

From their research into the "good ol' boy" (GOB) subculture of small southern towns, Dominguez and Lundgren discovered not only actual GOBs but also a pervasive ideology that affects their socialization. This ideology is a blending of class consciousness, racism, and sexism. The *projection* of a common working-class image prevents the development of overt questioning regarding the unequal distribution of rewards and resources in the community. GOB subculture keeps subordinates in their place. To succeed within such a subculture, subordinates must ingratiate themselves to literal GOBs due to the informal power network. Moreover, such ingratiation must involve continual and personal display of the proper opinions and behavior. This process acts strongly to maintain and stabilize the subculture while simultaneously excluding the "wrong" persons from access to power.

In recent years, the expression itself—good ol' boy—has spread to nonsouthern regions of the United States through the process of cultural diffusion. The context of usage is in relation to the use of informal power—the good ol' boy network. This broader application diminishes some of the essence of the true good ol' boy. Informal power networks do not necessarily include the complete character type that actual GOBs express. What remains is the implication of power expressed through personal face-to-face interaction. Personal merit does not guarantee success or even social position maintenance; one must be favored by a GOB, and such favor depends upon the personal display of rather dubious qualities in the context of a democratic society.

Next we turn to analysis of a more sophisticated and far-reaching kind of power elite.

The Trilateral Commission: Work, Power, and Economics Interrelated

Inaugurated in July 1973, at the beginning of the OPEC oil crisis, the Trilateral Commission was developed primarily as a policy-oriented organization. The commission has sought to develop practical proposals for joint actions on major issues facing North America, Western Europe, and Japan (Trilateral Commission 1979). The commission's members are some 300 distinguished citizens from those three regions of the world. About one-fourth of the total members are from the United States, including businesspersons, labor union leaders, university professors, research institute directors, politicians, and media representatives (Sklar 1980, xi). Members include top executives of Exxon, General Motors, Ford, Coca-Cola, Bank of America, Cargill, Bechtel, General Electric, CBS, *Time,* Barclay's Bank, and Mitsubishi of Japan.

Once every nine months, the full commission gathers in one of the three regions to consider various task force (committee) reports and briefings on important global issues of the day. These subjects include the social and political implications of inflation, financial aspects of the oil crisis, prospects for peace in the Middle East, illicit corporate payments, coordination of global economic policies, and problems of nuclear energy and nuclear weapons proliferation (Trilateral Commission 1979).

The amount of *actual* power that the Trilateral Commission possesses has been ardently debated. Some critics see the commission as a secret plot by the Eastern business establishment to serve the interests of multinational corporations. Others see the commission as a scheme to subject the working people of the world to capitalist exploitation (Sklar 1980, xi). Gerard C. Smith, U.S. ambassador-at-large for non-proliferation matters, says that the purpose of the commission is "to seek a private consensus on the specific problems examined in the Trilateral analysis" (Sklar 1980, xii). In other words, the commission seeks to educate audiences in the three regions so that public opinion will come to reflect the private consensus.

In defense of the Trilateral Commission, banker and commission member David Rockefeller argues that the commission does not take positions on issues or endorse individuals for office. Instead, the commission is merely a group of concerned citizens interested in fostering greater understanding and cooperation among international allies (Sklar 1980, xii).

Regarding Rockefeller himself, TV columnist Bill Moyers has said the following:

David Rockefeller is the most conspicuous representative today of the ruling class, a multinational fraternity of men who shape the global economy and manage the flow of its capital. Rockefeller was born to it, and he has made the most of it. But what some critics see as a vast international conspiracy, he considers a circumstance of life and just another day's work (Sklar 1980, xii).

Thus, the debate regarding the *degree* of power and authority possessed by the commission continues.

Next we turn to discussion of problems in the area of American economics.

"Supply Side" Versus Keynesian Economics

Figure 6–2 illustrates some major differences between "supply side" economics, employed in the first three years of the Reagan administration, and Keynesian economics, which has characterized America since the Great Depression of the 1930s.

As figure 6–2 shows, supply-side economists favor cutting corporate and personal taxes and boosting business profits, in hope of producing new investments in industry and eventually more jobs and increased economic growth. Keynesian economists take a different route to economic expansion. They think that politicians should either lower individual taxes *or* raise federal spending to stimulate people to buy more goods and services, thus encouraging companies to expand output. Hence supply-siders, like economics professor Arthur Laffer, push for lower taxes and less government spending to reduce the rate of inflation, while Keynesians, such as economist John K. Galbraith, typically encourage greater spending to get more money flowing in the system to reduce unemployment.

Hence, it is not accidental that we have had less overall inflation and increased unemployment under the Reagan Administration, and higher rates of inflation coupled with less unemployment under earlier, Democratic (Keynesian) regimes. Democratic economists complain that supply-side economics aids only the rich, while Republican economists complain that Keynesian policies increase inflation, which hurts everyone. In either case, both the Western and the global economies have been suffering for some time from **stagflation,** which is a continuation of economic recession and high rates of inflation occurring simultaneously.

FIGURE 6–2. Two Theories for Getting the Economy Moving

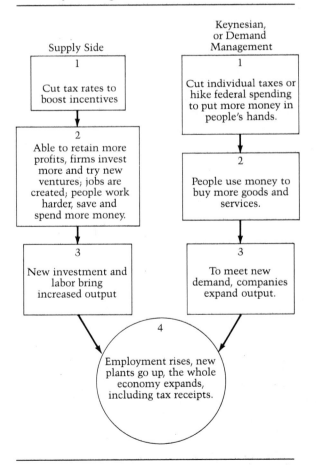

Data from *U.S. News and World Report,* 23 February 1981, p. 22. © 1981, U.S. News and World Report, Inc.

A typical U.S. unemployment line in 1984. The first three years of the Reagan administration brought lower overall rate of inflation and higher unemployment rates.

For economist Lloyd Dumas (1978), neither supply-side nor Keynesian economics will completely solve the problem of stagflation. This is primarily because neither of these conventional theories has addressed itself to the basic source of inflation, which is the relatively recent escalation in weapons expenditures. Dumas's reasoning is that the recent wave of inflation in the United States began *before* OPEC raised the price of a barrel of crude oil from $3 to $11 in 1974 (*Sierra Club Bulletin* 1975, 23). While some economists think the "energy crisis" triggered the occurrence of stagflation, Dumas argues that stagflation became noticeable around 1970—several years ahead of the sudden jump in oil prices. Federal expenditures for weapons and the military in excess of $200 billion a year seem to be contributing greatly to both inflation and recession.

Dumas singles out weapons expenditures as the root cause of our present economic woes for three reasons. The first reason is that the production and deployment of military weapons is highly *capital* intensive and not very *labor* intensive. That is, each weapon is so expensive, relative to the amount of labor required to build it, that not many jobs are created in weapons production. For example, a study that Employment Research Associates conducted (*United Press International* 25 October 1982) shows that every $1 billion spent on military purchases causes a loss of 18,000 civilian jobs, given how *consumers* would have spent the money. Hence, the 1981 military budget of $154 billion "caused a net loss of 1,520,000 jobs to the industrial and commercial base of the United States" (*United Press International* 25 October 1982). For the cost of *one* F–15 fighter plane, we could provide salaries for 1,000 teachers at $20,000 each (National Education Association 1983).

Dumas's second reason for viewing excessive military expenditures so negatively is that huge military budgets contribute to large federal deficits and high interest rates. Weapons production is a basic cause of inflation because it is funded with borrowed money, which today has to be paid back at very high interest rates.

Finally, military expenditures are problematic because at least 50 percent of federally funded scientists and engineers work on nonproductive weapons systems rather than for the productive civilian economy (National Education Association 1983). This represents a "brain drain" into the military and away from civilian technological innovation, which might lead to improved and diversified consumer goods production. In the area of *quality* consumer goods, we are losing out to countries like Japan and West Germany; insufficient capital is allocated to civilian technological innovation. Japan and West Germany spend proportionately much less on weapons and the military than America does, and inflation has not hurt them as much.

Laffer's supply-side economics has been increasingly discredited in many circles.

Economics departments of universities around the nation apparently have given up on supply-side economics and have stopped teaching courses based on that theory (*College Press Service* 7 April 1983). As economist Lester Thurow (*Newsweek* 1983, 62) expresses it:

The current economic disaster is not necessary. America has had six recessions between World War II and the onset of the current economic slowdown in the first quarter of 1979. They averaged only 11 months in duration and the longest was 16 months. . . . Those quick, vigorous recoveries did not happen by accident. Whenever government spotted a recession, it rushed to the rescue with lower interest rates, fiscal stimulus, jobs programs, and extended unemployment-insurance benefits. This time government has done none of those things quickly or vigorously enough, and with its failure to do so has turned what could have been a normal recession into a worldwide economic shutdown (*Newsweek* 1983, 62).

Despite the Reagan administration's professed disgust with the economics of John Maynard Keynes, the time has come to recognize that to get healthier and to create more jobs, the American economy needs lower interest rates and more "productive" federal spending for an extended period of time.

Finally, we turn to policy suggestions for overcoming some of our problems in the areas of economics, work, and societal elites.

ALTERNATIVE POLICIES FOR RESOLVING THE PROBLEM: CREATING BETTER WORK RELATIONS

Alternative Economics: Hazel Henderson

At a time when conventional economics seems to be failing us, economist Hazel Henderson is one of a small group of thinkers who are forging imaginative alternatives.

Henderson is an internationally published futurist and codirector of the independent Princeton Center for Alternative Futures. She is a director of the Council on Economic Priorities, a member of the U.S. Association for the Club of Rome (a group of concerned scientists), and an advisor to the Cousteau Society. One of Henderson's major concerns for the future is in the area of economics. She notes the following problems that some of our leading economists have not solved (Henderson 1978, 27–33):

1. Today's economists tinker with our disequilibrium economy, visualizing it as a fluid, equilibrium (balanced) system that can be managed with the simple hydraulics of aggregate supply and demand theory. These obsolete conceptual models now map a vanished system, monitor the wrong variables, and generate many statistical illusions. All mature industrial societies are in a process of transition from "hard energy path" to "soft energy path" economies. Hence, our most urgent task is to "remap" our economy, account for its structural evolution, and redesign our models and indicators more in accordance with today's social realities.

2. We are faced with the paradox that advancing technology in a free society systematically destroys the conditions required for free enterprise to function, and destroys the conditions required for voters in a democratic society to master sufficient technical information to exercise well-informed votes. For example, senators, congresspeople, or even the president—let alone the average voter—cannot fully master the inherent complexities of nuclear power.

3. It is paradoxical that in mature, industrial societies with highly complex technologies, free-market, laissez-faire (let nature take its course) policies become unworkable. Until we have devised public-choice systems adequate to manage the complexity we have created, we cannot proceed with the task of devising an economic alternative.

4. Another paradox for Henderson is the collapse of such traditional economic models as the Phillips Curve formulation of a supposed trade-off (i.e., inverse relationship) between unemployment and inflation. It is possible to demonstrate that the Phillips Curve is inoperative and that there are many other sources of inflation beyond wage costs (e.g., owners raising prices arbitrarily). Other sources of inflation are unanticipated social costs, soaring costs of maintaining coordination in the society, and our declining resource base and worsening population/resource ratio.

5. The paradox of greater efficiency in production, but less social and individual-consumer efficiency, leads to widespread social alienation. Efficiency is a highly subjective concept unless "time horizons and system levels are specified," i.e., efficiency for whom?

6. Paradoxically, increasing economic growth coexists with "structural" (built into the system) unemployment and having a significant proportion of our population under the poverty line.

Henderson's conclusion, in the face of these many contradictions, is that we must conserve our scarce and costly capital resources, and must now fully utilize our *human* resources. She adds, "Perhaps now is the time to recognize that the real factors of production are energy, matter and knowledge, and that the output is human beings" (Henderson 1978, 33).

New Types of Work: E. F. Schumacher and Amory Lovins

Changing the way we relate to one another in the area of economics will have consequences for work relations as well. Economist E. F. Schumacher and energy expert Amory Lovins have contributed new ideas for a more humane set of working conditions in Western society.

Schumacher, primarily in his book *Small Is Beautiful*, has contributed to making certain alternative life-styles acceptable to the conventional society. *Small Is Beautiful* has now been translated into all major languages

and has sold about a million copies (Harrison 1977, 32–39). Schumacher was a Rhodes scholar in economics, an economic adviser to the British Control Commission in postwar Germany, and the top economist and head of planning at the British Coal Board. Further, he was a close student of Mahatma Gandhi, nonviolence, and the environment (Schumacher 1973, 3).

Two of Schumacher's major contributions are his concept of **intermediate technology** and his work as director of the Scott-Bader Company, a successful plastics firm that turned control of management over to the workers. The idea of intermediate technology occurred to Schumacher as he toured India in 1961, advising the Indian Planning Commission on what to do about the surplus agricultural population that was flooding to the cities (Harrison 1977, 38–39). He realized that the "technology of Pittsburgh" would not fit into southern India, because background conditions of education and advanced technology were absent. The people of Indian villages would have to work with simple tools, such as the hand loom or the spinning wheel, rather than complicated machines.

This intermediate technology would be cheaper and would allow more workplaces to be created. It would use a minimum of nonrenewable resources and a maximum of locally available materials. It would be easy to operate, maintain and repair, and it would be *labor* intensive versus *capital* intensive (i.e., would rely on workers more than raw materials), because labor is available in the undeveloped areas in great quantities. Schumacher (1973, 179–80) explains:

If we define the level of technology in terms of "equipment cost per workplace," we can call the indigenous technology of a typical developing country—symbolically speaking—a £ 1-technology,[2] while that of the developed countries could be called a £ 1000-technology. The gap between these two technologies is so enormous that a

---

2. The symbol £ refers to the British pound, which is currently worth a little less than two U. S. dollars.

transition from the one to the other is simply impossible. In fact, the current attempt of the developing countries to infiltrate the £ 1000-technology into their economies inevitably kills off the £ 1-technology at an alarming rate, destroying traditional workplaces much faster than modern workplaces can be created, and thus leaves the poor in a more desperate and helpless position than before. If effective help is to be brought to those who need it most, a technology is required which would range in some intermediate position between the £ 1-technology and the £ 1000-technology. Let us call it—again symbolically speaking—a £ 100-technology.

Schumacher also points out that intermediate technology would be immensely more productive than the indigenous (native) technology, and it would also be immensely cheaper than the sophisticated, highly capital-intensive technology of modern industry.

Can Schumacher's ideas be applied to America? We conclude that intermediate technology might be applied to undeveloped and underdeveloped areas of the United States with great success. Here we have in mind employing people at intermediate technology levels in parts of Appalachia, on some American Indian reservations, and in the urban ghettos and barrios—where unemployment and underemployment rates are extremely high. Cabinetmaking and woodworking could be taken off the campus of Berea College, Kentucky, and taught to the people of the Appalachian hinterland. Isolated mountaineers could be encouraged to convert their stills from "white lightnin' " (moonshine) production to the production of alcohol to make gasohol.

Similarly, Native Americans could be encouraged to work with materials closer to their indigenous culture. For example, the buffalo could be reintroduced in place of Anglo cattle, which become entangled in fences and die during winter snows; more could be done with agriculture on the reservations, even if a profit isn't made; the older women and men could be employed to tell their grandchildren stories of the past so that the "cultural cup is not broken"; and

much of these activities could be funded through government grants in place of handouts, which do not seem to be working (Deloria 1969, 243–79). Further, poor black Americans and Mexican Americans could be put to work rebuilding the ghettos and barrios of our cities.

Schumacher was a trustee and later director of the Scott-Bader Company since the early 1950s, when he helped to draft its constitution. After thirty one years in business, Mr. Bader decided to introduce "revolutionary changes" into his company "based on a philosophy which attempts to fit industry to human needs" (Schumacher 1973, 275). He took on his former employees as his new partners, first drafting a constitution that would define powers and impose restrictions on the Scott-Bader Commonwealth.

When these changes were introduced, some predicted that a firm operating on the basis of collective ownership could not survive. The company, however, became even more successful. Over a twenty-year period, sales grew eightfold, net profits increased more than fourfold, total staff more than doubled, and bonuses amounting to more than $300,000 were paid to the staff (Schumacher 1973, 277). Similar cooperatives, such as the Weirton, West Virginia steel plant (*U.S. News & World Report* 1983b, 89), are being formed in the United States.

Further, after Youngstown Sheet and Tube Company was acquired by a conglomerate that soon merged with another conglomerate, the company's Campbell Works in Youngstown, Ohio was shut down, costing the area about 5,000 jobs. A broad-based community effort, with churches taking the lead, developed to create a community-owned corporation to reopen the works (*Unitarian Universalist World* 15 May 1979, 2).

Recently, the energy alternative suggestions of physicist Amory Lovins have been receiving national attention (*Birmingham News* 26 September 1978), including an invitation to the White House to spell out his ideas on the "soft energy path." Simply expressed, Lovins views our present large-scale energy system as the "hard path" method because it is an energy policy based on the eventual exhaustion of nonrenewable resources. The "hard path" involves operations such as nuclear power stations, big fossil-fueled power stations, large synthetic fuel plants for coal and shale, solar power towers, solar satellites, nuclear fusion, large monocultural biomass plantations, and perhaps ocean thermoelectric systems.

The "soft path" stresses diversity and smaller scale investments; it relies on renewable energy resources such as sun, wind, and water. Soft energy technologies include solar space and process heat, converting present farm and forestry residues to fuel alcohols and bio-gas, the use of wind and water for electricity, photovoltaic cells, and solar heat engines.

Lovins's concern over this country's continued use of "hard path" energy programs includes the economic dislocations of large-scale systems such as those that support our thermal (coal, oil and nuclear) power stations. As such stations get bigger, Lovins says, the proportion of time they do not work also gets larger—increasing from 10 to 35 percent. Lovins explains:

The picture gets worse. If one of these thousand-megawatt stations dies on you, it is like having an elephant die in the drawing room—you simply have to have another elephant standing nearby to haul the carcass away. You need a thousand-megawatt reserve margin to back you up. That costs a lot of money (*Birmingham News* 26 September 1978).

Instead, Lovins says, we should be building several stations of a few hundred megawatts each. Since they probably would not all fail at the same time, we would not need as much reserve margin as in the case of the thousand-megawatt stations. In practice, Lovins contends, these kinds of changes could allow us to do the same job for about one-third less new capacity. Further changes in the efficiency of substations could reduce that to about 60 percent to 70

percent less new capacity. These figures were discovered only recently, because "everyone had assumed they were negligible" (*Birmingham News* 26 September 1978).

Controlling Societal Elites

The power elites' exploitation of society is a problem area in which major changes will be difficult. However, we can recommend the following: (1) a crackdown on all types of white-collar crime, (2) making big business and big government accountable to the public, and (3) educating the public to act on its own behalf.

The idea of cracking down on white-collar crime isn't an innovative policy, since it is already being done to a certain extent. For example, the Justice Department has launched a policy to discourage price-fixing conspiracies (*U.S. News & World Report* 1978). The policy will now favor lenient treatment of corporations and their officers *who voluntarily expose their own antitrust violations*. Further, the FBI claims to want to change its image by going after white-collar criminals, mobsters, fraudulent land salespersons, and crooked politicians (*U.S. News & World Report* 1979a). Under orders from Washington, the FBI is concentrating on the worlds of organized and white-collar crime. Agents are particularly interested in politicians who sell out for bribes and other inducements.

In public agencies, accountability is to the public at large. Since its taxes pay the costs of production, the public should demand complete disclosure of how each tax dollar is spent, how time is spent, to whom the service is being rendered, and for what purpose. Thus, the demand for records and rules that account for their actions pushes public bureaucracies into efficiency. Public inefficiency is more visible; it cannot be absorbed in the cost of its product. In spite of citizen complaints about public agencies, business bureaucracies may be no more efficient than public bureaucracies. The level of inefficiency in the private sector, however, is not as visible. The problem with service-oriented systems is not one of applying better business practices but one of developing social structures that are better suited to the task. One of the future tasks of sociologists, social psychologists, and public administrators will be to devise more efficient social systems. Until this is done, we will probably remain burdened with the present over-bureaucratization.

Big business can be held accountable for its actions if the public urges enactment of an excess profits tax and an adequate energy policy. The authors of a study of multinational corporations say that "unless Congress acts to assert greater control over the giant firms, today's economic problems will grow progressively worse" (*Associated Press* 23 March 1975). Richard Barnet and Ronald Müller (*Associated Press* 23 March 1975), coauthors of *Global Reach*, insist:

We're going to see more and more instability, more and more inability of the government to control and manage the economy and more and more corporations whose interests and loyalties will increasingly transcend the United States.

If Barnet and Müller are right, corporations that fail to become accountable to the public could become nationalized (taken over and controlled by the federal government) in the future. Five major industries, including the utilities and oil companies, have been nationalized in the United Kingdom.

In our effort to focus on the accountability of big business, small-business fraud should not be overlooked. We need more ordinances like the one in Dallas, Texas, which prohibits car repair fraud (Seib 1978, 319–22). In the first three years after the passage of this ordinance, the Dallas Department of Consumer Affairs handled over 10,000 complaints. More than 190 of these complaints were serious enough to warrant prosecution.

Our final general policy suggestion is one of supporting the various consumer "watchdog" groups. Citizens need to be educated regarding what is happening to them at the hands of the military, big business, and big government. They need to listen to what Ralph Nader says about the extent of corporate fraud, and to what Barry Commoner and others are saying about deterioration of our natural environment.

Fortunately, some action is being taken. Consumer organizations, such as Common Cause, and other Washington lobbies have fought to have presidential elections publicly financed. They have also fought to repeal the oil depletion allowance, helped shatter an archaic and repressive seniority system in Congress, revealed large contributions from maritime unions and industry to members of Congress, and forced the House Ethics Committee to investigate unsavory land deals.

Much has been done recently to curb the excesses of societal elites. The question is, however, will it be enough and will it be done in time? Regarding the problem of creating new leadership, Tom Cummings of the University of Puget Sound's student association said:

The American people must be more demanding, and rightly so. A leader, in the words of the late Senator Hubert Humphrey, must be recognized as a statesman, and that person must have a stature which rides above prevailing political winds (*U.S. News & World Report* 1979b, 42).

SUMMARY

In this chapter, we have discussed people's reactions to the excesses of the rich and powerful, given a compact sociological analysis of the society's economic problems, and suggested alternative policies for containing elitist abuses of power and authority in the areas of work and economics.

We live in a highly technological society that values free competition, individualism, and political freedom. Yet excessive, uncontrolled competition can degenerate into open, societal conflict. Corporations, politicians, and white-collar individuals who mistake power for authority can abuse the freedom to control others. The result is continued inflation, white-collar crime, conflict between owners and workers, impersonality, and public alienation and apathy. Most of these social problems are contained within two larger problems: human greed and the lust for power. What is needed now in American society are higher social priorities and leaders who can enact them.

Freedom from control by others must soon replace economic and status domination. Cooperation must be placed at least on an equal level with competition and profit making in American life. We must pay more attention to the needs of the poor, elderly, sick, and alienated. Technology will have to be redirected toward producing life's essentials rather than tools of destruction. All these things—and more—will have to be done if we are to regain a view of America as a manageable and just society.

The last section of the chapter was devoted to presentation of alternative economic and energy policies that could enhance social survival in the foreseeable future. Certain of these societal policies are similar to ones practiced in various religiously oriented communes around the world. For example, E. F. Schumacher's concept of "intermediate technology" and his "economics as if people mattered" are practiced already by members of The Farm, a futuristic community in Tennessee. Further, the Scott-Bader Commonwealth has organizational features that are similar to an Amish or Hutterite colony.

After reviewing the major policy suggestions of Schumacher, Amory Lovins, and Hazel Henderson, we conclude that the world needs a drastic shift in life-styles—particularly in the economic, energy, and social justice areas—if we are to survive on a humane level. Further, these changes must take place soon if we are to recover our sense of society and survive until the twenty-first century. These and related problems are discussed further in chapter 15, "Energy, Civilization, and the Future."

STUDY QUESTIONS

1. How does the concept "good ol' boy" demonstrate the phenomenon of informal social power in a small town?

2. What alternative life-style policies are suggested for the larger American society at the end of this chapter and do you think they could work? Why or why not?

3. Discuss three policies suggested in the chapter for controlling societal elites. Which policy has the most appeal to you and why?

4. What unresolved paradoxes are contained within traditional economic theory, according to futurist Hazel Henderson?

5. According to Karl Marx, how does economic alienation under capitalism cause problems in the area of owner-worker relations?

6. Why does Amory Lovins argue that we must turn to the use of renewable energy resources in the near future?

REFERENCES

Associated Press. 23 March 1975; 1 September 1975; 2 November 1978; 13 December 1978; 8 March 1979; 2 June 1979; 7 January 1983; 29 March 1983.

Atlantic Nuclear Services. 1980. Questionnaire for steam generator support personnel.

Baran, P. A., and P. M. Sweezy. 1966. *Monopoly capital.* New York: Monthly Review.

Birmingham News. 26 September 1978.

Caudill, H. M. 1976. *A darkness at dawn.* Lexington, Ky.: Univ. of Kentucky Press.

College Press Service. 7 April 1983.

Consumer Reports. 1983. "CR judges the 1983 cars. (April).

Deloria, V., Jr. 1969. *Custer died for your sins.* New York: Macmillan.

Deming, A., and A. M. Field. 1976. Tanaka pays a price. *Time* (August): 57.

Domhoff, G. W. 1967. *Who rules America.* Englewood Cliffs, N.J.: Prentice-Hall.

Dumas, L. J. 1978. Why buying guns raises the price of our butter. *Christianity and Crisis* (27 November).

Emerson, R. M. 1962. Power and dependence relations. *American Sociological Review* 27: 32.

Flink, J. J. 1976. *The car culture.* Cambridge: MIT Press.

Gissen, J. with R. Behar. 1983. The Forbes four hundred. Forbes (Fall, Special Issue).

Halberstam, D. 1979. *The powers that be.* New York: Knopf.

Harrison, P. 1977. The legacy of E. F. Schumacher. *Human Behavior* (November): 32–39.

Henderson, H. 1978. *Creating alternative futures.* New York: Beckley Publishers.

Los Angeles Times. 27 March 1978.

Marx, K. 1964. *Economic and philosophical manuscripts of 1844.* New York: International Publishers.

McLaughlin, E. M. 1975. The power network in Phoenix: An application of smallest space analysis. *Insurgent Sociologist* 5 (3) (Spring).

Mills, C. W. 1956. *The power elite.* New York: Oxford Univ. Press.

———. 1946. *Small Business and Civic Welfare.* Report prepared for the Special Committee to Study Problems of American Small Businesses. 79th Cong., 2d Sess., S. Doc. 135.

Morgan, D. 1979. *Merchants of grain.* New York: Viking.

Nader, R., and M. Green. 1973. Owing your soul to the company store. *New York Review of Books* 20 (19).

Nader, R., and D. Ross. 1971. *Action for a change.* New York: Grossman Publishers.

National Education Association. 1983. *How can we safely cut the military budget?* (April).

Newsweek. 1979. America's new class. (May): 91–92.

———. 1983. A do-nothing government. (31 January): 62.

Parker, J. 1982. Walking wounded: The homeless in America. *Drug Survival News* 11 (3) (December): 14–23.

Phoenix Gazette. 24 February 1979.

Ratcliff, R. E. 1979. Banks and corporate lending: An analysis of the impact of capitalist class structure on the distribution of bank loan capital. Paper presented at the meeting of the Pacific Sociological Association, April.

Rothschild, E. 1979. Auto production—Lordstown. In *Crisis in American institutions,* ed. J. H. Skolnick and E. Curie, 330–42. Boston: Little, Brown.

Schumacher, E. F. 1973. *Small is beautiful.* New York: Harper & Row.

Seib, G. F. 1978. Dallas ordinance against car repair frauds. In *Crime at the Top,* ed. J. M. Johnson and J. D. Douglas, 319–22. Philadelphia: Lippincott.

Sierra Club Bulletin. 1975. (March).

Sklar, H. 1980. *Trilateralism.* Boston: South End.

Terkel, S. 1979. Women working. In *Crisis in American institutions,* ed. J. H. Skolnick and E. Curie, 343–58. Boston: Little, Brown.

Time. 1979 Release dated April 2.

———. 1983. Dirty tricks in Dallas. (7 March).

Town and Country. 1978. Release dated May.

Trilateral Commission. 1979. *The Trilateral Commission.* New York: Trilateral Commission.

Tussing, A. D. 1974. *Society* (11) 2 (January-February).

Unitarian Universalist World. 1979. (15 May).

United Press International. (27 February 1979; 9 April 1979; 3 September 1981; 25 October 1982).

U.S. Department of Transportation. 1981. *The car book.* Washington, D.C.: U.S. Government Printing Office.

U.S. News & World Report. 1978. Interview (23 October).

———1979a. As FBI charts a new course. (29 January).

———1979b. The generation gap takes a new look. (16 April).

———1982. Jobs: A million that will never come back. (13 September).

———1983a. Life in the depression belt. (21 March).

———1983b. When workers take over. (18 April).

Wall Street Journal. 8 April 1983.

Weber, M. 1947. *The theory of social and economic organization.* Trans. A. M. Henderson and T. Parsons. New York: Free Press.

Wooley B., and F. Reid. 1975. *We be here when the morning comes.* Lexington, Ky.: Univ. of Kentucky Press.

CHAPTER 7

Poverty and Class Conflict

CONTENTS

The American underclass

The barricades are seen only fleetingly by most middle-class Americans as they rush by in their cars or commuter trains—doors locked, windows closed, moving fast. But out there is a different world, a place of pock-marked streets, gutted tenements and broken hopes. Affluent people know little about this world, except when despair makes it erupt explosively onto Page One or the 7 o'clock news. Behind its crumbling walls lives a large group of people who are more intractable, more socially alien and more hostile than almost anyone had imagined. They are the unreachables: The American underclass.

The term itself is shocking to striving, mobile America. Long used in class-ridden Europe, then applied to the U.S. by Swedish Economist Gunnar Myrdal and other intellectuals in the 1960s, it has become a rather common description of people who are seen to be stuck more or less permanently at the bottom, removed from the American dream. Though its members come from all races and live in many places, the underclass is made up mostly of impoverished blacks, who still suffer from the heritage of slavery and discrimination. The universe of the underclass is often a junk heap of rotting housing, broken furniture, crummy food, alcohol and drugs.

. . .

Their bleak environment nurtures values that are often at radical odds with those of the majority. . . . Thus the underclass minority produces a highly disproportionate number of the nation's juvenile delinquents, school dropouts, drug addicts and welfare mothers, and much adult crime, family disruption, urban decay and demand for social expenditures. Says Monsignor Geno Baroni, [a former] assistant secretary of Housing and Urban Development: "The underclass presents our most dangerous crisis, more dangerous than the Depression of 1929, and more complex." The underclass is so totally disaffected from the system that many who would not themselves steal or burn or mug stand by while others do so, sometimes cheering them on.

Source: Time *29 August 1977.* © *Time, Inc., 1977.*

The no longer silent Americans

A great deal of rhetoric . . . has been directed to that portion of the American electorate alternately referred to as "the little people," "the silent majority" or "the forgotten Americans"—all euphemisms for the white, lower middle class of various ethnic backgrounds who appear to be most troubled, confused and angered by the rapidity of social change taking place around them. In spite of the welter of discussion, however, there has been relatively little systematic effort to understand the nature and extent of the problems underlying these fears and concerns. Yet such an examination is a vital necessity if we are to prevent the further polarization of American society along black-white [and class] lines.

Source: Bertram H. Gold, Introduction, in The reacting Americans, *ed. J. Maqidson (New York: Institute of Human Relations, 1970), pp. iii–iv.*

DEFINING THE PROBLEM: UNDERCLASS AND LOWER CLASS

The preceding statements on the poverty-stricken American underclass and the pressed lower middle class highlight two interrelated issues facing poor people. First, poverty in contemporary American society is a crushing daily reality for many citizens. Second, any attempts to end or further reduce the problems associated with poverty need to take into account the *social class* conflict that the strained circumstances of the lower middle class generate. In our changing high-technology society, hard work without skilled training no longer works well for most semiskilled middle-class members. Thus, as the poor try to break into the middle class, the lower-middle class tries to hold on to what they have.

Despite stagflationary and daily financial pressures, most middle-class members—particularly those of the lower-middle class—believe that the United States is overwhelmingly a middle-class society with a high standard of living (Jackman and Jackman 1982a, 1982b). Compared with our own cultural past and with most other nations, we are, in the words of economist John Kenneth Galbraith, an "affluent society" (Galbraith 1958). While this is generally true for the majority, millions of poor Americans have too little income. "Too little" income, as the economist Leon Keyserling notes, means "incomes far below the levels required to enable them to [experience] those minimum . . . standards which [most] people deem to be even barely adequate on the current American scene, with respect to food, clothing, housing, medical care, education, rewarding leisure, and a reasonable margin beyond what they spend" (Keyserling 1964, 15).

The irony in a democratic society, in which policy is generally based on majority rule, is that the minority of poor people may find themselves more isolated and in a more precarious social position than in a society in which most others are also poor. Poor people's sense of **relative deprivation** (feelings of deep resentment at unequal opportunity compared with others) is heightened in a deteriorating urban context in which most now reside. In such a setting, the poor can see and keenly sense their lack of opportunity compared with outer city and suburban residents. The closest neighbors they have are the pressed lower-middle class, who often view them as a threat. In this context, while the poor may not be part of the society's economic **division of labor** (an allocation of tasks to produce massive amounts of goods and services for most), they may create great disruption for the entire American urban society unless their life chances markedly improve.

The very middle-class nature of society is a central concern in any analysis of the poverty problem and what can be done about it. Cultural anthropologist Lloyd Warner expanded upon the narrow economic Marxian meaning of class. According to Warner and other contemporary class analysts, social "classes" are groupings of people with common social and economic (socioeconomic) positions in society (Warner 1960). The social class that each of us was born into influences our specific values, attitudes, and norms of behavior throughout life. The kind of neighborhood we grow up in, our educational aspirations, occupational goals, and opportunities, and every other aspect of our life-style are affected. At birth, we may live in an affluent suburb or on an overcrowded ghetto street, close to high-quality or dilapidated schools, in a neighborhood of general employment stability or one with chronic under- and unemployment.

In an increasingly credentials-oriented society, in which advanced educational training and degrees are often required to gain meaningful work in our automated, **cybernetic** (computer-controlled) economy, social class position at birth sharply increases or decreases the chance to achieve an economically stable life. Social scientists have long observed that the poor in modern society have become more desperate as their relative numbers decline and their lack of advanced technical, professional, or managerial training decreases the possibility of getting out of poverty. Since the late 1950s, American society has experienced organized civil rights movements that focused heavily on the poverty issue (Blauner 1969), major urban civil disorders that left hundreds dead, thousands injured, and millions of dollars of property damaged (Fogelson 1971), and an increasing violent crime pattern in large sections of our major cities (*Statistical Abstract of the United States* 1980, 184–86). These events have forced Americans to face the issue of poverty in society.

In the next section, we explore the recent historical recognition of poverty as a social problem that can be solved, and how traditional negative attitudes about the poor continue to influence what is, and is not, done about the problem. We then take up the social scientific research on the dimensions and consequences of poverty in society. The dilemma of "insular poverty" and class conflict in a generally upwardly mobile middle-class environment is a central concern. In the final section, we consider several major policy proposals designed to reduce or end the condition of poverty.

CONFRONTING THE PROBLEM: THE POVERTY ISSUE

Recognition of poverty is an age-old phenomenon. Yet, national recognition of poverty as a social problem is historically recent. Until the 1930s, the poor were generally held to be paupers or bums, often ignored. Any assistance to the poor tended to be through charity, often through activities of church groups (Carman and Syrett 1955, 222–23). At that time, poverty was so widespread that the idea that it could be eliminated was not seriously considered. In this day of average life expectancy beyond seventy and average family income of about $20,000, the condition of American life as historically recent as the turn of the century (U. S. Bureau of the Census, 1981) is

difficult to conceive. In 1900 the average American life span was forty-seven years (Population and the American Future, 1972). For an average week of more than six days, the *yearly* earnings of city factory workers were $566 for men, $307 for women, and $186 for children (Hourwich 1912, 298). Even controlling for inflation in recent years, this constituted near poverty-level living for the average worker at the time.

By the 1920s, medical advances and the sharply increasing capability to produce, through private enterprise assembly lines, more than subsistence-level existence for most, perhaps all, became an increasing reality. For the first time, a national perception existed that poverty was not inevitable. During the depression years of the 1930s, President Roosevelt observed that he saw "one-third of a nation ill-housed, ill-clad, and ill-nourished." With wide public support, much of his administration's domestic program was dedicated to reducing this high level of poverty. The Johnson administration's "war on poverty" in the 1960s—a period of general prosperity rather than recession or depression—further advanced the general belief that poverty was a social problem that could be eliminated. Yet, even as poverty has come to be recognized as a social problem, traditional values of viewing it as a problem for the poor to solve individually still influence what is done—or often what is not done—to resolve this pressing life syndrome. Playwright Eugene O'Neill characterized it as follows: "The child was diseased at birth, stricken with a hereditary ill that only the most vital men are able to shake off. I mean poverty—the most deadly and prevalent of all diseases." (Gordon 1978:183)

Looking Down at Those at the Bottom

Lower-middle class members are often in such pressed economic circumstances that they tend to express little interest in or patience with those who are even more pressed. The more affluent middle-class members are so far removed, both geographically in the suburbs as well as economically and socially, that the world of the poor seldom impinges on their daily consciousness. Consequently, short of media coverage on crime, ad hoc "tent cities" (which have included more of the unemployed lower middle class), and sporadic disruptive activities, the underclass poor are socially invisible in experiential terms.

The term *underclass* is an apt description of the actual condition of the poor because they are below others in a variety of generally valued attributes. Their income is less than others. Their schooling is below average. Their housing is smaller. Their ability to travel is less, and they can afford few of the amenities—restaurants, sport events, and theater—that most others can periodically enjoy.

The objective problems of this condition of life are pressing enough, including poorer physical health and a shorter life span (Gordon and Stephenson, 1980). The negative labeling of the poor by many in more advantaged social situations severely compounds these life condition problems of poor people. In classic social class studies of the 1930s and 1940s, hostile views toward poor people were found in different regions of the country. For example, Davis, Gardner, and Gardner reported in their study *Deep South* that most of those above the lower-lower poverty class used terms such as "No 'count lot'" and "shiftless people" (1941, 65) to describe the poor. At the same time, Warner and Lunt found in northern Yankee City studies that most people characterized the poor by such terms as "people just like animals, not worth a damn" and "people who scrape the bottom," (1941, 65). Consider the contrast of these negative terms with the admirable traits long considered most typical of Americans: "ambitious," "industrious," "materialistic," "efficient," and "practical" (Gilbert 1951; Gordon 1973; Katz and Braly 1933).

Assembly line workers are part of the middle class most vulnerable to finding themselves unemployed. The potential for losing their jobs to cybernetic computer-controlled production techniques is on the increase.

The Strained and Reacting Lower Middle Working Class

The social class position of protestors heavily influences the form and style that protest takes. The major violent racial disorders in the 1960s that resulted in thousands of injuries and millions of dollars in property damage in Detroit, Los Angeles, Newark, and other cities have been largely explained as a desperate response by many poor urban ghetto blacks whose lower-class position left them politically and economically powerless to change their segregated and relatively poor existence. (Fogelson 1971; National

Advisory Commission on Civil Disorders 1968, 35–108).

These race-related disorders were so extensive and damaging that relatively little national news coverage or public attention was directed at a parallel protest phenomenon. This protest was led by lower-middle class whites, often referred to as "the working class" in contrast with more affluent members of the middle class (Jackman and Jackman 1982b, 4). They generally live in neighborhoods closest to blacks and Hispanics who are pushing for integrated neighborhoods and schools. Ironically, many such whites believed, like blacks, that they were powerless to change what they perceived as a disruption of their homes, their lives, and their position in American society. Unlike most black protestors, these whites generally owned their homes; however, they were relatively small homes. Whites in this group tended to be financially pressed to make mortgage and other loan payments (Samuelson 1980, 82).

While not as damaging to life or property as the racial disorders, white rioting was nevertheless extensive enough to reveal deep-seated fears and anger that became increasingly evident in later years. Between 1964 and 1967, white rioting in protest to racial integration of their neighborhoods took place—not in the South where history would lead one to predict it—but in the northern urban communities of Brooklyn, sections of Chicago, in Cicero, Illinois, in the Kensington section of Philadelphia, and in Milwaukee (Friedman 1967). Like the socially combustible situation in which rioting blacks found themselves, white lower-middle class rioters also lived in crowded urban environments, the largest of them New York City. Pete Hammill, a native New Yorker, describes the situation with implications that go far beyond that city:

They call my people the White Lower Middle Class these days. It is an ugly, ice-cold phrase, the result, I suppose, of the missionary zeal of those sociologists who still think you can place human beings on charts. It most certainly does

not sound like a description of people on the edge of open, sustained and possibly violent revolt. And yet, that is the case. All over New York City tonight, in places like Inwood, South Brooklyn, Corona, East Flatbush and Bay Ridge, men are standing around saloons talking darkly about their grievances, and even more darkly about possible remedies. Their grievances are real and deep; their remedies could blow this city apart. (1969, 1–2)

What is the anger about? We have already noted some of the neighborhood, home, and family concerns. Generally, lower-middle class whites, and increasingly other middle-class members, view themselves as socially isolated between those more affluent in the suburbs and those in racial urban ghettos. They see themselves caught in extreme cross-pressures. On the one hand, lower-middle class members often cannot afford desirable suburban homes like those of the managerial and professional occupational classes. On the other hand, they see civil rights laws and special training programs designed to help the poor and racial minorities move into lower-middle class neighborhoods or even beyond them to the suburbs.

While they cannot afford a higher standard of living, members of the lower-middle working class earn too much to qualify for governmental assistance programs aimed at the lower-class poor. Seeing their personal and economic security threatened leads many of them to behave with what Franz Neumann calls "neurotic anxiety," in which they sometimes strike out against poorer victims in the social system (Neumann 1967).

Blaming the Victim

The generally negative view of poor people has had the effect of personally blaming the poor for circumstances in which they find themselves. As in the studies of Lloyd Warner and his associates, the poor were viewed as lazy and shiftless individuals. If small farmers went broke, it was because they did not work hard enough, not because large corporate farms could sell at much lower per-unit prices of any farm commodity. If coal miners were unemployed, it was their fault rather than the result of shifts to petroleum and other fuel resources. If Penn Central railroad workers were out of work, then they were at fault—even if the company went bankrupt after the construction of the St. Lawrence Seaway, which opened up inexpensive boat-shipping competition. This view is in sharp contrast with government loans to corporations facing bankruptcy, such as Penn Central, Lockheed Aircraft, or the Chrysler Corporation, which resulted in little negative public reaction. We apparently accept welfare for the rich while resisting and blaming the poor who request similar assistance under duress.

The process of blaming the poor for their circumstances, including blame from many in the lower-middle class who object to assistance programs that bypass them, has been applied to every aspect of their lives. As William Ryan observes,

the miserable health care of the poor is explained away on the grounds that the victim has poor motivation and lacks health information. The problem of slum housing [is] traced to the characteristics of tenants who are labeled as Southern rural migrants not yet "acculturated" to life in the big city. . . . From such a viewpoint, the obvious fact that poverty is primarily an absence of money is easily overlooked or set aside. (1978, 31)

Some poor individuals have both the capability and the opportunity to secure effective training or employment and to move out of a state of poverty into the opportunity system. When this is individually possible, the person who chooses not to move out of poverty represents a personal problem—not necessarily a social one. The depression years of the 1930s, however, made it clear to most Americans that certain times and circumstances prevented most poor individuals from getting out of poverty no matter how hard they tried. The economic and political forces they faced were too formidable to overcome individually. Millions of urban poor now face depression-level unemployment that averages over the 20 percent level as was the case in the 1930s for a much larger proportion of the population (Samuelson 1980, 80–82).

The increasing political recognition of poverty as a social problem issue is evident in the periodic "wars" against poverty since the 1930s. More people now than in the historical past concur with the view of C. Wright Mills:

When in a city of 100,000 only one man is unemployed that is his personal trouble, and for its relief we properly look to the character of the man, his skills, and his immediate opportunities. But when in a nation of 50 million employees, 15 million . . . are unemployed that is [a social] issue, and we may not hope to find its solution within the range of opportunities open to any one individual. (1959, 9)

No doubt many Americans still agree with the 1964 Republican candidate for president, Barry Goldwater, who then asserted: "The fact is that most people who have no skills have no education for the same reason—low intelligence or low ambition" (New York Times 16 January 1964). Republican Presidents Nixon and Ford and Democratic Presidents Johnson and Carter have been far less negative in their public statements about poor people. Since presidents are elected, they represent considerable public opinion. The election of President Reagan in 1980, with his proposals to substantially cut back on assistance programs for the poor, indicates that public opinion is fluid.

Relative Deprivation and Poor People's Views

So far we have concentrated on views of the poor by people who are not poor. What about the poor themselves? How do they view their situation in relation to others? To some extent, the answers to these questions depends on where poor people are located.

Poverty is more socially visible in urban

than in rural areas. Poor people's social protest is more evident in large cities. Poverty
in cities is not objectively more pressing
than poverty in rural areas and small towns.
The poverty of both black and white rural
poor has long been widespread. Millions of
rural residents live below the poverty level,
but the nature of small farming is to be independent and to live far from one's neighbors. In the past half century, most rural
poor found they could not make even minimum ends meet. They left the farms and
came to the cities seeking better opportunities, but with few occupational skills, they
are often unsuccessful. In cities, however,
the poor live closer to each other, can support each other's feelings and actions, and
can organize more effectively. These obser-

vations are supported by the research-based
concept of relative deprivation, one group
recognizing more sharply its own deprivation through close interaction with others
who are better off (Merton 1957, 227–34).

As poor people moved into the cities, a
syndrome occurred, which lends support to
the relative deprivation thesis. While the urban poor are generally better off than their
poor rural kin and with lower proportions in
a state of poverty (see table 7–1), they remain poor and have been involved in far
more extensive protest efforts against their
condition than have the rural poor.

Open sporadic violence in a hostile environment can be seen daily in crowded city
slum streets. Individual and gang violence is
indigenous to overcrowded poverty areas in

*Poverty is more socially visible in urban than in rural areas. The urban poor generally remain poor,
perpetuating the existing conditions and giving rise to social protest.*

all our large cities. Gerald Suttles catalogued the daily offenses from frustrated young residents in the high-unemployment Addams area of Chicago. The offenses included high rates of trespassing, carrying unlicensed weapons, heavy drinking, disorderly conduct, glue sniffing, turning on fire hydrants, shooting fire crackers, false alarms, and the more direct violence of street fighting, rape, murder, and property damage (Suttles 1974, 207–10).

This kind of daily living experience has given rise to major social protest. Indeed, one of the major aims of the civil rights movement of the late 1950s and 1960s was to end poverty. Symptomatic of this concern was that the 1963 march on Washington was characterized as a "civil rights" march, whereas the 1968 march on Washington was characterized as a "poor people's" march (Myrdal 1970, 210). Clearly, the marked sense of relative deprivation of the urban poor was also a major factor in the dozens of destructive riots that occurred in many of our large cities in the late 1960s (National Advisory Commission on Civil Disorders 1968). Whether on a sporadic individual or group level, or on the basis of organized social protest, many in the urban poor class in particular will continue to actively protest their state of poverty in either organized or disorganized fashion.

ANALYZING THE PROBLEM: THE CONSEQUENCES OF POVERTY

We have referred to the poor as the "underclass" and being at the "bottom." Such terminology draws upon social class analysis, which was stimulated by the work of cultural anthropologist Lloyd Warner and his associates in the 1930s, when he made his classic Yankee City study (Warner and Lunt 1941). Warner applied several measuring techniques to determine social class position, relying primarily on an occupational index that used the following categories: unskilled labor, skilled factory, skilled craft, management-aid, management, and professional.

Measuring the Lower, Middle, and Upper Classes

Warner's measurements of social class have been modified extensively since the 1930s, but his occupational criteria still provide a useful way of evaluating social class positions. These criteria make it possible to determine to what extent there are now proportionately more or less people at any given class level compared with ten, twenty, thirty, forty, or more years ago. Using the occupational index, Warner placed people in five major class strata: (1) *lower-lower* class

TABLE 7–1 Relative Poverty Levels in Selected Rural and Urban States, 1980

PREDOMINANTLY RURAL STATES		PREDOMINANTLY URBAN STATES	
Precentage of Population in Poverty		*Percentage of Population in Poverty*	
Alabama	17.9	California	11.3
Kentucky	18.4	Michigan	11.1
South Dakota	16.1	Ohio	10.5
Tennessee	17.0	Pennsylvania	10.5
	All States Average = 12.5		

Source: U.S. Department of Commerce, Provisional estimates of social, economic, and housing characteristics, states and selected standard metropolitan statistical areas, *1980 census of population and housing supplementary report* (Washington, D.C.: U.S. Government Printing Office, 1981), table P–4.

(the poorest people and, as discussed, viewed by the larger community as not respectable, lazy, often unemployed, and lacking in "good" middle-class virtues); (2) *upper-lower* class (who perform fewer of society's functional tasks and are viewed as poor but honest workers; these are semiskilled workers in factories, and service workers); (3) *lower-middle* class (some skilled workers, small businessmen, clerical workers, and lower-level white-collar workers); (4) *upper-middle* class (solid, highly respectable people but not "society"; these are substantial business and professional men and women who aspire to be upper class and who participate in community and civic activities); and (5) the *upper* class—wealthy people (*upper-upper* class if the wealth is inherited, influential merchants, financiers, or people in the higher ranks of their professions, such as surgeons or judges).

Warner diagramed his stratification findings based on these social class categories. Note that in figure 7–1 the diagram is shaped like a triangle, indicating larger numbers in the lowest social classes and fewer in the upper social classes. The pyramid that Warner first constructed in the late 1930s generally reflected social reality. More people were in the lower classes (lower-lower and upper-lower totaled well over half) than in the middle and upper classes (less than 41 percent of the total). The figure also indicates the changes in the American class pattern in the past generation. Next to Warner's 1940 proportions for each class level are the approximate proportions of these classes based on more recent data. No longer do the proportions become larger at lower levels of the scale; the largest group is now the middle class.

Fewer and More Isolated Lower-Class Members

Those in the upper and middle classes now far outnumber those in the lower classes. Further, upper- and middle-class members have occupations to which the American **work ethic** (a sanctioning of accepted and

FIGURE 7–1.   Growth of the American Middle Classes and Decline of the Lower-Class Proportions

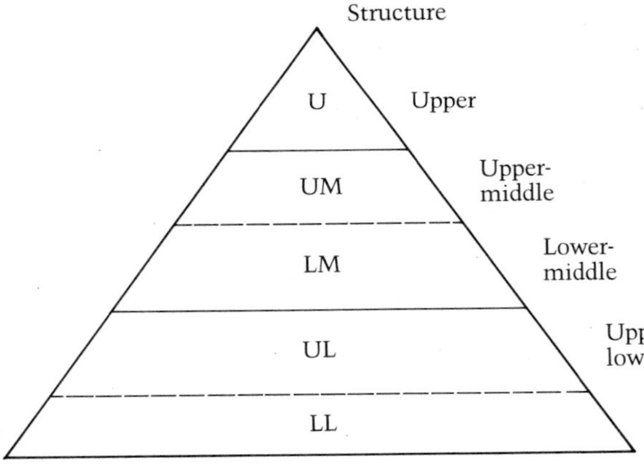

Occupational Status	Class Structure		1940[a] Yankee City Proportions	1980[b] Approximate U.S. Proportions
Managerial and Professional	U	Upper	3	15
Skilled Craft	UM	Upper-middle	10	25
Management-aid	LM	Lower-middle	28	25
Skilled Factor Semi-skilled	UL	Upper-lower	33	15
Unskilled	LL	Lower-lower	25	20
			99%*	100%

*The total percentage came to less than 100 percent because numbers were rounded off.

a, data from Lloyd Warner and Paul Lunt, *The social life of a modern community* (New Haven, Conn.: Yale Univ. Press, 1941), p. 225, table 7; b, data from *Employment and training report of the president* (Washington, D.C.: U.S. Government Printing Office, 1981) tables A–19 and A–21.

rewarded behavior) grants a high degree of desired **social status.** Since status involves the degree of social acclaim and prestige a given **social role** receives, high status brings admiration and respect. Conversely, as discussed earlier, low status results in lack of admiration, social rejection, and avoidance. Even for low-status individuals who move up, this low esteem has some continuing effects. A Stanford University study found that among freshmen, 32 percent of lower-class youth were socially withdrawn and isolated compared with 11 percent of those from other classes (Ellis, Lane, and Olesen 1963).

As noted in figure 7-1, those in the lower-lower class are generally unskilled workers. They tend to be in low-prestige occupations such as street sweeping, sharecropping, or janitoring. People in low-prestige occupations are often among those whose earnings are low and who are often unemployed, so that they compose the highest proportion of those in the poverty class. These lower-class members are a declining proportion of the total population, which has weakened the political position of those at the bottom. The lower-lower and upper-lower classes no longer have the social and political influence they had in the 1930s when their proportionate numbers in the population were greater.

Social Mobility and Immobility

A key question for the poor is whether the contemporary American stratification (social class) system is rigid or flexible. Is American society characterized by a closed *hierarchical class structure*, which prevents people from moving from one class to another, or by an overlapping *status continuum* (Landecker 1960), which allows for considerable upward **social mobility** from one class to another? Historically Americans have pinned their hopes on the idea that poor people can work themselves up the class ladder. Insofar as this was ever true, is it still so?

Those favoring the hierarchical class the-

sis argue that American society is now composed of distinct structural social class units that work to maintain some at the top and to keep others down at the bottom. Advocates of the status continuum hold that status differences in America are thought to be gradual and fluid, which enables members of the lower classes to move upward. Note the emphasis here on "upward" mobility. Given the value placed on achievement in America, most Americans at all class levels are encouraged either to maintain respectable class status or to move even higher (Williams 1970, 501–2). Downward movement is a subject of scorn. Thus, a manual laborer hopes to move to a white-collar occupation, but a white-collar jobholder rarely seeks a manual occupation.

The central issue here is whether upward social mobility is possible for most poor under contemporary social conditions. Emphasis is on the term *contemporary* because historically, except where racial prejudice was involved, a flexible upwardly mobile class continuum pattern has characterized American society. The complex issue of increasing versus decreasing social mobility in America is so closely related to the economic system that some main economic currents need to be considered to understand what is happening to poor people and many others, as those in the lower-middle class. In particular, advances in technology throughout this century affect the contemporary class system from top to bottom. Many of our class values are rooted in the open frontier society of our past.

The Frontier Effect on an Open Class System

One major influence in maintaining an open class sytem throughout the nineteenth century was the expanding frontier. The availability of vast lands west of the Mississippi served as an escape hatch for poor people trying to secure a better life. No matter how difficult life became for those in the lower strata of the society, new opportunities always existed in the relatively unsettled and undeveloped West. The moving frontier helped stabilize and maintain opportunity, a belief epitomized in Horace Greeley's famous advice, "Go west, young man, go west." Particularly in the nineteenth century, the existence of the frontier helped prevent a stagnant situation in the increasingly industrialized Northeast and Midwest. As the influential historian of the last century, Frederick Jackson Turner put it,

the existence of an area of free land, its continuous recession, and the advance of American settlement westward, explain American development. . . . This perennial rebirth, this fluidity of American life, this expansion westward with its new opportunities . . . furnish the forces dominating American character. (Wish 1960, 190)

Turner probably exaggerated the effects of the expanding frontier, and he neglected to assess its disruptive and impoverishing impact on native Americans and on Hispanics. Yet, much truth is contained in what he said. The presence and availability of a vast, sparsely developed frontier was a major force in facilitating upward social mobility for poor people.

At the same time, the development of automated manufacturing ensured a place in the economy for the masses of unskilled workers. Accordingly, these people were able to exercise effective political leverage. For example, in the depression years of the 1930s, they brought about adoption of such stabilizing measures as minimum wage laws, work safety standards, social security, and the right for labor union representatives to bargain with corporate owners on wages and work conditions (Schlesinger 1960). In effect, if a poor person could find a job, a series of laws were enacted that would protect his or her rights to secure employment and income through the retirement years. The problem for many of today's poor, as it is increasingly for semiskilled members of the lower-middle class, is the "if" in finding a productive job.

Since the 1930s, the upward mobility of the lower classes has accelerated mainly for those who were labor union members. For many young workers with few skills, however, a new development in technology—the **cybernetic revolution**—stopped upward mobility. Beginning in the 1940s, cybernetics—that is, automation coupled with computer control and analysis—rapidly increased productivity and simultaneously reduced the need for unskilled and semiskilled machine tenders (Michael 1962). Cybernation is such an advanced technological form of automation that it has changed the occupational status of millions in most major industries. A minority of workers are now in unskilled positions, and those who remain in those positions are in a precarious employment situation.

Table 7–2 shows the percentages of work-

TABLE 7–2. Percentages of Workers in Different Occupational Categories, by Race and Sex, 1981

OCCUPATION	ALL ANGLOS	ALL BLACKS	WOMEN
Professional and technical workers	16.7	13.9	17.0
Managers, officials, and proprietors	12.3	5.8	7.4
Clerical workers	18.5	18.4	34.7
Sales workers	6.8	3.0	6.8
Craftspersons	13.1	9.2	1.9
Operatives	13.3	19.2	10.5
Service workers	12.2	22.4	19.4
Laborers	7.1	8.1	2.3
Percentage of total population	88.0	8.0	51.0

Source: Employment and training report of the president (Washington, D.C.: U.S. Government Printing Office, 1981), tables A–19 and A–21.

ers in different racial and ethnic groups engaged as unskilled operatives and service workers in comparison with the percentage of workers in other, better rewarded occupations. Harvard economist Paul Samuelson points out that the ability of the economy to increase consumption, investment, and government spending influences the relationship of automation and cybernation to unemployment and to the economy in general (1980, 340–44). Not the worker, however, but forces largely outside the worker's individual influence control these alterations. Without major private or public efforts to train or retrain unskilled workers, they generally concentrate in poor sections of a community devoid of substantial training or upwardly mobile occupational opportunities. The result is pockets of poverty, or

what John Kenneth Galbraith refers to as "insular poverty," indicating conditions that make it unlikely that individuals can get off their impoverished "islands" without some assistance (1958, 326–327).

Computerized technology is now able to detect and correct breakdowns in equipment and to perform other processes with a minimum of human maintenance. What Donald Michael (1962) called the silent conquest of cybernation has resulted in a shift at the bottom of the stratification system from a continuum of overlapping classes to a structure with increasing rigidity. Even the great industrial unions in the American Federation of Labor and other industrial unions, which number over 20 million members, offer less worker protection. These unions no longer afford the protections or provide as

An example of rural poverty with little preparation for the children of the poor to prepare themselves for life in the high-technology twenty-first century.

much upward mobility for as many as they did during the automation period, when unskilled labor was in demand. The industrial unions have not been growing as rapidly as they had between the mid-1930s and mid-1950s; union membership gains have declined in recent years relative to the growth of the total labor force (see figure 7–2).

Dimensions of Poverty

The general upward shift in class status evident in figure 7–1 shows that an expanding economy benefits those who fill its functional needs. Also, unions more often protect the pressed and decreasingly needed (but currently more generally employed) semiskilled industrial workers. For workers (particularly the young and unskilled) who are not in the new work force of skilled technicians, professionals, and managers, unemployment and underemployment remain far above the national average.

The application of the Lorenz curve, an economic measure, provides one dimension of the position of the poor in relation to others. As figure 7–3 indicates, the Lorenz curve is a technique that graphically illustrates the degree of economic inequality in the society. The straight line in the graph represents absolute equality, i.e., where income is distributed equally throughout the population. No society has this characteristic. The question is, how far from income equality is the United States in relation to its own past? The curve represents the actual distribution of income. Note that if distribution of income were equal, then the lowest 20 percent of the population would earn 20 percent of the income. The lowest 20 percent of the population, however, actually earned only 5 percent of total income in both 1929 and 1979. Note further that beyond the lower 20 percent income population grouping, less inequality of income exists. Thus, except for the lower fifth of

FIGURE 7–2. Slowing Membership Growth of Labor Unions

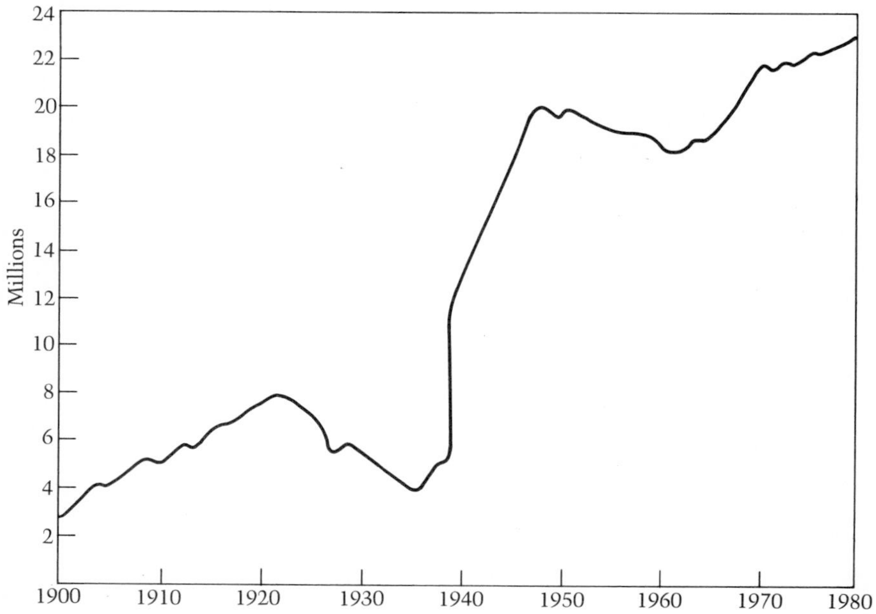

Data from U.S. Department of Labor, Statistical Abstract of the United States. (Washington, D.C.: U.S. Government Printing Office, 1980).

the population, a large majority of Americans have at least somewhat closed the income gap.

While there may be proportionately fewer people at the bottom of the scale now than in the past (see figure 7–1) the **Lorenz curve,** as a measure of how far real income distribution is from equal income distribution for all, provides some insight into their greater isolation from the rest of the American population. The relative position of the poor appears to be deteriorating—in **social distance** from other classes, in quality of education, in housing, and in other ways. Further, the actual decline in the proportion of poverty-level people in the society may not have declined as much as official governmental measures suggest. This can be explained as a consequence of the "dual market" system, whereby middle and upper classes participate in the "primary market" and poor participate in the "secondary market" of the

economic system. As Michael Piore explains,

the primary market offers jobs which possess several of the following traits: high wages, good working conditions, employment stability and job security, equity and due process in the administration of work rules, and chances for advancement. The . . . secondary market has jobs which, relative to those in the primary sector, are decidedly less attractive. They tend to involve low wages, poor working conditions, considerable variability in employment, harsh and often arbitrary discipline, and little opportunity to advance. The poor are confined to the secondary labor market. (1971, 91)

Federal poverty programs and some cooperative industrial efforts of the 1960s were designed to break into the secondary market where so many of the poor were located, particularly where those in racial and ethnic groups are concentrated (see table 7–2). By the end of the 1960s, official figures suggested a substantial drop in the proportion of those in a state of poverty. According to a 1969 Bureau of the Census report, the number of people living in absolute poverty dropped from near 40 million, or 22.4 percent of the population in 1959, to somewhat more than 25 million, or 12.8 percent of the 1968 population (U.S. Bureau of the Census 1969). These figures are based mainly on the effects of the rising price of food matched by income in constant dollars (what dollars would buy in 1959). The rise of 16.7 percent in the consumer price index for food between 1959 and 1968 was taken into account when computing the apparent decline in the number and proportion of those in a state of absolute poverty; but this single price index provides only a partial measure of the cost of living for the poor.

David Gordon (1972) obtained significantly different results using several other major cost factors. He noted that from 1959 to 1968, the cost of public transportation rose by 38.5 percent, medical care by 45.1 percent, and general services by 34.9 percent. He then calculated that the number in absolute poverty in 1968 was roughly 50

FIGURE 7–3. Comparing Income Inequality in 1929 and in 1979 by the Lorenz Curve

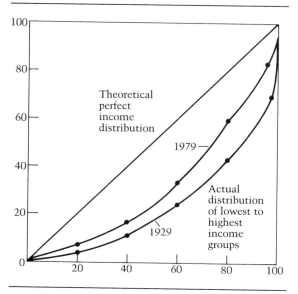

Note: for computation procedure, see Paul Samuelson, *Economics* (New York: McGraw-Hill, 1980), p. 81.

Data from U.S. Bureau of the Census, Money income of families and persons in the United States: 1979, *Current population reports,* ser. T-60, no. 121 (Washington, D.C.: U.S. Government Printing Office, 1981).

percent higher than the official estimates, or around 37.5 million persons—close to the lower 20 percent of the population that the Lorenz curve measured, rather than 12.5 percent as given in official figures (Gordon 1972, 99). Further, the 1980 census found a renewed growth of the American poverty class, although it was still not as high as before the 1960s programmatic assault on poverty.

ALTERNATIVE POLICIES FOR RESOLVING THE PROBLEM: THE POVERTY CLASS

In the case of poverty, as with other social problems, more than one social policy approach is possible. Here we shall consider several major policy approaches that are being tried or are being seriously considered. Given the political and social dynamics involved, the policies most likely to succeed in respect to the poor will take into account the developmental needs of people not in the poverty class, particularly those in the pressed lower-middle class.

Culture and Cycle of Poverty Theories

A number of theories have been advanced to explain why poor people are in a state of poverty. While each theory attempts to explain and predict poverty-related behavior, each theory also contains within it social policy implications about what can or cannot be done about the condition of the poor. Two alternative theoretical approaches are the *culture of poverty* thesis and the *cycle of poverty* thesis. Each theoretical approach focuses on people in the scarcity-based secondary market of our dual market system, as discussed previously.

Culture of poverty thesis.   A popular belief is that the poor have constructed an everyday way of life that enables them to survive within a poverty environment. This view suggests that the very survival traits that

poor people develop to adapt to their impoverished environment work against them in the general, more advantaged part of the society. Oscar Lewis, a leading exponent of this thesis, describes the immediate-survival pattern of the poor in these terms:

The culture of poverty is a subculture of western society with its own structure and rationale, a way of life handed down from generation to generation along family lines . . . a culture in the traditional anthropological sense that it provides human beings with a design for living, with a ready-made set of solutions for human problems. (1966, 19)

Most social scientists do not concur with the closed culture implications of the culture of poverty concept. The concept apparently suggests that poor people choose to maintain a pattern of early school dropouts, unskilled and underemployed labor, knowledge of welfare application assistance, and the like. Even regarding Oscar Lewis's own cross-cultural analysis (he studied Mexican and American poverty in particular), other analysts hold that poor people globally perpetuate these behavior patterns only when no alternative opportunities are available to them (Eames and Goode 1973).

Cycle of poverty thesis.   An alternative view to the culture of poverty is the idea of a *cycle of poverty*, which precludes poor people from breaking out of their impoverished circumstances. As sociologist George Wilber observes, people often inherit poverty in much the same manner as some people inherit wealth through no efforts of their own (Wilber 1973).

The cycle of poverty suggests that altering specific aspects of the poverty environment—such as providing more educational or job opportunities—would also alter the "culture" of poor people. The poverty cycle (see figure 7–4) would then be broken. According to the cycle thesis, dependence on the day-to-day survival syndrome of the "culture of poverty," without major interventive changes in the opportunity structure within that culture, is not likely to change the extent of poverty in American society. As one poor ghetto resident testified before the U.S. Commission on Civil Rights, "Just like you step into something, you just sink and you can't get out of it" (*The City* 1968).

Policy Proposals to End Poverty

Effective efforts to reduce and ultimately end poverty depend on an accurate assessment of why poverty exists. Most research analysts advance the "class structure" as opposed to the "class continuum" idea discussed earlier. The evidence cited in this chapter, including the effects of the cyber-

netic revolution, gives substantial support to the view that the poor of today generally cannot use unskilled occupational roles for upward mobility as did the poor of earlier generations.

We are faced with a situation in which a modern technological economy structurally excludes those in the lower class. Traditional self-help and charity measures aimed at those at the bottom do not help them. What is being done? What can be done? In his book *Poverty, U.S.A.* (1967), Thomas Gladwin provides a useful framework for considering specific policy steps that have been taken or have been proposed. Gladwin notes that if poverty is to be ended, specific

Such poor urban neighborhoods, with their high unemployment and low tax base for schools and other needs, are often viewed as the settings for the cycle of poverty thesis.

steps must be taken regarding the following four interrelated characteristics of poverty in American society: (1) poverty is being poor, (2) poverty is being despised, (3) poverty is being incompetent, and (4) poverty is being powerless. These simple-sounding propositions represent complex proposals. Let us consider the policy and program implications of these four points. Each set of proposals involves some mix of individual, private group, and governmental program efforts.

Poverty is being poor. That poverty is being poor is self-evident. What is not self-evident is *why* the poor *stay* poor. Although public opinion has shifted somewhat since the Great Depression of the 1930s, many middle-class Americans still adhere to the culture of poverty idea. The focus here is on the poor themselves. Evidence of this view in recent years relates to the wide acceptance of the aims of the civil rights movements for poor racial minority members. Many in the middle and upper classes supported the racial integration movement over the past two decades on the assumption that breaking down discriminatory barriers would be enough to ensure upward social mobility for blacks as well as for other poor people. The problem with this approach, as an old civil rights adage put it, is that racially integrating a lunch counter when you can't afford to buy lunch may be pointless.

In spite of the many criticisms leveled at it, the Moynihan report was the first major policy approach, in a nondepression period, that accepted the notion of necessary intervention to assist the poor. In his analysis, Daniel P. Moynihan, the senator who had previously served as a sociologist in the Kennedy, Johnson, Nixon, and Ford administrations, presented the idea that the lack of family cohesion among poor black families was the major factor inhibiting upward mobility. He advocated an end to the practice of excluding poor families with an able-bodied father at home from social welfare assistance (Moynihan 1965) (see figure 7–5). This practice, begun in the Great Depression, was designed to assist the most needy fatherless homes, but had the long-term effect of forcing many low-income fathers to leave their families for their wives and children to qualify for welfare assistance.

While touching on the need for intervention to help the poor, considerable doubt exists that the Moynihan thesis was correct

FIGURE 7–4. The Cyclical Nature of Intergenerational Poverty

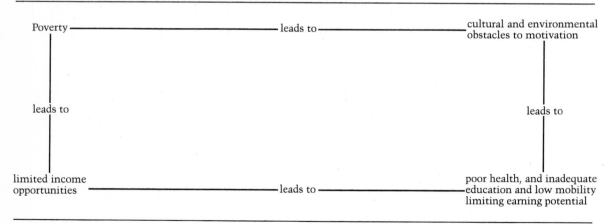

Data from Daniel P. Moynihan for the Council of Economic Advisors to President Kennedy (Washington, D.C.: U.S. Government Printing Office, 1963).

about the breakdown of black or other poor families as the basic problem among the poor. Research that Hyman Rodman (1959), Richard Della Fave (1980), and others conducted shows that the apparently disorganized form of much poor family behavior may represent the most effective survival solution to their problems of social and economic deprivation. The failure of poorly educated and unskilled individuals to succeed in the cybernetic age appears to be related as much to social forces in the larger society as to difficulties in the family structure of the poor. Insofar as an intergenerational poverty syndrome is often present in families, the cause may be more related to the larger economic, educational, and social conditions of the poor than to inherent characteristics of their family structures, their individual characteristics, or their culture. Keep in mind how often poor Americans before the cybernetic age were able to move up in social class status. Policies that fail to recognize the effects of these larger social conditions on the poor have little chance of success.

Since "being poor" means a lack of sufficient income, various *income maintenance* programs have increasingly been discussed. An example is a possible negative income tax approach in which all adults would file an annual income tax statement, but those falling below a prescribed poverty level would receive (rather than pay) graduated funds from the federal government if tied into a work incentive and job opportunity program (Moynihan 1973). Most such programs would constitute an extension of the Aid to Families with Dependent Children (AFDC) welfare programs, which have been in place since the 1930s. Perhaps in response to the explosiveness of poor urban ghettos, where civil disorders and high levels of daily violence are evident, proposals have been advanced that appear to cut across the conservative-liberal spectrum. Such proposals extend beyond the limited resources of the local communities where the poor are concentrated. The liberal Democratic administrations of Kennedy, Johnson, and Carter have advocated some of these proposals. The conservative Republican administrations of Nixon and Ford also advanced income assistance proposals for the poor. For example, Richard Nixon (along with Ronald Reagan), one of the most conservative presidents since Herbert Hoover, made the following policy suggestion in regard to welfare reform:

I propose that the federal government build a foundation under the income of every American family with dependent children that cannot care for itself —wherever in America that family may live. (Nixon 1970)

This and related proposals are reminiscent of the Moynihan report in its focus on family units rather than on individuals. Further, this proposal contained provisions on work requirements which, as some analysts believed, many persons with small children or those who were severely disabled could not meet (Turner and Stearnes 1976, 138–40). While such income-supporting programs have been suggested for more than a decade, little has been done in the way of practical implementation of such programs. Public opinion has been developing a Proposition-

FIGURE 7–5. Characteristics of Social Welfare Assistance Recipients

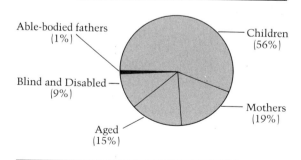

Note: Figures rounded as percentages vary slightly from year to year.

Data from U.S. Bureau of the Census and the Department of Labor.

13[1] tax-resistance orientation during this same period. Of those taxes people are willing to expend, programs for the poor are low on the priority list. Thomas Gladwin's second theme—the poor tend to be viewed with contempt—suggests the reason for this low priority.

Poverty is being despised.   Programs designed to increase the income of poor people by means of direct subsidy, job retraining programs, or by other means are not likely to be adopted so long as poor people are branded as undeserving. As David Matza observes:

The disreputable poor are the people who remain unemployed, or casually or irregularly employed, even during periods approaching full employment and prosperity; for that reason . . . they live in disrepute. (1966, 312)

This attitude strongly inhibits any such help to the poor as a guaranteed minimum income even when tied to work incentive programs, and works against other approaches designed to increase income of the poor. Poor people are an **out-group,** a group that experiences lack of acceptance from others. This is in contrast with those of higher socioeconomic status who tend to be **in-group** members—individuals who experience general acceptance and support (Merton 1957, 428–29). The result is the creation of a double standard. Thus, leaders of large bankrupt corporations like the Penn Central Railroad, the Lockheed Aircraft Corporation, or the Chrysler Corporation are not considered disreputable. These in-group societal members receive billions of dollars in public underwriting of their losses. In contrast, the disreputable poor out-group are often granted assistance grudgingly. The standard approach is that government "utilize[s] a 'means test' and demand[s] behavior which evidences a 'deserving poor'" (Miller and

Rein 1967, 513). In effect, we have created a system of *wealthfare* for the rich and *welfare* for the poor (see table 7–3).

The stereotypic hostility toward the poor has resulted in distortion of the objective situation of the poor. For example, in a typical Gallup poll, a majority of Americans said welfare should be cut, although less than one-fourth felt that tax cuts should be made in military defense or in other government programs. Pollster George Gallup made the following interpretive point about the wide gap between welfare beliefs and welfare reality:

Public perceptions about welfare "chiselers" may have influenced those who claimed welfare spending should be cut. As many as 36 percent of those polled in a recent Gallup survey believe 50 percent of those on welfare are cheating. *The fact is, however, that 90 percent of welfare recipients are unable to support themselves because they are aged, infirm or women with small children.* (*Arizona Republic* 25 February 1979) (italics ours)

Another objective problem with the work-means test approach is that the structure of employment in the American cybernetic economy is such that even if all the able-bodied adults were trained effectively, sufficient employment for the poor would still not be available, although their occupational problems would be far less severe. To understand this point, consider some observations that Nelson Rockefeller made while he was governor of the urbanized state of New York. Governor Rockefeller noted the need for advanced educational training for most people, including most of the poor, to be economically successful. He observed that his grandfather, oil tycoon John D. Rockefeller, was a school dropout at age fourteen, which would have precluded economic success to the same degree today. The governor reported that:

there were scads of unskilled jobs around in my grandfather's day. Now these kinds of jobs have gone the way of the buffalo. . . . Young people today need all the education, training and guid-

---

1. Proposition 13 was a tax limitation proposal passed in California in 1978. The proposition became a national byword to reduce all forms of taxation.

ance they can get. There are more opportunities than ever, thanks to our booming American economy, but not for those people without skills. (1966, 2)

Governor Rockefeller's state labor reports revealed that in New York state, over 700,000 adults were unemployed, and over 400,000 jobs were unfilled because too few skilled workers were available. Any work-means test for the poor would have to take this dilemma into account.

Programs for the poor are typically tied to notions regarding the willingness of the poor to work. What if no work is available, however, as was the case for so many during the Great Depression? The development of effective programs to end poverty is related to the attitudes and values of those in a position to support the programs. Reformers argue for more recognition that most poor are excluded from opportunity and for a revision of attitudes concerning the poor. Philip Wog-

oman, professor of Christian social ethics at the Wesley Theological Seminary, argues strongly for more objectivity in the handling of poverty programs:

One of the striking aspects of most welfare programs . . . is the expectation that the recipient will humbly acknowledge his indebtedness and properly express his gratitude to the giver. The outraged public response to the Welfare Rights Movement was revealing. More than anything else, the members of this movement [of poor people] sought to have their aid payments considered as a basic right, not as a gift, and it is believed that the recipients should be grateful to the givers . . . but [giving in such a manner] . . . leaves the humiliated poor in a scarcely improved condition. There is much to be said for an objective handling of the basic conditions of life, treating them rather as a basic human right. (1968, 76–77)

The minimum income proposal is not likely to get far as along as any gain that the poor make stigmatizes their marginally im-

TABLE 7–3.   The Welfare and Wealthfare Systems

	WEALTHFARE	WELFARE
(1) Source of Subsidy	Market purchases by government Government price policies Government export-import policies Government tax expenditures	Federal "grants and aids," supplemented by state and country subsidies
(2) Amount of Subsidy	Unknown for government economic policies, but probably at least 50 billion in tax expenditures	15–20 billion by federal, state, and local governments
(3) Recipients of Subsidy	Middle and upper income fifths; the more you make, the more you get	Bottom income fifth; the less you make, the more you get
(4) Stereotypes Associated with Recipients	Decent, hard-working people and/or clever entrepreneurs who know how to work the system	Lazy, immoral people who do not know how to manage their finances and who do not want to work
(5) Eligibility Requirements for Subsidy	Work for a large corporation which does a lot of business with government; belong to a large union or professional association; own large shares of stock in large corporations doing business with government; and have a good tax lawyer fill out complicated forms provided by government	Be close to starving; have kids; have a physical deformity; lose your job; or be old
(6) Monitoring of Recipients	Proclamations by President's Council of Economic Advisers on the "state of the economy"; spot checking by IRS	Frequent checking by "eligibility" worker who visits your home

Source: Jonathan H. Turner and Charles E. Starnes, *Inequality: privilege and poverty in America* (Pacific Palisades, Calif.: Goodyear, 1976), p. 152.

proved status. Indeed, such blame is one reason why the poor are excluded from the opportunity structure beyond minimum participation. Yet, practical as well as idealistic reasons exist for improving the condition of the poor. Both our secular democratic and our Judeo-Christian religious traditions hold to the dignity of every individual whatever his or her circumstances. This view aside, the poor, who are increasingly squeezed into deteriorating urban industrial centers, no longer suffer in silence. As Henry Ford II noted after the Detroit riots of 1967, "It is difficult to build automobiles in burned down factories." Further, as economist Paul Samuelson remarks:

For conscience's sake, we are impelled to help. Besides, history teaches us that men do not always starve quietly. (1973, 765)

Poverty is being "incompetent."   Along with their lack of income, the poor lack needed occupational skills. Given the problems college students sometimes have in se-

curing good jobs, even trained competence does not guarantee upward mobility. Still, training is clearly an increasing prerequisite and greatly increases the chances of improving one's economic status. Competence would lessen the rigidity of a system increasingly closed to those with little training. Lower-class members would be provided with the skills to take advantage of the opportunities that are available to others in a system generally still open for most.

Two primary routes to occupational competence on the part of the poor are available: education for children and training or retraining for adults. Since the future is with the young, let us consider education first. If a lessening of polarization by class and by ethnicity is to take place, then the educational system will be a major mechanism in the process. In American society, the belief has long been held that widespread opportunity for schooling is the best way to avoid a rigid class structure (Brookover and Gottlieb 1964, 177). This old ideal has become wide-

"I'm terribly sorry, sir, but in the process of cutting out programs for the poor we inadvertently cut out a program for the rich."

spread as we have moved from a **gemein-schaft** (small-town) society with continuity of occupations and life-styles from one generation to the next to a **gesellschaft** (metropolitan) society with intergenerational discontinuity of occupations. As the society becomes increasingly based on secondary rather than on primary ties, and as it becomes credentials oriented, education becomes more than ever the road to betterment for the poor.

Unfortunately, the poor quality of the schools available to disadvantaged children either has remained static or has deteriorated, while the need for quality has grown (Silberman 1970; Uhr and Evanson 1982). Census data show that most middle-class people have moved out of the central cities, which have the heaviest concentrations of the poor. The limited resources of rural school districts mean that the rural poor are no better off. A nationwide study on equal educational opportunity that James Coleman (1968) conducted identified the social class status of families, the larger community setting, and high achieving student peers as influential factors in academic and later occupational success. Federal courts cited these findings in cases of controversial court-ordered busing of children from poor to better quality schools (Pettigrew 1974).

The Elementary and Secondary Education Act (ESEA) of 1965 was the first major federal funding bill for schools below the college level. Funding under the act continues in the 1980s, although cutbacks have occurred (Weisman 1982). Such funding is designed to meet some of the problems and to stimulate communities and states to increase their support for schools in poverty-impacted areas. The major provisions of the act are intended to improve education as a source of opportunity for the young poor. These provisions include (Federal Role in Education 1966):

1. Federal aid for school operation and maintenance in districts where there are families with income under the federally designated poverty level;

2. Authorization of grants for the acquisition of school library resources, textbooks, and other printed instructional materials for the use of children and teachers; and

3. Authorization of grants to the states for supplementary educational centers and services and to establish model school programs.

In many ways, the ESEA turned out to be more a statement of aims than an actual benefit for poor schoolchildren. Public schools rely heavily on local property taxes for their support. The declining worth of property and lack of substantial new construction in poor school districts has resulted in an erosion in the local support of schools attended by the poor. Federal funding under ESEA has not offset the sharp decline in local tax support. An important caveat is that effective educational programs are predicated on poor children having sufficient home support through governmental work and aid programs if necessary for good nutrition and care needed for growth and development (Uhr and Evanson 1982).

While the future is with the young, what about the immediate problems of the adult poor? Helping only the young in impoverished communities is only minimally effective. The social stability of a poor neighborhood and an entire community clearly involves enabling poor adults to stabilize their lives as well. To help meet the needs of the adult poor, Congress passed the Economic Opportunity Act (EOA) in 1965, which calls for the use of public schools and private businesses to rehabilitate and train unskilled adults.

Perhaps the best approach to transcending the occupational exclusion of the poor lies in some of the programs advanced to assist the one-third of the nation living in poverty during the Great Depression of the 1930s. During President Hoover's administration in 1932, the Reconstruction Finance Corporation was chartered. The RFC authorized millions of dollars in loans to save banks, railroads, building and loan associations, and other financial institutions (Schlesinger

1960, 225–26). By the end of the 1930s, during the Franklin Roosevelt administration, an alphabet soup of new government agencies to help the poor had been formed, including the AAA (Agricultural Adjustment Administration) to stabilize farm prices, the CCC (Civilian Conservation Corps) to employ young people and aid in the preservation of natural resources, the FHA (Federal Housing Administration) to offer low-interest loans to people endangered by foreclosure of mortgages on their homes, and the NLRB (National Labor Relations Board) to assist in collective bargaining between unions and employers—and many others.

Since the 1930s, the American economy, based on a mixed approach of governmental controls and free enterprise, has expanded greatly until the effects of the international OPEC oil cartel in the 1970s with renewed growth in the 1980s (Abelson 1983). Hence, arguing that the changes in the social system in the 1930s undermined the growth and economic potential of the society would be difficult. Quite the opposite is true. By the 1980s, the poor had become a smaller proportion of the population. The problems now facing Americans are largely a consequence of enormous economic expansion. This has meant greater dependence on foreign sources of raw materials such as petroleum, and on foreign markets for our products. This system of global interdependence has great potential benefits for ourselves and for others. The system, however, can reduce stability unless we use the potential skills of Americans in the lower strata to increase our competitiveness in the world economy.

Poverty is being powerless. The problem of starting new programs and expanding old ones may be difficult because of the relatively small poor population in American society today. Most poor people, individually and as a group, have been relatively powerless to change their circumstances. Political action also requires effort at other levels of society. Poor people's marches have been aimed at creating national pressure to expand such programs as those under the Elementary and Secondary Education and Economic Opportunity Acts, as well as to press for new programs like income maintenance. Such action often requires effort at the grass-roots level. Examples are rent strikes in Chicago that the late Saul Alinsky led, and those in New York City that Jesse Gray led, as well as organizing to elect sympathetic local leaders.

In practical social and political terms, what are the chances that a coalition of the poor will succeed? Any major moves to increase opportunities for the poor to achieve upward mobility may meet with a backlash from others, particularly the pressed lower-middle class, as they have in the past. These are times in which many call for a serious discussion of a constitutional convention to require a balanced federal budget. This approach could severely limit programs designed to assist the poor. In the last analysis the majority, who are above the poverty level, have a deep stake in assisting the poor out of their frustrating and defeating circumstances. After reviewing the research following the destructive civil disorders in many poor urban ghettos in the late 1960s, a report of the National Advisory Commission on Civil Disorders (1968) drew this warning conclusion, which is still relevant to conditions facing the poor in the 1980s:

None of us can escape the consequences of the continuing economic and social decay of the central city and the closely related problem of rural poverty. The convergence of these conditions in the racial ghetto and the resulting discontent and disruption threaten democratic values fundamental to our progress as a free society.

If none of us can escape, then supporting the multiple individual efforts and private and public programs needed to end the condition of poverty around us is to the self-interest of people at all social class levels.

SUMMARY

We have discussed the problem of poverty in the predominantly middle-class American society. As a consequence of new economic forces, the poor constitute in some important respects a more isolated "underclass" than the poor of past generations.

Poverty, the problem of too little income to maintain a minimum culturally acceptable standard of living, is an age-old phenomenon. More affluent members of the society have long expressed hostile views of the poor. Even with such hostility, poor people in the past had certain widespread means of improving their position in society. While relatively undereducated and possessing few work skills, until recent history great demand existed for unskilled labor on farms and in factories. Further, the relative proportion of poor people was larger in the past, thereby giving former generations of poor people more political leverage. New economic developments, particularly the **cybernetic revolution,** have resulted in a sharply declining need for unskilled labor while expanding the economic opportunities for those more educated and more occupationally skilled.

The contemporary social position of poor people is measurable by such means as Lloyd Warner's and more recent class analysts' **social class** measures and the **Lorenz Curve measure of wealth distribution.** Although we now have fewer poor people than in the past, millions still in that condition find themselves isolated. The poor are the continuing subject of negative **stereotyping,** which has the effect of "blaming the victim." While most poor are white, the long history of **discrimination** leveled toward racial minorities has left a higher proportion of blacks, Chicanos, and native Americans in a state of poverty. Black or white, the poor have increasingly been moving into cities in our urban society. Concentration in cities has made the poor more visible. Concentration also intensifies feelings of relative deprivation, leading to organized protest to combat today's "insular poverty," which leads to a "cycle of poverty." Poverty means being poor, despised, incompetent, and powerless.

Complicating the problems of the poor are the increasing problems of the not-so-poor lower-middle class. Many find their, often union-protected, jobs in jeopardy as the high-technology and service economy requires less reliance on semiskilled industrial workers. Many long stable families, neighborhoods, and ethnic groups find themselves increasingly pressed and competitive with poor people for new training and job opportunities.

The lower class and lower-middle class conflicts have not yet resulted in a coalition to establish new programs. Increased organized protest and pressure of the poor and of the not-so-poor, however, have resulted in general public recognition of the problems of being poor. Largely in response to organized protest, an increasing number of private and public programs have been proposed to reduce or end poverty in American society. Prominent proposals are income maintenance plans, negative income tax, better quality schools, and job training for adults.

Changing the view of the poor as disreputable violators of the work ethic will increase the likelihood that these and related proposals will be put into more active effect than before. The goal is to end widespread impoverishment, a state once believed inevitable but no longer necessarily so.

STUDY QUESTIONS

1. How are the concepts of *relative deprivation* and *class conflict* related to each other?

2. Compare the old southern rural racial caste system of the past with urban insular poverty problems. Why are some of the effects of these two issues similar?

3. How could a declining proportion of people in a state of poverty leave those still poor in a more difficult set of circumstances than poor people in the past?

REFERENCES

Abelson, A. 1983. Up and down Wall Street. *Barron's National Business and Financial Weekly* (11 April).

Arizona Republic. 25 February 1979.

Blauner, R. 1969. Internal colonialism and ghetto revolt. *Social Problems* 16:393–408.

Brookover, W., and D. Gottlieb. 1964. *A sociology of education.* New York: American Book Co.

Carman, H. J., and H. C. Syrett. 1955. *A history of the American people,* vol. II. New York: Knopf.

The City. 1968. Testimony. (January): 14–15.

Coleman, J. 1968. *Equal educational opportunity.* Washington, D.C.: U.S. Government Printing Office.

Davis, A., B. Gardner, and M. Gardner. 1941. *Deep South.* Chicago: Univ. of Chicago Press.

Della Fave, R. 1980. The meek shall not inherit the earth. *American Sociological Review*: 955–71.

Eames, E., and J. Goode. 1973. *Urban poverty in a cross-cultural context.* New York: Free Press.

Ellis, R., W. C. Lane, and V. Olesen. 1963. The index of class position: An improved intercommunity measure of stratification. *American Sociological Review*: 271–77.

1966. *Federal role in education.* Washington, D.C.: U.S. Government Printing Office.

Fogelson, R. 1971. *Violence as protest: A study of riots and ghettos.* New York: Anchor.

Friedman, M. 1967. Kensington, U.S.A.: A social scientist's understanding analysis of the causes of white backlash. *La Salle Quarterly* (Fall): 1–5.

Galbraith, J. K. 1958. *The affluent society.* Boston: Houghton Mifflin.

Gilbert, G. M. 1951. "Stereotype persistence and change among college students." Journal of Abnormal and Social Psychology 28:245–255.

Gladwin, T. 1967. *Poverty: U.S.A.* Boston: Little, Brown.

Gold, B. H. 1970. Introduction. In *The reacting Americans: An interim look at the white ethnic lower middle class,* ed. J. Maquidson, iii–iv. New York: Institute of Human Relations.

Gordon, L. 1973. "The fragmentization of literary stereotypes of Jews and of Negroes among college students." *Pacific Sociological Review* 16:411–425.

———. 1978. *Sociology and American Social Issues.* Boston: Houghton Mifflin.

Gordon, D. 1972. *Theories of Poverty and the Underemployed.* Lexington, Mass.: D.C. Heath.

Gordon, R. and L. Stephenson 1980. "Medical deprivation and area deprivation." *Proceedings of Applied Geography* 3:286–297.

Hammill, P. 1969. The revolt of the middle class. *New York Magazine* (14 April): 1–2.

Hourwich, I. 1912. *Immigration and labor.* New York: G. P. Putnam's Sons.

Jackman, M., and R. Jackman. 1982a. *Class awareness in the United States.* Berkeley: Univ. of California Press.

———. 1982b. Class awareness: Social class is a major source of group identity for most Americans. *Institute of Social Research Newsletter* (August): 4–5.

Katz, D. and K. W. Braly 1933. "Racial stereotypes of 100 college students." Journal of Abnormal and Social Psychology 23:280–290.

Keyserling, L. H. 1964. *Progress or poverty.* Washington, D.C.: Conference on Economic Progress.

Landecker, W. 1960. Class boundaries. *American Sociological Review* 25: 868–77.

Lewis, O. 1966. The culture of poverty. *Scientific American* 4: 19–25.

Matza, D. 1966. The disreputable poor. In *Social structure and social mobility in economic development,* ed. N. Smelser and S. M. Lipset, 312–13. Chicago: Aldine.

Merton, R. 1957. *Social theory and social structure.* New York: Free Press.

Michael, D. 1962. *Cybernation: The silent conquest.* Santa Barbara: Center for the Study of Democratic Institutions.

Miller, S. M., and M. Rein. 1967. Poverty, inequality and policy. In *Social problems,* ed. H. Becker, 426–516. New York: Wiley.

Mills, C. W. 1959. *The sociological imagination.* New York: Oxford Univ. Press.

Moynihan, D. 1965. *The Negro family: The case for national action.* Washington, D.C.: U.S. Government Printing Office.

———. 1973. *The politics of a guaranteed income.* New York: Vintage.

Myrdal, G. 1970. Backlash, privilege, and pressure. In *Poverty in affluence,* ed. R. Will and H. Vatter, 210–12. New York: Harcourt, Brace.

Neumann, F. 1967. *The Democratic and Authoritarian State.* New York: The Free Press.

National Advisory Commission on Civil Disorders. 1968. *Report of the National Advisory Commission on Civil Disorders.* New York: Bantam.

New York Times. 16 January 1964.

Nixon, R. 1970. Welfare alternatives. In *Poverty in affluence,* ed. R. Will and H. Vatter, 204. New York: Harcourt, Brace.

Pettigrew, T. 1974. Race, schools, and riots in Boston. *New Society* (28 November): 538–40.

Piore, M. 1971. "The dual labor market; theory and implications," in D. Gordon, ed., *Problems in Political economy: an urban perspective.* Lexington, Mass.: D.C. Heath.

1972. *Population and the American future.* New York: Signet.

Rockefeller, N. 1966. Drop-outs: one man's answer. *This Week* (23 January): 2.

Rodman, H. 1959. On understanding lower-class behavior. *Social and Economic Studies* 8: 441–49.

Ryan, W. 1978. The art of savage discovery. In *Social problems: Institutional and interpersonal perspectives*, ed. K. Henry, 31–34. Glenview, Ill.: Scott, Foresman.

Samuelson, P. 1973. *Economics.* New York: McGraw-Hill.

———. 1980. *Economics.* 2d ed. New York: McGraw-Hill.

Schlesinger, A. Jr. 1960. *The politics of upheaval.* Boston: Houghton Mifflin.

Silberman, C. 1970. *Crisis in the classroom: The remaking of American education.* New York: Random House.

Statistical abstract of the United States. 1980. Washington, D.C.: U.S. Government Printing Office.

Suttles, G. D. 1974. *The social order of the slum.* Chicago: Univ. of Chicago Press.

Time. 1977. The American underclass: Destitute and desperate in the land of plenty. (29 August): 14–15.

Turner, J., and C. Stearnes. 1976. *Inequality: Privilege and poverty in America.* Pacific Palisades, Calif.: Goodyear.

Uhr, E., and E. Evanson. 1982. Social child support: An antipoverty program for the eighties. *Focus* (report of the University of Wisconsin–Madison Institute for Research on Poverty) (Fall and Winter): 1–5.

U.S. Bureau of the Census. 1969. Poverty in the United States, 1959 to 1968. *Current population reports,* ser. p–60, no. 68. Washington, D.C.: U.S. Government Printing Office.

———. 1981. Money income of families and persons in the United States: 1979. *Current population reports,* ser. T–60, no. 121. Washington, D.C.: U.S. Government Printing Office.

Warner, L. 1960. *Social class in America.* New York: Harper Torchbooks.

Warner, L., and P. Lunt. 1941. *The social life of a modern community.* New Haven, Conn.: Yale Univ. Press.

Weisman, S. 1982. Reaganomics and the president's men. *New York Times Magazine* (24 October).

Wilber, G. L. 1973. Determinants of poverty. In *Poverty: New perspectives.* ed. G. Wilber, 8–9. Lexington, Ky.: Univ. of Kentucky Press.

Williams, R. 1970. *American society: A sociological interpretation.* New York: Knopf.

Wish, H. 1960. Turner and the moving frontier. In *The American historian,* 181–208. New York: Oxford Univ. Press.

Wogoman, P. 1968. *Guaranteed annual income: The moral issue.* Nashville: Abington.

CHAPTER 8

Crime and Punishment

CONTENTS

Crime finally takes a pause

The surge of lawbreaking that has plagued the nation for two decades may be slowing down.

The Federal Bureau of Investigation reported on April 7 that serious crime remained at about the same level in 1981 as in the year before. By contrast crime had jumped 9 percent in 1979 and 9 percent more in 1980.

Many experts attributed the trend in part to population changes. "Babyboom babies are growing older and coming out of the crime-prone age groups," said Eugene Doleschal of the National Council on Crime and Delinquency. "As we as a nation grow older, crime will go down."

How long will the slowdown continue? Many experts believe crime rates might remain stable until the 1990s, when the number of young people in the population is expected to be on the rise again.

Another reason why crime may be slowing: Courts have been sending more lawbreakers to prison and keeping them locked up for longer terms.

Yet Gresham Sykes, a University of Virginia sociologist, noted that crime touched nearly 30 percent of U.S. households in the Census Bureau's 1980 survey and has yet to actually drop. He warned: "If the recession continues and unemployment goes up, crime may begin another climb."

The plateau in the overall crime rate results mostly from a steady level of property crimes—which outnumber violent crimes 9 to 1—against a population increase. While murders, assaults and rapes dropped slightly, robberies rose 5 percent. Thus, violent crimes increased by 1 percent.

The following table shows the ten cities with the highest and lowest 1981 rates of murder, rape, robbery and assault among the nation's 50 largest cities:

Source: U.S. News & World Report, 19 April 1982, p. 13. © 1982 U.S. News & World Report, Inc.

Highest Rates of Violent Crime

Cities	Violent Crimes Reported	Rate per 100,000 Residents
Newark	12,320	3,742
Miami	11,211	3,231
Boston	14,071	2,499
Atlanta	10,579	2,489
St. Louis	10,364	2,287
Washington	14,468	2,269
Baltimore	17,737	2,254
New York	156,946	2,220
Cleveland	12,429	2,166
Oakland	7,037	2,074

Lowest Rates of Violent Crime

Cities	Violent Crimes Reported	Rate per 100,000 Residents
Austin	1,545	447
Omaha	1,583	508
Honolulu	1,965	538
Milwaukee	3,424	538
San Antonio	4,651	592
Indianapolis	4,539	648
San Jose	4,122	648
Nashville	3,087	677
Tulsa	2,681	743
San Diego	6,593	753

Source: U.S. News & World Report, 19 April 1982, p. 13.

DEFINING THE PROBLEM: FORMS OF CRIME AND DELINQUENCY

This chapter incorporates both conflict and interactionist perspectives to explain a societal problem: crime in America.

Just as 1981–82 was associated with an apparent decline in some types of drug use in America (see chapter 2, "Drug Abuse"), a general leveling off in major crime rates characterized the same time period (U.S. Department of Justice 1981, 36). The article at the beginning of this chapter indicates a decline in rates for three of four types of violent crime. Rates for **murder,** defined as "the willful (non-negligent) killing of one human being by another"; **forcible rape,** defined as "the carnal knowledge of a female forcibly and against her will"; and **aggravated assault,** defined as "an unlawful attack by one person upon another for the purpose of inflicting severe or aggravated bodily injury," all declined between 1980 and 1981 (U.S. Department of Justice 1981, 6–19). The only violent crime in the FBI's crime index that showed an increased rate between 1980 and 1981 was robbery.

In August 1982, the FBI (U.S. Department of Justice 1981, 36) said that 13,290,300 U.S. crimes were reported for 1981 compared with 13,295,400 crimes reported for 1980. The **overall crime rate,** which relates the yearly number of reported crimes in the larger society to the total population (per every 100,000 persons), was down 2 percent from 1980—the first decline since 1977. The 1981 FBI crime statistics also marked the first time since 1976 that the total number of crimes had leveled off. That is the good news in the crime area.

The bad news is that the *overall crime rate in America is still very high* compared with other countries of the world, such as the United Kingdom, and our crime rates may remain high well into the future. In 1981, a violent crime occurred every twenty four seconds in America, a murder every twenty-three minutes, and a forcible rape every six minutes (see figure 8–1). Arson has become such a widespread and serious problem that it was added to the FBI's crime index as an eighth category in 1981.

While the article that began this chapter reports that the number of all violent U.S. crimes increased by 1 percent between 1980 and 1981, noting that the rates of both violent crime and property crime were down in 1981 (U.S. Department of Justice 1981, 36) is somewhat comforting. Further, in the property crime category, motor vehicle theft decreased by 4 percent and burglary dropped 1 percent in the same time period.

Why Crime and Delinquency Are Social Problems

Considering time frames of several years (see figure 8–2), however, the overall rate for reported crimes increased 15 percent between 1977 and 1981, and 61 percent between 1972 and 1981 (U.S. Department of Justice 1981, 36). Hence, sociologists and criminologists continue to regard the extent of crime in society as a major social problem. Social scientists are also concerned that handguns were employed in 50 percent of all U.S. murders in 1981 (U.S. Department of Justice 1981, 12). Further, arguments led to 42 percent of all murders in our society, while 17 percent occurred as a result of felonious activities such as robbery and rape (U.S. Department of Justice 1981, 12).

In the study of crime and delinquency, several areas of inquiry are especially important. One area involves the distinction between crime and deviant behavior. Criminologists (scientists who study crime) tend to define **crime** as any violation of the criminal law; they see crime as a legal concept. The sociological position with respect to all types of deviance is somewhat different. Sociologists tend to define **deviant behavior** as a violation of *any* conduct norm in human society. Hence, deviance is viewed in relation to general norms, rules, or expectations versus specific, written laws in the society.

Another area of inquiry relates to the issue of labeling people. Are criminologists concerned with explaining law violations or with the labeling of persons as "criminals?" This question has been debated for years and remains unresolved. Recently, however, a shift in sociology has occurred, from the study of individual criminal behavior to an emphasis on studying the processes by which this behavior comes to be defined as criminal or delinquent. In spite of their long tradition of focusing on criminal behavior, criminologists now contend that studying the criminal alone can never settle the issue of what constitutes crime. If we want to know something about crime, they say, we must study social control systems or processes. Analysis of the criminal justice system must include police conduct and misconduct, relationships among personnel

of the criminal and juvenile courts, how prisons are organized, and what effect they have on inmates (Cohen 1978, 154). Hence, to define crime, we must investigate interrelated topics ranging from individual behavior to how those who define it as criminal perceive behavior.

A third area of inquiry concerns informal controls outside the criminal justice system. This includes all the measures individuals take to reduce their vulnerability to crime: private police services, guard dogs, "block watching," locks, guns, and other protective devices. These responses are facets of the societal reaction to crime, and they are interrelated in ways that have hardly been explored.

Traditionally, criminologists have been concerned with the crimes of both "respect-

FIGURE 8–1.   FBI Crime Clock 1981

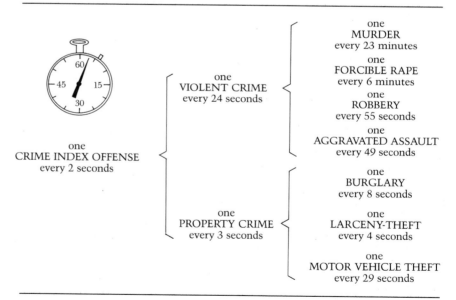

Note: This figure should be viewed with care. It represents the annual ratio of seven of the eight index offenses to fixed time intervals. Being the most aggregate form of *Uniform Crime Report* data, it is designed to convey the annual *reported* crime experience in America by showing the relative frequency of occurrence of seven index offenses.

Data from U.S. Department of Justice, Federal Bureau of Investigation, *Crime in the United States, 1981 uniform crime reports* (Washington, D.C.: U.S. Government Printing Office, 1981).

able" and "nonrespectable" citizens. The criminal law, however, now identifies "artificial persons" as well, such as corporations, governments, labor unions, patriotic groups and sport teams (Cohen 1978, 154–55). Although these collectivities (i.e., institutional groups) have been involved in crimes historically, comparatively little work has been done to explain collectivity crime, and even less attempt has been made to control it. This and other types of crime are discussed in the next section.

Types of Crime

Predatory crimes, or "acts that have victims who suffer loss of property or some kind of physical harm" (Lauer 1982, 189), represent one major category of all crime. Less than 10 percent of all predatory crime involves such violent acts as murder, rape, robbery, or aggravated assault (U.S. Department of Justice 1981). Thus, property crime is much more common than violent crime, but the public tends to think of violent crime as being more serious.

The FBI's crime index includes eight major **felonies** (serious violations of the criminal law). In addition to the four types of violent crime mentioned above, the index covers burglary, larceny-theft, motor vehicle theft, and arson. Because the index does not include all types of predatory crime, it cannot be used as an indication of the *total* amount of crime in America. Fraud, collectivity crime, and organized crime—each of which will be defined below—are types of white-collar (middle-class) crime that are excluded from the crime index.

The exclusion of white-collar crimes from the crime index makes it *appear* that lower income and minority individuals commit the majority of crime in the United States. Homicide rates, for example, are generally higher in lower income and minority neighborhoods. When all offenses are considered together, however, including white-collar crimes, the majority of offenders arrested are white, male, and over twenty-four years of age (*U.S. News & World Report* 5 March 1979, 42).

White-Collar Crime

In a now-famous article, criminologist Edwin Sutherland (1940, 1–12) defined **white-collar crime** as a violation of delegated or implied trust. He wrote of two major categories of white-collar crime: (1) misrepresentation of asset values, as in the case of computer fraud, and (2) duplicity in the ma-

FIGURE 8–2.   Crime Index Totals Between 1977 and 1981

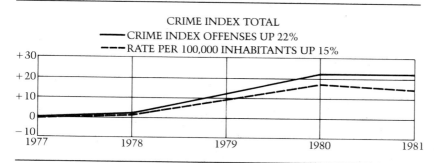

Data from U.S. Department of Justice, Federal Bureau of Investigation, *Crime in the United States, 1981 uniform crime reports* (Washington, D.C.: U.S. Government Printing Office, 1981).

nipulation of power, or the "double cross." The latter occurs when a white-collar offender holds two antagonistic positions, one a position of trust that is violated in the interest of the second position. One example is a city council member who violates the trust inherent in that position by using privately gained information to sell real estate or stock as a sideline. Financial loss from such white-collar crime is often less important than damage to social relations. Violation of public trust leads to public *distrust*, which lowers morale and can produce social disorganization on an ever-larger scale.

According to Sutherland (1940, 7–8), white-collar crime is encouraged when a community is not organized solidly against this type of behavior. In Sutherland's day, little organized public resentment existed against white-collar crime. This was because white-collar criminals tended to be segregated from other criminals; they were not regarded as "real" criminals either by themselves, by the general public, or by criminologists. Today, Ralph Nader and other consumer advocates argue differently, and public concern with white-collar crime is growing. C. Arnholdt Smith, an eighty-year-old millionaire, was sentenced to three years in jail when a jury found him guilty of four counts of state income tax evasion and one count of grand theft (*Arizona Republic* 11 June 1979). Banker John Cristo, Jr., was convicted in federal court on eighteen counts of bank fraud, and was sentenced to a minimum of eighteen months in jail and a fine of $90,000 (*Arizona Republic* 11 June 1979). Cristo had persistently overdrawn his personal account at a bank he controlled. The Smith and Cristo convictions underscore current public resentment of white-collar crime.

Public resentment is only one consequence of white-collar crime; alienation is another. People become alienated from the larger society when they learn that the high prices they pay for everything from natural gas to cleaning up the environment are partly due to white-collar crime.

Collectivity Crime

As mentioned earlier, **collectivity crime** is a special form of white-collar crime, in which "artificial persons," such as corporations and labor unions, violate criminal laws (Cohen 1978, 154). The question is, what kind of actor acts *collectively?* This seems like a contradiction in terms, because collectivities themselves do not act. Individuals act on behalf of corporations and labor unions, and these abstract collectivities can be held responsible for the action of individuals. Ford Motor Company was indicted on criminal charges related to a Pinto automobile crash in which three teenage girls died. The jury said that Ford knew the Pinto fuel tanks were unsafe but did nothing to correct them (*Associated Press* 14 September 1978). Ford has been named in almost fifty other Pinto-related civil suits that are pending in various courts.

Many types of collectivity crime take place in America. Land fraud is a collectivity crime that affects individuals as well as businesses that invest in real estate. Sociologist Robert Snow analyzed the complexities involved in the vast land fraud in Arizona during the past decade. Snow (1978, 68) found that

the land development and real estate market in Arizona represent a "boom market mentality" . . . which is based on individuals' beliefs in the "greater fool theory." This belief supports the gullibility and acceptability of purchasing land and other forms of real estate at vastly inflated prices in the hope that there will be another "greater fool" who will pay even more in order to "beat inflation" and make a profit on his investment.

Arizona land fraud swindles involve virtually all levels of the "legitimate" business community, including banks, title companies, realtors, developers, contractors, and advertising and media persons (Snow 1978, 68). Land fraud swindles and other high-level financial scams in Arizona, Florida, and Utah also involve billions of dollars taken annually from the general public.

Controlling these fraudulent business operations is difficult when so many people are caught up in the emotions of a "boom market mentality."

Computer crime is defined in current criminological literature as criminal behavior by means of manipulating electronic data processing (Nycum 1975, 444). Computer crime is one of the faster growing types of white-collar and collectivity crime. It is highly profitable, and criminals perceive it as less risky than other crimes. Means as simple as a home push-button telephone can gain access to some computers.

Computer crimes typically fall into one of the following categories: (1) financial crimes, (2) property crimes, (3) information crimes, (4) theft of services, and (5) vandalism (Bequai 1976, 22–30). *Financial crimes* are those in which the computer is used for financial processing, such as payrolls, accounts payable and receivable, and storage of financial data files. In computer *crimes involving property*, the criminal places orders with the computer for merchandise or other property for resale. *Information crimes* take the form of unauthorized access to computer systems via a remote terminal to alter data or physically confiscate programs or files or both. *Theft of services* refers to the use of a computer for personal gain at a company's expense. *Vandalism* involves intentional damage to computers, data files, data tapes, or other related equipment.

Very few computer "rip-offs" are ever detected. The largest known to date is the $2 billion Equity Funding scandal, in which twenty-two insurance company employees were convicted of "inventing" 56,000 fake policies for resale to other insurance companies. Another computer crime involved the programming of Penn Central computers to divert 277 freight cars to an isolated Illinois railroad siding, where both cargo and cars were plundered. Further, a nineteen-year-old electronics wizard gained access to Pacific Telephone and Telegraph terminals and ordered $1 million worth of supplies over a period of nearly two years without being detected (*Time* 8 August 1977, 53).

The small amount of computer crime that is detected (estimated at 1 case out of every 100 "rip-offs") is never publicly disclosed. According to IBM's Robert Courtney, "It's generally accepted in this business that about 85 percent of detected frauds are never brought to the attention of law-enforcement people" (Alexander 1974, 146). The computer criminal, once detected, is often required only to make restitution with no jail sentence. The courts realize that computer records can be altered easily, both before and after they are entered into the computer. Hence, the courts are reluctant to admit such records as evidence in most cases, which makes prosecution of computer criminals difficult.

Organized Crime

The most familiar example of organized crime in America is the so-called Mafia. The Mafia has been described as a "secret organization, rooted in a Sicilian tradition of violence, held together by ethnic solidarity, and operating outside the law" (Bassis, Gelles, and Levine 1982, 465). Sociologist Donald Cressey (1969) described a nationwide network of twenty-four crime "families" that reportedly deal in various illegal "service crimes." These crimes include such activities as importing and selling drugs, gambling, prostitution, loan sharking, and extorting money from legitimate businesspersons, under the guise of offering them "protection."

What is not clear about organized crime, and what probably accounts for so few sociological studies of it, is that no one really seems to know exactly *what it is or where its boundaries end*. In other words, the organized crime phenomenon is problematical, in and of itself. Are we speaking of a few underworld families and individuals in given cities and sections of the country, or are we talking about a national network or conspiracy of underworld figures over an extended period of American history? Anthropologist Francis Ianni (Bassis, Gelles, and Levine 1982, 465) maintains that assertions of government officials produce most of the evidence of a national, ethnically based crime organization.

Another related question is, where does institutional, corporate crime (*U.S. News & World Report* 6 September 1982, 25–30) leave off and underworld, organized crime take over? With the many recent allegations about linkages among legitimate business, political and sport figures, Hollywood personalities, and underworld individuals, "telling the players without a program" becomes increasingly difficult.

Nevertheless, recent events in the United States support suspicions regarding organized crime networks. For example, the relative ease with which hoodlums make huge profits by illegally dumping toxic wastes (*Chicago Tribune* 15 March 1983) raises questions about possible mob links to politicians responsible for protecting our environment (*Washington Post* 16 January 1983). Further, when Allen M. Dorfman recently became Chicago's gangland victim number 1,081 since 1919 (*Newsweek* 31 January 1983, 27), his murder raised questions about what happens to those closely associated with the Cosa Nostra (Our Thing). Insurance man Dorfman was murdered in a Lincolnwood, Illinois parking lot on 20 January 1983. His insurance agency and other companies reaped large payments from the Teamsters union for processing pension checks, health and welfare benefits, and other payments at what investigators charged were inflated rates.

Juvenile Crime

Studies made of the careers of some adult offenders generally show the importance of juvenile delinquency as a forerunner of adult crime. These studies support the conclusion that the earlier in life a juvenile is arrested or detained for an offense, the more likely

he or she is to be involved in criminal activity as an adult. A recent study that sociologist Lyle Shannon conducted, however (*United Press International* 30 August 1982), also indicates that predicting which teenagers will grow up to be adult criminals is generally impossible.

For many types of crime, including property crimes, the peak age of criminality occurs below twenty-four years of age. The fifteen- to seventeen-year-old group is the highest for burglary, larceny, and auto theft, and for these offenses, fifteen-year-olds are arrested more often than persons of any other age (*U.S. News & World Report* 5 March 1979, 42).

Part of the recent increase in American

Four young members of a New York gang. Not all such gangs are involved in crime and delinquency. Some are formed for social reasons, others for the mutual protection of gang members.

crime is due to the large number of young people who moved into the ten- to twenty-nine-year age group between 1960 and 1970, for this age group has the highest arrest rates for violent crime. Hence, much of the recent increase in violent crime can be attributed to more young people moving into adolescence rather than to the society as a whole. Research indicates that youth gangs commit about 15 to 20 percent of the major crimes in some American cities.

Gang Delinquency

Albert Cohen (1955) employs the anomie (normlessness) approach in explaining "lower-blue-collar-class" gang delinquency. He is especially concerned about the random, nonutilitarian (non purposeful) destruction of property that some lower-class gang delinquents perpetrate. Cohen thinks that members of these gangs engage in destructive behavior because they perceive that their opportunities in society are blocked. Gang members lack the education and skills to compete successfully for secure positions in the job market. Hence, they react *indirectly* against more successful, middle-class authority figures by destroying property that conventional members of society own. Cohen's (1955, 24–35) "reaction formation" concept is a major part of his anomie theory of gang delinquency.

In contrast with Cohen, anthropologist Walter B. Miller (1958) takes the value conflict approach in explaining gang delinquency. In his view, gang delinquents aren't "reacting" against anyone when they destroy property; they are simply carrying out the "focal concerns" (values) of lower-class culture. Miller (1958, 5–6) writes:

In the case of "gang" delinquency, the cultural system which exerts the most direct influence on behavior is that of the lower class community itself . . . rather than a so-called "delinquent subculture" which has arisen through conflict with middle class culture and is oriented to the deliberate violation of middle class norms.

For Miller (1958, 6–13), the focal concerns of lower-class culture are trouble, toughness, smartness, excitement, fate, and autonomy. "Trouble" relates to the issue of either getting into trouble or staying out of it. The concept of "toughness" means physical prowess as opposed to weakness. "Smartness" pertains to the ability to outsmart or outfox others as opposed to being conned by them. "Excitement" involves thrill seeking versus taking life as it comes. "Fate" is similar to fatalism, the idea that personal outcomes are predestined. Lastly, "autonomy" means freedom from external constraint, such as that which conventional authority figures impose.

Guided by these focal concerns, some lower-class gang youth attempt to con the police and terrorize neighborhoods. According to Miller, most of them are aware of the law-violating nature of this behavior. They are neither mentally ill nor physically or mentally defective. Why, then, do gang members commit these crimes? Miller thinks that a need for belonging and social status that they aren't receiving elsewhere motivate street-corner gangs. Acting out focal concerns becomes a way of achieving a sense of status and belonging. Miller (1958, 18) concludes:

1. Following cultural practices which comprise essential elements of the total life pattern of lower class culture automatically violates certain legal norms.

2. In instances where alternate avenues to similar objectives are available, the non-law-abiding avenue frequently provides a greater and more immediate return for a relatively smaller investment of energy.

3. The "demanded" response to certain situations recurrently engendered within lower class culture involves the commission of illegal acts.

Cohen's response to Miller would be to point out that *only a small proportion of lower-class youth become gang delinquents.* Hence, the focal concerns of lower-class culture cannot be *causing* gang delinquency. If they were, *all* lower-class youth would become delinquents. Miller might counter Cohen, however, with the argument that lower-class values might be a contributing factor in generating gang delinquency.

Middle-class Delinquency

Middle-class delinquency appears to be part of the general teenage culture in America. Many delinquent activities are an extension of the "normal" growing-up process in our society. These activities include partying, gambling, hot rodding, and sexual experimentation, which are part of the socialization of young persons and usually end as maturity begins. According to sociologists Joseph Scott and Edmund Vaz (1969, 115–16), "The bulk of middle class delinquency occurs in the course of customary nondelinquent activities and falls within the limits of adolescent group norms."

Media presentations give much less emphasis to middle-class delinquency than to lower-class delinquency. One reason is that middle-class delinquency seldom has the "gang" properties of lower-class delinquency, which the media can sensationalize. Another reason for this discrepancy may be that middle-class delinquents do not often come to the attention of juvenile authorities. According to Myerhoff and Myerhoff (1967, 124), "white-collar" delinquents may engage in as many antisocial activities as do lower-class youngsters. A combination of factors, however, particularly the specific form of delinquency, may interact to prevent these activities from coming to the attention of the authorities. Generally, the lower-class gang delinquent is perceived as more of a threat to society than the middle-class delinquent and is more likely to be arrested for the same type of behavior.

Interpretation of Crime Rates

Criminologists encounter a number of problems while attempting to estimate crime and delinquency rates from official records.

Official crime statistics can be extremely unreliable. Criminologists Edwin Sutherland and Donald Cressey (1966, 3) explain: "It is impossible to determine with accuracy the amount of crime in any given jurisdiction at any particular time. Obviously, a large proportion of crimes committed go undetected, others are detected but not reported, others are reported but not officially recorded."

Victimization studies, which poll actual victims of crime, show much higher rates of crime than official records—evidence that much crime goes unreported to the police. Rape victims, for example, are reluctant to subject themselves to the embarrassment of police questioning, and to reliving the attack during a subsequent trial. Similarly, people who have had con artists take money from them may be reluctant to admit their gullibility to the police or anyone else. Thus, official figures tend to underreport almost every type of crime and delinquency.

Another problem with official crime data relates to changing definitions of crime on the part of both the police and other law-enforcement agencies. The police, for instance, may arbitrarily change the definition of a bicycle theft from stealing a whole bicycle to stealing any part of a bicycle. This type of change has been known to increase the rate for this type of crime by several hundred percent in less than a year. Further, the public may decide that smoking marijuana should be changed from a felony crime to a misdemeanor. When this happens, a corresponding change in arrest rates for marijuana use takes place. The public may also become aware of some social condition, such as child abuse, that may have been occurring for a considerable time. The new awareness creates a new category of criminal behavior, and the rates for that type of crime may "increase" rapidly.

Finally, official sources of data, such as the FBI's *Uniform Crime Reports* and crime index, include only eight major felony crimes. Hence, many kinds of crime in the society do not appear in this report, and no uniform system exists for reporting either municipal police records or what transpires among the various juvenile courts. In spite of these limitations, sociologists must work with official statistics because sometimes they are the only data available for analysis.

The next section focuses on the issue of societal response to the problem of crime.

CONFRONTING THE PROBLEM: SOCIETAL CONCERNS ABOUT CRIME

As noted previously, Americans are concerned about the extent of crime and delinquency. The *Uniform Crime Reports* inform them that their society is becoming increasingly lawless. Various media also contribute to the public's concern about apparent increases in rates of crime and delinquency. Public opinion polls reveal increasing societal awareness of and concern over these problems. Ironically, this increased public awareness may have the effect of further increasing crime rates as people begin to report "suspicious" behavior that may have gone unreported in the past. Hence, the labeling process that results from "seeing" criminal behavior everywhere can create deviance and can become a social problem in itself.

Social scientists also uncover the subjective aspects of public awareness of crime when they publicize the findings of certain types of research. Sociologist Peter Rossi studied Baltimore residents to find out how they view the relative seriousness of different types of crime (Williams III 1974). Rossi asked his representative sample of 200 respondents to rank various offenses from most serious to least serious.

1. "Bribing a public official" was considered less serious than "buying stolen goods."
2. "Beating up an acquaintance" was among the least serious offenses and was more acceptable than "beating up a stranger."

3. "Beating up a spouse" was somewhat more acceptable than "beating up a policeman."
4. "Killing a pedestrian while exceeding the speed limit" was considered far less serious than "making sexual advances to young children" (Williams III 1974, 18).

Rossi's data also reveal that in general, forcible rape was considered more serious than killing someone in a bar, hijacking a plane was rated more serious than assassinating a public official, and using heroin was considered more serious than a public official accepting bribes.

Relativistic Versus Absolutistic Responses to Crime

Rossi's study demonstrates that a great deal of relativism (subjectivity) is involved in how individuals define the seriousness of crime. The position of the **moral relativist** is that no obvious moral meaning exists in the universe (Lofland 1969, 24). The relativist views good and evil as individual value judgments. Investigations of behavioral differences within and between societies reveal that people define and respond to specific behaviors in different ways (Pfuhl 1977, 267). This variation in response suggests the widespread operation of cultural and moral relativism in contrast with absolute (universal) cultural and moral standards (Pfuhl 1977, 267). For the **absolutist,** however, universal standards exist that serve as criteria for judging the difference between deviant and nondeviant behavior.

Criminologists also stress that community response to mass killers and child molesters tends to be absolutistic. Names of mass murderers, such as Richard Speck, Charles Whitman, Benjamin Smith, Juan Corona, David Berkowitz, Theodore Bundy, and John Gacy may come to mind. The response to these deviants by criminologists is frequently more relativistic, however. Berkowitz, for example, may have perceived that others rejected him—especially women his own age. As one writer put it:

Around dating bars in Fort Lauderdale, Fla., Berkowitz was remembered as a quiet listener who would timidly attempt to join animated conversation, inject a few comments with his bemused smile, *quickly be cut out of a group as an odd duck* [italics ours], retreat, then try futilely to strike up a conversation with others (*Time* 22 August 1977, 23).

If others labeled Berkowitz negatively for years, as interactionist theory seems to suggest, some of his general hostility against society could have been displaced against his thirteen victims.

Societal reaction against crime and delinquency is not limited to mass killers and child molesters, some of whom are killed in prison by other prisoners. Robbery, burglary, and muggings also take their toll on people's psyches. An elderly couple who had been robbed several times committed suicide because "they couldn't put up with the criminal situation in the Bronx" (*United Press International* 7 October 1976). Apparently, the couple was distraught over having been mugged twice near their apartment.

We have spent some time looking at crime in an anecdotal (biographical) way. The next section presents a sociological analysis of the problem.

ANALYZING THE PROBLEM: DOES THE PUNISHMENT FIT THE CRIME?

Sociological Theories of Crime and Delinquency

Theories of crime and delinquency tend to fall into three major categories: functional consensus theory, conflict theory, and interactionist theory.

Consensus theory, like Robert Merton's anomie theory, holds that most persons in society are motivated to achieve essentially the same set of cultural (material and nonmaterial) goals. In America, these goals are job prestige, money, marriage and family, a home, a summer home, and perhaps several automobiles. According to Merton (1957, 131–94), all members of our society are expected to want to achieve these goals of the American dream. Not all persons in our society, however, have the same set of means to achieve these cultural goals. People in the working classes, for example, are born into a social context that may make them less able to compete with the rich in the areas of family background and economic support for educational advancement. Hence, this discrepancy between goals and means, due to the social class structure of the society, places a greater strain on the lower classes to deviate in various ways. This "structural strain," as Merton (1957, 146ff.) calls it, may pressure a higher proportion of lower-class people to select illegitimate means to achieve society's cultural goals. This anomie, or normlessness, may even lead some persons to reject society's conventional goals as well as its legitimate means.

Further expansion of Merton's theory of conformity and deviance may be useful. When people reject societal goals and legitimate means to achieve those goals, they may become dropouts or retreatists. If they reject both goals and means, however, and then attempt to replace the cultural goals and means with new ones, they may become rebellious revolutionaries. Ritualists tend to overemphasize legitimate means, so that they lose sight of the cultural goals. Examples of ritualism include petty bureaucrats and some teachers and administrators. Innovators, like members of the Mafia, relate positively to the cultural goals of money and prestige, but reject legitimate means (e.g., education) for achieving those goals. Conformers embrace both conventional goals and means. Hence, in Merton's theory, everyone but the conformists are deviant in one way or another. Table 8–1 summarizes the variations in behavioral response to goals and means in Merton's theory.

The **conflict theory** approach is largely opposed to consensus theory. Conflict theorists, like Walter B. Miller, suggest that deviance is not so much a problem of disparity between societal goals and means and the subsequent feelings of blocked opportunity, but one of a difference in values. Individuals acquire these subcultural values from families, neighborhoods, peer groups and certain significant others in their lives. According to conflict theorists, values come into conflict in society because not all subgroups in the society have the same set of cultural values. Hence, values that the individual internalizes (learns) come to influence personal norms (rules) that control behavior. If shooting heroin or using cocaine is "in" among one's peers (friends), one may be persuaded to deviate in this particular way.

An example of the **interactionist** perspective is Edwin Sutherland and Donald Cressey's (1974, 75–76) differential association theory of crime, mentioned in the Prologue. The theory holds that *criminal behavior is learned in much the same way as noncriminal behavior.* The learning process is the same, but what comes to be valued is different. For example, white-collar criminality may be learned in direct or indirect association with those who already practice the behavior. Those who learn this type of criminal behavior may become isolated from frequent and intimate contacts with law-abiding behavior. Whether a person becomes a criminal or a delinquent depends on the frequency and intimacy of his or her contacts with deviant or nondeviant behavior. In some communities, structural and social pressures to deviate are greater. Differential association results in crime because this type of community is not organized solidly against a given type of deviant behavior (Sutherland and Cressey 1940, 1–12). In other words, the subcultural values in one type of community may encourage a kind of criminal or delinquent behavior that would not be tolerated in another community. Massage parlors and pornography shops are discouraged in some neighborhoods and encouraged or at least tolerated in others.

Research Results

Which perspective tends to be supported by sociological research—Albert Cohen's anomie theory of delinquency (derived from Merton's general anomie theory) or Walter Miller's conflict theory of delinquency? The answer is that evidence supports both theories. Each scholar seems to have some of the truth about gang delinquency in his particular theory.

Gang Delinquency Findings

To resolve some of the differences between anomie and conflict explanations of gang delinquency, sociologists Robert Gordon, James Short, and Desmond Cartwright (1963) tested the theories of Cohen and Miller. The researchers used six different samples of young respondents: a sample of black and one of white lower-class gang

TABLE 8–1. A Typology of Modes of Individual Adaptation

MODES OF ADAPTATION	CULTURE GOALS	INSTITUTIONALIZED MEANS
I. Conformity	+	+
II. Innovation	+	−
III. Ritualism	−	+
IV. Retreatism	−	−
V. Rebellion	±	±

Source: Robert K. Merton, *Social Theory and Social Structure* (Glencoe, Ill.: Free Press, 1957).

members; a sample of black and one of white lower-class, semidelinquent, nongang members; and a sample of black and one of white middle-class, nondelinquent, nongang boys. With the use of a special attitude scale, an attempt was made to differentiate the various groups.

Inferring from Cohen's concept of the gang's "reaction formation" against middle-class values, Gordon, Short, and Cartwright hypothesized that a higher degree of negativism toward middle-class values would characterize the delinquent groups. Gordon, Short, and Cartwright's (1963, 113) attitude scale afforded the respondents an opportunity to express bitterness and contempt toward middle-class values and norms. A group of items was also used to test Miller's concept of lower-class "focal concerns." These items included the phrases *smart-sucker, lucky-unlucky,* and *exciting life-boring life.* If Miller's conflict approach were correct, lower-class gang and semidelinquent boys would evaluate lower-class focal concerns more highly than middle-class boys would evaluate them. If Cohen's anomie theory of gang delinquency were correct, all of the samples would not equally endorse middle-class values.

Gordon, Short, and Cartwright found that *all six groups tended to place an equally high value on the middle-class life-style* (Gordon, Short, and Cartwright 1963, 117). This finding was unexpected regarding Cohen's reaction formation concept, as Gordon, Short, and Cartwright had hypothesized that the delinquent groups would be relatively "cool" toward middle-class values.

Other data supported Miller's hypothesis that gang and lower-class boys would evaluate lower-class images of life more highly than middle-class boys would evaluate them. Gang boys evaluated lower-class focal concerns more highly than did nongang boys, and gang and lower-class boys evaluated lower-class focal concerns more highly than did middle-class boys. This finding supports Miller's conflict theory contention that the values of lower-class boys are dis-

tinguishable from those of middle-class boys. Other research, however (Short 1965, 56–57), on legitimate and illegitimate "opportunity structures" (means) lends support to Cohen's concept of a possible reaction formation in gangs. One solution to this dilemma would be incorporating Miller's conflict approach with Cohen's anomie theory in subsequent research. Since both perspectives seem to have merit, criminologists ought to combine the best aspects of the anomie and conflict theories into a more adequate, single theory of gang delinquency.

Middle-class Delinquency Findings

A study of male delinquents in a Los Angeles suburban school district (Shanley, Lefever, Welty, and Rice 1969, 230–41) identified three student groups as (1) aggressive (i.e., assertive) students, (2) nonaggressive underachievers, and (3) a control group of well-adjusted students who were neither socially aggressive nor academically underachieving. Statistical analysis revealed striking differences in the percentage of police contact for the three groups. Seventy-three percent of the aggressive students had police records, 26 percent of the nonaggressive underachievers had records, and only 12 percent of the well-adjusted group had police records.

Given the relatively high rate of police contact for the aggressive group, the relationship between the police contact rate and the socioeconomic status of the aggressive group was studied. Analysis revealed an unexpectedly high incidence of police contact for all three social classes (i.e., upper, middle, and lower) *within the aggressive group.* Seventy-seven percent of the middle-class aggressives and 74 percent of the upper-class aggressives had at least one police contact. Further, the average numbers of police contacts for the delinquent subgroups of each student type were 3.8 for aggressives, 2.2 for underachievers, and 1.6 for the well adjusted. These findings suggest the usefulness of an aggressive versus a passive subclassification. Finally, much of the delinquent behavior of nonaggressive and well-adjusted middle-class adolescents may represent only a temporary deviation from conventional behavior.

Along this same line of reasoning, sociologists Pamela Richards, Richard Berk, and Brenda Forster (1979) contend that much middle-class, suburban delinquency may be viewed as a form of leisure or play. Using self-reported data, they examined age and sex patterns in overall middle-class delinquency, as well as vandalism, shoplifting, and drug use. They found that the concepts of peer influence and delinquency as leisure are more highly correlated with vandalism, shoplifting, drug use, minor theft, and running away from home than are boredom and feelings of inadequacy, which are often cited in the earlier delinquency literature. The concept "anger at authority figures" also seems to play a systematic role in patterns of minor vandalism (Richards, Berk, and Forster 1979, 99). Further, the alleged male character of delinquent property damage was challenged in this study, as Richards et al. (1979, 98) found that girls were often as likely to admit vandalism as boys.

Finally, regarding the issue of potential social class differences in delinquency, an increasing number of researchers who use self-reported measures versus delinquency rates conclude that there are few real differences in the delinquent activities of lower- and middle-class respondents (Richards, Berk, and Forster, 1979, 5). Apparently, social class biases inherent in official statistics have made class associations with delinquent activities appear greater than they really are.

The next section analyzes the criminal justice system and explores some of its injustices.

The Criminal Justice System

The purpose of criminal law and the justice system is to control human behavior and enforce penalties or other sanctions against deviant individuals and collectivities. Although crime is a major social problem in many Western nations, the United States has the reputation of being one of the most lawless major powers in the world. As we mentioned earlier, many U.S. crimes reported to the police are never recorded. In other words, crimes frequently are settled out of court through mutual agreement between the parties involved. These reported offenses are not taken to court because of lack of evidence, lack of interest on the part of potential prosecutors, or dismissal after a warning from police or the prosecutor's attorney (Becker 1966, 206–10).

Most crimes that authorities note result in an arrest procedure. After the arrest, the police must bring the accused person before a magistrate for a preliminary hearing. At this hearing, the magistrate must determine whether the crime has been committed and whether proper cause to suspect the accused is present. During the preliminary hearing, a majority of arrest cases are disposed of and no convictions occur. Less than half of all persons arrested on felony charges are convicted, and only one in five go to prison (U.S. News & World Report 1 November 1982, 35).

Injustice in the Judicial System

Along with excessive leniency, numerous other examples of injustice exist in the American judicial system. According to Uniform Crime Reports, the upper social classes tend to show lower overall crime rates than do the lower social classes. For political reasons, however, fewer arrests of upper-class persons take place, and this bias affects the validity of crime data presented by social class affiliation. Offenders in the upper income classes are known to buy their way out of arrests and convictions. Those familiar with the American court system concede that people in the upper income groups can avoid arrests and convictions more easily than those in the lower income brackets (Chambliss 1975).

Poorer offenders, because of ignorance of their rights, can be more easily pressured into confessions through threats and intimidation. Their status in the community usually protects the more educated groups, and because of their superior knowledge of how the system works, they can less easily be forced into admission of guilt without adequate evidence.

Bail practices constitute another area in which poorer and less educated persons tend to suffer. Bail is normally exacted "for the sole purpose of securing the attendance of the defendant in court" (Pfuhl and Zabezensky 1972, 409). Research, however, indicates this is not always the case. For example, a study of bail practices in Phoenix, Arizona suggests a relationship between type of legal representation (private attorney or public defender) and pretrial release of the accused. Since the *Gideon* v. *Wainwright* decision (1963), competent legal counsel must represent all persons facing felony charges. An attorney usually represents those able to afford a private attorney immediately following the time of arrest. The poor, without counsel at the time of arraignment (where the prisoner is told of the charges), are asked to recite a pauper's oath before the presiding justice. Then, the presiding judicial officer appoints a public defender to represent the prisoner.

Regarding the relationship between type of legal representation and pretrial release of the accused, Pfuhl and Zabezensky (1972, 424–25) theorized that

the accused who is able to hire his [or her] own attorney has a distinct advantage over others in securing pretrial release. The fact that someone is present at an administrative proceeding who is intimately involved in the judicial process and who may intercede directly . . . would seem to facilitate the securing of favorable conditions for release. The indigent accused, on the other hand, must await the arraignment procedure before having counsel assigned and must further await review of the case by such counsel before release may be considered.

In actuality, Pfuhl and Zabezensky (1972, 425) discovered that 56 percent of the defen-

dants who retained legal counsel at their own expense had gained release by the time of arraignment. Only 20 percent of the legally indigent, however, had secured release[1] by the time of arraignment. In the period between arraignment and preliminary hearing by the court, an additional 17 percent of those having retained private attorneys were released, and an additional 14 percent of those having a court-appointed attorney gained release. "Overall, between arrest and preliminary hearing, 73 percent of those defendants with private counsel secured release by some means, while only 34 percent of those with court appointed counsel secured release" (Pfuhl and Zabezensky 1972, 426).

Pfuhl and Zabezensky (1972, 427) also found that while retained (private) and court-appointed attorneys represented Caucasians about equally, the majority of Mexican-American, black, and other minority defendants must rely on court-appointed attorneys. This finding is consistent with the observation that minority group members generally have lower incomes. Most members of minority groups, then, are probably without the advantage of privately retained attorneys during the bail procedure.

Indeterminate prison sentences are another example of injustice in the American justice system. By this, we mean the wide discretion that judges and parole boards exercise in determining a convicted person's sentence. This results in greatly varying sentences for essentially the same types of crime (*U.S. News & World Report*, 1 November 1982, 35). A study of sentencing practices in Washington, D.C. shows wide variation in imposing penalties for serious offenses (*United Press International* 25 December 1978). The study found that more than one-third of the adults surveyed who were convicted of offenses involving a weapon were given probation or a suspended sentence. The only areas in which a rela-

---

1. *Release*, as used here, means making bail (money that a bail bonds person advances).

tively high degree of uniform sentencing was found were felony homicides and first-degree murder. Another study shows that slayers of whites are more likely to face execution than slayers of nonwhites (*Associated Press* 18 March 1979). Further, an exhaustive study of larceny and assault sentences (Dershowitz 1978, 239) reveals that in state courts, "74 percent of blacks convicted of larceny were sentenced to prison, while only 49 percent of whites with similar records were imprisoned."

Some of the blame for this type of disparity can be attributed to indeterminate sentencing, since it is the job of any legislature under that kind of sentencing to set only minimum and maximum sentences (Dershowitz 1978, 239). Reasoned debate over, for example, what sentence a "typical" bank robber should be given seldom takes place.

We have only begun to uncover the extent of injustice in the American court system. The next section discusses a related topic—police corruption and brutality that exist within many law enforcement agencies.

Police Corruption and Brutality

Why does **police corruption** exist, and how does it express itself? Police corruption can be described as any corrupt act that an officer commits for personal rather than for organizational interests (Sherman 1974). Most police corruption expresses itself in the form of bribery—money taken for services to the individual or other compensation for services rendered (*U.S. News & World Report* 1 November 1982, 46). This external type of corruption involves police behavior such as taking bribes in exchange for protecting certain dance halls and singles bars. The Mafia and other organized crime elements offer the police bribes if they will overlook such crime activities as drug sales, gambling, and prostitution (*U.S. News & World Report* 1 November 1982, 46). The money collected for these services either is kept by individual officers or, if several officers are involved, is kept in a "kitty" and distributed at the end of the month.

Internal corruption can occur within the structure of the police force itself. Here, payments are given to individuals for promotions, better shifts or assignments, or even for hiring. A large proportion of the corruption that occurs within major police departments appears to be located in the vice squads, where officers are confronted with numerous situations in which they have opportunities to receive bribes. Moreover, vice squad officers have very little direct supervision when they are on the job. Thus, they perceive that they can take bribes with only a very low probability of being caught.

The police are frequently accused of brutality as well as taking bribes. Jonathan Neumann was a new court reporter for the *Philadelphia Inquirer* when he noticed that murder suspects regularly testified that the police had beaten them (*Time* 1 May 1978, 36). Officials never investigated these accusations, however. This situation galled Neumann and William Marimow so much that they began asking pointed questions of people in high places. The two reporters then produced a well-documented series of articles that exposed police brutality and led to the indictment of fifteen Philadelphia police officers (*Time* 1 May 1978, 36). Later, seven more police officers were arrested, and two others pleaded guilty to departmental misconduct charges. The reporters' four-part series contains many examples of the police beating and harassing suspects and their friends and relatives. Some victims were hospitalized for injuries sustained during interrogation. In one case, "police raided a house without a search warrant, arrested a murder suspect without an arrest warrant, and beat four members of his family" (*Time* 1 May 1978, 36).

More recently, the Police Department in Richmond, California—already under a federal court decree to improve its treatment of minorities—was accused in the choking death of a black suspect. This was the *fourth* controversial death of a black person involving Richmond police over a two-year period.

The Prisons

Injustice is also pervasive in America's prisons and other detention facilities. Prisons as we know them today did not originate until the late 1600s and early 1700s, both in England and in America. Early practices in England, for example, were highly punitive even for minor offenses such as stealing a loaf of bread. Harry Allen (1975, 18) explains:

Corporal and capital punishment were the rule; executioners in sixteenth and seventeenth century Europe had at least thirty different methods to choose from. These ranged from hanging and burning at the stake to breaking on the rack. Public punishment and degradation were commonly prescribed for even minor offenses. Imprisonment served only as a preface to some gory punishment, carried out in the name of justice.

During this period of physical punishment in England, the Church began to establish its own method for dealing with offenders. Because the Church did not allow its courts to impose death sentences, it developed institutions called "penitentiaries" where people could pay their debts to society (Fogel 1975, 4). Even though the Church had initiated the establishment of a prison system, Britain temporarily chose to retain earlier punishment methods. They still favored the older practice of exiling and transporting prisoners to their colonies.

In America, the colonists initially copied English laws and punishment practices. No major changes in the treatment of convicts were brought about until 1682 when William Penn invoked the idea of institutional confinement as a punishment for serious crimes. His ideas were set down in what is known today as the "Great Law of 1682," which in part reads as follows:

[E]very County within Pennsylvania . . . shall build or cause to be built in the most convenient place in each County . . . a sufficient house, at least twenty foot square, for Restraint, Correction, Labor and Punishment of all such persons as shall be thereunto committed by law (Fogel 1975, 11).

This was the first time in America that any stand had been taken regarding the *imprisonment* of offenders in place of physical punishment for crimes.

While the original motivation for prisons in place of physical and capital punishment was a humanistic one, much of what happens to prisoners in today's penitentiaries is inhumane. Inmates are exposed to such problems as overcrowding, drug traffic, coercion into homosexual relations, and power struggles between racist subgroups. Let us look briefly into each of these problem areas.

Overcrowding.   American prisons are becoming increasingly crowded, and as a result, many states are facing lawsuits (*U.S. News & World Report* 1 November 1982, 47). These lawsuits are based on the Eighth Amendment, which prohibits cruel and unusual punishment. The problem of prison overcrowding is a fact. Yet, some people believe that overcrowding is not a problem. In 1973, the National Advisory Commission on Criminal Justice Standards and Goals said, "We already have more prison space than we need . . . there is no need to build additional institutions . . . for at least 10 years" (Flanagan 1975, 21). Many states followed the commission's advice and are now in trouble.

The need for more prison space is evident in all of the states—particularly in the South. Florida recently had 200 prisoners living in tents, and some states are converting ships into prisons (Marshall 1976, 5). Six thousand prisoners overcrowd Illinois prison facilities. Some inmates cannot shower regularly because of inadequate facilities. That Illinois is one of the states being charged with violating the Eighth Amendment is not surprising.

Southern Michigan Prison is the world's largest walled penitentiary. The prison was originally built for 5,700 inmates, but now houses over 6,000 prisoners. Over 100 men sleep in stairwells, and 35 healthy men live in the prison infirmary (*U.S. News & World Report* 28 November 1977, 76). This type of overcrowding negatively affects prisoners, guards, and prison administrators. An associate warden at North Carolina's Central Prison seems resigned to the overcrowding. He says, "There's no such thing as capacity around here. We put up whoever and whatever comes in" (*U.S. News & World Report* 28 November 1977, 78). Overcrowding leads to frustration, hostility, riots, and even murder. Because of the shortage of space, young first-time offenders are sometimes forced to stay in cells with hardened prisoners. Psychologists have found a relationship between prison over-crowding and complaints of illness such as high blood pressure, back-pain, nausea, rashes, and asthma (McCain, Cox, and Paulus 1976, 283–90). The United Nations suggests that each inmate needs sixty five square feet of living space, but the average inmate at one North Carolina prison has only twenty-five square feet.

Prison overcrowding reached its culmination at the New Mexico state penitentiary near Santa Fe in the spring of 1980, when inmates overpowered four guards and turned the prison into what reporters termed "hell on Earth" (*Arizona Republic* 27 February 1983). In all, thirty-three prisoners died at the hands of other inmates, and at least ninety prisoners were seriously injured in the riot. Twelve guards were held hostage, and some of them were beaten, stabbed, and sexually molested. Witnesses said "execution squads" of prisoners tortured and murdered other inmates, particularly those said to be informers. According to a New Mexico attorney general's office report, the prison was overcrowded and understaffed at the time of the riot. Prisoners had reportedly been receiving badly prepared food, inadequate nutrition, and poor medical and dental care.

Drugs. The drugs used in prisons are typically the same as those available on the streets: amphetamines, barbiturates, narcotics, and hallucinogens. Pushers are similar to those who sell drugs outside the prisons. They can provide fairly large quantities of drugs, which are sometimes bought with regular currency. Cigarettes, however, are the main monetary system that prison inmates use. When one inmate has accumulated many cigarettes, he is considered wealthy and can buy drugs as well as other amenities. Drugs find their way into correctional institutions through many channels. Channeling them through corrupt guards is the most common way. Identifying these guards is not very difficult for inmates, as the guards soon develop a reputation for dealing in drugs. Drug traffic represents a highly profitable business for some guards. This can be reassuring to convicts using drugs because they know these guards are not apt to report them to prison authorities. Drugs are also channeled into the prisons through local merchants who have access to the prisons when they deliver goods. A merchant who is "on the take" can store various drugs in cans of vegetables for example. This practice, which might involve several merchants, is difficult to detect. Inmates

Aftermath of riot at New Mexico state penitentiary. Prison overcrowding in America leads to frustration, riots, and even murder.

who work in prison hospitals sometimes pilfer drugs from hospital supplies (V. L. Williams 1974, 74). Finally visitors sometimes smuggle drugs to prisoners in the visiting area.

In federal prisons, inmates and their visitors are not fully separated from each other, and are sometimes grouped together in a single room with only limited supervision. Along with the passage of drugs from visitors to inmates, sexual activities and other privileges can often be arranged.

Homosexuality. Prisons are the largest single-sex institutions in North America today, which tends to have negative consequences for both male and female prisoners. In this kind of environment, sexual activities are usually restricted to sex dreams, masturbation, and homosexual contact with other inmates, including homosexual attacks on unwilling persons. Because of their incarceration, prisoners are forced to adapt to their situation. Thus, much prison homosexuality is *situational* rather than authentic or preferred. Some inmates may engage in homosexual activity for commercial reasons alone. By providing such services, these prisoners can obtain cigarettes, drugs, and extra food.

Racist-oriented power groups. Although racial subgroups are a problem in most prisons (Jackson 1970, 157–58), several new power groups are emerging within and outside of prisons in the western and southwestern United States. The participants include the Aryan Brotherhood, the Mexican Mafia, and a smaller group, the Black-Americans (*Associated Press* 1 January 1978). The Aryan Brotherhood is a racist group that whites control, while the Mexican Mafia is a group that Mexican-American prisoners dominate. The main fight for prison dominance seems to be between members of the Aryan Brotherhood and the Mexican Mafia, with the smaller group, the Black-Americans, staying in the background. Prison officials have

been fighting a losing battle to control these groups and to contain their violence.

Much violence in the prisons is never reported through the media, and some violence is never reported to prison officials. Oddly, the bulk of prison racial violence seems directed against members of the same racial group. This may be done to keep members in line and to maintain the power structure of each group. For example, Bruno Chavez tired of being a member of the Mexican Mafia in Los Angeles and wanted to get out. This was a fatal mistake; members of his own power group reportedly stabbed him twelve times (*Associated Press* 1 January 1978). Law officials investigating the case said, "It's a blood in, blood out organization. . . . You've got to spill someone's blood to get in. They spill yours if you try to get out" (Associated Press, 1 January 1978).

Juvenile Detention

Prisons for young people are called reformatories, detention centers, and juvenile halls, but they are all prisons nonetheless. They function much like adult prisons in that they "hold" people for the legal process; however, they differ in that rehabilitation is a stated objective of juvenile detention.

Legal reference to a *child* or *juvenile* means a person under the age of eighteen years. In Arizona, for example, an individual must file in writing any complaint of delinquent conduct, and that person must sign the complaint. The complaint is then referred to the juvenile probation officer that the court in question assigns. The probation officer records the complaint and investigates the facts to see whether they warrant bringing the young person into the court's jurisdiction. If a youth acknowledges his or her responsibility for the delinquent act, and the probation officer says that court action is not necessary, the youth may be referred to other agencies or to the parents or guardians.

A child may be detained only if reasonable grounds indicate (1) that otherwise he or she will not be present at any hearing, (2) that he or she is likely to commit an offense injurious to himself or herself or others, (3) that he or she must be held for another jurisdiction, or (4) that the interests of the young person or the public require custodial protection. No youth is to be held in detention for more than twenty-four hours unless a petition alleging his or her delinquent conduct has been filed *and* unless the court orders detention after the hearing. Once the youth is detained, however, he or she is already a part of the criminalization process. That is, the juvenile court has already negatively labeled the youth. Following a finding of delinquency, the young person is subject to the orders of the court regarding either probation or criminal prosecution.

Young people can go to jail or detention for offenses that would not convict adults—for instance, truancy and incorrigibility. They may even be detained because of parental abuse or being a witness to a crime. Hence, juvenile detention facilities sometimes serve as dumping grounds for many poor and troubled children. Many of these young people should be placed in other types of institutions. Counties without local jails or special juvenile detention facilities, however, continue to send some children to adult penal institutions for temporary custody. Goochland County, Virginia, for example, has sent its juvenile detainees to a maximum security cellblock within the Virginia State Farm, an institution for adult prisoners (Goldfarb 1975, 289). Further, a Law Enforcement Assistance Administration survey revealed that on a given day, 7,800 juveniles were being held in 4,000 adult jails (Goldfarb 1975, 291).

ALTERNATIVE POLICIES FOR RESOLVING THE PROBLEM: HOPES FOR REHABILITATION

This section examines three alternative policy areas: (1) delinquency prevention and control, (2) crime prevention and control,

and (3) revisions in the criminal justice system.

Delinquency Prevention and Control

Most delinquents abandon their criminal behavior after they leave adolescence. About 78 percent of all youths eventually stop their delinquent behavior despite whatever punishment, treatment, or controls American society exercises over them (McCord, McCord, and Zola 1959, 157–60). These "spontaneous" reformations are not totally accidental. Certain factors in a delinquent's early home background play an important part in his or her reformation. For example, delinquents raised by loving mothers who have been undisciplined and reared in neighborhoods with relatively low crime rates, and who had noncriminal fathers are most likely to reform in adulthood. In other words, despite their delinquent records, such children grow up in emotionally warm, noncriminal environments.

For those already on the road to delinquency, however, Rahway State Prison in New Jersey has started a program called Juvenile Awareness, Project Help, which involves the use of prisoners to counsel delinquents. The Oscar-winning documentary "Scared Straight" is based on this program. The prisoners meet several times a week with fourteen- to sixteen-year-olds who have had problems with the law. The inmates describe humiliations, dangers, and the unhappy and dangerous life in prisons, and a corrections officer takes the youths on a tour of the prison, including the solitary confinement cells. Essentially, the goal of the program is to "scare" the youths into "going straight." Prison analysts have labeled the "Scared Straight" documentary "deceptive," arguing that thirteen of the seventeen juveniles in the film came from an upper-middle class suburb outside New York City (*United Press International* 30 April 1979). In spite of recent criticisms, statistics indicate the effectiveness of the Rahway Juvenile Awareness Program. Out of the first 300 juveniles who had attended the program, only 4 were arrested on new charges (Gaylin 1977, 102).

Other delinquency prevention programs include Youth Service, Inc., the Boys' Clubs of America, Big Brother and Big Sister programs, and a project out of Tucson, Arizona called VisionQuest. Youth Service, Inc., is a child welfare agency that houses, all over the United States, children with serious problems who need a place to live. The Boys' Club works with all boys—not just those who are troubled. The Boys' Club tries to prevent boys from becoming negatively labeled as social outcasts. Its special areas of support include tutoring and reading programs, counseling, physical education, outdoor experiences, "rap" sessions, and citizenship projects such as the Big Brother program, which encourages older men to help boys who lack parental guidance.

VisionQuest tries to help juveniles whom state agencies, courts, and foster homes have failed to reach (*Arizona Republic* 10 January 1983). The program involves such events as 700-mile covered wagon trips through the Southwest, and living in tepees. The idea is to reform delinquent boys and girls by getting them off the streets and into the wilderness. This program is said to be successful with seven or eight out of every ten teenagers (*Arizona Republic* 22 March, 1979).

At a time when juveniles are responsible for much of the serious crime in this country, the legal system's neglect of the troubled child could have very serious consequences. Fortunately, one sociologist has found that as police officers mature, they are less likely to prescribe severe sanctions for dealing with delinquents (Roper 1969, 88).

Adult Crime Prevention and Control

The American public appears in a punitive mood. One Gallup poll showed that 62 percent of Americans are in favor of the death penalty (*Time* 18 September 1978, 54).

Much of this vindictiveness relates to the 300 percent increase in the nation's crime rate over the past two decades, even though a part of this increase is due to more efficiency in reporting crimes (*Time* 18 September 1978, 54). Silent Witness and Crime Stop programs tend to make the public even more aware of crime. These projects involve descriptions of unsolved crime, broadcast on radio and television in the hope that citizens will come forward anonymously with information that might help solve the crime. Informants are paid as much as a thousand dollars for information that results in a conviction (*Arizona Republic* 11 December 1978).

Regarding capital punishment, sociologists and criminologists are fairly well convinced that no causal relationship exists between homicide rates and whether or not a state has retained the death penalty. These scholars question the idea of the death penalty as a deterrent to homicide. One method of testing the deterrent effect of the death pen-

Gas chamber at a California prison. Few executions have taken place in the United States since 1967, but some states are now reinstituting capital punishment.

alty is to compare murder rates in states that have abolished the death penalty with states that have retained it (Sutherland and Cressey 1960, 292). Sociologist Karl Schuessler did such a comparison and found that most states that have abolished the death penalty have slightly lower murder rates than adjoining states that have retained the death penalty. According to Sutherland and Cressey (1960, 293), "The significant difference is not between states which have the death penalty and those which do not, but between the different sections of the country, regardless of whether the states have or do not have the death penalty."

Another method of testing the deterrent value of the death penalty is by comparing, in the states that have abolished the death penalty, homicide rates before and after abolition of capital punishment. The general finding here is that states that abolish the death penalty have no unusual increase in homicide rates (Sutherland and Cressey 1960, 294–95). Still another study indicates that the largest murder rate increases tended to occur in states with a poor record of capturing and convicting killers (*Associated Press* 24 October 1977). Further, it is now apparent that "those states in which the actual use of capital punishment ceased during the 1960s experienced no greater increase in the murder rate than did the states that did not have capital punishment in the first place" (*Associated Press* 24 October 1977). States that still maintain capital punishment in the face of this quantity of evidence may be more interested in vindictiveness than in deterrence.

Few executions have taken place in the United States since 1967. Thus, a better test of the deterrent value of the death penalty might be a comparison of *premeditated* homicides (first-degree murder convictions), rather than spontaneous homicides, against states that do and do not have the death penalty. If capital punishment has any deterrent value at all, it might be reflected in lower rates of premeditated (planned) homicides for states that either have retained or have reinstated capital punishment.

Since capital punishment does not seem to work as a general deterrent to homicide, are other policy alternatives available for dealing with those who commit murder? One psychologist has suggested the construction of jail-hospital facilities, where doctors can study violent offenders to determine what makes them volatile (*Phoenix Gazette* 8 February 1978). If such studies were successful, prediction of violent crimes might be possible. In the interim, life imprisonment without chance for parole might serve as a more effective deterrent to homicide than capital punishment.

Alternatives to Prison

Those who have committed less serious adult and delinquent crimes could be sent to halfway houses (group homes) rather than to prisons. The halfway house retains offenders in a far less violent, residential community setting. This alternative is seldom used either with adult offenders or with delinquents (*Arizona Academy* 1975). The development of the halfway house is based on the logic that the motivation to stay away from crime is strongest at the moment of release from a correctional institution. Yet, recidivism relapse into criminal behavior is highest during the immediate postrelease period, possibly because society tends to reject former prison inmates. Inmates need a gradual reentry into the community. Some writers describe the halfway house as the "decompression chamber" of the correctional system.

John Ehrlichman, who went to prison for his role in the Watergate scandal, once said that prison agencies must begin to offer alternatives to jails because they serve as a "training ground" where convicts refine their criminal techniques (*Arizona Republic* 4 December 1982).

Other alternatives to prison exist for those adults and children who have committed less serious offenses. A new development is the use of improved diet for both delinquents and adult convicts (*United Press International* 18 October 1982). The discovery was recently made that 90 percent of criminals in custody have hypoglycemia—low blood sugar—because their previous diets contained junk foods, alcohol, and drugs. The major villain in the usual diet of criminals seems to be sugar, which is known to cause bizarre behavior in some individuals. Hence, Los Angeles County is trying to wean delinquents and adult convicts away from junk food and sugar and onto a more nutritious diet. The diet program has cost taxpayers nothing, but it is too early to tell if it is having positive effects. In a similar diet program with delinquents in Ohio, however, the behavior of these youths "changed strikingly" after they were switched to a high-protein diet in place of sweets and starches.

Revision of the Criminal Justice System

Revisions in the criminal justice system include policies to deal with such problems as plea bargaining, incompetent judges, excessive leniency and/or severity, indeterminate sentences, police corruption, and negative conditions in the prisons not already discussed.

Modern treatment in crime control is based on the theory that punishment should fit the offender and not the offense. This, plus overcrowded conditions in the prisons, leads to **plea bargaining,** which occurs when the offender pleads guilty to a lesser offense rather than standing trial on the original charge (National Commission on Criminal Justice Standards and Goals 1973). A code adopted in Arizona creates a lesser chance of this happening. The legislature in that state noted a 65 percent rate of repeated offenses and adopted a code that gives a mandatory minimum prison term for the repeat offender (*Arizona Republic* 7 March 1978). Under this law, no possibility of probation exists for the repeat offender, and the inmate is eligible for parole only after a time established by the state legislature.

Much needs to be done in the areas of police corruption and brutality as well. In Philadelphia, a local district attorney has created a special unit to prosecute police misconduct, and the police department has strengthened the civilian complaint procedure (*Time* 1 May 1978, 36). Earlier, the U.S. Civil Rights Commission held hearings on the Philadelphia police. From time to time, these and similar steps will have to be taken in other major cities. With respect to bribery, situations in which the police are exposed to easy bribes need to be eliminated or brought under control. Investigative units, either governmental or police directed, can help with this work.

Conditions in the prisons constitute a major problem area in the American justice system. There are numerous obstacles to solving the overcrowding problem in U.S. prisons. The most serious roadblock is that taxpayers may not approve the funds necessary for building new prisons. The public wants criminals in jail, but doesn't want to pay for new facilities.

Still another obstacle to immediately reducing prison overcrowding is the great length of time it takes to build modern prisons. Public works projects take a long time to complete. Meanwhile, local jails are becoming overcrowded, and judges are increasingly reluctant to grant probation and parole. Some prisoners are being put into educational programs in minimum security prisons and into work-release programs which means that inmates can commute back and forth between the prison and their work (*Arizona Republic* 24 October 1982). Reduction in unemployment would also reduce prison overcrowding. A U.S. Bureau of Prisons study indicates that when the rate of unemployment increases or decreases, prison population follows the same pattern, allowing for a 15-month time lag (Marshall 1976, 6). The immediate choice, however may be between building more prisons and letting some criminals go free.

Prison officials and guards are aware of homosexual behavior in prisons, which will continue as long as no outlets are available for heterosexual behavior. Some prisoners engage in homosexual relations because they are seeking meaningful human contact. On the outside, they may have been functioning heterosexually; inside, they turn to homosexuality as a means of validating masculine self-conceptions. This causes problems for prison personnel, such as sexual jealousy and violence among prisoners. A policy in which periodic home visits could be arranged might be a way to relieve this problem. Presently, the social structure of American prisons does not encourage such sexual outlets.

Prison power groups are a problem both to prison officials and to prisoners themselves. Knifings inside prisons are not a rare occurrence, and violence seems to be a way of life for many prisoners. Some attempt must be made to break the stranglehold that prison gangs have on other inmates. Isolating the leaders of the various power groups, controlling movement of different types of contraband, and possibly limiting the population size of the prisons are all policies that have been suggested.

Some have maintained that no person can endure the prison system in America and come out unchanged. Unfortunately, the rehabilitation system appears bankrupt, and many prisons are turning from a philosophy of reform to one of punishment.

SUMMARY

The FBI *Uniform Crime Reports* make it appear that the crime rate is soaring, although part of the reason may be that people are becoming increasingly aware of crime. Nonetheless, Americans are concerned about the changing quantity and quality of violent crime in the society. Unfortunately, delinquent gangs are involved in about half of the serious crime that occurs in the United States.

An examination of sociological theories of crime and delinquency indicates that criminologists have no adequate, single theory to explain the various types of deviant behav-

ior. Evidence can be gathered to support both anomie and value conflict theories of crime, and some validity seems to be in both perspectives. Sociological interest in middle-class delinquency is relatively new compared with "lower-blue-collar-class" gang delinquency. Considerable injustice exists in the American justice system, including police corruption and brutality, intolerable conditions in the prisons, unfair sentencing, and similar problems in the area of juvenile detention.

With respect to policy alternatives, some positive steps have been taken in the areas of delinquency prevention, crime prevention and control, and the criminal justice system. These steps include the affirmation of children's rights, housing delinquents separately from adult offenders, revisions within the court system, the use of halfway houses, and other alternatives to prison. The federal penal system is no longer stressing rehabilitation as its primary goal for prisons, however. The federal mood is one of longer, more punitive sentences and less probation and parole.

We suspect, however, that more prisons and more prisoners will not mean less crime and delinquency in American society. Simply caging people, who have not committed violent crimes, in penal institutions may not be the answer. Our present criminal justice system and police acting as vigilantes are not answers to the crime problem either, because they do not address the causes of crime. The causes of much serious crime and delinquency involve such problems as discrimination, lack of education and housing, and unemployment and inadequate medical care for many people in our society.

STUDY QUESTIONS

1. How do both the media and social scientists contribute to the public's concern about apparent increases in rates of crime and delinquency? Is this concern justified or not?

2. Contrast the positions of the moral relativist and the moral absolutist regarding deviant behavior in American Society.

3. Contrast the various categories of computer crime in society. Why is computer crime so difficult to detect?

4. Contrast Albert Cohen's explanation of gang delinquency with that of Walter B. Miller. Which theory is best supported by sociological research?

5. Discuss four major types of problems that tend to arise in American prisons.

6. What policies are recommended to cope with crime and delinquency in America? Which policies might be the most successful and why?

REFERENCES

Alexander, T. 1974. Waiting for the great computer rip-off. *Fortune* (July): 146.

Allen, H. F. 1975. *Corrections in America: An introduction*. Beverly Hills: Glencoe.

Arizona Academy. 1975. The problem of crime in Arizona—How do we solve it? Arizona State University.

Arizona Republic. 7 March 1978; 11 December 1978; 22 March 1979; 11 June 1979; 24 October 1982; 4 December 1982; 10 January 1983; 27 February 1983.

Associated Press. 24 October 1977; 1 January 1978; 14 September 1978; 18 March 1979.

Bassis, M. S., R. J. Gelles, and A. Levine. 1982. *Social problems*. New York: Harcourt, Brace.

Becker, H. 1966. *Social problems*. New York: Wiley.

Bequai, A. 1976. Computer crime: A growing and serious problem. *Police Law Quarterly* (October).

Chambliss, W. J. 1975. Toward a political economy of crime. *Theory and Society* 2 (2) (Summer).

Chicago Tribune. 15 March 1983.

Cohen, A. K. 1955. *Delinquent boys: The culture of the gang*. Glencoe, Ill.: Free Press.

———. 1978. Introduction: The study of crime, items for an agenda. In *Major social issues*, ed. J. M. Yinger and S. J. Cutler. New York: Free Press.

Cressey, D. R. 1969. Theft of the Nation: The structure and operations of organized crime in America. New York: Harper & Row/Colophon.

Dershowitz, A. 1978. Let the punishment fit the crime. In *Readings in sociology*. Guilford, Conn.: Dushkin.

Flanagan, J. J. 1975. Overcrowding in today's prisons. *American Journal of Correction* 37(6) (November-December).

Fogel, D. 1975. *We are the living proof*. Cincinnati: Anderson.

Gaylin, J. 1977. Two answers—tougher words. *Psychology Today* (May): 102.

Gideon v. Wainwright, 372 U.S. 335 (1963). For a full discussion of this case see Anthony Lewis, *Gideon's Trumpet* (New York: Vintage Books, 1966).

Goldfarb, R. 1975. *Jails*. Garden City, N.Y.: Anchor.

Gordon, R. L., J. Short, and D. S. Cartwright. 1963. Values and gang delinquency: A study of street corner groups. *American Journal of Sociology* 69 (September).

Jackson, G. 1970. *Soledad brother*. New York: Bantam.

Lofland, J. 1969. *Deviance and identity*. Englewood Cliffs, N.J.: Prentice-Hall.

Marshall, E. 1976. Population explosion. *New Republic* (5 June).

McCain, G., V. C. Cox, and P. B. Paulus. 1976. The relationship between illness complaints and degree of crowding in a prison environment. *Environment and Behavior* 8(2) 283–90.

McCord, W., J. McCord, and I. K. Zola. 1959. *Origins of crime*. New York: Columbia Univ. Press.

Merton, R. K. 1957. *Social theory and social structure*. Glencoe, Ill.: Free Press.

Miller, W. B. 1958. Lower class culture as a generating milieu of gang delinquency. *Journal of Social Issues* 14: 5–19.

Myerhoff, H. L., and B. G. Myerhoff. 1967. Field observation of middle class gangs. In *Middle class juvenile delinquency* ed. E. L. Vaz, 124. New York: Harper & Row.

National Commission on Criminal Justice Standards and Goals. 1973. *Report of the National Commission on Criminal Justice Standards and Goals*. Washington, D.C.: U.S. Government Printing Office.

Newsweek. 1983. A gangland hit in Chicago. (31 January).

Nycum, S. H. 1975. Computer abuses raise new legal problems. *American Bar Association Journal* 61: 444–48.

Pfuhl, E. H. 1977. Deviant behavior. In *Sociology and social issues*, 2nd ed., ed. R. A. Hardert et al., 267.

Pfuhl, E. H., and M. Zabezensky. 1972. The price of liberty: Bail practices in Phoenix justice courts. *Law and the Social Order* (3): 409.

Phoenix Gazette. 8 February 1978.

Richards, P., R. A. Berk, and B. Forster. 1979. *Crime and play: Delinquency in a middle class suburb*. Cambridge, Mass.: Ballinger.

Roper, B. S. 1969. Attitudes of police officers concerning causation and disposition of juvenile delinquents. Master's thesis, Arizona State University.

Scott, J. W., and E. L. Vaz. 1969. A perspective on middle class delinquency. In *Readings in juvenile delinquency*, ed. S. Cavan, 115–16. Philadelphia: Lippincott.

Shanley, F., J. Lefever, D. Welty, and R. E. Rice. 1969.

The aggressive middle class delinquent. In *Readings in juvenile delinquency,* ed. S. Cavan, 230–41. Philadelphia: Lippincott.

Sherman, L. W. 1974. *Police corruption: A sociological perspective.* Garden City, N.Y.: Anchor.

Short, J. 1965. Perceived opportunity: gang membership and delinquency. *American Sociological Review* 30: 56–57.

Snow, R. 1978. The golden fleece: Arizona land fraud. In *Crime at the top,* ed. J. M. Johnson and J. D. Douglas, 133–50. Philadelphia: Lippincott.

Sutherland, E. H., and D. R. Cressey. 1940. White-collar criminality. *American Sociological Review* 5(1) (February): 1–12.

———. 1966. *Principles of criminology.* Chicago: Lippincott.

———. 1974. *Principles of criminology.* 2d ed. Philadelphia: Lippincott.

Time. 1977. The nation (8 August).

———. 1977. Computer capers. (22 August).

———. 1978. The cop tamers. (1 May).

———. 1978. On crime and much harder punishment. (18 September).

United Press International. 7 October 1976; 25 December 1978; 30 April 1979; 30 August 1982; 18 October 1982.

U.S. Department of Justice. Federal Bureau of Investigation. 1981. Crime in the United States. *Uniform crime reports.* Washington, D.C.: U.S. Government Printing Office.

U.S. News and World Report. 1977. Crisis in the prisons: Not enough room for all the criminals. (28 November).

———. 1979. No more kid gloves for young hoodlums (5 March): 42.

———. 1982. Crime finally takes a pause. (19 April).

———. 1982. Ethically, "society expects more from a corporation." (6 September).

———. 1982. American justice: Abc's of how it really works. (1 November).

Washington Post. 16 January 1983.

Williams, G. III. 1974. How criminal is crime? *Science Digest* (July): 18–23.

Williams, V. L. 1974. *Convicts, codes and contraband: The prison life of men and women.* Cambridge, Mass.: Ballinger.

CHAPTER 9

Physical and Mental Health

CONTENTS

Now it's Medicare that may go bust

Just as Congress is moving to rescue Social Security pensions, new fears are surfacing over medicare, the government's health-insurance program for 30 million Americans.

The Congressional Budget Office sounded the alarm in late February. If no action is taken, the CBO said, Social Security's 41-billion-dollar health-insurance trust fund that pays hospital costs under medicare will become "exhausted" sometime in 1987. After that, the red ink would grow rapidly, reaching 73.8 billion in 1995.

"If you think we face serious deficit problems with Social Security," says Senator Bob Dole (R-Kans.), chairman of the Finance Committee, "you're in for a bigger surprise when you look down the road at medicare."

Already, the fund's balance is dropping fast. It stood at 8.3 billion dollars at 1982's end, down from 18.7 billion a year earlier. A major part of the sharp decline resulted from last year's transfer of 12.4 billion from medicare's trust fund to the old-age-and-survivors fund to assure timely payment of Social Security benefit checks.

Still, medicare is facing several basic financing problems.

Among them—

■ Skyrocketing health-care costs. In 1982, the health-care component of the consumer price index jumped 11 percent, almost triple the overall inflation rate. Hospital costs attributable to medicare beneficiaries are projected to rise at an average annual rate of 13.2 percent between now and 1995, according to the CBO, much faster than other prices.

■ Higher hospital-admission rates and changes in medical-care practices affecting the elderly. New medical procedures are continually entering the mainstream, and "many of them are expensive," says the CBO.

For instance, coronary-artery-bypass surgery, still in its experimental stages in 1970, "is now a common procedure," the CBO said. Medicare's reimbursements for hospital care alone could reach $20,000 per bypass patient this year, health experts estimate.

■ The population is living longer. The number of persons age 65 and over is expected to grow by 2 percent a year through 1995. This means more elderly people will be using medicare.

■ While outlays shoot ahead, income to the health trust fund, which comes from payroll taxes, is being eroded by the slow economy. Each 1 percent rise in the unemployment rate reduces the fund's income by about 1 billion dollars a year, say congressional economists.

So far, few changes are on the drawing board to alleviate medicare's problem. President Reagan's 1984 budget tries to clamp down on federal health-care spending. But one Reagan proposal, aimed at saving 2 billion dollars next year, is drawing heavy fire from the elderly. It would require medicare patients to foot more of the bill themselves.

While Congress debates Reagan's plan, the CBO notes that even "bolder measures" are necessary to keep medicare afloat. Increased competition between medical providers and tighter eligibility requirements are two ideas.

Other suggestions include raising payroll taxes and using general tax dollars from the Treasury. But those potential panaceas would face heavy opposition, pointing up the fact that easing the strains on medicare may be difficult.

Source: U.S. News & World Report, 7 March 1983, p. 87. © 1983 U.S. News & World Report, Inc.

DEFINING THE PROBLEM: HIGH COSTS AND INADEQUATE HEALTH CARE

Medicine, "the art of preventing, caring for, and assisting in the cure of disease and care of the insured" (Clayton 1981), has progressed a great deal during the twentieth century. Medical science has learned to alleviate suffering through new anesthetics, terminate severe illness by using modern drugs, prevent crippling with vaccines, and postpone untimely death through modern surgical and medicinal techniques (Rutstein 1976).

Even though the American health care system has many types of facilities and a variety of doctors with different treatment philosophies, problems are found throughout the system. During the past few decades, progressive depersonalization and intense striving for financial success have placed great stress on our haphazard system of medical care. Accelerating depersonalization and economic competition cannot continue indefinitely in the medical field. The term *medical care* implies personal attention and service for everyone, the loss of which would be detrimental to our society (Rutstein 1976). Because the continued existence and well-being of humankind is dependent upon the health care available to all of us, the availability of efficient, cost-effective, personalized, and quality medicine is crucially important.

Problems in the Health Care System

To plan and organize a better American health care system, we must identify the problems associated with the current medical system. In this chapter, we focus on societal problems and employ an economic conflict perspective.

The largest and most threatening problem is the high cost of medical care and its inaccessibility to some people. Organizations such as Blue Cross and Blue Shield, private insurance companies, the Social Security Administration, welfare departments, and federal and state governments finance and, in effect, control American medical facilities—hospitals, emergency centers, and health clinics (Rutstein 1976). New information, specialization, and highly technical advancements have increased medical costs immensely, so that they now threaten the structure of the average family's finances. The prospect of hospital admission not only causes people anxiety and fear but also threatens their financial survival (Rutstein 1976).

Since 1967, overall medical costs have more than tripled in America, and hospital daily rates have more than quintupled. Total health care expenditures in the United States have risen from $27 billion, or 5.3 percent of the gross national product in 1960, to $247 billion, or 9.4 percent of the gross national product in 1980 (*Business Week* 1982, 58). Thus, the health care industry has become the nation's third largest employer after civil service and retailing.

Further, a study conducted by the Institute of Medicine estimates that 100,000 of the nation's 980,000 hospital beds may be unnecessary (*U.S. News & World Report* June 1982, 81). Considering that each bed costs about $85,000 to construct (Illich 1976), a considerable amount of funds are being wasted.

Other problems with the present medical system include the overspecialization of doctors, overuse of diagnostic procedures, and the business-minded attitude of many doctors. A study done in the New England states (Wennberg and Gittelsohn 1982) found that in one community, *70 percent of the women had had a hysterectomy, while in a nearby community, only 25 percent of the women had had the same operation.* The populations were similar in their overall general health and economic status. The researchers concluded that "the amount and cost of hospital treatment in a community have more to do with the number of physicians there, their medical specialties and the procedures they prefer than with the health of the residents" (Wennberg and Gittelsohn 1982).

Additionally, the policies of hospital boards and administrators, regulatory agencies, and providers of medical insurance provide incentives for doctors to perform more extensive medical procedures than are sometimes necessary. Some insurance plans will not cover certain diagnostic tests but will cover extensive surgery. Therefore, instead of providing a thorough diagnostic examination, the physician will opt for exploratory surgery (Wennberg and Gittelsohn 1982).

Although advances in medical technology have helped many to live longer and more comfortable lives, some negative effects from modern technology have also occurred. The most recent generation of physicians and paramedics has been indoctrinated with the overriding importance of new technology (Koop, 1982, 35). This situation has produced doctors who use potent and sometimes dangerous methods without a proper understanding of the risks involved (Macy 1971). Consequently, the growth of a particular type of medical technology has given rise to a somewhat inhumane, uncaring (in the sense of involvement with the patient) type of medical care (Macy et al. 1971).

Additionally, the mechanization of hospitals has distributed responsibility for patients over a wider area. Patients no longer have personal, comforting care, and no single person has sole responsibility for the patient, which has proved detrimental to the patient's well-being (Macy et al. 1971).

Deinstitutionalizing the Mental Hospitals

The system's lack of responsibility for the average medical patient also extends into the area of mental health care. The case of Lawrence Steubig demonstrates our point. Steubig was arrested and charged with the theft of six candy bars. His case was never heard in court; instead, he was found incompetent to stand trial and was committed to a state mental hospital, where he spent the next thirty four years of his life (*United Press International*, 2 March 1980). Steubig was involuntarily committed to the institution and was never released because he was said to suffer delusions of grandeur and a psychiatrist diagnosed him as a paranoid schizophrenic. Similarly David Tom, a Chinese immigrant, was confined for over 30 years in a series of Illinois state mental hospitals, apparently because he couldn't speak English (*Associated Press*, 1 January 1984).

New drugs and advances in brain research have revolutionized psychiatry, yet mental patients are still abused in institutions and are abandoned on city streets. Due to Medicare, Medicaid, and federal legislation that says that harmless individuals can no longer be detained in mental hospitals, former mental patients now find themselves residing in boarding homes, cheap hotels, and other "halfway houses" such as private centers for alcoholics and the indigent and retarded. Owners of these centers often appear less interested in caring for their residents than they are in gaining control of their residents' Social Security and Medicare checks. Hence, the mental health profession is taking a second look at **deinstitutionalization**—the rapid discharge of patients from state mental institutions into surrounding communities without follow-up treatment. Over a ten-year period, the number of patients in public mental institutions dropped by more than 65 percent, from 427,709 in 1969 to 146,772 in 1978, and the trend continues as officials reduce hospitalization to save money (Trafford 1979, 49).

CONFRONTING THE PROBLEM: PUBLIC CONCERN FOR THE QUALITY OF HEALTHCARE

Physical Health Care

The misuse of advanced medical technology leads society to question, "Is modern medicine worth its price?" Since the medical system cannot afford to utilize all of the technology available, the system must be certain that choices from among the various methods and equipment are useful. Dr. Harvey V. Fineberg of the Harvard School of Public Health cautions, "The main problem with technology is that procedures and techniques are accepted and widely used without any studies to assess their effectiveness, safety and long-term impact" (*U.S. News & World Report* 15 September, 1980, 53).

The rising costs of technology have affected the entire nation. Average coronary bypass surgery costs $15,000, and with 100,000 procedures performed a year, the total annual cost is $1.5 billion. Many other costly technological advances in medicine have been made. Maintaining the life sup-

port system for a premature baby costs about $100,000, and kidney dialysis exacts $30,000 per year, per patient (*U.S. News & World Report* 15 September 1980, 54). Even the value of intensive care units (ICUs) within hospitals is being questioned. Some physicians say that the ICU may be overused and that many patients should not be there. In one study of ICU patients over a fifteen-month period, 49 percent needed monitoring during only the first sixteen hours of treatment (*U.S. News & World Report* 15 September 1980, 54).

The term **iatrogenic** means "induced by a physician." More commonly, **iatrogenesis** refers to an injury that a patient suffers as a result of a physician's intervention (Illich 1976). Because diagnostic tests and proce-

A deinstitutionalized mental patient sits for hours in Chicago's Uptown area. This once vital neighborhood has become a psychiatric slum for about 10,000 ex-patients. Psychiatrist Thomas Szasz is opposed to involuntary institutionalization of persons for "mental illness," but rapid deinstitutionalization of mental hospitals has its problems too.

dures involve a certain risk, the most common setting for iatrogenesis occurs in medical testing. A physician will order a test to gain knowledge, screen for disease, avoid missing something, or more commonly, as a precaution against a potential lawsuit (Preston 1982, 236).

In most hospitals, routine diagnostic tests such as laboratory tests and radiological (X-ray) procedures are money-makers (*U.S. News & World Report* 15 September 1980). Thus, the financial incentives are in the direction of overtesting, that is, unnecessary testing. A U.S. Senate subcommittee on health estimated that more than 30 percent of the 240 million x-ray procedures done in 1977 (at a cost of $6 billion) were unnecessary. Further, one cardiologist estimated that 90 percent of electrocardiograms benefited neither the patient nor the physician (Preston 1982, 236).

Excessive medical testing has proven harmful to many patients. In one study of patients who were treated with a needle, tube, or catheter, 14 percent had at least one complication due to the test. Also, in an analysis of biopsies, 32 percent of the persons tested showed no significant results from the biopsy, but developed further complications from the biopsy surgery (Preston 1982, 237).

Overdiagnosis, excessive surgery, and harm from therapy have increased the overall risk of health care and have, in effect, increased the overall cost of routine health care (Preston 1982, 238). The current physical health care system has many problems. If an alternate system is not developed soon, the future of American medicine and health may be grim.

Mental Health Care

Sometimes psychiatrists are their own severest critics. Thomas Szasz (1974b, 109–12), for instance, has long insisted that "mental illness" per se does not exist—only "normal problems of living" and faulty ways

of responding to others. E. Fuller Torrey, another radical[1] psychiatrist, concedes that schizophrenia may be a brain disease, but also argues that these diseases can be treated with only a handful of drugs that general practitioners or internists could administer (*Time* 2 April 1979, 74). R. D. Laing (1967, 100–30), a Scottish psychiatrist, thinks that schizophrenia exists but that, in many cases, it is only a different way of viewing reality.

Even traditional mental health workers are uncertain that they can tell the "sane" from the "insane." In one experiment, D. L. Rosenhan (1973, 250–58) and some assistants pretended to be hearing voices and had themselves hospitalized. Once admitted, the researchers behaved normally and told the staff that the symptoms had disappeared. Many of the real patients realized that the impostors were sane, partly because the researchers kept taking notes. The staff, however, did not detect their "normalcy," and the researchers were kept in the hospitals for periods ranging from seven to fifty two days. Rosenhan (1973) concluded: "any diagnostic process that lends itself so readily to massive errors of this sort cannot be a very reliable one."

Criticisms of the Medical Model of Diagnosing and Treating Mental Disorders

Szasz, Laing, and other radical psychiatrists have reacted against the **medical model** of psychiatry which says that mental or emotional problems are disorders and should be treated like *physical* ailments. They also argue against the impersonality of the mental health industry and against the misapplication of the medical model of health and illness to people who are personally troubled but may not be ill in a physical sense. For

---

1. As used here, the term *radical* means being anti- or unconventional rather than politically radical.

Szasz and Laing, the concepts *mental health* and *mental illness* are mostly subjective and lack either a rational foundation or an empirical (observable) justification. As Laing (1967, 104) says, imputing a hypothetical disease of unknown cause and undiscovered pathology to someone is wrong unless he or she can prove otherwise.

Szasz and Laing's argument against traditional psychiatry and its use of the medical model is based on the unique legal authority of the physician-psychiatrist in subordinating the patient to his or her will. This includes defining the patient's "problem" and forcing the patient to accept that definition to obtain release from the mental institution. Still, people are often committed to mental hospitals for failing to play appropriately their expected roles attached to status positions (e.g., wife or husband) that they occupy in the community. When this behavior surpasses eccentricity (merely being "odd"), others' lives are rendered unpredictable. For example, failure to successfully play one's role as a breadwinner may lead to commitment to a mental hospital.

Regardless of our traditional societal response to eccentric behavior, the problem of turning former mental patients loose on the streets remains, where some cannot adjust to social expectations. Neither mental hospitals nor boarding homes appear the ideal answer. Dr. Eugene Feigelson (*U.S. News & World Report* 19 November 1979, 49), chief of psychiatry at Brooklyn's Downstate Medical Center, says:

The time has come to reconsider the notion of humane institutionalization—not necessarily in hospitals but in special residential facilities in the community for those patients for whom the prospect of independent living is a fantasy.

One way to gauge societal reaction to any social problem is to consider what the media report about that problem area. Television and newspapers present exposés about abuse and neglect of patients in state mental hospitals. Those who have worked in the wards of public mental hospitals tend to confirm these stories (Smith 1978). Mental health workers report that both staff and fellow patients sometimes beat and sexually abuse patients. Staff members sometimes bribe patients in various ways for sexual favors and to enhance discipline over other patients. Patients are also threatened with such devices as wet towels or a bar of soap inside two socks, which can be used to "persuade" them without leaving cuts or lasting marks. Other magazine and newspaper articles (*Phoenix Gazette* 5 February 1980) tell us that patients who are released from mental hospitals are "ignored and forgotten by a system unable to cope with their needs."

Another type of public reaction to mental disorder is depicted in such classic films as *David and Lisa*, in which bystanders make derogatory remarks about mental patients while they are waiting at a train station. Some of the patients, who are on an outing from a private hospital, shout back at their accusers to show their sensitivity to being referred to as "crazy."

An example of societal callousness toward mental disorder is depicted in *A Woman Under the Influence*, a highly regarded film about a housewife's eccentricities. In this film, the woman's husband and his family fail to understand the reasons for her non-normative behavior. The family's insensitivity reinforces the wife's tendency to react to the monotony of everyday life in unpredictable and non-normative ways.

Ken Kesey's novel *One Flew Over the Cuckoo's Nest* is another classic statement on the mental hospital as a **total institution**—any organization that has complete control over the individual. "Big Nurse" (Nurse Ratched) symbolizes the bureaucratic impersonality and rigidity of the total institution. The hero-patient, McMurphy attempts to "humanize" Big Nurse, and undermine the system by turning patients against staff.

When Sigmund Freud founded psychoanalysis, he did not suspect that he was setting in motion a chain of events that would result in the construction of a huge, self-regulating, self-perpetuating mental health industry—an industry created, regulated, and run often for the benefit of those who control it. In the words of psychiatrist Ronald Leifer (1969), "Psychiatric thought tends to express, justify, and advance the purposes and programs of organized psychiatry." Psychiatric thought and activity do not necessarily concern themselves with the needs of those who seek psychiatric help. Many troubled individuals have found relief in "therapeutic" encounters of all kinds, both individually and in groups, but the owners and managers of the mental health industry have also inflicted incalculable misery and anguish on many trusting, powerless individuals.

Psychotherapists who create categories of mental illness may help other mental health workers identify the bases for patients' symptoms or complaints. Psychotherapists however, also engage in a negative labeling process when they invent medical model terminology and apply it to troubled patients. Visiting a psychotherapist's office is not necessarily a sign of sickness; it may be exactly the opposite. Acknowledging internal or external difficulties and seeking help to alleviate them are signs of strength—even courage—and represent highly intelligent behavior, not necessarily mental illness.

ANALYZING THE PROBLEM: WHAT SOCIAL SCIENTISTS SAY ABOUT HEALTH CARE

Physical Health Care

Americans take for granted that every person is entitled to the benefits of any scientific discovery, professional skill, and institutional resource that can promote health, treat disease or disability, or prevent untimely death.

Unfortunately, the cost of medical care cannot be expanded indefinitely; an upper limit to health care costs must be established. Reaching this upper limit will cause the establishment of new priorities in medicine, and federal entitlement programs such as Medicare and Medicaid may not exist in the future. Change has already taken place with the development of organ transplants. Currently, ability to pay is the sole determining factor in establishing who is eligible for organ transplant surgery (Rutstein 1976).

Two major factors influence changes in costs in the medical system. Medical technology, the first factor, improves the ability to maintain or restore health, thus improving human productivity and reducing further demands on the social system. Conversely, medical technology is often expensive and is not always dependable. For example, the acquisition and maintenance costs of some laboratory equipment may outweigh its ben-

efits of being faster and more accurate than the humans it replaces. A balance must be present in the trade-off between the costs of technology and its effectiveness (Donnabedian 1976).

The second factor that raises medical costs is a captured consumer (patient) market. Simply stated, this means that the producers of medical care—chiefly pharmaceutical companies and physicians—can raise prices, and the consumer is forced to pay higher fees because of a lack of alternative means to good health (Donnabedian 1976).

The rising demand for health care has affected the market for hospitals, which are supposed to be nonprofit. To run a hospital, administrators must balance three major concerns: (1) a perceived standard of quality, below which medical care should not be permitted to fall, (2) the hospital's ability to respond to the demand for care, and (3) the need to survive financially (Donnabedian 1976).

Currently, operating the level of hospital occupancy at a maximum is the easiest way to balance these concerns. Thus, hospitals that are struggling to balance their budgets are crowded, creating dangerous problems such as the inability to maintain an adequate nursing staff with limited budgets (Macy et al. 1971). Keeping patients longer than necessary and admitting patients unnecessarily is common practice to keep the hospitals full (Donnabedian 1976).

Another reason for today's staggering medical prices is the government's inefficient and wasteful health care spending. In 1981, the United States government spent $80 billion on health care. Two substantial parts of the government's budget, Medicare ($39.1 billion) and Medicaid ($16.9 billion), are considered entitlement programs, available only to eligible people (Ehrenreich 1982, 587).

Further, one of the largest "entitlements," often overlooked when calculating governmental health care spending, is general tax benefits. Individual taxpayers can deduct

medical expenses and charitable contributions to health agencies from their taxable incomes. Individuals also do not have to pay taxes on health premiums, and nonprofit hospitals are exempt from a variety of taxes. In 1981, the sum of these tax exemptions was $23 billion. In effect, *current entitlement programs provide billions of dollars to persons who are not in true need*" (Ehrenreich 1982, 586).

Hospitals and doctors are not the only ones who profit from the vast expenditures that governmental entitlements and health insurance payments provide. Drug companies and medical, electronic, and health equipment suppliers also collect the available funds (Ehrenreich 1982, 588). Health care providers absorb an unnecessarily large part of federal spending for health care. The federal government has made considerable effort to reduce wasteful government spending in other areas. Recent budget cuts, however, do little to reduce medical costs or improve health care.

Another reason for recent increases in medical costs is that hospitals tend to be inefficient and wasteful. Many hospitals do not buy standard items in bulk or shop for the lowest prices; they buy when items are needed and when it is convenient. For example, if bought wholesale, a bottle of 500 aspirin tablets can cost $.38; however, some hospitals are paying $2.66 or more for the same amount (*U.S. News & World Report* 21 April 1980, 81).

Mental Health Care

According to the American Psychiatric Association's publication *The Chronic Mental Patient*, approximately 1.5 million mentally disabled Americans are living in the community, and another 1.8 million are in mental hospitals or psychiatric nursing homes (Trafford 1979, 49). The majority are diagnosed as having schizophrenic psychosis, a condition that affects roughly 1 million of the 3 to 4 million Americans who are considered victims of severe mental disorder

(Trafford 1979, 49). **Psychoses,** in general, refer to any of a number of behavioral conditions characterized by patients' lack of contact with social reality and by deep psychological depression, that is, overwhelming sadness. **Schizophrenia,** as first described by Swiss psychiatrist Eugen Bleuler, is a type of psychosis characterized by a person's withdrawal from social interaction. Other types of psychoses are also characterized by depressed behavior, but not necessarily by withdrawal from others. How various types of psychoses have been characterized is discussed later in this chapter.

Other than the psychoses, two other major classifications of mental disorder exist. **Neuroses** refer to various types of compulsive behavior that appear characterized by "free-floating" or constant anxiety—a type of persistent anxiety that appears to have no observable basis. Conversely, "normal" anxiety can usually be related to some actual threat in the individual's environment (Horney 1950, 24–69). While the person characterized as psychotic is said to lack social contact with reality, the person behaving in neurotic ways is in contact with reality but doesn't enjoy it. Hence, the person suffering from a neurosis frequently does not have to be hospitalized, because he or she makes a marginal adjustment to society (see figure 9–1).

What are some examples of neurotic behavior? The various phobias are supposedly indicative of neurosis. Agoraphobia is the fear of being in public places. People who suffer from agoraphobia fear going out alone or traveling alone or both. In severe cases, they never leave the house (Klein 1980, 69). Agoraphobics experience a kind of anxiety expressed in panic attacks. The number of Americans suffering from various kinds of anxiety attacks is unknown, since few community surveys with follow-up psychiatric evaluations have been done that would give us an accurate idea of the prevalence of anxiety disorders (Klein 1980, 69).

Psychosomatic disorders, a third major category of mental disorder, are "impair-

ments in physiological functioning that result from the individual's emotional state" (Lauer 1978, 161). The more serious forms of psychosomatic disorders are thought to include hypertension and high blood pressure, migraine headaches, severe asthma, and certain types of colitis. The term *psychosomatic* implies a continuum of interactive causation, i.e., external (social) factors can cause physiological changes and vice versa.

Regarding cross-cultural prevalence, the three major types of mental disorder are reported as a problem in all societies. Most modern societies regard behavior such as talking to one's self, laughing at inappropriate times (such as at a funeral), regarding one's self as an animal, refusing to eat for long periods of time, and engaging in fits of violence as symptoms of insanity or mental illness.

What else is known about mental disorder from a sociological point of view? First, everyone sometimes reflects symptoms of mental disorder. Remembering this point is more useful than thinking rigidly of types of mentally ill people (i.e., psychotics, neurotics, and psychosomatics). Today, the staffs (doctors, nurses, ward attendants, and social workers) in most mental hospitals deal with patients in terms of their relative depression (mild to severe) rather than labeling patients as neurotic and psychotic. Standard diagnos-

FIGURE 9–1.   The Spectrum of Depression

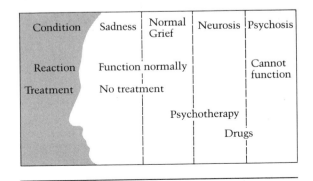

Data from *U.S. News & World Report,* 24 January 1983, p. 39.

tic categories, however, are applied to people when they are committed to the hospital and are defined as mental patients. Further, most people hospitalized for mental illness suffer from depression (sadness), although this is not true in every case, as in the patient characterized by manic (overactive) behavior.

A second point is that certain behaviors that formerly passed for neuroses or psychosomatic disorders are now being explained as chemical disorders. Some types of anxiety attacks and assorted bodily complaints are now attributed to such physical conditions as hypoglycemia or low blood sugar (Roberts 1967, 38–39) and postnatal depression due to mothers losing estrogen after childbirth.

Third, sociologists have found that mental disorder is more difficult to treat when depressed people come to enjoy the role of psychiatric patient and do not want to give up the status of that role to "get better." Psychiatrist Thomas Szasz (1974b, 100) states it this way: "For the mental patient's family and society, mental illness is a 'problem'; for the patient himself it is a 'solution.' This was Freud's great discovery. Psychoanalysts now ignore this, and psychiatrists deny it." Hence, getting some patients to give up their dependency on psychiatrists and/or mental hospitals can sometimes be a problem for the larger society.

Because the individual-oriented, psychoanalytic approach is inadequate to explain mental disorder on a social interactional level, we now focus on social scientists who have emphasized structural factors related to mental disorder. Gregory Bateson, R. D. Laing, Thomas Szasz, William Glasser, and Thomas Scheff represent a sociopsychological approach to mental disorder.

The Sociopsychological Approach to Mental Disorder

The sociopsychological approach to mental disorder is an alternative to the medical model and psychoanalysis. In this perspective, the focus is on learning factors, language patterns, and situational contexts, rather than on organic factors.

Social psychologists believe that some types of mental disorder relate to faulty communication patterns in families, inconsistent socialization, and depressing social situations that arise in daily life. The emphasis is on the broader social context of people's problems. To social psychologists, attributing mental or emotional problems or both to some hidden, internal condition such as the unconscious is another example of blaming the victim. Once a person is labeled or "tagged" in this way, it is very difficult to remove the stigmatization at some later point in time.

Psychiatrist Thomas Szasz, more than a number of others, seems to personify the basic themes of radical psychiatry. Simply expressed, Szasz (1974a, 37) views mental disorder as a defective strategy in living, not as a sickness for doctors and psychiatrists to cure. Problems diagnosed as mental illness (e.g., confusion, guilt, anxiety, alienation and some crimes) are problems encountered in living. They may be behavioral, social, or legal problems, Szasz maintains, but they are not diseases and should not be treated as diseases or discussed as such.

Szasz also attacks the practice of involuntary hospitalization of the mentally ill—a practice related to the problem of defining mental illness. If mental illness does not exist in the sense that it is conventionally used (i.e., a "sick" mind that medicine or therapy can cure), then no justification exists for confining or treating anyone involuntarily (against their will) for such problems. Szasz (1974b) states it this way:

Mental illness is a myth whose function is to disguise and thus render more palatable the bitter pill of moral conflicts in human relations. In asserting that there is no such thing as mental illness I do not deny that people have problems coping with life and each other. . . . Mental hospitals are the POW camps of our undeclared and unarticulated civil wars. . . . If a man says he is talking to God, we say he is praying. If he says God is talking to him, we say he is schizophrenic.

In other words, Szasz favors voluntary help, but is against false psychiatric definitions and coercive treatment. In his view, for example, rapists, child molesters, and murderers have broken the law and should be imprisoned in jails—not mental hospitals (although what advantage jails would have over mental hospitals is not clear). Szasz views the notion of temporary insanity as an excuse; hospitals should not be jails, nor doctors jailers. According to Szasz (1970, 113–39) no one should ever be incarcerated in any way unless a crime has been committed and the person is found guilty through the courts. Szasz thinks, however, that some

psychiatrists can help certain people who come to them voluntarily. People can change their attitudes and behavior not through the techniques associated with involuntary psychiatric treatment, but by help with clarifying life goals and patterns of personal conduct (*Cincinnati Horizons* 1975, 10).

Szasz's ideas have many critics, especially within the psychiatric establishment. For example, the most common question that students raise is, "What do you do in the case of a person who is a danger either to himself or herself or to others, but who also does not appear to be a criminal?" That question was asked of Professor Szasz (1980)

Once a person is labeled "mentally ill," it is difficult to remove the stigma. Instead of being sick, many such persons are simply troubled with life's problems. Even among psychiatrists, there is much confusion over the various meanings of the term mental illness.

at a public lecture. His response was that the question itself is evidence of the negative and pervasive influence of medical model terminology. According to Szasz (1980) the phrase *danger to himself or herself or others* constitutes a labeling of others "similar to the police state mentality that existed in Nazi Germany." Szasz's statement clearly shows that he is a passionate believer in individual rights and freedoms.

When asked if the medical model could be modified so that it could be used to help people, Szasz (1980) responded that "the 'medical model' means a host of different things to different people." People now employing the medical model sometimes misuse authority. "The idea of a pure, scientific, medical model that could do such things as locate the causes for schizophrenia" (Szasz 1980) would be a good aspect of the model. The political aspect of the medical model that is detached from individuals is a bad idea, however. For Szasz (1980), treatment then becomes "a kind of religion," which gives excessive power to some representatives of the medical care system.

Laing's "Politics of Experience"

Another sociopsychological view is found in the work of theorist and psychiatrist R. D. Laing. R. D. Laing (1967, 100–30) presents a different but equally radical critique of the medical model and of traditional psychiatry. He contends that the conventional concept of insanity ought to be rejected. Instead of a sickness, mental disorder may be an alternative and equally valid strategy for living, through which some people make the best possible adjustment to an unworkable life situation. Laing's inspiration for this unorthodox view of insanity is based partly on anthropologist Gregory Bateson's (1956) "double-bind" theory of schizophrenia. During research in New Guinea, Bateson discovered that the local people were caught in a no-win situation that was destroying their identity. This double-bind situation in-

volved the tribal people's desire to retain a cultural practice (transvestism or cross-dressing) that neutralized dangerous rivalries, while missionaries and the government objected to such practices. The local people were "damned if they did," and at the same time were "damned if they didn't."

Bateson later applied his double-bind hypothesis to families of diagnosed schizophrenics in an attempt to explain their disturbed patterns of communication. In four research settings in America, Bateson found (Laing 1967, 114) that all persons diagnosed as schizophrenic were part of a wider family network of extremely disturbed patterns of communication. This finding is matched in Laing's (1967, 114) research with persons diagnosed as schizophrenic. A situation of double-bind family communication that might encourage schizophrenia is one in which the child receives repeatedly conflicting signals from one or both parents. For instance, a jealous mother may describe women to her son in alternately positive and negative ways.

In over 100 cases in which Laing (1967, 114–15) "studied the actual circumstances related to the social event when one person comes to be regarded as schizophrenic," he found without exception that the behaviors, that are labeled schizophrenic constitute "a special strategy that a person invents in order to live in an unlivable situation." In this situation, the person comes to feel that he or she cannot act without suffering conflicting pressures and demands. If Laing (1967, 115) is correct, the social system and its inconsistencies, rather than single individuals within it, is the appropriate object of study.

In spite of the seemingly disturbed language patterns of schizophrenics, Laing contends that the language makes sense for the schizophrenic patient and within the social and family context where the disorder arises. He also thinks that the speech of schizophrenics has meaning for those who take the time to learn about the previous experiences of these patients and who will listen to them with an open mind (Robertson 1980, 351).

Regarding the possibility of organic factors underlying schizophrenia, Laing (1967, 104) writes:

Most but not all psychiatrists still think that people they call schizophrenic suffer from an inherited predisposition to act in predominantly incomprehensible ways, that some as yet undetermined genetic factor . . . transacts with a more or less ordinary environment to induce biochemical-endocrinological changes which in turn generate what we observe as the behavioral signs of a subtle underlying organic process.

Laing now thinks, however, that the ultimate causes of mental disorder may lie in the sociocultural context, not in brain chemistry. In other words, the emotional state of the individual (due to the social context) may influence brain chemistry, which may in turn influence behavior (*Granta* 1977, 4–8). This explanation is consistent with some recent findings in physiological psychology. David Rosenthal (1970) found that the offspring of two schizophrenic parents has about a 35 percent chance of becoming schizophrenic. Hence, the data that his method gathered seem to support the notion that a tendency for schizophrenia to develop can be transmitted genetically. Relatives of a schizophrenic offspring, however, share not only genes but also common social experiences. Further, a schizophrenic parent's behavior could be highly disturbing to a developing child. Thus, both social and biological factors may be involved in schizophrenia.

Other biological studies of schizophrenia lend indirect support to Laing's interactional explanation. John Neale and Gerald Davison (1978, 371) reviewed the major studies of schizophrenia in twins and found the following concordance (agreement) rates:

The concordance rates reported in the several studies of identical twins range with great variability from 0 to 86 percent. The rates of concordance for the fraternal twins range from 2 to 14 percent. Concordance for the identical twins

is generally greater than that for the fraternal, but it is always less than 100 percent. This is important, for if genetic transmission were the whole story of schizophrenia and one twin was schizophrenic, the other twin would be guaranteed a similar fate because MZ [monozygotic, or "one-egg"] twins are genetically identical.

Possible biochemical causes of schizophrenia have also been explored, but at present no biochemical theory has widespread support (Neale and Davison 1978, 375–76). This is true even though certain brain-altering drugs, such as the phenothiazines (e.g., Thorazine) have a tranquilizing effect on schizophrenics, and lithium carbonate has been effective in treating persons who suffer from manic-depressive symptoms (Neale and Davison 1978, 377, 559).

Glasser's "Reality Therapy"

William Glasser (1975) is also opposed to conventional psychiatry and argues for replacing it with what he terms "reality therapy." Like Szasz, Glasser (1975, 52–54) opposes the traditional concept of mental illness as sickness because it tends to relieve the patient of responsibility for his or her behavior. Instead, reality therapy encourages and helps the person with problems to act in mature, responsible ways. Ethical standards and discipline are important parts of Glasser's approach. Unlike most psychoanalysts, Glasser does not think it does much good to delve into a person's past or to try to examine unconscious conflicts. The past cannot be changed, and a patient cannot become involved with the therapist by excusing his or her behavior on the basis of unconscious motivations. A basic difference between reality therapy and most other approaches is that reality therapy contains a greater degree of interpersonal involvement between client and therapist.

Other requirements of reality therapy include encouraging patients to face reality honestly and to fill the need to love and be loved. The following conversation between

Glasser and a depressed patient demonstrates, in part, how reality therapy works:

Glasser: What are you doing about (your depression)?
Patient: Nothing, I just sit at home.
Glasser: Is this helping?
Patient: No, but I can't do anything else because I feel so bad.
Glasser: Well, if you won't cheer up and you won't do anything, it looks like you'll be depressed the rest of your life.
Patient: I didn't come here to hear that.
Glasser: Then let's take a look at your behavior and see where it can be changed (*Arizona Republic* 14 February 1979).

By avoiding the concept of mental illness and instead calling attention to the patient's past lack of responsibility, reality therapy defines the present situation much more precisely. It is perhaps easier to start by changing behavior than to change depressive feelings; and as behavior becomes more positive, the feelings improve (*Arizona Republic* 14 February 1979).

If a medical analogy applies to some interpersonal problems, it is not illness but ethical weakness (Glasser 1975, 56). Reality therapists challenge their patients to face social reality. Glasser admits that reality therapy does not always work, but his counseling is an effort to help clients make better, more adaptive plans for their future behavior.

ALTERNATIVE POLICIES FOR RESOLVING THE PROBLEM: BETTER PHYSICAL AND MENTAL HEALTH CARE

Physical Health Care Policy Alternatives

The earlier analysis of physical health care problems indicates that in order to deliver better medical care in the future, an alternate method to contain costs must first be developed. Prepayment for medical care provides assurance of necessary care for the patient and economic well-being for the health care providers. The major problem in developing any alternative payment system is devising a plan that allows the most advantages with the fewest drawbacks.

If doctors, hospitals, and nursing homes were required to provide medical services on a system of prospective reimbursement, health care costs could be reduced substantially. Government programs of Medicaid and Medicare could provide hospitals with a set amount of money at the beginning of the year and make hospitals stay within that budget (Walsh 1982).

By introducing competition into the American health care system, new incentives might reduce the present 18 percent yearly increase in medical care costs. The idea here is twofold. First, the concept rewards people for shopping around for cost-effective programs. Second, the system provides incentives for doctors and hospitals to save on costs (*Changing Times* 1982). Not only is the prepayment alternative feasible, but also many such plans are in effect today, and their results seem promising. Several of these programs are described next.

Health Maintenance Organizations (HMOs) provide competitive and comparative marketing incentives for potential patients. The plans operate on a prepaid principle with few or no deductibles. HMO plans also provide easily available services for patients and encourage early detection and treatment of minor ailments. Currently, any qualified company with twenty-five or more workers living near an HMO can use the HMO plan. While HMOs differ in how they are arranged and in how they deliver care and pay doctors, most of them are effective because the prepaid plan reduces unnecessary health care and ultimately saves money (*Changing Times* 1982, 61).

Individual Practice Associations (IPAs) provide the convenience of prepaid care without the patient having to change doctors. Basically, a premium income established at the beginning of each year pays the IPA physicians. The premium is usually a certain percentage below their standard fee. The IPA, then, is essentially a bookkeeping operation for doctors and patients. If medical care is not centralized, the IPA will contract a medical facility in which the doctor can provide care for patients who are on the IPA plan (*Changing Times* 1982, 61).

Preferred-provider organizations offer the same amount of coverage at roughly the same price as the HMO plan, with premiums approximately sixty dollars per month. While HMOs usually have their own doctors, and patients may have a two-hour wait for service, preferred-provider organizations allow patients to keep their own doctors and avoid the long wait for service.

Most prepaid health care programs eliminate deductibles and co-payments, offer increased benefits, have lower administrative costs, pay claims quickly, and deal with health care providers who offer much lower rates than nonparticipating providers (*Changing Times* 1982, 61).

Another medical policy alternative relates to national health care insurance. Estimates indicate that from 18 to 25 million Americans have no form of health insurance. According to 1980 statistics, private insurance paid 25.6 percent of the nation's total health care bill, federal and state government paid 38.8 percent, and individuals paid 32.4 percent (Koop 1982, 36). Further, most of the current insurance plans are "depression-era dinosaurs" and should be considered extinct (Straith 1982, 32). When a large percentage of patients are insured industrially or have expensive comprehensive coverage, some patients have little financial interest in either medical payments or premiums. Thus, patients and doctors have little motivation to assist in controlling costs (Straith 1982, 32). The second major step in controlling health care costs, then, would be to devise an alternate insurance plan that places some of the financial burden for containing medical costs on both the patient and the doctor, and one that is available to everyone—including indigents.

Because a large part of the federal health budget is spent on people over sixty-five, an important part of providing better medical care at lower costs is to develop more efficient care for the elderly. One plan, currently being used in both France and Germany, provides home-care programs and day-care centers for the elderly. This plan allows families to function normally while keeping their relatives at home (Walsh 1982, 67).

Another alternative to nursing homes, currently being used in the United States, is a medical team consisting of a physician and a nursing staff who regularly visit elderly patients. The team provides routine medical treatment, friendship, and help with patients' practical needs. Not only does this program save a considerable amount of money, but also it has proven beneficial to elderly patients.

Preventive Medicine

Modern medical science spends billions of dollars treating the *results* of disease and illness, and very little on the science of preventive medicine. Currently, millions of dollars are being spent each year on cardiological procedures. A large majority of the treated patients are overweight, heavy smokers, and mild to heavy drinkers. They are being treated for heart attacks, strokes, and hypertension. Since the perfection of open-heart surgery, thousands of Americans are opting for a dangerous, expensive operation a few years later instead of committing themselves to a more active exercise program and better overall health habits earlier in life.

In the face of health care costs that have increased astronomically, and because the risk of inadequate care has also risen, the need for less dependency on highly technical, expensive medical procedures seems clear.

Regionalizing Health Care Services

In devising future medical systems, regionalization of medical care services and avoidance of the present haphazard distribution of hospitals are important. Studying the distribution of a community's population while keeping geographic boundaries in mind could be helpful.

An estimation of the medical needs of the community or surrounding areas should be made before any medical center is constructed. This would avoid the wasteful duplication of specialist resources. Not all hospitals, for example, need an expensive, highly technical diagnostic instrument such as the CT (computerized tomography) scanner. Because these instruments are so expensive and require a large amount of maintenance, a number of medical centers can share them. Further, smaller communities do not need large multiroom hospitals with highly technical equipment. Small, primary, emergency care centers would be more than adequate in most cases.

To contain health care costs, keeping a precise inventory of medical resources is important. Not only would this procedure avoid wasteful stockpiling of resources, but also medical centers could assess their needs and order bulk items wholesale. Medical centers could also pool together when purchasing medical essentials.

America also has a great need to establish group practice, community medical centers. These group practice centers would have complete rosters of essential and ancillary medical personnel. The centers would provide modern yet cost-effective primary care, emergency services, general surgical needs, and most important, preventive holistic medicine. Instead of having a third-party insurance company reap a portion of the medical profits, however, the insurance plan could be established directly through the community medical center. Businesses, corporations, and individuals could set up local

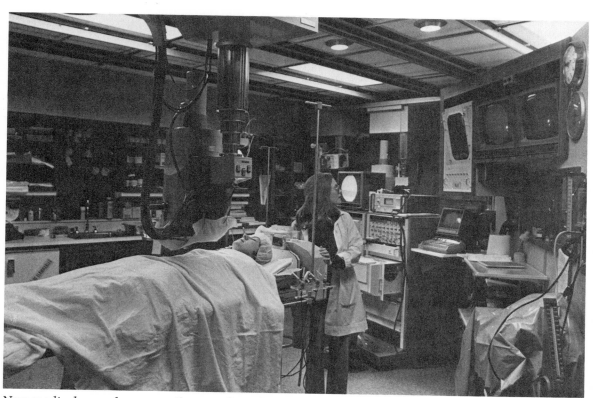

New medical procedures contribute to skyrocketing health-care costs. Some medical tests are unnecessary, and not all hospitals need highly technical diagnostic equipment.

health care plans for their specific needs. Government-funded programs such as Medicare, Medicaid, and Social Security could also establish prepaid medical plans for their older beneficiaries. Such centers not only could utilize profits to help maintain the level of quality care, but also funds could be available to voluntarily care for indigent people.

Mental Health Care Policy Alternatives

Psychiatrists Szasz, Laing, Glasser, and others all seem to favor new policy that would eliminate medical model mentality by not allowing people with interpersonal problems to be considered ill in the physical sense.

As Szasz has pointed out, what is termed mental illness is actually behavior that psychiatrists and other representatives of the system disapprove of. This labeling of people, or "stigmatization" as Erving Goffman (1961) calls it, becomes a value judgment in place of a true medical diagnosis. Moreover, labeling people "mentally ill" may contribute to their problems. This is the contention of Thomas Scheff (1966), who theorizes that mentally disordered people are social deviants of a special type. They have violated certain "residual" or taken-for-granted norms, such as the norm that indicates we should not laugh at inappropriate times. If the person continues the inappropriate behavior, he or she may come to be labeled "mentally ill." If the labeling of others' eccentricities by the so-called normal (conforming) public could be lessened, the creation of mental illness might be diminished greatly.

Another policy issue is Szasz's concern over the confusion between mental illness and behavior that violates the law. According to Szasz (1966, 11–82), if you break the rules or infringe on another person's rights, you should be jailed. No escape through such concepts as temporary insanity would be possible. If a crime is committed or a law broken, the violator would be punished according to the law. Presently, however, a psychiatrist may testify as an expert witness for the defense, as in the trial of John W. Hinckley, Jr., and swear that the accused is insane or was temporarily insane at the time of the crime.[2] Individuals can presently purchase any kind of expert psychiatric testimony they can afford.

Hinckley's shooting of Ronald Reagan, however, has sparked a recent drive to tighten the insanity plea. The American Psychiatric Association, for example, wants to reduce the role of psychiatrists at trials and toughen the release of those acquitted by reason of insanity (*U.S. News & World Report* 31 January 1983, 12).

Laing's (1967) complaints against the medical model are similar to those of Szasz. For Laing, the medical model permits the more powerful to control certain individuals under the guise of providing them with medical care. Explaining patients' protests as the madness of minds that do not recognize their own illnesses can then dismiss patients' objections to coercion. In mental hospitals, the chief administrator is usually a psychiatrist, and the medical degree he or she holds can serve to justify confinement, security, and surveillance as medical activities. If Laing and Szasz had their way, these policies would be changed immediately.

Glasser's (1975, 55) criticism of the medical model is based on the widely accepted concept of mental illness. This is the belief that "people can and do suffer from some specific, diagnosable, treatable mental illness, analogous to a specific, diagnosable, treatable physical illness." According to Glasser, this concept is inaccurate, and the inaccuracy is a major roadblock to proper psychiatric treatment. It misleads the doctor, patient, and those concerned with both of them into the false belief that the doctor's job is to treat some definite condition,

2. The M'Naghten decision, which says people are fit to stand trial only if they understand the charges against them, the nature of the proceedings, and can assist counsel in their defense, makes this type of psychiatric excuse possible.

after which the patient will get well. This by no means suggests that psychotherapists are evil or inhumane. Rather, it suggests the opposite—they are human and therefore subject to making errors that can compound human misery and anguish. Some psychiatrists are beginning to perceive the vast and intricate mythology of their profession, while most still cling to the mantle of authority with which their profession has been vested.

In spite of the growing criticism of medical model policy, its advocates continue to practice according to its terms. This may be due to the belief among those in power that people with mental and emotional problems are truly sick, in that their unconventional behavior is thought to have an underlying physical cause. If this is eventually shown to be true, then holding mentally (physically) ill persons responsible for their behavior will be even more difficult.

Community Mental Health Programs

The last major policy area relates to suggestions for reforming institutional care of the mentally disordered. What new policies are being tried? First, a move to get deinstitutionalized mental patients into multiservice community programs is in progress. Reportedly, these community mental health programs would cost no more (about $27,000 a year per patient) than state hospitals, and the level of care would be much better (*U.S. News & World Report* 28 May 1979, 67). Currently, about two-thirds of all mental patients are living in their respective communities without adequate care. Only about half of these patients continue to take medication after being discharged from mental institutions, and fewer than one-fourth are involved in formal outpatient programs. Legislation is needed to ensure that the chronically ill no longer face either unnecessary institutionalization or inadequate care in the community.

Also needed in this area is legislation that will clearly designate who is responsible for the aftercare of mental patients. Meanwhile, services need to be provided that will prevent or delay the total institutionalization of mentally disordered people. This would ensure that state mental hospitals do not contain anyone who does not require constant care within an institution. If funds were available, hospitals could also provide outpatient and aftercare services to the mentally disordered (*Phoenix Gazette* 14 February 1979).

Both inpatient and outpatient treatment are directed toward building the patient's confidence. Inpatient therapy, at a public mental hospital, assumes that the patient came from a troubled environment and that he or she needs a more rational, stable atmosphere. Outpatient therapy assumes that the patient needs to be kept within his or her home situation. Here, the patient learns to cope with his or her normal environment as it is; and the patient does not undergo the trauma associated with leaving familiar surroundings (Peszke 1975, 125–32). Inpatient treatment implies that the patient cannot cope with his or her old environment and needs the more relaxed and sheltered atmosphere of the psychiatric hospital (Gralnick 1975). While the medical model perspective still dominates most inpatient facilities, a gradual shift to the sociopsychological approach in the diagnosis and treatment of mental patients apparently has already been made.

The value of the hospital community itself, as a therapeutic force beyond individual psychotherapy, is another vehicle for change in the treatment of mental disorder (Jones 1953). Patient groups in a psychiatric ward exert a therapeutic influence on some patients whether or not the hospital fosters the development of such relationships. Nurses, attendants, and other personnel aid in the rehabilitation of patients whether or not they receive encouragement and direction from the medical staff (MacDonald and Daniels 1956, 148). Ward physicians may or may not extend their participation beyond the privacy of the therapy hour. Adequate development of the therapeutic community influence of both patients and staff requires continued effort by the senior medical staff and nursing personnel.

In *Humanizing the Psychiatric Hospital*, Alexander Gralnick (1975) suggests a firm yet flexible approach based on the patients acknowledging the importance of staff in the treatment of their illnesses. He encourages the use of group therapy to get patients to relate better to their problems. The objective of group therapy is to help patients explain and articulate their problems more openly. By using the therapeutic community in the inpatient situation, the hope is that the controlled environment will enhance the value of the therapy. The combination of group therapy, psychoanalysis, and controlled contacts with the patient means this treatment is essentially continuous. Thus, developing a therapeutic community on a psychiatric ward is not easy to accomplish.

An important hybrid concept in patient treatment policy is that of the work village (Koegler and Brill 1967). While a work village at first appears as inpatient therapy, a closer look shows a combination of inpatient and outpatient types of treatment. Although the patient is confined in barrackslike housing, he or she is afforded more responsibility and freedom than would be found in a conventional inpatient hospital. The major premise of the work village is that through work and acquisition of marketable skills, the mentally disturbed individual may become more community oriented and less antisocial.

Although Hollingshead and Redlich's (1958) study of social class and mental illness is now more than twenty five years old, we still discover that middle-class people are treated with "talking" therapy and lower-class people with shock treatments. Hispanics sometimes use Brujas and medicas (healers) and other traditional approaches to treat their problems, while native Americans use the sweatlodge to purify their minds and bodies to regain harmony with nature.

Similarly, modern psychiatric centers seem to have developed multiple treatment strategies. These diverse strategies range from full-time inpatient care to weekend-only outpatient care in community mental health centers. The assumption is that total institutionalization is more negative than the mental disorder itself. Rather than the medical model's attempt to cure the patient, the newer idea is to get the person operating in a social context as much like the external world as possible. Day or night care and the use of halfway houses are favored over twenty-four-hour care. The patient is expected to return for treatment but for increasingly shorter time periods, after which he or she can be turned over to community programs.

SUMMARY

This chapter has dealt with defining, confronting, analyzing, and suggesting alternative policies for our physical and mental health care problems. Although it will take the combined effort and sacrifice of both the providers and the consumers of medical care, providing cost-efficient, personalized, quality health care is possible for our medical care system. In spite of the high costs mentioned earlier, some Americans are still getting quality medical care. Health care costs, however, are being shifted to those patients who can pay. Thus, as Medicare and Medicaid payments decrease, insurance premiums must increase to compensate for the loss. One of the wealthiest countries in the world, the United States, ought to be able to supply quality physical and mental health care to all of its citizens.

Specifically, this chapter presented such mental health topics as the difficulty of defining mental illness, especially the concept of schizophrenia; deinstitutionalization of patients from mental hospitals; the relationship of psychoanalysis to the development of the medical model of treatment; Szasz, Laing, and Glasser's attacks on the medical model and traditional psychiatry; the sociopsychological approach to mental disorder; and reforming institutional care of the mentally disordered through increased community involvement.

Mental disorder is a highly complex and controversial social problems area. Until psychiatrists, medical doctors, and social scientists can agree on what the various forms of mental disorder are and their exact causes, offering reliable, safe, and just policies for helping those now labeled "mentally ill" will be difficult.

As promising as Glasser's reality therapy may sound, it too has weaknesses. The approach may work well for disorders related to faulty learning and the inability to get along with others. For organic problems, however, in which the disorder can be treated only by removing the underlying physical cause, reality therapy is inapplicable. In criticizing the medical model and conventional psychiatry, keeping in mind the distinction between disorders that have a physical basis and those that have a social basis is necessary. Those whose problems arise from interpersonal or social-situational factors may have the capacity to change their behavior through appropriate counseling and the support of significant others. Asking people who may suffer from underlying biological deficiencies to face social reality, however, as Szasz and Glasser appear to advocate, is not realistic. If the more serious forms of mental disorder are found to have predominantly organic causes, then psychiatric treatment may be of little help. In the long run, no single policy can be advanced to confront the many aspects of the problem of mental disorder.

STUDY QUESTIONS

1. What is the medical model approach to mental and emotional disorder, and why are some social scientists currently attacking it?

2. What is the sociopsychological approach to mental disorder, and how does it differ from the medical model approach of many conventional psychiatrists?

3. Write a brief essay in which you contrast the major ideas of Thomas Szasz with those of R. D. Laing on the issue of involuntary commitment of people to mental hospitals.

4. How do conflict and interactionist theories help us to understand problems in the areas of physical and mental health care?

5. What two factors are mainly responsible for the rise in costs of American physical health care? What policies might help alleviate the influence of these two factors?

6. What is meant by deinstitutionalization of public mental hospitals, and how has it created problems for former patients and for the larger society?

REFERENCES

Arizona Republic. 14 February 1979.

Associated Press. 1 January 1984.

Bateson, G., D. Jackson, J. Haley and J. Weakland, 1956. Toward a theory of schizophrenia. *Behavioral Science* 1(4) (October).

Business Week. 1982. The spiraling costs of health care. (February): 58–64.

Changing Times. 1982. Big changes ahead in how we buy health care. (March): 60–63.

Cincinnati Horizons. 1975. Szasz—Psychology's prolific polemicist. *Cincinnati Horizons* 4(4) (March): 10.

Clayton, T. L. 1981. *Taber's Cyclopedic Medical Dictionary.* Philadelphia: F. A. Davis.

Donnabedian, A. 1976. *Benefits in medical care programs.* Cambridge: Harvard Univ. Press.

Ehrenreich, J. 1982. Where the health dollar really goes. *The Nation* (15 May): 586–88.

Glasser, W. 1975. *Reality therapy.* New York: Harper & Row.

Goffman, E. 1961. *Asylums.* Garden City, N.Y.: Anchor.

Gralnick, A. 1975. *Humanizing the psychiatric hospital.* New York: Jason Aronson.

Granta. 1977. R. D. Laing interview by Ian Robertson. Cambridge University (October).

Hollingshead, A. B., and F. C. Redlich. *Social class and mental illness: A community study.* New York: Wiley.

Horney, K. 1950. *Neurosis and human growth.* New York: W. W. Norton.

Illich, I. 1976. *Medical nemesis.* New York: Pantheon.

Jones, M., A. Baker, T. Freeman, J. Merry, B. A. Pomryn, J. Sandler, and J. Tuxford, 1953. *The therapeutic community.* New York: Basic.

Klein, D. F. 1980. When panic strikes: Helping anxiety victims. *U.S. News & World Report* (2 June).

Koegler, R., and N. Brill. 1967. *Treatment of psychiatric outpatients.* New York: Meredith.

Koop, C. E. 1982. Why you're healthier and paying more for it. *U.S. News & World Report* (June): 35–37.

Laing, R. D. 1967. *The politics of experience.* New York: Ballantine.

Lauer, R. H. 1978. *Social problems and the quality of life.* Dubuque, Iowa: Wm. C. Brown.

Leifer, R. 1969. *In the name of mental health.* New York: Science House.

MacDonald, J. M., and M. L. Daniels. 1956. The psychiatric ward as a therapeutic community. *Journal of Nervous and Mental Disease* 124(2) (August): 148ff.

Macy, J., 1971. *Medical history and medical care.* London: Oxford University.

Neale, J. M., and G. C. Davison. 1978. *Abnormal psychology.* New York: Wiley.

Peszke, M. A. 1975. *Involuntary treatment of the mentally ill.* Springfield, Ill.: Charles C. Thomas.

Phoenix Gazette. 14 February 1979; 5 February 1980.

Preston, T. 1982. Warning: Doctors can be dangerous to your health. *Cosmopolitan* (October): 236–39.

Roberts, S. E. 1967. *Exhaustion: Causes and treatment.* Emmaus, Pa.: Rodale.

Robertson, I. 1980. *Social problems.* New York: Random House.

Rosenhan, D. L. 1973. On being sane in insane places. *Science* 179 (January 19): 250–58.

Rosenthal, D. 1970. *Genetic theory and abnormal behavior.* New York: McGraw-Hill.

Rutstein, D. D. 1976. *The coming revolution in medicine.* Cambridge: MIT Press.

Scheff, T. J. 1966. *Being mentally ill: A sociological theory.* Chicago: Aldine.

Smith, R. 1978. My experiences working at a state hospital. Unpublished paper. Arizona State University.

Straith, R. E. 1982. How to reduce medical and insurance costs. *Consumer Research Magazine* (April): 32–34.

Szasz, T. 1966. *Psychiatric justice.* New York: Macmillan.

———. 1970. Involuntary mental hospitalization. In *Ideology and insanity,* ed. Szasz, 113–39. Garden City, N.Y.: Anchor.

———. 1974a. *The myth of mental illness.* New York: Harper & Row.

———. 1974b. *The second sin.* Garden City, N.Y.: Anchor.

———. 1980. Mental health: Behavioral science or behavioral control? Paper presented at Arizona State University.

Time. 1979. Psychiatry on the couch. (2 April).

Trafford, A. 1979. Mental patients: A "forgotten minority" in the U.S. *U.S. News & World Report.* (19 November): 49.

United Press International. 2 March 1980.

U.S. News & World Report. Latest in health. 1979. (28 May).

———. 1979. Mental patients: A forgotten minority in U.S. 19 November.

———. 1980. Cost of hospital care in U.S.—Opposing views on major issues. (21 April).

———. 1980. Is modern medicine worth its price (15 September): 53–54.

———. 1982. New health hazard: Being out of work. 14 June.

———. 1983. Tomorrow. 31 January.

Walsh, W. B. 1982. Why cost of health care won't stop rising. *U.S. News & World Report* (8 March): 67–68.

Wennberg, J., and A. Gittelsohn. 1982. Variations in medical care among small areas. *Scientific American* 246 (April): 120–26.

CHAPTER 10

Racial and Ethnic Relations

CONTENTS

Miami already was "loaded gun" before McDuffie case pulled trigger

By George Esper

Death and destruction kept an appointment in Miami, an apocalypse of racial wrath that simmered for a dozen years, then exploded into the streets.

The trigger was the verdict a week ago by an all-white, middle class jury in Tampa, 250 miles away, that freed four white former police officers charged in the Miami beating death of a black insurance executive, Arthur Lee McDuffie, 33.

But the gun had been loaded ever since the big Miami riots of 1968 with grievances over a lack of job opportunities perceived as more than benign neglect, over justice they believed was unjust.

"People are waiting patiently, waiting to receive some benefit of their citizenship," said City Attorney George Knox, a black. "They had been waiting all this time. By virtue of the McDuffie verdict, people just spontaneously determined they could not take any more. The verdict was the most vivid expression of complete indifference."

The jury returned its decision at 2:36 p.m. Saturday, May 17, after deliberating for less than three hours.

"In God's eyes, they're guilty. God will take care of them," cried out the mother of the slain man.

Alex Marrero, 26, wept. Of the four former officers, he had faced the most serious charge—second degree murder.

"I knew God's justice would take care of my boy." Marrero's mother, Julia, sobbed. "He is innocent."

It was the beginning of the carnage.

Death ran a haphazard, maddening course. Whites, blacks, Latins, innocents—some whose lives took tragic twists when they unknowingly wandered into the battle zone—were among the 15 persons killed and nearly 400 injured.

Benny Higdon, 21; his brother-in-law, Robert Lee Owens, 15; and a friend, Chuck Brecker, 14, were returning from a fishing trip when blacks dragged them from their car and beat them to death.

Jeffrey Kulp, 22, and his brother, Michael, 18, both white, were returning home from the beach when a brick smashed through a window of their car. The vehicle skidded out of control and crushed a by-stander, 11-year-old Shanreka Perry.

Jeffrey Kulp was shot, paralyzed from the waist down with brain damage. His ears were sliced off and his tongue cut out.

"Even though some of the people in the neighborhood gave varying reasons to justify why the riots occurred, all the ones I talked to said that there was no excuse for the brutality in these cases," Sgt. Mike Gonzalez reported.

White shoot-and-run snipers firing from roving pickup trucks gunned down three blacks, Thomas Reese, 34; Eugene Brown, 38; and Andre Dawson, 14.

The riots were the worst in the history of the county.

Three black men were killed and more than a score of others injured during the riots of August 1968.

A study reported that police hostility toward blacks and black frustration over losing jobs to Cuban refugees in the 1960s were among the causes of the earlier rioting.

"Simmering frustration is putting it mildly," Knox said.

He said there is legitimate

criticism of the administration of justice for blacks.

No criminal charges were brought against a white officer who shot and killed an unarmed black youth.

In another case, he said, plea bargaining resulted in a sentence of probation and psychiatric evaluation for a white highway patrolman who admitted sexually molesting an 11-year-old black girl.

In a third case, he said, police drug agents who mixed up their addresses and mistakenly raided the home of a black schoolteacher weren't prosecuted.

But the most blatant miscarriage of justice, blacks said, was the McDuffie case.

McDuffie's life was one of ups and downs. His driver's license was suspended in 1975. He was cited at another time for driving with expired license plates.

Just before last Christmas, he and his former wife had decided to remarry. They were planning to spend Christmas with their two children.

But Christmas never came for McDuffie.

Shortly before midnight, December 17, McDuffie left a friend's home riding a borrowed motorcycle.

A police report filed by one of the defendants said McDuffie was traveling more than 100 mph trying to avoid arrest for running a stop sign.

The prosecution charged that the police officers clubbed McDuffie to death, then tried to cover it up by trying to make his injuries look accidental.

Three officers granted immunity from prosecution testified that as many as eight policemen circled McDuffie and reached over each other to pound him with night sticks and heavy flashlights.

They testified that Marrero smashed McDuffie three times on the head with his night stick, then, as McDuffie sat motionless, battered him three more times.

Marrero testified that he hit McDuffie, an ex-Marine and black-belt karate expert, in self-defense.

Janet Reno, Dade County State Attorney, came under criticism for the way the case was handled. She denied accusations that her office tilted justice.

David H. Fisher, who served as foreman of the jury, said the Public Safety Department bungled the investigation.

Source: Associated Press 25 May 1980.

DEFINING THE PROBLEM: DOMINANT AND MINORITY GROUP RELATIONS

Certain events so dramatize a problem that they spark widespread concern. The spring 1980 Miami race riot was one such event. To blacks and whites alike, the more than a dozen deaths, hundreds of injuries, and millions of dollars in property damage were reminiscent of the damaging racial rioting in the 1960s in such cities as Cleveland, Detroit, Los Angeles, Newark, and Philadelphia (National Advisory Commission on Civil Disorders 1968). The events in Miami highlighted that in American social life in the 1980s, racial conflict is still a smoldering problem that has not yet been resolved since the open confrontation days of the 1960s.

The intensity of our interracial problems

is not new. The issue has been developing for generations and captured the interest of sociologists. American society is so diverse racially, ethnically, and religiously that intergroup relations became a focus for early sociological research. Much of the history of intergroup relations has been a series of problems, from the days of slavery and exclusion of native Americans from their traditional lands to the restrictive immigration acts early in this century, aimed at keeping out Latin Americans, Orientals, and southern and eastern Europeans.

For many in America, the constitutional ideal of equal rights for every citizen has fallen short of attainment. Certain groups have been "more equal" than others—particularly white male Protestants, who have been the most influential group in this society (Baltzell 1964). Controversy and conflict

The racial rioting in Miami in the 1980s was reminiscent of similar rioting in many cities in the 1960s. Such rioting is symptomatic of some continuing intergroup strains within American society calling for conflict resolution.

have resulted, since no group is willing to accept second-class citizenship. In recent years, strong feelings have arisen among blacks, Hispanics, native Americans, women, and other groups about their unequal treatment and unequal opportunities. Of these groups, the national distribution of blacks, length and depth of minority experience, and prolonged research on the black American experience make a useful central focus on intergroup conflict. We also include references to other groups, however, who have long been excluded systematically from optimal opportunities and who make up part of America's culturally pluralistic society (see table 10–1).

TABLE 10–1. General Characteristics of Persons of Selected Ethnic and Racial Groups in the United States

ETHNIC GROUP	NUMBERS IN MILLIONS	PERCENTAGE
Total population	203.2	100.0
Female	103.9	51.1
Male	99.3	48.9
Native (born) of native parentage	169.6	83.5
White	146.2	71.9
Persons of foreign stock:		
Second generation in U.S.	24.0	11.8
First generation in U.S.	9.7	4.7
Second generation from:		
United Kingdom	1.8	.9
Canada	2.2	1.1
Ireland	1.2	.6
Germany	2.8	1.4
USSR	1.5	.7
Poland	1.8	.9
Italy	3.2	1.6
Mexico	1.6	.8
First generation from:		
United Kingdom	.7	.3
Canada	.8	.4
Ireland	.3	.1
Company	.8	.4
USSR	.5	.2
Poland	.5	.2
Italy	1.0	.5
Mexico	.8	.4
Persons of Spanish origin:		
Mexico	9.1	4.5
Puerto Rico	4.5	2.2
Cuba	.5	.2
Racial groups:		
White	177.7	87.5
Black	22.6	11.1
American Indians	.8	.4
Asian:		
Japanese	.6	.3
Chinese	.4	.2

Note: The ethnic breakdown reports prepatory to the 1980 U.S. census are complex, including both single and multiple ethnic ancestries, further rating the ethnic pluralism of American society. (See U.S. Bureau of the Census, Ancestry and language in the United States, *Current population reports*, Ser. P-23, no. 116 (Washington, D.C.: U.S. Government Printing Office, November 1979).

Source: U.S. Department of Commerce, Population of the United States, *Current population reports*, ser. P-23, no. 49 (Washington, D.C.: U.S. Government Printing Office, 1974) p. 93.

Generally, hostile attitudes toward minority groups are based on **prejudice** (negative preconceptions). Prejudice often results in **discrimination** (unequal treatment) against **minority** members who, because of discrimination, are lower in status and politically weaker than the majority of the population. These attitudes and practices have periodically resulted in a form of applied social Darwinism, in which some people hold the belief that they are racially superior. Many Americans thus face a moral dilemma in which practices of inequality often contradict the general American creed of equality.

An influential early twentieth century natural history **assimilation** model held that over time, minority group members became part of the equal opportunity system. As race riots of recent years and the difficult fight to secure an equal rights amendment for women show, such a linear, progressive model for racial and sexual minorities has been simplistic. Various forms of **segregation** persist, in which minority members are excluded from various social settings. Minorities have responded by mounting civil rights movements to challenge the racial, sexual, and ethnic status quo. These **social movements** have produced sufficient results, so that now a sociological debate ensues as to whether social class affiliation is currently more significant in American society than racial or other minority status is.

We must consider ways to break down social barriers confronting minorities if we are to come closer to fulfilling the American ideal of equal opportunity and treatment. This chapter discusses some of the crucial issues involved, including educational and affirmative action employment programs and busing to achieve racial integration in public schools. We also consider a number of subjective and objective intergroup developments. For all the minority-dominant group conflict in American society, a trend toward intergroup conflict resolution is evident.

CONFRONTING THE PROBLEM: PREJUDICE, DISCRIMINATION AND THE AMERICAN CREED

Prejudice and Discrimination as Conventional Wisdom

Many minority groups exist in American society. Given parental socialization, educational awareness, and mass media exposure, it would be unusual for any American—young or old—to be unaware of this social fact. Minority discrimination has existed for so long and has been recognized so widely that to many Americans, it is an accepted—if not always acceptable—social condition and a part of conventional wisdom—until open conflict develops. Why some people belong to minority groups and others do not may not be as evident. Why do female, black, or Chicano babies, for example, hold minority status at birth and thus grow up with multiple social barriers that most white male babies will never confront?

Since the position of minorities involves the status of people in racial, religious, ethnic, sexual, and other groupings, first considering what constitutes individual and group **status** in society is useful. Hoult (1969, 316) presents a summary of various sociological definitions of status:

Status involves the degree of social acclaim and prestige a role receives. High status brings admiration and respect, and is a source of positive attraction. Conversely, low status results in lack of admiration, social rejection, and avoidance.

The minority problem that many Americans face is that certain ascribed group quality characteristics, including race, sex, religion, and national origin, have been considered to have either high or low status, independent of such achieved performance status factors as education and income. A number of lower status minority groups have not been afforded the opportunities that go with higher status. Whites still tend to be of higher status than blacks, Anglos of higher status than Chicanos, northern Europeans of higher status than southern Europeans, and males of higher status than females.

Prejudicial attitudes and discriminatory actions. The major difficulties that minority status people face are based on prejudice and discrimination directed at them. These two concepts are so often coupled that their distinct meanings are sometimes lost. Prejudice may be positive, but here refers to hostile prejudgments and attitudes toward blacks and other minority group members, regardless of their personal qualities or achieved social position. Using the term *ethnic* to represent various types of minorities, Harvard psychologist Gordon Allport indicates some of the dynamics of prejudice in this generic definition:

Ethnic prejudice is an antipathy based upon a faulty and inflexible generalization. It may be felt or expressed. It may be directed toward a group as a whole, or toward an individual because he [or she] is a member of that group. (1958, 10)

For reasons we will explore below, people do not always act on their prejudices. When they do, they engage in discrimination, which constitutes clearer damage to minorities. The damage is more evident because discrimination involves overt action (beyond unexpressed feelings), in which minorities are subject to unfavorable treatment on the basis of race or some other minority group characteristic. As sociologist Brewton Berry writes:

Discrimination touches upon every phase of life. Subordinate groups are often restricted in their use of hotels, restaurants . . . intermarriage is opposed. . . . In the economic realm members of minority groups . . . are effectively excluded from many occupations, they are the "last to be hired, and the first to be fired." (1965, 341)

Based on prejudice and discrimination in all areas of American social life—close interpersonal relations, education, job opportunities, availability of housing, and other normal activities—blacks and other minorities have been treated as if they were inherently inferior to others.

Social Darwinism Revisited

When prejudice and discrimination combine, the result has often been a form of **racism,** which is the doctrine that the genetic inheritance of a designated group determines their human capabilities. In this doctrine, certain (usually dominant) groups hold to the belief that they are intellectually, socially, or morally superior. The German Nazis believed they were superior beings compared with Jews. The American Ku Klux Klan believes that whites are superior to blacks. Based on such racist beliefs, the Nazis killed millions of Jews, and Klan-like beliefs resulted in the enslavement and later segregation of millions of blacks.

Early twentieth century social scientific theories—now largely rejected—gave credence to racist doctrines. British sociologist Herbert Spencer (1877) and American anthropologist William Graham Sumner (1906) advanced the doctrine of Social Darwinism. Social Darwinism held that in the laissez-faire (free) law of competition in society, the fittest acquired the most wealth and social influence. People from groups that held relatively more affluence and influence found scholarly support for their racial superiority beliefs.

The result of racial superiority doctrines went beyond black-white relations. After World War I when job competition was keen, a move that white Protestants largely supported took place, in an effort to keep southern and east European immigrants out of the United States on the grounds that they were racially inferior. In *The Passing of the Great Race*, anthropologist Madison Grant (1916) advanced the view that in Europe "the amount of Nordic British and north European blood in each nation is a very fair measure of its strength in war and standing in civilization" (1916, 175). Further, as Harvard geologist Robert DeWard argued in the successful effort to keep out large numbers of Italians, Poles, and other southern or eastern Europeans by the Immigration Acts of 1921 and 1924, "it is in the highest degree 'ungenerous' in us, the custodians of the future heritage of our race, to permit to land on our shores mental, physical and moral defectives, who not only lower the standards of our own people, but will tremendously increase all future problems of public and private philanthropy" (DeWard 1919, 516).

If such racism was a problem for white ethnic groups, it was a disaster for blacks, who have experienced longer and deeper opposition based on their racial characteristics. Even though slavery was eliminated by the Fourteenth Amendment after the Civil War, its racist symbolic meaning has continued into the present. For most blacks, full emancipation has not yet become a reality. The southern "Jim Crow" segregation laws—based on the prejudicial beliefs of black incompetence—stimulated millions of blacks to migrate to the expanding industrial cities of the North. This movement was so extensive that by 1970, over half the black population lived in the North and West (U.S. Department of Commerce 1970).

The new hereditarians. In recent years, a group of analysts has emerged, which James Vander Zanden (1983) aptly describes as the "new hereditarians." Prominent among these analysts—often referred to as sociobiologists or biosociologists—are sociologist Lee Ellis (1977), educational psychologist Arthur Jensen, and biologist E. O. Wilson (1975). They take the position, reminiscent of Spencer and Sumner, that most human behavior can be explained on the basis of genetic inheritance rather than by social and environmental influences. Among these analysts, the work of Arthur Jensen (1980) has received an extensive amount of public media attention, based on his 1969 article in the *Harvard Educational Review* in which he advanced the now discredited thesis that most blacks score below average on standard IQ tests because of their genetic limitations.

For over a decade, many researchers have analytically discredited Jensen's racial competency doctrine. (Goldberg 1975; *Harvard Educational Review* 1969). Yet, Jensen's 1980 book, *Bias in Mental Testing*, appears to present the same case as his earlier work. He uses standard national survey data on IQ test results for black and for white children (see figure 10–1).

Such national sample analysis of black and white children does not control for the effects of such social factors as income of parents, community environment, quality of schools available, and related environmental forces. Jensen and other new hereditarians argue that socioeconomic factors would have little effect on genetically based racial or ethnic inheritance. Most social scientific analysts in this area of research, however,

FIGURE 10–1.   IQ Test Results for Black and White Children, Based on Standard National Survey Data, 1980

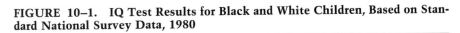
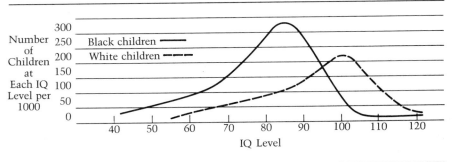

Data from Arthur Jensen, *Bias in mental testing* (New York: Free Press, 1980).

challenge this assertion on the following grounds.

First, Jensen's research assumes that blacks and whites constitute discrete, separate races. After intensive research, Theodosius Dobzhansky (1962) and other leading geneticists have concluded that no evidence exists that humanity ever consisted of uniform or pure races, or that any people now living—black, white, or Oriental—came from such races.

Second, the selection of environmental data in Jensen's research is also scientifically questionable. For example, the initial premise in Jensen's *Harvard Educational Review* (HER) article is that educational opportunity has been effectively attempted in American society; therefore, blacks and whites may now be considered as having equal advantages educationally, which enables valid IQ comparisons. Jensen states at the beginning of his article that "compensatory education has been tried and apparently has failed" (1969, 1). As Harvard sociologist Thomas Pettigrew and others noted also in the HER and elsewhere, however, the concept as well as the practice of compensatory education for economically poor black children began in most school districts only after passage of the Elementary and Secondary Education Act of 1965, which includes provisions for prekindergarten and other compensatory programs. Programming began in 1966 and has experience severe funding restrictions due to taxing limitations. These limitations were among the aftereffects of the post–Vietnam War and OPEC-induced stagflationary period that lasted into the 1980s. By reasonable standards of evaluation, "compensatory education" for black children in educationally disadvantaged areas cannot be considered, as Jensen states, to have "been tried and . . . failed."

Third, Jensen's work generally lacks an indepth analysis. This discrepancy is perhaps seen most clearly in the two polar examples of IQ capability reported (figure 10–1). Although the thrust of Jensen's analysis is the apparent demonstration that blacks are in-

herently less capable, he asserts that American-born Jews are genetically superior because they attain higher IQ scores than do other groupings of whites. The problem with this assertion is that the foreign-born generation of Jews that is not evaluated in the article scored below average on standard IQ measures (Hirsch 1926). The foreign-born Jewish generation presumably had the same genetic capabilities as did their offspring.

In sum, Jensen and other new hereditarians have not made a convincing case with regard to race and ability. Cultural-environmental influences appear to explain more of the variance in performance than genetic racial or ethnic inheritance does.

The self-fulfilling prophecy and racial competence. The public impact of Jensen's work may be more consequential than the work itself. If many people believe that blacks, women, or members of any other group are genetically less capable, even though objective evidence negates this thesis, then real consequences can develop in the form of a *self-fulfilling prophecy*. Sometimes called the **Thomas theorem,** the self-fulfilling prophecy in which false beliefs can lead to real consequences can be seen in numerous situations in daily life, including educational achievement in the classroom. W. I. Thomas (1928, 1931) developed his theorem after observing the negative achievement results of Polish immigrant children early in the century, when other children and teachers labeled them as incompetent.

In a study titled *Pygmalion in the Classroom*, Robert Rosenthal and Lenore Jacobson (1968) described the self-fulfilling prophecy in action. Teachers were told that according to a test that was supposed to predict children's potential, certain children were likely to do well in class. The test had no such predictive powers, but because teachers believed the predictions, they treated the children according to their supposed abilities. Those who were expected to do well *did* do well, and many showed remarkable improvement in their test performances. In addition, the researchers found that because of teacher prejudice, gains of minority children were more grudgingly acknowledged.

The teachers in the Rosenthal and Jacobson study, like many adults and children, were reflecting widely held popular beliefs about racial and ethnic competency. Educator Charles Silberman pinpointed the problematic consequences when he observed that, ". . . expectation [s] can and [do] quite literally affect a student's *performance*" (1970, 83). This problem is more than educational in our American credentials-oriented society in which good jobs and higher educational achievement increasingly go together.

In one of the national media articles on Jensen's research, two *Newsweek* reporters summed up the possible Thomas theorem effects of the social Darwinistic notions involved when they noted that "Jensen's ideas are . . . bound to renew the debate over race and genes. An uglier prospect is that they may lend themselves to those who would chip away at the fundamental principle of equal opportunity" (Sewall and Lee 1980, 59). This last prospect again raises the American moral dilemma regarding race and the ideal of equality of treatment.

Myrdal's American Moral Dilemma Thesis

The history of racial prejudice and discrimination in American society, which officially prides itself on equality of all citizens, has stimulated one of the most extensive and influential national sociological studies. In the late 1930s and early 1940s, the Carnegie Foundation sponsored the first societywide in-depth analysis of race relations in America. Swedish socioeconomist Gunnar Myrdal, who worked with a team of American sociologists, headed the investigation. The results were published in 1944 in the monumental *An American Dilemma*, a book that was later expanded and updated. Myrdal developed the thesis that the major conflict in

American race relations is moral; that is, the egalitarian values of the culture are at odds with the unequal treatment afforded black people. As Myrdal observed:

Though our study includes economic, social, and political race relations, at the bottom our problem is the moral dilemma of the American—the conflict between his moral valuations on various levels of consciousness and generality. The "American Dilemma" referred to in the title of this book is the ever-raging conflict between, on the one hand, the valuations preserved on the general plane which we shall call the "American Creed," where the American thinks, talks, and acts under the influence of high national and Christian precepts, and, on the other hand, the valuations on specific planes of individual and group living, where personal and local interest; economic, social, and sexual jealousies; considerations of community prestige and conformity; group prejudice against particular persons or types of people; and all sorts of miscellaneous wants, impulses, and habits dominate his outlook. (1944, xvii)

Myrdal argued that interracial tensions cause whites to have allegiance to two contradictory values: that all people are created equal and that whites are genetically superior to blacks. As a solution to this value conflict, he proposed the need to adopt exclusively the first value, which he identified as the American creed as expressed in the Declaration of Independence.

Myrdal's identification of a moral dilemma that whites experience makes an assumption with which not all analysts agree. Overt prejudice and discrimination may be lessening (Bogardus 1968; Gordon 1982; Karlins 1969), suggesting decreased hostility toward blacks and other minorities. Yet, considerable evidence suggests that for many Anglo-Americans, continuing prejudice toward blacks, Chicanos, and other minorities does not constitute a moral dilemma. Recent studies document that white Anglo-Americans often express little interest in opening up equal educational or job opportunities to large numbers of long-excluded minorities (Lieberson 1980; Steinberg 1981). Further, open violent white hostility has been expressed in urban areas, as in the Miami account in the beginning of this chapter (*Associated Press* 25 May 1980), and in small-town settings, as in the case of white officials' hostility toward black church members in Miracle Valley in southern Arizona (*Arizona Republic* 31 March 1983).

Insights into how many Americans can both hold values of equal treatment for all and practice unequal treatment for some is provided in studies designed to test the American dilemma thesis. Westie (1965) and DeFleur and Westie (1958) reported on two studies—one community based and the other university based. In both studies, community people and university student respondents were asked to agree or disagree with the general value statement "Everyone in America should have equal opportunity to get ahead" (a general American creed value). The community people sampled were then asked specific general value application questions. A typical one was "I would be willing to have a Negro as my supervisor in my place of work" (a specific application of the American creed value). Similarly, the university students sampled were asked specific value application questions, including the following interrelated ones: "I will pose for a photograph . . . with a Negro person of the opposite sex with the following restrictions on its use: I will allow this photograph to be used only in laboratory experiments where it will be seen only by professional sociologists. Signed _____. I will allow this photograph to be shown to hundreds of university students as a teaching aid in sociology classes. Signed _____. I will allow this photograph to be published in my home town newspaper as part of a publicity report on this research. Signed _____." While over three-quarters of the community people and the university students accepted the general value, about only half accepted the specific application of the value. Only a minority of white students were willing to allow a newspaper photo of themselves with a black person. That many

whites could agree in general with the egalitarian American creed while refusing to apply it to blacks—or other groups with minority status—creates a profound dilemma for blacks and other minorities.

Merton's explanatory model. How and why are some people consistent and others inconsistent in what they say and what they do about the American creed? Many people not only contradict themselves with regard to the general and specific application of the creed but also often contradict themselves in expressing specific prejudicial attitudes without engaging in discriminatory behavior or vice versa. Sociologist Robert Merton (1949, 1967) provides an analytical model that helps untangle this complex of prejudice and discrimination in relation to the American creed. Merton's model, which is a logically constructed typology of possible responses, illustrates the varying prejudicial attitudes and discriminatory behavior patterns found in society (see table 10–2).

Merton started with the traditional American creed value that all people are created equal. He then outlined various attitude and behavior possibilities, all of which are found in society. Only Type I, the unprejudiced nondiscriminators, and Type IV, the prejudiced discriminators, are consistent in their actions and expressed attitudes. Type I people are all-weather liberals, many of whom can be found among activists in civil rights movements. Type IV people are all-weather illiberals, many of whom adhere to the segregationist credo that opposes equal treatment of racial minorities under any circumstances (Vander Zanden 1983).

Type II and Type III people behave in a manner opposite to their expressed personal attitudes and values. By considering actual examples, gaining insight into what factors result in such an apparent contradiction is possible. Type II unprejudiced discriminators are fair-weather liberals who operate expediently to get along or to gain profit. This process was seen in a Wayne State University project in Detroit in the 1960s on assessing white resident attitudes about racially changing neighborhoods. A researcher reported that on one block, everyone said that they would be willing to sell their home to a black person or family but would not do so because it would offend their neighbors. Similarly, the unwillingness of corporate managers to hire or promote minority members may stem from fears of negative consequences from their allegedly more prejudiced associates and superiors.

Similar factors seem to operate in the attitude and behavior discrepancies of Type III respondents—the prejudiced nondiscriminators, or fair-weather illiberals. As with the Type II respondents, expediency is often involved. Many racially prejudiced army officers conformed to President Truman's 1948 order to desegregate the armed forces, and businesspersons and labor leaders operating under lucrative government defense and other contracts often desegregate only under the threat of losing these contracts if they do not comply.

Examining the social pressures activating a situation before interpreting what people say and do is therefore necessary. In race and other minority relations, the disparity between the egalitarian American creed and actual practice has led to tensions and conflict not only with blacks but also with Asian-Americans, Chicanos, native Americans, women, and other groups with minority status.

ANALYZING THE PROBLEM: THE CONSEQUENCES OF MINORITY GROUP STATUS

Park's Natural History Assimilation Model

In the 1920s, Robert Park advanced one of the most influential theories about the nature of minority-dominant relations. Park, a member of the first American Department of Sociology at the University of Chicago, held that all racial and ethnic minorities pass through a "natural history" of sequential or irreversible stages (Park 1949). In this natural history model, any given racial, religious, or ethnic group initially meets other groups through *contact*; contact in a community setting results in *competition*; various forms of economic and political competition cause *conflict*; the costs of conflict to all groups produce adjustments or *accommodation*; and in the final process, group members are culturally meshed, i.e., *assimilation* takes place.

The natural history model appears to ex-

TABLE 10–2. Varying Prejudicial Attitudes and Discriminating Behavior in American Society

	ATTITUDE DIMENSION: PREJUDICED (−) AND UNPREJUDICED (+)	BEHAVIOR DIMENSION: DISCRIMINATOR (−) AND NONDISCRIMINATOR (+)
I. Unprejudiced nondiscriminator	+	+
II. Unprejudiced discriminator	+	−
III. Prejudiced nondiscriminator	−	+
IV. Prejudiced discriminator	−	−

Note: The value of being unprejudiced and the behavior of being nondiscriminatory constitute the American creed.

Source: Robert Merton, Discrimination and the American creed, in *Discrimination and the national welfare*, ed. R. MacIver (New York: Harper & Row), pp. 100–110.

plain well the experience of most ethnic (nationality) and religious groups in American society. The model does not appear to apply as well in other respects, e.g., where minority status is based on race and sex. Park built his model on observations of ethnic and religious groups in Chicago, which paralleled what other analysts had observed elsewhere. For example, Lloyd Warner documented the occupational assimilation process of several ethnic and religious groups in a New England community (Yankee City) from the mid-nineteenth century to the beginning of the twentieth century (Warner and Lunt 1941, 39–43). Warner used six occupational classes and assigned numerical weights to each: (1) unskilled labor—1, (2) skilled factory—2, (3) skilled craft—2.5, (4) management aid (e.g., foremen in factories or salespersons for businesses)—3, (5) management—4, and (6) professional—5. An occupational index was constructed for each ethnic and religious group; the higher the index, the higher the average status and income. Table 10–3 illustrates Warner's findings. Note that most groups—Armenians, French, Irish Catholics, Jews, and Poles—advanced their occupational index over time, so that their final overall ethnic index was close to that of native white Protestants. Those ethnic groups that did not advance their index—Italians and Greeks—experienced large immigration during the time period assessed and have since shown similar

occupational assimilation into relatively higher status positions (Glazer and Moynihan 1971; Rosen 1959).

The movement away from index 1 (the lowest occupational class) is particularly relevant for members of these groups, as the economic division of labor in American society increasingly phases out most categories of unskilled labor needs. Further, as chapter 7 on poverty and class conflict documents, many members of these ethnic and religious groups are faced with continuing strains in American society. Still, the level of occupational and general assimilation for racial minorities and women has been substantial, as Park predicted in his natural history model.

Problems with the Natural History Model

Although the natural history model appears to apply well to many groups, questions have been raised about this optimistic assimilationist formulation. The questions have not entirely negated Park's model but have forced reconsideration of the theory both conceptually, as in its stage-by-stage sequence of relations, and in its application to black and other contemporary minorities.

Sociologist Amitai Etzioni notes major problems with the model in its capacity to explain and predict intergroup relations. Etzioni argues that the Park model is not suf-

TABLE 10–3. Occupational Status Indexes of Yankee City Ethnic Groups, by Decades

GROUPS	1850	1864	1873	1883	1893	1903	1913	1923	1933
Irish	1.62	1.72	1.74	1.76	1.84	1.94	2.14	2.31	2.52
French					1.95	2.10	2.14	2.23	2.24
Jews							3.10	3.22	3.32
Italians							2.32	2.29	2.28
Armenians							2.46	2.51	2.56
Greeks								2.53	2.34
Poles								1.88	1.97
Russians									1.95
Total ethnics									2.42
Total natives									2.56

Source: W. Lloyd Warner and Leo Srole, *The social systems of American ethnic groups* (New Haven, Conn.: Yale University Press, 1945), table 2, p. 60.

ficiently specific to be clearly tested. As he notes about Park's often used term *eventually*,

if an ethnic group is not assimilating . . . it has not yet reached the stage of assimilation. "Eventually" . . . every . . . group will be assimilated. As no time interval is mentioned and the sociological conditions under which the process of assimilation will take place are not spelled out, the whole scheme becomes unscientific. (Etzioni 1959, 25)

Two major critical questions about Park's model are related to time and to the inevitability of sequential contact-to-assimilation experiences of all groups. Let us consider the time factor first. Many groups—including blacks, Chicanos, native Americans, and women—were held to have low minority status in Warner's study and other early twentieth century studies, just as such ethnic and religious groups as Irish Catholics, Greeks, and Jews did. Yet, contemporary minorities have experienced prolonged minority status more than a generation after the latter groups have assimilated by most attitudinal and behavioral measures. The inevitability assumption is also dubious. For instance, the Nazi program in Germany reversed the long-term trend toward Jewish assimilation in that society (Shirer 1960). This consideration raises Etzioni's point about the need to specify conditions under which assimilation does or does not occur.

In spite of these limitations, Park's model remains useful in evaluating the relative positions of various groups in society. Further, as sociologist Stanford Lyman notes, Park's racial and ethnic cycle formulation has "focused critical attention on a significant aspect of intergroup relations" (1968, 20).

From De Jure to De Facto Segregation

The continuing effects of discriminatory practices (and the conflict stage of Park's model) can be seen in the degree of *segregation**, the separation of people on the basis of racial or other group characteristics. Perhaps the clearest example of continuing seg-

regation is the case of American blacks. After the post–Civil War Compromise of 1877, white southern politicians developed a campaign to dehumanize blacks among the line of their former slave image (Friedman 1970). Most blacks lived in the South then, and northern politicians increasingly acquiesced to southern proposals. The result was a wide assault on individual blacks and segregated exclusion of blacks from white neighborhoods, schools, jobs, and other areas of social life, leading to treatment that was separate but not equal. The races were separated in schools, employment, housing, and interpersonal relations, as well as in the initial focus of the Supreme Court's concern: mass transportation.

Encouraged by judicial doctrine, southern (and some northern) states moved to sepa-

This 1961 photo of a black woman being arrested in St. Louis for attempting to use a "white women" only facility represents de jure, legal, segregation which by congressional and court actions is no longer constitutional. Yet, the segregationist values represented have not entirely disappeared.

rate the races de jure, by a variety of specific laws. Such legally based segregation was less extensively practiced in the North and in the West, but restrictive covenant clauses in the deeds of private houses, which restricted their sale to whites, or more restrictively, to white Christians only, were common. Moreover, housing developments in which Federal Housing Administration (FHA) mortgage money was involved were racially segregated on the grounds that racial homogeneity was essential to a neighborhood's financial stability. This argument is fallacious. Researchers have documented that except for brief panic-selling periods of a few weeks or months duration, the evidence is substantial that housing values tend to *increase* in racially integrated neighborhoods (Laurenti 1960). Still, the FHA was reflecting popular beliefs, and in accordance with the Thomas theorem, if people believe something to be true, the consequences that follow these beliefs are real. One such consequence is that while more recent court decisions have largely ended de jure segregation enforced by law, other forms of segregation have emerged.

All legally sanctioned segregation has ended. Beginning in the 1920s, the National Association for the Advancement of Colored People (NAACP) initiated over a dozen judicial challenges to segregation (Ivy 1964, 285). The key decision was the *Brown* case of 1954, which reversed the *Plessy* decision of 1896, in which the Supreme Court had upheld the racist doctrine of "separate but equal." Citing social scientific evidence gathered since the *Plessy* decision, the Court held unanimously that schools racially segregated by laws were inherently unequal. Thus, the Court ended any sanctioning of the de jure segregation of public schools. By judicial extension in more recent years, this new position ended legally sanctioned segregation on virtually all levels of racial interaction, as indicated by the Court's response to a case challenging Virginia's antimiscegenation (racial intermarriage) law. In 1967, the Supreme Court held that Virginia's law banning marriage between members of different races was unconstitutional. This decision had the effect of nullifying similar laws in twenty other states (*New York Times* 13 March 1966).

Most of these decisions were aimed at the South, where a body of law supporting segregation existed. In the North and the West, de jure racial segregation did not exist to the same extent. Yet, the degree of de facto segregation, supported by practice rather than by law, developed as extensively as in the more rural South (Taeuber and Taeuber 1969).

In effect, blacks along with other often poor racial minorities have faced continuing institutional racism. They experience the dual frustration of being blocked from jobs on the grounds that they are unqualified and of being discouraged and intimidated in their efforts to find housing. Since they are prevented from buying suburban housing, blacks also lose access to new jobs in the growing suburban areas. Not informed about such jobs and lacking transportation to them, most blacks are thus confined to older city neighborhoods with inferior schools, inferior housing, and other problems.

The consequences of continuing segregation, and of the minority status of racial and other groups, are different in urban than in rural areas. People live closer together in cities, so they are able to communicate their discontents more regularly and extensively. The result is social conflict (Coser, 1967). These discontents are expressed in a variety of organized and unorganized ways, but always constitute a challenge to the dominant society.

Civil Rights Movements and Countermovements

Exclusion from the American system of equal treatment and opportunity for some minority groups has been so long and extensive that many in these groups have questioned Park's "natural" assimilation assumption. This reaction has particularly been evident among blacks, Hispanics, native Americans, and women. Many people in each of these groups have been active in minority-led *social movements* . . . —organized protest efforts to secure more equal treatment and opportunities. These movements have forced more open intergroup conflict than would occur during individual interaction in daily activity. The aim of such social movements is to challenge the status quo and to increase the range of educational, job, and other opportunities in American society. These social movements are a continuing process, and those in more dominant groups, who perceive social movements as threats to their more advantaged position in society, have produced countermovement activity.

Smelser's value-added social movement model. Sociologist Neil Smelser's (1962) "value-added" theory of collective behavior provides a useful framework in which to consider how social movements came into being and what effect they have had. Smelser documents that many—perhaps most—social movements appear to go through six stages. Generally, the chances for a major social movement, including a minority-led civil rights movement, increase as one stage leads to or produces another (the value-added concept). (Some analysts, however, have noted that not all social movements go through the sequence of stages that Smelser identifies.)

The first stage is *structural conduciveness.* In civil rights movement terms, the migration of blacks from spread-out rural areas of the South to densely populated urban neighborhoods in large northern cities is an example of structural conduciveness; that is, many more blacks were in closer interaction with each other. Such a condition increases daily communication and possibilities for organized activity.

The second stage of the value-added model is *structural strain.* This occurs when members of a group find their position at a disadvantage compared with others. Thus, blacks in an urban ghetto area are aware that they have been largely de facto segregated, with the result that their schools are older and more crowded than other schools, the public roads in their neighborhoods receive less repair than in other areas, their employment opportunities are less, and so on. Just as many women view their household role as a strain in their attempt to establish successful careers, structural strains increase the possibility of a social protest movement.

In the third stage, a *generalized belief* emerges. Leaders, often with **charismatic** qualities of mass appeal, articulate the feelings of many group members who have experienced structural conduciveness and structural strain. Leaders such as Martin Luther King, Jr., in the black community, Gloria Steinem among women, and Cesar Chavez among Chicanos articulate generalized values calling for change. Often, the values are drawn from the general society and applied to a particular minority group. For example, taking up the language of the Declaration of Independence: "We hold these truths to be self-evident, that all men are created equal," black leaders often add the words *that all black men and white men*, and feminist leaders often add the words *that all men and women*, while keeping intact the rest of the generalized belief that all are created equal under the law and in the opportunity system.

The fourth stage involves *precipitating factors* that dramatize and confirm the generalized belief. A classic example of a precipitating factor occurred in 1955, a year after the Supreme Court ruled in the *Brown* case that de jure racial segregation in schools was unconstitutional. In Montgomery, Alabama, a black women—Rosa Parks—refused to move to the back of a segregated bus to give a white woman her seat as required by local law and custom. The bus driver had Mrs. Parks arrested. Led by Dr. Martin Luther King, Jr., the black community of Montgomery organized a successful boycott of the city's buses in response to this event. Within a year, the buses of Montgomery were integrated. In this case, the precipitating event launched Dr. King and his organization, the Southern Christian Leadership Conference (SCLC), into national prominence (Vander Zanden 1983, 365–68).

In the fifth stage, *mobilization* of participants for action occurs. For example, by the 1960s the Montgomery bus boycott and other related precipitating factors resulted in such older black organizations as the National Association for the Advancement of Colored People (NAACP) and the Urban League actively supporting the more aggressive efforts of SCLC in agitating for reform. Other black-led organizations began to emerge, of which the Student Non-Violent Coordinating Committee (SNCC) and the Congress of Racial Equality (CORE) were particularly active. These organizations generally mobilized by employing an aggressive nonviolent strategy, using such tactics as sit-ins in segregated restaurants, marches in segregated neighborhoods, voter registration drives in predominantly black precincts, boycotts, the active search for white allies, and a variety of other tactics (Bell 1968, 29–45). The aim of these tactics was to change both the legal guarantees of protection of racial minority members and the larger society's racial attitudes and practices. The black-led rights mobilization period culminated in the 1963 march on Washington, D.C., which drew over 200,000 participants (Waskow 1967, 236). Such mobilization was paralleled in the Chicano community by the emergence of the *la raza* (the race) migrant labor and other protest movements (Alvarez 1973), as well as the American Indian Movement (AIM) (Josephy, Jr. 1971) and the National Organization for Women (NOW) (Giele 1978), among others.

The last social movement stage in Smelser's value-added model is the operation of *social control*. The developments in this stage are designed to deflect and control the social movement. Social control efforts can take many forms. In a successful social pro-

test movement, both minority protesters and members of the dominant society may find it advantageous to work out an accommodation. An example is found in the efforts of black civil rights leaders to secure major civil rights legislation and in the willingness of many white leaders to support such legislation as a way of ending disruptive protest activities. One result was the Civil Rights Act of 1964, the most comprehensive civil rights legislation since the end of the Civil War. This act guaranteed that the same standards for voter registration would be applied to all citizens in federal elections, and prohibited discrimination on account of race, sex,[1] religion, or national origin by businesses serving the public. The act also included a provision ensuring fair employment practices by employers or unions with twenty-five or more employees or members.

The last stage—social control—in a social protest movement process may or may not result in a new, more accepting normalization of relations between protesters and others. In the case of the black-led civil rights movement, the accommodation has been partial. One new conflict situation emerged when many whites organized in countermovements to oppose the Civil Rights Act of 1964 and other civil rights acts. The mid-1960s and 1970s witnessed such developments as the emergence of George Wallace's American Independent Party, which began by denouncing the Supreme Court's desegregation *Brown* decision and sharply opposing all civil rights legislation. The third reemergence of the Ku Klux Klan with its Nazi-like racial superiority doctrine also occurred during this time (Lipset and Raab

---

1. The term *sex* was added to this major civil rights legislation by Tennessee Senator John Stennis in mockery and as part of his opposition during congressional debate on the legislation. Congresswoman Martha Griffith of Michigan took this addition seriously and formally added the term *sex* to the Civil Rights Act in the House of Representatives. In the end, sex indeed became one of the group bases of civil rights protection in the comprehensive Civil Rights Act of 1964.

1970). On the other side, many blacks were increasingly frustrated by the combination of new civil rights laws designed to protect their rights and the continuing deterioration of their ghetto communities, schools, and job opportunities. Many were further exasperated by the relatively large number of blacks drafted to fight and risk death in Vietnam (King, Jr. 1967).

By the mid-1960s, this combination of white countermovement activity and black ghetto frustration over de facto segregation and deteriorating living experiences produced a new dimension of sometimes violent interracial relations. A series of violent events ensued, among them the blowing up of an all-black church in Birmingham, Alabama, which killed four children attending Sunday school. This event occurred just two weeks after the famous August 1963 march of over 200,000 on Washington, D.C., at which Dr. Martin Luther King delivered his most famous speech, "I Have a Dream"

(Waskow 1967, 238). Black outrage soon broke through the tenuous social control efforts, and many in our large cities still remain in a state of continuing social strain.

The J-Curve and Race Riots

As we look back at the black social protest movements of the 1960s from the perspective of the 1980s, some insights can be gained into the ongoing nature of intergroup relations in American society. While the black-led movement was earliest and most extensive, the mass protests of Chicanos, women, and students served as social flashpoints that made clear the widespread dissatisfaction of large groupings of Americans.

Americans in the 1960s were witness to the process sociologist James Davies identifies as the "J-curve of rising expectations" (Davies 1969). The J-curve (see figure 10-2) is a concept based on the social conflict processes Davies found in his studies of major

FIGURE 10–2.   Need Satisfaction and Rebellion: the J-curve

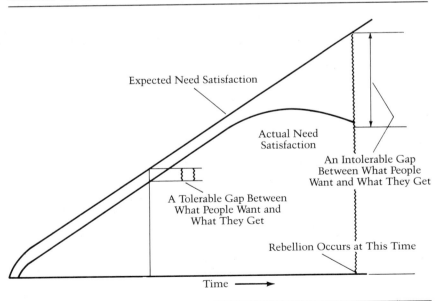

Data from James Davies, The J-curve of rising expectations and declining satisfactions as a cause of some great revolutions and contained rebellion, in *Violence in America*, ed. H. D. Graham and T. R. Gurr (New York: Bantam, 1969), p. 691.

revolutions (particularly the French and Russian revolutions) and applied to the black rebellion and student antiwar protests of the 1960s. In essence, the J-curve describes what occurs when masses of people in a social protest movement develop rising expectations that are not matched by the rate of improving conditions. In the case of the black protest movement, a number of major gains had been made by the early 1960s. These gains included the Supreme Court's 1954 *Brown* decision desegregation based on an NAACP court challenge of segregated schools, the passage of the Civil Rights Act of 1964, and the establishment of new job training and educational programs.

Such successes resulted in a sharp rise in the expectations of still more opportunities and a better life for millions of blacks. Some gains did occur. Black employment went up, educational levels advanced, and poverty among blacks went down (Farley 1977). Yet, the massive extent of black ghetto deterioration, coupled with the limited resources available for reconstruction programs after entry into the Vietnam War, produced an increasing gap between expectations and reality (Smith 1971). A sense of **relative deprivation** (feelings of opportunity deprivation compared with others) became pervasive in the black community. Further, while de jure legal segregation had ended, de facto segregation intensified as middle-class whites moved into suburbs beyond city limits.

The result was a series of disorganized, **anomic** (normless) protests in the form of race riot rebellions. In 1964, disorders broke out in Jacksonville, Florida, Jersey City, and New York City. Then in August 1965, in the Watts section of Los Angeles, a race riot resulted in thirty-four deaths, hundreds of injuries, and $35 million in damages. Over the next two years, a number of cities in all sections of the nation experienced similar racial disorders. Tampa, Cincinnati, Atlanta, and Newark were among the hardest hit. In July 1967, Detroit experienced the worst racial riots in the history of the nation and

the worst rioting any American city had seen since the Irish draft riots in New York City during the Civil War. The Detroit riots left forty-three dead, over a thousand injured, over seven thousand arrested, and at least $50 million in property damaged and destroyed (National Advisory Commission on Civil Disorders 1968).

Although they were typically unplanned, spontaneous events, the racial civil disorders became so extensive that researchers increasingly began to identify them as "violence as protest" (Fogelson 1971). Stokely Carmichael and other black leaders expressed the need to establish black power to secure their rights and to secure programs that would offer them real opportunities to exercise those rights (Carmichael and Hamilton 1967). While moderate black leaders, including Martin Luther King, Jr., and others who had organized the 1963 march on Washington, continued to urge nonviolent means to secure their rights, more militant leaders such as Eldridge Cleaver and Huey Newton of the Black Panther Party urged people to use *any* effective means. Moderate or militant, black leaders were united on one issue: They wanted major improvement in the status of blacks in American society.

The black-led civil rights movement stimulated and paralleled other protest movements, notably the Chicano, native American, and women's movements. In the last section of this chapter, we examine some of the major achievements of these minority movements. Resistance, sometimes referred to as the "backlash," has also been substantial as many white males perceived a lessening of their future security and opportunity. These mixed developments call for examination.

The Inclining or Declining Significance of Race: The Wilson-Willie Debate

As we move along in the decade of the 1980s, signs indicate that racism continues to be a major phenomenon in American society. This chapter's opening excerpt on the

1980 Miami race riots, which hostile actions against blacks precipitated, is symptomatic of the kind of racial antipathy reminiscent of the 1950s and 1960s. As detailed in the next section, however, new major federal legislation protective of the rights of blacks, Chicanos, women, and others with minority status is an established fact. Educational achievement levels and average income have gone up substantially for minority members, although they still remain well below those for most white males.

The question of whether blacks now confront exclusion from maximum opportunities because of their race, or Chicanos because of their ethnicity, or women because of their sex has been addressed by William Julius Wilson, the first black to chair the prestigious Department of Sociology at the University of Chicago. In his book *The Declining Significance of Race* Wilson (1978a) presents the view that social class has become more important than race in determining black life chances in American society.

Charles Willie of Harvard, another prominent black sociologist, takes issue with Wilson's social class thesis. Willie acknowledges that blacks have made substantial progress, noting, for example, that the proportion of black to white male professionals has increased from one-half to two-thirds (Willie 1978, 14). Willie stresses the point, however, that in all major respects—housing, residential and school de facto segregation, and income levels—most blacks and other minorities are in a severely disadvantaged position when compared with whites (see table 10–4).

Wilson's social class argument rests on the contention that blacks who attain high educational achievement no longer face pervasive exclusion from managerial and professional opportunities, as earlier generations of blacks did. Wilson points to the increase of blacks attending colleges and universities (from less than 350,000 in the mid-1960s to over 1 million by the late 1970s). He notes that young college-educated black adults now earn as much as their white counterparts. On this basis, Wilson concludes that racism, which would exclude even highly educated blacks from higher status and higher income positions, is clearly on the decline.

Yet, Wilson agrees with Willie on a crucial point about the current effects of a long history of racism, stating that "one of the legacies of the racial oppression in previous years is the continued disproportionate black representation in the underclass" (Wilson 1978b, 19). The degree to which Wilson's class thesis rather than Willie's race thesis is correct will determine the

TABLE 10–4. Persons Below the Poverty Level, by Race and Ethnic Origin of Household Head, for the United States, 1980

ETHNIC ORIGIN	NUMBER BELOW POVERTY LEVEL (in thousands)	PERCENTAGE BELOW POVERTY LEVEL
All persons	29,640	13.0
White	20,049	10.2
Black	8,555	32.5
Spanish origin	3,566	25.7

Note: The average poverty threshold for a family of four persons was $8,414 in 1980. The poverty threshold varies with geographical location depending on the cost of living in a locale and is updated each year to reflect changes in the annual average consumer price index.

Source: U.S. Department of Commerce, characteristics of the population below the poverty level, *Current population reports: Consumer income* (Washington, D.C.: U.S. Government Printing Office, 1981), table B.

likely willingness of nonblack Americans to implement policies designed to equalize treatment and opportunity for people regardless of their race, ethnic background, or sex.

ALTERNATIVE POLICIES FOR RESOLVING THE PROBLEM: ACHIEVING INTERGROUP ACCOMMODATION

Breaking Down Structural Barriers

The reform legislation of the 1950s and 1960s was designed in large measure to break down the structural barriers facing minorities. These barriers were multiple, including the massive movement of the white middle class from the large cities to separate governing suburbs with their separate school systems and expanding industrial parks. The protest movements, coupled with the strong presidential leadership of Lyndon Johnson, led to public support for civil rights legislation. Acts were passed in 1964 and 1965 that continue to provide the legal basis for achieving a number of the aims of the civil rights movement, with specific programs to achieve equality of opportunity in education, jobs, and other areas.

The Civil Rights Act of 1964 was followed by other acts passed in 1965 which addressed the programatic goals of the civil rights movement. The Economic Opportunity Act funded the training of unskilled blacks and others to secure good jobs in a rapidly changing cybernetic economy. The Elementary and Secondary Education Act was designed to stimulate more funding for quality education for poor, young blacks and others with low incomes.

These reform acts of the mid-1960s led to a series of court decisions and presidential executive orders aimed at implementing effective programming mandated by Congress. Controversy and mixed results have ensued as many nonminority members perceived a threat to their relatively more secure social and economic position.

Cutting Issues: School Busing and Affirmative Action Programs

That economic opportunity for minorities has a long way to go is evident from the data shown in table 10–4 which reveals a substantially higher percentage of blacks and Spanish Americans below the low-income level. To accelerate equal opportunities for minorities, a number of policy initiatives were advanced in the 1970s. Of these, two policies have received particular public attention and have generated considerable controversy. One such policy has been court-ordered school busing, designed to end not only the old southern de jure (legal) segregation but also de facto (social practice) segregation. Another such policy initiative was based on a series of affirmative action presidential orders in the Johnson and Nixon administrations.

The busing issue. The school desegregation busing decisions developed after the Supreme Court began to raise constitutional questions in a number of decisions that noted that racial segregation was not limited to the schools of the South. The Court's concern with the Fourteenth Amendment's equal rights protection clause was heightened by the unequal educational opportunities evident in racially segregated black schools. In this respect, the Coleman Report, based on a national study, concluded that poor, low-achieving blacks as well as poor whites would have to interact with high-achieving students to attain equality of educational opportunity (Coleman et al. 1966).

The NAACP, as part of that organization's civil rights activities, led court efforts to enforce busing. Court orders to bus children for school desegregation purposes met violent white opposition in Boston, Pontiac, and other cities. President Richard Nixon, reflecting public opinion, declared his opposition to the busing of children to achieve racial integration and urged steps to offset court decisions requiring such busing

(Pinckney 1973, 352). In 1976, President Gerald Ford advised his attorney general to place a test case on busing before the Supreme Court. The result limited busing to solitary school districts, thereby preventing busing between predominantly black cities and predominantly white suburbs. Then, also in 1976, James Coleman challenged his own Coleman Report by testifying in a Senate committee session that in his opinion, the Court's position in support of busing had become a major factor in driving whites out of large cities. In rebuttal, Reynolds Farley and other demographers noted that busing—in which less than 3 percent of court busing orders resulted in community protests—had *not* resulted in whites moving to

suburbs at any faster rate in cities under busing orders compared with those cities where no busing was occurring (Farley 1975). For all the conflicts, as the society moved into the 1980s, court-ordered busing and increased federal aid to poverty area schools had become an established technique to advance the status of minorities.

The affirmative action issue.   Affirmative action programs are designed to admit minority group members, long excluded by formal and informal means, to good schools and good jobs. Some white males charge that the practice amounts to reverse discrimination (Glazer 1975). Test cases before the Supreme Court have modified but not

This anti-busing protest in Boston is similar to those in some other cities where middle class whites organized to stop court-ordered busing designed to socially integrate public schools.

negated the constitutionality of affirmative action programs. Two such cases involved college professional programs, and one involved employment practices in a large industrial corporation.

The two college cases were the 1975 *De Funis* decision and the 1978 *Bakke* decision. In the *De Funis* case, a white male student whose entry scores were higher than some blacks who had been admitted was not accepted in the University of Washington Law School. In the *Bakke* case, a similar situation developed with regard to the University of California at Davis Medical School. Some complicating aspects were present in these cases, e.g., De Funis eventually entered and graduated from law school, and Bakke was over thirty years old when he applied for medical school entry. Focusing on the main issue, the Court held that affirmative action programs designed to bring more blacks, women, and other minority status people into the opportunity system were constitutional. The Supreme Court, however, ruled that specific numerical quotas—specifying 10 percent, 20 percent, or any specific proportion of minorities—were unconstitutional.

In the area of work, a key case was that of the 1979 *Weber* decision. Weber, a white male, worked at a Kaiser Aluminum plant, where about 40 percent of all the workers were black, but only 2 percent of the skilled, highly paid workers were black. The company began its own training program, and about half of those admitted were black. Weber was not admitted to the program and sued Kaiser. The Court, however, rejected Weber's reverse discrimination contention but, modifying its stand in *De Funis* and *Bakke*, held that where the racial—and by implication sexual or ethnic—imbalance was as great as at Kaiser, then general numerical goals were acceptable for a period of time.

Public opinion is influential in the effectiveness of affirmative action programs. If public opposition is massive, programs would be difficult to enforce if only because politicians opposed to enforcement would be elected to office, and in the extreme case, a constitutional amendment could be passed ending such programs. Public opinion polls in the late 1970s suggest that the Supreme Court's position of accepting affirmative action programs without specific numerical quotas is generally supported (Robertson, 1980, 230). When white males are asked about their view of quotas for minorities in professional programs, about three out of four are in opposition. When the issue of quotas is removed, however, the opposite result occurred, with about three out of four supporting or accepting affirmative action programs.

Objective Indicators of Accommodation

Signs of upward socioeconomic mobility of minorities. The relatively higher unemployment rates and continuing lower economic status of minorities sometimes obscure their real advances. Since the beginning of the civil rights movement in the 1950s, the gap in real income and occupational status between black and white males and between females and males has narrowed. With reference to black men, a sign of future equity is that in the late 1950s, no age group of black men had average earnings that were two-thirds of white male average earnings. Yet, by the late 1960s, black men between twenty-five and forty-five averaged two-thirds of white male earnings. Most important for the future, young black males between twenty and twenty five increased their average earnings from 64 percent to 91 percent of average white male earnings. A reflection of this growing black economic capability is the greater percentage in annual growth in number of households—a measure of home ownership. According to a U.S. census, the percentage increase for blacks during the prosperous 1960s continued well into the stagflationary 1970s, suggesting the saliency of Wilson's as opposed to Willie's thesis about racism, discussed earlier. The household growth pattern is summarized in table 10–5.

A similar pattern of upward mobility is evident among women. Between the mid-1960s and early 1970s, the proportion of professional and technical female workers doubled from 7 to 14 percent, and the number of female managers also doubled from 2.6 to 5 percent (U.S. Department of Commerce 1968, 64; 1973, 173).

If white middle-class males accept these trends based on equal treatment, then we can expect some resolution and accommodation of intergroup conflict. Noting that such trends slow down in periods of economic recession, such as the country experienced through most of the 1970s, is important. In such periods, unemployment rates are high, ranging up to 10 percent generally, but are considerably higher (over 20 percent) for young city-dwelling blacks. As we have discussed, such experiences intensify a sense of hopelessness and increase crime rates and violent protest orientations. One way in which a sense of hopelessness and its accompanying feelings of powerlessness are being overcome is in the increasing political influence that minorities have acquired.

Increasing political influence. The likelihood of minority socioeconomic gains being maintained and advanced is related to the political influence that minorities are able to exercise. Besides the jobs that the govern-

ment offers and the effect on the laws of the land, government (through defense expenditures and many other ways) is directly involved in billions of dollars' worth of private corporate production. At the big-city and community levels, an ironic consequence of the migration of middle-class whites to the suburbs has had one major benefit for blacks: it has enabled them to exercise political power in a way reminiscent of the Irish, Polish, and other ethnic power blocs of a half century ago (see table 10–6).

By the 1970s, Cleveland, Detroit, Los Angeles, and Newark, among other cities, elected black mayors for the first time in history. The election of Mayor Thomas Bradley in Los Angeles, where voting-age blacks constituted less than 20 percent of the population, demonstrated that significant numbers of whites were willing to accept blacks in a position of high status and influence. The more controversial election of Harold Washington in Chicago still needed white support in that city, with a large but minority black population (*New York Times* 9 April 1983). More generally, city-based blacks, by exercising political power, can pressure suburbanites on certain issues. Suburban communities are linked to central cities in many ways, including water and transportation systems, and in a variety of business enterprises. Political bargaining between blacks and whites resembles the bargaining that once took place between immigrant and dominant groups. Chicanos are increasingly attaining the same position in such southwestern cities as Albuquerque, Houston, Phoenix, and Tucson, as are Puerto Ricans in New York City.

These advancements are sometimes hampered, however. In some cities (as in Miami), minorities such as blacks and Cubans may be in conflict with each other. Probably more consequential is that in earlier times (as discussed above), all bargaining parties including the dominant Anglos lived within the city. Thus, minorities of the past were more directly effective than current minorities can be in applying political pressure on

TABLE 10–5. Percentage of Household Growth in the United States, by Race, 1960 to 1976

	AVERAGE INCREASE IN HOUSEHOLDS (%)	
	1960 to 1970	*1970 to 1976*
Whites	1.9	2.3
Blacks	2.4	3.3

Sources: U.S. Department of Commerce, *Current population reports*, PC(2)–4a (table 2), PC(2)–4a (table 3), ser. P–20, no. 311 (table C) (Washington, D.C.: U.S. Government Printing Office, 1960, 1976).

the more dominant white middle class now located in suburbs.

Even with this qualification, minority control of city government in many of the largest U.S. cities constitutes real political leverage. One apparent effect of such leverage can be seen in interview results with eighteen black and twenty-five white political and economic leaders in Detroit, the city that experienced the most damaging race riot in American history and where a black mayoral administration has been in place for over a decade. On a five-point optimism-pessimism scale about the future of the city, in which +2 means "very optimistic" and −2 means "very pessimistic," the results were as follows (Gordon 1983, 131):

	+2	+1	0	−1	−2
Blacks	44%	56%	0%	0%	0%
Whites	12%	64%	12%	4%	8%

With these black leaders now in positions of political influence, it is noteworthy that both they and the white leaders had shifted their universally pessimistic assessment about the state of race relations from the riot-ridden late 1960s. On a six-point scale on the state of race relations, in which +3

means "improving considerably" and −3 means "deteriorating considerably," the results were as follows (Gordon 1983, 132):

	+3	+2	+1	−1	−2	−3
Blacks	11%	22%	50%	11%	6%	0%
Whites	4%	8%	64%	24%	4%	0%

Minorities other than urban blacks and Hispanics are also organizing. While the feminist drive for the Equal Rights Amendment (ERA) met substantial resistance, thirty-five states had ratified the ERA by 1980, thereby ensuring equal protection of the law in most states. Women began to run for and get elected to office around the nation. By the mid-1970s, over 600 of the approximately 7,500 state legislators were women (*AAUW Journal* 1975, 10). Further, when Congress created over 100 new federal judgeships in the late 1970s, President Carter appointed more blacks and women to lifetime federal judgeships than all other presidents combined (*Associated Press* 10 August 1980). Political activity is also growing among native Americans, the elderly, and the handicapped. Although this activity is still minimal, it is a sign of change.

TABLE 10–6. Percentage of Black Population in the Ten Largest Cities, 1980

	PERCENTAGE OF TOTAL POPULATION	BLACKS AS A PERCENTAGE OF TOTAL VOTING-AGE POPULATION[a]
New York	27	24
Los Angeles	17	15
Chicago	39	34
Philadelphia	35	31
Houston	29	26
Detroit	63	58
Dallas	29	26
Baltimore	54	49
Washington, D.C.	70	64
St. Louis	45	49

[a]*Voting-age population* refers to persons eighteen years old and over.

Sources: U.S. Department of Commerce, "Standard metropolitan statistical areas and standard consolidated statistical areas: 1980, *1980 census of the population supplementary reports* (Washington, D.C.: U.S. Government Printing Office, October 1981), table 1; and U.S. Department of Commerce, "Age, sex, race, and Spanish origin of the population by regions, divisions, and states, 1980, *1980 census of the population supplementary reports* (Washington, D.C.: U.S. Government Printing Office, May 1981), table 2.

Subjective Indicators of Accommodation

The revolution in minority self-image and self-expression.   Kurt Lewin (1948), a social psychologist, documented that minority members often accept the negative definition of themselves that dominant groups have developed. Blacks, Chicanos, women, and other minorities no longer tend to accept such definitions. The minority reaction is epitomized in the popular black expression that "black is beautiful," a slogan that is also a rallying concept.

Consequences of this self-expression are visible in attempts to secure equal status and power. These attempts may create initial social conflict but also provide the basis for mutual intergroup respect. As we have noted, the black power movement is finding practical expression in big-city politics. Other related consequences are the fight for the passage of the ERA, led by women, Mexican Americans' *la raza* (the race) efforts to organize Chicano migrant laborers into effective unions, the American Indian Movement's (AIM) efforts to pressure the federal government to allow native Americans to run their own affairs on their reservations, and the Puerto Rican Independence Movement, aimed at gaining independence or statehood for that American protectorate.

Accompanying these developments has been what sociologists Robert Perrucci and Marc Pilisuk call "the revolution in expression" (1971, 561), which extends from moderates to radicals. An example from the high-activity period of the 1960s' civil rights movement is found in the words of Eldridge Cleaver who, as a Black Panther Party advocate, stated that

blacks are looking on and asking tactical questions. They are asked to die for the system in Vietnam. In Watts they are killed by it. Now— Now!—they are asking each other in dead earnest: Why not die right here in Babylon, fighting for a better life like the Viet Cong? If these little cats can do it, what is wrong with big studs like us? (1968, 137)

Malcolm X, who broke from the Black Muslims, and Stokely Carmichael and H. Rap Brown of the Student Non-Violent Coordinating Committee (SNCC), among other radical leaders, used similarly strong language. One of the effects of such aggressive expression, coupled with mass expressions of black discontent, was to move nonviolent black leaders to confront whites with the need to accept change. As Roy Wilkins, a spokesman of the long established NAACP, which has the largest black membership of any civil rights organization, stated:

In his drive, the Negro citizen will use every available weapon short of violence. No sector of race relations, North or South, will escape the pressures. As with any other population of its size there will be differences on methods, on priorities, and on the degree of concentration. There will be no differences on objectives, except for that minute minority which rejects integration into American life. (1963, 44)

Since these statements of the 1960s, one of the continuing signs of changing self-expression is the insistence of many minorities on creating their own name designations. The United States census now includes the designation *black* as well as *Negro*. A corollary of this development is the increasing use of the term *Chicano* for Mexican-Americans and the use of the words *he or she* in publications rather than the generic *he*, which many see as no more a generic term for all people than *she* is. These name designations appear to represent a step toward individual and group self-determination, a well-established American value.

Signs of more accepting attitudes toward minority groups.   What about the subjective indicators among the more dominant members of the society? While white male backlash and violent efforts to prevent integration of schools and housing have sometimes occurred, clear signs are also evident that people accept minority group members more than they did in the past. Over the last half century, the social distance between most whites and others has narrowed. A measure of this is the **Social Distance Quotient** (SDQ) that Emory Bogardus (1968) devised. Bogardus formulated a list of statements representing varying degrees of social intimacy or distance. He asked samples of Americans, mostly white Protestants of British or northern European ethnic heritage, to check off those classifications to which they would willingly admit members of a given group. The social distance quotient was based on the average of the following seven ratings: to close kinship by marriage (1 point); to my club as personal chums (2 points); to my street as neighbor (3 points); to employment in my occupation (4 points); to citizenship in my country (5 points); as visitors to my country (6 points); would exclude from my country (7 points).

Thirty ethnic, religious, and racial groups were listed in Bogardus's first sampling in 1926. Reliable information on trends in social distance is available because samples were again drawn in later years. The results of the 1926, 1946, and 1966 samples are provided in table 10–7. Note that while the rank remains similar, with blacks and other

Such scenes of blacks and whites, men and women working successfully and cooperatively together are more and more the norm in American society. Over the last half century, the social distance between most whites and others has narrowed.

racial minorities at the bottom, the total distance that white Anglo-Americans and others place between themselves and others has narrowed considerably. In 1926, the Americans surveyed listed five groups, including blacks, which they would not welcome as neighbors. By the mid-1960s, most people no longer expressed such a feeling about any group, as reported by Gallup and Harris polls that confirm the persistence of this trend.

College students, who will occupy influential economic and social positions, have expressed similar attitudes. Samples taken among college students between the 1930s and 1970s show a sharp drop in negative and hostile perceptions of minorities (Gilbert 1951; Gordon 1973; Katz and Braly 1933). For example, regarding negative traits attributed to blacks in these studies, all declined sharply—"superstitious" dropped from over 80 percent to less than 15 percent, "lazy"

TABLE 10–7.   Changes in Racial and Ethnic Social Distance

1926 SAMPLE OF 1,726 THROUGHOUT U.S.		1946 SAMPLE OF 2,053 THROUGHOUT U.S.		1966 SAMPLE OF 2,605 THROUGHOUT U.S.		
Cultural Group	SDQ*	Cultural Group	SDQ	Cultural Group	SDQ	
1. English	1.06	1. Americans (U.S. white)	1.08	1. Americans (U.S. white)	1.07	
2. American (U.S. white)	1.10	2. Canadians	1.16	2. English	1.14	
3. Canadians	1.13	3. English	1.23	3. Canadians	1.15	Primarily
4. Scots	1.13	4. French	1.47	4. French	1.36	British
5. Irish	1.30	5. Irish	1.56	5. Irish	1.40	and
6. French	1.32	6. Swedish	1.57	6. Swedish	1.42	Northern
7. Germans	1.46	7. Scots	1.60	7. Norwegians	1.50	European
8. Swedish	1.54	8. Germans	1.61	8. Italians	1.51	
9. Hollanders	1.56	9. Hollanders	1.63	9. Scots	1.53	
10. Norwegians	1.59	10. Norwegians	1.66	10. Germans	1.54	
11. Spanish	1.72	11. Finns	1.80	11. Hollanders	1.54	
12. Finns	1.83	12. Italians	1.89	12. Finns	1.67	
13. Russians	1.88	13. Poles	2.07	13. Greeks	1.82	Primarily
14. Italians	1.94	14. Spanish	2.08	14. Spanish	1.93	Southern
15. Poles	2.01	15. Greeks	2.09	15. Jews	1.97	and
16. Armenians	2.06	16. Jews	2.15	16. Poles	1.98	Eastern
17. Czechs	2.08	17. Czechs	2.22	17. Czechs	2.02	European
18. Indians (Amer.)	2.38	18. Armenians	2.33	18. Indians (Amer.)	2.12	
19. Jews	2.39	19. Japanese-Amer.	2.34	19. Japanese-Amer.	2.14	
20. Greeks	2.47	20. Indians (Amer.)	2.35	20. Armenians	2.18	
21. Mexicans	2.69	21. Filipinos	2.46	21. Filipinos	2.31	
22. Mexican-Amer.	—	22. Mexican-Amer.	2.51	22. Chinese	2.34	
23. Japanese	2.80	23. Turks	2.52	23. Mexican-Amer.	2.37	Primarily
24. Japanese-Amer.	—	24. Russians	2.56	24. Russians	2.38	Nonwhite
25. Filipinos	3.00	25. Chinese	2.68	25. Japanese	2.41	Racial
26. Negroes	3.28	26. Japanese	2.70	26. Turks	2.48	Groups
27. Turks	3.30	27. Negroes	2.74	27. Koreans	2.51	
28. Chinese	3.36	28. Mexicans	2.79	28. Mexicans	2.56	
29. Koreans	3.60	29. Indians (from India)	2.80	29. Negroes	2.58	
30. Indians (from India)	3.91	30. Koreans	2.83	30. Indians (from India)	2.62	

*Social Distance Quotient

Source: Emory S. Bogardus, Comparing racial distance in Ethiopia, South Africa and the United States, *Sociology and Social Research* 52:152 (1968).

dropped from about 75 percent to about 25 percent, and "stupid" dropped from about 20 percent to about 5 percent in different recent samples. The same trend was evident in opinions about ethnic and religious groups. In the latest studies, Italians were no longer generally viewed as "revengeful" nor Jews as "sly."

The general shift toward the acceptance of minority groups and individual members of those groups may be a major accommodating factor in ensuring true equality of treatment and opportunity. This factor is based on the assumption that American society will be able to stabilize its economy as new energy sources are developed. Conditions will need to improve sufficiently for minority group members before the emergence of a new J-curve of rising expectations and declining opportunities. The adaptive history of American society offers hope. An accommodating sign of the times for many long-excluded groups is the following statement from a bulletin of a major university—reflective of most large private enterprise policy statements, as well:

It is the policy of The University of Michigan that no person, on the basis of race, sex, color, religion, national origin or ancestry, age, marital status, handicap, or Vietnam-era veteran status, shall be discriminated against in employment, educational programs and activities, or admissions. (*University of Michigan Today* 1983)

SUMMARY

In American society, open **conflict**—including the resolution of conflict—helps us interpret the relations between minority and dominant groups. **Prejudice** and **discrimination** that blacks, Chicanos, native Americans, and other minority group members experience also shed light on racial and ethnic relations. Theories that the "new hereditarians" advanced have rekindled popular beliefs in the genetic superiority of white Anglo males. Most social scientific research does not support these beliefs, yet such be-

liefs lead to the Thomas theorem, which holds that even false beliefs can lead to real consequences.

Early century natural history assimilationist theories appear to fit well for European ethnic groups who have largely moved into the middle class. Racial prejudice is much deeper in American society, however. Educational, housing, and occupational de facto segregation continues for many racial minority members, as well as for Chicanos, women, and other minority members long excluded from the society's opportunity system. This segregation has constituted an American dilemma in which the American ideal of equality of opportunity and the practice of inequality come into conflict.

Civil rights movements led by blacks, Chicanos, native Americans, and women over the past two decades have changed intergroup relations in the society. Legal reforms have resulted, including passage of such federal measures as the comprehensive Civil Rights Act of 1964 and the Elementary and Secondary Education Act. Recent signs of white middle-class resistance to such minority challenges are evident in the organized opposition to court-ordered busing for school desegregation and to affirmative action policies designed to bring more blacks and other minority members into new educational and occupational settings.

Even with resistance, a number of objective and subjective indicators of social mobility advancement and more general acceptance of minority group members are evident. The scope of the problem is such that both continuing intergroup conflict and the need for conflict resolution remain high on the society's social agenda.

STUDY QUESTIONS

1. In your observations, what are ways in which some people express prejudicial attitudes but do not discriminate, while others do not appear personally prejudiced but do discriminate against minority group members?

2. What minority-led social movements are going on today? Who are their leaders, and toward what goals are they striving?

3. English is full of black and white imagery, with the term *black* often taking on negative connotations and *white* positive connotations. What effects do you think this usage has had on racial minority members and on white Anglo self-images?

4. Lewis Coser poses the question, why is it that when a group is long denied legitimate outlets for expressing dissent, subsequent intergroup conflict tends to be more intense and dysfunctional than it might originally have been?

5. Based on the experience of different racial and ethnic groups, what points can you marshal to support or to dispute the idea that American Society has been a racial and ethnic melting pot?

REFERENCES

AAUW Journal. 1975. Where women stand. (November): 10.

Alvarez, R. 1973. The psycho-historical and socioeconomic development of the Chicano community in the United States. *Social Science Quarterly 14:* 920–42.

Allport, G. 1958. *The nature of prejudice.* New York: Anchor.

Arizona Republic. 31 March 1983.

Associated Press. 25 May 1980; 10 August 1980.

Baltzell, D. 1964. *The Protestant establishment: Aristocracy and caste in America.* New York: Random House.

Bell, I. P. 1968. *CORE and the strategy of non-violence.* New York: Random House.

Berry, B. 1965. *Race and ethnic relations.* Boston: Houghton Mifflin.

Bogardus, E. 1968. *Social distance.* Yellow Springs, Ohio: Antioch.

Brown vs. Topeka, Kansas Board of Education 1955. 349 U.S. Supreme Court 294.

Carmichael, S., and C. Hamilton. 1967. *Black power.* New York: Random House.

Cleaver, E. 1968. *Soul on ice.* New York: McGraw-Hill.

Coleman, J., et al. 1966. *Equality of education opportunity.* Washington, D.C.: U.S. Government Printing Office.

Coser, Lewis 1967. Continuities in the Study of Social Conflict. New York: The Free Press.

Davies, J. C. 1969. The J-curve of rising expectations and declining satisfactions as a cause of some great revolutions and contained rebellion. In *Violence in America,* ed. H. D. Graham and T. R. Gurr, 690–730. New York: Bantam.

DeFleur, M. L. and F. R. Westie 1958. Verbal attitudes and overt acts. *American Sociological Review 23:* 667–673.

DeFunis vs. Odegaard 1974. 416 U.S. Supreme Court 312.

DeWard, R. 1919. Americanization and immigration. *American Review of Reviews* LIX: 513–16.

Dobzhansky, T. 1962. *Mankind evolving.* New Haven, Conn.: Yale Univ. Press.

Ellis, Lee 1977. "The decline and fall of sociology: 1975–2000." American Sociologist 12: 56–66.

Etzioni, A. 1959. The ghetto: A reevaluation. *Social Forces 37:* 255–62.

Farley, R. 1975. White flight to suburbs not caused by busing. *Information: Quarterly Journal of the National Institute of Education* (Fall): 1.

———. 1977. Trends in racial inequalities. *American Sociological Review:* 189–208.

Fogelson, R. 1971. *Violence as protest: A study of riots and ghettos.* New York: Anchor.

Friedman, L. 1970. *The white savage: Racial fantasies in the post-bellum South.* Englewood Cliffs, N.J.: Prentice-Hall.

Giele, J. Z. 1978. *Women and the future.* New York: Free Press.

Gilbert, G. M. 1951. Stereotype persistence and change among college students. *Journal of Abnormal and Social Psychology:* 245–54.

Glazer, N. 1975. *Affirmative discrimination: Ethnic inequality and public policy.* New York: Basic.

Glazer, N., and D. Moynihan. 1971. *Beyond the melting pot: The Negroes, Puerto Ricans, Jews, Italians, and Irish of New York City.* Cambridge: MIT and Harvard Univ. Press.

Goldberg, A. 1975. Statistical inference in the great IQ debate. *Institute for Research on Poverty Discussion Papers.* Madison, Wis.: Univ. of Wisconsin Press.

Gordon, L. 1973. The fragmentization of literary stereotypes of Jews and of Negroes among college students. *Pacific Sociological Review* 16: 411–25.

———. 1982. Sample results of racial and ethnic stereotyping among American and British college students. (Sabbatical research project at Arizona State, Lancaster, and London Universities).

———. 1983. Aftermath of a race riot: The emergent norm process among black and white community leaders. *Sociological Perspectives* 26: 115–135.

Grant, M. 1916. *The passing of the great race.* New York: Charles Scribner's Sons. 1979. *Harris Poll report on affirmative action.* Cited in I. Robertson, *Social Problems* 1980, p. 230. New York: Random House.

Harvard Educational Review. 1969. Critique of Arthur Jensen's IQ and scholastic achievement thesis. (Spring–Summer).

Hirsch, D. M. 1926. A study of natio-racial mental differences. *Genetic Psychology Monographs:* 231–406.

Hoult, T. F. 1969. *Dictionary of modern sociology.* Totowa, N.J.: Littlefield, Adams.

Ivy, J. 1964. Highlights in school desegregation. *The Crisis* (May): 285–89.

Jensen, A. 1969. How much can we boost IQ and scholastic achievement? *Harvard Educational Review* (Winter): 1–123.

———. 1980. *Bias in mental testing.* New York: Free Press.

Josephy, A. M., Jr. 1971. *Red power: The American Indians' fight for freedom.* New York: McGraw-Hill.

Karlins, M., T. Coffman, and G. Walters 1969. On the fading of social stereotypes: studies in three generations of college students. *Journal of Personality and Social Psychology* 13: 1–16.

Katz, D., and K. W. Braly. 1933. Racial stereotypes of 100 college students. *Journal of Abnormal Psychology* 23: 280–90.

King, M. L., Jr., 1967. *Where do we go from here: Community or chaos?* New York: Harper & Row.

Laurenti, L. 1960. *Property values and race.* Berkeley: Univ. of California Press.

Lewin, K. 1948. *Resolving social conflicts.* New York: Harper & Brothers.

Lieberson, S. 1980. *A piece of the pie: Blacks and white immigrants since 1880.* Berkeley: Univ. of California Press.

Lipset, S., and E. Raab. 1970. *The politics of unreason: Right-wing extremism in America, 1790–1970.* New York: Harper & Row.

Lyman, S. 1968. The race relations cycle of Robert E. Park. *Pacific Sociological Review* II: 16–22.

Merton, R. 1949. Discrimination and the American creed. In *Discrimination and the national welfare,* ed. R. MacIver, 100–110. New York: Harper & Row.

———. 1967. *On theoretical sociology.* New York: Free Press.

Myrdal, G. 1944. *An American dilemma: The Negro problem and modern democracy.* New York: Harper & Row.

National Advisory Commission on Civil Disorders. 1968. *Report of the National Advisory Commission on Civil Disorders.* Washington, D.C.: U.S. Government Printing Office.

New York Times. 13 March 1966; 9 April 1983.

Park, R. 1949. *Race and culture.* New York: Free Press.

Perrucci, R., and M. Pilisuk. 1971. *The triple revolution.* Boston: Little, Brown.

Pinckney, A. 1973. The black American. In *Outsiders: U.S.A.,* ed. D. Spiegel and P. Keith-Spiegel, 347–70. New York: Holt, Rinehart & Winston.

Plessy vs. Ferguson 1896. 163 U.S. Supreme Court 537.

Regents of the University of California vs. Bakke 1978. 438 U.S. Supreme Court 265.

Rosen, B. 1959. Race, ethnicity and the achievement syndrome. *American Sociological Review* 24: 47–60.

Rosenthal, R., and L. Jacobson. 1968. *Pygmalion in the classroom.* New York: Holt, Rinehart & Winston.

Sewall, G., and E. Lee. 1980. Jensen's rebuttal. *Newsweek* (14 January): 59.

Shirer, W. 1960. *The rise and fall of the Third Reich.* New York: Simon & Schuster.

Silberman, C. 1970. *Crisis in the classroom: The remaking of American education.* New York: Vintage.

Smelser, N. 1962. *Theory of collective behavior.* New York: Free Press.

Smith, R. 1971. Disaffection, delegitimation and consequences: Aggregate trends for World War II, Korea and Vietnam. In *Public opinion and the military establishment,* ed. C. Moskos, 230–38. Beverly Hills: Sage.

Spencer, H. 1877. *Principles of sociology.* New York: Appleton-Century-Crofts.

Steinberg, S. 1981. *The ethnic myth: Race, ethnicity, and class in America* New York: Atheneum.

Sumner, W. G. 1906. *Folkways.* Boston: Ginn.

Taeuber, K., and A. Taeuber. 1969. Negro residential segregation in the United States cities. In *Negroes in cities,* ed. K. Taeuber and A. Taeuber, 28–68. New York: Atheneum.

Thomas, W. I. 1928. *The child in America: Problems and programs.* New York: Knopf.

———. 1931. The relation of research to the social process. In *Essays on research in the social sciences.* Washington, D.C.: Brookings Institution.

University of Michigan Today. 1983. Policy statement. (Spring). Ann Arbor: Univ. of Michigan Press.

U.S. Steel Workers of America AFL-CIO, CLC vs. Weber 1979. 443 U.S. Supreme Court 193.

U.S. Department of Commerce. 1968. *Manpower report of the president.* Washington, D.C.: U.S. Government Printing Office.

———. 1970. The social and economic status of the black population in the United States. *Current population reports.* Washington, D.C.: U.S. Government Printing Office.

———. 1973. *Manpower report of the president.* Washington, D.C.: U.S. Government Printing Office.

Vander Zanden, J. 1983. *American minority relations.* New York: Ronald.

Warner, L., and P. Lunt. 1941. *The social life of a modern community.* New Haven Conn.: Yale Univ. Press.

Waskow, A. 1967. *From race riot to sit-in.* New York: Anchor.

Westie, F. 1965. The American dilemma: an empirical test. *American Sociological Review* 30: 527–538.

Wilkins, R. 1963. Emancipation and militant leadership. In *100 years of emancipation,* ed. R. Goldwin, 25–46. Chicago: Rand McNally.

Willie, C. V. 1978. The inclining significance of race. *Society* (July–August): 10–15.

Wilson, E. O. 1975. *Sociobiology: The New Synthesis.* Cambridge, Mass.: Harvard University Press.

Wilson, W. J., 1978a. *The declining significance of race.* Chicago: Univ. of Chicago Press.

———. 1978b. The declining significance of race: Revisited but not revised. *Society* (July–August): 11–21.

CHAPTER 11

Gender Roles in Transition

CONTENTS

The myth of equality: Compelling reasons to support the NOW legal defense and education fund

FACT: According to the U.S. Department of Labor, median earnings for full time workers age 16 and over were $301 per week. But white males earned $371, white females earned $234, and Hispanic females earned $203. (1)

FACT: Almost one female-headed family in three is poor; about one in eighteen families headed by a man is poor. (2)

FACT: In 1981, the number of children with mothers at work (31.8 million) was larger than the number of children with mothers at home (26.3 million). (3)

FACT: A study tracing child support payments by ex-husbands over 10 years showed 42% of these fathers didn't make a single payment in the first year. By the tenth year, 79% were making no payments. (4)

FACT: In 1980, total direct costs to raise a child in the U.S. were estimated at $85,163 through four years of college, or $72,894 to age 18 (moderate cost). (5)

FACT: One half of all women work in just 20% of over 440 occupational categories. They are 98% of all nurses, 98% of all receptionists, 97% of all secretaries. (6) (3)

FACT: Under the current job classification system a government secretary is paid less than a government parking lot attendant. Child care workers' salaries are on a par with dog pound attendants. (7)

FACT: More than one third of candidates for MBAs this year are women, but only 5% of executives in the top 50 companies are women. (8)

FACT: The majority of college students are women (6.2 million women, compared to 5.8 million men), yet women are only 25% of full-time college faculty and they are clustered at the lower professional ranks. (9)

FACT: Because of child bearing and rearing responsibilities, many women take time out from paid employment. Since most pension plans contain stringent requirements that workers be employed by the same employer for a long period of time, women who drop out of the paid labor force to take care of their families may forfeit contributions they may have made and find themselves ineligible for any benefits. (10)

FACT: As a result of pervasive job segregation and failure of the law or employers to reform pension coverage to take appro-priate account of women's child rearing responsibilities, women are half as likely as men to be employed in positions covered by private pension plans. (11)

FACT: Seventy-eight percent of all U.S. counties had no identified abortion service provider in 1980, and 28% of women of reproductive age lived in these counties. (12)

FACT: Between 18% and 23% of Medicaid eligible women who would have obtained abortions when Medicaid funding was available instead carried their pregnancies to term when that funding was cut off. (12)

---

(1) *Employment News,* Vol. III, #8; (2) National Advisory Council on Economic Opportunity, Twelfth Report, August 1980; (3) *New York Times,* 8/2/82; (4) L. Weitzman, "Legal Regulation of Marriage: Tradition and Change," *California Law Review;* (5) T. Espenshade, *Raising a Child Can Now Cost* $85,000; (6) Mary Rubin, "Women and Poverty," *Research Summary from Business and Professional Women's Foundation,* Series #4; (7) Ellen Goodman, "Earning Less for Women's Work," *Washington Post,* 10/16/78; (8) Jay Cocks, "How Long Till Equal-

ity?", *Time,* 7/12/82; **(9)** "On Campus with Women," *Association of American Colleges,* June 1978; **(10)** President's Commission on Pension Policy, *Working Papers: Working Women, Marriage, and Retire-ment* 36 (1980); **(11)** President's Commission on Pension Policy, *An Interim Report* 7 (1980); *Consultation on Discrimination supra* n. 20 at 473–75; **(12)** S. Henshaw, J. Forrest, E. Sullivan, C. Tietze "Abortion Services in the United States, 1979 and 1980," *Family Planning Perspectives,* Vol. 14, No. 1.

Source: NOW Legal Defense and Education Fund mailing, November 1982.

DEFINING THE PROBLEM: STRUCTURED SOCIAL INEQUALITY

"The Myth of Equality," which begins this chapter, outlines a number of inequities in contemporary American society. These inequities affect women in a variety of roles, the majority of which are family related. As shown in chapter 3, many ideals about the family and its members are not matched by the realities. This chapter discusses the inequalities in sex and gender roles that go beyond family relationships—inequalities that are problematic not only to individuals but also to society as a whole.

What Are Roles?

To understand sex and gender roles, a common definition of the term *role* itself must be introduced. A role is a pattern of behavior that individuals typically perform in specific situations. To some extent, the expectancies (norms) for the behavior patterns of role occupants are based on status within a given group. Consider, for example, the teacher-student status differential. Teachers and students are expected to attend classes and to be on time. Students, however, are not expected to select study materials, to prepare lectures, or to give tests; those behaviors are part of the typical role pattern for teachers. The status hierarchy, in the teacher-student case, is based on differences in expertise and responsibility.

Now consider the family as another social group. The nuclear family—usually consisting of parents and a child (or children)—contains several status relationships based on differences in age and sex. In the *authoritarian* view, the father is the head of the family. Sons, who are expected to become husbands and fathers, have higher status than daughters. The mother is the father's helpmate and is second in command. Daughters, who are expected to become wives and mothers, share the second-rank status assigned to their mothers. Children of either sex have lower status than parents of either sex. The authoritarian view defines roles of males and females in relatively narrow terms, primarily on the basis of sex. In the *equalitarian* view, mothers share the same status within the family as fathers. The status differential between parents and children is based on differences in expertise and responsibility—not on whether the individuals are male or female.

Expectancies for behaviors, in either of the views above, include ideas about the rights and obligations that roles carry with them. In their roles as parents, siblings, and children, family members may conform imprecisely to the behaviors we expect. When behavior departs too far from our expectancies, however, we often feel confused and angry, and try to bring the norm violators into line with our definitions. The authoritarian view provides little latitude in role definitions, and departures from conventionality are likely to be seen as disturbing. The equalitarian view, however, provides considerable latitude in role definitions, and unless they are extreme, departures from conventionality are unlikely to be viewed as disturbing.

To authoritarians, equalitarians seem to violate status arrangements that are believed essential to the continuance of family life. To equalitarians, authoritarians seem to cling to outmoded, impractical, and even destructive status arrangements, given a rapidly changing world.

The terms *traditional* and *modern* are popularized versions of the authoritarian/equalitarian distinction, but these terms are misleading. *Traditional* alludes to the way things were in a past, stable society, and *modern* alludes to the way things are in a present, rapidly changing society. In reality, role and status definitions have changed along with societal conditions throughout history. In the Victorian era, for example, the sexual roles of men and women were reversed. As historian Florence Rush tells us:

Woman was previously seen as the source of sin and man the embodiment of virtue, but when the exploding industrial economy required undisguised aggression and conquest, this order was conveniently reversed. Men appropriated sin, sexual lust and ambition as inherent positive masculine traits and assigned women, now defined as innately pure, passive and asexual, as the guardians of religion and morality. Wifehood and motherhood were glorified and it became a man's duty to protect (or exclude) "the angel in the house" from the nasty business of money making, politics, and world affairs. (1980, 67–68)

This example indicates why the terms *authoritarian* and *equalitarian* are preferable to *traditional* and *modern*. Although we will continue to use the first pair of terms in this chapter, students should be aware that in the public sphere, the second pair of terms is most often used.

Authoritarians link expectancies for behavior to the sex of the individual occupying a role; equalitarians see no necessity for linking role behavior expectancies to sex. Our language structure, however, is somewhat confusing with regard to the terms we apply to various roles. Some work-related words are conventionally linked to sex (e.g., mailman), although it makes no difference which sex performs the work (e.g., mail carrier). Some family-related words are sex-neutral (child or spouse), but others are sex-specific (brother or aunt). Although these constructions are merely a matter of linguistics and vary among languages, common usage of and familiarity with sex-specific words sometimes lead to the belief that the words represent the "natural order" of work or family arrangements.

The term *sex role*, for instance, should be applied only to patterns of behavior that only one or the other sex *can* perform. In common usage, however, the term is often incorrectly applied to patterns of behavior that are believed appropriate to only one or the other sex. The preferable term for behaviors seen as sex-appropriate is *gender role*. This chapter is more concerned with gender roles than with sex roles, for instance, the behavior of nursing mothers or sperm donors (see Gould and Kern-Daniels 1977).

Gender role is somewhat difficult to explain. As previously noted, the term refers to behavior or to role occupancy that is conventionally thought to be sex-appropriate. The term *gender* is used to indicate the relative masculinity or femininity of a role or of role performance, and refers to the qualities, traits, or characteristics of roles or their occupants. It would be virtually impossible to think of the sex role of nursing mother as masculine, or the sex role of sperm donor as feminine. For almost all other roles, however, conventional distinctions are made between male and female roles, and between masculine and feminine role performances. When roles or expectancies for role performance are assigned in this way, without regard to the desires or the accomplishments of the role occupant, sociologists call these **ascribed** roles. Roles occupied on the basis of something one has done, or on the basis of requirements one has met, are called **achieved** roles. Gender-role distinctions are ascribed, and in the authoritarian view, are sex linked. Equalitarians, however, see these ascriptions as arbitrary and potentially or actually destructive, since they restrict the range of human functioning and lead to personal and social misery.

Gender-Role Stereotypes

The authoritarian view of masculinity and femininity has been the conventional, or prevailing view. For most Americans, this view has been the guideline by which behavior was judged to be either normal or deviant. In this view, exceptions to men's masculine behavior might be permitted under unusual circumstances (for example, a man may cry when a parent or close friend dies). The man who is more expressive than the masculine ideal allows under usual circumstances, however, would be suspect. His behavior might be called effeminate, and ridiculed or stigmatized (Goffman 1963). Similarly, if women took on "men's work" during wartime, permission might be granted under the unusual conditions. Women who wished to retain such positions in a postwar world, however, might be called masculine and unnatural.

To equalitarians, authoritarian views of "normalcy" are unthinking conformity to arbitrary status arrangements (Chafetz 1974:4). In the equalitarian view, the best possible world would be one in which individuals' roles and role performances would be based on achievement, not ascription (1974:x). Thus, men who develop competency at child-care and women who develop competency in competitive careers are seen as flexible, adaptive persons whose achievements are suited to the changing demands of the contemporary world (Sinnott, 1974:144). Sex-linked gender ascriptions, in this view, are **masculinist** (derivatives of our long history of male dominance or patriarchy, and of its correlate, the inferiorization of women) (Tripp, 1976:38).

Stereotypic views of masculinity and femininity, currently widespread in our society, describe the real—not just the desired or expected—characteristics of boys and girls and of men and women. As sociologists Judith Bardwick and Elizabeth Douvan (1980, 56–57) point out, *individuals* may more resemble the stereotype of the other sex, but *group* differences between the sexes bear out the stereotypic portraits. Equalitarians argue that this resemblance is the result of socialization—the process through which social identity is learned from parents and other sources that influence the young. Authoritarians do not deny the importance of socialization. They argue, however, that the correspondence between stereotypes and reality is due to biological programming, or to God-given masculine-feminine differences, or both. According to Bardwick and Douvan, the conventional version of masculinity includes at least the following qualities:

independence, aggression, competitiveness, leadership, task-orientation, assertiveness, innovation, self-discipline, stoicism, activity, analytic-mindedness, objectivity, courage, unsentimentality, rationality, confidence, and emotional control (1980, 56).

Femininity, on the other hand, includes at least the following "opposite" qualities:

dependence, passivity, fragility, low pain tolerance, non-aggression, noncompetitiveness, inner orientation, empathy, sensitivity, nurturance, subjectivity, intuitiveness, yieldingness, receptivity, inability to risk, emotional lability and supportiveness (1980,56).

The conventional assignment of these and other characteristics to each sex provides a ready-made guide for training the young. The fact that we *must* be trained casts doubt on both the biologically programmed and God-given authoritarian arguments, although the need for *some* guidelines is societally necessary, as sociologists Peter Berger and Hansfried Kellner explain:

While there are individual biographical differences making for differences in . . . specific individuals, there exists in society an overall consensus on the range of differences deemed to be tolerable. Without such consensus, indeed, society would be impossible . . . since it would lack the ordering principles by which alone experience can be shared and conduct can be mutually intelligible (1980, 164–65).

Berger and Kellner's statement does not imply that the consensus we have is the only one possible or that consensus on what constitutes masculinity and feminity must be universal (which it is not). The guidelines for behavior may be *any* set of guidelines, as long as they are shared within any given society.

The socialization process of early childhood, however, is insufficient to keep males behaving in masculine ways and females behaving in feminine ways, as conventionally defined. According to Berger and Kellner (1980, 165), each of us needs ongoing validation of our identity, especially from **significant others** (people of importance to us, whose opinions we value). Ongoing validation sustains the plausibility and stability of the world as it has been defined for us. If we were truly certain that reality as we have learned it is both inevitable and universal, we would not need to have the conventions we live by or our social identities repeatedly confirmed. Validation of our identities is rewarding, however, and rewards sustain our motivation to behave in ways that ensure additional rewards.

Liberation Movements

Over the past twenty years, segments of the population have determined that conventional constructions work against rather than for human interest. Native Americans, Blacks, and other racial and ethnic minority groups, for instance, forged separate identities in which they could take pride, and proclaimed their disavowal of the dominant white male power structure that defined them as second-class citizens. During this time, the women's liberation movement resurfaced. Feminists asserted their refusal to accept authoritarian definitions of their "place" in society and of their behavior. They began to redefine themselves, based on the realities of their own lives.

Authoritarians accused feminists of creating a war between the sexes. Feminists (of both sexes) claimed that a long-standing war had been raging under an artificially placid surface of conventional masculinity/femininity definitions, perpetuated by the **double standard** (one set of rules for women, another set of rules for men). Authoritarians warned that feminists would destroy the family. Feminists contended that families have not been very healthy settings for either women or children, since both have been at the mercy of male-favoring norms.

Because feminism has been visible and vocal since the early 1960s, it is less well known that a parallel movement aimed at freeing men from authoritarian restrictions on their lives also began in the late 1960s. This men's liberation movement has generated a considerable body of literature. In 1974, political scientist Warren Farrell wrote his doctoral dissertation on the effect of the women's liberation movement on men's attitudes, and also in 1974, Farrell published *The Liberated Man*. A number of other writers soon followed Farrell's lead, their works dealing with ways in which authoritarian prescriptions for gender roles have impaired males' capacities to exercise the full range of their potential. Many of their books and articles indicate that authoritarian status arrangements are not only limiting to men but are also destructive, and virtually all works credit feminists for beginning the movement toward freedom from ascribed roles and behaviors (Fasteau 1974; Fein 1974a, 1974b; Goldberg 1976, 1979; Harrison 1975; Levine 1976; Petras 1975; Pleck and Sawyer 1974).

The authoritarian-equalitarian distinctions displayed in this section are not merely fodder for a quarrel between advocates of differing points of view. The ideological struggle is one in which each side sees the other as the source of a massive social problem. Equalitarians call for changes that would remove "antiquated roles and barriers to improved human alliances" (Nichols 1975, 20). Authoritarians call for programs to "strengthen morals" so that "right" ways of living may be perpetuated. The issues extend far beyond whether gender attributes are sex linked or sex interchangeable, innate or learned, reaching into virtually every aspect of economic, political, and social life.

As the following section illustrates, not every society defines gender-role behaviors in the same way. No matter how definitions vary, however, questions of normalcy versus deviance, based on beliefs in either sex linkage or sex interchangeability of behavior, underlie a power struggle whose effects are experienced by every member of society.

CONFRONTING THE PROBLEM: ARE GENDER AND SEX LINKS UNIVERSAL?

About half a century ago, the pioneering studies of anthropologist Margaret Mead drove a wedge into beliefs that our conventional sex-gender linking is universal. Mead's (1969) work included a study of three New Guinea villages within a 200-mile radius. The tribes she studied and first described in 1935 were the Tchambuli, the Arapesh, and the Mundugumor.

The Tchambuli villagers showed strong differences between the sexes; however, the characteristic behaviors and attitudes of men and women were opposite to those that our society conventionally assigns. Tchambuli men were "artistic, gossipy, delicate, and emotional; women were the major economic providers and were energetic, managerial, and unadorned" (Yorburg 1974, 27).

Among the Arapesh, Dr. Mead discovered that *both* men and women were "gentle and maternal, oriented toward the growth of all living things" (Yorburg 1974, 26). Sociologist Betty Yorburg summarized Mead's findings about the Arapesh as follows:

Aggressiveness, competitiveness, and possessiveness were strongly discouraged for both sexes, and gentleness, passivity, emotional warmth, and versatility were non-sex-typed, ideal personality traits. Sex typing was also minimal in the area of child care, which was defined as the work of both men and women. Both sexes were regarded as having identical sex drives; they were equally free and equally likely to initiate sexual intercourse. (1974, 26)[1]

---

1. Yorburg's term *sex typed* has the same meaning as our term *sex linked*.

Is this woman's executive role threatening to anyone or to conventional values? Authoritarians say it is; equalitarians say it isn't.

In short, gender characteristics did not differentiate between Arapesh men and women. Both sexes behaved in what we would conventionally call womanly or feminine ways.

The Mundugumor villagers were also undifferentiated by gender characteristics, but in a different way from the Arapesh. Yorburg summarizes Mead's findings about the Mundugumor:

[B]oth males and females were violently aggressive, insatiably acquisitive, and equally rivalrous. . . . Dr. Mead feels that only the great wealth and natural resources of this society enabled it to exist at all, characterized as it was by universal hostility and distrust. Both sexes hated openly and loved aggressively (1974, 27).

In summary of her study of the three New Guinea groups, Mead offered the following conclusion.

[M]any, if not all, of the personality traits which we have called masculine or feminine are as lightly linked to sex as are the clothing, the manners, and the form of headdress that a society at a given period assigns to either sex. . . . the evidence is overwhelmingly in favor of the strength of social conditioning (Yorburg 1974, 260).

If masculinity and feminity, as we conventionally define them, are sex linked because they are biologically programmed into humans, the Tchambuli, Arapesh, and Mundugumor (and other people whose gender prescriptions differ from our own) would be impossible to explain. Mead's work has been questioned by later anthropologists (*Newsweek* 14 February 1983) but this is not surprising, since ethnographers' work is often criticized by later workers in the same field. Moreover, Mead was female and, as sociologists John N. Edwards and Patricia Kluck remark, ethnographies written by men "are overwhelmingly couched in etic terms, unduly imposing an outside observer's (strictly male) view on native life" (1980:322) (The emic view, in contrast, is the view of a society's insiders.).

If the biological programming explanation fails in the face of the gender-characteristic distribution that Mead and others have discovered, one might still argue that because of peculiar sociocultural factors (e.g., economic political, or both), the instinctive differences between men and women in Mead's villages were severely repressed. In this view, such factors could account for the feminization of Tchambuli men and the masculinization of Tchambuli and Mundugumor women. Proving such an argument rests on the ability to demonstrate that there *are* instinctive (biologically determined) characteristics of men and women.

Are Gender Characteristics Instinctive?

The very definition of *instinct* defies the argument that some characteristics are biologically determined. Instincts are innate (i.e., inborn, unlearned) behaviors that are linked to species survival. If we use the same definition of *instinct* (*Webster's Third New International Dictionary*) that applies to other life forms, the term refers to *complex, species-wide, species-specific* responses to stimuli, which are *uninhibitable* (unalterable by reasoning processes). Complex behavior examples are found, for instance, in the work patterns of ants or bees; species-wide characteristics are those found in all normal (unimpaired) members. Species-specific means, for instance, that spiders (arachnids) respond to their need for food by spinning webs and not by hunting, as wolves (canids) do. Finally, a behavior pattern that is uninhibitable means that once the behavior pattern has begun as a response to the stimulus that triggered it, the pattern continues even when obstacles are placed in its way. This latter aspect of instincts alone argues against the belief that biologically programmed differences between men and women could be suppressed.

Even among those who grant that almost no human behavior fits the definition of instinct, the idea that women have a built-in maternal instinct persists. Almost as strong is the related belief that all men welcome male offspring. Among the Mundugumor, however, women showed no maternal inclinations whatever. They "dreaded pregnancy, nursed unwillingly, and violently rejected their daughters" (Yorburg 1974, 27). Mundugumor men virtually hated their sons (Chafetz 1974, 8). In our society, psychologist Herb Goldberg relates that

as far back as 1923, Ruth Read of Columbia University published an article in which she interviewed eighty-seven pregnant women. She asked if they were happily anticipating their babies. Seventy-five percent of them said "no," and gave many different reasons. Of those who answered "yes," a number did so only because their religion deemed motherhood a duty. (1976, 15)

Contemporarily, Barbara Lusk Forisha reminds us that "the number of children who are neglected, battered, and abused . . . stands as evidence against the 'naturalness' of the maternal instinct" (1978, 349). As Forisha points out, evidence exists that women (and females of other species) *learn* to be mothers, although not all women learn equally well.

Among those who have studied such matters, consensus favors Mead's conclusion that social conditioning, as it varies from society to society, is the main factor that produces gender differences. Humans have an enormous range of possible behavioral traits, and have the ability to take on roles of all kinds (Brenton 1966, 49–50). Our human capacity to adapt suggests that no single pattern of gender-role behavior is innate (Nichols 1975, 58). Thomas Ford Hoult's *Dictionary of Modern Sociology* (1969, 165) cites the following scholarly conclusions on the topic of human instincts.

Human instincts, viewed as behaviors, are . . . either reflexes . . . or they are habits modified by learning, and hence not instincts at all by the usual definition (T. Newcomb, *Social Psychology*, 1950).

And:

Instinct theories of human behavior which were once popular among behavioral scientists have virtually disappeared as the pervasive role of

learning has been increasingly studied and as the social generation of new needs has been stressed (A. Lindesmith and A. Strauss, *Social Psychology*, 1968).

In spite of the foregoing, there is still some occasional argument about infant suckling behavior, which some say is instinctive but others say is merely a reflex. Students may wish to consider infant suckling behavior in terms of the definition provided above, in order to form their own conclusions.

In gender-related behaviors, each sex has the capacity to behave in ways that social convention has assigned to the other sex. Men can be gentle and sentimental, and women can be aggressive and competitive. Such behaviors are not abnormal, perverse, or anti-instinctual; *all that is required is the permission and encouragement for such be-*

As social conditions change, men and women adapt by taking on role behaviors that may have been considered deviant under earlier conditions. Housecleaning is a task that more and more men are sharing equally with women.

haviors in the process of growing up in one's particular society (Yorburg 1974, 27).

Observable Masculinity-Femininity Differences

Well-learned beliefs about the sex-gender link that is conventional in contemporary American society are extremely resistant to change, since they are linked to beliefs about the correctness of our own identities. Those who hold such beliefs state that masculinity-femininity characteristics are observable in everyday life. These observers are only partially correct, and their assertion appears based on **selective perception**—perception that "emphasizes some aspect of the situation to the neglect of others to the extent that gross distortions occur" (Harriman 1965, 176).

When psychologists Janet T. Spence and Robert L. Helmreich (1978) measured masculinity, femininity, androgyny (high scores on both masculinity and feminity), and undifferentiated responses (low scores on both masculinity and femininity) of heterosexual college students, they found the distribution shown in table 11–1.

Males who scored high on conventional masculinity (66 percent) include 32 percent of the men who also scored high on femininity (in the androgynous category). Females who scored high on conventional

femininity (59 percent), include 27 percent who also scored high on masculinity.

The effects of socialization are represented in Spence and Helmreich's findings. As conventionally defined, most men show masculine characteristics, and most women show feminine characteristics. Socialization, however, is clearly not 100 percent effective. Also of interest is that virtually equal proportions of men and women (40 percent and 41 percent, respectively) scored high on the characteristics of the other sex.

Socializing agents, usually parents, typically make every effort to ensure that children will adopt the characteristics considered appropriate to their sex:

It is the custom to wrap the newborn baby in either a pink or blue blanket, depending on its sex as determined by the appearance of the genitalia. From this moment on, the child's maleness or femaleness is constantly reinforced. It is difficult, then, to determine the extent to which the child's learning of his [or her] sex role may be influenced by underlying biological predispositions (Hamburg and Lunde 1966, 15).

Reinforcement of sex-linked gender differences continues throughout life, but is particularly intensive during early childhood. Many elements (including televised portrayals) contribute to teaching the child how to behave as a "real boy" or as a "real girl." Notice that in the quotation from Hamburg and Lunde, the term "sex role" is used, where gender role is the correct term. (Old habits die hard.) Sex (male/female) does not need reinforcement; gender (masculinity/femininity) does.

Hamburg and Lunde refer to "underlying biological predispositions" as possibly influencing a child's gender characteristics. What they mean are not instincts but are innate drives, hormonal influences, or need dispositions that may influence masculinity and femininity (Chafetz 1974, 4). Only within the past twenty-five years have researchers undertaken the serious study of sex-related innate factors and have abandoned the older

TABLE 11–1. Percentages of Masculinity, Femininity, Androgyny, and Undifferentiated Scores of Heterosexual College Students

PERCENTAGES OF RESPONSES		
	Males	*Females*
Masculine	34	14
Feminine	8	32
Androgynous	32	27
Undifferentiated	25	28

Source: Janet Spence and Robert Helmreich, *Masculinity and femininity* (Austin: University of Texas Press, 1978) p. 53.

Freudian notion that "biology is destiny" (McCoy 1977, 157). As we review the findings of this line of research, keep in mind that investigators view any innate or hereditary factors as "predisposing" and not as "determining" (Sargent 1977, 147).

Male and Female

This review begins with a brief summary of what is known about male- and femaleness (Skolnick 1978, 180). Chromosomal composition, which is XX in females and XY in males, is determined by whether the father's fertilizing sperm cell contains the larger X or the smaller Y chromosome. Since the mother can contribute only the X chromosome, the fetus will be male if the father contributes a Y chromosome, and a female if he contributes an X chromosome. In male fetuses, the gonads will develop as testes, and in female fetuses as ovaries. Hormonal composition will also differ, producing more androgen and other male hormones in one case, and more estrogen, progesterone, and other female hormones in the other. When the infant emerges from the womb, we declare it to be a member of one or the other sex, and the process of social conditioning begins.

Since socialization into gender identity begins at birth, making it difficult if not impossible to distinguish possible hormonal influences from socialization influences, researchers have studied the newborn and infants of other species. These studies are also problematic, however, since hormonal influences are mediated by the brain, and differences in structure and functioning of the brain between humans and other species must be taken into consideration. Ruth Bleier, an experimental neuroanatomist and specialist in brain research, has outlined some of the human-nonhuman brain differences.

The part of the brain that distinguishes humans from other species is the cortex (outer surface layers); in humans, the cortex is of larger volume and area. In other species, much of the cortex is "primary receiving area," but in humans, more than half of the cortex consists of "association areas"—areas that "provide the substrate for the infinite variety" of human responses (Bleier 1976, 64). These differences contrast humans with the relatively stereotypic responses of species in which the cortex is less complex, writes Bleier. Those differences alone make it clear that generalizations to humans from research conducted on other species are probably unwarranted or at least hazardous. In any case, work with other species has provided inconclusive or mixed results so far. Bleier's work leads her to conclude that in spite of the "obvious and clearcut physical differences between the sexes that are related to different levels of estrogens and androgens," it is the cortical mechanisms, as manifested in learning and culture, that "come to be dominant as determinants of human behavior" (Bleier 1976, 68–69). Finally, Bleier cautions that if there is any biological determination of human behavior, we will never be able to know what it is until we can control both cultural determinants and researcher bias—and we are not likely to be able to control either of these.

Interesting insights into the gender-sex question in humans are provided by sociologist Arlene Skolnick's discussion of **transsexualism**—"the belief of a seemingly normal male or female that he or she is actually a person of the opposite sex" (1978, 178). Two well-publicized cases are those of tennis star and opthalmologist Renee Richards and newspaper writer Jan Morris. These former men were transformed into women by surgical procedures. As Skolnick remarks, transsexualism indicates that even maleness and femaleness are not automatic effects of anatomy or hormones. Like Richards and Morris, she states, the rest of us also *construct* our sexual selves through experience and over time, "but if the final outcome is in accord with our anatomical equipment, the temptation is to attribute our destiny to biology" (1978, 179).

Keep in mind that transsexuals Morris, Richards, and countless others believed they were imprisoned in bodies that were of the "wrong" sex, but that they never doubted what *sex* they were. In contrast, their *gender* identification was with the other sex. Their desire for congruence was great enough that they were motivated to undertake lengthy and irreversible sex transformations. Most of the rest of us, similarly, have no doubts about what sex we are. Still, as Skolnick points out, there are some individuals who are born with the anatomical characteristics of both sexes (hermaphrodites, or "intersexed" persons). Studies of these people, and of those who have sexual abnormalities of other kinds, have led to a striking finding: "children with the same anatomical structures could be assigned to *either* sex, and grow up to be a psychologically 'normal' member of that sex (Skolnick 1978, 181–82) (italics ours).

As Margaret Mead (1969, 281) has argued, "The existence in a given society of a . . . sex-determined, sex-linked personality penalizes in greater or lesser degree every individual born within it." Yet, some important aspects of our lives *are* affected by sex (XX or XY differences). For example, E. C. Pierson (a physiologist) and William V. D'Antonio (a sociologist) note that the ratio of male to female conceptions is estimated at 160:100, but that by the time of birth, the male to female ratio of live births is almost equal. The male XY chromosome combination "appears to weaken the human structure, thus making it more vulnerable to malfunctioning than that of the female XX combination" (1974, 8–9).

According to Pierson and D'Antonio, although it is more difficult to produce and maintain a viable (healthy) male than a female (males' muscular strength is offset by biological weakness), this does not mean that females are superior to males in any except a survival sense.

The Original Female and Subsequent Changes

Elizabeth Davis's historical text, *The First Sex* (1972), claims that males are mutations of the original female. Davis points out that women's reproductive organs are far older than men's and far more highly evolved:

Even in the lowest mammals, as well as in woman, the ovaries, uterus, vagina, etc., are similar indicating that the female reproductive system was one of the first things perfected by nature. On the other hand, the male reproductive organs . . . vary as much among species and through the course of evolution as does the shape of the foot—from hoof to paw (1972,34).

Moreover, says Davis, man is but an "imperfect woman"; she cites geneticists and physiologists who state that "the Y chromosome . . . is a deformed and broken X chromosome." How could this have happened? Davis suggests that some type of genetic disaster—a catastrophe possibly involving disease or radiation bombardment from the sun—caused the male mutation. In any case, "maleness remains a recessive genetic trait like color-blindness or hemophilia with which it is linked" (1972, 35).

Whether Davis's argument is accurate, the certainty remains that during the first six weeks of fetal life, all of us are female. Reproductive biologist Ashton Barfield (1976) points out that the XY constitution produces changes in the seventh week of intrauterine life. The production of androgen is involved in this process; without it, development as a female proceeds (1976, 63).

Bodily differences in females and males are greatly influenced by environment and culture—for example, the extent to which good nutrition is provided, physical activity and practice of skills are emphasized, and norms for performance are applied. Activities and cultural prescriptions, however, cannot account for the lower viability of male fetuses—a fact that some attribute to the dose of androgens released in the embryonic male (Oakley 1972), "widening the range for error in the developing organism" (Forisha 1978, 52). Others believe that the longer maturation period and higher metabolic rate of males may lie at the root of many of their weaknesses (Barfield 1976, 68–69). Finally, there is the possibility of immunological incompatibility between some male fetuses and their mothers, which may be related to productions controlled by genes on the Y chromosome (Singer, Westphal, and Niswander 1968). This would explain the spontaneous abortion (miscarriage) of greater numbers of male fetuses, as well as the larger number of male stillbirths. This effect might also cause nonlethal damage to the male fetus, producing mental and physical defects in later life (Williams 1977, 124).

These considerations are related to what researcher John Money (1973) has called a "broadly applicable principle of female precedence," and the fact that many more male than female fetuses are conceived may be "nature's way" of compensating for the greater vulnerability of the male (Forisha 1978, 52). The problematic area of research that has focused on male-female similarities and differences following birth, is examined next.[2]

Nature Versus Nurture, and Sex Preferences

Psychologist Kay Schaffer's review (1980) of relevant studies suggests that the tendency to prefer male children demonstrates the cultural assumption that males are more valuable than females, based on the influence of "sex roles and stereotypes" (1980, 6). This influence, Schaffer observes, is even more apparent once babies are born; "Parents tend to have different expectations for sons and daughters from birth, even though

information about the infants is minimal," and fathers' expectations tend to be even more stereotypic than those of mothers' (1980, 6). Here is some of Schaffer's evidence.

Fathers of baby daughters spend more time talking to them than to their infant sons, and show more apprehension over their little girls' well-being (Pedersen and Robson 1969; Rebelsky and Hanks 1971). The parents of newborns who were not objectively different from one another in birth weight, length, or any other physical or neurological characteristic were interviewed within twenty-four hours of the babies' births. (The study included thirty pairs of first-time parents, none of whom reported medical problems during pregnancies or deliveries. All babies had been carried full term.) Fathers described their daughters as more inattentive, delicate, and weak than mothers did, and fathers rated their sons as stronger, better coordinated, and more alert than mothers rated them. Schaffer's report of this study (Ruben, Provenzano, and Luria 1974) also relates that

parents of the girls described their infants as little, beautiful, pretty and cute more often than parents of boys, while parents of boys described their infants as big more often than did parents of girls.

As these and other similar studies make clear, parents' expectations are attributed to their children on the basis of sex and not on the basis of the infants' actual characteristics. Sociologist Laurel Walum (1977:40) reports a study in which five young mothers were presented with "Adam," a 6-month-old dressed in blue overalls. A second group of mothers were given "Beth," a 6-month-old wearing a pink frilly dress. "Compared to Adam, Beth was smiled at more often, offered a doll to play with more often, and viewed as 'sweet' with a 'soft cry';" but *Adam and Beth were actually the same child.*

Early months of life are clearly not free of gender training. This involves "differences

2. For a discussion of methodological problems involved in the study of infant sex differences, see I. H. Frieze, J. E. Parsons, P. B. Johnson, D. N. Ruble, and G. L. Zellman *Women and sex roles: A social psychological perspective* (New York: W. W. Norton, 1978), pp. 73–75.

in expectations, names, behavioral responses, apparel, toys, furniture styles, and games" (Davidson and Gordon 1979, 9), among other differences. This training for masculinity or femininity moves the young child along a path that is conventionally believed to confirm, but actually creates, gender identity linked to sex.

Socialization continues throughout life. Prescriptions for behaving in ways considered socially appropriate are modified as we move from girl to woman, from boy to man, and as we take on new roles and discard older ones. We do not expect individuals to fully live up to conventional gender ideals. In certain areas, we also allow greater lati-

Does this father's behavior indicate his maternal instinct? His paternal instinct? Any instinct? Studies have shown that fathers of baby daughters tend to spend more time talking to them than to their infant sons.

tude for one sex than the other. We tolerate, for example, rowdy, tomboyish girls, but exert considerable effort to keep boys from developing "sissy" behavior. We also make exceptions for "eccentric" behavior for certain adults whose public image of manliness or womanliness is thought to be beyond question. A football hero like Roosevelt Grier, for instance, may take up needlework without incurring negative comment. In general, however, such unusual behaviors are permitted to members of the highest and lowest social classes only (who have the least to lose by departing from conventionality), or to individuals in glamorous occupations. For the vast majority, conformity is emphasized and departures from norms are negatively sanctioned.

Research evidence indicates that parents' beliefs in differences between male and female children leads to socialization practices that coincide with those beliefs. A well-publicized case in point comes from a study that John Money and Anke Ehrhardt (1975) reported. The researchers describe the case of one of a pair of twin brothers who was raised as a female from the age of seventeen months onward—a decision made following a surgical accident that left the boy without a penis. By age five, Money and Ehrhardt note, the mother of the twins reported that her "daughter" was very feminine in every way, but her son, she said, was typically masculine (active, messy, rejected housework, and copied his father's behavior). Money and Ehrhardt suggest that parents give clues to their children regarding expected behaviors and attitudes "without conscious effort, routinely" (1975, 50).

Although the male human is less viable at all stages of life than the female is, males are more highly prized. This prizing does not appear based on the reality of males' greater vulnerability (their more tenuous hold on life) but on the belief that they are stronger, naturally the dominant sex, the protectors of females and the young, the primary economic providers, and the authorities in science, law, religion, art, and in virtually every other sphere of life. For the most part, men play out these roles as they are trained to do. Similarly, most women are socialized into accepting an inferior status.

When individual adults depart from the boundaries marking the range of conventionally defined gender-role norms, culturally approved ways exist for bringing such "strays" back into line. Most typically, it is only when individuals band together in groups, inspired by a common conviction that "the Emperor has no clothes," that change on a large scale can come about. Throughout history, individuals have departed from convention. Some, like Joan of Arc, (who donned a suit of armor and led an army) have been allowed to do so—at least for a time. Others have been persecuted for their differences. As sociologists Davidson and Gordon have observed, being born female or male is associated with the opportunities and limitations one may expect in life. Further,

if the powerful segments of a society are to maintain their power without the use of force, it is necessary that people believe that the opportunities and the limitations on their lives are at least unavoidable and at best desirable. Socialization serves as an efficient means to impose values and norms on the individual. It is perhaps the most effective method of social control because the individual regulates and polices his or her own behavior. . . . Internalization of the values of a system through the socialization process is a powerful way to perpetuate that system. Thus, *socialization into the acceptance of different opportunity structures, rights, rewards, and limitations for men and women works to the benefit of those who profit from current arrangements of economics and power* (1979, 11) (italics ours).

In the next section, we undertake the analysis of those powerful segments of society to which Davidson and Gordon refer. Our analysis focuses on what the power structure is, how it developed, and what profit it gains by perpetuating conventional definitions of masculinity and femininity.

ANALYZING THE PROBLEM: PATRIARCHY AND ITS CONSEQUENCES

Earlier, we proposed that today's conventional definitions of gender are not traditional. Rather, definitions change from time to time along with social circumstances. Prior to the 1920s, for instance, before American women gained the right to vote, "self-respecting" women did not smoke or drink in public places. Modesty and quiet demeanor were the hallmarks of "ladies." Radical changes occurred in women's behavior, however, in part an effect of their new political personhood. During the Roaring Twenties, some women took up styles of behavior and activities that would have been unthinkable for their sex only a few years earlier.

What *is* traditional almost everywhere is a status difference between men and women. Our long history of male dominance and female dependency underlies gender differentials and the double standard. In spite of challenges over the centuries, status arrangements have generally remained intact. The following section examines some of the characteristics of the patriarchal tradition and presents theories that attempt to account for its origin and its persistence.

The Patriarchal Tradition

Patriarchy is an *hierarchical* (stratified) arrangment in which one group (males) is defined as superior and the other (females) is defined as inferior. In patriarchal societies, men wield power and control the opportunity structure, and limits are placed on the opportunities available to women. Both C. A. Tripp (1976, 38), a psychologist-historian, and Mary Daly (1973, 3–4), a philosopher-theologian, point out that in male-dominated societies, the inferiority of women rather than the superiority of men is emphasized. Tripp and Daly also note that women, for the most part, either have not protested their inferiorization or have consented to their low status and victimization (Daly 1973, 2; Tripp 1976, 38), a statement that indicates the effectiveness of socialization into masculinist beliefs. Both Daly and Tripp provide a number of examples of how religious organizations in various societies (including our own) define women as inferior to men and perpetuate what Daly calls an "exploitative sexual caste system" (1973, 2). We are indebted to these writers for the following illustrations.

Buddhists hold that women embody all the snares spread for men by "the Tempter." Mohammed saw all women as a "calamity" to all men. The Hebrews believed that women were the source of all evil and death. St. Paul wrote that Adam was not deceived and hence was innocent; his woman, Eve, was the transgressor. The **misogyny** (woman hatred) of the Christian church fathers is further demonstrated by St. Augustine's opinion that women are not made in the image of God; by Thomas Aquinas and his followers' definition of women as "misbegotten males"; and by Martin Luther's comment that Adam was created to be the lord over the earth's creatures, but that Eve spoiled it all.

As recently as 1971, women have been banned from church choir lofts because their presence might "despoil" the church (Tripp 1976, 40–41). In the early 1970s, the Roman Catholic church reaffirmed its position that women's bodies were not under their own control by launching "all-out warfare against the international movement to repeal anti-abortion laws" (Daly 1973, 3). Daly summarizes these and many other aspects of antifemale religious ideology:

Patriarchal religion has served to perpetuate all of these dynamics of delusion, naming them "natural" and bestowing its supernatural blessings upon them. The system has been advertised as "according to the divine plan." . . . [T]he entire conceptual systems of theology and ethics, developed under the conditions of patriarchy, have been products of males and tend to serve the interests of sexist society (1973, 3–4).

How did masculinist-sexist interests come to be dominant? Two major sociological theories attempt to account for how societies divide into groups with power and groups with no power. The first of these theories is called the functionalist approach.

Functionalist Theory and its Assumptions

In the functionalist view, every society has certain "functional imperatives"—tasks that must be performed so that the society survives. Some roles in society are seen as more directly related to fulfilling the functional imperatives than others. Such roles are also thought more demanding and difficult than others. Individuals capable of occupying these important roles are relatively scarce; thus, those who fill key roles are given power, privilege, and prestige. These rewards encourage those who perform special survival-related tasks to continue performing. Thus, according to functionalists, the unequal distribution of power in a society perpetuates order and stability within the social system (Davis and Moore 1945).

Although this theory seems to make sense, it cannot account for many aspects of social organization. For example, a major survival task of any society is its capacity to pass on knowledge to each new generation. The functionalist theory suggests that those who transmit knowledge are rare and that those who can perform this function will be encouraged and rewarded. Most teachers, however, are underpaid and are not honored, powerful people. Similarly, if we look at primitive societies and consider the survival tasks necessary for their perpetuation, childbearing, childrearing, and defense against enemies are roles clearly related to survival. Yet women, the childbearers and primary childrearers in most societies, have not been accorded power, privilege, or prestige on a par with men, the primary defenders (in the military sense) of most societies.

A second theoretical perspective—conflict

theory—also attempts to account for the persistence of status inequities.

Conflict Theory and its Assumptions

Conflict theory maintains that all societies define some goods and services as scarce and valuable. Those who gain control over such goods or services tend to want to retain that control, since those who have it also tend to have power, privilege, and prestige. As power consolidates in the hands of the few, others, who experience relative lack of power (i.e., control over either their access to resources or the lives of others to gain access to resources), are motivated to oppose those holding power. Thus, the unequal distribution of power tends to perpetuate conflict in social systems (Coser 1956; Dahrendorf 1959).

This theory, too, seems to make sense. The goods and services defined as scarce and valuable may include the functional imperatives that functional theorists refer to, or they may be arbitrary. In the novel *Lord of the Flies* (1954), for instance, author William Golding describes a group of young boys stranded on an island and their efforts to set up a workable society. The boys agree to define possession of a conch shell as not only a scarce and valuable resource but also the very symbol of power, privilege, and prestige in their society.

The conflict theory approach accounts for both stability and change in social systems and provides a way to understand the distribution of power and its accompaniments. The power to define what the world is like and how it operates is precious. One or more out-groups will, from time to time, attempt to gain that right for themselves. With regard to the sexes, the struggle over the right to define is what psychologists Tavris and Offir (1977) have called "the longest war." In their view, status arrangements that favor one sex over the other have always produced conflict between men and women.

Contemporary writers have offered other explanations, some of which appear to be

justifications of the **status quo** (things as they are) or arguments favoring changes in traditional status inequities. In their effort to explain how male dominance came into being and why it has persisted, some contend that patriarchy has always existed; others contend that matriarchies were the original arrangement, but that when men took power, they destroyed almost all records of **matriarchy**, (a form of social organization in which power and authority are vested in females), erasing knowledge of a system that did not favor males.[3]

Power and authority (the ability to produce desired behavior in others without the use of force) have been considered in both conventional and scientific realms to have been the province of men. Recently, sociologist John N. Edwards and anthropologist Patricia Kluck (1980) have warned that (1) definitions of patriarchy are problematic and, in any case, are Westernized notions that may have no validity in other cultures, (2) methods by which the assessment of "universal patriarchy" are made are also problematic, especially since most investigators have been male interviewers of male informants, (3) the evidence available in support of universal patriarchy is dubious, especially in the light of such societies as Dahomey,[4] where *all* power and authority was shared by male and female pairs of ministers, and (4) the "scenario" that depicts "man as the hunter and woman as the keeper of the home fires," (1980, 327) used to describe patriarchal arrangements and supporting the belief in universal patriarchy, is highly suspect. Edwards and Kluck write that this scenario provides the basis for the belief in a division of labor by sex,

---

3. For male- and female-favoring contemporary writers, see Tiger (1970); Morgan (1972); Gilder (1975); and Davis (1972). See also Friedl (1975), for an argument that anthropologists have unearthed no evidence for the existence of matriarchies, and Davis (1972) for documentation that contradicts Friedl's argument. A balanced treatment of the issues is provided in Richmond-Abbott. (1983)

4. Dahomean society was made up of several West African kingdoms.

giving males the control of the public, political domain and relegating women to childbearing and housekeeping tasks. . . . Constructed by men mostly of another era, but widely prevalent today, this conjecture of evolution has been—if not patently—at least covertly self-serving . . . . Such a perspective offers a ready justification for those who prefer that women be homemakers . . . . exempt . . . . from any substantial involvement in affairs of power and authority (1980, 328).

Edwards and Kluck show through an examination of several societies that hunting (by males) is not and has not been universally valued over gathering (by females), and such work efforts are not always divided by sex in the way indicated (1980, 327–32). "Until universal patriarchy is expunged from

our body of conventional wisdom, our analyses will remain distorted, if not completely erroneous" (1980, 333). The important question, however, according to Edwards and Kluck,

is not whether men are always dominant but under what conditions do varying degrees of dominance exist? Promising starts have been made along these lines with investigators examining economic variations, in particular, and a host of other structural variables—types of marriage, residential patterns, and the like—which may affect male and female statuses. . . . But even this tack may be only a beginning in furthering our understanding. For while statuses tend to be interdependent, perfect consistency is seldom realized. To the extent that this is the case, future research needs to be directed to the different domains in which dominance emerges and to the

One of the effects of a belief in universal patriarchy is to justify keeping women out of positions in which they might have access to power and authority. Edwards and Kluck state that "until universal patriarchy is expunged from our body of conventional wisdom, our analyses will remain distorted, if not completely erroneous."

specific conditions under which it occurs (1980,33–34).

Edwards and Kluck not only point a finger at the tendency of male anthropologists to cast research in a light favoring the belief in patriarchy as universal; they also note that perhaps the best known American sociologist, Talcott Parsons (1955), a structural-functionalist, theorized in a rigid and inflexible way about the sexes. Parsons postulated that men's roles were "instrumental" but women's roles were "expressive" (Edwards and Kluck, 1980:334fn).

This chapter later picks up the "economic variations" thread to which Edwards and Kluck have directed our attention.

Creativity

In Western society, men not only have dominated all major social institutions (the family, religion, economics, politics, the military, and others) but also have controlled access to the written word. If women have created or invented aspects of the material or social worlds, male historians have told us little or nothing about it. Yet, some suggest that women's capacity to create life is the mysterious, even "supernaturally" powerful difference between the sexes that inspired men to subjugate women (Campbell 1959; Hays 1964; Sanday 1981). (The role of males in the process of creating life could hardly have been understood among primitive humanoids, since birth is far removed in time from the act of sexual intercourse.) Given this powerful capability of women and the higher proportion of male deaths at all ages, how might men have allayed their fear and awe of the powers of the female majority? Let us consider three possible courses of action.

First, men might band together and allocate to themselves whatever goods and resources they could, removing women from access to them. Control over food, shelter, protection from enemies, sacrificial (for the gods) ceremonies, and virtually all other life-sustaining activities might serve as a counterweight to female powers.

Alternatively, the magical powers of women could be given credence through acts of worship and deference, by elevating women to divine or semidivine status. Women, however, would then become all-powerful.

A third course—a combination of the first two options—might be preferable. In this alternative, the "divide and conquer" principle could come into play. Women could be divided into two groups, thus minimizing the effects of their numerical majority. "Good" women who were nurturing (kinswomen, mothers, or potential mothers) could receive help and protection from men in exchange for limiting their ambitions and activities. "Bad" women who refused such limits would receive minimal or no help—even if they bore infants. Women of the "good" group would be accorded derivative status (Daly 1973, 2) as a function of their relationships with male protectors; women of the "bad" group would be fully exploitable. With power and authority thus gained, acceptance of male-favoring definitions of the world could be readily enforced.

This scenario is not imaginary. The good girl-bad girl distinction is male defined and persists today with no good boy-bad boy parallel (Crosby 1979, 212–13). Of man's desire to create on a par with women or beyond it, it has recently been said that "the machine is man's daughter, born without help of a mother"[5] ("Meanings of Modern Art," 1980). A history of male creativity has elevated men to almost godlike status and has diminished the meaning of female creativity in all spheres. Nonconforming women, in American history as well as in European, have been called witches and have been sub-

---

5. Parthenogenesis—the ability to produce offspring without the collaboration of a member of the other sex—is a feat beyond the capacity of most women although it occurs in nature among females of other species (deBecker, 1969; Michelmore, 1964; *Newsweek*, 1980; *Time*, 1980) and is quite common in many religious traditions (e.g., the Virgin Mother of Christianity).

jected to torture and death because men said that they were the devil's disciples. In *Entertaining Satan* (1982), historian John Demos reports that the accused were usually middle-aged women with few or no children—especially those who strove for individualism (against the prevalent requirement of neighborliness and cooperation). New England Puritans, writes Demos,

> regarded themselves as participants in a cosmic struggle between the forces of God and of Satan for control of the universe. History was, by their lights, a theatre of unceasing warfare—grand in scale, terrifying in character, and fraught with the gravest consequences for all concerned (Strouse 1982).

Beyond religious traditions that support conventional gender-role definitions, the au-

thority and power that the mental health professions—especially psychiatry and psychoanalysis (Nichols 1975, 63–64; see also chapter 9)—wield in our own time have perpetuated status inequalities. In assessing mental health, the standards by which all are judged are the attributes assigned only to males. The attributes assigned to females (weakness, dependency, passivity, and so on) are taken as signs of emotional disturbance, if not of mental disorder (Walum 1977, 8–10). Sigmund Freud, often called the father of psychoanalysis, once asked, "What do women want?"—a question to which he did not know the answer, although most of his patients were women. In *Powers of the Weak*, author Elizabeth Janeway provides the answer to Freud's question: "What women want is a world that offers more

The answer to Freud's question, "Women—what do they want?" is "options," similar to those historically available only to men. Among these are options to do work of one's own choosing.

than two choices—male role, female role, and nothing else" (*Universal Press* 11 July 1980).

Economic Variations

Are there societies in which control over goods and resources have made a difference either in dominance or in the definition of gender roles? A reconsideration of the Arapesh, Tchambuli, and Mundugumor societies, to which anthropologist Margaret Mead introduced us, is instructive.

Among the Tchambuli (where our conventional gender roles were reversed), women controlled the means of production and the wealth of the village, and provided the bulk of the work necessary to produce that wealth. Among the Mundugumor (where both men and women were conventionally masculine), the village was so rich in natural resources that acquisitive and materialistic as the villagers were, neither group could gain control over the available abundance. The Arapesh (whose men and women were conventionally feminine) lived in a subsistence economy; little wonder that both sexes were devoted to the nurturance of all living things.

The extremely different experiences of these three societies, with regard to dominance, economics, and gender definitions, provides a clue that economic variations may be at the base of status arrangements. Thus, the widespread existence of male dominance may be a function of common economic conditions in the beginnings of many societies, and its persistence today grounded in primitive beliefs and behaviors regardless of their current impracticality. Historian Tripp writes:

Ancient fears and prejudices have a way of reasserting themselves in each new generation. Certainly most of the really serious charges against women live on—weaving themselves ever more subtly into the very fabric of modern mores on which the claims of emancipation are writ large. . . . [A]ll too clearly from the distant past the jungle drums continue to beat out the message: that women are dangerous (1976, 41–42).

If most men and women in any society are conditioned to want and to respond to conventionally defined versions of each other, Tripp wonders why they do not enjoy each other's company more. Many believe that marriage is optimally a relationship of intimacy beyond that which is possible in any other partnership. Intimacy, however, requires trust (Larzelere and Huston 1980). Trust, in turn, is possible only between equals. Dominant-submissive status arrangements undermine the possibility of genuine intimacy between men and women.

Today, rules prescribing different behaviors and opportunities for men and women perpetuate ancient antagonisms between the sexes. Sociologist Laurel Walum (1977, 143) suggests that status inequality will continue until two interrelated changes take place. First, men and women will need equal access to the control and distribution of scarce goods and services. Second, men and women will need equal responsibility for childrearing. To these changes, we add a third—which both may assist in bringing about the first two changes and also may be an outgrowth of them: Men and women will need to be socially rewarded for their abilities to display characteristics and qualities that conventionally have been rewarded in one sex and not the other.

The final section of this chapter considers these recommendations for change as solutions that may transcend the archaic and dehumanizing restrictions that have plagued the lives of both men and women.

ALTERNATIVE POLICIES FOR RESOLVING THE PROBLEM: TRANSCENDING GENDER ROLES

Men's liberationist Jack Nichols addresses the need for change and tells men that

being born into a culture was once sufficient for role implementation and fixation. Until recently, men did not question the traits expected by their culture. . . . That this is no longer the case is beyond dispute. . . . *His long-established roles, if he clings to them too tenaciously, threaten to make him at best a ponderous and absurd burlesque, at worst a menace* (1975, 58–59) (italics ours).

Nichols points out that roles are already changing. *Androgyny* (a term created by combining the Greek root words for male and female—*andr-* + *gynē*) is becoming the ideal. Over a decade ago, researchers L. J. Ellis and P. M. Bentler (1973) reported that descriptions of the "ideal male" and the "ideal female" were alike (androgynous). Not long afterward, psychologists Helmreich, Spence, and Holahan (1979) also found that men and women gave similar (androgynous) descriptions of the "ideal self." Correlates of the androgynous ideal self include androgynous identification of the self, high social competence, and high self-esteem (Spence, Helmreich, and Stapp 1975). The subject of androgyny will be further discussed toward the end of this chapter, since the topic is relevant to the third of our recommendations for transcending conventional gender roles. First, however, we consider the two changes that Walum (1977) has recommended: (1) equalization of access to goods and services and (2) equal responsibility for childrearing.

Concerning equality of rights and obligations in general, women have not been defined as equal to men in the Constitution, and the attempt to add the Equal Rights Amendment is an effort to remedy that long-standing omission. That women should need to wage a national struggle to establish their equality is perhaps the best evidence of their unequal status. The simplicity of the wording of the Equal Rights Amendment makes clear how basic a right is being sought. In its entirety, the amendment reads:

Section 1. Equality of rights under the law shall not be abridged or denied by the United States or by any state on account of sex.
Section 2. The Congress shall have power to enforce, by appropriate legislation, the provisions of this article.
Section 3. This amendment shall take effect two years after the date of ratification.

Equal Access to Goods and Services

Some have argued that the Equal Rights Amendment (ERA) is unnecessary, since women already have equal rights with men. They cite, for instance, the Civil Rights Act of 1964, which made employment discrimination against women illegal. Despite that act, however, women still earn only sixty-two cents for every dollar that men earn in comparable occupations. Moreover, notwithstanding the Civil Rights Act, the wage discrepancy reflects an actual *loss* in female earning power across the years since 1955 (Bonk 1980).

In education, as in the job market, sex stereotyping continues, routing women into less lucrative fields of employment. For these and other reasons, "many women who have a single means of employment are forced to hold a second paid job and a third inside the home to counterbalance the wage differential and to make ends meet" (Bonk 1980, 9).

Prior to the Civil Rights Act of 1964, state laws had banned women from occupations such as mining and prohibited certain job activities such as overtime work (which pays well) or heavy lifting (which women—especially mothers—had always done in the home). Mining is difficult, risky work, but pays three times more than jobs such as factory seamstress or nurse's aide. Despite the 1964 act, it took a sex discrimination suit in 1974 to ensure women's right to work in the mines. Women miners, however, are still frequently victimized by sexual harassment, inadequate safety protection, and lengthy waits for advancement (as compared with male miners) (*Newsweek* 19 April 1982). The director of the Coal Employment Project, an equal rights group, has noted that women are also often given the heaviest, dirtiest, entry-level jobs (1982, 18).[6]

Even in the highest paid jobs, women's earnings are generally much lower than

---

6. Unless we are discussing professional sperm donors or professional wet nurses, almost no work that men have done has not been done by women and vice versa. (Miller and Swift 1977, 47)

those of men. Further, "when the full job range is expanded to include low-paying levels, the wage gap is even more severe" (*National NOW Times* April 1982, 2). The same source provides the following highlights regarding earning discrepancies.

■ Lawyers: Women attorneys earn $407 weekly, while men in the same profession earn $574;

■ Elementary and secondary school administrators: Women earn $363 weekly compared with $520 for men;

■ Computer specialists: The average weekly salary for men is $488, $133 more than is paid to women;

■ Bookkeepers: Women comprise 91 percent of this profession and earn an average of $222 to men's $320;

■ Retail salesclerks: Women in this field are paid $154 compared with $229 paid to men;

■ Nurses, dieticians, and therapists: Women comprise 91 percent of this profession and earn $18 less per week than do men in the same jobs.

The average woman will spend twenty-five years of her life holding a paid job outside her home, and the number of married women working outside the home outnumbers full-time homemakers (Bonk 1980). Governmental policies and educational or employment practices that discriminate against women clearly have negative effects on the whole society. As one man stated, "I am the son of a woman and the brother of a woman. Their happiness is my happiness, their misery, my misery. The interests of the sexes are inseparably connected, and in the elevation of the one lies the salvation of the other" (*New Woman* 1980). In addition, most men are also the husbands of women, and many are fathers of daughters.

Although we have barely skimmed the surface of sexual inequality, our illustrations, we believe, indicate the need for social restructuring represented by the Equal Rights Amendment. We turn now to the second of Walum's recommendations.

Equal Responsibility for Childrearing

As chapter 6 discussed, our vision of the ideal American family is far from the reality. Full-time homemakers and caretakers of children are no longer the majority of wives and mothers. Given these facts, the persistence of employment policies that discriminate against women and the lack of day-care facilities for their children are highly wasteful and impractical. By amending our Constitution to ensure equality of opportunity, America will move toward matching existing conditions, a move that other advanced societies have already made.

Rosalyn F. Baxandall (1975), who has studied the history and development of day-care programs in the United States, points out that in our country, the provision of day care is seen as something like welfare—an aid to the "poor mothers" who must meet certain tests before their children can be included. Baxandall suggests that the only way day care can be made available without stigma is to treat it as a free public utility.

If overcoming prejudices against day care is difficult, how much more difficult may it be to overcome the male prejudice against doing work that is conventionally assigned to women—in this case, sharing childrearing responsibilities? Men have been slow to accept responsibility for any conventionally defined "women's work" because of its connection with inferior status. Times are changing, however, in this regard, as a "60 Minutes" report on house-husbanding (25 October 1981) indicated (see also Nieves 1978; Roache 1975). Although men may face prejudice and ridicule for crossing the sex-segregated job market line, more men are doing so today:

The Urban Institute, a research group in Washington, recently estimated that the number of male secretaries rose 24% to 31,000 in 1978 from 25,000 in 1972, while the number of male telephone operators over the same span rose 38%, and the number of male nurses, 94%. Labor experts expect the trend to continue (*Wall Street Journal* 25 February 1981).

Unlike women miners, however, "men in traditional female jobs often move up the ladder fast" (*Wall Street Journal* 25 February 1981).

Some (still isolated) employers are now granting paternal as well as maternal leaves when children arrive (Fein 1974a). The Ford Foundation now allows fathers up to eight weeks of paid leave to spend time with their newborn or adopted children (Sloane 1982a), based on the belief that childrearing should be shared. "Such a practice is common with employers in several European countries," writes Sloane, but is still novel in the United States (1982a, 12).

An underlying problem is that of governmental support for paternal leave, day care, and other childrearing aspects. As social critic Ellen Goodman has argued, the Reagan administration was quick to protect the rights of the unborn (i.e., in supporting the Hatch Amendment, which "would let Congress and the states prohibit or restrict abortions as they saw fit") but reluctant to protect the born (e.g., by quickly prohibiting defective infant formula from being marketed). The government, Goodman contends, pronounced itself profamily, but ended that policy beyond the delivery room (1982, 11).

Minimal gains have been made, however. The U.S. Department of Labor for instance, has become the first federal employer to allow up to two years of unpaid childrearing leave for both men and women, with the same or a comparable job guaranteed on return.

In the private sector, men worry about their masculine image, their virility, and even about their position of primacy in the family if they take on homemaking or childrearing. As a survey that two major advertising agencies conducted not long ago concluded, "It's easier for men to accept the possibility of women as brain surgeons than to release their wives from the drudgery of laundry and cleaning the bathroom" (*National NOW Times* November–December 1982, 2). Occasionally, fear of a female political takeover is expressed. In view of male overrepresentation in politics, however, this is a baseless fear. (Although women comprise more than 51 percent of the population, they hold less than 10 percent of all elective offices—and only 1 percent of the seats in the U.S. House of Representatives.) Survey researcher Daniel Yankelovich believes that in spite of the men's liberation movement, the division of housework (including child care) has changed very little. "My feeling is that future change is not going to focus on housework until there's more equality on the job front" (Sloane 1982b, 10).

Ratification of the ERA (the first bill introduced in the U.S. House of Representatives in January 1983), which would open opportunities that the Civil Rights Act of 1964 has not accomplished, is perhaps the most important single route to transcending gender-role stereotypes. Support for the ERA in the House (230 sponsors) is now greater than it was at its original introduction (210 sponsors). Passage in the House of Representatives seems assured at this writing, although the fate of the ERA in the highly conservative Senate appears problematic. In 1983, National Organization for Women (NOW) President Judy Goldsmith stated about the Senate:

The Republican leadership must choose whether they will stand with the president and the 1980 party platform which repudiated the ERA, or whether they will support full constitutional rights for women. The choice they make will be a major factor in determining what happens at the polls in 1984 (*National NOW Times* January–February 1983, 1).

In the 1980 elections, to which Goldsmith referred, right-wing Christian coalitions (among them, a group called the Conservative Caucus) mounted a strong effort to block passage of the ERA (*ERAmerica* 1980) and to sustain male dominance in every sector.

Whether the struggle for equality will end with success or suffer defeat concerning ratification of the ERA, its continuance appears inevitable. Liberated women and men have been working toward equality for both sexes virtually since the founding of this nation.

Not Unisex but Androgyny

The traits associated with the conventional definition of masculinity have always been more attractive to women than the traits associated with the conventional definition of femininity have been to men. In the late 1960s, however, America's young men began to wear longer hair and jewelry (a trend that older men later took up), and women during the same period donned blue jeans and work shirts. On his visits to college campuses in the mid-1970s, men's liberationist Jack Nichols became convinced

that males . . . are decidedly more gentle in outward manner than their counterparts ten years ago. There is no reason to call them feminine or to call the decisive young women I have observed masculine. Instead, both sexes are simply beginning to adopt characteristics once thought to belong to one sex or the other. (1975, 60)

Nichols calls arguments against sexual equality and role variation "unimaginative," since they assume that people cannot transcend their bodies when changing circumstances require transcendence. "This concept of mind hardly leaves any room for creativity, or, conceivably, for survival" (1975, 62).

The unisex trend and its outgrowth, the trend toward androgyny, are recognitions of a link between the fates of men and women. Gains for one sex do not imply losses for the other, as opponents argue. Rather, the trend toward androgyny promotes what sociologists Davidson and Gordon (1979) have called a "human liberation" perspective—a synthesis of attributes within individuals. The term *unisex* refers to similarity of styles in clothing and hairdressing; androgyny, in contrast, encompasses the whole being.

Historian Peter Filene (1976) credits the various social movements of the 1960s with the beginnings of androgyny. The 1960s were a time when activists of both sexes stepped out of their old conventional roles and took on (at least for the time) the challenge of seeing what the world looked like through different eyes. Movements such as those for black, Chicano, native American, and gay rights, as well as the antiwar protest, involved people in such a way that androgyny was presaged. Sharing of social and political spheres and maximizing the potentials of both sexes, we believe, are necessary before unadaptive conventional arrangements and definitions can be overcome. As Davidson and Gordon state, "Proponents . . . see 'the enemy' as a system rather than as individuals . . . and current versions of stratification, based on arbitrary distinctions such as gender would be eliminated" (1979, 15).

Psychologist Herb Goldberg writes that

feminism has been a trauma for some men only because they have reacted defensively, trying to accomodate to the woman while being castigated for being exploiters and chauvinists. These were accusations he could not see beyond. While she was busy defining her new role, he was busy trying to adjust to it rather than redefining his. While she reexamined and rejected aspects of her roles as wife and mother and passive-supportive figure, he was unable to challenge the preconceptions and presumptions of his roles as father, husband, active dominator, and so on.

Perhaps the single most valuable contribution of feminism has been the way it has chipped away at men's fantasies about women. Today, it is the destructive woman, consciously or unconsciously intent on controlling . . . men, who feeds on his regressive, pathetic desire to see himself as the dominant superman. In return for these false ego strokes, he assumes responsibility for her. As a result, his emergence out of the gender nightmare is aborted, and he remains a posturing caricature (1979, 188–89).

Goldberg asserts that men who grasp the meaning of feminism will be able to free themselves from destructive compulsions to perform. "The growth of men depends on the growth of women, and vice versa, in order for the sexes to experience the full potential of themselves and each other" (1979, 189–90). The price of falling back into the conventional way of relating, Goldberg maintains, would be a destructive gender fantasy that annihilates possibilities for full personhood.

Psychologist Sandra Bem (1972) characterizes androgynous people as those who have a wider range of capabilities than those who are predominantly masculine or feminine (regardless of sex). In two experiments, Bem found that psychologically androgynous people showed a high level of independence in stressful situations and displayed more adaptability and flexibility. What Bem (1974, 1975) and others who study androgyny have called masculinity and femininity, however, is based on conventionally ascribed gender characteristics. Studies of androgynous people, then, indicate less about how masculine or feminine they are and more that they are high in such qualities as self-reliance and assertiveness as well as gentleness and understanding.

For women, androgyny without equality may have negative consequences. Frieda Adler (1975) has noted that pressures associated with gender identity convergence (androgyny) make girls more vulnerable to delinquency than boys are. The androgyny trend is an ambiguous one for young women because, according to Adler, "while they are urged toward equality of education and community participation on one level, they also encounter discrimination and are urged to reject their intellect on another level." Coupled with the usual strains of early adolescence, such ambiguities may influence girls to turn to drinking, stealing, gang activity and fighting, or into prostitution and

Some men have resisted sharing childcare with women, but others have responded to the opportunity with pleasure.

drug addiction (1975, 94–95). Thus, until full equality is established, the lag between social circumstances and identities may create negative consequences.

In contrast, for those at later ages, androgyny has been linked to survival itself. Gerontologist Jan Dynda Sinnott's review of relevant research leads to the conclusion that "a person's ability to show life-span variations in gender roles is an indication of a general flexibility which is associated with more successful aging and a longer life span" (1979, 144). Although Sinnott uses the term *sex roles* for what we have called gender roles, the meaning of the following passage is clear.

At birth, the individual behaves androgynously. Sex roles diverge in middle childhood, converge again in the working period of the early twenties, and diverge again during the child raising period. When children have grown, roles again converge. This changing lifetime pattern suggests that . . . roles are not central to identity and that the adaptive individual usually functions with the ability to modify sex roles and other roles when needed (1979, 148).

Another gerontologist, David Guttman, compared men and women in a number of cultures. Even though the cultures were different from our own, Guttman found that developmental changes occurred in a predictable sequence, leading to the "normal androgyny" of later life (1979:152). He contends that any developmental pattern such as gender-role changes in later life "is an evolved outcome . . . an adaptation to species survival."

All that apparently remains is to understand the difference in outcomes of perpetuating stereotypic sex-linked gender distinctions and restrictions, on the one hand, and of training ourselves and our children for full adaptive functioning and changing our institutions to implement full functioning, on the other hand. The latter approach is the road to satisfying, happier lives and to survival.

SUMMARY

The costs of perpetuating conventional versions of masculinity and femininity are great. They create problematic relationships between men and women, and their perpetuation is linked to institutions that promote inequalities that serve neither sex. Providing a social environment in which equal rights, responsibilities, and opportunities are assured can improve the quality of life and enhance individual survival.

This chapter has contrasted the conventional view of gender roles (authoritarian) with the equalitarian view. Through a review of the anthropological and sociological literature, we have seen that definitions of status arrangements and gender roles are neither universal nor instinctive. A learning approach explains the perpetuation of stereotypical male and female behaviors and attitudes. The arrangements and behaviors found in nonhuman animals cannot be transposed to humans because of the great differences in brain structure and function between species.

Chromosomal composition (XX and XY) does have consequences for humans. In particular, males are the more vulnerable sex, contrary to cultural beliefs that created and have sustained the idea of female inferiority.

The power differential that favors males in the patriarchal tradition has been examined through differing theoretical frameworks, and the large role of religions in perpetuating male dominance has been displayed. We have also looked at some of the consequences of superior-subordinate relationships between the sexes.

Regarding options for the future, three interrelated policies have been examined, along with their consequences. We have also noted the problematic nature of change and the worries it creates in those who are less able to adapt. The active pursuit of equality between the sexes and of shared childrearing responsibilities has been shown to produce people whose self-esteem is high and who benefit in a number of ways throughout life.

Progress toward assimilation of the sexes is under way. One barrier to more rapid change is language itself. Language, however, is changing in response to new images, and the division of labor is becoming somewhat less segregated by sex.

How soon will full assimilation occur? The women's suffrage movement lasted seventy-two years—from 1848 (when the first women's rights convention met) to 1920 (when the Nineteenth Amendment became part of the Constitution). In our time, the ERA is not yet ratified.

The prospect of equality is growing stronger, however. More women work outside the home today than ever before in our history, and although their wages are still low compared with men's wages, women are wage-earning, voting participants in the political process. National organizations promoting equality for men and women, although underfunded, are at work. A consciousness of the intertwined fate of the sexes has emerged. Perhaps the current effort at equality will succeed more quickly than earlier efforts have. The day may not be far off when all new parents will proudly announce additions to the family with the words *It's a person!*

STUDY QUESTIONS

1. We have stated that conflict theory explains the origins and persistence of patriarchy better than functionalist theory does. Using the general view of either theory, explain any other cultural institution or institutionalized practice (e.g., democracy, racism, or social stratification).

2. The terms *authoritarian* and *equalitarian* have been used to describe value systems with regard to gender roles. Could we substitute the terms conservative and liberal for the same purpose? How might the latter terms be more, or less, appropriate?

3. Think of any joke dealing with relationships between the sexes. Is it masculinist or feminist?

4. It has been argued both that the ERA would not require unisex bathrooms and that it would require them. Amplify either side of this argument.

5. Why do men and women refer to each other as the "opposite" sex? Is there a better designation? Why is it better?

6. We have maintained that stereotypes of masculinity and femininity are created and sustained in the socialization process. Who or what does this socializing?

REFERENCES

Adler, F. 1975. *Sisters in crime.* New York: McGraw-Hill.

Bardwick, J. M., and E. Douvan. 1980. Ambivalence: The socialization of women. In *Marriage and family in a changing society*, ed. J. M. Henslin. New York: Free Press.

Barfield, A. 1976. Biological influences on sex differences in behavior. In *Sex differences: Social and biological perspectives*, ed. M. S. Teitelbaum. Garden City, N.Y.: Anchor, Doubleday.

Baxandall, R. F. 1975. Who shall care for our children? The history and development of day care in the United States. In *Women: A feminist perspective*, ed. J. Freeman. Palo Alto, Calif.: Mayfield.

Bem, S. 1972. "Where have all the androgynous people gone? Paper presented at the UCLA Symposium on Women, May.

———. 1974. The measurement of psychological androgyny. *Journal of Consulting and Clinical Psychology* 42(2): 155–62.

———. 1975. Sex role adaptability: One consequence of psychological androgyny. *Journal of Personality and Social Psychology* 31(4): 634–43.

Berger, P. L., and H. Kellner. 1980. Marriage and the construction of reality. In *Marriage and family in a changing society*, ed. J. M. Henslin. New York: Free Press.

Bleier, R. H. 1976. Brain, body, and behavior. In *Beyond intellectual sexism: A new woman, a new reality*, ed. J. L. Roberts. New York: David McKay.

Bonk, K. 1980. The wage gap. *National NOW Times* (August): 8–9.

Brenton, M. 1966. *The American male.* New York: Fawcett World Library.

Campbell, J. 1959. *The masks of God: Primitive mythology.* New York: Viking.

CBS. 1981. "House-husbanding in America", Report on "60 Minutes" (25 October).

Chafetz, J. S. 1974. *Masculine/feminine or human? An overview of the sociology of sex roles.* Itasca, Ill.: F. E. Peacock.

Coser, L. 1956. *The functions of social conflict.* New York: Free Press.

Crosby, J. F. 1979. Reclaiming our sexuality: Owning ourselves. In *Choice and challenge: Contemporary readings in marriage.* 2d ed., ed. C. E. Williams and J. F. Crosby. Dubuque, Iowa: Wm. C. Brown.

Dahrendorf, R. 1959. *Class and class conflict in industrial society.* Stanford, Conn.: Stanford Univ. Press.

Daly, M. 1973. *Beyond God the Father: Toward a philosophy of women's liberation.* Boston: Beacon.

Davidson, L., and L. K. Gordon. 1979. *The sociology of gender.* Chicago: Rand McNally.

Davis, E. G. 1972. *The first sex.* New York: Penguin.

Davis, K., and W. Moore. 1945. Some principles of stratification. *American Sociological Review* 10 (April): 242–49.

deBecker, R. 1969. The Other Face of Love (M. Crosland and A. Daventry, translators). New York: Grove.

Demos, J. P. 1982. *Entertaining Satan.* New York: Oxford.

Edwards, J. N., and P. Kluck. 1980. Patriarchy: The last universal. *Journal of Family Issues* 1(3): 317–37.

Ellis, L. J., and P. M. Bentler. 1973. Traditional sex-determined role standards and sex stereotypes. *Journal of Personality and Social Psychology* 25: 28–34.

ERAmerica. 1980. For full and permanent equality . . . the Equal Rights Amendment. Publication of ERAmerica, Washington, D.C.

Farrell, W. 1974. *The liberated man.* New York: Random House.

———. 1974. The political potential of the women's liberation movement as indicated by its effectiveness in changing men's attitudes. Ph.D. diss., New York University.

Fasteau, M. 1974. *The male machine.* New York: McGraw-Hill.

Fein, R. A. 1974a. Men and young children. In *Men and masculinity,* ed. H. Pleck and J. Sawyer. Englewood Cliffs, N.J.: Prentice-Hall.

———. 1974b. Men's experiences before and after the birth of a first child: Dependence, marital sharing, and anxiety. Ph.D. diss., Harvard University.

Filene, P. G. 1976. *Him, her, self: Sex roles in modern America.* New York: Mentor, New American Library.

Forisha, B. L. 1978. *Sex roles and personal awareness.* Morristown, N.J.: Scott, Foresman.

Friedl, E. 1975. *Women and men: An anthropologist's view.* New York: Holt, Rinehart & Winston.

Gilder, G. 1975. *Sexual suicide.* New York: Quadrangle, New York Times Book Co.

Goffman, E. 1963. *Stigma: Notes on the management of spoiled identity.* Englewood Cliffs, N.J.: Prentice-Hall.

Goldberg, H. 1976. *The hazards of being male: Surviving the myth of masculine privilege.* New York: Signet.

———. 1979. *The new male: From macho to sensitive but still all male.* New York: Signet.

Golding, W. 1954. *Lord of the flies.* New York: G. P. Putnam's Sons, Perigee.

Goodman, E. 1982. At large. *National NOW Times* (April): 11.

Gould, M., and R. Kern-Daniels. 1977. Toward a sociological theory of gender and sex. *American Sociologist* 12(November): 182–89.

Guttman, David 1979 Individual adaptation in the middle years: Developmental issues in the masculine mid-life crisis. In J. Hendricks and C. D. Hendricks (eds.), Dimensions of Aging: Readings. Cambridge, MA: Winthrop.

Hamburg, D. A., and D. T. Lunde. 1966. Sex hormones in the development of sex differences in human behavior. E. E. Maccoby. In *The development of sex differences,* ed. Stanford Conn.: Stanford Univ. Press.

Harriman, P. L. 1965. *Handbook of psychological terms.* Totowa, N.J.: Littlefield, Adams.

Harrison, J. 1975. A critical examination of research on "masculinity/femininity" and a proposal for an alternative paradigm for research on psychological differences and similarities between the sexes. Ph.D. diss., New York University.

Hays, H. R. 1964. *The dangerous sex: The myth of feminine evil.* New York: G. P. Putnam's Sons.

Helmreich, R., J. T. Spence, and C. Holahan. 1979. Psychological androgyny and sex-role flexibility: A test of two hypotheses. *Journal of Personality and Social Psychology* 37(10): 1634.

Hoult, T. F. 1969. *Dictionary of modern sociology.* Totowa, N.J.: Littlefield, Adams.

Larzelere, R. E., and T. L. Huston. 1980. The dyadic trust scale: Toward understanding interpersonal trust in close relationships. *Journal of Marriage and the Family* 42(3): 595–604.

Levine, J. 1976. *Who will raise the children? New options for fathers (and mothers).* New York: Lippincott.

McCoy, N. L. 1977. Innate factors in sex differences. In *Beyond sex roles,* ed. A. G. Sargent. St. Paul: West.

Mead, M. 1969. *Sex and temperament in three primitive societies.* 2d ed. New York: Dell.

Michelmore, S. 1964. Sexual Reproduction. New York: Natural History Press.

Miller, C., and K. Swift. 1977. *Words and women: New language in new times.* Garden City, N.Y.: Anchor, Doubleday.

Money, J. 1973. Developmental differentiation of femininity and masculinity compared. In *Sexism: Scientific debates,* ed. C. Stoll. Reading, Mass.: Addison-Wesley.

Money, J., and A. A. Ehrhardt. 1975. Rearing of a sex-reassigned infant after traumatic loss of the penis. In *Sex, male; gender, masculine: Selected readings in male sexuality,* ed. J. Petras. Port Washington, N.Y.: Alfred.

Morgan, E. 1972. *The descent of woman.* New York: Stein & Day.

National NOW Times. 1982 Wage gap persists even in highest paid jobs. (April): 2.

———. 1982. Women's work not properly rewarded. (November–December): 2.

———. 1982. ERA reintroduced in House with Massive support. (January–February): 1.

New Woman. 1980. (September–October): 12.

Newsweek. 1980. A fishy formula for changing sex. September 15:70.

———. 1982. Women coal miners: The struggle goes on. (19 April).

———. 1983. In search of the real Samoa. (14 February): 56.

Nichols, J. 1975. *Men's liberation: A new definition of masculinity.* New York: Penguin.

Nieves, A. L. 1978. Diary of a sane househusband. *Friends Journal* 24(2): 12–13.

Oakley, A. 1972. *Sex, gender, and society.* London: Maurice Temple Smith.

Parsons, T., and R. F. Bales. 1955. *Family, socialization and interaction process.* Glencoe, Ill.: Macmillan.

PBS. 1980. "Meaning of modern art." Public Broadcasting System presentation (July 13).

Pedersen, F., and K. Robson. 1969. Father participation in infancy. *American Journal of Orthopsychiatry* 39(3): 466–72.

Petras, J. W., ed. 1975. *Sex, male; gender, masculine: Selected readings in male Sexuality.* Port Washington, N.Y.: Alfred.

Pierson, E. C., and W. V. D'Antonio. 1974. *Female and male: Dimensions of human sexuality.* Philadelphia: Lippincott.

Pleck, J., and J. Sawyer. 1974. *Men and masculinity.* Englewood Cliffs, N.J.: Prentice-Hall.

Rebelsky, F., and C. Hanks. 1971. Fathers' verbal interaction with infants within the first three months of life. *Child Development* 42: 63–68.

Richmond-Abbott, M. 1983. *Masculine and feminine: Sex roles over the life cycle.* Reading, Mass.: Addison-Wesley.

Roache, J. 1975. Confessions of a househusband. In *Sex, male; gender, masculine: Selected readings in male sexuality,* ed. J. W. Petras. Port Washington, N.Y.: Alfred.

Rubin, J., F. Provenzano, and Z. Luria. 1974. The eye of the beholder: Parents' views on sex of newborns. *American Journal of Orthopsychiatry* 44(4): 512–19.

Rush, F. 1980. *The best kept secret: Sexual abuse of children.* New York: McGraw-Hill.

Sanday, P. 1981. *Female power and male dominance.* Cambridge: Cambridge Univ. Press.

Sargent, A., ed. 1977. *Beyond sex roles.* St. Paul: West.

Schaffer, K. F. 1980. *Sex role issues in mental health.* Reading, Mass.: Addison-Wesley.

Singer, J. E., M. Westphal, and K. R. Niswander. 1968. Sex differences in the incidence of neonatal abnormalities and abnormal performance in early childhood. *Child Development* 39:103–22.

Sinnott, J. D. 1979. Sex role inconstancy, biology, and successful aging. In *Dimensions of aging: Readings,* ed. J. Hendricks and C. D. Hendricks. Cambridge, Mass.: Winthrop.

Skolnick, A. 1978. *The intimate environment: Exploring marriage and the family.* 2d ed. Boston: Little, Brown.

Sloane, B. K. 1982a. In brief. *National NOW Times* (March): 12.

———. 1982b. In brief. *National NOW Times* (November–December): 10.

Spence, J., and R. Helmreich. 1978. *Masculinity and femininity.* Austin: Univ. of Texas Press.

Spence, J., R. Helmreich, and J. Stapp. 1975. Ratings of self and peers on sex role attributes and their relation to self-esteem and conceptions of masculinity and femininity. *Journal of Personality and Social Psychology* 32: 29–39.

Strouse, J. 1982. New England's witching time. Review of *Entertaining Satan,* by John Putnam Demos. *Newsweek* (20 December): 81.

Tavris, C., and C. Offir. 1977. *The longest war: Sex differences in perspective.* New York: Harcourt, Brace.

Tiger, L. 1970. *Men in groups.* New York: Vintage, Random House.

Time. 1980 Leapin' lizards. February 18:50.

Tripp, C. A. 1975. *The homosexual matrix.* New York: McGraw Hill.

Universal Press. 11 July 1980.

Wall Street Journal. 25 February 1981.

Walum, L. R. 1977. *The dynamics of sex and gender: A sociological perspective.* Chicago: Rand McNally.

Webster's third new international dictionary. Unabridged, S. V. "instinct." Springfield, Mass.: G. & C. Merriam.

Williams, J. H. 1977. *The psychology of women: Behavior in a biosocial context.* New York: W. W. Norton.

Yorburg, B. 1974. *Sexual identity: Sex roles and social change.* New York: Wiley.

PART III

The Question of Survival

This section raises some serious questions about the existence of humankind in the near future. We must be made to realize that if the world were to end today through nuclear holocaust, all human endeavor would end as well. And, for many of us in the social sciences, there is nothing less feasible than the prospect of being dead. The theme of Part Three is that unless *all* of us—scholars and nonscholars alike—address ourselves to a number of survival problems *now*, the future of the social world as we know it is in jeopardy. The problems discussed in this section are both societal and global in nature, and the theories employed to analyze them are functional, conflict, and (macro) interactionist. Due to the *speed* of social change, the ways in which we view these problems are constantly changing.

Chapter 12 deals with sociological concerns over uncontrolled population growth in many parts of the world, particularly in the technologically less developed areas. This type of growth is a *social* problem because of the strain it places on all life support systems, including air, water, food, land, and energy.

Chapter 13 explores the crisis of the cities and what is being done about it. The urban crisis is a worldwide phenomenon with economic, political, social and cultural dimensions. It includes problems ranging from mass unemployment, migration, and eco-

nomic default to normative and psychological breakdown. Life in the larger cities of the world isn't what it used to be, and urban renewal programs have been largely a failure. More time and care will have to be taken in designing cities of the future.

Chapter 14 focuses on the global problem of war and peace and its relationship to such factors as social inequality and governmental policies. Many countries of the world are now at war and, therefore, ways must be found to reduce tensions and de-fuse the international atmosphere of cold war terror.

Finally, in Chapter 15, we discuss prospective future energy sources and their potential consequences for civilization *in the long run*. The creative use of renewable resources to produce energy would improve the quality of our lives and that of posterity. Following the advice of Welsh lyric poet Dylan Thomas, we need to "rage against the dying of the light."

CHAPTER 12

Population, Environment, and Resources

CONTENTS

China's growth taking heavy toll on environment

NEW YORK—China is causing widespread and serious damage to its environment in its efforts to quadruple its economic output in the next 20 years, according to a survey of the published writings of more than a score of Chinese scientists.

Vast forest areas have been denuded, lakes and streams have been polluted, and substantial soil erosion and loss of arable land have occurred, the survey reports, as China has expanded and upgraded its farms, factories and utilities.

The consensus among the scientists, writing in official scientific and political papers published in Chinese journals, is that the environmental deterioration poses a serious threat to their nation's physical well-being and hence to its social stability.

The survey, to be published in the October issue of the *Bulletin of the Atomic Scientists,* was done by Dr. Vaclav Smil, a professor of geography at the University of Manitoba in Winnipeg, Canada.

Smil said that when taken separately, these accounts by reputable Chinese researchers "are worrisome enough." But when taken together, he added, "the dimensions and implications of China's environmental degradation" are devastating.

Smil said about 800 million people among China's estimated population of more than 1 billion are rural inhabitants. Yet, he said, only about a tenth of the fuel needs of these rural residents is furnished by coal, the only readily available fuel. He cited reports that show that people make up their fuel shortage by using every available source of material that could be burned: stumps, roots, branches, bark, twigs and leaves from trees, grasses, dried sod, animal dung and dried sweet potatoes.

In addition to the demands on trees for fuel use, huge forest areas have been cleared for agriculture.

Smil said China, as a result of its "grain first" policy, is producing about 70 percent more grain annually than it did in the 1950s. But, he said, increasing population literally has eaten up the output, so there has been no improvement in the low food-energy intake of the average Chinese diet.

"So taking the 'easiest way out' by expanding grain production," he said, "has not only destroyed forests but has extended to conversion of grasslands and filling of lakes, resulting in higher soil-erosion rates and widespread ecosystemic disruption."

Source: New York Times 3 October 1982.

DEFINING THE PROBLEM: WORLD POPULATION GROWTH

China is not the only country with population growth pressures and environmental problems. According to the "1983 World Population Data Sheet," only two countries—West Germany and Denmark—showed a decrease in population compared with their previous year's populations (Population Reference Bureau 1983). Thus, the problem of human population growth, environment, and resources has *international* dimensions. Although representatives of France, the United Kingdom, and the Soviet Union, among others, sometimes state that their populations are not growing fast enough, these nations are the exception and not the rule.

The world now experiences about 80 million more births than deaths each year (Population Reference Bureau 1983). This means that the human population expands by almost exactly the total of the United States population every three years. Further, the present world population of over 4.6 billion persons is expected to double in about forty years. This is a spectacular growth rate, particularly when one considers that it took much of human history for the world population to reach 1 billion persons by 1830, but only another 100 years for it to reach 2

This photo shows how we have been "feathering our own nest," ecologically-speaking, over a long period of time. America is a land of contradictions, with many yet-to-be-solved social problems.

billion persons in 1930—primarily due to *declining death rates*. Declining death rates and increased life expectancy are generally attributed to increased food sources (nutrition), development of commerce and transportation, changes in industry and technology (including development of public health and sanitation systems), and increased control of infectious diseases, *in that order*.

After the Second World War, death rates fell even more rapidly, birth rates remained high—especially in technologically undeveloped areas—and world population "exploded." It reached 3 billion thirty years later in 1960 and 4 billion only fifteen years later in 1975 (Zero Population Growth 1978b). By the year 2000, world population is expected to reach a little more than 6 billion (see figure 12–1). Continued world pop-

ulation growth, especially in the undeveloped countries) is a serious social problem because of the strain it places on already overtaxed life support systems, such as air, water, food, and energy resources.

Some population biologists (Ehrlich 1971) think that the world's present population—4.6 billion persons—is three to seven times as many people as the planet can support permanently. In their view, the world is already overpopulated. We are expending nonrenewable resources at an enormous rate to support the present world population at a less than acceptable level in many areas. Viewed this way, the overall growth rate is astronomical.

To further complicate the issue, at least two kinds of growth rates are calculated. One rate adds numbers to the previous year's population; the other takes into ac-

FIGURE 12–1. History of World Population Growth

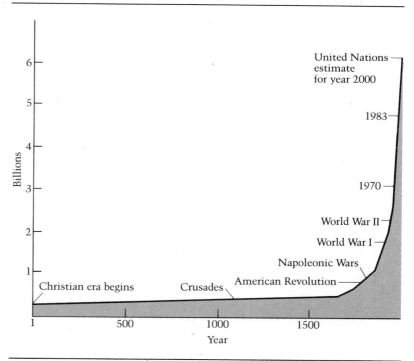

Data from Griffin, Paul F., ed. *Geography of Population: A Teacher's Guide*. Published for the National Council of Geographic Education Belmont, CA Fearon Publishers, 1969.

count the added population's potential to pollute the environment. For example, India is growing at a rate of 2.1 percent per year compared with a little less than 1 percent for the United States. India, however, has much less capacity to contaminate the environment than the United States does. America's per capita power consumption is fifty times greater than that of India. The impact on the environment of the average American baby, regarding nonrenewable resources, is 300 times greater than that of the average Indian or Indonesian baby. Thus, the growth rates in the "overdeveloped" countries—the United States, Japan, the Soviet Union, and other Western European nations—are more serious environmentally than the numerically higher growth rates in undeveloped countries like India and Pakistan. Population growth in countries like India and Pakistan, however, also indirectly causes greater contamination in the American environment, since the United States has to produce more food and other products that rapidly growing populations in Third World countries need.

On the more positive side, growth rates are declining slightly in fifty-six of the world's most populous countries. Recent data (Population Reference Bureau 1983) show that India's yearly rate of natural increase declined from 2.5 percent per year in 1976 to 2.1 percent in 1983, and the U.S. rate of natural increase has now dropped to .7 percent per year. Even with these lower rates of increase, however, India added about 15 million people in 1983, and the United States added about 1.6 million. Moreover, world population continued to grow at a rate of 1.8 percent in 1983. Given a 1.9 percent per year increase in world population between 1970 and 1976, while food production increased only 2.4 percent per year, the world population growth problem is clearly far from solved (Zero Population Growth 1978b).

The problem is even clearer considering that during the same time period, the *less developed countries* (LDCs) gained only 3 percent of the increased food production, while the *more developed countries* (MDCs) gained 1.4 percent per year (Zero Population Growth 1978b). In the poorest countries, such as those in South Asia, the Middle East and most of Africa, harvests per person actually declined.

In a global sense, **zero population growth** (ZPG) will occur when births equal deaths, and the number of people doesn't increase or decrease from one generation to the next. In a national sense, zero population growth also involves migration: births plus immigration must equal deaths plus emigration to achieve ZPG. Whether ZPG will be achieved in the near future depends on a number of other factors related to population growth pressures. These factors are such emotionally charged problem areas as family planning, sex education, teenage pregnancy, sterilization and abortion, infant mortality, average length of life, and social inequality related to health care and social welfare. That peoples' subjective attitudes are *polarized* concerning these and other population issues will become clear in the discussion that follows.

CONFRONTING THE PROBLEM: ATTEMPTS TO CONTROL GROWTH

No global social problem, other than war, has attracted more public attention during the decades since World War II than the world's "population explosion" (Tsui and Bogue 1978, 3). As every reader of newspapers and news magazines knows, people are taking sides on this and related issues such as food problems, environmental deterioration, and the long-term energy depletion crisis. Various positions have been taken regarding the question of whether world population growth constitutes a serious social problem. Hence, value conflict theory is the major explanatory perspective used in this chapter.

The English clergyman Thomas Malthus was the first important voice raised against uncontrolled world population growth. Contemporary followers of Malthus are referred to as neo-Malthusians; those who oppose Malthus's theories of population growth are called anti- or non-Malthusians. Both neo-Malthusians and anti-Malthusians abound today, just as they did in the late 1700s when Reverend Malthus wrote his *First Essay on Population.* In that book, Malthus took issue with philosopher William Godwin, who had argued that problems of overpopulation surely would be solved because humankind was "perfectable." Malthus also disagreed with economist Adam Smith, who argued that problems of population growth, inequality, and the food supply would be solved through the natural operation of the economic marketplace.

Smith assumed that every increase in profit or capital (resources) in a society would somehow benefit *all* workers and improve the living conditions of the poor (Malthus 1960). Conversely, Malthus made no assumptions regarding ultimate population growth, equality versus inequality, and the food supply. He found that industrially developed societies controlled their population growth somewhat better than undeveloped societies did. Malthus's (1960, 5) basic theoretical argument was that "the power of population is indefinitely greater than the power in the earth to produce subsistence for man" (and woman). The premises upon which this "dismal theorem" is based are: (1) food is necessary to existence and (2) sexual reproductive activity is necessary and will remain almost constant over time (Malthus 1960, 76).

Preventive Versus Positive Checks on Population Growth

Malthus concluded that future population growth could be reduced either by "preventive checks," such as late marriage, no marriage, and avoidance of sexual intercourse, or by nature's "positive checks," such as famine, disease, and war, which he predicted would follow each sharp increase in popula-

tion growth. Malthus obviously had no way of predicting the future influence of the preventive checks to which he was morally opposed, such as contraception and abortion.

Today, anti-Malthusians criticize Malthus not for any lack of logic in his theory but for his oversimplified mathematical model of "people production" versus food production. Malthus contended that if unchecked, population tends to continue doubling or to grow geometrically (as in the sequence 1, 2, 4, 8, 16, . . .), while food production tends to grow only arithmetically (as in 1, 2, 3, 4, 5, . . .).

While Malthus's dismal theorem has not held for many technologically advanced countries of the world, many undeveloped countries of the world still cannot produce enough food for their own people. Even Japan, a highly industrialized nation, is forced to import almost half its total food supply and nearly all of its fossil fuels. Japan is an island about the size of California, with a population more than one-half the U.S. population (119 million for Japan compared with 232 million for the United States in 1982).

Margaret Sanger and the Birth Control Movement

Thomas Malthus was not the only voice advocating population control. The founder of the birth control movement was the American nurse Margaret Sanger. She wanted family planning to be available to everyone because, as a public health nurse, she had seen too many women die from crudely performed abortions (Stewart 1956, 47). Sanger was also opposed to women being used as breeding machines and having too many babies born too close together. In 1916, she founded America's first planned parenthood clinic. This event resulted in a series of jailings for her violation of the Comstock Law, which prohibited the dissemination of birth control literature and materials.

Margaret Sanger defied, and finally overcame, what she believed to be an outmoded

Margaret Sanger was the founder of the Birth Control Movement in America. H. G. Wells, British historian and novelist, once said of Mrs. Sanger: "When the history of our civilization is written, it will be a biological history, and Margaret Sanger will be its heroine."

law that had negative consequences for women. She endured a number of hardships to make birth control information available to all who wanted and needed it. After her death in 1966, British historian H. G. Wells said of Mrs. Sanger, "When the history of our civilization is written, it will be a biological history, and Margaret Sanger will be its heroine" (Lader and Meltzer 1969, 163).

What Anti-Malthusians Say about World Population Growth

As we indicated earlier, not everyone agrees with the Malthusian position on world population growth pressures. Writer Joseph Breig (1971, 13–15) even argues that "overpopulation is a myth." Rather than being overpopulated, he maintains, the world is in

a state of economic imbalance. Breig (1917, 13) believes that the populations of undeveloped nations are "insanely maldistributed" and that they are without leadership in social systems that need drastic reform. Similarly, the USSR and the People's Republic of China argued until recently that no world population growth problem existed. To admit to such a problem would be to undermine socialist ideology, which argues for redistribution of wealth to solve most social ills. More recently, however, mainland China has enacted a vigorous family planning program that has decreased its yearly rate of population growth to 1.5 percent per annum (Population Reference Bureau 1983). Even at this lower rate of increase, however, China is adding at least 15 million persons to each year's previous population.

Some individuals argue against human population control for still other reasons. The Roman Catholic and Mormon church hierarchies around the world, as well as various Anabaptist communes such as the Hutterites and Amish, are indirectly against population control, since they are morally opposed to any artificial means of family planning. These groups, however, are not opposed to "natural" means of birth control, such as abstinence (no sexual activity) and the so-called rhythm method (avoiding sex during the wife's fertile period). The problem with these methods is that people do not always plan the size of their families, and the family-planning methods they use do not always work. The result is often unwanted children and additional population pressure for the society.

Abortion, Sterilization, and Family Planning

Minority group members and the poor are sometimes anti-Malthusian regarding the question of birth control. Blacks are aware of the sterilization of Jews in Nazi Germany for "eugenic reasons" and are suspicious of family-planning agencies (official birth control programs) in their communities. Birth control centers are often concentrated in poor neighborhoods, and a disproportionate share of black people live in such areas. This concentration has led some blacks to proclaim that family-planning programs are aimed at black **genocide** (the destruction of an entire race or group of people).

Erma Craven, a black social worker, is not opposed to birth control programs in general. She has distributed birth control literature and information in Milwaukee and other cities as part of her work. She is, however, strongly opposed to the use of abortion as an "after-the-fact" type of birth control. Ms. Craven contends it is "elitist, racist and genocidal to be pro-abortion" and charges that abortion on demand is a program of genocide against racial minorities (*Phoenix Gazette* 24 January 1978). A sociological study by Charles V. Willie (1971,1) indicates, however, that only a minority of blacks associated family-planning programs with a plot to eliminate blacks (*Ebony* 1973; *Essence* 1973a, 1973b; *Jet* 1973). Nevertheless, the sensitivity of some members of minority groups to birth control programs shows that population policies must be directed at all sectors of society if they are to be effective.

The abortion issue has generated much emotion and even some violence. An article in *Newsweek* (1978b, 33) expressed the problem:

Last week it was a fire set in a lavatory at the Akron, Ohio, Women's Clinic. Two weeks before that, a man splashed gasoline around the operating room of the Concerned Women's Clinic in Cleveland, tossed in a match and caused $30,000 in fire and smoke damage—injuring a nurse and terrifying sixteen patients. Over the past year, other women's clinics in St. Paul, Fairfax, Va., Omaha, Burlington, Vt., Cincinnati, Columbus and elsewhere have been subject to bombings, vandalism, disruptive pranks, physical threats to personnel, intimidation of patients—the common denominator being that all the targets are places where legal abortions are performed.

Newsweek also said that national anti-abortion leaders deplore this "intermittent

thuggery." The article indicated, however, that the recent outbreaks of violence may have been sparked by a seminar titled "How to Disrupt an Abortion Clinic," given at a prolife national convention in Boston in 1976 (*Newsweek* 1978b, 33). Apparently, prolife groups have adopted a wide variety of activist tactics, including marches, picket lines, sit-ins, and the use of films and literature that appeal to the emotions. The films typically display six-month-old fetuses sucking their thumbs and moving around in the mother's womb, although fetuses are not usually aborted after the first three or four months. Prolife advocates see abortion as premeditated murder. Specifically, they are

The abortion issue has generated much emotion and even some violence. Prolife groups have adopted a wide variety of activist tactics that are designed to appeal to the emotions.

opposed to the estimated 40 million abortions performed worldwide every year (Zero Population Growth 1978b).

Recently, anti-abortion (prolife) groups have been getting their way more often than not. In June 1977, the Supreme Court ruled that while states may not ban abortions, they are not required to pay for nontherapeutic abortions. Further, in the fall of 1977, Congress enacted the Hyde-Michel amendment prohibiting the use of federal Medicaid funds for most abortions (*Newsweek* 1978a, 32). In states that do not provide funds, abortions are more difficult for poor women to obtain, although some county governments are still willing to foot the bill, and some private clinics have reduced their fees. Thus, the Hyde-Michel amendment has had little impact on the abortion rates. Many states continue to provide funds for abortion, including states with the heaviest concentrations of the poor.

Anti-abortion forces therefore push for even more legislative change. For example, the so-called Human Life amendment would impose a ban on *all* abortions and some of the most widely used forms of birth control. Further, the Human Life Federalism amendment that Senator Orrin Hatch sponsored would give *both* Congress and the states the power to outlaw all abortions (Planned Parenthood 1983).

The greater danger in all of this, according to prochoice groups, is that a large percentage of the nearly 1 million women who need or want abortions every year may turn to dangerous "home remedies" to induce abortion. If a physician cannot be found to perform an illegal abortion, many women may turn to back-alley abortionists. Before the Supreme Court's 1973 decision to legalize abortion, illegal abortion was the leading cause of maternal death. Today, the maternal death rate from legal, first trimester abortions is only 1.7 per 100,000 abortions compared with 14.6 pregnancy deaths per 100,000 live births (National Abortion Rights League 1978). If the anti-abortion forces continue to get their way, illegal

abortion may again become a leading cause of maternal death. In addition, safe abortions for the poor, teenagers, and rural women may become a thing of the past. With or without violence, the abortion struggle has been characterized by an intensity similar to that of the antiwar movement of the 1960s.

Voluntary sterilization has been a much less controversial issue. Approximately 85 million persons worldwide have voluntary sterilization operations yearly; of these, 600,000 are American women (*Arizona Republic* 19 February 1978). India turned to voluntary sterilization as a method of birth control after efforts to introduce the rhythm method failed due to inadequate education. India's voluntary sterilization program involved male heads of families who had already fathered two or three children. This program resulted in several million sterilizations per year and was funded largely by American aid. Transistor radios or cash gifts of up to fifty dollars were offered as incentives for voluntary sterilization. Although these rewards may seem minimal, they represent sizable incentives in India, where per capita gross national product is equivalent to only $253 dollars per year in the United States (*Population Reference Bureau* 1983).

Sterilization became a controversial issue when India shifted temporarily to an involuntary program in the fall of 1976. This program attempted to increase the yearly number of sterilizations and thereby further reduce the birth rate. Indira Gandhi, who was then prime minister, her son, Sanjay, and Dr. D. N. Pai ordered compulsory sterilization for the state of Maharashtra on an experimental basis. The idea was to limit families to three children; however, an exception permitted a couple with three children of the same sex to have a fourth and final try for a child of the other sex (*Los Angeles Times* 10 October 1976). By spring 1977, the Indian people were openly resisting the coercive aspects of the mass sterilization program. Bloody rioting occurred in several states, and India's Muslim minority feared that the program was an attempt at genocide by the Hindu majority (*Wall Street Journal* 4 February 1977, 24). According to the Indian government, compulsory sterilization was a success, although India continues to add about 14 million persons annually to its population (Population Reference Bureau 1983).

Infant Mortality and Social Inequality

America has one of the highest per capita gross national product (GNP) averages in the world, yet fourteen other countries have lower infant mortality rates than that of the United States (Population Reference Bureau 1983). This fact is often puzzling; however, the explanation is connected to our highly competitive and individualistic economy. Our relatively high infant mortality rate reflects a health care system that is inadequate, expensive, and inaccessible to many people (see chapter 9).

Presently, the U.S. infant death rate is 11.4 per 1,000 live births; Japan and Sweden have infant death rates of only 7 per 1,000 live births. In comparison, Africa has an infant death rate of 120 per 1,000 live births. The **infant death rate** measures mortality in the first year of life. It is computed by relating the annual number of deaths of infants under one year of age to the annual number of live births, and is expressed as the number of deaths per 1,000 live births yearly in a society. The infant death rate is the most sensitive indicator available regarding social welfare and health conditions in any society. That the United States has a higher crude death rate than Japan is due partly to our higher infant death rate. Differences in access to prenatal and postnatal health care apparently contribute to the differences in rates. Further, infant death rates in the United States and many other societies are higher for nonwhites than they are for whites (U.S. Bureau of the Census 1977, 70).

Another meaningful statistical comparison is one that compares life expectancies at birth with race and sex. Our interest here is in average length of life by race, since most readers already know that women outlive men in the United States by a margin of several years. That nonwhite males can expect to live only 63.6 years compared with 69.4 years for white males may reflect social inequality in health care. Nonwhite females can expect to achieve 72.3 years compared with 77.2 years for white females (U.S. Bureau of the Census 1977, 66). Since nonwhite females, however, have a *higher* life expectancy than white males, sex is also an important factor in life expectancy.

Part of the racial differences in average length of life may be due to the rising costs of medical care. Blacks, and other nonwhites such as American Indians, with an average life expectancy of only forty-six years (Native American Rights Fund 1983), cannot afford the level of medical treatment that more affluent white Americans take for granted. Cancer, for example, takes an increasing toll on blacks compared with whites. In the past twenty-five years, the overall cancer rate for blacks rose 8 percent, while it dropped 3 percent for whites (*Associated Press* 18 February 1979). During the same period, cancer death rates for blacks increased 26 percent compared with 5 percent for whites. This indicates that health programs aimed at the general population often miss blacks, many of whom are locked into poverty in the urban ghettos. These differences in death and disease rates will continue as long as social inequality exists within and between societies.

ANALYZING THE PROBLEM: POPULATION GROWTH PRESSURES

The modern population growth problem contains dimensions of which Thomas Malthus in the 1790s and Margaret Sanger in the 1920s probably did not conceive. The problem consists of many diverse problems, and the problem emphasized depends on who does the defining. As we pointed out, some developed countries such as the Soviet Union and France point to their slow rates of growth, or to a lack of numbers in the younger age groupings (see figure 12–2) to show that they are "underpopulated." Few sociologists, however, will argue that a population growth problem does not exist on a worldwide basis.

Greatly lowered death rates in the LDCs have widened the gap between the now variable factor of mortality (deaths) and the nearly constant factor of fertility (births) in many of the LDCs. It is a paradox that the largest stumbling block to worldwide economic development is the early successes of

the natural and biological sciences. Drastically lowered death rates were brought to the LDCs when the MDCs such as the United States sent them more and better food, medicine, insecticides, and better sanitation techniques.

Meanwhile, nothing was done to lower birth rates in the LDCs to bring them in line with rapidly declining death rates. The result was population "explosions" in most of the LDCs that received aid from Western countries. Lowering death rates appeared humanitarian at the time (although motives were political and economic as well); however, lowering birth rates at the same time would have been much better for the LDCs in the long run. The human population explosion is the result of declining death rates combined with continuing high birth

FIGURE 12–2. Population Age Pyramids: Developed and Developing Regions, 1975 and 2000

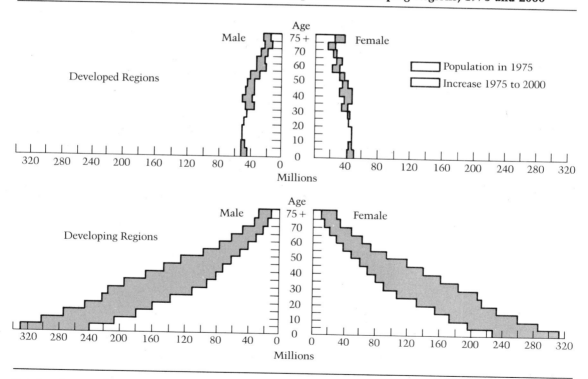

Data from Jean van der Tak, Carl Haub, and Elaine Murphy, Our population predicament: A new look, *Population Bulletin* 34 (5): 6 (December 1979).

FIGURE 12–3. Summary of the Human Population Explosion in Various Countries of the World

Crude Birth Rate, about 1980

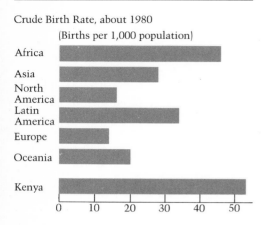

Crude Death Rate

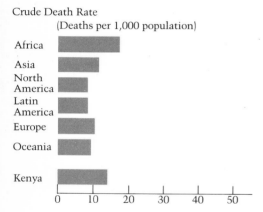

Rate of Natural Increase*

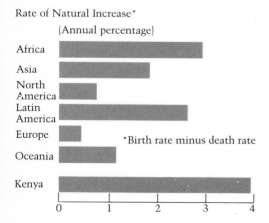

*Birth rate minus death rate

Data from Population Reference Bureau, *Intercom/3 8* (10) (October 1980).

rates in many parts of the world (see figure 12–3).

Birth Rates, Death Rates, and Migration

Numbers of births (fertility), deaths (mortality), and migrants (immigration and emigration) determine the size and growth of a population. In social systems terms, births and immigration are *input*, while deaths and emigration are *output*. In discussing human fertility, distinguishing it from fecundity is necessary. **Fecundity** is the potential for reproduction and is based on the number of women in the childbearing years of fifteen to forty-four. **Fertility** refers to the actual reproductive performance of women regarding numbers of children born in a given time span.

The single most important source of population data for the United States is the national census, which now will be taken every five years. Although by law everyone is supposed to respond to the census, some groups are underenumerated (undercounted) by the census. This undercounting of about 3 to 5 percent of the total population is due to some people not having permanent addresses; therefore, the census takers cannot locate them. Central city people and migrant workers are hardest to locate and have the highest rates of underenumeration. Still, the U.S. census is thought to be one of the most accurate in the world.

Vital statistics reports are the next most important source of population data. These reports provide a way of computing the population between censuses by adding the number of births and immigrants to the previous census and subtracting the number of deaths and emigrants. Vital statistics are kept in the government documents section of libraries.

Although various aspects of population data are important to sociologists, the crude birth and death rates, along with the infant death rate, are sufficient for a basic understanding of world population growth problems.

The **crude birth rate** measures the number of babies born in one year per 1,000 of the total population and is calculated as follows:

$$\text{Birth rate} = \frac{\text{Number of births per year}}{\text{Population}} \times 1{,}000$$

Similarly, the **crude death rate** is the number of deaths in one year per 1,000 of the total population and is calculated as follows:

$$\text{Death rate} = \frac{\text{Number of deaths per year}}{\text{Population}} \times 1{,}000$$

To obtain both crude birth and death rates, a fraction is multiplied by 1,000. This is done so that the rates can be expressed in whole numbers (e.g., 14), which are easier to understand than decimals are (e.g., .014).

Demographic Transition: A Natural Lowering of Birth Rates

Demographic transition occurs in an industrial society when it passes from a stage of population growth to a stage in which the rate of growth is declining. In the first stage—typically prior to industrialization—a society's birth rate is only a little higher than its death rate, and population growth is slow. The second stage of growth is caused by either a gradual or a sudden lowering of death rates, particularly the infant death rate. The third stage of population decline is due to a gradual lowering of the crude birth rate, which is then brought closer to correspondence with previously lowered death rates. The United States, Canada, Japan, and all of Western Europe have completed transition to lower birth rates and lower percentages of population increase per year. Periods of explosive population growth are usually associated with a drastic reduction in death rates rather than with increases in birth rates, which tend to remain fairly stable until (or unless) transition is completed.

Examples of stage-one areas of the world include western, eastern, and central Africa; specific countries include Haiti, Bolivia, Nepal, Cambodia, and Indonesia. Malthus's "positive checks" of famine, disease, and war produce high death rates in these areas and suppress rates of population growth.

Examples of stage-two areas include most of Asia—especially Southwest and Southeast Asia—and most of the countries of Latin America. Relatively high birth rates in these areas indicate that preventive checks are not being employed to any great extent. This situation may later lead to positive checks. Family planning is made more difficult in most of the stage-one and stage-two LDCs because of the political instability.

Stage-three countries such as the United States, France, and Japan have completed transition to birth rates that are almost as low as their death rates. India and other stage-two countries have not been able to lower birth rates nearly as rapidly as they have lowered their death rates. The following discussion may help to explain why the LDCs have had less success in lowering their birth rates than the MDCs have had.

First, a country must have agricultural surplus, that is, surplus food before it can industrialize, accumulate capital, and experience a natural (gradual or unforced) lowering of birth rates. Family size began to shrink in Europe and in the United States long before birth control pills or family-planning campaigns existed. In the United

States, childbearing rates declined 60 percent between 1800 and the 1930s (Zero Population Growth 1978b). During that period, the United States became industrialized. America can now produce more than enough food for its total population with less than 5 percent of its labor force working on farms. In many of the LDCs, 60 percent to 70 percent of the labor force is employed in agriculture; still not enough food is produced for all of the people.

Second, when a country produces an agricultural surplus and is accumulating capital, the released labor force can migrate into towns and cities and help industrialize them. Industrialization further refines agricultural technology, which is then applied back to the land for even greater yields with less labor. This process is cyclical and mutually reinforcing which allows more and more farm workers to migrate into the cities. The society becomes more industrial and urban and less agricultural as the cyclical process continues.

Third, continued urbanization and industrialization is tied to the rise of a larger middle class. This group is relatively better educated and generally has higher career expectations for its children, which is a strong motivation for smaller family size in the Western industrial nations. Since better education is what the middle class wants for its children, family planning and smaller families are important to them. Contraception began in the cities with the middle and upper classes and has always been greater in the cities. Conversely, the LDCs are preindustrial and rural, have a smaller middle class, and therefore have less incentive for family planning. Birth control is contrary to rural tradition that says that large families bring security and a source of inexpensive labor. These values change slowly, even in the face of intense educational programs.

A fourth variable is the influence of the Judeo-Christian ethic in Western industrial society (Weber 1958). Values derived from that tradition have encouraged the expression of individualism, competition (goal achievement), thrift, and hard work in countries such as the United States. Caste or slavery systems, however, provide less motivation for individual competitiveness and technical innovation. Further, many LDCs have stratification systems in which little chance for upward social mobility exists. Among other capital resources, such as an abundance of high-quality land, LDCs may also lack entrepreneurs (investors)—people who risk their money to make even more money. This almost fanatical spirit of rationality, thrift, ambition, and productivity appears lacking in many of the LDCs.

Demographic transition theory does not fit the population patterns of many LDCs and most totalitarian societies. Petersen (1975) argues that the underdeveloped nations and totalitarian societies exhibit patterns of fertility, mortality, and migration that make them difficult to analyze along the lines of traditional demographic transition. Typically, underdeveloped countries "buy" Western health programs and medical technology, and "instantly" reduce death rates. Totalitarian societies intervene and significantly affect population dynamics through such policies as family subsidies, state-controlled abortion, national health insurance, forced migration, and immigration or emigration restrictions.

Given the Western model of demographic transition, many of the LDCs seem to have settled in stages one or two of demographic transition, and have not experienced a natural (gradual) lowering of birth rates. Thus, we need to consider policy alternatives that might encourage an artificial (imposed) lowering of birth rates. First, however, we present an analysis of the relationship between population dynamics and environmental problems.

Population Growth and Eco-Catastrophe

A little over two decades ago, biologist Rachel Carson's *Silent Spring* (1962) became a controversial best-seller and spearheaded the environmental movement. This book produced the initial awareness of the consequences of contaminating the environment at dangerous rates. Yet, 1.8 million copies later, pesticide use has not declined. Overall pesticide and other chemical use in the United States has continued to climb, although DDT and other chemicals that linger in the environment have been banned or restricted (*United Press International* 3 October 1982). The pesticide industry surpassed $3 *billion* in annual sales in 1978, while in 1953, annual pesticide sales were estimated at $118 *million* (*United Press International* 3 October 1982).

How much have we learned from Rachel Carson and other environmentalists about pollution? Public opinion polls indicate that more people are becoming aware of the delicate relationship between population growth and the environment. Increased membership in such conservation-minded groups as Zero Population Growth (ZPG), the Sierra Club, and the Wilderness Society—partly in reaction against the questionable policies of former Secretary of the Interior James Watt—indicates the public's growing sensitivity to environmental problems.

Much educative work is still necessary regarding the danger of **eco-catastrophe,** defined as the human attack on the support systems that sustain our lives. For example, radioactive strontium 90, released into the air through nuclear explosions, returns to earth in rain or as fallout and eventually works its way into our bones. Regarding strontium 90, marine biologist Jerome Lowenstein (Reader, Hardert, and Moulton 1980, 71) points out:

One-half of the mammoth dose of strontium 90 released into Bikini lagoon on July 25, 1946, still circulates in the waters of the earth, being cycled and recycled through the shells of mollusks, the bones and teeth of fishes and their predators, including man. In the year 2006, one-quarter of the original dose will still be radioactive somewhere in the environment, or in ourselves.

Similarly, chemicals sprayed on croplands, forests, and gardens lie in the soil, enter living organisms, and are passed along in a poisonous chain reaction. In addition, some of these chemicals pass into underground streams, mix with air and sunlight, and combine into new forms that kill vegetation, sicken cattle, and harm those who drink from once pure wells. Much of this pollution is irreversible.

A situation involving dioxin pollution is a case in point (*Associated Press* 23 February 1983). **Dioxin,** a chemical by-product of herbicide production, causes kidney, spleen, and liver ailments in laboratory animals. The chemical was mixed with waste oil and sprayed on streets in the St. Louis suburb of Times Beach and in other areas of the United States to control dust over a decade ago. The dioxin used came from a plant that produced the controversial herbicide Agent Orange during the Vietnam War. Although the effect of dioxin on humans is unclear, in February 1983 the federal government agreed to spend $33.1 million to buy the *entire town* of Times Beach, Missouri and relocate its residents to protect them from dioxin contamination (*Associated Press* 23 February 1983). This is the first time the American government has bought out a contaminated town, although the federal government and New York State each spent about $7.5 million to buy 660 homes in a ten-block area around the former Love Canal chemical dump in Niagara Falls, New York (*Associated Press* 23 February 1983). Similar compensation may have to be paid to residents of a Denver, Colorado subdivision, whose neighborhood was contaminated by radioactive plutonium from nearby Rocky Flats nuclear weapons plant (*Arizona Republic* 24 April 1983).

Finally, overpopulation affects our quality of life in other ways. Diminishing resources, especially loss of plant and animal life, is a worldwide issue. The destruction of forests and grasslands is happening throughout Asia and in parts of South America, including Brazil. Regarding wildlife, Africa has turned its guns against its native animals (*U.S. News & World Report* 1980, 74–75). From crocodile to cheetah to elephant, that continent's wildlife is being tracked down and slain—usually for a profit. The number of mountain gorillas in Zaire and Rwanda has been reduced by 50 percent since 1960, and over the past decade, 90 percent of the rhinoceroses in Kenya, Uganda, and northern Tanzania have been slain (*U.S. New & World Report* 1980, 74).

Still other signs of imminent eco-catastrophe are present. In the whaling industry, for example, hunters are killing smaller and younger whales in increasingly larger numbers and not allowing time for replacement of fully grown adults (Hardert et al. 1977, 133). Peruvian anchovy fishing may be coming to an end. Most ocean fish that return to fresh water to breed, such as salmon, may soon become extinct. Their breeding streams are so dammed up and polluted that their powerful homing instinct leads them only to death. As the annual yield of fish from the sea decreases, malnutrition and starvation can be expected to increase.

American farmers are not using water and other resources in the most ecologically advantageous ways. By **ecology** we mean the interrelationship of all organisms to all of the environment in terms of subsistence. Too many farmers have depleted their land of many of its natural nutrients, and are using biocides and nitrogen fertilizers to make up for the lack of natural nutrients. Because of this depletion of natural minerals, and because of bad land and water management in the past, the land is in danger of erosion.

U.S. farmers prefer unstable monocultural planting, which encourages various insects to devastate whole fields of cropland. This practice leads farmers to use massive amounts of pesticides on their crops in an effort to produce high yields. If farmers planted *various* crops on the same plot instead, one type of insect could not destroy the entire field. Because monocultural planting is easier in the short term, however, the practice continues. Energy expert Hunter Lovins (1983) suggests that the use of chem-

ical biocides and petroleum-based fertilizers are only short-term answers. In the long run, insects become resistant to the pesticides, and costs for farmers steadily increase.

Regarding the issue of water mismanagement, agriculture uses about 90 percent of the water consumed in the United States (Lovins 1983). Most American farmers use the irrigation method, in which considerable water is lost to evaporation into the atmosphere. In the sprinkling system method, evaporation occurs, too. Much of the water flowing through the system never reaches the plants. Lovins favors the so-called drip method as the most practical (efficient) irrigation method, because little water is lost to evaporation in this method. If most U.S. farmers shifted to the drip method, our underground water tables would not drop as quickly, and aquifers could be replenished more easily.

A Bankura family sits in the street in rags and eats leaves that they have picked from the countryside. Bankura, some 200 miles from Calcutta in West Bengol is an area of India that has been badly hit by famine.

Environmentalist Wallace Stegner (Sierra Club 1983) sums up many aspects of our population and environmental problems:

Something will have gone out of us as a people, if we ever let the remaining wilderness be destroyed; if we permit the last virgin forests to be turned into comic books and plastic cigarette cases; if we drive the few remaining members of the wild species into zoos or into extinction; if we pollute the last clean air and dirty the last clean streams and push our paved roads through the last of the silence, so that never again will Americans be free in their own country from the noise, the exhausts, the stinks of human and automotive wastes. And so that never again can we have the chance to see ourselves single, separate, vertical and individual in the world, part of the environment of trees, rocks and soil, brother to the other animals, part of the natural world and competent to belong to it.

A recent estimate (*U.S. News & World Report* 1983) claimed that cleaner air and water alone will cost us $690 billion in the near future.

Population Pressure and the Food Supply

One of the major social problems of our times is the imbalance that exists between world population growth and the food supply. The severity of the problem is becoming more apparent, and our inability or unwillingness to provide food, domestically and abroad, is increasing steadily. Of our own country, one of the wealthiest in the world, it has been said (Schwartz-Nobel 1981) that "30 million Americans are going hungry and starvation is at epidemic levels." What is the situation, why has it been ignored, why does it exist, and what can we do?

Affluence, Poverty, and Food

"Since the beginning of agriculture until quite recently, nearly all of the growth in demand for food stemmed from population growth" (Brown and Eckholm 1974, 36). Rising consumption has begun to contribute to growing food demands. Rising affluence is now beginning to take a sizable share of our available food—at the expense of poorer nations. Affluence has been more responsible for the gap between food supply and demand than population growth has. For many nations, increasing their food production to meet their rapidly growing population has been problematic enough. In addition, however, they now have to compete for food with the rising affluence of developed nations that use their disproportionately large share of the world's food inefficiently.

Affluence typically refers to the diet that is prevalent among Western industrial countries. The diet is noted for its inefficiency both in nutrition and in food waste. The affluent diet is composed mainly of animal proteins and fats in the form of meats and dairy products, as well as a high amount of refined flour, sugar, and processed foods. The inefficiency in the affluent diet lies in how whole grains are used. For example, grain use has increased substantially among the developed nations; however, whole grains are almost absent in the affluent diet. This discrepancy is due to the majority of whole grains being consumed indirectly in the form of meat from grain-fed livestock. Conversely, diets in underdeveloped nations are comprised mainly of *directly consumed* cereals. That is, in less developed nations, each person has about 400 pounds of grain available per year. This grain must be consumed *directly* to meet the minimal energy needs. In contrast, the average North American uses nearly a ton of grain (Brown and Eckholm 1974, 36), only 200 pounds of which are consumed directly.

How significant is this conversion of grain into meat? First, grain supplies are finite in any given year; if some nations consume more, others will have to consume less. Second, grain for livestock is mainly available to developed nations who have the wealth to buy a disproportionately larger share of available grains. Grain hoarding has a tremendous worldwide impact. For example, "about a tenth part of the grain fed to beef cattle in 1974 could have met the entire grain shortfall in Asia that same year" (Dumont and Cohen 1980, 138). Additionally, the grain surplus produced in North America in 1976 could have fed India's 600 million people.

Converting large amounts of grain energy into smaller and less nutritious forms of food energy is extremely wasteful and irresponsible regarding human food needs. Producing one pound of meat requires thirty pounds of cattle feed, and the costs for this conversion are paid by the world's poor, who are consequently forced to eat less. In view of wide-scale malnutrition and hunger, livestock feeding epitomizes the disproportionate consumption and waste of richer nations. Food experts Frances Lappé and Joseph Collins (1978) have estimated the amount of food that would be available per person if affluent individuals and nations were to become more responsive to the world's needs: "If cereals were not fed to food animals, and if the per capita allocation of these grains were equalized, there would be roughly 5,000 calories per person per day" (see figure 12–4).

Presently, one-third of the world's grain is fed to livestock. The United States, however, converts two-thirds of its grain into

FIGURE 12–4. Energy Loss in Use of Land for Meat Production

Land Use	Food Product	Calories
1 Acre Wheat	Bread	800,000
1 Acre Grazing	Meat	200,000
	Energy Loss	600,000

Data from John A. Scharffenberg, *Problems with meat* (Santa Barbara, Calif.: Woodbridge, 1979), p. 64.

meat. Even during the worst year on record for wheat, 56 million tons of grain were fed to cattle while world famine escalated to new heights. "Overall, the richer countries, . . . give more grain to their livestock each year than is available for the combined human and animal populations of the poorer countries" (Dumont and Cohen 1980, 137). If affluence continues to rise, we can expect world famine to intensify in the future. Competition that increasing consumption generates will undoubtedly put prices out of reach for most of the world's poor.

The average person in the United States now consumes 250 pounds of meat per year, or about 5 pounds per week. This figure represents a doubling of meat consumption over the past generation. We have recently seen the beginning of a leveling in U.S. animal protein consumption. This leveling has largely been related to the medical community's recent acknowledgement of the growing evidence of the adverse effects of a meat-centered diet. The biggest danger Americans face from the affluent diet, nevertheless, is not to their health but in *global* consequences. Meat consumption has remained extremely high despite its recent leveling, and other nations have unfortunately not learned from our mistakes. As they become increasingly industrialized, their more nutritious native diets are being replaced with diets high in meat content. The Soviet Union and Japan are the two most recent converts to our inefficient diet. The Soviets in particular are giving a new meaning to the word *waste*. Their livestock feeding methods have surpassed the United States in inefficiency.

In short, we can expect affluence to become an increasing source of conflict between the developed and the developing nations as their populations begin to skyrocket, as major food-producing nations begin to reach their yield ceilings, as needed resources become stretched to their limits, and as famine escalates to unimagined heights.

ALTERNATIVE POLICIES FOR RESOLVING THE PROBLEM: WORLD POPULATION GROWTH, THE ENVIRONMENT, AND RESOURCES

Because food supply will become a major problem in the years ahead, special consideration and time will have to be focused on Third World nations—where our greatest potential for increasing food production lies. Additionally, moral questions will have to be resolved concerning rights and assurances for all nations to have access to world food supplies. Three major proposals for accomplishing these goals include establishing an international food council, promoting small farm progress, and implementing family-planning programs.

Family-planning Policies

More than one-third of the world's population today is under age fifteen. This means that by about 1990, potential new parents will number nearly 1.5 billion. In the LDCs, 65 percent of the people are younger than twenty-five years. As Zero Population Growth (1978b, 2) expresses it, "Youth is the engine that will drive future population growth."

How many children will future parents have, and how many *should* they have? Demographers (sociologists who specialize in the study of population problems) use the total fertility rate (TFR) to illustrate the lifetime number of children per woman. The **total fertility rate** is "a measure of childbearing that projects the lifetime number of children that would be born per woman if all women had children at the prevailing rates of a given year" (Zero Population Growth 1978b, 2). In countries where birth control is practiced only rarely, the TFR has been five to eight children per woman. In several European countries, Canada, and the United States, the TFR is already below 2.1.

In a low death rate society like ours, a

TFR of 2.1 is called "replacement-level fertility." This means if American couples continue to have an average of 2.1 or fewer children, there will eventually be only enough births in a generation to replace the preceding generation. In areas where more people die in infancy and youth, higher TFR is needed to replace the mothers' generation. In either case, zero population follows several decades after a country reaches replacement level, because the mothers' generation is still alive while its children and grandchildren are reproducing their own offspring. As Zero Population Growth (1978b, 2) states:

It can take 70 years of childbearing at that rate (TFR) before growth slows to a halt. If, by a miracle, the world reached replacement-level childbearing tomorrow, 2.5 billion more people would still be added before growth halts.

The World Bank has calculated that "for every decade of delay in reaching replacement level, the ultimate world population will be 15 percent larger" (Zero Population Growth 1978b, 2). What can be done to control this type of world population growth pressure? The following policies warrant careful consideration.

Agricultural Policies

First, agricultural efficiency needs to be increased in the LDCs to make them efficient at farming. Some LDCs do not have the quality and quantity of land found in North America. They do not have the luxury of extensive cultivation in which crops can be rotated and fields can be left dormant for a time to regain nutrients. Instead, cultivation in many of the LDCs is intensive, and the land is being used constantly. What is needed is more and better fertilizers and less monocultural (single crop) planting.

The MDCs could also increase aid to the LDCs in the form of money and high-quality fertilizers. Temporarily, the money could be used to import food when crops run

short. Some argue that the MDCs already provide too much aid to the LDCs. The late economist E. F. Schumacher (1975, 195), however, provides the following statement to refute that argument:

If we take the total of Western aid, after eliminating certain items which have nothing to do with development, and divide it by the number of people living in the developing countries, we arrive at a per-head figure of rather less than £ 2 [about $4.00] a year.

Second, agricultural production in certain Third World countries could be increased. With better land management, motivation, and agricultural technology, South America, for example, could produce more of its own food. The inflating costs of food, rent, and transportation, however, make it difficult for even middle-income people to live in countries like Brazil and Ecuador, which have exploding populations.

Third, if more people everywhere became vegetarians, less nutrition would be lost in raising cattle and pigs, and more would be available for people. Also, much high-quality protein, in the form of fish, is expended on the world's pets. If less protein were expended on dogs and cats in the MDCs, more of this food would be available to those who are presently starving in both the MDCs and the LDCs. If more people became vegetarians, according to food expert George Borgstrom, the world's population could be fed adequately (Zero Population Growth 1978b, 2). If world population growth remains unchecked, however, approximately 1 billion people will be going hungry in the next decade.

Fourth, the so-called **green revolution** (Brown 1970) is another method of increasing the world food supply. The method refers to the use of high-yield crops in the same land area where low-yield crops have been planted in the past. This method alone is not the answer; very few green revolutions have been successful in the long run. The introduction of the potato into Ireland was a green revolution. For a time, this effort helped sustain the Irish population, but the potato blight brought famine and death to about 1 million of the Irish. Two million others saved themselves only by migrating to other countries.

Numerous other biological, economic, social, and political reasons indicate why green revolutions are not the total answer to the food supply problem. Green revolutions are not a source of the high-quality protein needed for balanced diets. High-quality protein is expensive and is frequently in short supply. The protein that is not in short supply is often poorly distributed. To underscore the seriousness of the world food supply problem, consider that no growth in world food production occurred in 1969, while world population grew by 2 percent. Norman Borlaug, recipient of the 1970 Nobel Peace Prize for work in high-yield wheat research, maintains that the food supply approach *by itself* is not a total solution to the problem. Too many people are still coming into the world too quickly (*Arizona Republic* 16 May 1971).

A massive reduction in world population growth would be the most helpful, but other steps must also be taken. High-yield foods require efficient transport and storage systems. Such systems are needed in the LDCs to conserve food between the harvest and the table. An estimated one-third of the total food supply to these countries spoils before it reaches the hungry. Insects, rats, and mold contribute to the spoilage.

Political Responses to Population Growth Pressures

In 1960, only India and Pakistan had governmental policies related to reducing population growth (Zero Population Growth 1978b, 4). According to the Population Council, thirty-five nations had official antigrowth policies by 1977 (Zero Population Growth 1978b, 4). Much work, however, still needs to be done. Sixty-six nations have no official

population policies, and eight countries have restrictions *against* family planning.

Some demographers, such as Kingsley Davis, think that more persuasive political programs must be adopted (Zero Population Growth 1978b, 5). Yet, overzealous coercion raises human rights issues and is questionable in effect. Recall India's drive for involuntary male sterilization in 1976, which contributed to the defeat of Indira Gandhi's government. Countries with population growth problems must be encouraged to bring their own houses in order. China, for example, has an antigrowth strategy that includes annual birth rate goals, free contraceptives for men and women, free sterilization and abortion, delayed marriage, and discouragement of premarital sex. Similarly, Japan cut its birth rate in half—mainly through abortion—only six years after World War II (Azumi 1978, 256). Governmental action needs to be taken in Malaysia, where older couples want an average of 4.7 children, and in Africa, where the desire is for an average of 6 children.

Voicing concern over the population problem through letters and phone calls to the president and members of Congress is helpful. The sponsorship and passing of bills in Congress is another way to work politically within the system. For example, Congressmen Michael J. Harrington of Massachusetts and Richard L. Ottinger of New York introduced a bill to establish an explicit American population policy (Zero Population Growth 1978a). Mexico, which has a low death rate (6) and a relatively high birth rate (32), has experienced a complete turnaround in population policy (Population Reference Bureau 1978). In an effort to halt its population explosion, the Mexican government launched its first education campaign to encourage family planning. The $130 million per year program aims at reducing population growth from 2.6 percent per annum to 1 percent by the year 2000. Dr. Jorge Martinez Manatou, the project's health coordinator, says, "We should have started 20 years ago; we are 20 years too late" (*Associated Press* 15 January 1978). Meanwhile, Mexico's current population of 76 million is straining its life-support systems. Housing is scarce, food supplies are dropping, and unemployment is on the rise.

Continuing Traditional Policies

Along with political change, continuing traditional contraceptive policies is necessary. The number of couples worldwide using birth control soared from 147 million in 1970 to 250 million in 1977, according to the Agency for International Development (Zero Population Growth 1978b). Voluntary sterilization is the most popular method of birth control, with 80 million users in 1977. Birth control pills, foams and jellies, condoms, and intrauterine devices (IUDs) are also widely used. Sterilization appears to be gaining popularity among families with two children. The estimated 40 million abortions performed worldwide each year also greatly reduce world population growth.

Other traditional policies include family-planning education and tax incentives to encourage smaller family size. Family-planning education could be extended to the public schools if religious and political barriers were removed. Tax incentives are already employed to encourage people to use solar energy devices in some states. Similarly, tax relief could also be given to parents who limit the size of their families. At present, our tax system rewards people for contributing to world population growth problems.

Some anti-Malthusians still oppose all measures to control population growth. They argue that industrialization of the LDCs is the best approach to the problem. The mineral resources of the world are being depleted, however, which prevents the LDCs from industrializing. How the LDCs will modernize in the face of declining, non-renewable resources such as fossil fuels remains to be seen. Conversely, the MDCs must either "de-develop" or face the prospect of poisoning life-support systems.

What some anti-Malthusians have apparently failed to consider is that the development of smaller families is related to specific aspects of social and economic development. Improved infant health care and smaller family size, for example, enable women to obtain an education and locate work. When people have hope for the future—for themselves and for their children—they tend to limit family size.

SUMMARY

Population growth pressures and environmental deterioration are related problems for most of the world. The world population problem is how to produce, in the LDCs, the social, economic, and political changes that have lowered birth rates in the MDCs. In demographic transition, stage-two countries like Brazil, India, and Mexico have not had the industrial and cultural changes that would naturally motivate their people to practice family planning. While their death rates were drastically lowered through aid from Western nations, their birth rates remain relatively high.

Some LDCs were able to cut their death rates in half in less than a decade. The same decrease can be achieved with birth rates if the proper controls are applied. People in preindustrial nations, however, still tend to want traditionally large families because they believe that many children represent safety and security.

That the ecosystem of the earth can continue to support the 8 billion people we are expected to have in the next forty years is increasingly doubtful. We are faced with world population growth trends that cannot continue into the next century without catastrophe. Each additional million people causes a heavier drain on world resources.

Regarding population growth and food problems, many alternative sources of food for the world exist, such as high-quality vegetable protein products and soya protein to replace animal protein in diets. Food *scar-*

city is not the problem per se; that is, food *could* be much more abundant. Political, social, and economic inequalities are what maintain world hunger. If famine is to be eradicated, an overhaul of our free market food trade system will first be necessary. In short, food will need to become regarded as a human right—not a privilege.

STUDY QUESTIONS

1. Trace the history of world population growth from 1776 to 1983. What factors are most directly related to this pattern of growth?

2. Explain how demographic transition experienced in the industrial societies could lower the population growth rates of·some other societies to manageable levels. Why is it said that demographic transition theory does not fit the population patterns of many LDCs and most totalitarian societies?

3. Why is bringing about fertility planning in many of the less developed countries of the world so difficult? Provide examples from this chapter.

4. Why does value conflict theory seem to be the most appropriate perspective for understanding world population problems?

5. Explain the relationship between population growth pressures and the food supply in many of the less developed countries of the world.

6. Explain how uncontrolled population growth can and does bring about eco-catastrophe.

REFERENCES

Arizona Republic. 16 May 1971; 19 February 1978; 24 April 1983.

Associated Press. 15 January 1978; 18 February 1979; 23 February 1983.

Azumi, K. 1978. The mysterious drop in Japan's birth rate. In *Social problems: Institutional and interpersonal perspectives*, ed. K. Henry, 255–59. Glenview, Ill.: Scott, Foresman.

Breig, J. A. 1971. Overpopulation is a myth. *U.S. Catholic Jubilee* (May).

Brown, L. 1970. *Seeds of change: The green revolution and development in the 1970's.* New York: Praeger.

Brown, L., and E. P. Eckholm. 1974. *By bread alone.* New York: Praeger.

Carson, R. 1962. *Silent spring.* Greenwich, Conn.: Fawcett.

Dumont, R., and N. Cohen. 1980. *The growth of hunger.* Boston: M. Boyars.

Ebony. 1973. Sterilization: Newest threat to the poor. (October). 150–156.

Ehrlich, P. 1971. *The population bomb.* New York: Ballantine.

Essence. 1973a. Is abortion black genocide? (September).

———. 1973b. A Montgomery tragedy. (September).

Hardert, R. A., H. A. Parker, E. H. Pfuhl, and W. A. Anderson. 1977. *Sociology and social issues.* Hinsdale, Ill.: Dryden Press.

Jet. 1973. Black youngsters are sterilized by Alabama agency (July): 12–15.

Lader, L., and M. Meltzer. 1969. *Margaret Sanger: Pioneer of birth control.* New York: Crowell.

Lappé, F. M., and J. Collins. 1978. *Food first.* New York: Ballantine.

Los Angeles Times. 10 October 1976.

Lovins, H. 1983. Water and agriculture problems. Paper presented at Arizona State University (Spring).

Malthus, T. 1960. *Population: The first essay.* Ann Arbor: Univ. of Michigan Press, Ann Arbor Paperbacks.

National Abortion Rights League. 1978. *Newsletter.* (June).

Native American Rights Fund. 1983. Save a fish—spear an Indian. *Newsletter* (Spring).

Newsweek. 1978a. (6 February).

———. 1978b. (13 March).

Petersen, W. 1975. *Population.* New York: Macmillan.

Phoenix Gazette. 24 January 1978.

Planned Parenthood. 1983. (pamphlet) (810 Seventh Ave., New York, NY 10019).

Population Reference Bureau. 1978. Mexico's population policy turnaround. *Intercom* 33 (5) (December).

———. 1983. *1983 World Population Data Sheet* (April).

Reader, M., R. Hardert, and G. Moulton. 1980. *Atom's eve: Ending the nuclear age.* New York: McGraw-Hill.

Schumacher, E. F. 1975. *Small is beautiful.* New York: Harper & Row.

Schwartz-Nobel, L. 1981. *Starving in the shadow of plenty.* New York: McGraw-Hill.

Sierra Club. 1983. Membership renewal advertisement.

Stewart, M. S. 1956. *Problems of family life and how to meet them.* New York: Harper & Row.

Tsui, A. O., and D. J. Bogue. 1978. Declining world fertility: Trends, causes, implications. *Intercom* 33(4) (October): 3.

United Press International. 3 October 1982.

U.S. Bureau of the Census. 1977. *Statistical abstract of the United States.* Washington, D.C.: U.S. Government Printing Office.

U.S. News & World Report. 1980. Africa turns its guns against its animals. (8 December).

———. 1983. Cleaner air and water—Can we afford $690 billion? (28 February).

Wall Street Journal. 4 February 1977.

Weber, M. 1958. *The Protestant ethic and the spirit of capitalism.* New York: Charles Scribner's Sons.

Willie, C. V. 1971. A position paper. *Population Bulletin* (selection no. 37).

Zero Population Growth. 1978a. *National Reporter* 10(5) (June–July): 1.

———. 1978b. *National Reporter* 10(10) (December): 1.

CHAPTER 13

The Urban Crisis

CONTENTS

Detroit riot area makes a comeback in the 1980s

The nation's worst urban riot erupted on Detroit's 12th street in July 1967, and when the shooting and looting stopped after four days, 43 people were dead and the surrounding Virginia Park area lay in ruins. Fifteen years later, 12th Street is finally making a comeback, largely as a result of the efforts of local residents, who last month celebrated the opening of a community center and shopping plaza. "We've brought 12th Street back to life," says Herschel Richey, president of a citizens' group called Virginia Park Community Investment Associates, Inc. "It sure gives me a good feeling to see people walking along that street again."

Since the riots destroyed almost every shop on 12th Street . . . residents have had to walk several miles for groceries and other supplies. "If the area was going to survive," says Richey, "we needed a shopping plaza. But people said we'd never be able to do it, and we called the project 'Mission Impossible' ourselves." It wasn't long after the VPCIA raised $90,000 seed money by selling construction bonds, holding raffles and passing the hat, that Mayor Coleman Young helped arrange for more than $1 million in city grants. The Equitable Life Assurance Society provided the rest of the money needed with a $1.5 million loan.

Even with construction under way, the VPCIA had difficulty luring businesses to the high-crime neighborhood. They finally calmed the fears of shopkeepers by organizing an "anticrime squad" to patrol store aisles and report shoplifting or other disturbances to store managers and the police. Today the plaza boasts the largest Farmer Jack supermarket in Detroit and a dry cleaner, hardware store, beauty salon, drugstore and three restaurants. "We want these stores to stay," says Richey.

"We're here to make sure that crime doesn't run them out again."

. . .

The area's main need now is housing. There are still nearly 200 empty lots—some the size of an entire city block—and hundreds of the houses left standing desperately need repairs. The VPCIA has arranged with the city for home-improvement loans at 3 percent interest and has supervised construction of more than 400 federally funded town-house and apartment units. The council is now working on 70 single-family houses—the first such homes built in the neighborhood in more than 50 years. Rebuilding is a slow process, says executive director Fred Durhal, Jr. "But we've learned patience. I only hope it doesn't take another 15 years."

Source: Newsweek 6 December 1982.

DEFINING THE PROBLEM: URBAN LIFE AND THE STRUGGLE TO BE HUMAN

Why are the mayors all quitting?
Why are the cities all broke?
Why are the people all angry?
Why are we dying of smoke?
Why are the streets unprotected?
Why are the schools in distress?
Why is the trash uncollected?
How did we make such a mess?

> Author anonymous
> Cited in L. Gordon, *Sociology and American Social Issues* (Boston: Houghton Mifflin, 1978), p. 297.

The interest in cities is a reflection of the global concern with urban living. Worldwide, thirty times as many people as in 1800 now live in cities with populations of 100,000 or more, although the total world population has only quadrupled in that time (Semenoick 1966; United Nations 1980). The rapidity with which this global *urbanization** process has occurred has caused major adjustment problems at every level of the social system. The result has been an era in which social solidarity of the type existing in small-community settings with strong intergenerational kinship ties is declining or is already nonexistent.

This worldwide urban reality has been developing for a longer time in the United States than in most other societies. In the United States, the major shift to cities early in this century initially produced among many individuals and whole groups a widespread sense of **anomie** and "marginality," a social condition in which one "does not quite 'belong' or feel at home" (Stonequist 1937, 1942). The ideas of social anomie and marginality are based on the findings of Robert Park and other urbanologists in the influential "Chicago School" of sociology (the first major sociology department in the United States), and appeared less than two decades after the United States census of 1920 first reported that most Americans lived in urban areas (see table 13–1). By mid-

century, urban researchers were finding that a second and third generation of American urban dwellers were exhibiting fewer signs of marginality, including stronger primary and more stable secondary relations (Axelrod 1956; Komarovsky 1946; Rogers 1961).

Since mid-century, changing urbanizing trends have generated new and complex problems. One symptom of urban life problems is indicated on table 13–1, which shows that since the census began in 1790, the 1980 census was the first to indicate that a lower proportion of Americans resided in urban areas than in the previous decade. The urban adjustment problems of our now overwhelmingly urban society are evident in the following social facts about American society today, reported by the U.S. Bureau of the Census and other standard sources of information. Divorce rates have been growing twice as fast as marriage rates, pockets of chronic intergenerational ghetto-area underemployment and poverty are evident in every big city, and de facto residential and educational **segregation** on the basis of race and class is increasing. Analysis of any urban area must deal with a complex of these and related problems facing people in the modern world as it now exists and is rapidly developing.

In such a context, there are so many problems to solve that approaching them from more than one disciplinary point of view is important—whether it be that of sociology, history, psychology, political science, economics, geography, or any other single field. An interdisciplinary approach is necessary to assess the problems people experience in the modern urban condition. Although the material that follows is primarily sociological, many references are made to urban research in other disciplines. The aim is to develop the kind of perspective that can lead to consideration of new urban strategies and policies. We are at a point of urban development when new approaches to urban life and urban planning appear crucially necessary. In recent years, a number of individual, private, and public ideas and efforts have been advanced to generate new community environments. The idea is to meet the numerous and diverse interests of individuals and cultural groups living in our metropolitan areas.

As we explore the urban crisis, it will become clear that the most pressing issues exist within the old, large-city boundaries rather than in their surrounding suburbs. This is true for a wide range of problems including those listed in the opening section poem. Concentrated in the cities are the issues of increasing racial and economic segregation, of schools with increasing needs and declining tax bases to meet those needs, of traffic congestion, air pollution, and rising rates of violent crime. Yet, the picture is not all bleak. The cities remain the center of commercial development. They are also the home of many great universities, the setting for much of our art, theater, and music, and

the place where citizens of different cultural heritages can interact. In addition, the cities are so strategically located geographically, economically, and politically that their vitality is closely linked to the health and welfare of the entire society. Indeed, virtually all large cities are experiencing pockets of neighborhood revitalization as in the news report in the beginning of this chapter. This process is often called "regentrification," in that some upper-income individuals and families have moved back into central large cities. As yet, this movement is small but noteworthy. Urban problems remain large.

This chapter takes up three dimensions of the urban crisis. Each dimension can be formulated as a question. First, how do Americans view their cities with all their attendant problems? Second, what objective consequences do we face as a result of our—

TABLE 13–1. U.S. Urban Population as a Percentage of Total Population by Regions, 1790–1980

	U.S. TOTAL	NORTHEAST	NORTH CENTRAL	SOUTH	WEST
Current SMSA[a] urban definition:					
1980	74.8	84.9	70.9	66.8	82.5
1970	75.6	86.7	71.8	66.0	83.4
1960	69.9	80.2	68.7	58.5	77.7
1950	64.0	79.5	64.1	48.6	69.5
Previous urban definition:					
1960	63.0	72.8	63.9	52.7	66.1
1950	59.6	75.4	61.1	44.6	59.9
1940	56.5	76.6	58.4	36.7	58.5
1930	56.1	77.6	57.9	34.1	58.4
1920	51.2	75.5	52.3	28.1	51.8
1910	45.6	71.8	45.1	22.5	47.9
1900	39.6	66.1	38.6	18.0	39.9
1890	35.1	59.0	33.1	16.3	37.0
1880	28.2	50.8	24.2	12.2	30.2
1870	25.7	44.3	20.8	12.2	25.8
1860	19.8	35.7	13.9	9.6	16.0
1850	15.3	26.5	9.2	8.3	6.4
1840	10.8	18.5	3.9	6.7	b
1830	8.8	14.2	2.6	5.3	b
1820	7.2	11.0	1.1	4.6	b
1810	7.3	10.9	0.9	4.1	b
1800	6.1	9.3	b	3.0	b
1790	5.1	8.1	b	2.1	b

[a]*Standard Metropolitan Statistical Area* (includes suburbs around central cities).

Source: U.S. Department of Commerce, *Standard metropolitan statistical areas and standard consolidated statistical areas: 1980 census of the population,* Report PC80-S1-5 (Washington, D.C.: U.S. Government Printing Office, October 1981), table 5.

often negative—views of cities and of the contemporary complex of problems evident in our cities? Third, what options do we have to achieve urban environments that are attractive, appealing, and stabilizing?

The first section of this chapter focuses on the American small-town heritage. This heritage has been carried over to a considerable extent into our suburban communities. One consequence is a massive neglect of our deteriorating central big cities, which now harbor a disproportionate number of our society's poor and racial minorities. The second section takes up the objective social situation that has developed out of the issues raised in the first section. The pressing problems that have been generated in our cities are of import not only to the people in

cities but also affect the stability of entire metropolitan areas. Here, we consider what constitutes "urbanism" and "suburbanism" and how the latter excludes many city inhabitants from the opportunity structure of American society. The makeup and operation of "community power" is a central issue here. The third section takes up the pressing need for comprehensive urban planning in a society that no longer has an open frontier. The societal movement toward a national, regional, and metropolitan planning ethic has been developing since the 1960s, and parallels earlier such developments in other urbanized societies. An assessment is made of prospects for various urban policies and plans. These include large-scale private and public urban renewal

There is considerable life in deteriorating city neighborhoods, but unless re-development occurs these children are most likely looking toward a bleak future.

efforts, as well as smaller scale urban home-steading and neighborhood gentrification de-velopments.

CONFRONTING THE PROBLEM: THE URBAN CRISIS

There is little question that Americans are generally aware that our big cities are in trouble. Gallup and Harris polls repeatedly remind us of how we perceive our cities. Ask about cities and be prepared for a litany of charges about poor schools, bad housing, violent crime, ghetto poverty, declining job opportunities, and deteriorating public ser-vices. As our anonymous poet asked, How did we make such a mess?

City Images through a Small-town Prism

The combination of massive, big-city prob-lems and the small-town rural heritage of American society have combined to produce a widespread negative view of urban life. Let us consider that heritage and its continuing influence. When the first U.S. census was taken in 1790, nineteen out of every twenty people lived in the rural countryside. The most urban society of the time was Great Britain, with whom Americans had engaged in a bitter struggle for independence. Thomas Jefferson expressed a widely held opinion when he made the observation that "I view cities as pestilence to the morals, the health and the liberties of man" (Bloom-berg 1967, 359).

Jefferson's agrarian, ideal community set-ting and his distrust of large cities is still evident today. Popular television programs, calendar photo scenes, political campaign rhetoric, and the like reflect this cultural at-titude. We look with nostalgia to the open-ing frontier, to breathing room, limited regulation of our lives by others, and clean air and water. The big city is often viewed

as the opposite of these desired goals: the absence of freedom, health, and opportunity.

As historian Frederick Jackson Turner ob-served, a key influence was the West and its frontier (Wish 1960). The West was open country where farms could be started and small towns settled. Urbanization in the United States has happened so fast that life in the revered small town has been a vivid and positive memory for many, who recall for their children, grandchildren, and friends a time of apparent simplicity, stability, and warmth. Sociologists Robert and Helen Lynd reported the recollections of a physician in Muncie, Indiana, which in the nineteenth century was still considered the West:

> The log farmhouse of his father was sealed inside without plaster, the walls bare save for three prized pictures of Washington, Jackson, and Clay. All meals were cooked before the great kitchen fireplace, corn pones and "cracklings" and bread being baked in the glare of a large reflector set before the open fire and by tallow dips; there was great excitement later when the first candle mold appeared in the neighborhood. Standard time was unknown; few owned watches, and sun time was good enough during the day. . . . When the fire went out on the family hearth the boy ran to a neighbor's to bring home fire between two boards; it was not until later that the first box of little sticks tipped with sulfur startled the neigh-borhood. . . . Social calls were unknown, but all-day visits were the rule, a family going to visit by horseback. . . . Social intercourse provided a highly important service; there were no daily pa-pers in the region, and much news traveled by word of mouth. (1929, 11–17)

This kind of idealized, small-town life does not fit the reported experiences of many any more than the "mean street" im-age of city life reflects the experiences of many city dwellers.

Myth and Reality

The Jeffersonian belief that the city was evil and that the countryside nurtured all civic virtues was a social construction of reality that never fully reflected life in big cities or in small towns. Even while Jefferson decried large cities, much of the social momentum and leadership for the democratic movement he so strongly supported was generated in the three largest cities of the day, populated at the time by several hundred thousand residents each: Philadelphia, New York, and Boston. Further, in the society from which the United States emerged, the movement toward parliamentary reform and advancement of individual rights was centered in the major urban area of London (Churchill 1956, 163).

Yet, in modern industrialized urban America, the influence of our traditional rural heritage has remained strong. Weary city dwellers, who can afford to, seek alternatives daily. Even the anti-establishment hippie movement of the late 1960s and early 1970s reflected traditional, small-community values by spawning thousands of rural communes (Kanter 1972). Thoreau's *Walden* (or *Life in the Woods*) still sells well. Films about returning to the wilderness are popular. The Jeffersonian rural farm ideal and aversion to large urban centers is indeed evident (see table 13–2).

TABLE 13-2.   Actual and Preferred Community Settings

	WHERE DO YOU LIVE NOW? (%)	WHERE WOULD YOU PREFER TO LIVE? (%)
Open country	12	34
Small town or city	33	30
Medium-sized city or suburb	28	22
Larger city or suburb	27	14

Source: Based on a national public opinion survey by the Opinion Research Corporation in 1971 conducted for the Commission on Population Growth and the American Future, as reported in *Population and the American future,* a U.S. government sponsored study (New York: American Library, 1972), p. 36.

How accurate is this image of country versus city? To some extent, we are dealing with qualitative, subjective values about the "good life" and cannot be as precise in answering this basic question as we could in determining the exact amount of air pollution per square kilometer in one community compared with another. Nevertheless, it appears that small-town views are exaggerated historically and do not reflect some current, small-town realities. Indeed, urban analyst C. W. Griffin attributes part of our deteriorating urban environment to the frontier approach to keeping up the town. As Griffin sees it, many of our urban ills are directly related to our small-town frontier heritage and lead to a "tragedy of the urban commons." As Griffin describes it:

Pollution and many other wasteful evils associated with urban growth and industrialization stem from the persistence of the frontier ethic in a drastically altered world totally unsuited for it. The inexorable mechanism at work is called *The Tragedy of the Commons* by biochemist Garrett Hardin. Consider a pasture open to all the commons. At a primitive, sparsely settled frontier stage of civilization, while the pasture or range offers a relatively bountiful feed supply, the community's herdsmen can use it freely without social distress. But once the grazing herds reach the critical number corresponding to the commons' food-supply capacity, an inexorable process of deterioration sets in, unless the rules for the commons' use change drastically.

The reason the rules must change derives from a basic conflict between *individual vs. social* interests. To the individual herdsman, the addition of one animal to the herd represents a potential gain of plus 1, since he alone profits from the sale on an additional animal. The cost to the herdsman, however, is only a trivial fraction of minus 1, since all the herdsmen on the commons share the costs of one additional animal's grazing. Thus each herdsman, acting in his own self-interest, like Adam Smith's rational economic man, adds another, and another animal to his herd. There is an incentive to increase one's herd without limitation in a world of limited resources. . .

Illustrations of the tragedy of the commons are

ubiquitous. Public resources—water, air, and, to a lesser degree, land—are prime examples of a fixed, limited commons subjected to growing demand by a growing population. In a more restricted sense, privately distributed energy resources—electric power, fuel oil, natural gas, and gasoline—each represent a commons. With the widening gap between supply and demand for our diminishing fossil-fuel reserves, we confront a tragedy of the commons that requires more efficient ways of reducing consumption and apportioning the use of these increasingly scarce resources. According to a recent federal study of apartment energy use, tenants in master-metered buildings consume 35% more electrical energy than tenants in individually metered buildings, where instead of sharing your waste with other tenants and the landlord, you pay for your own personal consumption. Master metering creates an energy commons, encouraging profligate waste.

Any exhaustible resource or service whose use is not economically regulated tends inevitably toward the tragedy of the commons. Free parking spaces, free use of crowded streets and highways promote congestion, air pollution and general inefficiency. New York's unmetered water supply encourages energy waste. It is never in an individual's economic interest to replace the washer in a dripping faucet; it is cheaper to share the cost of leakage with millions of other taxpayers (1974, 14–15).

Today, small towns have their alienated marginal groups as do big cities. Just as blacks, Chicanos, and other minorities or poor whites are often exluded from many of the opportunities available to middle-class whites in cities, small towns also have their **out-groups** that their neighbors do not accept. Arthur Vidich and Joseph Bensman provide us with an insight. In the small town of Springdale in upper New York State, they found a situation reflective of many other small towns. In Springdale, farmers of Polish background, and small farmers more generally, were excluded from much of the township decision-making process, and their interests were underrepresented: "The political biases of the [township board] are revealed in the condition of specific roads and in the location of

good roads. These biases reflect those forces in the community, the prosperous farmers, who can make the board act" (1958, 157).

The warmth of small-town life does not always envelop those who do not fit the pattern. Nobel prizewinning novelist Sinclair Lewis made this point in his novel *Main Street* (1920). The protagonist, Carol Milford, is conversing with Maud Dyer, a community social leader. Mrs. Dyer is critical of Mrs. Mott, wife of the superintendent of schools, who wishes to improve the old schoolhouse and upgrade the quality of schooling:

Oh, so Mrs. Mott has got you going on her school craze! She's been dinging at that till everybody's sick and tired. What she really wants is a big office for her dear bald-headed Gawge to sit around and look important in. Of course I admire Mrs. Mott, and I'm very fond of her, she's so brainy, even if she does try to butt in and run the Thanatopsis [ladies' book discussion club], but I must say we're sick of her nagging. The old building was good enough for us when we were kids! I hate these would-be women politicians, don't you? (1920, 133)

The year of this book, 1920, was one of profound changes in the society. Recall that this was the year the U.S. census first found that a majority of Americans were living in cities. Also in that year, Lewis found a new urban audience that was beginning to identify with life in cities and to question their former ways. This process continues. To avoid the tragedy of the commons, the challenge is how to balance traditional, individualistic values with the need to cooperate for a good life in highly populated urban environments.

The suburban compromise. To a considerable extent, the massive movement from cities to the suburbs constitutes a compromise. Even with decentralizatin of much production, many workers are tied directly or indirectly to jobs that large corporate and governmental centers in metropolitan areas generate (Holcomb and Beauregard 1981, 70–72). As such, these workers are not in a position to act on their value preference to live in open country or a small town. Yet, when people move to a suburb near a big city, their life-style expresses nostalgia for the small-town ideal.

The research literature on this phenomenon is substantial since the movement to the suburbs following World War II (Palen 1981, 161–63). Examples include Sylvia Fava's "Suburbanism as a Way of Life" (1956), William Newman's "Americans in Subtopia" (1957), *Levittowners: Ways of Life and Politics in a New Suburban Community* (1967), and J. R. Seeley, R. A. Sims, and E. W. Loosley's study of the Toronto suburb of Crestwood Heights (1974). The general small-town yearning and the desire of suburbanities to keep their social distance from the "Big City" is clearly stated by Seeley, Sims, and Loosley:

There is . . . a subtle but decided line drawn between Crestwood Heights and Big City. The vary

name 'Crestwood Heights' expresses to perfection the 'total personality' of the community, particularly in its relation to the metropolis of which it is part. That name suggests, as it clearly meant to do, the sylvan, the natural, and the romantic, the lofty and serene, the distant but withdrawn; the suburb that looks out upon, and over the city, not in it or of it, but at its border and on its crest. The name is a source of pride, a guide for differential conduct . . . but first and foremost a symbol evoking difference. Crestwood Heights is bound inescapably to Big City by many ties, but the proximity of the heterogeneous metropolitan area provides chiefly a foil against which Crestwood Heights can measure its own superiority and exclusiveness, core of its communal identity. (1974, 219–20)

There are problematic consequences of this combination of suburban community development and attitudes of indifference, even antipathy, toward the "Big City." The large cities of our modern society have declined in their ability to provide sufficient

For all the problems large cities confront, there remain areas of neighborhood stability with positive social relationships.

job opportunities and services for their residents (Berry 1981, 55–56). The result is a series of growing crime, racial tension, pollution, and related problems that city residents primarily face. The social and economic costs of these problems are increasing.

ANALYZING THE PROBLEM: CONSEQUENCES OF THE CONTEMPORARY URBAN CONDITION

The Upward and Outward Syndrome

Our largest cities developed during the industrialization of society in such a way that people initially settled close to the central downtown business district. Commercial concentration began there, often near port facilities. As more people were attracted to the job opportunities in the growing cities, those whose earnings went up sufficiently were able to leave the crowded hustle and bustle of central-city living. They moved outward toward the city limits and then into the more spacious suburbs. Ernest Burgess's concentric zone model (see figure 13–1) presents this general process for the city of Chicago in the 1920s. Later analysts have noted variations of the same basic process in many other cities (Farley et al. 1978; Harris and Ullman 1945; Hoyt 1939).

Since the outward movement toward the suburbs has been observed for over a half century, what about this trend is new and problematic for big cities? The massive size of the outward movement in recent years is what has raised concern. Until mid-century, the city-to-suburban movement was steady, but most people, including the important middle-class taxpayers, continued to live within big-city limits from New York to Los Angeles. By the 1970s, however, most people in the thirty-three urban areas with 1 million inhabitants or more—areas that the U.S. Census Bureau calls Standard Metropolitan Statistical Areas (SMSAs)—were liv-

ing in the suburbs around big cities (see figure 13–2). This outward movement trend began after World War II. As a result the mass of middle- and upper-income SMSA residents now live outside city limits in suburbs where most of their business and taxes go.

The suburbs have not entirely escaped growing urban life problems. By the 1970s and early 1980s, central-city deterioration was spilling over into a number of older suburban communities located close to large central cities. The picture of comfortable suburban living was now qualified, with about 7 percent of the suburban population below the poverty line (Palen 1981, 180). Although this percentage was less than half the proportion of the average central-city population living in poverty, the suburban proportion translates into millions of people who live in deteriorating community environments at subsistence levels.

This developing suburban blight points up what happens when neighborhoods and communities are abandoned rather than preserved. The condition is a warning signal to those suburban communities that still feel safely removed from urban decline when the economic and social stability of cities and their suburbs are actually highly interdependent. Recognition of this reality has been slow in developing.

Chocolate Cities, Vanilla Suburbs[1]

In an article entitled "Chocolate City, Vanilla Suburbs" (1978), researchers Reynolds Farley and his associates at the University of Michigan's Institute of Social Research reported on the high degree to which most residents in the city of Detroit were black, while most people living in the surrounding suburbs were white. This same pattern has been found in metropolitan areas through-

---

1. A popular tune, "Chocolate City with Vanilla Suburbs" (Malbix/Ricks Music, RMI, 1976), well describes this theme.

out the society (U.S. Department of Commerce 1981a).

Segregation, the separation of minority group members from others based on race, has been increasing. The *Report of the National Advisory Commission on Civil Disorders* warned in 1968 that American society was moving toward two societies—one black and one white. While considerable differentiation exists between suburbs and in different areas of big cities, the basic pattern is that large cities are becoming increasingly black, and most suburban areas are remaining predominantly white. This

FIGURE 13–1. The Concentric Zone Model of City Growth

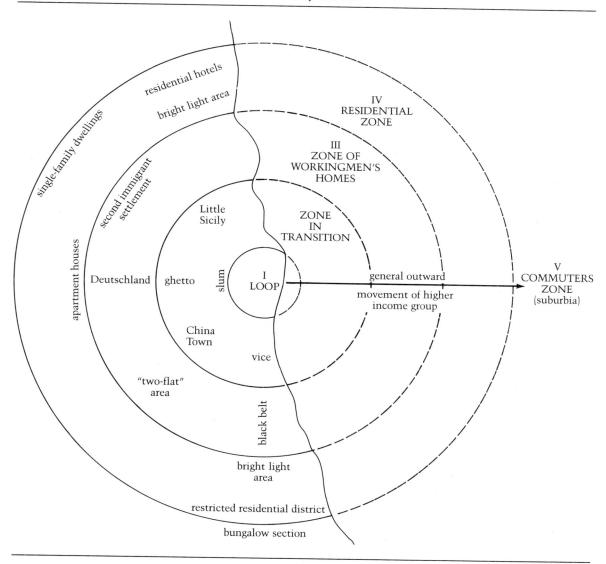

Adapted from Ernest Burgess, The growth of the city, in *The city*, ed. R. Park and E. Burgess (Chicago: University of Chicago Press, 1925), p. 55.

pattern is paralleled in southwestern urban areas like Houston, Phoenix, and Los Angeles, with heavy Chicano Hispanic, and black concentration in central cities, and in New York City where many Puerto Rican Hispanics reside.

Are the causes of such racial residential separation a matter of mutual black, Hispanic, and other minority agreement with whites to live in separate residential areas? Farley and the Michigan team attempted to answer this fundamental question. Their findings suggest that long-observed, hostile white attitudes toward racial minorities persist and, unless changed, indicate continuing and deepening interracial conflict between our predominantly black cities (along with some predominantly black suburbs) and the numerous predominantly white suburbs. While this discussion focuses on the urban black-white pattern that is national, it is important to keep in mind similar segregation problems with Hispanics, native Americans, Puerto Ricans, and other minorities.

Farley asked a **random sample** (in which every sampled interviewee had an equal chance of being selected as anyone else in

the population) of black and white Detroit-area residents the following three questions.

1. Is residential segregation largely the result of misperceptions about the ability of blacks to afford housing in the greater Detroit area (specifically in predominantly white middle class areas of cities and suburbs)?

2. Is residential segregation mainly the result of black preferences for segregated neighborhoods?

3. Is residential segregation mainly the result of white preferences for segregated neighborhoods? (1978, 35)

In response to the first question, the findings reveal that over a third of the black families could afford to move into white middle-class suburbs. Further, this housing market fact was generally known to both blacks and whites. Given these findings, we might well predict a yes response to the second question. That is, perhaps blacks live in all-black neighborhoods and stay away from white suburbs because that is what they

FIGURE 13–2. City, Suburban, and Nonmetropolitan Population, 1950 to 1980. *The greatest concentration of population in the United States is now outside central cities in surrounding suburban communities.*

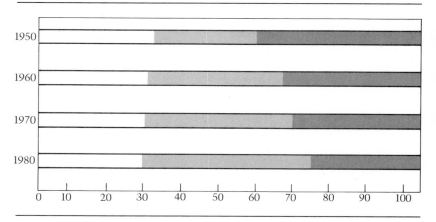

Data from U.S. Bureau of the Census, *Census of the population, 1980, supplemental reports* (October 1981), p. 1.

Note: □ *Inside central cities* ▨ *Outside central cities* ▪ *Outside SMSAs.*

generally prefer. Some years ago, Louis Wirth observed that ethnic and racial group concentrations were in part voluntary, thereby serving the interests of preservation of a common culture (Wirth 1928). For example, Jewish neighborhoods developed in part because Orthodox Jews, as well depicted in the movie *The Chosen* (1982), believed that the synagogue should be within walking distance from their homes. Yet, since the days of Wirth's analyses in the 1920s and 1930s, most Jews, like most Irish Catholics, Italians, Poles, and other predominantly white ethnic groups have dispersed considerably and moved toward or into the suburbs. Further, in addition to about half the black families being able to afford suburban housing, Farley found that "a majority of black respondents not only favor residential integration but they do so because of a belief in racial harmony rather than a belief that services are better in mixed neighborhoods" (1978, 71).

White Resistance to Suburban Integration

The general racial minority desire for interracial community harmony and residential integration has long been observed (Farley et al. 1978; Schnore, Andre, and Sharp 1976; Taeuber 1975). Yet, while over a third of black families had middle-class incomes sufficient to move into generally desired suburban communities, less than a tenth actually moved into the suburbs (U.S. Department of Commerce 1981b).

While the beginning of some black movement into some suburbs is apparent, their predominant absence is a reflection of racial attitudes and discriminatory practices. White attitudes that perpetuate avoidance of black neighbors is evident in the Farley study. Recall that the third question asked of white respondents related to both black and white families, all of whom were middle class and shared similar educational levels of achievement and occupational status. Yet, most whites saw areas open to any blacks, including those of the middle class,

as undesirable. Note the results in figure 13–3. In a neighborhood block of fifteen homes, if one home is occupied by a black family, then 24 percent of white respondents indicated that they would be "uncomfortable," and 27 percent more would not consider moving into such a minimally integrated neighborhood. Should black families occupy five of the fifteen homes, almost three-quarters—73 percent—of the white respondents would not be willing to move into such a neighborhood. No wonder, then, that the few suburbs to which blacks have moved have tended to become predominantly or all black (Schnore, Andre, and Sharp 1976; Taeuber 1975).

Given these negative white attitudes, why both poor and middle-class blacks tend to see the causes of urban racial tensions in the same basic way is understandable. Note in table 13–3 that every income class of blacks in Detroit similarly perceived the causes of the 1967 racial riots (National Advisory Commission on Civil Disorders 1968, 107–8). All samples of blacks, regardless of social class, saw the causes of urban racial conflict as stemming from poor housing, lack of jobs, poverty, and police brutality. This finding contrasts with that of whites, who were prone to identify the causes of black rioting as "too much welfare," "black teenagers," and "black nationalism" (Warren 1971, 145). The evidence is strong that these findings are reflective of a national pattern. They indicate that the continuation of largely exclusive white suburbs is both a consequence and a continuing cause of interracial tensions in metropolitan areas throughout the country.

Ghettos and Civil Disorder

While the problems that middle-class blacks face are socially and psychologically substantial, the most severe problems in large cities are concentrated in their decaying central cores. It is there that poor blacks nationally, Chicanos in the Southwest, Puerto Ricans in New York City, and other poor minorities as well as poor whites are increasingly concentrated. With the general white middle-class movement to the suburbs, large cities have been experiencing tax declines to support their schools and basic fire, police, schooling, and other services. Perhaps most immediately troublesome to poor blacks and others in the cities is the outward shift of jobs beyond city limits. For example, between the mid-1940s and late 1960s the cities' average of manufacturing, retail and wholesale trade, and selected services declined from over two-thirds to about half, while the suburbs increased their share in the distribution of jobs correspondingly (Gold 1972, 450). With jobs developing outside the cities and more of them requiring higher levels of formal educational training, the cities' poor increasingly tend to be locked in, or structured out.

One major consequence is the development of large, ghetto slum areas in every big city. The term *slum* has long been used to designate areas of a city that early Chicago School analysts called "zones of deterioration" (Burgess 1925, 55). When slum areas concentrate particular groups such as blacks, Chicanos, Puerto Ricans, or poor whites, the term **ghetto** is often used to designate such an area with its multiple serious social problems facing the people who live there. The term *ghetto* originally referred to a place in medieval Venice where the Jewish settlement was forced to live. In modern times, the term is no longer limited in its application to the Jewish people. As Louis Wirth observed in his book *The Ghetto*, "It has come into use in recent times as a common noun—a term which applies to any segregated racial or cultural group" (1928, ix–x).

FIGURE 13–3. **Attractiveness of Neighborhoods of Varying Racial Composition for White Respondents**

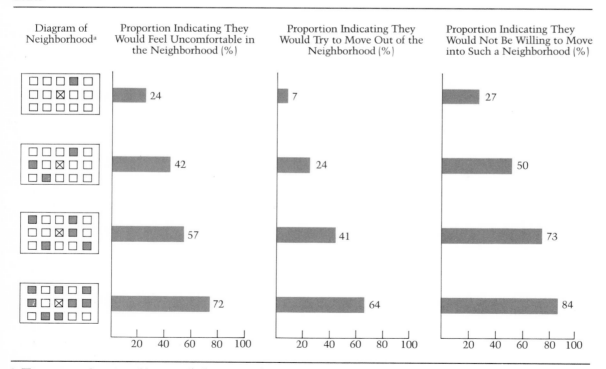

Diagram of Neighborhood[a]	Proportion Indicating They Would Feel Uncomfortable in the Neighborhood (%)	Proportion Indicating They Would Try to Move Out of the Neighborhood (%)	Proportion Indicating They Would Not Be Willing to Move into Such a Neighborhood (%)
	24	7	27
	42	24	50
	57	41	73
	72	64	84

[a] ⊠ represents location of homes of white respondents; ■ represents location of homes of black families.

Data from Reynolds Farley et al., *Chocolate city, vanilla suburbs: Will the trend toward racially separate communities continue?* (Ann Arbor: University of Michigan Institute of Social Research, 1978).

The ghetto areas that Chicago School researchers and others originally analyzed a half century ago largely contained white ethnic groups. These groups faced much **prejudice** and **discrimination,** but less so than racial minorities have faced throughout the history of American society (M. Gordon 1978). Further, the American economy was in great need of unskilled labor early in this century. In contrast, such labor is experiencing a declining need today. Membership in unskilled and semiskilled labor unions has grown more slowly than the growth of the total labor force (Samuelson, 1980). While contemporary black, or white, urban ghetto residents have similar low educational and skill characteristics when compared with the ghetto residents early in this century, their services are no longer in great demand.

Under these circumstances, ghetto residents' feelings of social isolation and alienation are widespread, producing a state of civil disorder that may destabilize entire cities and eventually whole metropolitan areas if not alleviated. The term *civil disorder* conjures up the dramatic form of disorders seen in urban race riots. Race riots, however, are only one form of civil disorder. Another, perhaps even more consequential form, is the daily civil disorder that goes on without dramatic media notice but destroys the viable basis of a residential community. Both forms of disorder need to be taken into account (L. Gordon 1971, xiii–xvi).

The *Report of the National Advisory Commission on Civil Disorders* (1968) documents how damaging riotous racial disorders in our cities can be. The commission reported both the wide extent and the clustering of injury and property loss in the following terms.

In its study of 75 disturbances in 67 cities the Permanent Subcommittee on Investigations of the Senate Committee on Government Operations reported 83 deaths and 1,897 injuries. Deaths occurred in 12 of these disturbances. More than 80 percent of the deaths and more than half the injuries occurred in Newark and Detroit. In more than 60 percent of the disturbances, no deaths and no more than 10 injuries were reported.

Substantial damage to property also tended to be concentrated in a relatively small number of cities. Of the disorders which the Commission surveyed, significant damage resulted in Detroit ($40–45 million), Newark ($10.2 million), and Cincinnati (more than $1 million). In each of nine cities, damage was estimated at less than $100,000.

TABLE 13–3.   Selected Riot Causes as Perceived by Detroit Area Blacks Following a Major Race Riot—Rank Ordered

LOW-INCOME RIOT-AREA SAMPLE[a]	UPPER-INCOME NORTHWEST-AREA SAMPLE[b]	MIDDLE-INCOME DETROIT-WIDE SAMPLE[c]
Police brutality	Poor housing	Police brutality
Poor housing	Lack of jobs	Poor housing
Lack of jobs	Poverty	Lack of jobs
Poverty	Police brutality	Poverty
Disappointment with white public officials	Disappointment with white public officials	Disappointment with white public officials
Teenagers	Teenagers	Teenagers
Black nationalism [d]	Black nationalism	Black nationalism
	Too much welfare	Too much welfare

Source: Donald Warren, Community Dissensus, in *A city in racial crisis,* ed. L. Gordon (Dubuque, Iowa: Wm. C. Brown, 1971), p. 145.
[a]437 respondents.
[b]188 respondents.
[c]392 respondents.
[d]"Too much welfare" not listed in this survey.

What we have said should not obscure three important factors. First, the dollar cost of the disorder(s) should be increased by the extraordinary administrative expenses of municipal, state and Federal governments. Second, deaths and injuries are not the sole measures of the cost of civil disorders in human terms. For example, the extent of dislocation of people—though clearly not quantifiable in dollars and cents—was a significant factor in Detroit, the one case in which many residences were destroyed. Other human costs—fear, distrust, and alienation—were incurred in every disorder. Third, even a relatively low level of violence and damage in absolute terms may seriously disrupt a small or medium-sized community. (1968, 115–16)

The commission report then noted an American urban reality of the late 1960s that persists in the 1980s:

Segregation and poverty have created in the racial ghetto a destructive environment totally unknown to most white Americans.

What white Americans have never fully understood—but what the Negro can never forget—is that white society is deeply implicated in the ghetto. White institutions created it, and white society condones it. (1968, 2)

Such reporting on racial riots and their underlying causes is useful in providing insights into the causes and potential control of collective disorder. Civil disorders in this respect serve as social flashpoints for long-simmering intergroup conflict. Pointed up is the existence not only of immediate civil disaster situations but also of the larger cultural disaster that daily characterizes the precariousness of life in an urban ghetto. What young and old residents alike experience in crowded ghetto-area slum streets is open sporadic violence in a hostile environment. In this environment, most people live in what Ernest Burgess referred to as "submerged regions of poverty, degradation, and disease, and their underworlds of crime and vice" (1925, 54). Claude Brown's (1966) description of his childhood experiences in the streets of Harlem indicates the impact on the **socialization** of young people.

You might see somebody get cut or killed. I could go out in the street for an afternoon, and I would see so much that, when I came in the house, I'd be talking and talking for what seemed like hours. Dad would say, "Boy, why don't you stop that lyin'? You know you didn't see all that. You know you didn't see nobody do that." But I knew I had. (1966, 429)

Indeed, he had seen it. In this manner, many of the ghetto young are socialized into perpetuating a deteriorating and deadly life pattern. Where street violence rates are high, unemployment is severe, and housing and schooling are poor, the emotional toll is high. One consequence is that almost half of ghetto residents are so emotionally distraught that their ability to perform everyday jobs or other tasks is impaired (Srole 1972, 1978). (See table 13–4 for a comparison of typical low-income and high-income residents.)

Are designated urban ghetto "zones of deterioration" inevitable? Not necessarily. Ghetto conditions can get much worse, or

TABLE 13–4. Distributions on Mental Health Classification of Top and Bottom Strata: Socioeconomic Range of Midtown Manhattan Study Respondents

	HIGHEST SOCIOECONOMIC RESPONDENTS (%)	LOWEST SOCIOECONOMIC RESPONDENTS (%)
Well	30.0	4.6
Mild symptom formation	37.5	25.0
Moderate symptom formation	20.0	23.1
Impaired	12.5	47.3

Source: Leo Srole, Mental health in the metropolis: The Midtown Manhattan study, 3d. ed. (New York: New York University Press, 1978), p. 309.

they can be reduced or ended. The historical
and contemporary evidence suggests that
ghettos and their inhabitants are in a state
of dynamic change. How they change is
strongly related to what big cities continue
to mean to most Americans—particularly
suburban Americans—and to the effectiveness of comprehensive private and public
decision making. As for the people of the
city ghettos—black, brown, and white—that
they would welcome a chance to improve
their life prospects has long been known. As
Ernest Burgess observed about the people of
Chicago's Black Belt and other segregated
urban groups, "all . . . [are] . . . obsessed
with the vision of a new and better world"
(1925, 56).

Does City Living Breed Alienation?

Does the complex of social problems that
the urban minorities and the poor experience suggest a deeper problem for all who
live in cities? The anomic loss of small-
town-like social roots and alienation from
others in urban life as theorized by Park,
Burgess, Wirth, and other Chicago School
sociologists may have been a characteristic
of early urbanization. This included the immigrants' quest for new roots as early century ethnic ghettos formed.

By mid-century, analysts began to find
that most city people were not in an alienated anomic state generally characterized by
impersonality, anonymity, and secondary
social relations (Axelrod 1956; Rogers 1961).
Most people had informal relations that
were likely to be personal, close, and intimate. The report of Bell and Boat on four
neighborhoods in San Francisco was typical.
In all four neighborhoods, whether of high
or low income and many or few family ties,
most people participated in informal social
relations at least once a week (Bell and Boat
1957).

The question of how alienating the city is
depends on the kind of city-living experiences people have. Gans identifies three
types of urban dwellers who have generally

In the midst of deteriorating areas around old
downtown city sections, many cities are
encouraging new commercial development. One
such development, pictured here, is the new
Renaissance Center in Detroit.

favorable experiences and two types who
have generally alienating experiences (Gans
1962). Those adjusting well to city life include *the cosmopolites,* the professionals,
corporate managers, and intellectuals who
find economic and cultural benefits in the
city; *the singles,* generally those in their
twenties and early thirties who find initial
jobs and social opportunities, including marital partners; and *the ethnic villagers,* often
found in working-class, family-oriented
neighborhoods in close proximity to those of
the same ethnic and religious background.
Two alienated urban dweller types that
Gans identified are *the deprived,* mostly
poor racial minorities in ghettos, and *the
trapped,* those who want to move to the
suburbs but cannot afford to do so, and remain close to ghetto zones of deterioration.

While the city scene is a mixture, it can

be said that urban living does not necessarily seem to breed alienation or to be as generally destructive as our stereotypes suggest. As we take up policy considerations on solving the pressing problems of cities, keeping clear the realities of urban living will be useful. In part, such city problems as poverty, intergroup conflict, and the powerlessness of some individuals and groups are found in most communities, small or large. We associate them chiefly with cities only because most people live in metropolitan areas. Other problems such as air pollution and traffic congestion appear native to urban living.

The importance of solving the complex of city problems lies in the contemporary nature of our society. As Protestant theologian Harvey Cox (1965) stated in *The Secular City*, Americans and their institutions, including churches, must come to terms with the reality that American society is and will remain primarily urban.

ALTERNATIVE POLICIES FOR RESOLVING THE PROBLEM: THE URBAN FUTURE

Our Stake in the Urban Condition

Our stake in the urban condition is clear from the demographic facts of life in American society. Recall the discussion early in this chapter about the predominant urban trend in the United States since 1920. By 1960, every region in the country, including the formerly rural South, was mostly urban (see table 13–1). Further, projections of American population growth and distribution indicate that by the year 2000, 85 percent of Americans will be in metropolitan areas (Commission on Population Growth and the Urban Future 1972). Thus, the present pattern of city and, especially, suburban living is intensifying.

The major urban problem—our open-country preferences notwithstanding (see table 13–2)—is not likely to be a "standing room only" syndrome. The mass American

land spaciousness has resulted in an actual lessening of urban densities since the late nineteenth century (Elazar 1969). Instead, the ironic problem of separate suburban and city-living patterns is that our daily lives are lived in such small-unit social spaces that the larger reality of metropolitan economic, political, and social interdependence is often not keenly felt. This is particularly so for the relatively more secure and comfortable suburbanites. The result of minority racial and low-income group concentration in cities and others in suburbs results in what sociologist Joseph Gusfield (1976) calls "social segmentation." Additionally, suburbanization has been so extensive since the 1950s that social segmentation is now evident in different kinds of working-class, middle-class, and other types of suburbs (Berger 1974).

As blacks and whites as well as middle-class and lower-class concentrations are increasingly estranged from informal or formal social, economic, and political ties in one community setting, the likelihood of community polarization of attitudes increases. Such polarization makes it difficult to effectively coordinate interdependent metropolitan needs in such basic areas as water purification and supply, road and mass transit needs, traffic control, and environmental pollution. Further, the deterioration of job and educational opportunities within central cities increases the number of discontented people in the urban setting. The combination of urban-living awareness, mass media exposure, and limited opportunities results in a marked sense of **relative deprivation,** which produces various forms of individuated destabilization (as evident in table 13–4) and the potential for protest movements that can challenge the entire society (Davies 1969).

The stake of city residents in the urban future is easily discernible. Looking beyond the daily aspects of the generally more advantageous suburban living is also useful. In this perspective, the stake of people throughout metropolitan areas in the future of central cities becomes clear. Whether it be in the safety of getting to jobs in a big city, or in the traffic safety and road efficiency of the area, or in the larger economic and political stability costs involved, the future is intimately tied to suburban *and* central-city conditions that meet the community needs of people throughout the metropolitan area.

What Hope for Our Cities?

Since the big cities of our society from coast to coast are in the greatest state of complex problems, let us focus primarily on the question of whether the cities have a realistic basis for a hopeful future. Ever since the national focus on urban renewal created by Title I of the 1949 Housing Act, Americans have been increasingly concerned with urban problems.

The situation is not that so many more urban problems exist now than there were in our cities in the past. Rather, the urban experience is so general now for so many Americans that signs of increasing leadership and general awareness of urban problems are evident, if not yet awareness of the need to work on both immediate and long-range solutions. The national Urban Coalition of civic, religious, labor, business, and other voluntary associational interests has developed beginning in the 1960s (*City* 1968). The coalition's rationale rests on a point made by Milton Eisenhower, chair of the National Commission on the Causes and Prevention of Violence. Regarding daily violence and disorder in urban ghettos, Eisenhower observed: "Disenchantment with governmental institutions and disrespect for law are most prevalent among those who feel that they have gained least from social order and the actions of government." (Institute of Human Relations 1970, 3).

With an eye to policies that might reverse the deteriorating inner-city trend, one Urban Coalition member, the American Jewish Committee, conducted a national city-by-city survey to determine problems and needs of the large number of urban poor.

The following facts were revealed (Institute of Human Relations 1970, 5).

1. Welfare benefits are much too low and in many states fall far below the poverty level as set by the federal government.
2. There is widespread hunger and malnutrition in the poor areas of cities, and there are large numbers of hungry school children who do not eat even one good meal a day.
3. Poor people receive inadequate care when ill, and almost no preventive medicine. Dental care is nonexistent for large numbers of poor people, both adults and children.
4. There are too few day care facilities to accommodate the children of relief recipients who could be trained for work or referred for employment if their youngsters were cared for.
5. The personal dignity of relief recipients is often violated and their rights frequently infringed upon. Many poor people are unaware of their rights under the law.
6. The urban poor often pay more for goods and services and there is inadequate consumer protection for poor people.

This kind of evaluation and awareness has led to new comprehensive approaches to the complex of city problems. While the concept of *comprehensiveness* has been extensively developed in respect to urban problems, the practical implementation of such approaches has not yet developed.

An Urban Systems Approach to Planning

The history of private, unplanned growth in American cities and suburbs has resulted in many physical, social, and economic problems. Increasingly, policies have developed involving governmental and privately planned programs. These programs have been evident in various forms since the New Deal of the 1930s, as aspects of urban renewal (Greer 1965; Holcomb and Beauregard 1981). As a consequence of American society's small-town and frontier heritage, large-scale coordinated planning—long evident in Great Britain and other geographically smaller urban societies (Gist and Fava 1974, 658–67)—was not part of the American urban renewal process until the 1960s. Private economic interests in the past seldom participated in community-wide planning, nor, until recent years, have local or federal governments. The urban programming that did develop tended to be isolated. Some federal and local funding programs were developed for schools, others for building expressways, others to offer welfare assistance to the unemployed and unskilled urban poor, and still others focused on slum clearance and low-cost housing. (The latter was a specific aim of the Housing Act of 1949 and the Urban Renewal Agency, which was set up originally in the 1930s.)

What has been the result of these past, fragmented efforts? Unfortunately, for those in greatest need of genuine urban renewal, the consequences of such programs have often been social disaster. As Scott Greer succinctly observed about uncoordinated urban renewal projects by the 1960s:

At a cost of more than three billion dollars the Urban Renewal agency (URA) has succeeded in materially reducing the supply of low-cost housing in American cities. Like highways and streets, the program has ripped through the neighborhoods of the poor, powered by the right of eminent domain. From Boston to Portland, Oregon, hundreds of American cities and citizens are involved. (1965, 3)

This assessment by a widely respected urban analyst points up the basis for the movement toward new, more comprehensive, urban problem-solving approaches.

Systems theory and model cities. An emerging sociological perspective on the problem of bringing about constructive change in metropolitan areas is based on *systems theory* (Berry 1981; Buckley 1967). In essence, systems theory holds that modern society is an intricate, interrelated system in which balance cannot be maintained by working on only one problem at a time.

Priorities may have to be chosen, and these may vary from city to city, but it is unlikely that any one priority in any city can be dealt with effectively if all others are neglected. The roots of systems theory in structural-functionalism are clear. Also, conflict theory with its emphasis on social class interests has elements of a comprehensive systems approach. (See Overview.)

Aware of the growing complex of urban problems, Congress enacted the Demonstration Cities Act in 1963 (generally known as the Model Cities program), beginning with a two-year appropriation of $1 billion (Stewart 1966, 11). This program has continued in some form each year since its enactment. The program is designed to respond to and stimulate local city and suburban governments and private individuals and groups to develop a model city plan to halt deterioration and to advance urban community life. Once a plan is developed by a wide variety of city-based (and often suburban) citizens and organizations, funding can then be secured from the federal government to match local government, private corporate, and other community-approved funding sources. The federal commitment varies with the state of the economy and the amount of administrative support. To qualify, a city administration must document the involvement of various local citizen interests in the development of any given city's model plan. This means that representatives of a wide variety of business, labor, civil rights, and other community interests must be given the opportunity to express their views about what is needed for urban redevelopment.

The Model Cities policy program offers a practical illustration of how urban systems analysis may work as well as why it has not yet worked as envisioned. The approach itself grew out of political pressures. The black-led civil rights movement of the late 1950s and early 1960s forced both industry and government to develop new policy approaches. A need was perceived to stabilize the urban economic environment. Corporations such as the Ford Motor Company, the

Chase Manhattan Bank, and the Xerox Corporation began for the first time to seriously recruit employees from the poorest sections of the city (Lief 1971, 147–48). New preschool and other educational programs were started in urban poverty areas, and a multitude of other programs were initiated (Gist and Fava 1974, 657–58).

The many governmental and private programs that are a part of any given model city plan are designed to create a better urban life for all in the metropolitan area. The old, fragmented approach in which programs were developed independently of each other was clearly ineffective. If a preschool program was begun while a city's tax support for its regular school program was declining, then quality education was not advanced. If jobs for minorities opened up in suburban industrial parks but no mass transit was available to get to those jobs, then occupational opportunities for ghetto residents were not advanced. The model city approach is based on the understanding that a metropolitan area—and indeed all modern society—is part of a single social system. Such a system requires a continuing exchange about needs and how to fulfill them (Blau 1964).

Comprehending the interdependence of cities and suburbs and of various individuals and groups on each other is difficult enough.

Through systematic urban planning, a number of cities have been able to revitalize deteriorating areas. The example here of such a development is Boston's Faneuil Hall Market Place.

Effectively implementing comprehensive urban program approaches is even more difficult. Public and private resources are limited. Each individual and group approaches any comprehensive urban plan at least partially, if not solely, from their own interest perspective. Vying for any particular program—for schools, jobs, roads, water, or another need—may hamper or negate another program. Which program gains initial ascendancy is often a matter of who can exercise more community power than another.

Community power and fractured model cities programming. **Community power** is the ability of certain individuals and groups to exercise relatively greater political and economic decision-making influence within a community. The exercise of such power in respect to model city programming helps explain why this comprehensive approach has not yet resulted in programs that are much different than the fragmented policy approaches of the past.

To illustrate the general problem, let us consider the model city plan and its implementation in Detroit, one of the first cities to develop a comprehensive plan under the Demonstration Cities Act. Here, in order of community-determined planning priorities, is a list of programs that were developed for the urban plan in Detroit (Gordon 1978, 326–28):

1. Slum clearance of dilapidated buildings in the inner city,

2. Development of low-cost housing for people displaced by slum clearance,

3. Development of improved public schooling in poverty-impacted neighborhoods,

4. Development of job-training programs for unskilled adults,

5. Development of low-cost metropolitan mass transit to enable inner-city dwellers to work in the suburbs and to ease the mobility of suburbanites into the central city,

6. Stimulation through zone variances and tax incentives for new commercial construction within the central city, particularly the downtown area (an early form of what came to be called "enterprise zones" in the 1980s),

7. Encouragement of public officials to build, within the older sections of the city, new county and local government offices,

8. Development of middle- and high-cost apartments and housing units to attract back into the city some of those who had moved to the suburbs, and

9. Construction of new expressways to reduce the congestion of auto traffic.

By the 1980s, this comprehensive plan of the mid-1960s was only partially implemented in Detroit; this has also been true in other cities (Holcomb and Beauregard 1981). What happened? The program priorities of the earlier period were largely reversed. Here we see community power as it has *actually* operated. For cities to develop the many proposals necessary to meet the needs of the heterogeneous individuals and groups in residence was one matter. To implement programs in a coordinated and effective manner for all was—and is—another matter.

Available model cities funding has been limited for Detroit and for other cities as a consequence of multiple factors, including global developments such as the economic effects of the Vietnam War and the OPEC oil cartel, as well as cities throughout the nation vying for funded programs. The traditional community power factors came into play in these circumstances. As a result, in city after city, many needed projects of the less influential and poor city residents have been delayed while projects that more powerful interests favored were developed. Thus, in regard to the nine points previously listed for Detroit, after slum clearance (1), the next steps the city took related to expressway construction (9), the development of high-cost apartments on the waterfront (8), and the stimulation of new downtown governmental structures and commercial enterprises (6 and 7). In short, the priority list was reversed as soon as the local community power structure began to influence the city plan.

The fragmented way in which model cities planning has been implemented has worked to the immediate benefit of large cities' dominant groups, with little effectively done with respect to the urban poor and dispossessed. A compounding problem for effective model cities programming is the reduction of tax funds as a consequence of the late 1970s middle-class tax revolt, sparked by passage of Proposition 13 in California. A suburban "no growth" syndrome has been developing that serves to limit low-income resident movement into the suburbs and restricts the general tax funding available for central-city redevelopment (Huttman 1979). The result on intracity redevelopment is well summarized by Bennett Harrison who observes that

urban renewal programs almost invariably *reduce* the welfare of the poor, who are displaced from the city, find[ing] it almost impossible to afford the new housing constructed on the old sites, and—because of racial and class segregation in the non-ghetto housing market—find it difficult to obtain housing elsewhere to replace what they have lost. As a result, they move in with friends and relatives in the ghetto, increasing congestion and consequent pathologies even further. . . . The uprooted residents are seldom adequately compensated for their property. Moreover, small businesses are also uprooted, as are churches and community centers—the "glue" of the neighborhood. These commercial and institutional linkages are especially fragile and difficult to reproduce in the new areas into which the dislocated citizens are forced. (1974, 144–45)

Harrison's characterization makes a telling point. The city is often not renewed for all its inhabitants but only for those who see immediate material capital as more important than long-range human capital. For the profiteer, a viable environment for others is expendable.

Renewing urban renewal.   The urban issues in American society in the 1980s raise the question of whether comprehensive solutions are possible. How can particularized

vested interests be marshaled to support community-wide development in our metropolitan areas? The most likely solutions appear to lie in the combination of what Alan Shank (1970) calls "political power and the urban crisis." The Urban Coalition, as discussed, was formed in the late 1960s to help counter the political weakness of racial minorities and others with great needs in our cities. Stimulated by such traditional civil rights groups as the NAACP and the Urban League, this ongoing coalition secured the public support of a variety of business, labor, and religious leaders, as well as the open support of the mayors of major cities including New York, Chicago, Philadelphia, Boston, Atlanta, and Phoenix (*City* 1968).

Since the founding of the Urban Coalition in the late 1960s, the fragmented implementation of urban renewal projects has resulted in a series of new city efforts at rehabilitation. Some signs of new life in cities are visible. Boston's Quincy Market has again been turned into an attractive shopping area, which draws thousands for daily shopping in its minipedestrian mall (Morehouse 1978, 3). Detroit's multimillion dollar New Renaissance Center has brought big business back into the downtown area within sight of nearby housing slums (Gordon 1978, 327). Cincinnati's new efficient city manager planning administration has reduced deficits while maintaining services (*Arizona Republic* 27 February 1978). The problem is that these and other cities face, on a smaller scale, the "on balance" problems of New York City: For all these positive developmental steps, there is still more deterioration than there is redevelopment. Although reduced somewhat since then, by the mid-1970s New York City's short-term debt reached over $6 billion, and the city borrowed about $500 million a month to convert old, maturing debts to new loans (Lalli 1975, 8). The costs of basic governmental services—schools, police, fire protection, road repair, and welfare costs—cannot yet be met in our older cities, and new Sun Belt cities like Houston and Phoenix are increasingly feeling the pressures (Berry 1981).

In effect, turning our cities toward a stable future will take increasingly comprehensive programs, both private and governmental. Given the continuing problems in accomplishing this goal, noting the 1960s testimony of Martin Luther King, Jr., before a Senate subcommittee dealing with urban problems is of continuing policy relevance in the 1980s:

It will be necessary to form on a national scale some type of union of slum dwellers. A quality of leadership and organization that is rooted in the slums and designs the techniques of struggles uniquely suited for action there . . . [T]he racial minorities and urban poor generally . . . will not do it alone, but they will not permit it to be done without them. This should be a basis for constructive collaboration between white and Negro, government and citizen, not in some distant time, but in the immediate present with all its emergencies that urgently call for creative statesmenship, risks of radical action and confidence that the bonds uniting humanity are stronger than the hostilities separating them. (1966, 2979)

Effective community power mechanisms for bringing programs to the deteriorating core of American's cities will not alone solve the problem. Dr. King'a point, though, is that it is a necessary precondition before the many problems spelled out in the Demonstration Cities Act can be faced. Even with universal commitment to urban planning and development, major controversies will persist. Some individuals, like Jane Jacobs (1961), will challenge the total destruction and clearance of slum districts rather then reconstructing them. Conflicts will arise among the urban poor about whether to press for low-cost housing and other needs in their slum neighborhoods or for resettlement in other parts of the city or in the suburbs. Yet, these are issues that can be dealt with once resources for and commitment to urban planning and city reconstruction are available. The internationally respected urban planner C. A. Doxiadis stated the matter well:

Personally, I am convinced that the root of all problems in our cities lies in our minds, on our loss of belief in man and in his ability to set goals and to implement them.

We can never solve problems and tackle diseases unless we conceive the whole. We cannot build a cathedral by carving stones but only by dreaming of it, conceiving it as a whole, developing a systematic approach, and then working out the details. But dreaming and conceiving are not enough. (1967, 14)

To put a complex set of problems simply, the cities in American society cannot be revived as viable communities until a shift in national priorities and a shift in governmental and private resources take place. Since the cities are strategically located, their vitality is closely linked to the health and welfare of the entire society. Revitalization of our cities, however, has the further advantage of alleviating a host of other social problems found within their deteriorating areas.

SUMMARY

In the twentieth century, American society has undergone a transformation from being a predominantly rural to being a predominantly urban society. The first major sociology department in the United States, the Chicago School, undertook the study of the processes and consequences of urbanization. Urban developments and urban problems have been of continuing concern.

What many analysts call the "urban crisis" is primarily a concern with the deterioration of large central cities and the effects of such deterioration on suburban communities and life generally in American society. The Jeffersonian rural values have influenced social policy toward our large cities, where the lower-income and minority group members have increasingly been concentrated.

Middle-class population trends have resulted in the major growth of suburbs outside large city limits. These trends have given rise to urban theories including the concentric zone theory, which points to the processes of increasing segregation of urban populations by social class and by race. Lower-income racial groups have viewed themselves increasingly isolated from the educational and economic opportunity structure of the American social system. Organized protest and disorganized civil disorder rioting have been two consequences of such isolation in urban ghettos. These disorganized protests resulted in the *Report of the National Advisory Commission on Civil Disorders,* which provided a detailed overview of policy needs to stabilize and redevelop our large central cities from New York to Los Angeles.

Some sporadic city redevelopment, such as the regentrification of selected old city sections, is in process. There is, however, increasing urban policy analysis consensus on the need for a systemwide private and public approach if our major cities are again to be viable, attractive places for people from all social class ranks. Such a systems approach holds that businesses will not locate in an urban area with deteriorated housing, and families will not be attracted without good schools, transportation, and neighborhood safety. As outlined in the Model Cities program, a number of economic, housing, educational, transportation, and related developments need to occur at the same time for any single city development to succeed. A problem in successfully securing a coordinated approach lies in community power—who has it and how it is exercised, in the interest of some or in the interest of the entire community.

STUDY QUESTIONS

1. What social problems are found within cities because they are found in all community settings?

2. What social problems appear native to big cities?

3. Why is it unlikely that suburbs can be insulated from the deterioration of large central cities?

4. Do you believe suburbanites are aware of their relationship to the city?

5. According to table 13–3, all social class levels of blacks tended to agree on the causes of the Detroit race riot. Since members of different social classes often differ in their views, how do you account for no class differences in this case?

REFERENCES

Arizona Republic. 27 February 1978.

Axelrod, M. 1956. Urban structure and social participation. *American Sociological Review* 21: 13–18.

Bell, W., and M. Boat. 1957. Urban neighborhoods and informal social relations. *American Journal of Sociology* 63: 391–98.

Berger, B. 1974. Myths of American suburbia. In *The sociology of community,* ed. C. Bell and H. Newly, 228–398. London: William Cowles & Sons.

Berry, B. J. L. 1981. *Comparative urbanization.* New York: St. Martin's.

Blau, P. 1964. *Exchange and power in social life.* New York: Wiley.

Bloomberg, W. 1967. Community organization. pp. 259–425 in H. Becker, ed., *Social Problems.*

Brown, C. 1966. *Manchild in the promised land.* New York: New American Library.

Buckley, W. 1967. *Sociology and modern systems theory.* Englewood Cliffs, N.J.: Prentice-Hall.

Burgess, E. 1925. The growth of the city. In *The city,* ed. R. Park and E. Burgess, 17–62. Chicago: Univ. of Chicago Press.

Churchill, W. 1956, *A History of the English-Speaking Peoples,* Volume II. New York: A Time-Life Publication.

City. 1968. Bi-monthly review of urban America. Vol. 2(1) (January).

Cox, H. 1965. *The secular city: Secularization and urbanization in theological perspective.* New York: Macmillan.

Davies, J. C. 1969. The J-curve of rising and declining satisfactions as a cause of some great revolutions and a contained rebellion. In *The history of violence in America,* ed. H. D. Graham and T. R. Gurr, 690–730. New York: Praeger.

Doxiadis, C. A. 1967. The coming era of ecumenopolis. *Saturday Review* (18 March): 11–14.

Elazar, D. 1969. Smaller cities in metropolitan society: The new American "towns." Center for the Study of Federalism. Working Paper no. 9. Philadelphia: Temple Univ. Press.

Farley, R., H. Schuman, S. Bianchi, D. Colasanto, and S. Hartchett. 1978. Chocolate city, vanilla suburbs: Will the trend toward racially separate communities contine? Ann Arbor: University of Michigan Institute of Social Research Working Paper.

Fava, S. 1956. Suburbanism as a way of life. *American Sociological Review* 21: 34–37.

Gans, H. 1962. *The urban villagers.* New York: Free Press.

———. 1967. *The Levittowners: Ways of Life and Politics in a New Suburban Community.* New York: Free Press.

Gist, N., and S. Fava. 1974. *Urban society.* New York: Crowell.

Gold, N. 1972. The mismatch of jobs and low-income people in metropolitan areas and its implications for the central city poor. In *Population distribution and policy,* ed. S. Mazie, 450. Volume V of *Report of the Commission on Population Growth and the American Future.* Washington, D.C.: U.S. Government Printing Office.

Gordon, L. 1971. *A city in racial crisis.* Dubuque, Iowa: Wm. C. Brown.

———. 1978. *Sociology and American social issues.* Boston: Houghton Mifflin.

Gordon, M. 1978. *Human nature, class and ethnicity.* New York: Oxford.

Greer, S. 1965. *Urban renewal and American cities.* New York: Bobbs-Merrill.

Griffin, C. W. Jr., 1974. *Taming the last frontier: A prescription for the urban crisis.* New York: Pitman.

Gusfield, J. 1976. *Community: A critical response.* New York: Harper & Row.

Harris, C., and E. Ullman. 1945. The nature of cities. *The Annals of the American Academy of Political and Social Science* 242: 7–17.

Harrison, B. 1974. *Urban economic development: Suburbanization, minority opportunity and the condition of the central city.* Washington, D.C.: Urban Institute.

Holcomb, H. B., and R. A. Beauregard. 1981. *Revitalizing cities.* Washington, D.C.: Association of American Geographers.

Hoyt, H. 1939. *The structure and growth of residential neighborhoods in American cities.* Washington, D.C.: U.S. Federal Housing Administration.

Huttman, E. 1979. Social inequality and the "no growth" movement: A further barrier to low income families' entry into desirable residential neighborhoods. In *Urban life and the struggle to be human,* ed. A. Mayer and L. Gordon, 191–97. Dubuque: Kendall/Hunt.

Institute of Human Relations. 1970. What hope for our cities? Background memorandum. New York: Institute of Human Relations.

Jacobs, J. 1961. *The death and life of great American cities.* New York: Random House.

Kanter, R. M. 1972. *Commitment and Community:*

Communes and Utopias in Sociological Perspective. Cambridge, Mass.: Harvard University Press.

Komarovsky, M. 1946. The voluntary associations of urban dwellers. *American Sociological Review* 11: 686–698.

King, M. L. Jr., 1966. *Testimony before Senator Abraham Ribicoff's Senate Subcommittee on the Federal Role in Urban Affairs, Part 14.* Washington, D.C.: U.S. Government Printing Office, 2979.

Lalli, F. 1975. A defense of the big banks. *Harper's Weekly* (29 September): 8.

Lewis, S. 1920. *Main Street.* New York: Harcourt, Brace.

Lief, D. 1971. Community consensus as a goal: Seeking constructive change. In *A city in racial crisis,* ed. L. Gordon, 146–51. Dubuque, Iowa: Wm. C. Brown.

Lynd, R., and H. Lynd. 1929. *Middletown.* New York: Harcourt, Brace.

Morehouse, W. 1978. Halls slow downtown downtowns. *Christian Science Monitor* (27 July): 3.

National Advisory Commission on Civil Disorders. 1968. *Report of the National Advisory Commission on Civil Disorders.* New York: Bantam.

Newman, W. 1957. Americans in subtopia. *Dissent:* 256–266.

Palen, J. J. 1981. *The urban world.* New York: McGraw-Hill.

Rogers, W. 1961. Voluntary associations and urban community development. *International Review of Community Development* 7: 140–41.

Samuelson, Paul. *Economics.* New York: McGraw Hill.

Schnore, L., C. Andre, and H. Sharp. 1976. Black suburbanization 1930–1970. In *The changing face of the suburbs,* ed. B. Schwartz, 69–94. Chicago: Univ. of Chicago Press.

Seeley, J. R., R. A. Sims, and E. W. Loosely 1974. Crestwood Heights. pp. 218–227 in C. Bell and H. Newby, ed., *The Sociology of Community.* London: William Clowes & Sons.

Semenoick, A., 1966. World population growth, 1800–1965 (projected to 2000). chart. *Fortune* (June): 110.

Shank, A. 1970. *Political power and the urban crisis.* Boston: Holbrook.

Srole, L. 1972. Urbanization and health: Some reformulations. *American Scientist* 60: 576–83.

———. 1978. *Mental health in the metropolis: The Midtown Manhattan study.* 3d ed. New York: New York Univ. Press.

Stewart, M. 1966. *Can we save our cities? The story of urban renewal.* Public Affairs Pamphlet no. 374. Washington, D.C.

Stonequist, E. 1937. *The Marginal Man.* New York: Charles Scribner's Sons.

———. 1942. The marginal character of the Jews. p. 297 in Graber and S. Britt, ed., *Jews in a Gentile World.* New York: Macmillan.

Taeuber, K. 1975. Racial segregation: The persisting dilemma. *Annals of the American Academy of Political and Social Science* 442:87–96.

United Nations. 1980. *Demographic yearbook*. New York: United Nations.

U.S. Department of Commerce. 1981a. Persons by race and Spanish origin and housing unit counts for standard metropolitan statistical areas: 1980. *1980 census of the population supplementary reports*. Washington, D.C.: U.S. Government Printing Office, October.

———. 1981b. Standard metropolitan statistical areas and standard consolidated statistical areas. *1980 census of the population*. Report PC80-S1-5. Washington, D.C.: U.S. Government Printing Office.

Vidich, A. and J. Bensman 1958. *Small Town in Mass Society*. New York: Anchor.

Warren, D. 1971. Community dissensus: Panic in suburbia. In *A city in racial crisis*, ed. L. Gordon. Dubuque, Iowa: Wm. C. Brown.

Wirth, L. 1928. *The ghetto*. Chicago: Univ. of Chicago Press.

Wish, H. 1960. Turner and the moving frontier. In *The American historian*, New York: Oxford.

CHAPTER 14

War, Peace, and Government

CONTENTS

Teaching alternatives to war is the real 'basic'

By Colman McCarthy
The Washington Post

WASHINGTON—Can peace be taught? And learned?

Earlier this year, a teacher at School Without Walls, a progressive Washington high school, invited me to her classroom to find out.

We had common feelings about education, including the idea that if it was time to get back to the basics, as all the commissions and President Reagan are now saying, then the most basic subject of all is peace.

The teacher and I agreed: Unless America educates its children in the heroes, history and philosophy of nonviolence and peacemaking, then the children haven't been educated at all.

We have merely processed one more generation that will continue to settle disputes among individuals and nations with fists, guns, armies or nukes.

Come teach the course, my friend said. I agreed, provided an interest among the students was present.

There was. Twenty-five sophomores, juniors and seniors enrolled in the twice-weekly 2½-hour seminar.

The difficulty in creating a curriculum for a peace studies course is the breadth and richness of the available literature.

Martin Luther King Jr.'s essay, in which he wrote "the choice is nonviolence or nonexistence," could take years for a full and properly reverential analysis. A lifetime is needed to study the thought of Gandhi.

The children seemed amazed by the diversity of men and women who have both written about pacifism and committed their lives to it.

The amazement was understandable. With exceptions, the schools promote the study of wars, not resistance to them.

Yet for every Napoleon or Caesar in our history there is a Eugene Debs, William Penn, Tolstoy, Camus, Erasmus, Henry Miller, Sean O'Casey, Norman Thomas and A. J. Muste who advocated resistance against militarism.

Every class, we read aloud excerpts from a fundamental text, ranging from Thoreau's *On the Duty of Civil Disobedience* to a Martin Buber essay. The students then wrote about the texts.

From *All Quiet on the Western Front* by Erich Maria Remarque, we read the scene in which the French soldier has knifed the German soldier and is in the trench with the body.

The passage led several students to reach deep inside themselves. One girl, who plans to enter the military after graduation, wrote that "I know I want to die for my country, but I'm no longer sure if I will or can kill for my country."

The excerpt and the class, she wrote, "have shown me another side—a side I believe the soldier in the story never realized before then. And that is the actual fact of killing not just 'Russians' but 'people' very much like ourselves."

Throughout the weeks of concentrated reading and writing, I emphasized one theme: Alternatives to violent solutions exist and that, if individuals and nations can organize themselves properly, moral force is always stronger than violent force.

Some students opened their minds to this immediately. They understood Gandhi: "Nonviolence is the weapon of the strong."

Others had doubts, which I encouraged them to express. They did, repeatedly: Nonviolence and pacifism are beautiful theories but in the real world there are the muggers and the Soviets.

All I asked of the "realists" was to think about life's two risks. Do you depend on violence or nonviolence to create peace?

The history of pacifism leads

to one conclusion, that the risk of injury, defeat and death from the use of well-planned nonviolent protest is much less than the risks run by using instruments of hate or annihilation.

The children didn't need to get into their heads what was already deep in their hearts: the haunting awareness that their future is threatened by the nuclear wipeout. Why should that world, some asked, be elevated as the real one?

In my childhood, the fear of bombs and the enemy was dealt with in school drills. The bells rang for an "air-raid practice" and we dove under the desks until "the planes" passed. Then the class resumed.

Nothing was discussed—not the lunacy of our leaders, nor our compliance. If we had fears, we held them inside.

This generation wants a healthier approach. It wants to read, write and talk about the alternatives, and then act on them. It wants the basics.

DEFINING THE PROBLEM: WAR, DOMINATION, AND ABUSES OF POWER

War, domination, and abuses of power are among the more pervasive and critical of social issues. They raise fundamental questions about our humaneness and constitute the most immediate threats to the continuation of purposeful life on our planet.

This chapter discusses some of the major connections between and among various forms of political violence in an effort to discover how their negative effects might be lessened. We shall suggest that humans may have evolved to the point in their shared existence where war, repression, and perhaps even the pursuit of power itself have become obsolescent.

CONFRONTING THE PROBLEM: AT THE CROSSROADS

War and other types of societal violence have reached epidemic proportions in the twentieth century. Newspapers relate stories of outbreaks of armed conflicts, kidnappings of national symbols, and indictments of once-respectable business leaders or politicians. The details change and the occasions vary—rich against poor, men against women, nation against nation, weak against strong—but the pattern remains constant: dependency, domination, violation, exploitation, too often followed by sudden death.

A Century of Total War

Unlike earlier epochs, ours has been termed a century of total war (Aron 1955). Struggle seems to be incessant and everywhere; it blurs previously held distinctions between soldiers and civilians, and is directed as much against people's minds as their bodies. Three kinds of evidence support this appraisal.

Lethal violence. The twentieth century has had more than its share of battle-related destruction, made particularly savage by the development and use of weapons of mass destruction against civilian populations (see table 14–1). In the past four decades alone, more than 100 major international wars and revolutions have been fought, at an estimated direct cost of 25 million lives and several trillions of dollars (Beer 1981; Center for Defense Information 1979a, 1979b, 1983; Sivard 1974, 1982). Military regimes now crowd the global political landscape (Kidron and Smith 1983), and once-thriving democratic societies are consumed by their perceived security needs (Sivard 1982). At any given time, approximately 25 million people dress out in the military uniforms of the world's standing armies, and another 50 million serve in paramilitary units such as reserves and specially equipped riot police (Sivard 1979).

Children in many societies learn to locate themselves in history by the wars their relatives have fought: World Wars I and II, the Russian and the Chinese revolutions, and the many wars of national independence that hastened the collapse of the European empires after 1945. Military indoctrination has seemingly become a rite of passage, an accepted part of growing up, in the modern age (Rosenblatt 1983).

War and the preparation for war have also become one of humanity's most important businesses. Transnational and domestic corporations profit from it (G. Adams 1981) (see table 14–2), minorities use it as a means of upward mobility by enlisting in its armies, and technicians find in it a source of income and status. Each year, for example, the world's military budget is several times greater than the total amount of money spent trying to eradicate world hunger, illiteracy, disease, and other disabling legacies of global poverty. Much of humanity's scarce research and development funds and its skilled pool of scientists and engineers are diverted into designing, testing, and manufacturing the world's guns, tanks, planes, missiles, thermonuclear devices, and biochemical weapons (Sivard 1980, 1982).

Additional evidence of the century's political violence is recorded in the many cases of **state terrorism** (totalitarianism), revolutions, and assassinations of public officials that have become yearly occurrences in the contemporary world. Each generation seems to produce its concentration camps and enemy lists, its victims and executioners, its Mohandas K. Gandhis and its Idi Amins. Political prisoners are now held captive in large numbers globally (Amnesty International 1975), and as recent events suggest, political surveillance is becoming as much a fixture of political life in democracies as in openly oppressive regimes (Donner 1981).

This "poor, nasty, brutish and short" war (Hobbes 1957) is not aimed at public figures alone. It affects the daily lives of ordinary people, and its circumstances for many have come to resemble a "war of all against all" (Graham and Gurr 1969; Hobbes 1957). Subcultures of physical violation and brutality, directed against both persons and property, exist in many societies. Parts of city slums are frequently burned and looted. Environments are raped and polluted. Armed intimidation is used by professional criminals and police alike. Drug-related muggings, accidental shootings, property thefts, and countless forms of family violence are commonplace. Many Americans can now expect to be affected by crime during their lifetimes.

Domination. Less physical, but no less damaging, are the various ways in which people's freedom and personal integrity are undermined in the modern world. In recent years, many individuals and groups have concluded that their interpersonal arrangements have become **structurally violent** (unjustly organized) (Galtung 1964, 95–119), intended to produce and sustain disabling inequalities among people and their interests (Schroyer 1973). For instance, feminists have made many individuals conscious of the pervasiveness of domination in much of the past and present language behaviors of the western world (Lakoff 1975; Miller and Swift 1977), and many critics of the computer revolution (Weizenbaum 1982) have questioned whether an emerging information society will bring us closer to peace or merely turn social intercourse into sound and fury signifying nothing.

Domination and resistance to domination have become familiar themes in contemporary life. Today, many organizations and interpersonal relationships are affected by charges of exploitation and manipulation. The modern nation-state system, public and private bureaucracies, domestic and international corporations, the courts, big science and higher education, organized medicine and welfare, human habitats, sports, and sexual attitudes have all been accused of creating zero-sum situations (Thurow 1981)—circumstances in which some people *are made* to win only because others *are made* to lose (Green and Massie 1980).

"It's not how you play the game," a popular American football coach said, inverting the familiar democratic baseball ethic, "it's whether you win or lose." One may suspect that behind each IQ test, each doctor-patient relationship, each automobile sale, and each inequality lies the urge for *social control*, the attempt by some people to increase their power by decreasing others' freedom.

Modern governments often embody this practice by creating or magnifying otherwise avoidable social conflict. They prompt people to fight for interests that are not their own, and encourage them to sacrifice concrete life for abstract causes. For example, many Americans and Russians seem willing to struggle for a capitalism or communism they neither practice nor understand, and some Arabs and Israelis contemplate the destruction of entire races out of ancient hatreds and for reasons of state.

Today, nation-states have become centers where violence is institutionalized and domination legitimated (Falk 1975). Seemingly, they are places where power-brokers gather either to fight over limited economic and information resources or to create scarcities

TABLE 14–1. A World At War

LOCATION OF CONFLICT	DATE CONFLICT BEGAN	WARRING PARTIES	NUMBER OF TROOPS (estimated)
MIDDLE EAST/PERSIAN GULF			
Afghanistan	1978	Afghan government & Soviet forces vs. Islamic & anti-Communist guerrillas	25–35,000 105,000 90–100,000
Iran	1978	Iranian government vs. separatist and anti-government guerrillas	235,000 active; 35,000 paramilitary* 20–100,000+
Iraq	1979	Iraqi government vs. separatist and Shiite Muslim guerrillas	342,000 active; 12,000 paramilitary* 5,000
Iraq & Iran	1980	Iraqi government vs. Iranian government	342,000 active; 12,000 paramilitary* 235,000 active; 35,000 paramilitary*
Israel & Lebanon	1948	Israeli government vs. Palestinian guerrillas	174,000 active; 4,500 paramilitary* 10,000
Lebanon	1975	Christian Lebanese vs. Muslim Lebanese	100,000 (all factions)
North Yemen & South Yemen	1950s	North Yemen government vs. South Yemen government	32,050 active; 20,000 paramilitary* 26,000 active; 15,000 paramilitary*
Pakistan	1972	Pakistan government vs. separatist and anti-government guerrillas	478,000 active; 109,000 paramilitary* 5,000+
Syria	1976	Syrian government vs. Sunni Muslim guerrillas	225,500 active; 9,800 paramilitary* 4,000
Turkey	1974	Turkish government vs. left-wing, right-wing, and separatist guerrillas	569,000 active; 120,000 paramilitary* hundreds
ASIA			
Burma	1948	Burmese government vs. Communist & separatist guerrillas	179,000 active; 73,000 paramilitary* 30–50,000
China & Vietnam	1979	Chinese government vs. Vietnamese government	200–300,000 150–200,000

FOREIGN SUPPORT	TYPE OF FOREIGN SUPPORT	NUMBER KILLED (estimated)
USSR	Arms, 105,000 troops	
		100,000+
China, Pakistan, US, Saudi Arabia, Egypt	Arms	
		4–26,000
Iraq	Arms	
		NK†
Iran, Syria	Arms	
Saudi Arabia, Jordan, Egypt, Morocco	Arms, money	
		80–100,000
Syria, Israel, Libya, North Korea	Arms	
US	Arms	
		10,000+
Syria, Arab States	Arms, 30,000 Syrian troops	
Israel	Arms	
		80,000+
Arab States	Arms	
Saudi Arabia, US	Arms	
		1,000+
USSR, East Europe	Arms, advisers	
US, France, China	Arms	
		9,000+
USSR	Arms, advisers	
		5,000+
Jordan	Arms	
US, W. Europe	Arms	
		6,000+
W. Europe, US	Arms	
		Thousands
China	Arms	
		47,000+
USSR	Arms, advisers	

TABLE 14–1. (continued)

LOCATION OF CONFLICT	DATE CONFLICT BEGAN	WARRING PARTIES	NUMBER OF TROOPS (estimated)
East Timor (Indonesia)	1975	Indonesian government vs. Fretilin guerrillas	269,000 active; 82,000 paramilitary* 300–6,500
India	1947	Indian government vs. separatist guerrillas	1,104,000 active; 260,000 paramilitary* 5,000+
Kampuchea	1970	Samrin government & Vietnamese forces vs. anti-government guerrillas	20,000 180,000 30–63,000
Laos	1975	Laotian government & Vietnamese forces vs. anti-government guerrillas	48,700* 40–60,000* 8,000
Malaysia	1945	Malaysian government vs. Communist guerrillas	99,100 active; 90,000 paramilitary* 2,000+
North Korea and South Korea	1950	North Korean government vs. South Korean government	784,000 active; 798,000 paramilitary 601,600 active; 9,520,000 paramilitary
Philippines	1972	Philippine government vs. Communist & Muslim guerrillas	112,800 active; 110,500 paramilitary 4–10,000 & 8–20,000
Thailand	1965	Thai government vs. Communist & separatist guerrillas, drug warlords	233,100 active; 53,000 paramilitary* 6–14,000
AFRICA Angola	1975	Angolan government vs. anti-Communist guerrillas	37,500 active; 169,000 paramilitary* 15,000+
Chad	1965	Chad government (Habre) vs. various anti-government armies	4–8,000 5,000+
Ethiopia (Eritrea)	1962	Ethiopian government vs. separatist Eritrean guerrillas	250,500 active; 169,000 paramilitary* 45,000
Ethiopia & Somalia (Ogaden)	1962	Ethiopian government & anti-Somali guerrillas vs. Somali government & separatist Ogaden guerrillas	250,500 active: 169,000 paramilitary* & several hundred 62,550 active; 29,500 paramilitary* & 10,000

FOREIGN SUPPORT	TYPE OF FOREIGN SUPPORT	NUMBER KILLED (estimated)
US, W. Europe	Arms	
		100–250,000
USSR, France, UK	Arms	
		Thousands
Vietnam	180,000 troops	
USSR	Arms, advisers	1972–1978: 1–4 million
China, Thailand	Arms, sanctuary	1979–1982: 3,000+
Vietnam	40–60,000 troops	
USSR	Arms, advisers	
China, Khmer Rouge	Arms	10–50,000
US, W. Europe	Arms	
China	Arms	NK (less than 100/year)
China, USSR	Arms, advisers	1950–1953: 1,900,000
US	39,000 troops, arms	1954–1982: 1,100+
US	Arms	
		50–100,000
US	Arms	
China	Arms	NK (hundreds each year)
USSR, Cuba, East Germany	Arms, 20,000 Cuban troops, 1000 Soviet advisers, 2,500 East German advisers	Thousands
South Africa	Arms, troops	
France, Sudan	Arms	
Libya	Arms, troops	20,000+
USSR, Cuba Iraq, Syria	Arms, 1400 Soviet advisers, 13,000 Cuban troops Arms	30,000+
USSR, Cuba	Arms, 1400 Soviet advisers, 13,000 Cuban troops	
US, Italy, China	Arms	25,000+

TABLE 14–1. (continued)

LOCATION OF CONFLICT	DATE CONFLICT BEGAN	WARRING PARTIES	NUMBER OF TROOPS (estimated)
Mozambique	1978	Mozambique government vs. right-wing guerrillas	21,600 active; 6,000 paramilitary* 3–5,000
Namibia	1966	South African government vs. Namibian (SWAPO) guerrillas	28–33,000 3–5,000
South Africa	1970s	South African government vs. Black nationalist guerrillas	81,400 active; 145,500 paramilitary* 3–4,000
Uganda	1981	Ugandan government vs. revolutionary guerrillas	5,000 active; 6,000 paramilitary* 1,000
Western Sahara	1975	Moroccan government vs. Polisario guerrillas	40–60,000 15,000
Zimbabwe	1980	Zimbabwe government vs. anti-government guerrillas	63,000 active; 11,500 paramilitary* 2,000+
LATIN AMERICA Argentina	1976	Argentine government vs. left- and right-wing guerrillas	180,500 active; 43,000 paramilitary* several hundred
Colombia	1978	Colombian government vs. left- and right-wing guerrillas	67,800 active; 50,000 paramilitary* 4–6,000
El Salvador	1977	El Salvador government & right-wing groups vs. left-wing guerrillas	16,000 active; 9,000 paramilitary 10,000
Guatemala	1967	Guatemalan government & right-wing groups vs. left-wing guerrillas & Mayan Indians	19,000 active; 11,600 paramilitary* 5–6,000
Honduras	1970s	Honduran government vs. left-wing guerrillas	11,700 active; 3,000 paramilitary* several hundred
Nicaragua	1981	Nicaraguan government vs. right-wing guerrillas & Miskito Indians	21,500 active; 5,000 paramilitary* 10,000 & 2,000

FOREIGN SUPPORT	TYPE OF FOREIGN SUPPORT	NUMBER KILLED (estimated)
USSR, Cuba	Arms and advisers	1,000+
South Africa	Arms	
Angola	Arms, sanctuary	8,000
Mozambique, Angola, Black African nations	Arms, sanctuary	NK (low)
Tanzania	Troops	Hundreds
Libya?	Arms	
US, France	Arms	7–10,000
Algeria, Libya, Mauritania	Arms, sanctuary	
UK, North Korea	Arms, North Korean advisers	1,000+
W. Europe, Israel, US	Arms	1976–1979; 5–7,000 1980–1982: NK (low)
US, France, Israel, West Germany	Arms	Hundreds
US, Israel, France	Arms and US advisers	30,000+
Nicaragua, Cuba?	Arms	
US, France	Arms	1967–1974: 20–40,000 1979–1982: 12–22,000+
Cuba?	Arms	
US, UK	Arms	NK (low)
Nicaragua, Cuba?	Arms	
France, Cuba	Arms	Hundreds
US, Honduras, Costa Rica	Arms, sanctuary	

TABLE 14–1.   (continued)

LOCATION OF CONFLICT	DATE CONFLICT BEGAN	WARRING PARTIES	NUMBER OF TROOPS (estimated)
Peru	1980	Peruvian government vs. left-wing guerrillas	135,500 active; 25,000 paramilitary* 500–1,000
EUROPE Italy	1970	Italian government vs. left- and right-wing guerrillas	370,000 active: 205,000 paramilitary* several hundred
Northern Ireland	1969	British government & Protestant Irish paramilitary groups vs. Irish Catholic nationalist guerrillas	11,600 British troops & 15,000 Protestants 400–500
Spain	1960s	Spanish government vs. Basque separatist guerrillas	347,000 active; 105,000 paramilitary* several hundred

*Not all troops are engaged in combat.
† = Not Known.

Source: Center for Defense Information, *Defense Monitor* XII (1) 14–15 (Washington, D.C.: Center for Defense Information, 1983).

where none exist. Without superpowers, it is said, there would be no superwars. Without the desire to discipline large populations and large land masses, there might be fewer bureaucracies and fewer police to enforce fewer rules (Beer 1981; Schumacher 1973). Without a power elite abusing its trust, there might be more enlightened discussion and easier resolution of public issues.

As some theorists remind us, all semipermanent, complex social organizations, including governments, tend toward oligarchy (Michels 1968). They are ruled by, and act for, the few who reach decisions that reflect their own limited perspectives and aspirations. Today's military-industrial-information complexes are not exceptions to this rule. In their desire to retain power, they seek security against external threats and internal disturbances of all kinds. They raise armies to protect themselves against the former, and use words—and when words fail, police—to defeat the latter.

Ideology.   Modern elites often rely on the power of language rather than the force of arms to legitimate their rule (Mueller 1975). In order to govern large populations for any length of time, they must convert brute force into, if not consent, at least acquiescence.

Aware that what people do is a reflection of what they think (Boulding 1956) and that human thoughts are framed in symbols (Langer 1957), modern political elites seek to control the behavior of their citizen-subjects by dominating their image systems (Edelman 1964). Hitler's "Big Lie" about Nazi superiority and the Soviets' efforts at brainwashing their critics through selective arrests, psychiatric imprisonment, and exile are examples of the effectiveness of twentieth century experiments in mind control.

More subtle techniques of **mentacide** (the killing of intelligence) have been perfected in affluent societies. There, combinations of media, money, and information control rou-

FOREIGN SUPPORT	TYPE OF FOREIGN SUPPORT	NUMBER KILLED (estimated)
USSR, France, US, Italy	Arms	100+
Libya?	Arms	NK (low)
Libya?	Arms	2,200
Libya?	Arms	NK (less than 100/year)

tinely shape elections, make policy decisions, and manipulate public opinion (Jacobson 1980). Thus, relatively few noticed or protested when, in 1983, a beleaguered conservative government sought to pay the world's largest advertising agency $1.5 million to "sell" the Cruise and Pershing II nuclear missiles to the British public.

The object of all such propaganda campaigns is to prevent people from seeing what they are doing (Orwell 1971). By naming the atomic submarine the *Corpus Christi* and the MX missile the *Peacemaker*, U.S. military and political leaders may have deflected the attention of others, as well as themselves, from the destructiveness of these weapon systems (Hilgartner and Bell 1982).

When people cannot think clearly about their feelings and lives, they may be said to be acting *ideologically*, either confusing their preferences for reality (Bergmann 1951), or pursuing narrow economic or other situational interests at the expense of the public interest (MacRae 1961; Marx and Engels 1934), or willingly destroying each other in the name of their national, racial, and sexual prejudices (Arendt 1953; Shklar 1965). Blinded to the consequences of their actions, people easily become "logical criminals" (Camus 1954), willing to kill each other on behalf of their abstractions rather than out of momentary passion.

The results of modern society's innovations in image manipulation are far-reaching, with human reason and imagination among the prime casualties (Mander 1978). Given the centrality of words to the formation of a coherent picture of reality, revolutionary and established political elites regularly vie to control both the content and the conditions of public debate. By so doing, they prevent citizens from taking charge of their own lives, liberties, and happiness. Thus, the mass media are frequently criticized for flattening rather than rallying human sensibilities (Mander 1978), serving

TABLE 14–2. One Hundred Companies Whose Subsidiaries Received the Largest Dollar Volume of Military Prime Contract Awards, Fiscal Year 1978

RANK	PARENT COMPANY	RANK	PARENT COMPANY
66	Aerospace Corp.	60	Johns Hopkins University
56	Agip Spa	28	LTV Corp.
32	Amerada Hess Corp.	77	Lear Siegler, Inc.
39	American Motors Corp.	6	Litton Industries, Inc.
21	American Telephone & Telegraph Co.	4	Lockheed Corp.
89	Atlantic Richfield Co.	91	Loral Corp.
64	AVCO Corp.	19	Martin Marietta Corp.
78	Beech Aircraft Corp.	90	Mason & Hanger Silas Mason Co.
40	Bendix Corp.	69	Massachusetts Institute of
86	Bethlehem Steel Co.		Technology
7	Boeing Co.	2	McDonnell Douglas Corp.
42	British Petroleum Co. Ltd.	93	Mitre Copr.
96	Burroughs Corp.	48	Mobil Corp.
61	Chamberlain Mfg. Corp.	65	Motorola, Inc.
81	Charles Stark Draper Labs, Inc.	99	Natomas Co.
13	Chrysler Corp.	84	Norris Industries, Inc.
53	Coastal Corp.	57	North American Phillips Corp.
88	Computer Sciences Corp.	15	Northrop Corp.
34	Congoleum Corp.	50	Ogden Corp.
71	Control Data Corp.	79	Pacific Resources, Inc.
98	Cubic Corp.	73	Pan American World Airways, Inc.
97	Day & Zimmerman, Inc.	45	Petroleos Mexicanos
82	Dupont E. I. de Nemours & Co.	16	RCA Corp.
58	E. Systems, Inc.	9	Raytheon Co.
72	Eastman Kodak Co.	49	Ret Ser Engineering Co.
68	Emerson Electric Co.	23	Reynolds R. J. Industries, Inc.
43	Engelhard Minerals & Chemical Corp.	94	Rich, Marc & Co.
33	Exxon Corp.	11	Rockwell International Corp.
30	FMC Corp.	47	Royal Dutch Shell Group
20	Fairchild Industries, Inc.	67	Sanders Associates, Inc.
26	Ford Motor Co.	52	Signal Companies Inc. (The)
63	General Cable Corp.	35	Singer Co.
1	General Dynamics Corp.	14	Sperry Rand Corp.
5	General Electric Co.	38	Standard Oil Co. of California
24	General Motors Corp.	76	Standard Oil of Indiana
46	General Telephone & Electronics Corp.	62	Sun Co., Inc.
41	General Tire & Rubber Co.	83	Sverdrup & Parcel & Associates, Inc.
51	Goodyear Tire & Rubber Co.	31	TRW, Inc.
55	Gould, Inc.	36	Teledyne, Inc.
10	Grumman Corp.	25	Tenneco, Inc.
59	Guam Oil & Refining Co., Inc.	22	Texas Instruments, Inc.
87	Gulf Oil Corp.	12	Textron, Inc.
74	Harris Corp.	70	Thiokol Corp.
44	Harsco Corp.	29	Todd Shipyards Corp.
54	Hercules, Inc.	85	Transamerica Corp.
92	Hewlett Packard Co.	100	United Industrial Corp.
17	Honeywell, Inc.	80	United States & South American
8	Hughes Aircraft Co.		Enterprises
27	International Business Machines Co.	3	United Technologies Corp.
95	International Harvester Co.	75	Vinnell Corp.
37	International Telephone & Telegraph Corp.	18	Westinghouse Electric Corp.

Source: U.S. Department of Defense, *100 companies receiving the largest dollar value military prime contract awards, fiscal year, 1978,* p. 7.

governments or their opponents as manipulative agents (Mills 1959), and distorting people's perceptions of reality (Greenstein 1967; McGinnis 1970).

When the media fail in their pacifying tasks, and political elites feel themselves threatened by the stirrings of the poor, the bored, or the oppressed, words can then be mobilized to stimulate violent deeds. Governments may then invent a "national emergency" to unite a restless people, or they may pit interest against interest by stigmatizing and criminalizing behaviors like homosexuality or marijuana use. In the modern world, the struggle to control people's languages has become a prime political act.

The Threat of Extinction

War in the twentieth century is total in a twofold sense: it can extinguish all of human life—bodies as well as minds. This is the central reality of the atomic age, and this is what makes modern politics so perilous. For the first time in history, people have acquired the power of total destruction. They have "become Death; the shatterer of Worlds." At any time, it is possible to put an end to human life through a computer malfunction, the miscalculation of a military planner, or the deranged act of a mundane politician. The past, present, and future can be eradicated, negating all of humanity's collective meanings (Schell 1982). Robbed of an assured posterity to sustain them, people may lose direction and helplessly rush toward the "unparalleled" catastrophe that Albert Einstein feared.

In the decades since the August 1945 atomic bombings of Hiroshima and Nagasaki, enough atomic, thermonuclear, and biochemical weapons have been produced to physically liquidate humanity several times over. As Lord Louis Mountbatten stated:

In the event of a nuclear war there will be no chances, there will be no survivors—all will be obliterated. . . . nuclear devastation is not science fiction—it is a matter of fact.

As he watched the first nuclear explosion at Alamagordo in the New Mexican desert in 1945, physicist J. Robert Oppenheimer recalled these words from the religious book, the Bhagavad Gita: "If the radiance of a thousand suns were to burst into the sky, that would be like the splendour of the Mightly One . . . I am become Death, the shatterer of worlds." The splitting of the atom, Albert Einstein remarked, has changed everything except our way of thinking and thus we drift toward unparalleled catastrophe.

The world now stands on the brink of the final abyss. Let us resolve to take all practical steps to ensure that we do not, through our own folly, go over the edge. (Strasbourg, 11 May 1979)

The destructive power currently available to military and political leaders is difficult to imagine and impossible to comprehend emotionally. What does it mean to say that the nuclear weapons nations currently possess enough destructive power to destroy humanity many times over, and that if these explosives were detonated it would be the equivalent of a second world war happening every second (Humphrey 1981) for between one and two hours? (Union of Concerned Scientists 1981; Physicians for Social Responsibility 1980). If they are to be comprehensible, the subjects of nuclear war and nuclear weapons must be conceived of in other ways—either in the sterilizing language of **megatons** (the equivalent of 1 million tons of TNT, or seventy times the size of the Hiroshima bomb) and megadeaths or, more appropriately, as the horror they are (Zuckerman 1982).

Nuclear weapons and nuclear war. In 1982, the world's nuclear weapons stockpile was equal to 16,000 million tons of TNT. This amount is more than 1 million times the destructive force of the Hiroshima bomb, and more than 5,000 times the total tons of munitions detonated in World War II, in which 40 to 50 million people lost their lives (Sivard 1982).

If only 10 percent of the 50,000 nuclear weapons were used in an exchange between the United States and the Soviet Union, an estimated 140 million Americans, 113 million Russians, and 800 million people worldwide would die outright. This compares with 1.1 million U.S. battlefield deaths counted from the Civil War onward, and 31.7 million Russian deaths from World War I onward (United Nations Association n.d.).

Soon after such an attack, most of the surviving human population would perish from:

1. *Physical injuries* suffered as a result of blast, heat, and radiation damage (Glasstone and Dolan 1977);

2. *The unraveling of the social infrastructure,* as industrial, agricultural, transportation, water, medical, communications, and governmental networks ceased working (Katz 1982; U.S. Congress 1979);

3. *Radioactive contamination of natural ecological systems,* as air, land, and water reserves were polluted, crops failed, and the ozone layer was depleted, causing blindness in animals and interrupting the reproductive cycle of all living things (Schell 1982);

4. *Interruption of the earth's biological and weather systems* as radioactive dust, smoke and fires blotted out the sun, causing a sudden sub-freezing "nuclear winter" (Sagan and Ehrlich 1983); and

5. *The collapse of human psychological systems,* as people experienced unbearable shock, grief, despair, disorientation, hopelessness, and an impaired ability to make and communicate symbols (R. Adams and Cullen 1981).

It is not so much that the survivors of a nuclear war would envy the dead, as President John Kennedy once remarked. The "survivors" would be survivors in name only. They would be in various stages of dying, able to postpone their demise for a few short years at most (Robert Jay Lifton in R. Adams and Cullen 1981).

The more bombs fired, the more unpredictable the results. For example, commercial nuclear reactors would likely melt down as communication systems were impaired, spewing more radioactivity into the environment than the detonations themselves produce. (Fetter and Tsipis 1981, 41–97). Missiles might also go randomly astray, making a mockery of all mass evacuation programs and rational civil defense planning. Other **synergistic effects** (where the sum is other and greater than its parts) can also be expected (see figure 14–1).

As sobering as these estimates are, they fail to convey people's responses to the sudden, violent ending of their lives. For those responses we may examine the statements of Japanese atomic bomb survivors (Osada 1982), the descriptive images of creative writers (Vonnegut 1974a, 1974b) and film-makers (American Broadcasting Company 1983; Concord Films Council n.d.; Union of Concerned Scientists 1982), or the reflections of the atomic scientists who first conceived of the Bomb (Grodzins and Rabinowitch 1963).

In the event of nuclear war people will not stoically cover themselves with a shovelful of dirt as the bombs begin to fall, as some U.S. officials have seriously proposed (Scheer 1982). More likely, they will wander aimlessly in the radioactive ruin of their lives (Hersey 1946).

FIGURE 14–1. Fallout Areas at One Hour and Twenty-Four Hours After Detonations

Fallout areas at 1 hour after detonation

Fallout areas at 24 hours after detonation

Data from the Union of Concerned Scientists, *The Threat of Nuclear War Convocation information sheet,* 11 November 1981.

The global arms race.   The terrifying prospect of a global arms race has transformed politics among nations. On the one hand, thermonuclear weapons have made the abolition of war essential (Pauling 1962; Sharp 1980); on the other hand, they have unleashed the processes that make such a war seem inevitable.

Seeking shelter from potential atomic attack, sovereign (independent) nation-states have built up prodigious nuclear and conventional arsenals to neutralize the weapons threat of others. They have joined rival military and economic alliances (e.g., North Atlantic Treaty Organization (NATO) and the Warsaw Pact), and have extended their spheres of interest and influence around the world. In the process, two nations—the United States and the USSR—have emerged as the first truly global military and political empires (Steel 1970). Their confrontational politics, known as the cold war (Yergin 1977), and their interventions in the domestic affairs of many nations have been the result (Klare 1981).

When faced with challenges to their interests, the United States and the USSR have either used the threat of nuclear war to maintain the peace (Chomsky 1982; Ellsberg 1981; MIT Conference 1982) or have inspired civil insurrections, political assassinations, ideological struggles, and authoritarian to totalitarian takeovers in clientele nations as a means of balancing their power (Klare and Arnson 1981).

Diplomatic efforts at building a peaceful international order have broken down accordingly, with militarily weaker nations seeking to free themselves from superpower dominance. A spiraling global arms race has ensued (Aldridge 1979). Some nations, like China and France, have developed nuclear weapons of their own. Others have moved to seal their borders and protect their natural resources against superpower penetration. Resurgent nationalism, the breakdown of the United Nations' peacekeeping mission, and a widening gap between rich nations and poor have ensued, aggravated in

large part by the poor's need to buy weapons from the very Northern Hemisphere countries that have impoverished and destabilized their societies (Pierre 1982) (see figures 14–2 and 14–3).

The costs of the global arms race have not been borne by developing countries alone, however. While they ranked first and second in national military expenditures in 1980, the United States and the USSR placed thirteenth and thirty-seventh, respectively, among the nations of the world in per capita spending on health services for their own citizens (Sivard 1983). Not unexpectedly, the $2 trillion six-year military budget of the Reagan administration could cost each U.S. household over $20,000—enough to keep the financially ailing Social Security system solvent for seventy-five years. As Swedish Nobel laureate Alva Myrdal has noted (1982) apparently all that humanity has managed to buy with its military dollars is less and less security at higher and higher prices.

The erosion of democracy. The constant threat of nuclear war has been expensive on another front as well. It has bred the national security state and a supporting set of values and behaviors that are proving inimi-

FIGURE 14–2. Shares of World *Exports* of Major Weapons, 1979–81, by Country

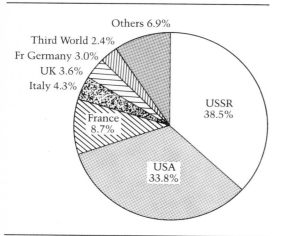

Data from the Stockholm International Peace Research Institute, *The arms race and arms control* (London: Taylor & Francis, 1982).

FIGURE 14–3. Shares of World *Imports* of Major Weapons, 1979–81, by Region

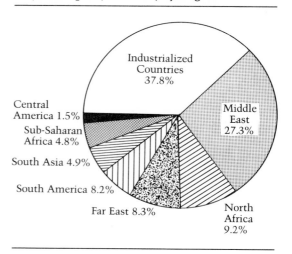

Data from the Stockholm International Peace Research Institute, *The arms race and arms control* (London: Taylor & Francis, 1982).

cal to the practice of democracy (Falk 1982). Concern for security has inflated military-industrial interests in previously democratic nation-states (Mills 1960) and has led to the establishment of standing armies in many nations, an arrangement universally feared by the makers of the democratic experiment (Bailyn 1967).

The quest for nuclear security has also encouraged domestic violations of human rights. Intelligence gathering, government denial of information vital to people's lives (under the stamp of "classified" or "top secret"), and surveillance of citizens have become familiar occurrences in many ostensibly democratic societies (D. Burnham 1983). Political demagoguery, often expressed through anti-Communist or national security slogans, has also become commonplace (Jezer 1982).

In brief, atomic politics has legitimated government lawlessness and abuses of power wherever they have appeared. For instance, in an effort to make the American nuclear weapons deterrent policy credible to Soviet leaders, former U.S. President Richard Nixon undermined the democratic electoral process, created a secret government within a constitutional one, treated critics of his Vietnam War strategy as enemies of the state, and resorted to lying and intimidation to conceal illegal and violent governmental acts in Southeast Asia and elsewhere (Schell 1976).

As suggested since, the Nixon presidency and democracy may have been casualties of the demands of nuclear diplomacy. In the years since President Nixon's forced resignation from public office, it has been revealed that several administrations regularly concealed the dangers of nuclear decision-making from the American public. In the 1950s, President Dwight Eisenhower's administration failed to warn civilians and soldiers of the medical hazards of above-ground nuclear weapons testing in the southwestern states (Rosenberg 1980). Presidents John Kennedy and Lyndon Johnson used the Federal Bureau of Investigation (FBI) (Navasky 1977) and the Central Intelligence Agency (CIA) as political police to harass opponents in the 1960s, and Presidents Kennedy and Nixon contemplated the first use of nuclear weapons in the Cuban missile crisis and during the Vietnam War in the 1960s and 1970s, respectively (Chomsky 1982; Ellsberg 1981).

If they had been confined to ruling groups alone, these and similar events might be regarded as aberrant behaviors in otherwise democratic cultures. Suspicion mounts, however, that much of the formal and informal educational systems upon which democracy ultimately rests (Dewey 1966) has surrendered to the authoritarian imperatives of the Bomb. In technological societies, knowledge is sought for power's sake and not for the wisdom it might bring. Science continues to be made "the prostitute of war," as British Nobel laureate Philip Noel-Baker once remarked, through its involvement in military contracts and its capacity for prediction and control of human behavior. Instruction in the humanizing arts and letters has diminished in favor of escalating military budgets. Whether the democratic ethos of liberty, equality, and tolerance can recover from a long period of economic starvation and social ostracism is uncertain.

Causes for concern.   Until the mid-1970s, nuclear weapons maintained an uneasy nuclear truce between the superpowers. Ironically, that truce was based on the assumption that neither the United States nor the USSR would start an atomic war if it feared destruction in a retaliatory attack. Military planners in America and Russia pursued various deterrent, balance of terror, and mutually assured destruction (MAD) strategies accordingly. Each country tried to build just enough nuclear weapons, along with the willingness to use them defensively, to convince the other that it had more to lose than to gain by starting a nuclear war.

These mutual deterrence strategies began to come apart in the mid-1970s, exposing humanity to its gravest survival peril since the nuclear age began. In a rapid succession of events:

1.   The United States and the Soviet Union began to lose control of the terms of nuclear weapons possession when nonaligned India secretly detonated a nuclear device in 1974. The materials used were derived from what had been heralded previously as India's Atoms-for-Peace program. Since then, the world has faced the prospect that a nuclear war might be initiated by any small nation or terrorist group and spread to the great powers (Heilbroner 1980).

2.   Around the same time (1973–74), the trilateral nations of the United States, Western Europe, and Japan (Sklar 1980) learned that their economies were vulnerable to oil interruptions in the Middle East (see chapter 15). In response, the United States declared that it was in its vital interest to protect the flow of oil in the Persian Gulf, thereby risking being drawn into a nuclear confrontation with the Soviet Union in that politically volatile region at some future date.

3.   In response to the Russian invasion of Afghanistan and the stationing of SS-20 missiles on its western borders, the United States abandoned its **détente** (live-and-let-live) policy late in 1979, and returned to an earlier, hard-line cold war rhetoric. Further, the U.S. Senate failed to ratify the SALT II arms control treaty negotiated with the Russians by the Carter administration, and Ronald Reagan was elected to the American presidency.

4. Throughout the early 1980s, the Reagan administration talked openly about fighting and winning a limited or protracted nuclear war. The administration moved to regain U.S. nuclear "superiority," and sought to place Cruise and Pershing II missiles in Europe. If launched, these and similar weapons systems could destroy military command centers on Soviet soil and reduce Soviet reaction time to a nuclear attack to six minutes. Critics contended that this short lead time would effectively turn over to computers the decision to move to nuclear war, and would encourage a Soviet first-strike, preventive attack.

5. When it bombed an experimental nuclear reactor under construction in Iraq (1981), Israel claimed the right of any nation to attack the nuclear installations of any other nation if it has reason to fear that its national existence is *potentially* threatened by nuclear developments in another nation-state. Subsequent UN sanctions of Israel proved more symbolic than real, thereby undermining the nuclear peacekeeping credibility of the International Atomic Energy Agency (IAEA).

6. To avoid nuclear war in the 1990s, both Soviet and American military advisers moved to militarize space, develop laser and other high-technology weapons systems to "neutralize" each other's nuclear forces, and otherwise engage in a diplomatically uncontrollable and economically bankrupting escalation of the arms race.

ANALYZING THE PROBLEM: WHY POLITICAL VIOLENCE?

Premonitions of disaster plus widespread social dislocation throughout the century have stimulated research into the ubiquity (perva-siveness) of political violence in the modern world. The results have brought the very foundations of civilization into question, and have suggested the need to reformulate presently accepted attitudes toward power and politics. The two basic perspectives that have emerged regarding the sources of contemporary warfare and domination are discussed next.

Violence in History

In the first view, the mounting threat of nuclear war is seen as the outcome of a long evolutionary process in which various forms of political violence are thought to result from the interaction between the individual and society. Anger and aggression, it is said, reside within the human personality and become activated (1) in circumstances of emotional or material (economic) deprivation, (2) wherever creative human energies are constrained by narrow societal roles, or (3) when societies themselves become stratified into various classes and castes.

Power and personality. Following the intellectual lead of Sigmund Freud, one group of analysts holds that individual and collective acts of violence, as well as the pursuit of political power itself, may be rooted in personality disorders or neuroses (Lasswell 1958, 1976)—products of repressed sexual desires directed inwardly against oneself or outwardly against others. Destructive behaviors and social institutions are thus seen as reflections of either distorted "instincts" or communications (Connerton 1978, 348–61; Mueller 1975), with particularly violent historical epochs regarded as the triumph of a deeply buried, universally held death wish (Freud 1958).

Where sexuality, power, and physical violation are confused—as frequently happens in technological societies—some might actually welcome a final thermonuclear "bang," either as a confirmation of their sexual prowess or as a release from overwhelming, sexually related guilt feelings. The more repressive the social system, this view contends, the greater the level of personal frustration and resulting violence (Freud 1958).

More recently, sociobiologists and others have located the inclination toward war and social domination in human nature itself. Humans, they believe, are genetically programmed toward either aggression (Lorenz 1970), hierarchy (Wilson 1975), territorial defense (Tiger and Fox 1971), or the genetic continuity of their species.

Like other animals, this theory suggests, humans pursue power, seek authority, and try to attain some degree of social discipline in order to survive. Unlike other species, however, humans improvise their social roles (Habermas 1979) and sometimes store up destructive resentments against those who impose restraints on their natural liberties (Adorno et al. 1950). In this view, interpersonal conflict and societal violence may be anticipated as a normal consequence of collective life.

A supporting view is offered by those who trace the origins of violent conflict to natural biological and temperamental differences said to exist among humans. Since no two people are exactly alike, the supposition is that some people may have a stronger will-to-power (Nietzsche 1974) and greater talent or intellectual endowments than others. Violence might thus occur whenever individuals fail to establish a dynamic equilibrium among unequals (Foucault 1980), and might turn into lethal conflict when common rules of behavior (civility) (Burke 1955) cannot be established, or when governments are unable to reconcile or neutralize people's inherent differences (Dahl 1956; Hamilton, Madison, Jay 1961.

Societal indicators. Whatever its source, the key to understanding political violence is social rather than individual, however. There is a universe of difference between fighting for status in a "state of nature" and in raising and provisioning an army. One set of actions requires social organization; the

Armaments don't give security

other does not. One cannot be prevented; the other can.

Ultimately, those who seek explanations for human aggression must look to learned social behaviors (Montagu 1966, 1968, 1976) or to the specific arrangement and content of societal roles and values as indicators of whether, and when, people will resort to collective violence. Minimally, social life amplifies, routinizes, and legitimates whatever primitive drives toward aggression people might have; maximally, it may cancel or override their destructive urges.

Cross-cultural studies of primitive people reveal them living in many different ways, sometimes with and sometimes without domination and other forms of violence. The recent discovery of the pastoral Tasaday tribespeople of the Philippines confirms earlier anthropological observations that people can, and sometimes do, live in peace (Nance 1975). Seemingly, peaceful coexistence occurs in nomadic situations in which hierarchies are very simple, slavery and class stratification are absent, political integration takes place at the family or most intimate community level, achievement norms are low, the accumulation of wealth is moderate, sexual satisfaction is high among all age groups, and egalitarian—as opposed to domineering—values are taught (Textor 1972).

As far as most students of the problem are concerned, war, domination, and violent behaviors are learned rather than inherited (Bramson and Goethals 1964). Passions may take over under battlefield conditions (Wills 1982, 281–302). Political violence in traditional societies, however, appears the consequence of social choices about human needs, such as expanding wealth (Lenski and Lenski 1982) or keeping populations in balance with available resources (Harris 1978) rather than any inherently wicked or evil trait that humans are sometimes alleged to possess.

Human limitations can be a source of destructive social conflict, however. Economic inequalities and inadequate responses to changing environmental demands may increase the occasions of war (see chapter 15) as societies attempt to generate wealth quickly or resolve population and resource problems. The nation-state system, recent anticolonial revolutions for bread, and earlier rebellions for political rights make this possibility more than evident (Arendt 1962).

Nowhere is this lesson clearer than in the modern nation-state system where unequal, sovereign nations compete for ascendancy in a world whose military, economic, and political problems often require global or local rather than national solutions. As recognized from the start of the nuclear age, without a common power to prevent them from going to war, these competitive nation-states cannot do much to deliver security, political liberty, or economic equality to their citizens.

It has been shown that domination and abuses of power increase in bureaucratic societies as well. People learn to obey impersonal rules and commands of superiors and become distanced from their actions. In these circumstances, they are likely to (1) treat each other either as objects or as functions rather than as individuals like themselves, (2) inflict physical pain on others when authority figures instruct them to do so, or (3) lose touch with the ways in which their rule-making decisions will have impact on people's everyday lives (Prosterman 1972, 45–134). In contemporary society, almost everyone has had occasion to be on the receiving end of a bureaucratic decision that seems rational by organizational standards but which damages concrete lives when abstractly applied (Reader 1972, 337–72).

Power Transformed

As instructive as the evolutionary perspective of abusive power is, it falls short of explaining what seem to be the distinguishing expressions of political violence in the twentieth century: the concentration camp, technological civilization, and the atomic bombings of Hiroshima and Nagasaki.

In response to these three phenomena, many contemporary social thinkers have suggested that both power and violence have been transformed in the modern world and that, accordingly, we live in an age of discontinuity where few lessons of the past apply. Nevertheless, by understanding the unique dynamics of recent political trends, the hope is that we may be able to avoid the tragedies that seem to await us.

Totalitarianism: From violence to terror. For many, modernity began at Dachau and Auschwitz and in the Russian Gulag Archipelago (Nazi and Soviet concentration camps, respectively) (Solzhenitsyn 1973; Steiner 1979). Totalitarianism continues wherever people are exterminated, tortured, or worked to death for no reason other than that they run afoul of prevailing political orthodoxies (Timerman 1981).

Whatever the causes, the twentieth century has seen the creation of new forms of government dedicated to the destruction rather than the improvement of life. Hitler and Stalin intended to kill not only their external enemies but also all who were not like themselves. The chilling images of resulting brutality are familiar to readers of George Orwell's fictional masterpiece on totalitarianism, *1984:* a boot stamping on a face forever, Room 101 where one's worst fears come true, the pursuit of power-for-domination's sake (Orwell 1971). Understand the dynamics of the concentration camp, it is said, and one may discover what is really novel in contemporary politics: its total randomness and terror.

For millions of victims of modern police states and death squads around the world, the experience has been the same: inhumane punishments for no discernible crimes, arrests by armed guards for no reason, physical beatings followed by transportation to the concentration camps, entry into barbed-wired compounds, then execution in gas chambers or self-dug ditches, depending on the whim of the camp commandant. For survivors of these initial executions, their experience is a living death whose only object is the mental and physical depersonalization of the individual (Cohen 1953; Wiesel 1972).

Students of the concentration camp experience believe that totalitarian dictatorships are characterized by random violence by authorities, an official ideology to which all must conform, a single political party loyal to a single leader, widespread spying and control of communications and armaments by governments or their agents, and the establishment of a permanent war economy as a way of ensuring the obedience of the masses (Friedrich and Brzezinski 1956). Terror is thought to be the lynchpin of the system. It has the twin effects of disorienting and isolating people's behavior and of subse-

quently reintegrating them into an undifferentiated mass committed to the principle of "Thou shalt kill" (Arendt 1953).

The success of totalitarianism lies in our inability to cope with the randomness of its leaders or with its excessive violence. Psychologically speaking, we are not equipped to deal with a reality in which planned killing takes place for no compelling reason.

All available evidence indicates that humans are creatures of meaning (Langer 1957) and that they will try to attach significance to events even when none may be said to exist. When confronted with a computer printout, people will make poetry from randomly programmed words; when exposed to the paintings of a chimpanzee, they will find beauty in them; and when marched to what for them were the gates of Hell, Jews and others will dispute why some have been handed yellow and others brown Stars of David armbands (Cohen 1953). Like Anne Frank's father, people find it difficult to grasp a reality of destructiveness and continue to do business as usual until it is too late either to fight or to flee the totalitarian system (Frank 1958).

In many respects, it is easier to explain the behavior of victims than of executioners in terroristic situations. Almost everyone can understand the paralytic and divisive effect that the sudden threat of physical violence can have on people. In 1966 an armed assailant entered the apartment of nine young Chicago nurses and killed all but one, who miraculously escaped by hiding under a bed. Had they banded together, these nurses might have disarmed Richard Speck. Terrorized as each was, however, and unable to accept the fact that they were all dead as far as their executioner was concerned, each nurse sought to survive individually and, in so doing, sealed her fate and that of her friends.

How does one account for the actions of Richard Speck or of those Nazis and Stalinists who ordered the mass executions of Jews and Communists, anti-Communists and kulaks, gypsies, homosexuals, Poles, and Jehovah's Witnesses? How does one explain the actions of those who carried out their commands? While one can intuit the rage and sense of destruction that might prompt ignorant and insecure fanatics to commit violent acts (Hoffer 1966), what motivates bureaucrats to give the order to eradicate an entire group of people?

Disturbingly, the answer may be *nothing*. The suggestion has been made that those who willingly carry out commands to kill an entire nation or group of people (genocide) may neither notice nor regret what they are doing. Apparently, this is what Hannah Arendt had in mind when she spoke of the "banality of evil" (Arendt 1965). The modern world, she surmised, may be filled with potential Adolph Eichmanns. Each of us has the capacity to do extensive damage under circumstances in which our power seems to be unlimited and an authority figure or leader supports our behavior. In social psychological terms, we may lose the capacity to place ourselves in the role of the other (Mead 1967) in such contexts. Our focus, then, turns to unemotional, technical questions such as how many Jews can fit in a boxcar rather than to ethical questions like "Should people be treated like cattle at all?"

Extermination camps have become familiar scenes in the twentieth century. Here, American GIs look on in horror at the legacy of Adolph Hitler's dream of a thousand year empire. The key to understanding the modern world may well lay in coming to terms with the dynamics of totalitarian rule.

Mass society: From terror to distraction. If physical terror is at the heart of totalitarianism, artificiality and manipulation are the hallmarks of **technological civilization** (a society whose most important products are its tools and techniques of production and consumption of goods, information, and services) (Barrett 1979; Ellul 1967). By destroying variety, continuity with the past, and immediate sensory contact with others, modern affluent societies randomize human experience and create the conformity of taste and opinion typical of **mass tyrannies** (systems of popular government that deprive individuals of their fundamental rights) (Mill 1956, Ortega y Gasset 1932).

In his last film, *Being There*, British actor Peter Sellers recreated the sterility and superficiality that are characteristic of daily life in much of consumer-oriented America. For the film's hero, Chance the gardener, no life is real and no event is noticed unless it appears on an ever-present television screen. Love, sexuality, friendship, and death have been replaced by the sort of distracted spectatorism (Livingston and Thompson 1966, 60–93) ordinarily associated with a visit to Disneyland: pleasant but not real.

The lifelessness beneath the surface excitement of technological civilization has resulted from two recent developments: (1) the mass production of goods and services (Galbraith 1980) and (2) an accelerated rate of technological change that has uprooted people from their pasts and has disoriented their behaviors (Toffler 1970).

Standardized products and new inventions have altered political and personal life in affluent societies in several significant respects. First, some technological advances have impoverished the public world. The same telephones, automobiles, and TV sets that enrich the private, material lives of today's suburbanites have also led to a decline of the city (Jacobs 1961), the loss of community (face-to-face encounters), and the decay of public services ranging from postal to mass transportation systems. Political activity has suffered accordingly and has been converted from an occasion of public celebration and interpersonal trust (Kariel 1972) into a struggle for power by impersonal nations, political parties, and pressure groups (Morgenthau 1974).

Quoting John Studenmaier, a Jesuit scholar, columnist Ellen Goodman (*Arizona Republic* 29 March 1983) points out that with the birth of the telephone in 1876, people "split voice from sight, smell and taste" and, for the first time, were no longer able to reach out and touch each other in the speech act. Organizational power—in this case, that of the telephone company—rushed in to widen and deepen the resulting social void.

Second, this general weakening of sensory (social) interactions among modern people has fostered reliance on large-scale organizations for one's version of reality, sense of identity, and economic livelihood (Riesman 1973; Whyte 1957), accounting perhaps for the persistence of **nationalism** (excessive devotion to one's country) and corporate loyalty in affluent societies.

The more institutions become essential to providing basic personal, economic and psychological needs, the more resistant they are to change and the restraints that people have traditionally placed on power and its uses. The lawless national (Hacker 1965) and transnational conglomerate has become a fact of modern life (Barnet and Muller 1974), as have politicians who rise above the Constitution by flexing their nuclear weapons muscles and overlooking white-collar crimes such as illegal dumping of dangerous chemical wastes and price gouging by oil company majors.

Finally, to deliver mass-produced homes, refrigerators, and insurance policies to an expanding body of consumers, modern economies have had to generate a class of technical and salaried workers (Burnham 1960; Galbraith 1971) skilled in the art of manipulation (Ellul 1967) and tied to anti-democratic tools and techniques necessary in the production and consumption of many new products (Schwartz 1983).

Consumer goods and services are often manufactured in impersonal, hierarchically organized factories and corporate situations. Sales campaigns are frequently manipulative. Computers may scramble people's reality either by misplacing information or by interrupting their private moments. Video arcades may reflect lessons of violence in game situations, and scientists, aerospace engineers, and corporate executives may become morally indifferent to whether the planes their decisions produce are used to deliver passengers or bombs.

In short, rapid technological change and the homogenized life-styles it brings has led to the creation of shallow, one-dimensional societies (Marcuse 1964). These monocultures cannot withstand much freedom or unplanned change, and must increase their control of nature and individuals to fulfill their promise of material abundance.

Affluent societies may not be able to resolve their ambivalent attitudes toward power and its uses. By creating economic prosperity for many, technological civilizations have indeed generated the preconditions for genuine freedom (Lipset 1981), as evidenced in the 1960s with the appearance of humanistic countercultures (Keniston 1968; Reich 1970; Roszak 1969). By reducing variety and destroying traditions, however, affluent societies may have equally rendered themselves unable to accommodate the very spontaneity that many of their technologies produce (Bronowski 1974).

In the 1950s and 1960s, some societies tried to resolve this tension between freedom and social control by reducing sexual repression and encouraging people to "do their own thing." Unexpectedly, the resulting sexual revolution and emergence of various liberation movements (Dolbeare and Dolbeare 1976) led many to question the domination and inequality on which much of the material wealth of modern societies seems to be based (see chapter 15). More recently, politicians in affluent societies have begun to use the threat of unemployment and atomic war as ways of reestablishing

the conformity of opinion and life-style they apparently require to generate mass affluence and to maintain their power.

In the final analysis, then, the use of psychological terror may have joined the use of physical terror as prime instruments of rule in the modern world (Bettelheim 1960).

Nuclear culture: From distraction to desocialization.   When the atomic bombs fell at Hiroshima and Nagasaki, many victims believed the world had ended (Hersey 1946; Lifton 1968). Faced with the sudden disintegration of familiar scenes of daily life and death everywhere around them (Committee 1981), people's senses began to unravel (Lifton and Falk 1982). Without warning, they had been cast into a universe of total power and with it, total meaninglessness (Japan Broadcasting 1977).

For years afterward, neither the survivors nor those who had dropped the bomb could make sense out of what had happened. The events of 6 and 9 August 1945 had seemingly impaired the workings of their senses, creating a "psychic numbing" (Lifton 1968) for victims and executioners alike. Only later did some come to realize that the **hibakusha** (atomic bomb survivors) had lived through not only their own deaths and those of their children but also the death of the whole of creation, much as had the **Musselmanner** (the desensitized survivors of Hitler's concentration camps). In a poem called "Give Back the Human," inscribed on a memorial stone at Hiroshima park, bombing victim Sankishi Tage described this feeling:

Give back my father, give back my mother;
Give grandpa back, grandma back;
Give my sons and daughters back.

Give me back myself.
Give back the human race.

As long as this life lasts, this life,
Give back peace
That will never end.
                          (Pacific War Research Society 1981, 272)

Among the victims, the ordeal created survivor guilt, an impaired ability to mourn the many dead, paranoia and, above all else, an impairment of normal feelings about death and dying. Death was now associated, as it has been for many since, with total annihilation (Lifton and Falk 1982).

This encounter with extinction cannot be understated; it may constitute the central psychosocial problem of our time (Schell 1982). Apparently, much of what makes life meaningful for humans is a confidence that others will mourn and remember them after they have died (Schell 1982). By attaching significance to death, people give meaning and direction to life. In situations of actual or imagined extinction, however, as is now present in our fear about nuclear war, there is only nothingness (Barrett 1962; Wild 1963), an existential encounter that the senses and spirit find difficult to process or withstand. When one lives with dread and without an assured posterity, all of life's projects seem futile and counterfeit. Creativity dies and purpose itself becomes unhinged.

Anger, denial, depression, and feelings of hopelessness and despair are among the initial reactions to one's own *personal* death and dying (Kubler-Ross 1974). Similar responses may have taken place at the collective, societal level under the constant burden of threatened thermonuclear extinction, followed by acceptance of the inevita-

Shigeko Sasamori, left, and Esuko Bundy, survivors of the atomic bombing of Hiroshima, testify before a U.S. Senate subcommittee hearing on the short- and long-term effects of radiation.

bility of nuclear war and death. A generation of psychic survivors of the atomic age may have relived the *hibakusha* experience and may have been desensitized, demoralized, and desocialized as a result.

Seemingly, many would-be nuclear victims and executioners gave up on social and human solutions to the problem of nuclear war in the post–World War II period. They hoped that the threat would go away if they ignored it, or concluded that the matter would be resolved by devising a foolproof military defense strategy against it. Recent findings indicate that American schoolchildren's psychic lives became distorted when exposed both to the prospect of nuclear devastation and to reassuring talk about survival. This inconsistency may have colored their attitudes toward both power and legitimate government, and may have led some to question the authority of institutions and societal arrangements that continue to preach the gospel of progress even under the cloud of nuclear destruction (Carey 1982). Others might welcome such an event as retaliation against a society that has left them futureless and powerless (Humphrey 1981).

Paradoxically, by training their children to kill any would-be intruders into their private bomb shelters, another group of potential nuclear victims—so-called **survivalists** (people who actively prepare to survive a nuclear war)—have begun to engage in acts of "anticipatory anomie" (Geiger 1981), in which they doubt the ability of *any* present or future *social* action to prevent calamity.

A similar desocializing process seems to be at work among nuclear war planners. Typically, those who prepare for nuclear war seem unable either to imagine the end of the world or to experience themselves as victims of their nuclear plans (Schecter and Schecter 1983, 63–73). They, too, have given up on collective solutions to the war problem, believing that a technical weapons "breakthrough" rather than a social or diplomatic solution is humanity's only hope of survival. Thus, Edward Teller, the father of the hydrogen bomb, and Herman Kahn, a

leading technological futurist, have both proposed that life will go on routinely in the aftermath of a nuclear war and that under certain circumstances, liquidating millions of innocent civilians in order to defend ill-defined notions of "freedom" and "progress" might be necessary (Lifton and Falk 1982).

Caught in the tyranny of their own illusions, many have come to think of atomic and hydrogen bombs as the latest in a long line of weapons that political and military elites traditionally use against faceless enemies as the occasion warrants (Frank 1982). Situations in which neither potential victims nor executioners are able to humanize their common circumstances may make nuclear war seem inevitable.

ALTERNATIVE POLICIES FOR RESOLVING THE PROBLEM: GIVING PEACE A CHANCE

Given the mounting threat of thermonuclear devastation, many have begun to reconsider the direction of their lives. Along with former U.S. Ambassador to the Soviet Union, George Kennan, they have come to believe there is "no hope, no fear, nothing to which we aspire, nothing we would like to avoid—which could conceivably be worth a nuclear war" (Kennan 1983). Confronted with premature death, as were the inmates of the concentration camps and the survivors of Hiroshima and Nagasaki, many have come to appreciate the wonder of life and are discovering ways of empowering themselves and their children to peacefully challenge and disarm the seemingly invincible centers of destruction.

The Theory and Practice of Nonviolence

Behind the mass sit-ins, concerts, and marches for disarmament—commonplace occurrences in an emerging global peace culture—is one of the most electrifying social forces in the twentieth century: countless personal decisions to renounce domination and to do one's part in ending **social injustice** (inequality) and political repression of all kinds (Sharp 1973a, 1973b, 1973c).

Personal responsibility and civil disobedience. At the core of today's peace movement is the threefold conviction that:

1. Violence in the modern world originates from oppressive economic and political regimes (systems), as well as from the behavior of some individuals (Mills 1960).

2. These tyrannical systems can be changed through personal, nonviolent action based on a love of creation and the decision to continue the life process into the distant future (Bishops' Statement 1983).

3. Only by accepting philosophers Bertrand Russell and Albert Einstein's advice to "remember your humanity and forget the rest" (Nathan and Norden 1981) can the nuclear age be outlived.

Today's peacemakers believe that individually and collectively, people are, or can become, meaningful and moral agents (actors) if given love, respect, and nurturing (Maslow 1968, 1973). They also believe that humanity is violated insofar as it is prevented from acting sociably (nonviolently) toward others (Reader and Wolf 1973). Some hold that humane action begins when individuals place themselves in harmony with the world, refuse to deliberately damage themselves and others, and are prepared to unmask—and sometimes suffer—the violence of their surroundings as confirmation of their ongoing commitment to the peaceful continuation of life (Bondurant 1965).

When confronted by destructive societal control and domination, humanity can be sustained by nonviolent action (Sibley 1963). Tacit (silent) support of, or consent to, tyrannical regimes can be withdrawn or withheld (de la Boetie 1975; Locke 1952), e.g., by not seeking employment in atomic weapons factories. Active resistance to the violent deeds of others can be undertaken by disobeying unjust (humanly destructive) laws

or arrangements (King, Jr. 1964; Rawls 1971), as did the Plowshares Eight in 1980 when they damaged the nose cones of two disarmed U.S. nuclear missiles. In refraining from any act that would diminish or threaten another's life, meaning and dignity are given to one's own life and the lives of others.

"I rebel, therefore we are," wrote French philosopher Albert Camus (1954), speaking for a tradition of nonviolent civil disobedients who, from the classical period onward, have suffered the wrath of the state and gone to jail or the executioner's block rather than forfeit their common humanity (Lynd 1966; Mayer 1966).

Nonviolent direct action. Responding to the unique problems of violence in the twentieth century, contemporary peacemakers have made significant additions to this ancient commitment to nonviolent resistance to tyranny.

First, in response to totalitarianism, mass society, and the prospect of nuclear annihilation, many have begun to hold individuals personally responsible for the violent deeds they commit in the name of impersonal organizations or abstractions, e.g., modern nation-states or the national security system. The Nuremberg principles, developed during the trials of Nazi war criminals at the close of World War II, established the rule that as ethical beings, all people must be held legally and morally accountable for their life choices, especially when they lead others to destruction. Planned **genocide** (the destruction of an entire race or group of people) has thus been made a crime in international law (Falk, Kolko, and Lifton 1971), and contemplated **omnicide** (the destruction of the human race) (Somerville 1976) is now gaining recognition as *the* major criminal act in today's society.

Second, peace activists have come to appreciate the effective and transforming role of collective, as distinct from isolated, acts of nonviolent civil disobedience in defeating entrenched systems of power (Gregg 1966;

Mother Teresa

Martin Luther King, Jr.

Dorothy Day

Gandhi (center)

Albert Einstein

Rosa Parks (center)

Modern peace activists have helped end colonialism (Gandhi); sparked a revolution in human rights (Rosa Parks, Martin Luther King, Jr.); worked among the world's poor (Mother Teresa); added a religious dimension to the struggle for social justice (Dorothy Day); and announced the obsolescence of violence in a nuclear age (Albert Einstein).

Sharp 1971) and in making politics (public life) a friendly place in which to operate (Kariel 1966, 1977).

Popular, nonviolent actions were useful in ridding India of British domination in 1947 (Erikson 1969), securing equal political rights for black Americans in the 1960s (King, Jr. 1964), and preventing the use of atomic weapons in Vietnam in the 1960s and 1970s (Ellsberg 1981). They also have proven essential in rebuilding a sense of political community and shared purpose among previously powerless and dispirited people, as the Solidarity Union experiment in Poland suggests.

Third, modern peace activists have invented "movement politics" as a way of retaining a sense of individuality and humanity as they act to save themselves and others from desolation (Reader 1967, Roszak 1969). As millions of people learned during the 1960s, and as many more have realized since, it did not take superhuman effort or the commitment of a lifetime to join hundreds of thousands at the Washington Monument in 1963 and again in 1983 to share Martin Luther King, Jr.'s dream of peace and social justice, or at Woodstock in 1969 for a weekend of counterculture music, or in the streets of the world's capitals in 1982 to protest an escalation of the nuclear arms race.

The key to building movement politics lies in a voluntary, impermanent assembly of individuals who participate equally in making decisions vital to their well-being. The need for hierarchy, bureaucracies, and elites in political decision making is reduced (Thayer 1973), and the practice of direct rather than representative democracy is encouraged (Megill 1970).

As these and similar events suggest, the effects of pooling many small, part-time, individual acts of conscience may prove decisive in the struggle for survival. For instance, it was small gatherings of citizens in New England town meetings in 1982 who rejected as foolish and dangerous U.S. government plans for wholesale evacuation of

populations in the event of a nuclear attack. In turn, they joined with others in villages and cities around the world to declare themselves "nuclear-free zones" in return for banishing all nuclear activities from their communities. By participating in consumer boycotts, refusing to pay taxes, withdrawing their labor from destructive activities, using their vote effectively, and engaging in pray-ins, peace vigils and fairs, and letter-writing campaigns, citizens of many countries have begun to put pressure on governments and corporate leaders for fundamental, nonviolent social change (Sharp 1973a, 1973b, 1973c).

Human rights and environmental ethics. Such nonviolent and creative efforts have persuaded many that humans are potentially "wonderful" and worthwhile beings (Haksar 1979) entitled to a life of equal dignity and respect (Williams 1962). If they are to become *fully* human, however, the common assertion is that people must be permitted to grow in peaceful social and environmental surroundings. This perception has sparked the contemporary environmental and human potential movements (Ferguson 1980) and has led many in the religious community to call for an end to domination in any form.

Globally, the human rights movement has sought to extend to all individuals political rights that were previously reserved to the few. At the same time, the guarantees of freedom of speech, press, assembly, petition, conscience, and movement have been recognized as being without substance unless backed by broadly based economic, health, welfare, and educational rights (Macpherson 1966). The 1948 United Nations (UN) Declaration of Human Rights (Leech, Oliver, and Sweeney 1973) not only guarantees all people protection of life, liberty, and security against arbitrary government but also states that everyone is equally entitled to the right to work, to be free of the fear of unemployment, and to secure whatever other economic, social, and cultural rights seem indispensible for human dignity and the free development of personality.

A more explicit linkage between political liberty and economic rights is drawn in the 1972 UN Declaration on the Environment, in which it is stated that quality of life considerations for this and future generations require nations to end **apartheid** (South African racial discrimination), racial segregation, and colonialism of all kinds (Fritsch 1980).

Sensitized to the pervasive effects of domination in modern life, many citizen groups worldwide have called for the rapid implementation of social, political, and economic equality measures, ranging from the ratification of the Equal Rights Amendment to the U.S. Constitution, to the promulgation of an environmental bill of rights that would guarantee clean air, land, and water to all, to the writing of laws that would extend legal protections to an otherwise defenseless physical environment against destructive human activities.

The connection among political rights, economic equality, and quality of life indicators is perhaps most clearly drawn in a number of recent studies (Brandt and Sampson 1980) that indicate that the basic threat to peace comes from an unequal distribution of wealth (see chapter 15). If, as these studies indicate, inequality is the prime source of conflict between nations and people, the rich Northern Hemisphere countries may have to implement a program that will quickly end world poverty and guarantee to this and future generations the full satisfaction of basic human needs of survival, labor, education, recreation and leisure, self-reliance, and participatory development (Tinbergen 1976).

Human rights activists have been joined in this view by many religious denominations which, in recent years, have recognized that peace (harmony and equality) requires the attainment of social justice. As significantly, under the threat of extinction, religious and ethical communities have recently modified the theory of "just war" developed during the Middle Ages, before total

destruction was possible (Bishops' Statement 1983); have reconsidered the morality of nuclear deterrence policies that commit nations and individuals to kill innocent civilians (Van Voorst 1983); and have returned to a more traditional view that if we are to survive, we must give up the pursuit of power in favor of love (sociability) (Cobb 1969).

Strategies for Survival

Working within this general intellectual context, the global "peace community" has adopted a number of short-term survival strategies which, it hopes, will reduce the threat of nuclear war and create a climate of opinion in which the pursuit of peace can again become a legitimate activity for diplomats and others (Barnet 1981; Wallis 1982).

Avoiding nuclear war. In an effort to deescalate the arms race and prevent an accidental or miscalculated nuclear war from starting, peacemakers have urged a number of proposals on U.S. and Soviet negotiators (Union of Concerned Scientists 1982). These include the following:

1. A bilateral (two-party) agreement, along the lines of SALT I and SALT II, that would set a lower limit on nuclear weapons holdings by the superpowers and ban the development of new and more dangerous weapons in the future;

2. Various nuclear weapons "freeze" proposals that seek a mutual and verifiable halt to the testing, production, and deployment of new nuclear weapons and delivery systems by the United States and the USSR;

3. A no-first-strike pledge by the United States, which would help defuse the possibility of nuclear war beginning in Europe in response to a conventional Soviet attack there;

4. A comprehensive nuclear test ban treaty that would effectively end the production of new nuclear weapons and bring the underground testing of such weapons to a close;

5. Various "deep-cut" proposals that would slash the number of nuclear weapons possessed by the United States and Russia by 50 percent or more, on the general understanding that both nations currently have nuclear weapons overkill capacities (Fallows 1982); and

6. A number of unilateral (one-party) nuclear weapons disarmament proposals that would permit either of the superpowers, acting alone and in advance of agreement with the other, to begin dismantling its nuclear weapons stockpiles (Wright 1965). For instance, either the United States or the Soviet Union could decide not to produce its weekly quota of nuclear weapons and challenge the other to do the same.

Additional peace proposals have been offered to reduce the chances of nuclear war beginning through the actions of other actual or potential nuclear weapons states, or by terrorist groups that might come into possession of the Bomb. By controlling the spread of fissionable (explosive) materials produced in the nuclear fuel cycle (see chapter 15) and providing meaningful leadership in resolving the world's social problems, both the United States and the USSR might be able to curb the proliferation (spread) of nuclear weapons (Beres 1980), and give the community of nations time to build a more stable and equitable economic and political order.

Curtailing abusive power. Other short-term survival suggestions are rooted in the conviction that power and the powerful must be restrained in their actions and placed under the **rule of law** (the conduct of politics according to established, known procedures, mindful of individual liberties).

At the institutional level, peace activists have attempted to extend traditional principles of **constitutionalism** (the limited, responsible use of political power) to regulate national and international power elites, and to find ways of reducing the total amount of destructive force available to their leaders.

Toward these ends, they have worked to place the war-making power of modern chief executives under legislative control; to reassert congressional and parliamentary authority over military budgets and arms sales; and to actively support moves to curtail the destructive power of public and private corporations (artificial persons) by converting their operations from military to civilian uses (Melman 1970, 1974).

"Think globally; act locally," has become the slogan of a generation of **devolutionists** (believers that "bigness is bad" and that "small is beautiful") who are committed to community and neighborhood building (Morris and Hess 1975) and participatory democracy (Stavrianos 1976).

Many peacemakers have given up on the personal pursuit of power and have begun to discover ways of persuading others that politics need not be a place of domination and constant struggle. By celebrating life publicly, a new generation of political actors—representative among them the Green Party in West Germany—have begun to make political activity less threatening and to re-create the spirit of "happy versatility" and amateurism on which democratic practices have historically been based (Thucydides 1934).

Peace education and democracy. Thus, a growing understanding has recently emerged that the prospects of ending war, domination, and abuses of power depend on our ability to link the lessons of peace to the lessons of popular government.

Based on the assumption that more wisdom exists in the minds of the informed many than of any few (Dewey 1966), and that no modern-day elite has either the skill or the ability to command survival, peace workers throughout the world have begun to humanize the educational processes in many societies (Ernest 1982, 2–12; Haavelsrud 1974; Henderson 1973). Their activities have ranged from offering peace studies courses in schoolrooms (Wehr and Washburn 1976) to teaching their children gentleness and nonviolence in their everyday life encounters (Benson 1981; Rabin 1982). Curricula on peace education now often include instruction on the causes and consequences of war and social conflict, analyses of the global political economy, brainstorming about possible and desirable alternatives to violence, and training in nonviolent action (Reid and Yanarella 1976).

Among the more tangible outcomes of such programs have been the development of nonnuclear defense strategies in a number of nations (American Friends Service Committee 1967; Boserup 1975; Roberts 1968) and the building of an identifiable worldwide peace network (*Peace Diary* Annual), which continues to generate the basic aesthetic symbols and humanistic expressions essential in the making of a nonviolent culture.

SUMMARY

War, domination, and abuses of political power may be understood from several sociological perspectives. Sometimes they express a society's attempt to meet the challenge of changing environmental circumstances, such as growing populations and dwindling resources. On other occasions, they result from conflicts over access to limited wealth and power. In still other situations, they constitute breakdowns in the ability of individuals and groups to communicate meaningfully.

Whatever perspective one adopts, we seem to have evolved to a point where increasingly destructive force has been placed in the hands of increasingly less sociable people. Accordingly, the ability to avoid disaster may not lie in centralizing power further as some propose (Heilbroner 1980). Life-sustaining changes may well depend on rekindling a neglected human interest among us (Sakharov 1968) and empowering people everywhere to act on behalf of their posterity

(Keyes n.d.) Certainly this is what Martin Luther King, Jr., had in mind when he said:

I refuse to accept the cynical notion that nation after nation must spiral down a militaristic stairway into the hell of nuclear destruction. I believe that unarmed truth and unconditional love will have the final word in reality. (*New York Times.* December 11, 1964:33).

STUDY QUESTIONS

1. In your opinion, what factors account for the destructiveness of social conflict in the modern world?

2. List as many social costs of war, domination, and abusive power as you can, and then indicate how the negative consequences of each might be lessened through appropriate political action.

3. In addition to the specific recommendations made in this chapter for reducing the chances of nuclear war, what other steps might be taken to eliminate the prospect of extinction?

4. What are the major roadblocks that stand in the way of building a peaceful world?

5. Can democracy withstand the security demands of the nuclear age? Explain your reasoning.

6. What major changes in personal lifestyle and social organization might a nonviolent society require?

REFERENCES

Adams, G. 1981. *The politics of defense contracting: The iron triangle.* New York: Council on Economic Priorities

Adams, R., and S. Cullen. 1981. *The final epidemic: Physicians and scientists on nuclear war.* Chicago: Univ. of Chicago Press.

Adorno, T., E. Frenkel-Brunswik; D. J. Levinson, and R. N. Sanford. 1950. *The authoritarian personality.* New York: Harper & Row.

Aldridge, R. C. 1979. *The counterforce syndrome: A guide to U.S. nuclear weapons and strategic doctrine.* Washington, D.C.: Institute for Policy Studies.

American Broadcasting Company. 1983. *The Day After* (November 20).

American Friends Service Committee. 1967. *In place of war: An inquiry into nonviolent national defense.* New York: Grossman.

Amnesty International. 1975. *The Amnesty International report on torture.* New York: Noonday.

Arendt, H. 1953. Ideology and terror: A novel form of government. In *The origin of totalitarianism.* New York: Harcourt, Brace.

———. 1962. *On revolution.* New York: Viking.

———. 1965. *Eichmann in Jerusalem: A report on the banality of evil.* New York: Viking.

Arizona Republic. 29 March 1983.

Aron, R. 1955. *The century of total war.* Boston: Beacon.

Bailyn, B. 1967. *The ideological origins of the American Revolution.* Cambridge: Harvard Univ. Press.

Barnet, R. J. 1981. *Real security: Restoring American power in a dangerous decade.* New York: Simon & Schuster.

Barnet, R., and R. E. Muller. 1974. *Global reach: The power of the multinational corporations.* New York: Simon & Schuster.

Barrett, W. 1962. *Irrational man: A study in existential philosophy.* New York: Doubleday.

———. 1979. *The illusion of technique: A search for meaning in a technological civilization.* Garden City, N.Y.: Anchor Press, Doubleday.

Beer, F. A. 1981. *Peace against war.* San Francisco: W. H. Freeman.

Benson, B. 1981. *The peace book.* London: Jonathan Cape.

Beres, L. R. 1980. *Apocalypse: Nuclear catastrophe in world politics.* Chicago: Univ. of Chicago Press.

Bergmann, G. 1951. Ideology. *Ethics* LXI (April).

Bettelheim, B. 1960. *The informed heart: Autonomy in a mass society.* New York: Free Press.

Bishops' Statement. 1983. The challenge of peace: God's promise and our response. NC Documentary Service, National Catholic News Service, Washington, D.C.

Bondurant, J. V. 1965. *Conquest of violence: The Gandhian philosophy of conflict.* Berkeley: Univ. of California Press.

Boserup, A. and A. Mack 1975. *War without violence: nonviolence in national defense.* New York: Schocken Books.

Boulding, K. 1956. *The image.* Ann Arbor, Mich.: Univ. of Michigan Press.

Bramson, L. and G. Goethals, eds. 1964. *War: Contributions from psychology, sociology, and anthropology.* New York: Basic Books.

Brandt, W., and A. Sampson, eds. 1980. *North/south: A program for survival.* Cambridge: MIT Press.

Bronowski, J. 1974. *The ascent of man.* Boston: Little, Brown.

Burke, E. 1955. *Reflections on the revolution in France.* Indianapolis: Bobbs-Merrill.

Burnham, D. 1983. *The rise of the computer state.* New York: Random House.

Burnham, J. 1960. *The managerial revolution.* Bloomington, Ind.: Indiana Univ. Press.

Camus, A. 1954. *The rebel.* New York: Knopf.

Carey, M. J. 1982. Psychological fallout. *Bulletin of the atomic scientists.* 38, (January): 20–24.

Center for Defense Information. 1979a. *A world at war.* Washington, D.C.: Center for Defense Information.

———. 1979b. *Defense information fact sheet.* Vol. XII (1).

———. 1983. *Defense information fact sheet.* Vol. VIII (10).

Chomsky, N. 1982. Commencement speech. Fordham University, 30 May.

Cobb, J. B., Jr. 1969. *God and the world.* Philadelphia: Westminster.

Cohen, E. A. 1953. *Human behavior in the concentration camp.* New York: Grosset & Dunlap.

Committee for the Compilation of Materials on Damage Caused by the Atomic Bombs in Hiroshima and Nagasaki. 1981. *Hiroshima and Nagasaki: The physical, medical, and social effects of the atomic bombings,* trans. E. Ishikawa and D. L. Swain. New York: Basic.

Concord Films Council. n.d. *Films for peace.* Catalogue. Ipswich, Suffolk, U.K.: Concord Films Council.

Connerton, P. 1978. *Critical sociology.* New York: Penguin.

Dahl, R. 1956. *A preface to democratic theory.* Chicago: Univ. of Chicago Press.

de la Boetie, E. 1975. *The politics of obedience: The discourse of voluntary servitude.* Montreal: Black Rose.

Dewey, J. 1966. *Democracy and education.* New York: Free Press.

Dolbeare, K., and P. Dolbeare. 1976. *American ideologies: The complex political beliefs of the 1970s.* Boston: Houghton Mifflin.

Donner, F. J. 1981. *The age of surveillance: The aims and methods of America's political intelligence system.* New York: Vintage.

Edelman, M., 1964. *The symbolic uses of politics.* Urbana: Univ. of Illinois Press.

Ellsberg, D. 1981. Introduction to *Protest and survive,* by E. P. Thompson and D. Smith. New York: Monthly Review.

Ellul, J. 1967. *The technological society.* New York: Random House.

Erikson, E. H. 1969. *Gandhi's truth: On the origins of militant nonviolence.* New York: W. W. Norton.

Ernest J. 1982. A call to the conscience of the university community. *Center Magazine* (February).

Falk, R. 1975. *A study of future worlds.* New York: Free Press.

———. 1982. Nuclear weapons and democracy. *Praxis International* 2 (1) (April).

Falk, R. A., G. Kolko, and R. J. Lifton. 1971. *Crimes of war*. New York: Random House.

Fallows, J. 1982. *National defense*. New York: Vintage.

Ferguson, M. 1980. *The aquarian conspiracy: Personal and social transformation in the 1980s*. Los Angeles: J. P. Tarcher.

Fetter, S., and K. Tsipis. 1981. Catastrophic releases of radioactivity. *Scientific American* 244 (4) (April).

Foucault, M. 1980. *Power/knowledge: Selected interviews and other writings*. New York: Pantheon.

Frank, A. 1958. *Diary of Anne Frank*. New York: Modern Library.

Frank, J. 1982. *Sanity and survival in the nuclear age: The psychological aspects of war and peace*. New York: Random House.

Freud, S. 1958. *Civilization and its discontents*. Garden City, N.Y.: Anchor/Doubleday.

Friedrich, C. J., and Z. Brzezinski. 1956. *Totalitarian dictatorship and autocracy*. Cambridge: Harvard Univ. Press.

Fritsch, A. J., ed. 1980. *Environmental ethics: Choices for concerned citizens*. New York: Anchor/Doubleday.

Galbraith, J. 1971. *The new industrial state*. Boston: Houghton Mifflin.

———. 1980. *American capitalism*. Armonk, N.Y.: M. E. Sharpe.

Galtung, J. 1964. A structural theory of aggression. *Journal of Peace Research* 1 (2): 95–119.

Geiger, H. J. 1981. Taped lecture, Physicians for Social Responsibility. Albuquerque, New Mexico.

Glasstone, S., and P. J. Dolan. 1977. *The effects of nuclear weapons*. Washington, D.C.: U.S. Department of Defense and the Energy Research and Development Administration.

Graham, H. D., and T. R. Gurr. 1969. *Violence in America: Historical and comparative perspectives*. A report to the National Commission on the Causes and Prevention of Violence. New York: Bantam Books.

Green, M., and R. Massie, Jr., eds. 1980. *The big business reader: Essays on corporations in America*. New York: Pilgrim.

Greenstein, F. I. 1967. *Children and politics*. New Haven, Conn.: Yale Univ. Press.

Gregg, R. B. 1966. *The power of nonviolence*. New York: Schocken.

Grodzins, M., and E. Rabinowitch, eds. 1963. *The atomic age: Forty-five scientists and scholars speak on national and world affairs*. New York: Basic.

Haavelsrud, M., ed. 1974. *Education for Peace: Reflection and Action*. United Kingdom: University of Keele.

Habermas, J. 1979. *Communication and the evolution of society*. Boston: Beacon.

Hacker, A., ed. 1965. *The corporation take-over*. New York: Doubleday.

Haksar, V. 1979. *Equality, liberty, and perfectionism*. Oxford: Oxford Univ. Press.

Hamilton, A., J. Madison, and J. Jay. 1961. *The federalist*, ed. J. E. Cooke. Cleveland: World

Harris, M. 1978. *Cows, pigs, wars and witches: The riddles of culture*. New York: Vintage.

Heilbroner, R. L. 1980. *An inquiry into the human prospect*. New York: W. W. Norton.

Henderson, G., ed. 1973. *Education for peace: Focus on mankind*. Washington, D.C. Association for Supervision and Curriculum Development.

Hersey, J. 1946. *Hiroshima*. New York: Knopf.

Hilgartner, S., and R. C. Bell. 1982. *Nukespeak: The selling of nuclear technology in America*. San Francisco: Sierra Club.

Hobbes, T. 1957. *Leviathan*. Oxford: Basic Blackwell.

Hoffer, E. 1966. *The true believer*. New York: Harper & Row.

Humphrey, N. 1981. Four minutes to midnight. *Listener* (29 October).

Jacobs, J. 1961. *The death and life of the great American cities*. New York: Random House.

Jacobson, G. C. 1980. *Money in congressional elections*. New Haven, Conn.: Yale Univ. Press.

Japan Broadcasting. 1977. *Unforgettable fire*. New York: Pantheon.

Jezer, M. 1982. *The Dark Ages: Life in the United States 1945–1960*. Boston: South End.

Kariel, H. S. 1966. *The promise of politics*. Englewood Cliffs, N.J.: Prentice-Hall.

———. 1972. *Saving appearances: The reestablishment of political science*. Boston: Duxbury.

———. 1977. *Beyond liberalism, where relations grow*. New York: Harper & Row.

Katz, A. 1982. *Life after nuclear war: The economic and social impact of a nuclear attack on the U.S.* Cambridge, Mass.: Ballinger.

Keniston, K. 1968. *Young radicals: notes on committed youth*. New York: Harcourt, Brace.

Kennan, G. 1983. *Nuclear delusions: Soviet-American relations in the atomic age*. New York: Pantheon.

Keyes, K., Jr. n.d. *The hundredth monkey*. St. Mary, Ky.: Vision.

Kidron, M., and D. Smith. 1983. *The war atlas: armed conflict, armed peace*. New York: Simon and Schuster.

King. M. L., Jr. 1964. Letter from Birmingham Jail. In *Why we can't wait* New York: New American Library.

———. 1964. Nobel peace prize address. *The New York Times*, December 11, p. 33.

Klare, M. 1981. *Beyond the Vietnam Syndrome: U.S. Interventions in the 1980's*. Washington, D.C.: Institute for Policy Studies.

Klare, M. T., and C. Arnson. 1981. *Supplying repression*. Washington, D.C.: Institute for Policy Studies.

Kubler-Ross, E. 1974. *On death and dying*. New York: Macmillan.

Lakoff, R. 1975. *Language and women's place*. New York: Harper & Row.

Langer, S. 1957. *Philosophy in a new key.* Cambridge: Harvard Univ. Press.

Lasswell, H. 1958. *Politics: Who gets what, when and how.* New York: Meridian.

———. 1976. *Power and Personality.* Westport, Conn.: Greenwood.

Leech, N. E., C. T. Oliver, and J. M. Sweeney. 1973. *The International Legal System.* Mineola, N.Y.: Foundation.

Lenski, G. and J. Lenski. 1982. *Human societies: An introduction to macrosociology.* 4th ed. New York: McGraw-Hill.

Lifton, R. J. 1968. *Death in life: Survivors of Hiroshima.* New York: Random House.

Lifton, R. J., and R. Falk. 1982. *Indefensible weapons: The political and psychological case against nuclearism.* New York: Basic.

Lipset, S. M. 1981. *Political man.* Baltimore: Johns Hopkins.

Livingston, J. C. and R. G Thompson. 1966. *The consent of the governed.* New York: Macmillan.

Locke, J. 1952. *The second treatise of government.* New York: Liberal Arts.

Lorenz, K. 1970. *On aggression.* London: Methuen.

Lynd, S. 1966. *Nonviolence in America: A documentary history.* Indianapolis: Bobbs-Merrill.

Macpherson, C. B. 1966. *The real world of democracy.* New York: Oxford Univ. Press.

MacRae, D. G. 1961. *Ideology and society.* London: Heinemann.

Madison, J., 1961. *The federalist,* vol. 10. ed. J. E. Cooke. Cleveland: World.

Mander, J. 1978. *Four reasons for the abolition of television.* New York: Morrow.

Marcuse, H. 1964. *One-dimensional man: Studies in the ideology of advanced industrial societies.* Boston: Beacon.

Marx, K., and F. Engels. 1934. *The German ideology.* New York: International.

Maslow, A. H. 1968. *Toward a psychology of being.* New York: Van Nostrand.

———. 1973. *The farther reaches of human nature.* Middlesex, England: Penguin.

Mayer, P., 1966. *The pacifist conscience.* Chicago: Henry Regnery.

McGinnis, J. 1970. *The selling of the president, 1968.* New York: Pocket.

Mead, G. H. 1967. *Mind, self, and society.* Chicago: Univ. of Chicago Press.

Megill, K. A. 1970. *The new democratic theory.* New York: Free Press.

Melman, S., ed. 1970. *Conversion of industry from a military to civilian economy.* New York: Praeger.

———. 1974. *The permanent war economy: American capitalism in decline.* New York: Simon & Schuster.

Michels, R. 1968. *Political parties.* New York: Free Press.

Mill, J. S. 1956. *On liberty.* Indianapolis: Bobbs-Merrill.

Miller, L., and K. Swift. 1977. *Words and women.* Garden City, N.Y.: Doubleday.

Mills, C. W. 1959. *The power elite.* New York: Oxford Univ. Press.

———. 1960. *The causes of World War Three.* New York: Ballantine.

MIT Conference. 1982. *The deadly connection: Nuclear war & U.S. intervention.* American Friends Service Committee (4–5 December).

Montagu, M. F. A. 1966. *On being human.* New York: Hawthorn.

———. 1968. *Man and aggression.* New York: Oxford University.

———. 1976. *The nature of human aggression.* New York: Oxford University.

Morganthau, H. J. 1974. *Politics among nations: The struggle for power and peace.* New York: Knopf.

Morris, D., and K. Hess. 1975. *Neighborhood power: Returning political and economic power to community life.* Boston: Beacon.

Mountbatten, L. 1979. "Strasbourg speech," Campaign for Nuclear Disarmament, London.

Mueller, C. 1975. *The politics of communication: A study in the political sociology of language, socialization, and legitimation.* New York: Oxford University Press.

Myrdal, A. 1982. *The game of disarmament: how the United States and Russia run the arms race.* New York: Pantheon.

Nance, J. 1975. *The gentle Tasaday: A Stone Age people in the Philippine forest.* New York: Harcourt, Brace.

Nathan, O. and H. Norden, eds. 1981. *Einstein on peace.* New York: Avenel.

Navasky, V. S. 1977. *Kennedy justice.* New York: Atheneum.

Nietzsche, F. 1974. *Geneology of morals and peoples and countries.* New York: Gordon.

Ortega y Gasset, J. 1932. *The revolt of the masses.* New York: W. W. Norton.

Orwell, G. 1971. *1984.* New York: National American Library.

Osada, Dr. A. 1982. *Children of hiroshima.* New York: Harper & Row.

Pacific War Research Society. 1981. *The day man lost: Hiroshima, 6 August 1945.* Tokyo: Kodansha International.

Pauling, L. 1962. *No more war!* New York: Dodd, Mead.

Peace diary. Annual. London: Houseman's.

Physicians for Social Responsibility. 1980. *The last epidemic: The medical consequences of nuclear weapons and nuclear war.* Videotape. Watertown, Mass.

Pierre, A. J. 1982. *The global politics of arms sales.* Princeton, N.J.: Princeton Univ. Press.

Prosterman, R. L. 1972. *Surviving to 3000: An introduction to the study of lethal conflict.* Belmont, Calif.: Duxbury.

Rabin, J. 1982. The children's campaign. *Commonweal* (February).

Rawls, J. 1971. *A theory of justice.* Cambridge: Harvard Univ. Press.

Reader, M. 1967. The politics of avoidance: on the contours of ambiguity. *Ethics,* 77 (4) (July) 268–284.

———. 1972. Watching the revolution uncork. *Politics and Society* 2 (3) (Spring).

Reader, M., and D. J. Wolf. 1973. On being human. *Political Theory* 1 (2) (May).

Reich, C. 1970. *The greening of America.* New York: Random House.

Reid, H. G., and E. J. Yanarella. 1976. Toward a critical theory of peace research in the United States: The search for an intelligible core. *Journal of Peace Research* XIII (4).

Riesman, D. 1973. *The Lonely Crowd.* New Haven, Conn.: Yale Univ. Press.

Roberts, A., ed. 1968. *Civilian resistance as a national defense.* Baltimore: Penguin.

Rosenberg, H. L. 1980. *Atomic soldiers: American victims of nuclear experiments.* Boston: Beacon.

Rosenblatt, R. 1983. *Children of war* Garden City, N.Y.: Anchor Press/Doubleday.

Roszak, T. 1969. *The making of a counter culture: Reflections on the technocratic society and its youthful opposition.* Garden City, N.Y.: Doubleday.

Sagan, C. and P. Ehrlich. 1983. *Conference on the long-term biological consequences of nuclear war.* Washington, D.C.: The World After.

Sakharov, A. 1968. *Progress, coexistence and intellectual freedom.* New York: W. W. Norton.

Schecter, J. L., and L. P. Schecter. 1983. The war planners. *Esquire* (January).

Scheer, R. 1982. *With enough shovels: Reagan, Bush and nuclear war.* New York: Random House.

Schell, J. 1976. *The time of illusion: An historical and reflective account of the Nixon era.* New York: Vintage.

———. 1982. *The fate of the earth.* New York: Knopf.

Schroyer, T. 1973. *The critique of domination: The origins and development of critical theory.* New York: Braziller.

Schumacher, E. F. 1973. *Small is beautiful.* London: Blond & Briggs.

Schwartz, D. 1983. Totalitarian tools: Preface to a theory. Paper presented at annual meeting of Southwestern Anthropological Association, 23–26 March, San Diego.

Sharp, G. 1971. *Exploring nonviolent alternatives.* Boston: Porter Sargent.

———. 1973a. Power and struggle. Part I of *The politics of nonviolent action.* Boston: Porter Sargent.

———. 1973b. The methods of nonviolent action. Part 2 of *The politics of nonviolent action.* Boston: Porter Sargent.

———. 1973c. The dynamics of nonviolent action. Part 3 of *The politics of nonviolent action.* Boston: Porter Sargent.

———. 1980. *Making the abolition of war a realistic goal.* New York: Institute for World Order. Pamphlet.

Shklar, J. 1965. The political theory of utopia: From melancholy to nostalgia. *Daedalus* (Spring).

Sibley, M. Q., ed. 1963. *The quiet battle: Writings on the theory and practice of non-violent resistance.* Garden City, N.Y.: Anchor Books, Doubleday.

Sivard, R. L. 1972–1983. *World military and social expenditures.* Annual. Leesburg, Va.: WMSE Publications.

Sklar, H. 1980. *Trilateralism: The trilateral commission and elite planning for world management.* Boston: South End.

Solzhenitsyn, A. I. 1973. *The gulag archipelago.* New York: Harper & Row.

Somerville, J. 1976. *The crisis: A true story about how the world almost ended.* San Diego, Calif.: Published by author.

Stavrianos, L. S. 1976. *The promise of the coming dark age.* San Francisco: W. H. Freeman.

Steel, R. 1970. *Pax Americana: The cold war empire and the politics of counter-revolution.* New York: Viking.

Steiner, J. 1979. *Treblinka.* New York: New American Library.

Textor, R. B. 1972. Characteristic of primitive societies correlated with warfare. In Prosterman, R. *Surviving to 3000: an introduction to the study of lethal conflict.* Belmont, Calif.: Duxbury.

Thayer, F. C. 1973. *An end to hierarchy! An end to competition.* New York: Franklin Watts.

Thucydides. 1934. Pericles' funeral oration. In *The Peloponnesian War.* New York: Random House.

Thurow, L. C. 1981. *The zero-sum society: Distribution and the possibilities for economic change.* Middlesex, England: Penguin.

Tiger, L., and R. Fox. 1971. *The imperial animal.* New York: Holt, Rinehart & Winston.

Timerman, J. 1981. *Prisoner without a name, cell without a number.* New York: Knopf.

Tinbergen, J. 1976. *Reshaping the international order.* New York: Dutton.

Toffler, A. 1970. *Future shock.* New York: Random House.

Union of Concerned Scientists. 1981. *The threat of nuclear war.* Briefing manual. Cambridge, Mass.: Union of Concerned Scientists.

———. 1982. *Solutions for the nuclear arms race.* Briefing manual. Cambridge, Mass.: Union of Concerned Scientists.

———. 1982. *Solutions to the arms race.* Organizing manual. Cambridge, Mass.: Union of Concerned Scientists.

United Nations Association n.d. *An educational exhibit about the effects and dangers of nuclear war.* Daly City, Calif.: United Nations Association.

U.S. Congress. Office of Technology Assessment. 1979. *The effects of nuclear war.* Washington, D.C.

Van Voorst, L. B. 1983. The churches and nuclear deterrence. *Foreign Affairs* (Spring).

Vonnegut, K. 1974a. *Cat's cradle.* New York: Dell.

————. 1974b. *Slaughter-house five.* New York: Dell.

Wallis, J. ed. 1982. *Waging peace: a handbook for the struggle to abolish nuclear weapons.* San Francisco: Harper & Row.

Wehr, P., and M. Washburn. 1976. *Peace and world order systems: Teaching and research.* Beverly Hills: Sage.

Weizenbaum, J. 1982. Playing with violence. *Fellowship* (September).

Whyte, W. 1957. *The organization man.* Garden City, N.Y.: Doubleday.

Wiesel, E. 1972. *Night.* New York: Avon.

Wild, J. 1963. *Existence and the world of freedom.* Englewood Cliffs, N.J.: Prentice-Hall.

Williams, B. 1962. The idea of equality. In *Philosophy, politics and society,* ed. P. Laslett and W. G. Runciman. 2d series. Oxford: Basil Blackwell.

Wills, G. 1982. Critical inquiry (kritik) in Clausewitz. *Critical Inquiry* 9 (2).

Wilson, E. O. 1975. *Sociobiology: The new synethesis.* Cambridge, Mass.: Belknap.

Wright, Q. 1965. *A study of war: An analysis of the causes, nature, and control of war.* Chicago: Univ. of Chicago Press.

Yergin, D. 1977. *Shattered peace: The origins of the cold war and the national security state.* Boston: Houghton Mifflin.

Zuckerman, S. 1982. *Nuclear illusion and reality.* New York: Viking.

CHAPTER 15

Energy, Civilization, and the Future

CONTENTS

TMI mothers' anxiety still above normal

By Patrick Young
Newhouse News Service

CAMBRIDGE, Mass. — Thirty months after the accident at the Three Mile Island nuclear power plant near Harrisburg, Pa., mothers who evacuated their young children continued to suffer higher-than-normal levels of severe anxiety and depression, according to a new study.

But the study cannot tell to what extent the mental problems were related to the March 1979 accident or to other factors such as the current economic recession, according to psychologist Herbert C. Schulberg of the University of Pittsburgh, one of three researchers directing the continuing study.

While the level of anxiety and depression had declined slightly among TMI-area mothers from that of a year after the accident, episodes of these mental problems more than doubled in a comparison group of women living around the Shippingport and Beaver Valley nuclear plants near Pittsburgh.

Among TMI-area mothers interviewed 30 months after the nuclear reactor accident, 12.4 percent had experienced severe anxiety or depression in the previous year, compared with 17.7 percent of the mothers living near the other two nuclear facilities.

"The rates at this time are not the matter of the TMI group going down, but the rate of depression and anxiety in the comparison group going up," Schulberg said.

He blamed that rise largely on fears generated by a sharp increase in unemployment in the Pittsburgh area.

The psychological scars left by the accident at the TMI-2 reactor—the worst ever in a U.S. nuclear power plant—have remained a major issue.

A presidential commission that investigated the accident concluded its most damaging and lasting health effect was "on the mental health of the people living in the area."

The study being conducted by Schulberg, Evelyn J. Bromet and David K. Parkinson began in late 1979 with funds from the federal government's National Institute of Mental Health.

They interviewed 311 mothers of young children who lived within 10 miles of Three Mile Island at the time of the accident nine and 12 months after the event. The number was increased to 413 during the interviews last fall, 30 months after the accident, and another round of interviews is now in progress.

Final data from the 30-month interviews were compiled Monday, and Schulberg reported the findings Thursday at a science writers' seminar sponsored by the non-profit Council for the Advancement of Science Writing.

Schulberg said the study was designed not to measure the lingering psychological effects on all area residents, but on two groups considered at high risk of suffering mental problems—mothers who evacuated and workers at TMI. Results of the 30-month worker interviews will be released later.

The women interviewed were asked a series of questions about their perceptions of TMI.

Among the TMI mothers, 50.2 percent said they thought Three Mile Island was currently dangerous; 52.7 percent said it was unsafe to live within 10 miles of a nuclear power plant; 58.8 percent said it was unsafe to live that close to TMI; 48.7 felt their family's health would be affected by living near TMI; and 42.8 percent thought the accident would cause health problems or abnormalities in future generations.

Source: Newhouse News Service 12 November 1982.

DEFINING THE PROBLEM: THE GLOBAL ECONOMIC CHALLENGE

While the details of the global energy puzzle change with some regularity, one constant remains. How and whether we can resolve the problem of generating sufficient wealth for this and future generations will decide the conditions of life on our planet for many years to come.

The problem is this: Can the projected economic needs of roughly 6 to 7 billion people be met by the year 2020 without experiencing thermonuclear war, environmental collapse, or social breakdown in the process? Stated slightly differently, can we survive into the next century without either reducing energy demands or altering the sources of energy supply on which we have come to depend since 1950? Many now realize that (1) human existence has become increasingly dependent on nonrenewable and polluting energy sources (coal, oil, and uranium) since the end of World War II, and (2) the demand for energy has increased several times faster than the population (see figure 15–1), which has climbed from roughly 2.5 billion worldwide to more than 4.5 billion today (Sivard 1979).

In general terms, we have recently

FIGURE 15–1. Energy Consumption and Population Growth in the United States from 1850 to 1978

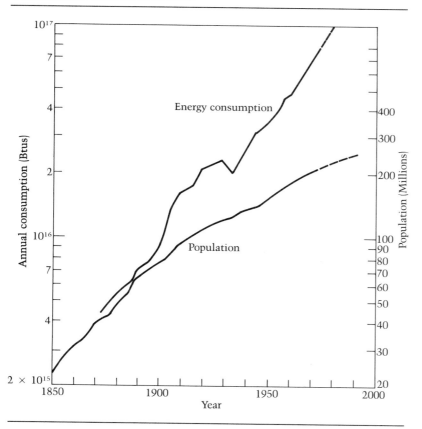

Data from Richard C. Dorf, *The energy fact book.* (New York: McGraw-Hill, 1981).

evolved to the point where we are trying to support the seemingly insatiable economic appetites of growing numbers of people by relying on progressively less sustainable energy sources. Unless substantive changes are made in our energy and economic decisions, the world is headed for a massive ecological or social collapse (or both) in the foreseeable future.

To be feared most is an outbreak of atomic war between the superpowers, unable to resolve energy and resource problems at home and seeking access to Middle East oil abroad. No less fatal would be the pollution of air, land, and water systems by nations and commercial interests intent on exploiting coal, oil, and uranium reserves to produce enough wealth to support burgeoning populations. A further worry is the probable rise in social conflict, accompanied by an increase in authoritarian governments, as disoriented people try to cope with skyrocketing energy prices, inflation, and unemployment. Should this happen, the circle of human destruction will have been completed, with increasingly frustrated citizens willing to give up their freedoms and to accept any technological insult in return for getting the energy they presently need.

The energy problem is not so much "natural" as it is social and political. We cannot and should not expect to solve all of our energy-related problems immediately if someone discovers an energy bonanza or invents energy-saving devices. No technological invention in itself can do much to halt the growth in population and energy demand, or to shift the world toward politically and economically sustainable energy sources, such as wind, water, sun, methane gas, and geothermal power. It must be understood that the energy we use and the way in which we use it is intimately tied to those social forces and values we have developed historically, and that desirable energy policies can be brought about only by reasserting control over the process of social evolution.

CONFRONTING THE PROBLEM: ENERGY, INEQUALITY, AND ENTROPY

Energy and Society

To say that one's energy choices and life prospects go hand in hand is to agree with sociologist Fred Cottrell (1955, 2) that the "energy available to man limits what he can do and influences what he will do." Energy use, in other words, sets the parameters of social action and helps differentiate one society or one social context from another (Odum and Odum 1976; White 1943, 335–56).

The connection between energy and society becomes apparent when we understand what energy is. Usually, **energy** is defined as the capacity to do work. Work, as sociologists understand, involves the ability to organize human labor, values, and resources (see chapter 6). Energy choices and social life, then, are fully intertwined, with any decision about energy use actually a decision about how people will arrange their economic, political, technological, and spiritual existence. For example, the invention of the steam engine in the nineteenth century not only gave rise to the widespread application of coal as a prime energy source but also created the structure of wealth and power associated with modern commercial societies, including the cultures of poverty encountered in the mining towns of Appalachia (Caudill 1963) and industrial England (Orwell 1958).

Energy use and social change. People have often anticipated the impact of energy changes in their lives. Traditionalists, like American Indians or present-day aborigines in Australia, have typically resisted temptations to enlarge their capacity to do work, and thus expand their command over nature and their neighbors, out of an understanding that organized labor would transform both their inner and their outer lives, usually in undesirable ways. Crazy Horse, an Oglala Sioux, expressed the view of hunting and gathering people everywhere when he told his Anglo-American conquerors:

You tell us to work for a living, but the Great Spirit did not make us to work, but to live by hunting. You white men can work if you want to. We do not interfere with you, and again you say, why do you not become civilized? We do not want your civilization! We would live as our fathers did and their fathers before them. (McLuhan 1972)

The ancient Greeks put the case similarly in their stories of how Prometheus' gift of fire so altered the human estate as to rival and anger the gods. Even contemporary people have generated insights into how they must enter a **Faustian bargain** (sell their souls to the devil) to assure themselves a limitless supply of nuclear energy (Weinberg 1979).

Many people in most societies grasp almost intuitively that any substantive change either in the source or in their access to, or use of, energy will usually be accompanied by changes in the pace, tempo, and material conditions of their daily lives. This change will also constitute a challenge to ruling elites and established belief systems by transforming what they and future generations will be able to do.

Should a new energy gate be opened or closed too abruptly, some realize that their

Much of civilization's history may be told in energy terms, with gains in humanity's ability to generate wealth frequently offset by its decision to exploit nature and groups of people to get the job done. A typical urban setting is likely to experience private opulence and declining quality of public life as a result.

personal lives may fall into disarray and that their societies may move toward disequilibrium—what many fear is happening today. Indeed, one useful way of thinking about social change and societal conflict is to consider both the outcome of significant expansion and contraction in the total amount of work available to a society (Rifkin 1980). This situation took place in post–World War II America with the introduction and, more recently, the contraction of cheap and abundant supplies of petroleum (Jezer 1982, 67–70 and pass.)—a finite and nonreplenishable energy resource. What oil made possible—the automobile, modern suburbs, shopping centers, and high spatial mobility—its sudden constraint now threatens to take away.

Accordingly, the most difficult problems in any energy consideration are usually human rather than technological—precisely because of the hidden societal dimensions behind them (Reader 1977). With every change in the energy source, we worry about the sort of lives we can reasonably expect to live as we move from one energy context to the next. What interests people now is which energy sources they can and should choose if they wish to retain or secure their lives, liberties, and happiness (see table 15–1).

Energy converters.   Work is accomplished using tools or techniques that convert less useful forms of energy into more useful forms. **Photosynthesis** is the technique plants use to convert the direct rays of the sun into natural sugar and oxygen. Amino acids and enzymes are the transformers that animals (including humans) rely on to warm their bodies and set themselves in motion. Unlike most other animals, however, we have invented a host of additional processes and techniques to increase our capacity to work. We have tamed animals, learned to turn wood into heat, water and wind into motion, coal into steam, and crude oil into the refined products that propel cars and planes. More recently, we have split the atom to produce large quantities of heat, radioactivity and electricity.

All human-produced energy converters have one thing in common. To exist, each requires varying degrees of social discipline, sometimes called **civilization** (technological decision making and hierarchical social organization) (MacIver 1931, 1965). Minimally, people must exercise a certain amount of social discipline to pick an apple from a tree and convert it into usable calories (Rousseau 1964). More frequently, we have had to organize each other to grow crops, build windmills, sail ships, drive steam and internal combustion engines, and power atomic reactors.

The properties of this work-amplifying tool—civilization—have become so commonplace that they pass unnoticed. The properties include hierarchy, centralized power and authority, division of labor, breakup of the human community into socioeconomic classes, mechanized production, wage and sometimes slave labor, and the enlargement of trade, communications, and value transactions beyond local communities (Mumford 1967, 186). Indeed, that civilization was *the* tool we invented and continue to use to enlarge our capacity to work is now evident. In its evolution we have (1) created the extremes of wealth and poverty within and between societies and (2) augmented those profoundly humanizing **cultural activities** (value-making) such as language, ritual, the arts, and "lived" knowledge of the world around us (Hall 1976).

Energy choices and social entropy.   While it has increased our productive capacities, civilization has become increasingly costly to operate with respect to energy, and may have become a major source of many of the environmental and economic difficulties we now experience. An instrument of programmed inequality and violence from its inception (Diamond 1982; Mumford 1967), only recently has civilization begun to consume more physical and human energy than is available to support it (Bohannan 1971).

Changes in the size, complexity, and reach of social organization have been reflected in both growing energy use (Adams 1981, 603–24) and physical and social pollution all along the civilizational line (Rifkin 1980). Seemingly, the chief beneficiary of each increase in productive capacity, power, technology, and communications has been **artificial or corporate persons** (institutions) rather than flesh and blood ones (Reader 1971, 337–62). Technical work, bureaucratic organization, abstract and rationalistic thinking, and a growing belief that the "system is the solution" have made the lives of individuals seem superfluous to the workings of what humanist Lewis Mumford (1967) calls the Megamachine. Thus, the tool that was supposed to liberate us has diminished us instead. For this reason, we may have to either transcend the inequalities civilization has created as we attempt to solve our energy and economic problems, or risk perishing (Bohannan 1971).

To understand why and how this situation has occurred, two points about energy and its uses must be appreciated. First, while we have often extracted more work out of an energy source than we have put into it, we have not been able to produce large surpluses in energy (Cook 1976) without usually causing some environmental damage or social dislocation (or both) in the process. This effect is reflected in the consumption of part of the earth's finite stock of limited resources or in the need for disciplined behavior, or usually both. Second, each time we convert *nonrenewable* (depletable) energy from one form into another, we "lose" part of that original stock for useful work in the future (Davis 1979, 7–8). The less efficiently we work, and the more energy conversions we make, the more effort we may have to expend the next time around to get the same job done (Georgescu-Roegen 1977; Rifkin 1980).

On the basis of this insight, some social scientists are coming to believe that in the course of building civilization, we may have speeded up the **law of entropy** (the second law of thermodynamics). This law describes the tendency of any closed energy system to decay toward "disorder, increased probability and loss of information" (Commoner 1976, 24). Some think the more complex or energy intensive (or both) the level of human-imposed organization, the greater both the physical and the social entropy—one measured in overpopulation and environmental pollution; the other measured in a declining quality of life, loss of spontaneity, and growing violence. In energy and economic terms, history is as much the story of poverty as progress, with material gains frequently offset by the impoverishment of human relationships and habitats.

This thesis is borne out in figure 15–2, which reflects the growth of cities as it relates to more air pollution and higher death rates from cancer and emphysema. Still other pollutants, such as lead contained in some gasoline products, could be affecting human intelligence, as recent studies indicate.

In boldest terms, the expansion of the human capacity to work has set in motion a seemingly never-ending spiral of exponential growth in population and affluence, inequality and poverty. Each increase in material wealth has eventually necessitated the introduction of new and progressively more energy-intensive and damaging technologies to meet the human survival needs of food, shelter, clothing, and information (Barney 1977; Brown 1978).

As the authors of the landmark *The Limits to Growth* study (Meadows 1972) wrote:

If present growth trends in world population, industrialization, pollution, food production, and resource depletion continue unchanged, the limits to growth on this planet will be reached sometime within the next 100 years. The most probable result will be the rather sudden and uncontrollable decline in both population and industrial capacity.

Similar warnings are contained in estimates about the world's affordable, and conse-

TABLE 15–1. An Inventory of Energy Sources

ENERGY SOURCES	POTENTIAL FOR FUTURE U.S. SUPPLY[1]	STATUS OF TECHNOLOGY[2]	ECONOMICS	ENVIRONMENTAL AND HEALTH IMPACTS
Nonrenewable Oil	8–35 yrs.[3]	Highly developed. Emphasis on improving inground resource recovery and offshore exploration and drilling.	High capital costs, especially for new technologies.	Offshore: oil spills, blowouts. Refineries: minimal air and water pollution, industrialization. Transportation by tanker and pipeline damaging to environment.
Oil Shale	Double the proved[3] reserves of domestic petroleum	Pilot model studies, both mining and in situ, completed.	Current technology not cost effective unless price of oil exceeds $21 a barrel.	Disposal of large quantities of spent shale; water scarcity; air pollution; possible carcinogenic effects on workers.
Coal	600 years[3]	Highly developed. Need for improved pollution control technologies.	High pollution control costs.	Soil erosion and stream pollution from stripmining; acid mine drainage; hazards to miners; air pollution (SO_x, CO_2 and possible "greenhouse effect").
Coal Gasification	—	Pilot stage.	High capital costs. Not cost effective unless price of oil exceeds $15–$20 a barrel.	Except for SO_x and metals, impacts of above are magnified, possible carcinogenic effects on workers.
Natural Gas	13–30 yrs.[3]	Highly developed.	Low cost due to controlled prices; minimal pollution.	Pipelines use large land area. Liquified Natural Gas (LNG) transport and storage may be hazardous.
Uranium Fission (LWRS)	30 yrs.[3]	Developed.	Operating costs competitive with fossil fuel plants; construction costs higher; future costs of uranium uncertain.	Storage of radioactive wastes; possibility of reactor accidents; thermal pollution.

Plutonium (Breeder (LMFBR)	Very large	Experimental.	Costs of uranium reprocessing, storage, decommissioning plant sites unknown.	Same as above; possible explosion; nuclear proliferation, sabotage.
Fusion	Very large	Experimental.	Low cost fuel; high cost equipment.	Possible leakage of tritium; radioactivity produced in reactor materials but less radioactive than LWR or LMFBR fuels.
Renewable				
Hydroelectric	Small	Highly developed.	Most potential sites already developed; high construction costs.	Damming affects land use patterns, fish and wildlife habitat, availability of water.
Geothermal	Small	Developed for dry steam; pilot stage for wet steam and dry rock reservoirs.	Capital and operating costs competitive with fossil fuel plants.	Land subsidence, minimal air and water pollution.
Wind	Small	Storage technology uncertain.	Capital costs uncertain.	Land use, esthetics; possible weather modifications.
Solar Heating/Cooling (H/C)	Large, but limited, by market potential	Commercially feasible.	Cost competitive with electric h/c systems; installation costs decreasing; indirect savings in pollution.	Aesthetics; possible weather modifications.
Solar Electric	Very large	Experimental.	Not cost competitive	Same as above.
Bioconversion	Small	Highly developed for small-scale timbering, organic waste burning.	Large-scale systems not yet demonstrated as cost competitive.	Aesthetics, impacts on land and water use, air pollution.
Ocean Thermal Energy Conversion (OTEC)	Large	Experimental.	High capital costs.	Aesthetics, possible climatic changes, navigation hazards.

1. *It is difficult to characterize the potential for nonrenewable sources in the same way as for renewable sources. Estimates for nonrenewable resources are based on proven reserves; estimates for renewable resources as well as the plutonium breeder and fusion are characterized as small or large potential in comparison with our total energy use.*

2. *The more experimental the technology, the less is known of its potential and its impacts.*

3. *Based on proven reserves at current rates of consumption.*

Source: "The Politics of Energy," The National Voter, League of Women Voters, Washington, D.C. Vol. 27, (2) (Summer, 1977): 4-5.

quently available, reserves of nonrenewable energy resources if current consumption patterns among the affluent continue to grow at projected rates (Barney 1980). The world may have to pay an unacceptable environmental and economic price for petroleum and coal by the year 2020 and in about 100 years, respectively, while probably experiencing intolerable social costs well before then (Meadows et. al. 1972).

What most studies do not mention is that any rapid, massive decline in either population or productive capacity will not likely take place with a whimper but with a thermonuclear bang. Thus, while enough time to shift away from increasingly polluting and nonsustainable energy sources still exists, (Lovins 1977a, 1977b), each year of delay makes the transition more difficult by increasing the amount of social and physical entropy that must be overcome to survive. As hope and meaningful life wane and as energy-related problems build, we may increasingly become less able to lavish the care and commitment on this planet that UN Ambassador Adlai Stevenson thought so

essential to its survival. This theme was in Stevenson's last speech before the United Nations.

Energy, Work, and Civilization

A prime reason why civilization has been such a disappointing energy converter can be found in the evolution of the work process itself (see chapter 6). Often, creative, humanizing activity has been systematically converted into routinized and meaningless labor to increase economic profits. This can be seen by (1) examining the growth of civilization in energy terms and (2) historically tracing the emergence of energy elites (see table 15–2).

Work and its discontents.   What usually passes for the history of work—and consequently the history of civilization—begins and in many respects is continued in the control of the energy source most basic to human existence: food. (Lappé and Collins 1979). As one recent environmental study (Barney 1977, 11) notes, "People need food;

FIGURE 15–2.   Bigger Cities, More Air Pollution, More Deaths

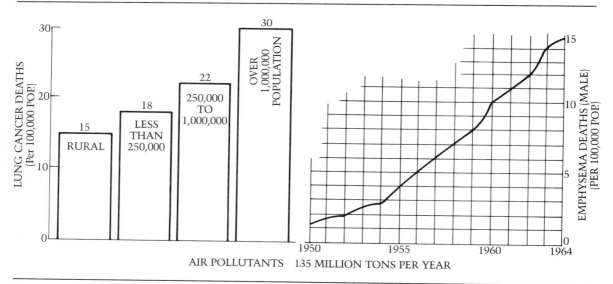

Data from Robert Theobald, *Habit and habitat* (Englewood Cliffs, N.J.: Prentice-Hall, 1972), p. 110.

raising food requires energy; energy production utilizes materials from the earth's crust; the extraction of these materials demands energy, and all of these activities depend upon the labor and ingenuity of people, who need food."

For the first nine-tenths of human history, people existed as gatherers and hunters either by eating wild berries, seeds, fruits, and tubers, or by hunting and fishing, or a combination of these activities (Cook 1976). For prehistoric people living in situations ranging from subsistence to relative natural abundance, organized work was intermittent, requiring little permanent social control or domination (see chapter 14). Many humanists and social scientists agree that

life among many prehistoric people was nomadic; that accumulations of wealth (property) were minimal, limited to what each person could carry; and that war, hierarchy, and interpersonal violence were either absent or ritualized (Harris 1979). In contrast, cultural or humanizing (work and play) activities were plentiful (Huizinga 1955), as the early and rich elaboration of speech and the arts of personal adornment, myths, rituals, and an intimate knowledge of nature suggest. Rather than living in a Hobbesian state of incessant conflict (Hobbes 1957), many anthropologists now believe that the everyday life of prehistoric people was egalitarian and cooperative enough to make the evolution of culture possible.

Fossil fuel production has taken an enormous toll on the physical environment. The use of coal has been responsible for acid rain and water pollution, as well as stripmining; and the use of oil as the energy base for modern civilization has led to photochemical smog and serious oil spills globally.

TABLE 15–2. The History of Energy Use

TIME	SOCIAL ORGANIZATION	ENERGY SOURCE	ENERGY ELITE	MAINTENANCE LEVEL 2,000 KILOCALORIES/ DAY/PERSON	PER CAPITA MAINTENANCE BEYOND (i.e. times) PRIMITIVE SITUATION
1.4 million yrs ago	Primitive	Fire	None	2,000	—
100,000 yrs ago	Gathering/Hunting	Fire	None/Impermanent	5,000	2–3
5,000 B.C.	Primitive Agriculture (Civilization)	Domesticated animals; human labor	Kings, priests, traders, scribes, military	12,000	6
1400 A.D. Europe	Advanced Agriculture	Wind, water, mines, metals	Feudal/church hierarchy; merchants/traders	25,000	12.5
1870 England	Industrial	Steam-power	Coal, steel, textiles, railroads, banks	75,000	38
1970 United States	Technological	Electricity, fossil fuels, (uranium)	Oil, multinationals, government, nuclear/technochip industries	230,000	115
Global Future	? ? ?	Solar? Other?	? ? ?	?	?

Source: Based on data supplied by Earl Cook, The flow of energy in an industrial society, *Scientific American* (September 1971).

Early peoples' cumulative knowledge of nature proved critically useful when their food base was either threatened by overuse, or as changing weather patterns forced them into more settled slash-and-burn agricultural and village communities. (Davis 1979, 7–8). In these new surroundings, traditional restraints on population control were weakened (Wilkinson 1973). Children became useful as field hands and herders for newly domesticated animals (Harris 1979), and the first signs of permanent social inequality may have appeared (Habermas 1979).

Crop planting produced temporary and small food surpluses and with them the rudiments of property and domination (Diamond 1982). As anthropologist Marvin Harris (1979) suggests, violence and hierarchy were amplified as some people succeeded in intensifying production, redistributing agricultural surpluses, and using their wealth and prestige to organize trading and military expeditions.

The move toward agricultural civilization was completed when these secondary producers gained control of the flow of food needed by primary producers who, for a variety of reasons, found it too difficult to migrate from these stable agricultural systems (Harris 1979). Civilization assumed its first recognizable form in the empires of Mesopotamia, Egypt, and Meso-America. In these and later empires, the status of agricultural workers changed to a permanent peasantry (Moore 1966), and a permanent ruling class emerged by virtue of its ability to efficiently control access to energy—often in the form of water (Wittfogel 1957).

As agricultural surpluses accumulated, a familiar historical pattern began to emerge. The greater the affluence and population increase, the greater the requirements for social discipline and more energy-using and polluting technologies to keep them going. Increases in population and affluence created pressure on the land and on societies to create even greater energy surpluses, leading to still more disciplined social organization and energy inputs, causing expansion, mi-

gration, wars, and ever-greater pressures to increase productivity (Wilkinson 1973).

Where agricultural societies were dependent on irrigation to water crops (as in the Aztec, Inca, and classical empires of the Tigres, Euphrates, and Nile Rivers) the centralization and magnification of economic, political, technological, and communications systems apparently took place swiftly. Bureaucracies and a military class developed early in these societies. In agricultural systems that were dependent on rainfall (as in Western Europe), the centralization of the energy supply, and therefore of most instruments of wealth and power, was delayed until the rise of a central administrative source. This source was the modern commercial nation-state, whose prototypes appear from the fifteenth century onward (Wallerstein 1974).

The introduction of taxation and the use of money as a universal standard of exchange and common denominator of all value were helpful in enlarging work and in spreading civilization (Marx 1964a, 1964b). These developments, however, also converted free workers and craftspeople into wage laborers who were made increasingly dependent for their existence on an emerging class of profiteers, tradesmen, money lenders, and administrators (bureaucrats). Land, labor, and capital were gathered in the hands of a rising commercial class committed to the belief that (1) the common stock of nature was destined for private use, (2) short-term profit taking was defensible, and (3) personal wealth and human worth were to be measured in monetary terms. Such beliefs opened up new energy choices and revolutionized the social fabric, ushering in the industrial age of capitalism and growth economies (Marx 1964a, 1964b).

These events, however, also destabilized both the physical and the economic order. On the economic front, profits were realized by opening new markets, securing unlimited access to cheap sources of raw materials and labor, and destroying an older ethic of limits or restraint. The instruments used to accomplish these tasks were (1) combinations of missionaries and traders who "taught" indigenous people the "virtues" of both work and the unlimited accumulation of wealth, while simultaneously subjecting them to taxation and the money economy; and, more recently, (2) nation-state politicians and transnational corporations who, as managers of economic development, continue to shatter whatever remains of traditional restraints imposed on economic growth (Barnet and Muller 1974). Only after contact with industrial-technological European and American-based colonial empires did rapid growth patterns in population, expectations, and poverty begin to plague "emerging" or "developing" nations (Commoner 1972).

Similarly destructive events were experienced elsewhere along the civilization line. Power was enlarged progressively, moved from tribe to nation-state, freed of most constraints, and placed in increasingly more impersonal, bureaucratic hands (Gerth and Mills 1958). The atomic bomb completes the general trend toward turning politicians into god-kings (see chapter 14). Human communications, originally a mutually creative act, became an instrument of elite manipulation designed to enlarge societies' capacity to work (Habermas 1979). Tools, once largely handcrafted for personal use and enjoyment, today are owned by others and routinely mass produced (Schumacher 1973).

Water, wind, wood, and sailing societies of the fourteenth through sixteenth centuries intensified the drift toward hierarchy. For the most part, societies of the High Middle Ages and the mercantile civilization of Tudor England were made possible by exploiting agricultural labor from the countryside. Governments sanctioned policies of confiscating the accumulated wealth of other cultures, often by enslaving their inhabitants (Cook 1976; Cottrell 1955).

Civilization and, with it, work assumed their present forms with the triumph in the nineteenth century of growth economies that took profit at the expense of nature,

posterity, and specific classes of people. In the early phase of the coal-based Industrial Revolution, the character of work was transformed through a number of mechanical inventions, the introduction of the factory system, and the creation of an industrial working class (the proletariat), which Karl Marx (1964a, 1964b) described as being alienated from its own labor.

With the twentieth century advent of technological civilization—which depends on oil for its energy supplies—salaried, clerical, and managerial employees began to replace the blue-collar working class as the most visible economic group (Ebenstein 1973). Work was routinized further in bureaucratic situations, and the now-familiar politics of mass society emerged, as discussed in chapter 14.

In the long, historical view of the evolution of the work process, consensus seems to be emerging on one essential point: Throughout the course of history, human activity has been extremely conflict-ridden despite (and perhaps because of) increases in human wealth. For Lewis Mumford (1967), technical work has replaced cultural work as the prime human activity. For Karl Marx (1964a, 1964b), alienated labor has replaced species-satisfying labor. For political philosopher Hannah Arendt (1959), humanity has moved from active and contemplative thought to work, to labor, and finally to empty or vacant time. For sociologist Max Weber (Gerth and Mills 1958), the organization of human activity has changed from the traditional to the charismatic to the legal-rational and bureaucratic.

Economic elites.   The quest for energy surpluses has also led to a marked increase in inequality. This inequality is reflected in the growth of energy elites and the preferential ways in which energy is used and wealth is distributed in modern societies (see table 15–3). As much as anything else, the history of civilization teaches that an intimate connection has always existed between the strategic position a group occu-

TABLE 15–3. Energy Consumption Per Capita in Twenty Most Populous Countries, 1980

COUNTRY	COAL EQUIVALENT (kilograms)
United States	10,410
Fed. Rep. of Germany	5,727
USSR	5,595
United Kingdom	4,835
France	4,351
Japan	3,690
Italy	3,318
Mexico	1,770
Brazil	761
Turkey	737
People's Rep. of China	619
Egypt	473
Thailand	371
Philippines	328
Indonesia	220
Pakistan	218
India	191
Vietnam	148
Nigeria	144
Bangladesh	46

Source: Based on an analysis of various United Nations sources.

pies along the energy-economic chain and what C. Wright Mills (1956, 296) called the **power elite** (i.e., those persons and attitudes within a society that habitually command, are habitually obeyed, and which habitually reap whatever wealth, power, and status rewards society can bestow (see chapter 6).

Among hunters and gatherers, the role of energy elites was limited. Almost all were equally engaged in providing an adequate food supply that was available and widely dispersed, and productive techniques about food gathering were commonly known and shared. Knowledge of the "secrets" of nature—of which berries to eat and which not to eat—was transmitted from generation to generation through the elaboration of speech and by involving everyone in the functioning of the community (Habermas 1979; Mumford 1967).

This situation was less the case in early agricultural societies where control of the food-energy cycle began to pass into the hands of proportionately fewer people. Indeed, the outlines of modern society and

modern energy-related ruling classes first became evident with the advent of stable agricultural communities, as astronomers, priests, scribes, traders, and warriors assumed importance by virtue of the critical position they occupied in the production, acquisition, distribution, knowledge, and processing of grain (Boulding 1964). Later, when financial capital came into play more openly, this early food elite was transformed into the now-familiar merchants of grain (Morgan 1980). These were the speculators, agricultural experts, agribusiness, governmental bureaucracies, grain elevator operators, shippers, packagers, and processors of foodstuffs—each of whose prototype first emerged in classical empires.

In time, agricultural, sailing, and lumber elites were supplanted by a new ruling class, the result of a wood crisis in medieval Europe. "King Coal" saw the emergence of the turn-of-the-nineteenth century captains of industry: bankers, textile, railroad, and steel magnates, as well as a new knowledge elite who adapted a secondary energy form—electricity—to a myriad of industrial and commercial uses.

Today's energy elite includes representatives of these early elites, now greatly expanded and operating on a global scale, along with a more contemporary aggregate of oil processing and distributing transnationals including Gulf, Texaco, Exxon, and Mobil Oil (Blair 1978; Sampson 1975), natural gas companies and utilities, and the combination of established commercial, financial, and energy interests which control domestic uranium reserves (see table 15–4). This power elite also includes most major governments, many of whose politicians, information specialists, and militaries continue their traditional role as promoters of economic growth, as indicated in chapter 14 (Anderson 1976).

Two important trends are found in the emergence of these energy-economic elites. First, they have become progressively more wealthy and powerful, and second, they continue to be immune from effective social controls, resulting in the disaffection and mistrust that ordinary citizens continue to display toward big government, big business, and big labor.

The Energy Crisis Restated

The pertinent facts in our present-day energy situation seem to be the following:

1. Most modern civilizations are held together by nonrenewable, environmentally and socially damaging, and centralizing energy sources (Lovins and Lovins 1982), and supporting elites, as reflected in today's patterns of wealth and power and the social problems they create.

2. Historically, each extension of the ability to work has been accompanied by the further spread of civilization's problems. These problems include inequality, violence, profits for some and environmental and social losses for many, growing energy inefficiencies, unemployment, and socially wasteful jobs (Grossman and Daneker 1979). Apparently, we have created social arrangements that are using increasing energy to produce diminishing humanly supportable results.

3. Serious discussion of energy-related problems has increasingly shifted away from the technical issue of how we can get more work for our dollars to whether and how we can make the transition from a high-intensity energy base to a lower intensity one without either depleting scarce resources or destroying ourselves in the process.

The control of oil has become the subject of economic and political maneuvering in the modern world. Here, a number of ministers from the Organization of Petroleum Exporting Countries (OPEC) gather to discuss the price of oil.

TABLE 15–4. Top Twenty Corporate Holders of Domestic Uranium Reserves (January 1976)

COMPANY	RESERVES (THOUSANDS OF TONS)	TOTAL U.S. RESERVES (%)
Kerr-McGee	145.0	21.0
Gulf Oil	80.0	11.6
United Nuclear	40.0	5.8
Continental Oil	25.0	3.6
Western Nuclear (Phelps Dodge)	22.5	3.3
Getty Oil	20.0	2.9
Utah International (General Electric)	17.5	2.5
Exxon	17.5	2.5
Anaconda	15.0	2.2
Phillips Petroleum	12.5	1.8
Rio Algom Mines	9.0	1.3
Reserve Oil & Mineral	5.5	.8
Union Pacific	5.0	.7
Sohio	5.0	.7
Union Carbide	4.0	.6
Pioneer Corp.	4.0	.6
Atlas	3.0	.4
Socal	3.0	.4
Ranchers Exploration	3.0	.4
Houston Natural Gas	1.5	.2
Federal Reserve	1.5	.2
American Nuclear	1.0	.1
Total U.S. reserves	690.0	100.0
4-Firm total	290.0	42.0
Oil companies	324.0	47.0

Source: U.S. Senate, Committee on Energy and Natural Resources, Petroleum industry involvement in alternative sources of energy. (Washington D.C.: U.S. Government Printing Office, 1977).

ANALYZING THE PROBLEM: BEYOND CIVILIZATION

Faced with potential shortfalls in nonrenewable energy supplies, one nation after another is being pressured to change its energy base to enlarge wealth once again. The use of uranium, and soon the human-made element plutonium, as prime fuels in the global energy stew (Gyorgy and Friends 1979) and the use of more sustainable solar-related technologies (Butti and Perlin 1980) are under discussion by policymakers.

The End of the Atomic Age

With atomic breeder reactors producing more plutonium fuel than they burn, some believe that satisfying energy demands for centuries to come may be possible. The general understanding is that a plutonium-based economy could extend fuel supplies for 1,500 to 2,000 years (Commoner 1976). Rising safety and economic problems, however, coupled with the growing fear that atomic energy will cement all of the unequal patterns of wealth and power found in civilization, have slowed nuclear development.

Atomic reactors are connected to a globally spreading nuclear fuel cycle which many believe humanity can neither sustain nor endure. In addition to serious economic and safety problems, a uranium-plutonium economy creates many social problems which have eluded solution.

As the number and location of radioactive transactions have expanded globally along with a spreading nuclear fuel cycle (see figure 15–3), so have the costly and dramatic accidents (Ford 1982a). These accidents have prompted scientists and citizens to call for (1) closing of all uranium mines, mills, enrichment and fuel fabrication facilities, reactors, and reprocessing plants and (2) finding permanent and safe storage for the world's growing stockpile of highly toxic, long-lasting radioactive wastes. Some fear that further commitment to the split (fissioned) atom as a way of producing electricity will require the creation of a worldwide energy technology that we can neither sustain nor endure (Reader, Hardert, and Moulton 1980).

Environmental-economic problems. Expanded reliance on **fission power** (energy derived by splitting the atom) intensifies many of the economic-environmental problems associated with the use of other nonsustainable fuels. Even so, such fuels may not be counted on to meet unchecked energy demands. Of all energy sources, atomic power is the least energy efficient (Science and Mankind 1976), among the most expensive (Miller 1976) when all safety and clean-up costs along the whole of the nuclear fuel cycle are calculated (Komanoff 1979, 14–17), and the least environmentally compatible once the recognition is made that atomic reactors heat up large quantities of water in their normal operation, thus jeopardizing aquatic life (Lovins 1977a, 1977b). They can also contaminate vast portions of the ecosystem now and through the future should radioactive spills occur anywhere along the nuclear pathway (Ford 1982b; Medvedev 1979).

Even if an expanding fuel cycle could operate without negative incident as it spreads to increasingly less technically mature parts of the world, the amount of money needed for nuclear hardware will seriously strain

FIGURE 15–3. The nuclear fuel cycle.

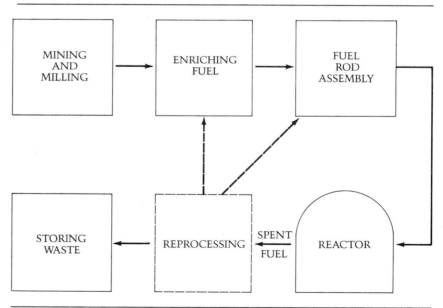

Data from Mark Reader, Ronald Hardert, and Gerald Moulton, *Atom's eve: Ending the nuclear age* (New York: McGraw-Hill, 1980), p. 6.

national economies. It would divert scarce capital from other life-sustaining needs such as housing, food, health care, and education (Hayes 1977).

The political problem. A second problem associated with a global atomic industry concerns the issue of nuclear weapons proliferation (Lovins and Lovins 1980), including the increased prospect of atomic war and nuclear-related acts of terrorism (Flood 1976). At present, six nations are known to have atomic weapons. The fear is that by 2000, forty to fifty nations could have nuclear weapons capability derived from their reactor programs. This capability could come from reprocessing plutonium from the spent (used) fuel generated at the site of each working reactor, or from enriching to bomb-grade quality the uranium used to fuel these reactors (Epstein 1975). That each year any standard 1,000 megawatt atomic reactor can generate enough plutonium to trigger between twenty to forty Hiroshima-sized bombs (Caldicott 1978) is now generally accepted. At recent rates of growth, the world may have produced more than 1 million

pounds of plutonium by the year 2000 (Tinbergen 1976). By then, any nuclear weapons nation will be able to start an atomic war against any other nation, as Israel's bombing of the Osirak reactor mentioned in chapter 14 suggests.

This realization has forced policymakers to give up their earlier confidence in "the peaceful atom." It has also created fear that should atomic weapons abound, a limited nuclear war, followed perhaps by a more universal holocaust, might occur by the end of this century (Barnaby 1976).

To prevent this possibility, the nuclear nations are trying to tighten international security controls over all spent reactor fuels and to increase surveillance by globally monitoring the entire nuclear fuel cycle (Beres 1980). These deterrent policies, however, probably cannot end the rush toward nuclear instability and tragedy. "Bad" governments and "irresponsible" terrorists are not pushing the world toward the thermonuclear brink. Rather, larger, unresolved energy problems, plus widespread social and economic inequality, continue to make possession of nuclear weapons and nuclear energy attractive (Reader 1978a, 3–11). Unless nonnuclear energy sources can be developed and social justice attained, some groups and governments will seek atomic power in all of its forms as a way of ensuring political, economic, and social parity (Poneman 1982; Pringle and Spigelman 1981). In other words, unless the nuclear "haves" give up their unequal lien on wealth and power, and the nonnuclear energy needs of all are guaranteed, the prospect of a world filled with atomic power plants and atomic weapons is likely to increase in the years immediately ahead. The chances of thermonuclear war and serious radioactive accidents will also increase (Reader, Hardert, and Moulton 1980).

Social questions. Worldwide increases in the quantities and handlings of radiation and the need to keep many of these cancer-producing substances out of reach for hundreds to thousands of years, sets up a third problem in uranium-related energy choices: Can we live with the fissioned atom at all? Further, can we build viable social systems to support nuclear power as a major energy source? In other words, can we hope to protect our lives, liberties, and happiness in a world filled with atomic reactors and weapons?

As long as the number of exchange points in the nuclear fuel cycle are few and the amount of radioactivity being handled is comparatively small, social problems connected to the fissioned atom are barely detectable. Once the decision to enlarge the nuclear commitment is made, however, as happened in the 1970s and as is projected for the 1990s, several potentially insurmountable problems appear.

1. *Health.* As demonstrated at Hiroshima and in the above-ground weapons testing program in the Pacific and the American Southwest, the most frightening thing about an errant atom is that it can kill (Freeman 1981; Wasserman 1982). Deaths from radiation among uranium miners have been several times higher than the national average (Union of Concerned Scientists 1975). Also known is that the threatened core meltdown at Three Mile Island in March 1979 could have killed thousands of people throughout the Eastern American seaboard (Ford 1982a); that the inhalation of plutonium in quantities as small as 1/10,000 of an ounce is usually fatal; and that theoretically by the year 2000, enough plutonium may be coursing the world's transportation arteries to kill off the whole of humanity (Tinbergen 1976).

Little dispute exists about the toxicity of high-level radioactive materials produced in the military and civilian nuclear program. A great deal of controversy exists, however, within the scientific and medical communities about the dangers of "low-level" radiation previously thought harmless in those quantities being produced at reactor sites (Gofman 1981).

The resulting medical uncertainties pose two troubling social problems. First, to what extent will the increased use of atomic power throughout the world, along with anticipated breakdowns, irrevocably damage life and contribute to premature deaths in this and future generations (Freeman 1981)? Second, will anxiety about the safe operation of the whole of the nuclear fuel cycle create a serious public mental health problem, and with what consequence? Social workers at the Three Mile Island accident, for example, report that nearby residents continue to experience psychic difficulties as a result of their ordeal (Cunningham 1982, 47–52). As Yale psychiatrist Robert Jay Lifton (1978, 46–51) and others have recently suggested, people lose their ability to become fully sensual and dimensional in the presence of a potential killer they cannot see, feel, hear, taste, or smell (Lifton 1979).

2. *Freedom.* Beginning with the atomic bomb, the destructiveness of the fissioned atom set up the need for extraordinary surveillance measures in human society and the growth, in peacetime, of a permanent national security state (see chapter 14). As the fissioned atom is increasingly used to generate electricity, people may forfeit their basic liberties as they develop machines to watch machines to watch people watching their lethal energy source (Reader 1978b, 22). Indeed, large-scale commitment to nuclear power may be incompatible with democracy as the rise in civil liberties violations reported in connection with the security demands of an expanding nuclear industry now indicates (Peterzell 1981; Warnock 1979). Surveillance of both nuclear workers and the public is beginning to rise in the United States and elsewhere (Jungk 1979). The American Civil Liberties Union has warned that any further expansion by the nuclear establishment could wipe out many basic liberties quaranteed by the U.S. Constitution (Glasser 1979).

As the film *The China Syndrome* suggests, atomic energy may create a social atmosphere of technological fascism and the need for a police state to run it. This possibility is why the U.S. government's prior censorship attempt of *The Progressive* magazine's hydrogen bomb story (1979) was worrisome. The suspicious circumstances surrounding the death of atomic worker Karen Silkwood, killed in an auto accident on her way to talk with a *New York Times* reporter about alleged safety violations at a plutonium processing plant in Oklahoma (Kohn 1975, 43–46 and pass. 1981), also troubled many.

3. *Equality.* As physicist Alvin M. Weinberg (1979), former head of the Oak Ridge laboratory, noted several years ago, people who make the fission commitment must also accept rule by a nuclear "priesthood" exerting "eternal vigilance" over the whole of the nuclear fuel cycle. Weinberg thought that this "Faustian bargain" was acceptable in return for a limitless supply of electricity. Others conclude that the decision to divide the world into nuclear "haves" and nuclear "have-nots" destabilizes rather than stabilizes social systems, stimulating the chances of accident and the prospect of thermonuclear war (Reader, Hardert, and Moulton 1980). Moreover, given the symbiotic relationship between energy and civilizational problems, that any elite, no matter how powerful, can amass sufficient skills to dictate the terms of human survival now and into the remote future is doubtful (Hertsgaard, 1983).

4. *History.* How can we hope to build societies to last however long it will take to make sure that radioactive materials do not back up into our lives in years to come (Reader 1978c, 39–44)? Twenty-four thousand years ago, the time it takes a pound of plutonium to decay to half a pound (its half-life), people were living in the Ice Age. If we choose to monitor lethal nuclear wastes for even a fraction of the time necessary to assure their safety, history may be brought to a standstill. This could happen if we force future generations to build a high-intensity energy civilization much like our own to do the job, and even then, it might fail. Meanwhile, we will probably not be able to live with greater doses of social control and less variety in our everyday lives as we try to protect ourselves against potential disaster. Finally, to what extent does the fission choice close out the possibility of substantive social change in the future, and how ethical is such a foreclosure?

Toward A Non-nuclear Future

Indications are growing that we may be able to avoid each of the economic, political, and social pitfalls posed by the split atom by pulling back from the nuclear brink. We have already slowed demand for nonrenewable energy sources in the affluent nations (see figures 15–4 and 15–5) and we could temporarily fine-tune the use of natural gas, oil, and coal to help ourselves through a difficult twenty to fifty-year transition period.

On the supply side, for example, each new discovery of natural gas and oil extends the time in which the conversion from a nonrenewable to a renewable energy system can occur. The judicious use of coal, plus the rapid implementation of renewable energy sources, may be able to fill the needs that natural gas and oil cannot meet.

The key to a sustainable energy future, however, seems to lie as much on the demand side as it does on the supply side of the equation. Pressure on the world's limited reserves of fossil fuels could be relieved, with attendant reductions in political tensions, if the United States and other technological societies were to implement extensive conservation, energy efficiency, and solar energy-related policies. If this were to happen, Americans, who comprise 5 percent of the world's population but who consume 30 to 40 percent of its nonrenewable energy resources, could save as much as 40 percent of the energy we use without experiencing insupportable life-style changes (Lovins 1977a, 1977b).

Sizable savings could be, and in some cases have been, realized by improving gasoline mileage performance in automobiles, using solar technologies for space heating and cooling, recycling or reusing materials (aluminum, garbage, and human waste), and altering the pattern of food production, distribution, and consumption (Fritsch 1977; Lappé 1975).

Why these changes have been delayed has less to do with available technologies than it does with existing inequalities and values created by civilization. Any fundamental change in the pattern of energy consumption in technological societies would threaten corporate profits and the power elite, as continued governmental and big-business commitment to nuclear power indicates.

Nuclear and other high-intensity energy options are even less appropriate in Third World countries where shortages in both capital and high-technology skills are real, where untapped and sustainable energy sources are often available, and where settlement patterns frequently make it uneco-

FIGURE 15–5. Average Household Energy Use, History and Projections, Midprice Scenario

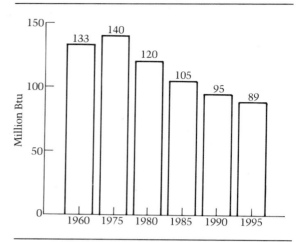

Data from U.S. Department of Commerce, Bureau of the Census, *Statistical abstract of the United States (1980)*; U.S. Department of Energy, Energy Information Administration, *State energy data report* (April 1980); and Energy Information Administration estimates for 1980.

FIGURE 15–4. Consumption of Electricity by Sector and Industry's 1975 Projections and History of Projections

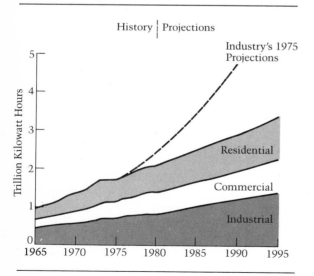

Data from: 1965–79: U.S. Department of Energy, Energy Information Administration, 1980 *Annual report to Congress*, Vol. 2; 1980: U.S. Department of Energy, Energy Information Administration, *Monthly energy review* (November 1981).

nomical to build power lines to deliver centrally produced electricity equitably.

Government and industry claims about the absolute necessity of following both the uranium and the oil routes must also be taken with a grain of salt, given that the actual need for petroleum and nuclear power has been systematically inflated in the recent past (Commoner 1979). Thus, while politicians and nuclear industry representatives were regularly claiming that 12 to 13 percent of electricity consumed in 1979 America was produced by the fissioned atom, they rarely added that this accounted for only 3 to 4 percent of the total energy used in the United States. This was little more than the amount of energy cut off to domestic consumption by the Iranian revolution. In addition, basic questions have been raised about the misuse and overdependency on electricity itself.

No guarantee exists that the world will survive without the fissioned atom and continued oil dependency, just as no guarantee exists that the world can survive with it.

Given the seemingly insurmountable economic, military, and social problems that accompany the widespread use of oil and fission power, however, a non-nuclear future seems preferable. This kind of future opens up the prospect of settling the energy-civilization crisis peacefully and sanely, and raises hope for survival.

ALTERNATIVE POLICIES FOR RESOLVING THE PROBLEM: DESIGNING SUSTAINABLE ECONOMIES

Culture Building

The move beyond technological civilization toward human cultures (Hall 1976) is well under way, as are the makings of sustainable, energy futures (Brown 1981). Many now agree with the late E. F. Schumacher that work need not be demeaning or social organization unequal and violent. We can live more modestly and cooperatively within smaller, more intimate contexts. By using tools more in keeping with our actual needs, we can overcome our self-centeredness while creatively and cooperatively producing those "goods and services needed for a becoming existence" (see "Buddhist Economics" in Schumacher 1973).

The redefinition of work and the reemergence of sociable, interpersonal—as distinct from functional—relationships are taking several forms. In industrial societies, many are coming to value the quality of life above "success" as socially defined, to labor less and to play more, to reduce impersonality at their workplaces and within their family units, and to insist on greater and more equal participation in those matters that affect their lives (The Simple Living Collective 1977).

This democratic trend is also evident on the organizational front. Resistance to "bigness" is hardening (Sale 1980). Spontaneous work teams, or "ad-hocracies" as Alvin Toffler (1970) called them, are challenging

bureaucracies for leadership by virtue of their growing ability to gather and use information (Henderson 1978, 1981). A visible move toward decentralization is taking shape in taxpayers' rebellions, the continuance of neighborhood "movements" (see chapter 14), and subgroup politics (women's, black, Chicano, native American, gay, Gray Panther, and community-control activities) in the United States (Lipnak and Stamps 1982). An equally vital drive exists toward cultural pluralism and local autonomy (devolution) throughout Europe.

Seemingly, various groups have decided to take survival matters into their own hands and to reverse many of those values on which technological civilization is based (American Friends Service Committee 1977). Increasingly, they wish to substitute love for power, interpersonal dialogue for bureaucratic commands, barter and exchange of services for the money-economy, and intermediate technologies for large-scale ones. Emergence of a new global energy consciousness and a set of supporting values associated with a "voluntary simplicity" movement (Elgin 1982) now promise to put many onto a renewable, peaceful energy path during the next century.

Goals for the Future

That the prospects for survival will remain dim unless we adopt and implement a whole-earth energy perspective (Ward and Dubos 1972) is now generally recognized. Basic to that perspective is a land ethic (Berry 1977) that acknowledges that (1) planet earth is humanity's only home into the foreseeable future and must be cared for accordingly (Leopold 1949); (2) each person and each generation must act as a trustee for, rather than owner of, the environment (Sax 1971; Stone 1974); and (3) physical and social life will continue to deteriorate as long as we consume the earth's finite stock of resources to maximize our wealth and power.

Energy ethics begins, then, with a conception of **intergenerational justice** (fairness toward the future) (Barry 1981). This involves a decision to try to use only those energy sources that are renewable, safe, nonpolluting, flexible, easily understandable, and hence accessible to all. It also means using energy sources that are nonviolent, job producing rather than machine dependent, matched to the society and the task to be served, and "pleasing to the senses and enjoyable to work with." (National Council of Churches statement in Reader, Hardert, and Moulton 1980) With sustainable sources such as these (see figure 15–6), we might be able to move toward a world of peace, environmental balance, social justice (fairness), and political liberty for each person in every generation (Mendlovitz 1975).

The prime advantages of using sustainable, "soft," or solar-related energy resources are twofold: (1) greater energy efficiency and (2) less social and ecological pollution as people are put in a position to cut those energy-related ties that now bind them to centralized energy producers and distributors (Illich 1974). If individuals and small communities were able to control benign energy sources, (e.g., by converting utility-controlled electric hot water heaters into rooftop solar heated ones), they could simultaneously lessen their dependence on centralized energy elites and realize sizable energy savings as well (Citizens Energy Project 1977; Okagaski and Benson 1979).

Implementation of a "soft," decentralized energy system in the United States, could reduce energy waste by 50 percent by the turn of the century, according to physicist Amory B. Lovins (1977a, 1977b). Savings could be realized by (1) eliminating distribution losses caused by transmitting electricity over power lines, (2) curtailing diseconomies of scale experienced when centralized power plants break down, (3) removing unwelcome overhead costs incurred by the utilities' need to maintain expensive bureaucracies to bill customers, (4) reducing financial losses suffered in an uncertain energy market, especially the nuclear one.

The major gains to be realized by chang-

ing to renewable energy systems, however, would be socioeconomic many believe (Barnet 1980; Barney 1980; Glenn 1979). If we could tap into the sun directly (Lyons 1978; Reece 1979), "thrift, simplicity, diversity, neighborliness, humility and craftsmanship" (Lovins 1977a, 1977b) might replace harsher civilizational values and life-styles, while avoiding many of those weighty social problems that will accompany an unnecessary coal, oil, or nuclear-dominated future. The soft-energy path, Lovins (Reader, Hardert, and Moulton 1980) notes, offers:

advantages for nearly every constituency at once: . . . jobs for the unemployed, capital for business people . . . savings for consumers, chances for small business to innovate and for big business to recycle itself, environmental protection for conservationists and better military security for the military, world order and equity for globalists, energy independence for isolationists, exciting technologies for the secular, a rebirth of spiri-

FIGURE 15–6 Classification of Renewable Energy Resources

Renewable or income energy resources may be classified as follows.

> *Solar*
>   Heating
>   Ambient
>   Man-induced
>   Power
> *Biological*
>   Plant food and feed
>   Animal food (meat, eggs, milk, cheese, fish)
>   Wood and other vegetable fuels
>   Night soil and other organic wastes
>   Animal and human power
> *Water*
>   Water mills to produce mechanical work
>   Turbine generators for electricity
> *Wind*
>   Windmills to produce mechanical work
>   Wind generators for electricity
> *Tidal*
> *Terrestrial heat flow*
> *Deuterium (quasi-income)*

(Deuterium from sea water, the potential fuel for fusion power reactors, is listed as a quasi-income resource because the reserves will be enormous if fusion power becomes a reality.)

Data from Earl Cook, *Man, energy, society* (San Francisco: W. H. Freeman, 1976) p. 54.

tual values for the religious, radical reform for the young, traditional virtues for the old, civil rights for liberals, local autonomy for conservatives.

National Energy Strategies

Typical of current national renewable energy strategies (Kendall and Nadis 1980; Stobaugh and Yergin 1979; Taylor 1979) are those advanced by some biologists and environmentalists in the United States and England (Commoner 1976, 1979; Goldsmith 1972) who are persuaded that a relatively smooth solar transition could be accomplished by approximately the year 2000. In America, for example, biologist Barry Commoner has urged farmers to produce food and energy-producing plants for use as "natural" fuels (methane gas); expanded

community efforts to cogenerate electricity, especially by trapping and using the waste heat given off by all engines and motors; and action by the central government to "pump prime" the solar economy by purchasing large quantities of **photovoltaic cells** (which transform the sun's rays into electricity), thereby driving down the price of solar technologies.

In this way, Commoner is convinced, the transition from a fossil fuel to a solar-based civilization could be made while retaining the mobility, urbanization, and daily lifestyle that modern Americans and others who aspire to an automotive civilization do not seem ready to surrender.

Commoner (1979) and others are also persuaded that centers of wealth and power might change in a solar America along with the direction of future energy decisions. A

Strange sights are likely to accompany the introduction of solar-related technologies as the world moves toward more sustainable energy sources. Here, a number of wind turbines are hooked into a centralized electrical grid system to provide power to nearby cities and towns.

solar strategy would cut into the military-energy companies' hold on American politics by putting coal, oil, and nuclear interests under the rule of law and eventually out of business. It would also shift the burden of natural gas production away from costly underground exploration to the farms and progressively place energy decisions and technologies in the hands of local communities and municipalities. This would take place as it becomes evident that energy economies are not to be realized by building larger rather than smaller solar units.

Echoing philosopher John Dewey's call for a **socialized** (democratically planned economy) America, Commoner proposes that in the future, all energy companies and utilities must have a public trust and be subject to public regulation. He concludes by noting (1979) that the nation is not poor in energy resources, but mismanaged. The question is not whether appropriate energy technologies can be developed but whether the United States is ready to be governed by social rather than by private interests.

A second influential national study, *Blueprint for Survival*, is aimed at British audiences but has wider applicability (Goldsmith et al. 1972). This study contends that energy policies are needed that minimize ecological disruption; force modern economies to produce fewer but more durable goods; stabilize population; rebuild a waning stock of varied plant, animal, and cultural life, and implement a new, decentralized social system. Sustainable energy choices can be assured by using the taxing and spending powers of the modern state to encourage greater energy efficiencies. These public "carrot-and-stick" policies could foster recycling and materials substitution while discouraging high-intensity energy-consuming industries (such as the plastics industry, perhaps, and agribusiness where overuse of herbicides, pesticides, and petroleum is the norm). The goal of these policies is to generate a network of interlocking, small rural communities.

The extent to which modern nation-states can or should be dismantled as the energy base of civilization changes is uncertain. Some people, like political scientists Richard Barnet of the Institute of Policy Studies and Richard Falk of Princeton, believe that the nation-state system must be supplemented, if not supplanted, by more enlightened global policies. Barnet (1980) and Falk (1975) argue that many energy-related decisions should pass into the hands of both (1) greater numbers of active local communities and neighborhoods and (2) a shifting international guidance center (rather than an autocratic world government). The latter might be composed of enlightened nation-state politicians, multinational and other business leaders, nongovernmental organizations, globally oriented and professional interest groups, private citizens, and the like (Falk 1975).

The desirability of completely deurbanizing life as the solar society nears completion is even less clear. Some believe that while it may be desirable to equalize wealth and power as nations move toward solar cultures, both the automobile and the city can and should remain as two of the central liberating forces in the post-modern world (Commoner 1979). Others, like psychobiologist W. Jackson Davis (1979), question the ability of a solar society to maintain any of the trappings of technological civilization for very long. Davis is convinced that the law of entropy, plus a low-intensity energy future, requires a return to village and rural life and a move away from urban-suburban existence, both of which are energy wasteful. Still others hold that low-energy civilizations tend to produce poverty, boredom, and stultifying social relationships (Cook 1976; Cottrell 1955), thereby debasing human life even further. As energy wasteful as they might be, this argument runs, some degree of urbanization and centralization will be needed in a solar society if we are to generate those cultural activities that seem pivotal for purposeful and humanly rewarding lives.

Whatever the outcome of this debate, the

likelihood is strong that any substantive political move toward more traditional, solar-based energy systems will strengthen the call for land redistribution in wealthy and poor nations alike. It would also enlarge the movement toward organic farming, changed diets, greater plant and animal diversity, and the greening of cities. It would slow rates of economic change and the pace of life as the bicycle and public transportation become commonplace. Less clear is the extent to which existing energy elites will be able to hold onto their privilege by centralizing and monopolizing access to the sun (Humphrey & Buttel 1982, 179–194; Munson 1979, 12–15; Reece 1979).

The Transition

Well before we may have to answer these questions, though, a transitional energy strategy must be developed that can keep us from thermonuclear war, environmental collapse, and technological fascism (Yergin and Halenbrand 1982). Given the continuing struggle between rich and poor, such a policy will probably include the following:

1. A global agreement (stated or not) to stop the sale, construction, and operation of all parts of the nuclear fuel cycle, with nations presently using fission power ending their use as quickly as the judicious use of fossil fuel (Easterbrook 1980, 20–30) and renewable energy sources will allow (Lovins and Lovins 1980);

2. A decision by one or more of the superpowers to begin a program of the staged and **unilateral** (one-party) reduction of nuclear weapons as a way of reducing international tensions and discouraging the nuclear have-nots from becoming the nuclear haves. The United States or the USSR might simply decide to challenge the other to "match" their weapons reductions (see chapter 14);

3. International negotiations aimed at settling the world's energy problem equitably and globally by (a) assuring industrial nations like France, Japan, and the United

States a temporary, uninterrupted supply of oil in return for meaningful energy conservation measures and abandonment of the nuclear alternative, and (b) delivering sufficient economic, social, and technological aid to the poorer nations to improve their standards of living by developing indigenous fossil fuel as well as renewable energy sources (Steinhart 1979);

4. Implementation in the industrial nations of thoroughgoing conservation, energy efficiency, and solar measures that are equitable for all citizens and that put people in control of both their energy resources and those corporations that deliver them. This might entail an end to energy profiteering and the "busting" of coal, oil, and nuclear trusts (Barnet 1980; Commoner 1979);

5. Renewed attempts to bring the world's population into equilibrium based on the understanding that sensible energy goals cannot be realized without it. It may be unethical to overload any single generation with more than its share of births when that means that future generations may be denied a turn at life; and

6. Extension of continuing, worldwide energy education programs designed to teach people everywhere basic energy lessons and skills (Terry and Witt 1976).

Whether this or a similar program is ratified in the years immediately ahead may depend less on the initiative of energy and governmental elites than on groups of individuals who, in their private resolves and public actions, decide to give up civilization's illusions and to live in peace with themselves and their physical surroundings. As naturalist Loren Eiseley put it: "The need is not really for more brains. The need is for a gentler, more tolerant people" (1957, 140).

SUMMARY

In recent years, many have realized that the human lifeline is not guaranteed into perpetuity and that the issue of survival is being, and will be, decided by this and the next generation. Both their wisest scientists and their everyday experiences tell them that the fate of the most promising life form in the known universe is presently in doubt (Reader and Wolf 1973). Many worry about the growing threat of atomic war, as nuclear reactors spread around the world, and the continuing prospect of environmental collapse under mounting pressure of too many people squandering our limited resources (see chapter 12).

Others no longer doubt that the paradoxical and undesirable need for total social control has been the prime carrying charge of the atom (see chapter 14) and that their security and freedom are being jeopardized by many of those technologies they have developed since the close of the Second World War. People have come to fear the sudden accident or miscalculation that kills off sizable numbers of people or poisons a part of the ecological system upon which life depends (see chapter 12).

For the most part, however, the forfeiture of one or more of our vital life-support systems—air, land, or water—is not likely to occur as the result of a single accident or mistake. Should we experience an irreversible environmental catastrophe, it will likely happen because we continue to lead lives in ways to which we and our supporting ecosystem have not yet become accustomed. One too many plant or animal species may be removed from the chain of life. One too many rivers or streams may be polluted with industrial, municipal, or agricultural wastes. More noxious fumes, chemicals, or radioactivity may be released than our lungs or genes can sustain. More garbage may be dumped onto the land than the earth can reprocess as happened at Love Canal in New York state and in the community of Times Beach, Missouri.

Hunger, poverty, disease, wars, other crimes of violence, natural disasters, volatile behavior, and psychic stress constitute additional threats to survival. The dehumanization and depersonalization of everyday life is reaching epidemic proportions in many parts of the world. In this century alone, large numbers of people have been killed, injured or made homeless through acts of war and cruelty (see chapter 14). If we believe that we can do little to change worsening conditions, we permit conditions to worsen even further by accepting our dehumanizaiton as "natural" and "inevitable."

If enough time and determination exist, we may be able to overcome these crises. We have, however, become dependent on a now-faltering and inflexible technological civilization. As petroleum, the wealth-producing base of modern society, dries up, it becomes increasingly clear that whether—and under what conditions—human life continues is being decided by the energy choices of those living today.

Indeed, we may have evolved to a point where civilization now stands against itself, denying to those who might save it the very cultural process of questioning and commitment essential for its salvation. Locked in a prison of our own making, what are we to do?

STUDY QUESTIONS

1. In this chapter, we have suggested that humanity may have evolved to a point where it must simultaneously transcend the atomic age and the harshness of civilization, or perish. Do you agree or disagree with this analysis? Why?

2. Understanding of the law of entropy may prove essential in evaluating energy and economic choices now and into the future. Explain the likely impact of this phenomenon on social life.

3. What are some of the major plusses and minuses associated with pursuing either a high- or a low-intensity energy path?

4. Why might resolution of the problem of social injustice prove critical in securing the goals of peace and environmental balance?

5. What policies might be pursued in the

immediate future to reduce the negative effects of current energy choices while improving the quality of life for sizable numbers of people?

6. What sort of energy-economic future would you prefer? Why?

REFERENCES

Adams, R. N. 1981. Natural selection energetics, and "cultural materialism." *Current Anthropology* 22 (6) (December 1981).

American Friends Service Committee. 1977. *Taking charge: Personal and political change through simple living.* New York: Bantam.

Anderson, W. 1976. *A place of power: The American episode in human evolution.* Santa Monica, Calif.: Goodyear.

Anderson, J. and J. Boyd. 1983. *Fiasco.* New York: Times.

Arendt, H. 1959. *The human condition.* Chicago: Univ. of Chicago Press.

Barnaby, F. 1976. World armaments and disarmaments. *Bulletin of the Atomic Scientists* 32)6).

Barnet, R. 1980. *The lean years.* New York: Simon & Schuster.

Barnet, R., and R. Muller. 1974. *Global reach: the power of the multinational corporations.* New York: Simon Schuster.

Barney, G. O., ed. 1977. *The unfinished agenda.* New York: Crowell.

———. 1980. *The summary report.* Vol. I of *The global 2000 report to the president of the U.S.,* New York: Pergamon.

Barry, B. 1981. *Intergenerational justice in energy policy.* Center for Philosophy and Public Policy. College Park, Md.: Univ. of Maryland Press.

Beres, L. 1980. *Apocalypse.* Chicago: Univ. of Chicago Press.

Berry, W. 1977. *The unsettling of America: Culture and agriculture.* San Francisco: Sierra Club.

Blair, J. 1978. *The control of oil.* New York: Random House.

Bohannan, P. 1971. Beyond civilization. *Natural History* (February).

Boulding, K. 1964. *The meaning of the twentieth century.* New York: Harper & Row.

Brown, L. 1978. *The twenty-ninth day.* New York: W. W. Norton.

———. 1981. *Building a sustainable society.* New York: W. W. Norton.

Butti, K., and J. Perlin. 1980. *A golden thread: 2500 years of solar architecture and technology.* New York: Van Nostrand.

Caldicott, H. 1978. *Nuclear madness: What you can do!* Brookline, Mass.: Autumn.

Caudill, H. 1963. *Night comes to the Cumberlands.* Boston: Little, Brown.

Citizens Energy Project. 1977. *Lifestyle index.* Washington, D.C.: Citizens Energy Project.

Commoner, B. 1972. *The closing circle: Man, nature, and technology.* New York: Knopf.

———. 1976. *The poverty of power: Energy and the economic crisis.* New York: Knopf.

———. 1979. *The politics of energy.* New York: Knopf.

Cook, E. 1976. *Man, energy, society.* San Francisco: W. H. Freeman.

Cottrell, F. 1955. *Energy and society: The relation between energy, social change, and economic development.* New York: McGraw-Hill.

Cunningham, A. M. 1982. Is there a seismograph for stress? *Psychology Today* (October).

Davis, W. J. 1979. *The seventh year: Industrial civilization in transition.* New York: W. W. Norton.

Diamond, S. 1982. Civilization and progress. In Falk, R., S. Kim, and S. Mendlovitz (eds.) *Toward a just world order* 1. Boulder, Colo: Westview.

Easterbrook, G. 1980. The energy crisis: How to end it. *Washington Monthly.* 12 (8) (October).

Ebenstein, W. 1973. *Today's isms: Communism, facism, capitalism, socialism.* Englewood Cliffs, N.J.: Prentice-Hall.

Eiseley, L. 1957. *The immense journey.* New York: Vintage.

Elgin, D. 1982. *Voluntary simplicity: An ecological lifestyle that promotes personal and social renewal.* New York: Bantam.

Epstein, W. 1975. *The last chance: Nuclear proliferation and arms control.* New York: Free Press.

Falk, R. A. 1975. *A study of future worlds.* New York: Free Press.

Flood, M. 1976. Nuclear sabotage. *Bulletin of the Atomic Scientists* 32 (8).

Ford, D. 1982a. *Three Mile Island: Thirty minutes to meltdown.* New York: Penguin.

———. 1982b. *The cult of the atom.* New York: Simon & Schuster.

Freeman, L. J. 1981. *Nuclear witnesses: Insiders speak out.* New York: W. W. Norton.

Fritsch, A. 1977. *99 ways to a simple lifestyle.* New York: Doubleday.

Georgescu-Roegen, N. 1977. *Energy and economic myths.* Pergamon.

Gerth, H. H., and C. Wright Mills, eds. 1958. *From Max Weber: Essays in sociology.* New York: Oxford Univ. Press.

Glasser, I. 1979. *Special alert letter.* New York: American Civil Liberties Union.

Glenn, B. 1979. *Humanistic Energy Choices.* Boulder, Colo.: Solar Energy Research Institute.

Gofman, J. 1981. *Radiation and human health.* San Francisco: Sierra Club.

Goldsmith, E., R. Allen, M. Allaby, J. Davoll, S. Lawrence 1972. *Blueprint for survival.* Boston: Houghton Mifflin.

Grossman, R. and G. Daneker. 1979. *Energy, jobs and the economy*. Boston: Alyson.

Gyorgy, A., and Friends. 1979. *No nukes: Everyone's guide to nuclear power*. Boston: South End.

Habermas, J. 1979. *Communication and the evolution of society*. Boston: Beacon.

Hall, E. 1976. *Beyond culture*. Garden City, N.Y. Anchor.

Harris, M. 1979. *Cultural materialism: The struggle for a science of culture*. New York: Random House.

Hayes, D. 1977. *Rays of hope*. New York: W. W. Norton.

Henderson, H. 1978. *Creating alternative futures*. New York: Berkley.

———. 1981. *The politics of the solar age*. New York: Anchor/Doubleday.

Hertsgaard, M. 1983. *Nuclear, inc.: The men and money behind nuclear energy*. New York: Pantheon.

Hobbes, T. 1957. *Leviathan*. Oxford: Basil Blackwell.

Humphrey, C. R. and F. R. Buttel 1982. *Environment, energy, and society*. Belmont, Calif.: Wadsworth.

Illich, I. 1974. *Energy and equity*. New York: Harper & Row.

Jezer, M. 1982. *The dark ages: Life in the United States 1945–1960*. Boston: South End.

Jungk, R. 1979. *The new tyranny: How nuclear power enslaves us*. New York: Grosset & Dunlap.

Kendall, H. W., and S. S. Nadis. 1980. *Energy strategies: Toward a solar future*. Cambridge, Mass.: Ballinger.

Kohn, H. 1975. The nuclear industry's terrible power and how it silenced Karen Silkwood. *Rolling Stone* (183) (27 March).

———. 1981. *Who killed Karen Silkwood?* New York: Summit Books.

Lappé, F. M. 1975. *Diet for a small planet*. New York: Ballantine.

Lappé, F., and J. Collins. 1979. *Food first: Beyond the scarcity myth*. New York: Ballantine.

Leopold, A. 1949. *A Sand County almanac*. London: Oxford Univ. Press.

Lifton, R. J. 1978. Death in life. *New Age* (June): 46–51.

———. 1979. *The broken connection*. New York: Simon & Schuster.

Lipnack, J., and J. Stamps. 1982. *Networking: The first report and directory*. Garden City, N.Y.: Doubleday.

Lovins, A. 1979. Energy Strategy: The Road Not Taken? in *Soft energy paths*. Cambridge, Mass.: Ballinger.

———. 1977. *Soft energy paths: Toward a durable peace*. Cambridge, Mass.: Ballinger.

Lovins, A., and L. Hunter Lovins. 1980. *Energy/war: Breaking the nuclear link*. New York: Harper & Row.

———. 1982. *Brittle power*. Andover, Mass.: Brick House.

Lyons, S., ed. 1978. *Sun! A handbook for a pre-solar decade*. San Francisco: Friends of the Earth.

MacIver, R. M. 1931. *Society, its structure and changes*. New York: Long & Smith.

———. 1965. *The web of government* (Rev. Ed.). New York: The Free Press.

Marx, K. 1964a. *Das Kapital*, ed. F. Engels. New York: International.

———. 1964b. *Economic and philosophical manuscripts of 1844*, ed. D. J. Struik, trans. M. Milliga. New York: International.

McLuhan, T. C. 1972. *Touch the earth: A self portrait of Indian existence*. New York: Outerbridge & Legard.

Meadows, D. H., 1972. *The limits to growth*. New York: New American Library.

Medvedev, Z. 1979. *Nuclear disaster in the Urals*. New York: W. W. Norton.

Mendlovitz, S. 1975. *On the creation of a just world order*. New York: Free Press.

Miller, S. 1976. *The economics of nuclear and coal power*. New York: Praeger.

Mills, C. W. 1956. *The power elite*. New York: Oxford Univ. Press.

Moore, B. 1966. *Social origins of dictatorship and democracy*. Boston: Beacon.

Morgan, D. 1980. *The merchants of grain*. New York: Penguin.

Mumford, L. 1967. *The myth of the machine*. Vol. 1. New York: Harcourt, Brace.

Munson, R. 1979. Ripping off the sun. *The Progressive* (Septemer).

Odum, H. T., and E. Odum. 1976. *Energy basis for man and nature*. New York: McGraw-Hill.

Okagaski, A., and J. Benson. 1979. *County energy plan guide book*. Fairfax, Va.: Institute for Ecological Policies.

Orwell, G. 1958. *The road to Wigan Pier*. New York: Harcourt, Brace.

Peterzell, J. 1981. *Nuclear Power and political surveillance*. Washington, D.C.: Center for National Security.

Poneman, D. 1982. *Nuclear power in the developing world*. Winchester, Mass.: Allen & Unwin.

Pringle, P., and J. Spigelman. 1981. *The nuclear barons*. New York: Holt, Rinehart & Winston.

The Progressive. 1979. "Born secret" the story behind the H-bomb article we're not allowed to print. Vol. 43 (5).

Reader, M. 1971. Watching the revolution uncork. *Politics and Society* 2 (3) (Spring).

———. 1977. *Energy: The human dimension*. Tempe, Ariz.: Center for Environmental Studies.

———. 1978a. Nuclear power and the history of the future. *Energy systems: Analyses for engineers and policy makers*, ed. J. E. Bailey. New York: Marcel Dekker.

———. 1978b. Political culture in the nuclear age: Atomic reactors and the threat to civil liberties. *Peace and Change* V (1).

———. 1978c. Everyday life in a nuclear future. *Christian Science Monitor* (17 August).

Reader, M., R. A. Hardert, and G. L. Moulton, eds. 1980. *Atom's eve: Ending the nuclear age*. New York: McGraw-Hill.

Reader, M., and D. J. Wolf. 1973. On being Human. *Political Theory* 1 (2) (May).

Reece, R. 1979. *The sun betrayed.* Boston: South End.

Rifkin, J. 1980. *Entropy: A new world view.* New York: Viking.

Rousseau, J. 1964. *The first and second discourses.* New York: St. Martin's.

Sale, K. 1980. *Human scale.* New York: Coward, McCann & Grorghegan.

Sampson, A., 1976. *The seven sisters.* New York: Bantam.

Sax, J. 1971. *Defending the environment.* New York: Knopf.

Schumacher, E. F. 1973. *Small is beautiful.* London: Blond & Briggs.

Science and Mankind. 1976. *Critical issues in science and society: The great energy debate.* Parts I and II. New York: Science and Mankind. (Sound-slide show)

Sherrill, R. 1983. *The oil follies of 1970–1980.* New York: Anchor.

The Simple Living Collective. 1977. *Taking charge: personal and political change through simple living.* New York: Bantam.

Sivard, R. L. 1979. *World energy survey.* Leesburg, Va.: World Priorities.

Steinhart, J. S., 1979. *Pathway to energy sufficiency: The 2050 study.* San Francisco: Friends of the Earth.

Stobaugh, R., and D. Yergin, eds. 1979. *Energy future.* New York: Ballantine.

Stone, C. D. 1974. *Should trees have standing?* Los Altos, Calif.: Wm. Kaufman.

Taylor, V. 1979. *The easy energy plan.* Cambridge, Mass.: Union of Concerned Scientists.

Terry, M., and P. Witt. 1976. *Energy and order.* San Francisco: Friends of the Earth.

Tinbergen, J. 1976. *Reshaping the international order.* New York: E. P. Dutton.

Toffler, A. 1970. *Future shock.* New York: Random House.

Union of Concerned Scientists. 1975. *Nuclear fuel cycle: A survey of the public health, environmental and national security effects of nuclear power.* Cambridge: MIT Press.

Wallerstein, I. 1974. *The modern world system.* New York: Academic Press.

Ward, B., and R. Dubos. 1972. *Only one earth: The care and maintenance of a small planet.* New York: Norton.

Warnock, D. 1979. *Nuclear power and civil liberties: Can we have both?* Washington, D.C.: Citizens Energy Project.

Wasserman, H., N. Solomon with R. Alvarez and E. Walters. 1982. *Killing our own.* New York: Delacorte.

Weinberg, A. M. 1979. Salvaging the atomic age. *Wilson Quarterly* 1 (3).

White, L. 1943. Energy and the evolution of culture. *American Anthropologist* 45: 335–56.

Wilkinson, R. G. 1973. *Poverty and progress: An ecological perspective on development.* New York: Praeger.

Wittfogel, K. 1957. *Oriental despotism.* New Haven Conn.: Yale Univ. Press.

Yergin, D., and M. Halenbrand. 1982. *Global insecurity: A strategy for energy and economic renewal.* Boston: Houghton Mifflin.

EPILOGUE

In Search of the Good Society*

CONTENTS

---

* With Con Alan Wilson.

The farm that keeps flowering

During the "flower power" days of the late 1960s and early '70s, communes sprang up around the country like weeds. Most have long since disbanded, but one—the Farm, in Summertown, Tenn.—has grown and prospered to the point where it now resembles a small town. It boasts 1,500 members as well as its own school, health clinic, recording studio and telephone company (known locally as Beatnik Bell). As the tenth anniversary approaches this fall, 46-year-old Farm leader Stephen Gaskin says: "I don't see any reason for us not to continue onward."

The Farm started with 300 West Coast hippies who traveled to Tennessee in a caravan of brightly painted school buses and who styled themselves the "Technicolor Amish." Members, who preach a blend of Christian and Zen philosophy, consider the Farm a "spiritual community"; the Internal Revenue Service apparently concurs, having granted it tax-exempt status as a monastery. But one religious practice nearly proved the group's undoing: growing marijuana for use during "communion" services. Although they protested that the marijuana was a "holy tool to allow us to experience reality," Gaskin and three fellow members were arrested and convicted. Lawyers for the Farm took the case all the way to the U.S. Supreme Court, which refused to review the decision, and the men spent a year in prison.

Since then, the Farm has agreed not to grow marijuana or to use it in public ceremonies, and when state authorities investigated the property last year, all they found was some ragweed growing in a watermelon patch. That's not to say some of the residents don't light up in private. "We are all hippies," notes longtime member Matthew McClure. "And most hippies would smoke a joint if it came along."

The Farm, which advocates marriage and childbearing, is largely self-sufficient: residents live in cottages in groups of two or three families and grow the food for their strict vegetarian diet. After the crops are processed in the Farm's flour mill or canning-and-pickling factory, they go to the Farm Free Market—where members help themselves to whatever they need. Operating expenses, which total $10,000 a week, are paid for with contributions from new members and income from the Farm's many businesses. These include a construction company, a health-food market and a publishing firm that prints Gaskin's teachings as well as a number of how-to-books. "We are making it mainly on the bookpublishing company," says Gaskin. "But we would like to see our electronics workshop branch out. We sell a radiation detector for $200, and we're trying to get that business off the ground before the Japanese sell one for $59.50."

According to Gaskin, Farm members are now concerned with "reaching outside ourselves." They have established their own relief organization, PLENTY, which has helped teach people in Guatemala and Africa to grow soybeans and improve water-management techniques. Another PLENTY project is closer to home: after members saw a documentary about the troubled South Bronx section of New York, they sent volunteers to the city to set up an auxiliary ambulance service.

As the Farm has expanded, so has its potential political clout; today members account for roughly 16 percent of the Summertown area population. Gaskin says the commune may put up two candidates for county offices in next year's election. "Our presence in the county could make a difference in Democrats getting elected," he notes. "Not that we are Democrats, but that is the party that is farthest left."

Source: Newsweek, 10 August 1981, p. 14.

CULTURAL CONTRADICTIONS IN CAPITALISM

In *The Cultural Contradictions of Capitalism*, sociologist Daniel Bell (1976, 53) wrote that Western technological society is now characterized by "a radical disjunction of culture and social structure" that may lead to its eventual decline. He fears that the bureaucratization (emphasis on rationality), impersonality, and efficiency of our social structure is coming into conflict with cultural traits, such as ideas of equality, individualism, hedonism (pleasure seeking), and permissiveness. The "contradiction," Bell states, is that capitalism, as a social and economic system, requires ever-greater applications of rationality, but capitalist culture places ever-greater emphasis on such values as "feeling," personal gratification, and self-fulfillment. Thus, he fears that capitalism may not survive the attitudes and values that have become associated with it as an economic system (Bell 1976, 281).

Bell's assessment of a "contradiction" between Western social structure and cultural values may or may not be valid. To us, apparently little contradiction exists between what has been a highly competitive, efficient, and *materialistic* production structure in Western Europe and America, and a pleasure-oriented, self-centered set of cultural values. In terms of priorities, both system and values are *impersonal* because neither is oriented toward the good of the society as a whole. If we cannot cope with the competitiveness, insecurity, and loneliness of the technological society in which we live (Slater 1976), then perhaps we should try changing it into a more *cooperative*, caring society.

For example, the economic production structure and the cultural values of agricultural communes such as the Farm in Summertown, Tennessee (Gaskin 1977) and certain other communities have this kind of internal consistency. These "intentional communities" are organized for group survival, and their cultural goals, values, and behavior all tend to reflect this same social concern. Hence, internal consistencies can exist between social structures and cultural values both in Western society and in more communal, agricultural subsocieties.

The Hutterites, for example, are one of the world's great social and economic experiments and the only religious, communal society (i.e., where all property is shared) with extended longevity. This community seems to defy some of the commonly held assumptions about social organization. Hutterite society is classified as a cooperative society as compared with Western industrial nations, which are competitive and individual oriented. Complexity, it appears, places severe strains on cooperative relations, and competitive relationships can dominate a society. If that is the case, humankind faces a serious dilemma, for as population increases and our relationships become more complex, the need for cooperation increases. Perhaps larger societies can learn something positive from Hutterite social organization.

While the Hutterites and the Farm continue to meet with great success, many of the older communal societies have disappeared. The Shakers, Oneida, and the Father Divine Movement (Kephart 1976), as examples, no longer exist in any active sense. Yet, hundreds of new utopian communities have formed and continue to form (Toffler 1980). The rise of intentional communities and cooperative living means that large numbers of people experience alienation in the larger, technological society.

The objective in this text has been to face our social problems as *challenges*, to develop an understanding of our present crises, and to suggest options for reducing or eliminating them. This objective also presents us with the opportunity to suggest ways in which future generations may avert some foreseeable crises. Clearly we are living in a time between the industrial and informational eras—a transition that makes these problems even more complex (Toffler 1980). This transition period encompasses the transformation of our present world social system and how we perceive it, to something else as yet unknown. In essence, we are experiencing a structural strain so great that the only possible outcome is the eventual disappearance of the present system (Wallerstein 1982, 1). It is this structural strain that has precipitated many of the problems and dilemmas that have been addressed in this text. Our capabilities and especially our organizations and institutions are experiencing stress points on many levels as the rate of change continues to accelerate. The social problems we confront are the symptoms of this inability to cope and to manage such complex phenomena.

OPTIMISTIC VERSUS PESSIMISTIC VIEWS OF THE FUTURE

In the quest for solutions to societal problems, the debate over outcomes has tended to polarize. We noted in the prologue that social scientists (sociologists, economists, and others) hold differing views as to how problems should be defined, analyzed, and resolved. In policymaking institutions and among social planners, we also see a range of opinions—from the very pessimistic to the very optimistic. Forecasts of a bright technocratic future, such as those advanced by Herman Kahn (1976), are at one extreme; at the other end of the continuum, we find the foreboding predictions of the "limits to growth" advocates such as the Club of Rome (Meadows et al. 1972). Is either of these views likely to be correct?

That neither extreme—Kahn's prophecies of superindustrial growth nor the vision that the Club of Rome advances—takes sufficient account of the complexities involved is likely. The radical vision of Karl Marx (i.e., his forecast of a revolution of the proletariat in the advanced capitalist societies) did not come to pass. Rather, history shows a virtual inversion of Marx's prediction for many parts of the world. Single-path forecasts of the future, whether optimistic or pessimistic, represent polar forms of sim-

plistic thought. Given levels at which choices are made—individual, interpersonal, organizational, institutional, societal, and intersocietal—and given differing decision-implementing power across levels, single-path forecasts are not likely to be borne out. History documents human choices among alternative possibilities. Any outcome is the product of many choices at many levels; any choice produces multiple outcome possibilities. These principles of "multicausality" and "multifinality" should be kept in mind in any discussion of social change.

SOCIOLOGY AND SOCIAL CHANGE

Social change has been defined as "any modification in the social organization of society in any of its social institutions or patterns of social roles" (Theodorson and Theodorson 1979, 284). Given that change *will* occur (i.e., no living system can remain in a static state), what concerns us are the possibilities for change that are survival enhancing. Our basic assumptions may need to be challenged and our frameworks for explaining social systems revised. Perceptions of the capacity for, pace of, and scale of change that were useful in earlier eras may be unrealistic for today's world.

As a starting point for understanding change in social systems, we reintroduce Ogburn's (1966) concept of "cultural lag" and briefly discuss Toffler's (1970) extension of Ogburn's concept, namely, "future shock."

The concept of cultural lag incorporates the observation that some parts of social systems change more rapidly than other parts. Basing his concept on the structural-functional assumption of interdependence of parts in any system, W. F. Ogburn noted that a rapid change in any part of a social system requires readjustment through changes in other parts. Modifications may result in a temporary disruption of the integration and continuity of the whole. Specifically, the material culture, through rapid advances in science and technology, changes more rapidly than does the nonmaterial culture (institutions such as the family, religion, and education, along with the values for which these institutions serve as carriers). The result is a lag between material culture change and nonmaterial or adaptive culture change.

Alvin Toffler's extension of Ogburn's ideas states that as we enter the postindustrial era, lags will not only affect our institutions but also will be directly experienced by individuals. As a result of the increased acceleration and complexity of social interaction and information flows, individuals must relate to the social environment in new ways in order to survive. Rapidity of change requires that we quickly "decontextualize and recontextualize," i.e., take apart our mental building blocks and put them back together in new ways. This process forces us to reevaluate and redefine our institutions, from the family to the nation-state, as well as to reevaluate and redefine the nature of our relationships at all levels of interaction. In the process, social problems that require social resolution become visible.

The many reevaluations, redefinitions, and adjustments that survival necessitates under future-shock conditions cannot be undertaken piecemeal. Rather, a framework and methodology are needed that can explain the intricately interconnected world system and encompass its effects on individual experience. If we can accept that we live in a transitional period, one in which "industrial modes" of thinking are being replaced by an "information mode," then it becomes apparent that old ideologies and old ways of problem solving may be inadequate for contemporary problems.

According to Toffler (1980, 46–56), industrialism gave rise to six interrelated principles that virtually "programmed" human behavior: centralization, concentration, maximization, specialization, standardization, and synchronization. These principles no longer serve us well. The system of

knowledge that powered industrial-mode thought was codified in the seventeenth century. The successes of the physical sciences led to efforts to discover a "social physics" (Randall 1940, 255). Science operated on the intellectual triumphs of thinkers such as Newton, Locke, and Descartes for the 300 years since.

Industrial-mode thought and our understanding of world systems were constructed by the analysis of component parts. The result was **atomization,** or specialization of knowledge, in which quantified measurement of smaller and smaller problems left us without a sufficient view of larger problems. The assumption had been made that the whole (e.g., the whole of society) could be understood by studying the parts (units of analysis) in isolation. Over the last few decades, however, this narrow, specialized mode of thought has been challenged by a "total, rather than fragmentary look at problems" (Ramo 1969, vi).

SYSTEMS THEORY AND THE GOOD SOCIETY

In the physical sciences, one of the spokespersons of this holistic view is Ilya Prigogine, who in 1977 won the Nobel Prize for his work in nonequilibrium thermodynamics. His "Theory of Dissipative Structures" (complex open systems) may prove as important a breakthrough in science, in general, as the theories of Einstein were to physics. The theory's purpose is to bridge the critical gap between biology and physics. This bridging requires locating the missing link between the physicist's belief in **entropy** (that the universe is running down or randomizing and that all organized patterns must eventually decay) and the biologist's understanding of **evolution** (that life continually gives rise to higher and more complex organization).

The crux of Prigogine's argument is that in a complex system, the parts of the system are in constant flux, always undergoing small-scale change due to internal or external stimuli or both. These changes or fluctuations, *left unchecked*, will break up the old equilibrium, resulting either in disorder and decay or in the creation of a wholly new structure at a higher level of complexity (Nicolis and Prigogine 1977). This new structure is more complex and differentiated and requires a greater amount of resources than the old structure to sustain itself. The theory strikes hard at "industrial thinking" and the "old causality" by contending that "chance" and "necessity" dominate change between periods of "predictive determinism." As Prigogine sums up, "The laws of strict causality appear to us today as limiting situations, applicable to highly idealized cases. The science of complexity leads to a completely different view" (Toffler 1980, 309).

This questioning of the laws of science, which serves as a foundation for our understanding of the universe, has not evolved in a void. Rather this new intellectual craftsmanship grew out of an awareness of the impossibility of fitting older explanations to structural transformations (physical, biological, and social). In this view, the social problems and processes of our complex and interrelated world system *cannot* be addressed by reducing nature to the simplicity of a reality governed by universal laws. A new framework of analysis is needed—one that does not postulate equilibrium as the "natural" state of existence; one concerned with interactions and "flows" as opposed to units and "stocks"; one dealing with the plurality and diversity of social life; one underscored by the realization that all science is created *by* humans *for* humans (Wallerstein 1982, 13–15).

General systems theory offers such a view. From a systems perspective, social problems are interconnected and overlapping, and the solution of one problem affects the solution of another (Churchman 1968, 4). In this view, major problems such as overpopulation, resource depletion, pollution,

and malnutrition form a web of interconnected concerns (Churchman 1968, 126). This interconnectedness must be faced by policymakers in their efforts to find solutions (Mason and Mitroff 1981, 4–5).

One of the key concepts of systems theory is that of feedback (information exchange). "Negative feedback" preserves equilibrium by dampening or suppressing change. "Positive feedback" amplifies change. From this perspective, the state of a system (relatively stable or involved in transformation) depends on the feedback exchanged between internal and external systems and subsystems. As Prigogine demonstrated with his mathematics of physical systems, systems theory indicates that social systems are never entirely stable, i.e., in perfect equilibrium or completely predictable. This applies at all levels and for all systems or subsystems observed.

How may these feedback mechanisms allow us to enhance our social environment? Our advances in information-communication technologies have ushered in the "information era." Unlike the previous "industrial era" with its focus on system components, new technological capabilities permit us to connect components into the larger, more complex systems they really are a part of and to enhance understanding of the whole. These technologies also enhance the operation of feedback mechanisms in both positive and negative communication flows. Thus, the means by which the transition itself is being fueled promises to propel our capacity to deal with change in the new age through the use of the same information-communication technologies. According to cybernetic (systems) information theory, since "intelligence" is a feature of any feedback system that has a capacity for learning, we may envision a "collective intelligence" evolving out of what Marshall McLuhan has called the "Global Village" (1962).

To operationalize (make real) this vision requires a fundamental shift in our ways of looking at social life. For instance, specialists must be supplemented with generalists who are oriented to diversity and change. Questions must be raised about the most obvious and simple assumptions, which requires our willingness to think in nonconventional ways. In the language of chemistry, the purpose in the use of our ingredients or resources must result in a "solution" and not a mere "mixture" in our efforts to resolve or manage social problems.

Insofar as this perspective is "radical," it poses a challenge to all disciplines within the social sciences. For example, economists "see" what their tools and measurements allow them to manipulate; they may not see how changes have affected their concepts. Barry Commoner (1976, 198–211) and others have emphasized the role of energy in our socioeconomic equation. But, since traditional supply and demand theory uses *current* supply and demand to determine current price, it cannot account for differences between renewable and nonrenewable supplies. Similarly, sociology must expand and understand developments in the areas of ethnic identity, gender consciousness, and racial pride that have unfolded in the wake of "melting pot" theories. New perspectives must be developed for understanding intangible and nonquantifiable factors of cultural values (Hawken, Ogilvy, and Schwartz 1982, 203–14). The fission of the social sciences in the industrial era must be transformed into a fusion in the information era to produce a "cultural economics."

The economics and sociology of information and knowledge are not the same as material goods and commodities (Bell 1973, ix–xv). In an information economy, as opposed to an industrial economy, value is increased not by labor but by knowledge. Marx's "labor theory of value" must now be replaced with a "knowledge theory of value." Knowledge is a *social* product, and unlike an industrial good that is consumed and used up, it remains with the producer even when it is sold. Hence, its effects are also synergistic, which means that the whole becomes greater than the sum of its parts. As management philosopher Peter Drucker has said:

The next economics may even attempt to be again both "humanity" and "science." It may base itself on the postulate that productivity—that is, knowledge applied to resources through human work—is the source of all economic value (Bell and Kristol 1981, 17–18).

DECENTRALIZATION, NETWORKING, AND THE "THIRD WAVE"

Our future may depend on using communication-information technologies to decentralize some of our traditional organizations and institutions. That upper limits have been reached regarding organizational inefficiencies stemming from sheer size has become apparent. Decentralization is the organizational counterpart to our ideological tradition of freedom and provides for our actual diversity of values, as well as for the opportunity to devise new norms (Naisbitt 1982, 97–130). Decentralization of organizations within institutions affirms, along with Toffler (1980, 261–62), that "small within big is beautiful."

Social relations created by new feedback linkages are not conducive to the old hierarchical organization of the industrial era. New social relations are evolving out of the inability of highly centralized organizations to cope with a world that is growing more diverse, pluralistic, and complex. As Marilyn Ferguson (1980, 62–63) has pointed out, new linkages or "networks" foster self-help, exchange information, change society, improve productivity, and share resources. Their structure permits information transmittal in quicker, more personal, and more energy-efficient ways. Such networking systems (called "matrix management" within corporations) are in their beginnings, but are capable of providing both vertical and horizontal—even multidirectional and overlapping—linkages. Jessica Lipnack and Jeffrey

Stamps (1982, 1–10) see networks as the human equivalent of "appropriate" technology. Networking procedures and skills are beginning to circumvent and decentralize the hierarchical structures of the industrial era, and to help solve its problems.

We stand at a "watershed" in world history in which our problems are so complex and our ability to gather and exchange information so advanced that for the first time, informed, democratic, and collective decisions are possible and necessary on a worldwide scale. In the words of leading systems theorist Ervin Laszlo:

We are part of an interconnected system of nature and unless informed "generalists" make it their business to develop systematic theories of the patterns of interconnection, our short-range projects and limited controlabilities may lead us to our own destruction (Lilienfeld 1978, 161).

In the social sciences, Max Weber's method of **verstehen** (understanding) must be continually employed, as we have attempted to employ it in this text. The role of knowledge continues to increase in importance and, as Prigogine and Stengers (1979, 281) have pointed out, "We are only at the beginning, at the prehistory of our insights."

REFERENCES

Bell, D. 1973. *The coming of post-industrial society: A venture in social forecasting.* New York: Basic.
———. 1976. *The cultural contradictions of capitalism.* New York: Basic.
Bell, D., and I. Kristol. 1981. *The crisis in economic theory.* New York: Basic.
Churchman, C. W. 1968. *The systems approach.* New York: Laurel.

Commoner, B. 1976. *The poverty of power.* New York: Bantam.
Ferguson, M. 1980. *The aquarian conspiracy.* Los Angeles: Houghton Mifflin.
Gaskin, S. 1977. *Volume one: Sunday morning services on the Farm.* Summertown, Tenn.: Book Publishing.
Hawken, P., J. Ogilvy, and P. Schwartz. 1982. *Seven tomorrows.* New York: Bantam.
Kahn, H. 1976. *The next 200 years.* New York: Morrow.
Kephart, W. 1976. *Extraordinary groups.* New York: St. Martin's.
Lipnack, J., and J. Stamps. 1982. *Networking: The first report and directory.* Garden City, N.Y.: Doubleday.
Lilienfeld, R. 1978. *The rise of systems theory: An ideological analysis.* New York: Wiley, Interscience.
Mason, R., and I. Mitroff. 1981. *Challenging strategic planning assumptions.* New York: Wiley, Interscience.
McLuhan, M. 1962. *The Gutenberg galaxy.* Toronto: Univ. of Toronto Press.
Meadows, D. H., D. L. Meadows, J. Randers, and W. W. Behrens III. 1972. *The limits to growth.* Washington, D.C.: Potomac Associates.
Naisbitt, J. 1982. *Megatrends, ten new directions transforming our lives.* New York: Warner.
Nicolis, G., and I. Prigogine. 1977. *Self-organization in non equilibrium systems: From dissipative structures to order through fluctuations.* New York: Wiley, Interscience.
Ogburn, W. F. 1966. *Social change.* New York: Dell.
Prigogine, I., and I. Stengers. 1979. *La nouvelle alliance.* Paris: Gallimard.
Ramo, S. 1969. *Cure for chaos: Fresh solutions to social problems through the systems approach.* New York: David McKay.
Randall, J. H. 1940. *The making of the modern mind.* Cambridge, Mass.: Houghton Mifflin.
Slater, P. 1976. *The pursuit of loneliness.* Boston: Beacon.
Theodorson, G. A., and A. Theodorson. 1979. *A modern dictionary of sociology.* New York: Barnes & Noble.
Toffler, A. 1970. *Future shock.* New York: Bantam.
———. 1980. *The third wave.* New York: Bantam.
Wallerstein, I. 1982. Crises: The world-economy, the movements, and the ideologies. Paper presented at Sixth Annual Political Economy of the World System Conference, University of Arizona, 15–16 April.

Glossary

Absolutist A person who believes that there are universal standards that serve as criteria for judging the difference between deviant and nondeviant behavior.

Achieved (role or status) Behaviors, attitudes, or social position (or a combination of these) assumed when an individual or group meets particular requirements (e.g., a women achieves the role and status of "wife" by behaving in specific ways, i.e., marrying, caring for her spouse).

Affirmative action Programs designed to admit minority group members to good schools and good jobs.

Ageism Discrimination for or against people solely on the basis of chronological age.

Aggravated assault An unlawful attack by one person upon another for the purpose of inflicting severe or aggravated bodily injury.

Aggression (Lorenz) "The fighting instinct (or drive) in beast and man which is directed against members of the same species."

Alcohol A central nervous system depressant, sometimes prescribed to aid sleep and digestion or to relieve pain.

Alcoholic A person addicted to alcohol.

Alienation (Seeman) Feelings of powerlessness, meaninglessness, cynicism, cultural estrangement, social isolation, and even self-estrangement.

Amphetamine-related psychedelics Includes DMT, LSD, mescaline and peyote, and psilocybin/psilocin, all of which have hallucinogenic effects on the user.

Amyl nitrite A cardiac stimulant once recommended for angina patients but now used by a small number of persons for the intense high it provides when inhaled.

Anarchy A loss of social and political control, especially in political government.

Androgyny Having characteristics (usually personality traits) of both sexes; containing the full range of human personality potential.

Anomic See Anomie

Anomie A condition of normlessness in society, in which some individuals' or groups' sense of social cohesion is broken or severely weakened; a loss of rules to guide personal conduct.

Antidepressant Drugs such as Elavil, Triavil, Tofranil, and Etafron, which have a sedating effect; also known as "uppers."

Apartheid South African racial discrimination.

Aristocratic power structures (Miller) Power structures in which a set of families tends to perpetuate itself.

Artificial or corporate persons Institutions.

Ascribed (role or status) Behaviors, attitudes, or social position (or a combination of these) arbitrarily assigned to an individual or group if that person or group meets specific requirements, irrespective of desires or accomplishments, e.g., a person born into the royal family line has high status.

Assimilation The absorption of one cultural group by another, although in the process, behavior patterns of the two (or more) interacting cultural groups become meshed.

Atomization Specialization of knowledge.

Authoritarian One whose mind is closed to new ideas and who advocates punitiveness as a response to perceived deviance.

Authority (Weber) A special form of legitimate power, in which members of a group or society agree that persons occupying given social statuses may exercise power over them in certain social situations.

Autism A form of childhood schizophrenia in which the child reacts to people as things to be manipulated rather than persons with whom to interact.

Autocratic power structure (Miller) Refers to the inherited power of a single person or family.

Barbiturates and other sedatives Central nervous system depressants considered more potent than minor tranquilizers, such as Nembutal, Phenobarbital, Seconal, Quaaludes, Doriden, and Placidyl.

Basic anxiety (Horney) The notion that every person is born isolated and helpless and that the infant has these feelings.

Behavior strategies (Horney) Ways in which people cope with the world as they strive for security.

Bilateral Reciprocally affecting two sides.

Blaming the victim (Ryan) An ideology for justifying a perverse form of social action designed to change society's victim—not society, as one might expect.

Buprenorphine A drug used in Europe as a painkiller.

Bureaucracy (Blau) A type of organization designed to accomplish large-scale administrative tasks by systematically coordinating the work of many individuals.

Bureaucratization The subdivisions of large, complex organizations in which each division has separate functions designed for maximum efficiency in accomplishing particular tasks.

Caste system Social stratification based on the ascribed status of individuals in differentiated, socially ranked groups. Members are encouraged to marry only among themselves.

Charismatic leadership Influence as an outgrowth of exceptional qualities of grace and/or sanctity attributed to a leader by a group.

Child abuse Refers to any type of psychological or physical injury inflicted on a child.

Child neglect Includes abandonment for long periods of time; lack of supervision; nutritional, medical, dental, and educational neglect; inappropriate or insufficient clothing; shelter and emotional neglect; and moral neglect (i.e., not providing ethical guidance).

Chiliasm The belief that the millennium is a hand, that we are near the Second Coming of Christ.

Civilization The techniques that people use to increase their productive capacities.

Class See Social class.

Cohort A group—actual or theoretical—whose members begin life or marriage (or some other life stage) at the same general time.

Collectivity crime (Cohen) A special form of white-collar crime, in which "artificial persons," such as corporations and labor unions, violate criminal laws.

Commitment (Kanter) "A person's willingness to carry out the requirements of a pattern of social action because he or she sees it as stemming from his or her basic nature as a person."

Communes "Intentional communities" that have values and norms that set them apart from the culture of the larger society.

Communion (Kanter) The "we-feelings" of brotherhood or sisterhood essential for continuation of a group in the face of obstacles and disagreements.

Community power The concentration or diffusion among groups and individuals of political and economic decision-making influence within a community.

Compliant personality (Horney) A personality trend in which people tend to "move toward others" (i.e., rely too much on others) as a way of relieving personal anxiety.

Computer crime Criminal behavior by means of manipulating electronic data processing.

Concentric zone theory Points to the processes of increasing segregation of urban populations by social class and by race.

Conflict A regulated or unregulated form of intense competition in which rival individuals and groups try to attain their goals by overpowering (sometimes physically) their competitors.

Conflict theory The assumption that social life is based on informal and formal conflict in a competitive struggle to protect and advance one's personal and group interests.

Conquest proprietorship Territory taken from one group of people through the use of force and violence by another group.

Consensus theory Holds that most people in society are motivated to achieve the same set of cultural (material and nonmaterial) goals.

Constitutionalism The limited, responsible use of political power.

Construct A hypothetical model that does not describe an actual aspect of the world, but is useful for analysis and interpretation of reality.

Cortex Part of the brain.

Counterculture The normative system of a group or a subsociety that contains a theme of conflict with the values of the larger society.

Crime (Jeffrey) A general sociological definition is that crime is a "violation of any conduct norm whatsoever."

Critical theory An examination of recurring problems and issues in traditional sociology.

Crude birth rate (Hardert and Parker) A rate that measures the number of babies born in one year per 1,000 of the total population.

Crude death rate (Hardert and Parker) A rate that measures the number of deaths in one year per 1,000 of the total population.

Cults (Richardson) Groups that are unhappy with life in the larger, conventional society and whose members seek to create a new social order. They are "usually small in size, informal, lacking in definite authority structure, and somewhat spontaneous."

Cultural activities Value-making activities such as language, ritual, the arts, and "lived" knowledge of the world around us.

Culture (Barnouw) "The way of life of a group of people," including "the more or less stereotyped patterns of learned behavior which are handed down from one generation to the next through the means of language and imitation."

Current use Refers to the percentage of respondents who report having used a drug during the month previous to the interview.

Cybernetics An advanced form of automation involving computer control and analysis in mass production; it has resulted in the elimination of most unskilled industrial jobs.

Deinstitutionalization Rapid discharge of patients from state mental institutions into surrounding communities.

Depressants Drugs such as barbiturates and other sedatives, minor and major tranquilizers, painkillers, and alcohol; also known as "downers."

Detached personality (Horney) A personality trend in which people "move away from others" (i.e., isolate themselves from others) sometimes to an exaggerated extent.

Détente A policy of live and let live.

Deviant behavior A violation of any conduct norm in human society.

Devolutionists Believers that "bigness is bad" and that "small is beautiful."

Dioxin Chemical by-product of herbicide production. Causes kidney, spleen, and liver ailments in laboratory animals.

Discrimination Unequal negative treatment of members of minority groups; forced upon them by dominant members of society.

Division of labor The formal or informal allocation of tasks to achieve group goals. Division of labor is particularly evident in complex production processes.

Dominance Refers to controlling resources or rewards in a given territory.

Double standard One set of rules for judging the behavior or attitudes or both of one sex and a different set of rules for judging the behavior or attitudes or both of the other sex, e.g., the double standard of morality (less stringently applied to men than to women).

Drug Any substance that has a chemical effect on the central nervous system.

Drug abuse (Lauer) The improper use of drugs or alcohol to the degree that the consequences are defined as detrimental to the user or society or both.

Drug tolerance The need to ingest more chemicals to reach the same high; develops with prolonged drug use.

Dysfunctional Antithetical to the interests of society as a whole.

Eco-catastrophe The human attack on the support systems that sustain our lives.

Ecology The interrelationship of all organisms to all of the environment in terms of subsistence.

Ecumenicism, ecumenical The joining of persons or groups whose views may be opposed, for some common goal, e.g., Catholics, Protestants, and Jews join in an ecumenical movement to overcome racial bigotry.

Ego (Freud) The rational or socialized part of the human mind.

Embezzlement A criminal violation of financial trust.

Energy The capacity to do work that involves the ability to organize both human labor and values.

Entropy In physics, the belief that the universe is running down or randomizing and that all organized patterns must eventually decay.

Ethology (Hardert) Broadly defined as "the study of animal behavior, in an evolutionary context, in application to human behavior."

Evolution The notion that life continually gives rise to more complex organization.

False consciousness (Marx) The human capacity for thinking and acting in ways that do not favor one's own position in society.

Family of orientation The nuclear family into which the individual is born or is socialized; also called "family of origin."

Family of origin See family of orientation.

Family violence Includes child neglect, child abuse, incest, wife battering, husband battering, and battering of the elderly, including parent abuse.

Faustian bargain To sell one's soul to the devil.

Fecundity The potential for reproduction based on the number of women in the childbearing years of fifteen to forty-four.

Fellatio A form of oral-genital sexual contact in which the penis is inserted into the mouth of another.

Felonies Serious violations of the criminal law.

Fentanyl A new synthetic narcotic that has been described as "worse than heroin."

Fertility Refers to the actual reproductive performance of women regarding numbers of children born in a given time span.

Fission power Energy derived by splitting the atom.

Food The energy source most basic to human existence.

Forcible rape The carnal knowledge of a female forcibly and against her will.

Functional consensus theory The theoretical approach to the operation of society that emphasizes the interdependence of institutionalized elements to the stability and maintenance of society.

Gay men Homosexual men who have publicly affirmed their sexual orientation.

Gemeinschaft Intimate, personal, primary relations that tend to be found in small communities.

Generalizability The degree to which specific information is applicable to similar but unstudied phenomena.

Gerontocracy   Control or rule over the rest of the society by its elder members; political-economic dominance by the old.

Gerontophobia   Fear of contact with older people.

Gesellschaft   Limited, impersonal, secondary relations that characterize much social interaction in large urban communities.

Gesture   That part of a behavioral act that stands for the total (implied) act.

Ghetto   A region or neighborhood of a city in which the predominant population is composed of an ethnic group whose members may encounter resistance if they attempt to move elsewhere.

Global   Comprehensive; all-encompassing.

Green Revolution (Brown)   A method of increasing the food supply by using high-yield crops in the same land area where low-yield crops have been planted in the past.

Heterogeneous   Groups or individuals whose characteristics are dissimilar or unalike, e.g., a male and a female are sexually heterogeneous; Caucasians and Asians are racially heterogeneous.

Hibakusha   Atomic bomb survivors.

Hierarchy   A set of persons or groups ranked according to the extent to which they exercise power or have privileges or both.

Homoeroticism   Sensual or sexual (or both) behaviors or attitudes between same-sex partners.

Homogeneous (homogeneity)   Groups or individuals whose characteristics are similar or alike, e.g., he and she are religiously homogeneous if both are Jewish, racially homogeneous if both are Caucasian.

Homophile   One who holds a positive attitude toward same-sex attraction or toward those who are attracted by members of their own sex.

Homophobia   Feelings of personal anxiety, disgust, and avoidance of homosexuals.

Homosexuality   Sexual interest in or sexual contact with a person of one's own sex.

Homosocial   The preference for or conduct of one's activity with members of the same sex, e.g., the Boy Scouts and Girl Scouts are homosocial organizations.

Human ecology   The research specialty dealing with the way people relate and adjust to their physical environment.

Humanist perspective in sociology   Argues that the purpose of sociology is to promote human understanding of social ills and to help reform society through the application of scientific knowledge.

Iatrogenesis (Illich)   Refers to an injury that a patient suffers as a result of a physician's intervention.

Id (Freud)   The aggressive, unsocialized part of the human mind.

Ideal type (ideal-typical)   A hypothetical idea of any phenomenon in which its most characteristic features are exaggerated; used to show a standard against which reality can be measured, but not used to mirror reality.

Idealism   Asserts that mind or spirit is basic to everything that exists; the body and material things are less important than mental processes.

Ideologies (Mills)   The particular sets of ideas that members of various groups use to explain things.

Infant death rate   Measures morality in the first year of life. Computed by relating the annual number of deaths of infants under one year of age to the annual number of live births, and is expressed as the number of deaths per 1,000 live births yearly in a society.

In-group   A group in which an individual believes that he or she belongs and is accepted.

Indexicality   Refers to the importance of the social context or immediate situation for determining the meaning or sense of any particular action or utterance occurring within it.

Innate   Inborn; unlearned.

Institutionalization   Phenomena established as part of a permanent system.

Insular poverty   Poverty based on the lack of educational and economic opportunities in certain areas and among certain groups which, in effect, locks many into a life of poverty.

Intergenerational justice (Reader)   A decision by those presently alive to try to use only those energy sources that are renewable, safe, nonpolluting, flexible, easily understandable and hence accessible to ordinary people everywhere; nonviolent, job producing rather than machine dependent, matched to the society and the task to be served, and "pleasing to the senses and enjoyable to work with."

Intermediate technology (Schumacher)   More productive than the native technology of most undeveloped countries, but also considerably cheaper than the sophisticated, highly capital-intensive technology of modern industry.

Intersubjective understanding   Takes place when people can share essential meanings about aspects of social reality.

Investment (Kanter)   The resources (e.g., time, energy, money, property and reputation) that a person provides a group.

Law of entropy (Commoner, Rifkin)   The tendency of any closed energy system to decay toward "disorder, . . . and loss of information."

Learned helplessness (Walker)   A type of dependency associated with the psychological reasons why battered women remain in violent relationships.

Lesbianism   Sexual attraction or sexual behavior between women.

Lifetime experience   Defined as the percentage of respondents who report ever having used a drug.

Longitudinal research Studies of behavior in a selected sample over an extended period of time or at several different points in time.

Lorenz curve A means of measuring income inequality (see figure 7–3).

Macrofunctional approach Studying whole societies or large systems within societies.

Major tranquilizers Drugs such as Thorazine, Compazine, Haldol, Mellaril, and Stelazine, also known as downers, used to reduce symptoms of psychosis, such as fear, hallucinations, and hyperactivity, and to treat alcohol withdrawal symptoms.

Marijuana Generally classified as a central nervous system drug; its proper subclassification is presently in dispute.

Marijuana use Refers to the smoking (or occasionally the eating or drinking) of the ground leaves, flowers, or upper stems (or a combination of these) of the Indian hemp plant *cannabis sativa*.

Masculinist An attitude favoring males over females; ascribing superior status across social institutions to males.

Mass tyrannies Systems of popular government that deprive individuals of their fundamental rights.

Master status A status that overrides other characteristics of individuals or groups, e.g., Ku Klux Klan members (seen by nonmembers) may be male, strong, and handsome, but their master status is "bigot."

Materialism Asserts that matter is the fundamental substance; the opposite of idealism.

Matriarchy A form of social organization in which power and authority are vested in females.

Median The middle score in a distribution of scores, e.g., 3 is the median in the series 1-2-3-4-5.

Medical model The belief system that says that mental or emotional problems are disorders and should be treated like physical ailments, inferring that the etiology or causation of mental disorder is primarily located in the psychology or the physiology of the individual.

Medicine (Clayton) The art of preventing, caring for, and assisting in the cure of disease and care of the ill.

Megaton The equivalent of 1 million tons of TNT, or seventy times the size of the Hiroshima bomb.

Mentacide The killing of intelligence.

Methadone maintenance A method of treatment aimed at replacing the addict's craving for heroin.

Methodological dualism (Gouldner) Argues for an (artificial) separation between the social scientist and the people observed; based on philosophical "dualism," which asserts that there are two ultimate (basic) substances: mind and matter.

Microfunctional approach Focusing on small groups within societies.

Milieu control (Lifton) The purposeful limitation of all forms of communication with the outside world, along with sleep deprivation and change in diet.

Military-industrial complex Power elites such as the military, big business, and big government.

Millennarian movements (Cohn) Societal movements that expect immediate, total, collective, and this-worldly salvation.

Mind-matter (or mind-body) problem Refers to the difficulty of distinguishing between the ideal world of the mind and the world of physical things.

Minor tranquilizers Drugs such as Valium, Librium, Equanil, Miltown, Dalmane, and Serax, which act as central nervous system depressants to reduce anxiety, tension headaches, and insomnia.

Minority Any group within a given population that is discriminated against by other members of the society.

Misogyny Hatred of women.

Monogamy A form of marriage in which each partner is permitted only one legal mate at a time. The ideal-typical form of monogamy lasts until the death of either of the partners.

Monolithic Power that is conceived as being centralized in the hands of a few people at both national and local levels.

Monopoly capitalism The ability of big business to make increasing profits by dominating various markets, which involves gaining control over sources of raw materials.

Moral entrepreneur A person with broad-based humanitarian concerns, who creates and enforces rules.

Moral relativist (Lofland) A person who believes that there is no obvious moral meaning in the universe; good and evil are viewed as value judgments by the individual.

Moral relativity The idea that there are no universal ethical or religious standards; directly opposed to the concept of moral absolutism.

Mortification (Kanter) The death of the old self and the birth of a new one.

Murder The willful (non-negligent) killing of one human being by another.

Musselmanner Survivors of Hitler's concentration camps.

Nationalism Strong devotion to one's country.

Negative income tax A tax system that provides individuals and family units below the taxable level enough additional income to exceed the poverty line.

Neolocal In a new location, as when a newly married couple settles somewhere away from the parental homes.

Neonate Newborn infant.

Nonrenewable Depletable.

Norm A behavioral expectation in a society that people will act or think in a defined way in a certain situation.

Neuroses   Refers to various types of behavior that appear to be characterized by "free-floating" anxiety, a type of persistent anxiety that appears to have no observable basis.

Nuclear (nuclear family)   Usually a married couple and their children, natural or adopted, who reside in the same place.

Omnicide   Contemplated destruction of the human race.

Out-group   Any persons who are not members of the group designated by the term *we;* especially, groups toward which "we" hold negative attitudes.

Overall crime rate   Relates the yearly number of reported crimes in the larger society to the total population (per every 100,000 persons).

Painkillers   A type of downer; they include narcotics such as codeine, heroin, and morphine, as well as synthetic narcotics such as Darvon, Demerol, Fentanyl, Methadone, Percodan, and Talwin.

Paradigm   General descriptions of the natural world that are seen by scientists as fundamental and self-evident.

Parataxic mode (Sullivan)   A type of social experience that lies between the prototaxic and syntaxic modes.

Patriarchy   A society in which males are dominant (especially older males); control over family members by the father.

PCP (Angel Dust)   Also sold under the names Cannabinal, Crystal, THC, Dust, TIC, TAC, Erth, Green, KW, KJ, Hog, and Sheets; commonly taken orally, smoked, snorted, and injected.

Pedophiles   Those whose primary sexual gratification involves contact with children.

Personality trends (Horney)   Behavior strategies that bring feelings of security, tend to be repeated, and become fixed in a person's behavior.

Phenomena   Things as they are perceived through our senses; each of us perceives a given phenomenon in a slightly different way.

Phenomenology   Defined as the study of phenomena generated by human consciousness.

Photosynthesis   The technique plants use to convert the direct rays of the sun into natural sugar and oxygen.

Photovoltaic cells   Cells that transmit the sun's rays into electricity.

Plea bargain (Report of the National Commission on Criminal Justice Standards and Goals)   An agreement in which the offender pleads guilty to a lesser charge rather than standing trial for the original charge.

Pluralism   The idea that larger social systems are made up of groupings of subsystems that are interdependent but retain some degree of separate identity.

Police corruption (Sherman)   Any corrupt act that an officer, or group of officers, commits for personal rather than for organizational interests.

Pornography   Often mistakenly equated in general usage with the term *obscenity* and is sometimes confused with the term *erotica.*

Power (Emerson)   "The ability to make others dependent."

Power elite (Mills)   Those persons and attitudes within a society that habitually command, are habitually obeyed, and which habitually reap whatever wealth, power, and status rewards society can bestow.

Predatory crimes (Lauer)   Acts that have victims who suffer loss of property or some kind of physical harm.

Prejudice   Negative opinions of persons or groups based on beliefs rather than on facts.

Primary relationship   A (usually two-person) relationship in which the parts (persons) are not interchangeable with others, even though others are capable of enacting the same role (e.g., one's mother and one's child).

Problematic theory   Includes such perspectives as symbolic interactionism, phenomenology, and ethnomethodology, all of which seek to discover the inherent meaning of human behavior.

Prostitution   Allowing sexual access in return for money, goods (such as drugs), or favors.

Prototaxic mode (Sullivan)   A type of social experience in which there is a minimal inner elaboration of thought.

Psychoses   Generally refers to any of a number of behavioral conditions characterized by patients' lack of contact with social reality and by deep psychological depression.

Psychosomatic disorder (Lauer)   Defined as "impairments in physiological functioning that result from the individual's emotional state."

Public   A large aggregation of people who share certain common interests.

Public opinion   The process (by voting or other means) by which members of a public express their opinions on issues of common interest.

Racism   Prejudice or discrimination (or both) against individuals or groups because of their racial origin; like ageism and sexism, racism ascribes like qualities and characteristics to persons *solely* on the basis of group membership.

Radical perspective in sociology   Argues that drastic social reforms are needed right away and that science may not be the answer to solving societal problems.

Random sample   A sample in which every member of the population being studied has an equal chance for selection, so that reasonable inferences may be drawn about the total population.

Rape (McCombie)   "A total attack upon the person which affects physical, psychological, and social well-being."

Reality (Roszak) "The boundaries of . . . the collective mindscape, the limits of sane experience."

Reference group A set of people whose standards (as perceived by any individual) are seen as particularly relevant to use as a basis for evaluating important aspects of that individual's life.

Reinforcement (negative or positive) The process or technique through which a response (to a stimulus) is strengthened, with the goal of producing desired behavior and eliminating undesired behavior.

Relative deprivation The condition in which individuals of similar status feel deprived in comparison with others whose social situation they perceive to be better.

Role The expected behavior pattern attached to a particular status position.

Role model Any person whose characteristics or behavior may be adopted by any other person (usually one whose status is lower than that of the role model).

Rule of law The conduct of politics according to established, known procedures, mindful of individual liberties.

Sacred Indicating the venerated, sanctified, and transcendent (regarding) (both religious and nonreligious phenomena).

Sacrifice (Kanter) The more it costs a person to be a member of a group, the more valuable he or she will consider it.

Sadomasochistic In which inflicting pain or having pain inflicted are experienced as pleasurable.

Sanction (social) A reward or penalty, as appropriate, for approved or disapproved behavior. Society uses sanctions to regulate its norms.

Scapegoat A person or group that is blamed for or persecuted (or both) for the troubles of any other person or group, e.g., the Jews were scapegoated by the Nazis.

Schizophrenia A specific form of psychosis characterized by a person's withdrawal from everyday social interaction.

Scientific perspective in sociology Maintains that the purpose of sociology ought to be doing quantitative (versus qualitative) research, testing hypotheses, confirming or rejecting theories, and adding knowledge about various subjects.

Scientology (Sanders) "A reincarnationist religion that claims to train individuals to experience past lives, to leave their bodies, and to achieve great power and immortality."

Secondary anxiety (Horney) A fear of loving others, which prevents love.

Secondary relationship A (usually two-person) relationship in which the persons are interchangeable with any other persons capable of playing the same role, e.g., clerk and customer.

Sects (Richardson) Similar to cults, but lacking the innovative element found in cults; they are "more authoritarian, voluntaristic, and elitist than cults."

Secular The worldly and nonspiritual; the rational and utilitarian (nonreligious).

Segmented pyramid (Dahl) A power structure with pluralistic blocks of power, as depicted by the idea of interlocking circles, similar to the symbol of the Olympics, with many nuclei of power.

Segregation Social or physical separation (or both) of minority group members from others in the society who wish to avoid social contact with them. Segregation may be de jure (supported by a variety of specific laws) or de facto (supported by social practice rather than by law).

Selective perception (Harriman) Perception that "emphasizes some aspect of the situation to the neglect of others to the extent that gross distortions occur."

Sex roles Sets of behaviors and attitudes thought to be appropriate to one or the other sex, or of which only one or the other sex is capable, e.g., wife, brother. Often misdefined as gender role.

Sibling A brother or sister.

Significant other A person (sometimes a group) on whose attitudes, values, and beliefs an individual (sometimes a group) places high value; often someone in a primary relationship, e.g., spouses may be each other's significant other.

Social change (Theodorson and Theodorson) Any modification in the social organization of society in any of its social institutions or patterns of social roles.

Social class A stratification system in which people are socially distinguished by income, education, occupational rank, family prestige, and related factors.

Social distance The limits placed by individuals and by group norms on social interaction with individuals and groups of different statuses. The social distance quotient, or Bogardus 7-point scale, is a measure of social distance between racial and ethnic groups.

Social distance quotient See Social distance.

Social injustice Inequality.

Social mobility The movement of people up or down the social class stratification system.

Social movement A process of seeking social change through the organized efforts of a group.

Social problem A condition described by someone, or by some interest group, as a problem; social problems are what people say they are.

Social role See Role.

Social status See Status.

Socialization The process through which group members learn to behave willingly according to the group's standards; the process through which social identity is acquired.

Socialize See Socialization.

Societal consensus Shared values.

Sociological imagination (Mills) "A quality of mind that allows some persons to develop a rational view of 'what is going on in the world and what may be happening within themselves.' "

Sociology The general science of the structure and

functioning of human social groups, cultures, societies, subcultures, and countercultures.

Sociology of knowledge The field that relates thought, thought systems, and ideas to the social matrix in which they arise.

Sodomy Any sexual intercourse that is thought to be unnatural, e.g., between same-sex persons (especially males). Usually anal intercourse.

Spoiled identity (Goffman) Refers to the feeling of ego deflation resulting from self-knowledge of one's physical and/or social imperfections.

Stagflation A continuation of economic recession and high rates of inflation occurring simultaneously.

Standard Metropolitan Statistical Area (SMSA) A measure of an urban population, which includes a large central city and surrounding suburbs.

State terrorism Random violence by totalitarian authorities.

Status A person's relative position within a group; includes a set of rights and obligations, and may involve either high or low rank.

Status quo Things as they are.

Stigma Any blemish, defect (or sign of a blemish or defect) that has serious negative consequences for an individual's social acceptance.

Stratified pyramid A power structure of varying levels from top to bottom, with the most power at the top and the least at the bottom.

Structural violence (Turner) Aggression expressed through institutional means in which people who have power and authority over others can either bestow or withhold rewards, goods, and services—even the necessities of life.

Subculture Refers to a sub-unit of people within a larger culture that has qualities that distinguish it from the larger culture.

Subjective Resulting from the feelings or thoughts of the one who is thinking, rather than from the attributes of the object that is thought of.

Subjectivity Refers to the degree of personal bias in viewing social "reality."

Suicide (Shneidman) The human act of self-inflicted, self-intentioned cessation.

Suicide intervention Relates to the treatment and care of a person during a suicidal crisis.

Superego (Freud) The conscience of the individual.

Surrogate A substitute; someone or something doing the work of or standing in the place of the actual or genuine element, e.g., a surrogate sex partner.

Survivalists People who actively prepare to survive a nuclear war.

Synergistic effect Effect created when the sum is other and greater than its parts.

Syntaxic mode (Sullivan) A type of social experience that involves a maximum of inner organization and elaboration of thought.

Technological civilization A society whose most important products are its tools and techniques of production and consumption of goods, information, and services.

Thomas theorem The proposition that if people believe something to be true, then real consequences will follow, often as a self-fulfilling prophecy.

Total fertility rate (Zero Population Growth) "A measure of childbearing that projects the lifetime number of children that would be born per woman if all women had children at the prevailing rates of a given year."

Total institution Any organization that has complete control over the individual.

Transcendence (Kanter) The experience of higher power and meaning residing in a movement beyond the life of a single person.

Transcendentalism The notion that to be critical of something, you have to be able to "transcend" it or stand outside of it.

Transsexualism "Crossing the boundary" between the sexes. Adopting the life-style, dress, and mannerisms of the other sex, with or without surgical intervention or hormonal treatment or both.

Transvestism See Transsexualism.

True believer One who has a deep need to belong to something larger than himself or herself.

Unilateral One-sided.

Urbanization Concentrated population growth that results in the development and growth of large cities and suburbs.

Utopia A set of ideas that promotes the interests of underprivileged groups in a given society, which locate their goals in the future.

Values How we think things ought to be.

Verstehen Understanding.

Victimization studies Studies that poll victims of crime.

Vigilantes Paramilitary groups who attempt to take the law into their own hands.

Violence (Steinmetz and Straus) "The intentional use of physical force on another person"; can also be used to connote coercion—hence, it has psychological as well as physical aspects.

White-collar crime (Sutherland) A violation of delegated or implied trust.

Work ethic Sometimes referred to as the Protestant work ethic; based on the idea that work and the acquisition of wealth is morally sanctioned activity.

Zero population growth Occurs when births equal deaths and the number of people does not increase or decrease from one generation to the next.

Name
Index

Subject Index

†